Shared Memory Application Programming

Concepts and strategies in multicore application programming

Shared Memory Application Programming
Programming
Concepts and strategies in multicore application programming

Victor Alessandrini

AMSTERDAM • BOSTON • HEIDELBERG • LONDON
NEW YORK • OXFORD • PARIS • SAN DIEGO
SAN FRANCISCO • SINGAPORE • SYDNEY • TOKYO

Morgan Kaufmann is an imprint of Elsevier

Morgan Kaufmann is an imprint of Elsevier
225 Wyman Street, Waltham, MA 02451, USA

Notices
Knowledge and best practice in this field are constantly changing. As new research and experience broaden our
understanding, changes in research methods, professional practices, or medical treatment may become necessary.

Practitioners and researchers must always rely on their own experience and knowledge in evaluating and using
any information, methods, compounds, or experiments described herein. In using such information or methods
they should be mindful of their own safety and the safety of others, including parties for whom they have a
professional responsibility.

To the fullest extent of the law, neither the Publisher nor the authors, contributors, or editors, assume any liability
for any injury and/or damage to persons or property as a matter of products liability, negligence or otherwise, or
from any use or operation of any methods, products, instructions, or ideas contained in the material herein.

British Library Cataloguing in Publication Data
A catalogue record for this book is available from the British Library

Library of Congress Cataloging-in-Publication Data
A catalog record for this book is available from the Library of Congress

For information on all MK publications
visit our website at http://store.elsevier.com/

ISBN: 978-0-12-803761-4

Working together
to grow libraries in
developing countries

www.elsevier.com • www.bookaid.org

Contents

Preface

This book proposes a pedagogical introduction to shared memory application programming. It grew out of several years of user training at IDRIS supercomputing center in France, and, more recently, at the PATC training program of the PRACE European infrastructure. It is designed to guide readers with a reasonable background in C-C++ programming, in becoming acquainted with current multicore programming environments, and in developing useful insights about threads. This book is therefore placed at an intermediate level; basic experience in multithreaded programming is of course welcomed, but not mandatory.

Multithreaded programming is today a core technology, at the basis of any software development project in any branch of applied computer science. There are, naturally, a number of excellent presentations of the subject. We tried to provide in this book a basic overview of the multithreading landscape, so that readers can start mastering threads, benefiting from the abundant references that push these subjects much further in several directions. It seems therefore appropriate to expose in some detail the pedagogical motivations and strategies adopted here.

PEDAGOGICAL OBJECTIVES

Software engineering practices have experienced a profound evolution in the last 25 years, since shared memory programming first showed up. From simple, monolithic applications designed to solve a specific problem, dealing with a simple parallel context, we moved toward software packages dealing with complex, multicomponent modules, sometimes running in distributed computational environments. Another major evolution in software engineering occurred in the mid-2000s when working processor frequencies—and the peak performance that comes with it—ceased to double every 18 months, because a power dissipation wall was hit. Today, the only way to increase performance is to increase the number of processors, and for this reason multithreading, which was initially a question of choice and opportunity, has become a mandatory software technology. Threads are definitely a part of the life of any software developer concerned with issues of efficient network connectivity and I/O, interoperability, computational performance and scalability, or efficient interactive access to an application.

In this diversified and rapidly evolving landscape, a rather broad view of the utilities and the strategic options proposed by the different multithreading libraries and environments seems to be an important asset for software developers. An overview of different libraries and programming environments operating on Unix-Linux or Windows platforms is proposed, underlining their often complementary capabilities, as well as the fact that there is sometimes benefit in taking advantage of their interoperability. The first chapters of this book develop an overview of the native multithreading libraries like Pthreads (for Unix-Linux systems) or Windows threads, as well as the recent C++11 threads standard, with the purpose of grasping the fundamental issues on thread management and synchronization discussed in the following chapters. A quick introduction to the most basic OpenMP thread management interfaces is also introduced at this stage. In the second part of the book, a detailed discussion of the two high-level, standard programming environments—OpenMP and Intel Threading Building Blocks (TBB)—is given.

OpenMP—which played a fundamental role in disseminating shared memory programming—is today a broadly adopted and well-established standard. Nevertheless, we believe that a more general presentation of the basic concepts of shared memory programming, showing the way they are declined in the various programming environments, is useful for learning to think creatively about threads, not about programming languages. True enough, OpenMP can cope with practically any parallel context in an application. But the implementations of the basic multithreading concepts by different libraries often incorporate additional features that enable, in some specific cases, a better match to the application requirements. Some libraries propose specific extended utilities. A few cases will be given in which C++11 or TBB utilities are profitably used to boost application performance. This does not mean, however, that software developers need to abandon their well-rooted habits and best practices, because most of the time different libraries coexist peacefully and inter-operate inside an application. Examples are proposed of utilities developed using native or basic libraries, but exploited, for example, in an OpenMP environment.

This book focuses on parallel and concurrent patterns and issues that commonly occur in real applications, by discussing useful programming idioms, potential pitfalls, and preferred best practices that are very often independent of the underlying programming environment. In any subject, however, complex, there is always a limited number of important concepts and ideas to be solidly grasped. Once they are mastered, the rest is information that can be easily integrated when needed. Being able to think creatively about threads is more important than knowing every possible detail about specific libraries. In training users, our purpose has always been to enhance their insights on threads and to broaden their understanding of the strategic design choices open to them. For this purpose, a substantial number of examples are proposed in each chapter, with commented sources. All, without exception, are applications of varying degrees of complexity that can be compiled, run, and modified if needed. Many examples involve input parameters that can be changed to better understand the code behavior. A special effort has been made to propose simple but realistic examples, dealing with common issues in application programming.

PROGRAMMING ENVIRONMENTS

This book is addressed to C-C++ programmers. Deep expertise in C++ is not required. True enough, a major step today is the increasing availability of a standard C++11 thread library, but we tried to avoid excluding C programmers. Two of the programming environments discussed here (C++11 and TBB) are C++ libraries, but most of the examples and applications only rely on the usage of C++ objects, an issue easily handled by C programmers. Some more advanced C++ features used by TBB or C++11—like function objects and lambda expressions—are discussed in annex B.

The role, scope, and potential usefulness of the different programming environments discussed in this book will be clarified as we go, but it is useful to take a first look at their relevance. We will henceforth call *native libraries* the multithreaded support provided by different operating systems: the Pthreads (Posix Threads) library for Unix-Linux systems and the Windows API (formerly called Win32 API) for Windows. These native libraries provide the primitives needed to construct multithreaded applications, as well as a number of useful utilities.

The C++11 standard has incorporated a complete set of multithreading facilities into the C++ Standard Library. This evolution was motivated by the obvious interest in boosting C++ to a thread aware programming language, to provide C++ programmers with the capability of disposing of a portable and efficient environment for refined code development. Performance was a basic requirement: the C++11 thread library is designed to support sophisticated system programming without the help of the more basic native programming interfaces. It provides the same basic services as the native libraries mentioned before, as well as a few other refinements and extensions aiming at facilitating code optimization. Given the increasing availability of fully C++11 compliant compilers—like GNU 4.8 or higher in Linux, and Visual Studio 2013 in Windows—we have incorporated C++11 threads in this book on the same footing as Pthreads or Windows threads.

Boost is a prestigious, portable, general-purpose C++ library providing powerful utilities in all areas of C++ software development. It includes a multithreading library fully compliant with the C++11 standard. In fact, Boost was the testing ground where the C++11 standard was developed. We will occasionally refer to some specific facilities proposed by Boost.

OpenMP and TBB are programming environments proposing high-level programming interfaces encapsulating the native libraries services or the very low-level operating system support for multi-threading, adding value and features. These environments are portable in the sense discussed above: the same programming interfaces with different implementations in different operating systems. The fundamental added value with respect to native libraries is the availability of high-level interfaces for thread management, synchronization, and scheduling, simplifying the programming and deployment of parallel applications. It would not be appropriate, however, to completely disregard the basic libraries on the basis that they are low-level environments. True enough, it takes a substantial amount of time and effort to implement a complex application with only the basic libraries. But they have indeed many features that are definitely not low level, easily accessible to application programmers. And, on the other hand, there are programming contexts that require subtle low-level programming even in a high-level environment like OpenMP, simply because the high-level tools required to cope with them are not proposed by the environment. This is the reason why we believe it is useful and instructive to keep a critical eye on the basic multithreading libraries.

There are other useful and efficient programming environments that are not discussed in this book, for portability reasons. OpenMP requires compiler support, but it is automatically integrated in any C-C++ compiler. TBB, instead, is a portable library not requiring compiler support. These environments are therefore fully portable. Another very attractive environment is Intel CilkPlus [1], with easy-to-use C-C++ programming interfaces, based on software technologies also adopted by TBB. CilkPlus, however, requires compiler support, traditionally provided by the Intel C-C++ compiler, which limits its portability. But the expected support in the GNU compiler may change the situation in the future. Last but not least, Microsoft has traditionally provided very strong multithreaded support for Windows, today implemented in a set of Concurrency Runtime tools, incorporating, among other things, the Microsoft Parallel Patterns Library (PPL) [2]. A close collaboration between Microsoft and Intel has established a large amount of compatibility between PPL and TBB.

Besides the basic libraries and high-level programming environments mentioned above, this book relies on another relatively small, high-level library we developed during the last few years, called vath. This library proposes some high-level, easy-to-use utilities in the form of C++ classes that encapsulate the low-level primitives provided by the basic libraries. Our initial motivation was to simplify the usage of the thread management utilities proposed by the native and basic libraries and to dispose of simple tools to cope with specific parallel contexts not easily handled in OpenMP. The specific added value that this additional library may provide will be discussed in later chapters. The point we want to make here is that it is as portable as OpenMP or TBB: the same programming interfaces are implemented in Pthreads (for Unix-Linux systems) and in Windows threads. And there is also a third implementation using the C++11 thread library. This book focuses on the use of this library, not on its implementation. However, for pedagogical reasons, a maximal simplicity programming style has been adopted in the source codes, in order to make it easily accessible to readers interested in taking a closer look at basic Pthreads, Windows of C++11 programming.

As far as the application examples are concerned, with the exception of a few cases in which our purpose is to show some specific feature of one of the basic libraries, we access Pthreads or Windows threads via portable code using the vath library. Most of the code examples have a vath version and an OpenMP version and, whenever relevant, a TBB version.

BOOK ORGANIZATION

Chapter 1 reviews the basic concepts and features of current computing platforms needed to set the stage for concurrent and parallel programming. Particular attention is paid to the impact of the multicore evolution of computing architectures, as well as other basic issues having an impact on efficient software development, such as the hierarchical memory organization, or the increased impact of rapidly evolving heterogeneous architectures incorporating specialized computing platforms like Intel Xeon Phi and GPU accelerators.

Chapter 2 introduces a number of basic concepts and facts on multithreading processing that are totally generic and independent of the different programming environments. They summarize the very general features that determine the way multithreading is implemented in existing computing platforms.

Chapter 3 introduces threads in detail. First, the programming interfaces proposed by Pthreads, Windows, and C++11 to create and run a team of worker threads are discussed, with the help of specific examples. Then, a portable thread management utility from the vath library is introduced, encapsulating the basic programming interfaces. Finally, a first look at OpenMP is taken to show how the same thread management features are declined in this environment. A few examples introduce some basic multithreading issues, like thread safety or thread synchronization. This initial part of the book adopts the traditional *thread-centric programming style* in which the activity of each thread in the application is perfectly identified.

Chapter 4 examines the thread safety issue for function calls: under what conditions a library function provides the correct, expected service when asynchronously called by several threads in a multithreaded environment? Random number generators are used as examples of functions that are not thread-safe. A detailed discussion follows, concerning the thread-specific storage tools proposed by different programming environments (OpenMP, TBB, C++11, Windows) in order to enforce thread safety in functions that are not by nature thread-safe. Best practices concerning the thread-specific storage tools are discussed.

Chapters 5 and 6 deal with the fundamental issue of thread synchronization. Two basic thread synchronization primitives – mutual exclusion and event synchronization – are introduced. Mutual exclusion deals with thread safety in shared data accesses, and in its simplest forms this primitive is easy to use in application programming. Chapter 5 examines in detail the mutual exclusion interfaces available in the five programming environments, underlining the different additional features proposed by each one of them. Then, atomic operations are introduced as an efficient alternative to mutual exclusion in some specific cases, and the way they operate in OpenMP is reviewed (an in-depth discussion of atomic operations is reserved to Chapter 8). Finally, the concurrent container classes provided by TBB are described. They correspond to extensions of the Standard Template Library containers having internally built-in thread safety, not requiring explicit mutual exclusion in their data accesses. This chapter concludes with a number of observations concerning mutual exclusion pitfalls and best practices.

Chapter 6 is concerned with event synchronization, namely, how to force a thread to wait for an event triggered by another thread (an event can be, for example, a change of value of some shared data item). A detailed pedagogical discussion of the event synchronization primitives in Pthreads, Windows, and C++11 is presented. However, direct use of these event synchronization primitives is indeed low-level programming, and they are never used as such in the rest of the book. They will show up encapsulated in higher level, easy-to-use vath utilities discussed in Chapter 9.

Chapter 7 focuses on the fundamental problem in shared memory programming: given the asynchronous behavior of threads and the hierarchical structure of the memory system, how can we know for sure that a shared data access retrieves the correct, expected data value? This problem leads to the notion of memory consistency model, and a simple, high-level discussion of the relevance of this concept is presented. This leads to the fundamental conclusion of this chapter: mutual exclusion, initially introduced to enforce thread safety in memory write operations, is also required to enforce memory consistency in memory read operations.

On the basis of the previous memory consistency concepts, Chapter 8 presents a rather detailed discussion of the powerful atomic classes proposed by C++11 and TBB, as well as the Windows atomic services. Besides the obvious use in replacing mutex locking, this chapter discusses the way they can be used to implement efficient, custom synchronization utilities. First, the discussion focuses on the way to enforce thread safety in shared data accesses, not using mutual exclusion: the so-called lock-free algorithms. Next, it is shown how the memory consistency constraints embedded in the atomic services are used to implement custom synchronization patterns based on "happens before" relations among operations in different threads. Two examples are proposed, implementing synchronization utilities incorporated in the vath library.

Chapter 9 presents an overview of high-level thread synchronization utilities incorporated in the vath library. They implement synchronization patterns common in applications programming (synchronized memory read-writes, Boolean locks, blocking barriers, reader-writer locks, concurrent queues) that are not immediately available in OpenMP. A pure OpenMP version of some these utilities is also provided. The discussion on the scope and impact of these utilities, as well as the examples proposed, is designed to significantly contribute to sharpen the understanding of thread synchronization pitfalls and best practices.

Chapters 10 and 11 are the core of this book: the presentation of the OpenMP and Intel TBB programming environments. The focus moves at this point to thread pool interfaces—the underlying architecture of both programming environments—where threads are created first and wait silently in a blocked state to be activated to execute a task. The traditional OpenMP programming model relies on a thread-centric pool, in the sense that there is a clear mapping between parallel tasks and threads, and it is possible to know at any time what every thread is doing. If more parallelism in needed in the applications, more threads are added to the pool. Nearly 10 years ago, an alternative programming model emerged, pioneered by Cilk [3], in which any number of parallel tasks are executed by a fixed number of threads, their execution being organized in an innovative way with a substantial amount of intelligence in the task scheduler itself. In such a task-centric environment, it is not possible to know what every individual thread is doing at a given time. TBB first implemented this model as a standalone library, and at about the same time OpenMP started to integrate task-centric software technologies in the 3.0 and 3.1 versions. The recent 4.0 version also makes a substantial step in this direction. Therefore, at this point readers are led to move progressively from thinking about threads to thinking about parallel tasks. The focus starts to move from thread centric to task-centric programming, particularly adapted to irregular, recursive, or unbalanced parallel contexts.

Chapter 10 presents a complete overview of OpenMP: the traditional programming model as well as a full discussion and examples of the new features incorporated in the latest OpenMP 4.0 release. Particular attention is given to the pitfalls and best practices related to the task directive. Besides the 4.0 extension of the task API incorporating a substantial number of additional task-centric features, the other major 4.0 extensions are also reviewed, like the cancellation of parallel constructs, thread affinity, and directives for vectorization and code offloading to external accelerators.

Chapter 11 concentrates on the TBB programming environment. TBB proposes a number of useful standalone utilities, already discussed in previous chapters. This chapter concentrates on the high-level TBB programming environment, based on a number of easy-to-use, STL like automatic parallelization algorithms that cope with a variety of different parallel patterns. Then, the discussion moves to a recent programming interface providing a simplified access to the most relevant features of the task scheduler, and several of the examples proposed in the OpenMP chapter are reexamined in this context. The discussion of the full task scheduler API is delayed to Chapter 16.

Chapter 12 discusses yet another thread management utilities: the SPool and NPool thread pool classes proposed by the vath library, implementing, respectively, a thread-centric or a task-centric programming environment. The SPool class has already been used to implement simple parallel patterns in previous chapters. Our motivation in developing these thread pools was not to compete with professional, well-established programming standards, but to benefit from some additional programming comfort in some specific cases not easily handled by OpenMP. Unlike OpenMP or TBB, thread pools are explicitly created by the user. An application can dispose of several independent pools, and parallel jobs can be submitted to all of them. Client threads that submit jobs are always external to the pools, but they are correctly synchronized with the jobs they submit. The task scheduler of the NPool utility is less refined than those implemented in OpenMP or TBB, but the pool can run most of the OpenMP or TBB examples proposed in the two previous chapters. These environment makes it very easy to run several parallel routines in parallel, and an explicit example of the added value they provide is presented at the end of the chapter.

The three following chapters discuss a few full applications taken from computational sciences, each one concentrating on one specific parallel context. The purpose here is to clearly understand the multithreaded architecture of the applications and the thread synchronization requirements that follow. We also look in detail at their scaling properties and at the impact on performance of excessive synchronization overhead. It is here that an example is met in which mediocre scaling properties are improved by the use of custom synchronization tools constructed with TBB or C++11 utilities. Chapter 13 discusses a molecular dynamics application—computing the trajectories of a set of interacting particles—exhibiting a substantial demand of barrier synchronization. Chapter 14 deals with data parallelism, developing two classical examples of domain decomposition in solving partial differential equations. Chapter 15 discusses pipelining, a kind of control parallelism totally different from data parallelism. Two complete pipelining applications are developed, one of them dealing with a image treatment problem. In all cases, vath, OpenMP and TBB versions of the code are proposed (which are sometimes very similar).

> The examples in Chapters 13–15 deal with simple but realistic scientific problems. However, a significant pedagogical effort has been made to make them accessible to readers not having a scientific background. Simple descriptions are provided of the relevance and interest of the problem, but the discussion concentrates on the solutions to the programming challenges raised by the application.

Last but not least, Chapter 16 deals with the programming interfaces enabling direct access to the TBB task scheduler. This subject, admittedly a rather advanced subject on task parallelism, is nevertheless interesting and relevant. It was often emphasized in preceding chapters that the event synchronization primitives and high-level utilities discussed in Chapters 6 and 8 are not adapted to be used in task-centric environments (TBB, NPool, or the OpenMP task API), because they are programmed inside parallel tasks, but they really synchronize the underlying executing threads. This is fine as long as a controlled, one-to-one mapping of tasks to threads is established. However, in task-centric environments this issue is handled by introducing specific task synchronization features in the task scheduler itself, enabling programmers to synchronize tasks, not threads. Chapter 10 covers a OpenMP 4.0 extension, based on the new depends directive, that goes in this direction. The TBB task scheduler API implements task synchronization by using advanced scheduler features to organize the way the parallel tasks are scheduled and executed. In Chapter 16, a number of task synchronization examples are provided. In addition, the task scheduler is used to explore possible optimization strategies designed to improve the performance of the molecular dynamics application discussed in Chapter 13.

Finally, a few more words about support software, which can be downloaded from the book site http://booksite.elsevier.com/9780128037614. There are, in early chapters, some examples that target specific Pthreads, Windows, or C++11 features. But the majority of examples access the basic library utilities through the portable vath library presented in Chapters 9 and 12. The examples are therefore fully portable, and it is up to the reader to decide what implementation to use. Annex A provides a complete description of the accompanying software, as well as detailed instructions for installation of the different software components, and for compilation and execution of the vath library and the code examples.

Biography

Victor Alessandrini After obtaining a PhD in Theoretical Physics in Argentina—where he was born—he spent several years as a visiting scientist, working in theoretical particle physics in different research laboratories in the United States and Europe, in particular, at the Centre Européen des Recherches Nucleaires (CERN) theory division. In 1978, he was appointed full professor at the University of Paris XI in Orsay, France. His basic interests shifted to computational sciences in the early 1990s, when he was the Founding Director of IDRIS supercomputing center in Orsay, which he directed until 2009. In 2004-2009, he coordinated the DEISA European supercomputing infrastructure, a consortium of national supercomputing centers that pioneered the deployment of high-performance computing services on continental scale. He is currently emeritus Research Director at "Maison de la Simulation," a CEA-CNRS-INRIA-University research laboratory providing high-level support to HPC. In 2011, he was named "Chevalier de l'Ordre National du Mérite" by the French Republic.

Acknowledgments

I am deeply indebted to my colleagues at IDRIS supercomputing center—in particular, to Denis Girou, Pierre-François Lavallée, and Philippe Collinet—for more than 20 years of sharing vision and insights in high-performance computing.

I have also benefited from the stimulating environment of Maison de la Simulation, and I am indebted to Edouard Audit for his warm support and Pierre Kestener for a critical reading of some of the book chapters.

I am also grateful to Arch Robison from Intel Corporation, for exchanges that sharpened my understanding of TBB.

INTRODUCTION AND OVERVIEW

1.1 PROCESSES AND THREADS

Multithreading is today a mandatory software technology for taking full advantage of the capabilities of modern computing platforms of any kind, and a good understanding of the overall role and impact of threads, as well as the place they take in the computational landscape, is useful before embarking on a detailed discussion of this subject.

We are all permanently running standalone applications in all kinds of computing devices: servers, laptops, smartphones, or multimedia devices. All the data processing devices available in our environment have a master piece of software—the operating system (OS)—that controls and manages the device, running different applications at the user's demands. A standalone application corresponds to a *process* run by the operating system. A process can be seen as a black box that owns a number of protected hardware and software resources; namely, a block of memory, files to read and write data, network connections to communicate eventually with other processes or devices, and, last but not least, code in the form of a list of instructions to be executed. Process resources are protected in the sense that no other process running on the same platform can access and use them. A process has also access to one or several central processing units—called CPU for short—providing the computing cycles needed to execute the application code.

One of the most basic concepts we will be using is the notion of *concurrency*, which is about two or more activities happening at the same time. Concurrency is a natural part of life: we all can, for example, walk and talk at the same time. In computing platforms, we speak of concurrency when several different activities can advance and make progress at the same time, rather than one after the other. This is possible because CPU cycles are not necessarily exclusively owned by one individual process. The OS can allocate CPU cycles to several different processes at the same time (a very common situation in general). It allocates, for example, successive time slices on a given CPU to different processes, thereby providing the illusion that the processes are running simultaneously. This is called multitasking. In this case, processes are not really running simultaneously but, at a human time scale, they advance together, which is why it is appropriate to speak about concurrent execution.

One special case of concurrency happens when there are sufficient CPU resources so that they do not need to be shared: each activity has exclusive ownership of the CPU resource it needs. In this optimal case, we may speak of *parallel execution*. But remember that parallel execution is just a special case of concurrency.

As stated, a process incorporates a list of instructions to be executed by the CPU. An ordinary sequential application consists of a single *thread of execution*, i.e., a single list of instructions that are bound to be executed on a single CPU. In a C-C++ programming environment, this single thread of execution is coded in the main() function. In a multithreaded application, a process integrates several independent lists of instructions that execute asynchronously on one or several CPU. Chapter 3 shows in detail how the different multithreading programming environments allow the initial main thread to install other execution streams, equivalent to main() but totally disconnected from it. Obviously, multithreading is focused on enhancing the process performance, either by isolating independent tasks that can be executed concurrently by different threads, or by activating several CPUs to share the work needed to perform a given parallel task.

1.2 OVERVIEW OF COMPUTING PLATFORMS

A computing platform consists essentially of one or more CPUs and a memory block where the application data and code are stored. There are also peripheral devices to communicate with the external world, like DVD drives, hard disks, graphic cards, or network interfaces.

Figure 1.1 shows a schematic view of a personal computer. For the time being, think of the processor chip as corresponding to a single CPU, which used to be the case until the advent of the multicore evolution, circa 2004, when processor chips started to integrate several CPUs. The data processing performance of the simple platform shown in Figure 1.1 depends basically on the performance of the CPU, i.e., the rate at which the CPU is able to execute the basic instructions of the instruction set. But it also depends critically on the rate at which data can be moved to and from the memory: a fast processor is useless if it has no data to work upon.

The rate at which the CPU is able to execute basic instructions is determined by the internal processor clock speed. Typically, the execution of a basic low-level instruction may take up to a few cycles, depending on the instruction complexity. The clock frequency is directly related to the *peak*

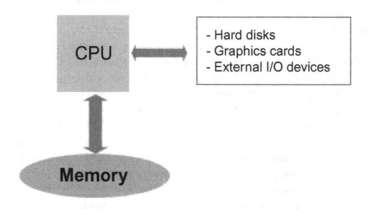

FIGURE 1.1

Schematic architecture of a simple computing platform.

performance, which is the theoretical performance in an ideal context in which processor cycles are not wasted. The original Intel 8086 processor in the late 70 s ran at 5 MHz (i.e., 5 millions of cycles per second). Today, processors run at about 3 GHz (3000 millions of cycles per second). This represents a 600× increase in frequency, achieved in just over 20 years.

Memory performance is a completely different issue. The time T needed to move to or from memory a data block of N bytes is given by:

$$T = L + N/B$$

where L is the *latency*, namely, the access time needed to trigger the transfer, and B is the *bandwidth*, namely, the speed at which data is moved once the transfer has started.

It is important to keep in mind that, in the case we are considering, moving data from memory to the processor or vice versa:

- The *bandwidth* is a property of the network connecting the two devices. Bandwidths are controlled by network technologies.
- The *latency* is an intrinsic property of the memory device.

It turns out that memory latencies are very difficult to tame. At the time of the 8086, memory latencies were close to the processor clock, so it was possible to feed the processor at a rate guaranteeing roughly the execution of one instruction per clock cycle. But memory latencies have not decreased as dramatically as processor frequencies have increased. Today, it takes a few hundreds of clock cycles to trigger a memory access. Therefore, in ordinary memory bound applications the processors tend to starve, and typically their *sustained performances* are a small fraction (about 10%) of the theoretical peak performance promised by the processor frequency. As we will see again and again, this is the crucial issue for application performance, and lots of ingenuity in the design of hardware and system software has gone into taming this bottleneck, which is called the *memory wall*

1.2.1 SHARED MEMORY MULTIPROCESSOR SYSTEMS

The next step in computing platform complexity are the so-called *symmetric multiprocessor* (SMP) systems, where a network interconnect links a number of processor chips to a common, shared memory block. Symmetric means that all CPUs have an equivalent status with respect to memory accesses. Memory is shared, and all CPUs can access the whole common memory address space. They are shown in Figure 1.2.

For reasons that will be discussed in Chapter 7, coherency in shared memory accesses prevents SMP platforms from scaling to very large numbers of CPUs. Today, shared memory systems do not exceed 60 CPUs. This limit will perhaps increase in the future, but it is bound to remain limited. These systems are very useful as medium-size servers. They can perform efficient multitasking by allocating different applications on different CPUs. On the other hand, a multithreaded application can benefit from the availability of a reasonable number of CPUs to enhance the process performance.

However, note that the SMP computing platforms are not perfectly symmetric. The reason is that a huge, logically shared memory block is normally constructed by using, say, M identical memory devices. Therefore, the SMP network interconnect is really connecting all N processor chips to all M memory blocks. According to the topology and the quality of the network, a given CPU may

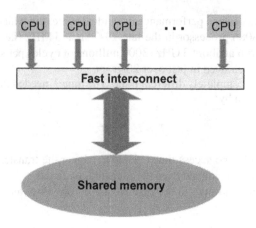

FIGURE 1.2

Symmetric multiprocessor shared memory platform.

not be at the same "effective distance" of all *M* memory blocks, and the access times may be non-uniform with mild differences in memory access performance. This kind of computing platform is called a NUMA (Non-Uniform Memory Access) architecture. This observation is sometimes relevant in multithreaded programming, because performance may be optimized by placing data items as close as possible to the CPU running the thread that is accessing them. This issue—placing threads as near as possible to the data they access—is called *memory affinity*. It plays a significant role in multithreaded programming.

1.2.2 DISTRIBUTED MEMORY MULTIPROCESSOR SYSTEMS

The only way to move beyond SMPs to large massive parallel computers is to abandon the shared memory architecture and move to a *distributed memory* systems, as shown in Figure 1.3. These platforms are essentially clusters of SMPs; namely, a collection of SMP computing platforms linked by

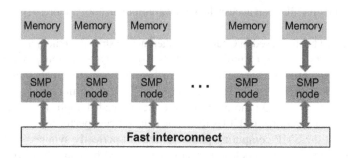

FIGURE 1.3

Distributed memory computing platform.

yet another, higher level network interconnect. Each SMP has its own private memory address space. When running a huge parallel application that engages several SMP nodes, CPUs in different SMP nodes communicate by explicit message-passing protocols.

The quality of these platforms as parallel platforms depends essentially on the quality of the network interconnect. Standard clusters integrate commodity networks, while more ambitious supercomputers tuned for extreme massive parallelism—like the IBM BlueGene systems—incorporate proprietary networks that support highly optimized point-to-point and collective communication operations. There is no limit to the scalability of these systems other than those arising from network performance. Today, systems incorporating several hundred thousands of CPUs are in operation.

Large parallel applications consist of independent processes running on different SMPs and communicating with one another via an explicit communication protocol integrated in a programming model, called the *Message Passing Interface* (MPI). Each process acts on its own private data set, and a number of synchronization and data transfer primitives allow them to communicate to other processes the updated data values they need to proceed. Programming these systems is more difficult than programming ordinary SMP platforms because the programmer is in general lacking a global view of the application's data set: data is spread across the different SMP nodes, and each autonomous process accesses only a section of the complete data set. However, on the other hand, MPI is the only programming model that can cope with scalable, massive parallelism.

1.2.3 MULTICORE EVOLUTION

Since the early 1970s the sustained evolution of silicon technologies has followed a trend initially underlined by Gordon Moore, one of the Intel founders: *the number of transistors that can be placed inexpensively on an integrated circuit doubles approximately every two years*, and observation that is known under the name of Moore's law. This exponential growth of the transistor count in a chip—arising from the smaller transistor sizes—generated a golden age in computing systems, not only because a given surface of silicon real state could accommodate more transistors, but also because the transistor performance increased with decreasing size: smaller transistors commuted faster—which meant faster chips—and used less working voltages and currents, i.e., less power.

A seminal paper written in 1974 by Robert Dennard and colleagues [4] at the IBM T.J. Watson Research Center, described the scaling rules for obtaining simultaneous improvements in transistor density, switching speeds and power dissipation. These scaling principles—known as Dennard scaling—determined the roadmap followed by the semiconductor industry for producing sustained transistor improvements. Table 1.1, reproduced from Dennard's paper, summarizes the transistor or circuit parameters under ideal scaling. In this table k is the scaling factor for transistor size.

The implications of Dennard scaling are obvious: reducing by a half the transistor size multiplies by 4 the number of transistors in a given area *at constant power dissipation*, and in addition each transistor is operating twice as fast. This is the reason why for more than three decades we enjoyed the benefits of automatic performance enhancements: processor working frequencies (and, therefore, their peak performance) doubled every 18 months. This was a very comfortable situation; it was sometimes sufficient to wait for the next generation of CPU technology to benefit from an increased applications performance. Parallel processing was mainly an issue of choice and opportunity, mostly limited to supercomputing or mission critical applications.

Table 1.1 Dennard Scaling Results for Circuit Performance	
Dennard Scaling	
Device or Circuit Parameter	**Scaling Factor**
Device dimension	1/k
Voltage V	1/k
Current I	1/k
Capacitance	1/k
Delay time per circuit VC/I	1/k
Power dissipation per circuit VI	1/k
Power density VI/area	1

This golden age came to an end about 2004, when a power dissipation wall was hit. As transistors reach smaller sizes, new previously negligible physical effects emerge—mainly quantum effects—that invalidate Dennard's scaling. Working voltages essentially stopped shrinking at this time, and today clock speeds are stuck because it is no longer possible to make them work faster. Moore's law still holds: it is always possible to double the transistor count about every 2 years, but shrinking the transistor size does not make them better, as was the case when Dennard scaling applied.

Today, the only benefits of shrinking transistor sizes are disposing of more functions per chip and/or lower costs per function.

For this reason, the last decade has witnessed the multicore evolution. Processor chips are no longer identified with a single CPU, as they contain now multiple processing units called cores. Since clock speeds can no longer be increased, the only road for enhanced performance is the cooperative operation of multiple processing units, at the price of making parallel processing mandatory. Virtually all processor vendors have adopted this technology, and even the simplest laptop is today a SMP platform. Multicore processor chips are now called *sockets*. The present situation can be summarized as follows:

- The number of cores per socket doubles every 2 years.
- Clock speeds tend to mildly decrease. In any case, they are stabilized around a couple of GHz.

It follows that the most general computing platform has the following hierarchical structure, as shown in Figure 1.4:

- Several cores inside a socket
- A few sockets interconnected around a shared memory block to implement a SMP node
- A substantial number of SMP nodes interconnected in a distributed memory cluster

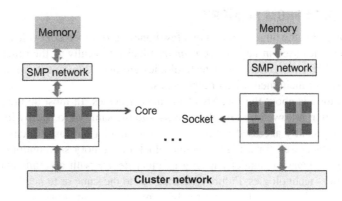

FIGURE 1.4

Generic cluster computing platform.

In such a system, three programming models can be implemented:

- Shared memory multithreaded programming inside a SMP node. From a programmer's point of view, the logical view of a SMP node is just a number of virtual CPUs—the cores—sharing a common memory address space. It does not matter whether the different cores are in the same or in different sockets.
- Flat MPI distributed memory programming across cores. In this approach, each core in the system runs a full MPI process, and they all communicate via MPI message passing primitives. It does not matter whether the MPI processes are all in the same or in different SMP nodes.
- A hybrid MPI-Threads model in which each MPI process is internally multithreaded, running on several cores. These MPI processes communicate with one another via the MPI message passing protocol.

This book covers the first programming model discussed above; namely, shared memory application programming on multicore platforms. Chapter 2 presents the different ways in which a multithreaded process can be scheduled and run on these platforms.

1.3 MEMORY SYSTEM OF COMPUTING PLATFORMS

A number of programming issues that will be encountered later on require a clear understanding of the operation of a computing platform memory system. As stated, one of the most important performance issues is the *memory wall*; namely, the mismatch between the processor clock and the high latencies involved in each main memory access. The memory system of modern computing platforms is designed to reduce as much as possible the memory wall impact on the application's performance.

1.3.1 READING DATA FROM MEMORY

The first observation is that the huge latencies of a few hundreds of processor cycles are a characteristic of the *sdram* technologies used in large *main memory* blocks, typically of the order of 2-4 gigabytes per core in current platforms. Other, faster technologies are available, but it would be prohibitively expensive to use them for main memories of these sizes.

The next observation is about the *locality* of memory accesses. In most applications, access to a memory location is often followed by repeated accesses to the same or to nearby locations. Then, the basic idea is to store recently accessed memory blocks in smaller but faster memory devices. When a memory location is accessed for a read, a whole block of memory surrounding the required data is copied to a *cache memory*, a smaller capacity memory device with a significantly lower latency, based on faster memory technologies. Future read accesses to the same or to nearby memory locations contained in the block will retrieve the data directly from the cache memory in a much more efficient way, avoiding costly main memory access. The memory blocks copied in this way are called *cache lines*.

Cache memories are significantly smaller than the main memory. It is then obvious that, when reads are very frequent, the cache lines will often be overwritten with new data, thereby invalidating previously cached data values. Various algorithms are used to choose the cache lines that are to be reused, with different impacts on performance.

These observations lead to a hierarchical multilevel memory system in which cache lines at one level are copied to a faster, lower level memory device. As long as data is read, it is retrieved from the lowest level cache memory holding a valid data value (we will soon discuss what a valid data value is). Figure 1.5 shows a typical organization of the memory hierarchy, exhibiting two intermediate cache levels—called L1 and L2—between the main memory and the *core registers*, which are the ultrafast memory buffers internal to the executing core, where data is deposited before being processed by the core functional units. Typically, core registers are 4(8) bytes wide for 32(64) bit architectures. It is important to keep in mind that current CPUs are *load-store architectures* in which data is *always* moved to core registers before being processed. Direct manipulation of memory locations does not occur in these architectures.

The L1 caches are rather small but fast memory blocks used both as data caches—to store the most recently accessed data—as well as instruction caches—to store the instructions to be executed by the core. Because they are partly used to store the instructions to be executed, the L1 caches *are never*

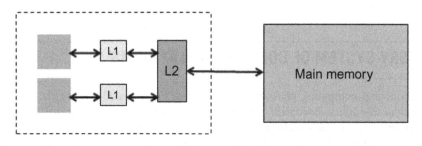

FIGURE 1.5

Hierarchical memory system.

shared: threads running on different cores have their own, proprietary instruction stack. The L2 caches, instead, only store data, and they may be shared by several cores. In most systems, there is yet another cache level—called L3—between the L2 caches and the main memory, but this is not critical to our discussion.

Typical values of cache lines are 128 (or more) bytes for L2 and 32 bytes for L1. Typical latencies are 4 cycles for the L1 cache, 12 cycles for the L2 cache, and roughly 150-200 cycles for main memory. This memory hierarchy enhances memory performance in two ways. On one hand, it reduces the memory latency for recently used data. On the other hand, it reduces the number of accesses to the main memory, thereby limiting the usage of the network interconnect and the bandwidth demand. Indeed, accesses to L1 and L2 caches do not require network activation because they are part of the processor socket.

1.3.2 WRITING DATA TO MEMORY

When a data value is changed in a processor register, the CPU must proceed to update the original main memory location. Typically, the new data value is updated first in the L2 cache, and from there on the network interconnect is activated to update the main memory. The following issues arise every time a new data value is updated in the L2 cache:

- First, the cache memory is no longer coherent with the main memory. How and when the main memory is updated is system dependent, but there is in most cases a time delay: the memory update is not *atomic* (instantaneous). Some systems choose to delay the writes in order to collect several data items in a *write buffer*, and then move them in a unique memory access in order to pay the big latency cost only once.
- Secondly, the updated cache memory is no longer coherent with other L2 caches in other sockets that may contain the old invalid value of the updated variable. The CPU that has performed the update must therefore inform all other CPUs engaged in the application that the relevant cache line is invalid, and that further reads of data in this cache line must get the data values from main memory. This is the *cache coherency issue*.
- Finally, because of the time delays in memory updates mentioned before, those threads that must get updated data values from main memory must know, in one way or another, *when the new updated values are available*. They must make sure that, in performing a read, they recover the last updated value of the target data item. This is the *memory consistency issue*.

These two issues—memory coherency and consistency—are analyzed in more detail in Chapter 7. It is obvious that the cache coherency mechanism requires a persistent communication context among sockets in a SMP platform, and this is the main reason why it is not possible to extend a shared memory SMP architecture into the massive parallel domain. It is just too expensive and unrealistic to try to enforce cache coherency among hundreds or thousands of sockets in a SMP node.

In discussing the performance and the behavior or several real applications in Chapters 13–15, we will have the opportunity to discuss how the memory access patterns impacts the application performance.

1.4 PARALLEL PROCESSING INSIDE CORES

The essence of multithreaded programming is the capability of coordinating the activity of several CPUs in the execution of a given application. In principle, whatever happens inside a single core is not directly relevant to multithreaded programming. However, it is extremely relevant to the overall performance of the application, and there are some capabilities of current CPU architectures that must be integrated into the developer's options.

There is an amazing amount of parallel processing inside a core. After all, millions of transistors operate concurrently most of the time. After translating the application code into basic assembler language, hardware, system, and compiler software cooperate to take as much as possible advantage of *instruction level parallelism*. This means running the basic instructions in parallel whenever it is possible to do so while respecting the program integrity.

Instruction-level parallelism is too low level to constitute a direct concern to programmers. But there are other parallel structures that are definitely worth their attention: hyperthreading and vectorization.

1.4.1 HYPERTHREADING

Hyperthreading is the CPU capability of *simultaneously* running several threads. This means, very precisely, that the core has the capability of interleaving the execution of instructions arising from different execution streams, while maintaining the program integrity. These different execution streams interleaved in hyperthreading are in general targeting different data sets, and Chapter 2 will explain how the multithreaded execution environment is organized in such a way as to make this possible.

Hyperthreading should not be confused with another feature also to be discussed in the next chapter: a core can service several threads by running them one at a time, in a round robin fashion, allocating CPU time slices to all of them. This is a very general operating system feature that has always existed in multithreading, enabling the possibility of over-committing threads on a given core. In this case, different threads access *successively* the CPU cycles. In a hyperthreading operation, they are *simultaneously* sharing CPU cycles.

The main reason for introducing hyperthreading capabilities in modern CPU architectures is to make better use of the CPU cycles, e.g., in accumulating efforts to beat the memory wall. If a thread needs to wait for memory data, there may be tens or hundreds of cycles wasted doing nothing. These cycles can then be used to run other thread instructions. Hyperthreading has different impacts on different architectures. In general-purpose CPUs, hyperthreading hides occasional latencies, and its impact on performance strongly depends on the code profile. However, there are more specialized architectures—like the IBM BlueGene platforms, or Intel Xeon Phi coprocessor discussed in the following—where for different reasons hyperthreading is required to benefit from the full single-core performance.

The name *hardware threads* is used to refer to the number of threads that a core can simultaneously execute.

1.4.2 VECTORIZATION

Vectorization is another parallel processing technique that enhances the single core performance. In a multithreaded environment, different threads execute different instruction streams acting on different data sets. This parallel pattern is called MIMD, meaning Multiple Instruction, Multiple Data.

Vectorization, instead, implements a totally different parallel pattern called SIMD—Single Instruction, Multiple Data—in which a single instruction operates on several data items in one shot, as is explained in detail below.

Let us consider a simple example, the execution of the operation a += b; where a and b are vectors of doubles of size N. This corresponds to the execution of the loop:

```
double a[N], b[N];
...
for(int n=0; n<N; n++)
   {
   a[n] += b[n];
   }
```

LISTING 1.1

Executing a vector operation

Figure 1.6 shows the internal CPU registers, where the target data for operations is stored. The scalar registers are 64 bits wide, and can hold a double. In the default scalar mode of operation, the vector addition is computed by adding one component at a time. The values of a[n] and b[n] are loaded into Ra and Rb registers, respectively. Then, the operation Ra = Ra+Rb is performed, and the value of Ra is copied to a[n].

Cores with SIMD capabilities have wide vector registers that can hold several vector components. In the Intel Sandy Bridge processor, vector registers are 256 bits wide, holding either four doubles or eight floats, and we speak in this case of four or eight SIMD lanes, respectively. Vector instructions can act simultaneously in one shot on all the SIMD lanes, boosting the floating-point performance. In vector mode, the loop above is computed by loading in RVa and RBv a block of four a[] and b[] components, and acting simultaneously on all of them.

Implementing wide vector registers in the core architecture is not sufficient. The capability of loading the wide vector registers as fast as the scalar registers is also required, which in turn demands an

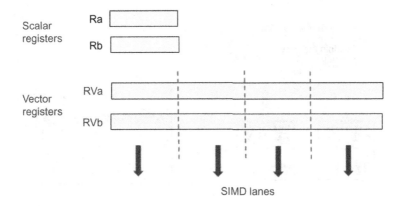

SIMD lanes

FIGURE 1.6

Scalar versus vector processing.

enhanced communication bandwidth between the core and the L2 cache. When the code profile is well adapted, vectorization can provide significant performance enhancements in computationally bound applications. Vectorization is re-examined in more detail in Chapter 10, when discussing the OpenMP 4.0 new vectorization directives. In Chapters 13–14, the impact of vectorization on real application examples is assessed.

1.5 EXTERNAL COMPUTATIONAL DEVICES

The last few years have witnessed impressive development of external computational devices that connect to a socket via the standard network interfaces for external devices. They act as a co-processor executing code blocks offloaded from the CPU cores, boosting the execution performance for suitable computationally intensive code blocks—called *kernels*—in the application. They are seen from the host CPU as another computational engine available in the network.

External computational devices are shown in Figure 1.7. They all have an internal device memory hierarchy as well as a large number of cores for computation. There are today two very different kinds of external devices: GPUs (Graphical Processing Units)—accelerator devices capable of executing basic computational kernels with very high performance and very low power consumption—and the Intel's Xeon Phi coprocessor.

1.5.1 GPUs

Initially, graphics accelerator cards—called GPUs, for Graphical Processing Units, used for rendering visualization images—were occasionally used to perform other computations that could be rephrased in terms of the graphical programming API. Working on a two-dimensional image—a two-dimensional array of pixels—is a highly parallel affair, because most of the time sets of pixels can be simultaneously updated. Graphics hardware and software are strongly data parallel. GPUs map the graphics algorithms to a large set of independent execution streams (threads) all executing the same operations on different sectors of the target data set.

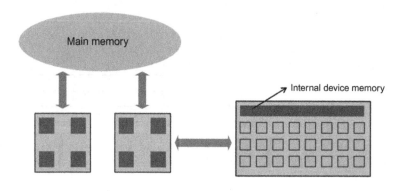

FIGURE 1.7

Generic external computational device.

A major step was taken in 2007 when NVIDIA Corporation realized the interest in allowing programmers to think of a GPU as a processor. Besides a substantial number of hardware improvements to reduce the gap between graphics accelerators and more standard computational engines, the CUDA C/C++ compiler, libraries and runtime software were introduced, enabling programmers to access the underlying data parallel computation model and develop applications adapted to this model. Graphics APIs were no longer needed to benefit from the GPU computing environment. Since then, the progress accomplished at the hardware and software levels is quite remarkable. Today, GPUs are very powerful computational engines, and part of their success is due to the fact that the computing cores, being very lightweight, beat the power dissipation wall providing an excellent ratio of computing power (flops) per dissipated watt.

When discussing GPU accelerators, the concept of *heterogeneous computing* is important, because the GPU computing engine's design requirements are different from those guiding CPU design. The CPU design is *latency driven*: making a single thread of execution as efficient as possible. A substantial amount of the silicon real state in a CPU is devoted to control logic—needed to implement instruction-level parallelism or to provide the low-level interfaces required to run an operating system—or to cache memories needed to optimize memory accesses. Further, CPUs have a limited number of cores. GPUs, instead, are *throughput driven*. They have today tens of thousands of *very lightweight* cores, each one involving very limited silicon real state because they are not intended to run an operating system. Indeed, GPU cores execute a restricted number of instructions for computation and synchronization with other cores. The code blocks they execute are offloaded from the application running in the main computing platform they are connected to. GPU cores are in absolute terms substantially less efficient than CPU cores, but the performance impact comes from their important number mentioned above, which provides a huge potential throughput. An application's performance strongly depends on its capability to take advantage of the important amount of potential parallelism offered by the GPU. The interest of heterogeneous computing lies in the possibility of executing parts of the application in a standard platform and offloading to the GPU the execution of code blocks adapted to its architecture.

The fundamental performance-limiting factor in GPUs is, again, the memory wall. Current GPUs have no direct access to the main memory, and the target data set must be offloaded to the GPU together with the code to be run. Then, output results must be returned to the master code running in the main platform. In this context, the real achieved sustained performance strongly depends on the application profile. Excellent efficiency is obtained only if a substantial amount of computation can be performed with a limited amount of data transfers to and from the host CPU. GPU architectures are nevertheless evolving very fast, and the possibility of directly exchanging data between different GPUs is available today. Substantial improvements are expected in the future concerning their access performance to the platform main memory.

GPU programming requires specific programming environments (CUDA, OpenCL, OpenACL) capable of producing and offloading code and data to the GPU. These programming environments have matured greatly in the last few years, facilitating the dissemination and adoption of GPU programming. An important recent evolution is the recent OpenMP 4.0 extensions incorporating directives for offloading data and code blocks to accelerators, which will be reviewed in Chapter 10.

Code executed in GPUs must conform to the target architecture capabilities. Threads running on the GPU cores *are not* the general-purpose threads, running on a general-purpose CPU, which are the main subject of this book.

Today there is vast literature on GPUs. A good reference providing a broad coverage of this subject is D. Kirk and W. Hwu book, "Programming Massively Parallel Processors" [5]. Other useful references are "The CUDA Handbook" by N. Wilt [6] and "CUDA by Example" by J. Sanders and E. Kandrot [7].

1.5.2 INTEL XEON PHI

Intel's Xeon Phi chip is very different from GPUs. Like GPUs, it must be connected to a CPU host and can communicate with it. However, *Intel Xeon Phi is really a complete SMP node*. Rather than integrating hundreds or thousands of very lightweight cores that execute a limited instruction set, Intel Xeon Phi incorporates today 60 normal CPU cores that all execute a full and improved x86 instruction set and run a complete Linux operating system. The Xeon Phi chip integrates today 8 GB of shared memory (extension to 16 GB will soon be available). In fact, the chip is just a huge SMP node that can even work as a standalone computing platform. The only point to be underlined is that the Xeon Phi cores only access the internal chip shared memory. The access to the main memory of the computing platform goes, as in the GPU case, through the external device network interfaces that connect to the master CPU in the computing platform.

Since the Intel Xeon Phi is an ordinary SMP node, standard programming models are used to compile and run applications. All the distributed memory (MPI) and shared memory programming environments (Pthreads, OpenMP, TBB) we will be discussing in this book operate "as such" inside the Intel Xeon Phi. If needed, these programming environments are completed with a few directives that offload code blocks for execution on the coprocessor, or vice-versa. In fact, the coprocessor has three modes of execution:

- The main application runs on the master CPU, and specific code blocks are offloaded for execution in the coprocessor
- The main application runs on the coprocessor, and specific code blocks are offloaded for execution in the master CPU. This is very useful, for example, to perform computationally intensive operations on the Intel Xeon Phi, while offloading I/O operations for execution on the master CPU.
- Standalone SMP node: the whole application is run on the Intel Xeon Phi.

A very useful and complete reference to the Intel Xeon Phi coprocessor is the "Intel Xeon Phy Coprocessor" book by J. Jeffers and J. Reinders [8]. The online Intel Xeon Phy documentation can also be consulted [9].

1.6 FINAL COMMENTS

This chapter has reviewed the basic technological concepts related to shared memory programming. A somewhat more detailed discussion is available in the early chapters of D. Gove book "Multicore Application Programming" [10].

Threads have been with us for a very long time. All current operating systems support multithreading, and threads are needed—even for programmers not concerned by parallel programming—to enhance the performance of interactive applications. We all see every day Web pages where several animations are running without interruption. Each one of these animations is a Java applet running as a thread. These applets are just sequential flows of control executing inside the application, which is the browser himself. When the browser runs on a single processor system, the operating system creates the illusion that the different animations are simultaneous in time. In fact, the different applets get, one at a time in a round-robin fashion, access to the processor for a short interval of time called a *time slice*. This time slice is very short—typically a few milliseconds—as compared to the time scale for human perception.

The multicore evolution, and the fact that the number of cores per processor chip will keep increasing in the foreseeable future, has neatly enhanced the impact of multithreading. This software technology is today the only way to take full advantage of the enhanced performance of current computing systems.

INTRODUCING THREADS

2.1 APPLICATIONS AND PROCESSES

Applications executed in a computing platform run as an operating system process, *which is the basic unit of resource allocation to an application.* Indeed, when the application starts execution, the operating system allocates a number of resources to the process:

- A protected fraction of the available memory. Protected means that no other process can access it.
- File handles required by the application.
- Access to communication ports and I/O devices.
- A share of the CPU cycles available in the executing platform (multitasking).

The process executes first some startup code needed to allocate the resources and set up the application environment. Then, it proceeds to execute the main() function provided by the programmer. Figure 2.1 shows the way in which the memory block allocated to the process is organized by the operating system. There are three distinct memory domains:

- A memory region where the program global variables are allocated. Global variables are those declared outside the function main(), and they are naturally allocated by the startup code before main() starts.
- Another memory region, called the *heap*, is reserved for the dynamic memory allocations the application may eventually perform. This is the memory allocated by the library functions malloc() in C or new in C++.
- Finally, there is a memory buffer called the *stack*, which is used to allocate the local variables defined inside main(), as well as the local variables involved in all the possible nested function calls originating from main(), as we will soon explain.

Pointers—initialized to point to the address of some memory block by malloc() or by the operator new—can be declared either as global variables or as local variables to main(). For a sequential process this is not important, but this difference becomes relevant for multithreaded processes.

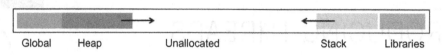

Global   Heap   Unallocated   Stack   Libraries

FIGURE 2.1

Memory organization in a sequential process.

2.1.1 ROLE OF THE STACK

The stack is a *container* in C++ language, used to store data, with a particular way of inserting or extracting data out of it. A clear understanding of its role is useful to understand a number of thread operation issues.

The stack operates like a pile of dishes: it is a LIFO (Last In, First Out) data structure where data can only inserted *(pushed)* or removed *(popped)* at the top. The stack buffer has an associated data item, the *stack pointer, SP*, which contains the address of the top of the stack. This address is of course increased (or decreased) when data is pushed (or popped). The addresses of the different data items stored in the stack are simply determined by their distances (offsets) to the stack pointer. When main() starts, its local variables are allocated in the stack.

There are several important reasons for using this kind of data structure for allocating local variables, having to do mainly with multithreading, that will be clarified later on. One important issue is the management of function calls. The discussion that follows captures the essential ideas, avoiding unnecessary complications. Details may differ across different computing platforms and operating systems.

When the compiler writes the code for a function, it assumes that its local variables are placed in a well-defined order—the order in which they have been declared inside the function code—in a stack. In the function code, their addresses are manipulated as offsets with respect to a *yet unknown* stack pointer. Indeed, at compile time the place in memory where the stack buffer will be allocated is not yet known. The compiler simply assumes that the correct SP address is stored in a specific, dedicated processor register. When main() starts, the stack memory address is known, and so is the stack pointer SP after the local variables have been allocated on the stack.

When a function is called, the following steps are taken by the process (see Figure 2.2):

- The return address where the code must resume execution after the function returns is pushed to the stack.
- The argument values that need to be passed to the function (represented by the first buffer following the return address in Figure 2.2) are also pushed to the stack.
- At this point, execution is transferred to the called function.

When the called function starts execution, it pushes all its local variables to the stack and performs its work (see Figure 2.2). The situation is now very much the same as before the call. The local variables of the running function are sitting just below the new stack pointer, and the argument values passed to the function are also sitting in a well-defined place on the stack, so that the function code can access them. The compiler has also determined their addresses in terms of their offsets with respect to the new stack pointer.

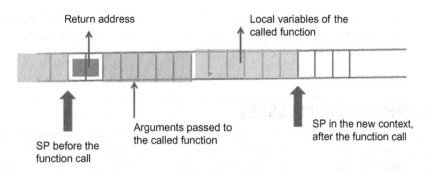

FIGURE 2.2

Behavior of the stack in a function call.

When the function returns, it destroys its local variables and the function arguments by popping them from the stack. After that, the runtime code pops the return address that was previously pushed by the caller and transfers control to this address. At this point, the original state of the caller stack is fully restored. It is clear that this mechanism is recursive, supporting nested function calls.

Application programmers do not really need to understand how function calls operate in the background, but this discussion is useful because it helps to better understand a few best practices required for multithreaded programming.

2.1.2 MULTITASKING

Multitasking is the capability of the operating system of running several applications at the same time. It is therefore deeply related to the OS capability for managing shared resources, and in particular for arbitrating conflicts resulting from resource over-commitment. In a multitasking environment, the totality of the computer's resources (memory, files, CPU time) are allocated to different applications, and they are managed in such a way that each one of them gets a share according to specific priority policies.

When CPU resources are over-committed, the operating system schedules the different active processes by performing a process switch at regular time intervals, distributing the available CPU cycles according to a well-defined priority policy. Multitasking is therefore the natural execution model of single or multiprocessor systems. It is the way several applications share the resources of a computing platform. Processes are, in fact, *highly autonomous and protected* independent execution streams. If a resource—CPU time, I/O device—is available to one of them, it may not available to the others. The operating system provides inter-process communication mechanisms, like pipes or signals. They are meant to enable communication *across* applications.

Switching among different processes naturally induces an execution overhead. Whenever a process switch occurs, all the process resources must be saved. If, for example, there are several open files, the file handles that identify each file, as well as the file pointers that identify the current positions inside each file, must be saved. The operating system is also forced to save all other information related to the state of the process (instruction pointer, stack pointer, processor registers, etc.) needed to reconstruct its state at a later time slice.

2.2 MULTITHREADED PROCESSES

Processes are, as we said, the basic units of resource allocation, but *they are not the basic units of dispatching*. Indeed, they are not doomed to live with only the initial execution stream encoded in the main() function: additional internal asynchronous execution streams, or *threads*, can be launched. This is done by the native multithreading libraries that come with the OS: the Windows thread API, or the Posix Threads library—Pthreads for short—in Unix-Linux systems. A thread is therefore *a single sequential flow of control within a program*. When mapped to different cores allocated to an application, these independent, asynchronous flows of control implement parallel processing.

Parallel processing relies on exploitable concurrency. There are a number of concepts that will be systematically referred to, and it is convenient to be precise about their meaning:

- Concurrency exists in a computational problem when the problem can be decomposed into sub-problems—called tasks—that can safely execute at the same time.
- Tasks are fundamental units of sequential computation. They are units of work that express the underlying concurrency in the application, providing the opportunity for parallel execution. Tasks that can be active at the same time are considered to be concurrent.
- Parallel execution occurs when several tasks are actually doing some work at the same point in time. This happens when they are simultaneously executed by several threads.
- Concurrency can be beneficial to an application, even if there is no parallel execution. This point is further discussed at the end of the chapter.

The application performance can naturally be enhanced if concurrent tasks can be executed in parallel, overlapped in time as much as possible. Threads provide the way to implement this fact. This is summarized by the following statement:

Threads execute tasks, transforming the potential parallelism expressed by the existence of concurrent tasks into real, mandatory parallelism implemented by their simultaneous execution.

One of the first things a programmer learns about programming is organizing and isolating tasks by subroutines or function calls. Indeed, we will see in the next chapter that, *in order to launch a new thread, a function must be provided that encapsulates the sequence of instructions to be executed by the thread*, in the same way the main() function displays the sequence of instructions to be executed by the initial thread in the process, called the *main thread*.

Threads are nevertheless more than functions. Function calls correspond to a *synchronous* transfer of control in the program. A standard function call is a very convenient way of *inserting* a set of instructions into an existing execution flow. Threads, on the other hand, correspond to *asynchronous* transfers of control to a new execution flow. The initial execution flow that launches the new thread

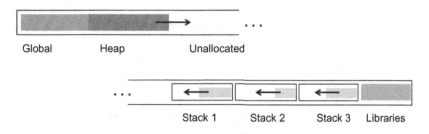

FIGURE 2.3

Memory organization in a multithreaded Unix process.

continues its own progress, and it is not forced to wait until the new thread finishes and returns (it may do so if needed, as will be explained in the next chapters).

2.2.1 LAUNCHING THREADS

Initially, a process consists of only one thread, the *main thread*. Next, the main thread can launch other threads by calling the appropriate library functions provided by the native libraries. From here on, there is absolutely no difference between the main thread and the other threads. Any thread can call again the appropriate library function and launch new threads. All the threads, no matter how they are created, are treated as equal by the operating system and scheduled in principle in a fair way. All these new execution streams are totally equivalent to the initial main() function. Threads can be thought of as asynchronous functions that become totally autonomous and take off *with their own stack*, where they manage their own local variables as well as their own nested function calls.

Threads share all the process resources *except the stack*. Each thread creation involves the creation of a new stack where the new thread function will allocate its local variables or the local variables of the functions it calls.

2.2.2 MEMORY ORGANIZATION OF A MULTITHREADED PROCESS

The memory organization in a multithreaded process is shown in Figure 2.3. The main difference with a sequential process is that there are now several stack buffers—one per thread—with a definite size. In fact, the stack size is one of the fundamental attributes of a thread. Default values are provided by the operating system, but they sometimes can be modified by the programmer, as discussed in the next chapter.

It is important to notice that:

- Global variables are *shared variables* that can be accessed by any thread.
- Local variables on the thread's stack are *private variables* that are only accessed in principle by the owner thread.

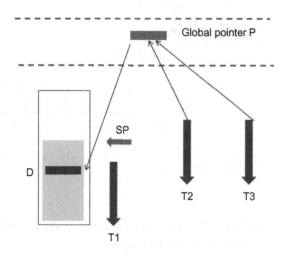

FIGURE 2.4

Publishing private data.

Notice also that dynamically allocated memory can be shared by all threads if it is referenced by a global pointer. Otherwise, dynamically allocated memory is only accessible by the thread that owns the pointer. This is the standard pattern for distinguishing between *shared* and *private* variables in multithreaded codes.

However, it would be wrong to conclude that it is impossible for a thread to read or modify data that is private to another thread. In fact, the owner thread can *publish* its local data by initializing a global pointer with its address. In Figure 2.4, a local data item is sitting in the thread T1 stack. This thread initializes a global pointer with the address of this private data item, and then threads T2 and T3 can use it to access T1's data item and eventually modify it. This mechanism is not unusual, and it will often be used later on to transfer data values across threads. However, as we will see when the time comes, it must be used with care.

2.2.3 THREADS AS LIGHTWEIGHT PROCESSES

We conclude therefore that each thread created inside the process has its own stack and stack pointer, as well as its own instruction list. However, all the other resources (global memory, files, I/O ports, . . .) allocated to the process are shared by all the threads.

A process may have more threads than available cores, and in this case CPU resources must be shared among threads: each one disposes of time slices of the available CPU time. However, switching among threads is much more efficient than switching among different processes. Indeed, since most of the global resources are shared by all threads, they do not need to be saved when the thread switch occurs.

To sum up:

- Threads are slightly more complex than ordinary method functions. Each thread has its own stack.
- Threads are simpler than processes.

Indeed, a thread can be seen as a sort of a "lightweight" process with simpler resource management, since the only data structure linked to the thread is the stack. It can also be seen as a function that has grown up and acquired its own execution context, i.e., its own stack.

2.2.4 HOW CAN SEVERAL THREADS CALL THE SAME FUNCTION?

In general, *threads call library functions*. In fact, several threads can call the *same* function. This means they all incorporate, somewhere in their code sequences, the function code (see Figure 2.5). Therefore, several threads can, at some time, find themselves *executing the same library function*. It is useful to take a close look at the way this happens.

Look at Figure 2.5, displaying two threads, T1 and T2, calling the same function, e.g., a function of the standard C or C++ libraries. These two calls are asynchronous, and they may or may not overlap in time. When called from T1 (or T2), the function will be operating on argument values and local variables that are in the T1 (or T2) stack. *These are two independent data sets*. However, there is only *one* piece of code for the function, sitting somewhere in memory. Now the question is, how can a unique suite of instructions operate simultaneously on two different data sets, and yet provide the correct results?

It is at this point that the stack properties play a role. The function body constructed by the compiler references all local addresses inside the function with the offset to an unknown stack pointer SP. Let SP1 and SP2 be the stack pointers of threads T1 and T2. The core running the thread T1 (or T2) has a stack pointer register SP holding the value SP1 (or SP2). When using a stack to manage

FIGURE 2.5

Two threads calling the same function.

local variables, switching the SP values switches a complete data set. The stack strategy to address local variables allows different threads to execute simultaneously the same function acting on different data sets.

A word of caution is needed here. Functions that are executed in a multithreaded environment must be *thread safe*, namely, they must be able to render the correct service to each caller even if they are called concurrently by different threads that are manipulating different data sets. *This is true only if the action of the function depends only on the arguments passed to it*. But this is not always the case. Some functions carry an internal state, persistent across successive calls, that also determines the outcome of the next function call. These functions are not thread safe, and the way to cope with this issue is the subject of Chapter 4.

2.2.5 COMMENT ABOUT HYPERTHREADING

As discussed in Chapter 1, hyperthreading is the capability of a core of *simultaneously* executing two or more threads. Figure 2.6 shows a core running two hardware threads. In this case, the two instruction sets are interleaved, and the core takes advantage of eventual delays in the execution of one of the threads to execute instructions of the other. In the Intel Xeon Phi, for example, decoding an instruction takes two cycles. The only way to try to obtain the execution of one instruction per cycle is running two hardware threads.

Once again, we have a core operating on two data sets. In this case, when hyperthreading is enabled, the core dedicates two registers to hold the stack pointer of the two stacks. In this way, each instruction hits its correct data target.

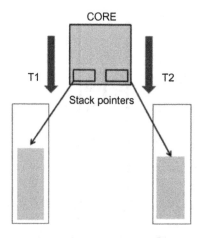

FIGURE 2.6

Single core running two hardware threads.

2.3 **PROGRAMMING AND EXECUTION MODELS**

It is useful to keep in mind the difference between *programming* and *execution models*:

- A programming model is the logical view that the programmer has of the application.
- An execution model is the precise way in which the application is processed by the target platform.

Programming models—like OpenMP, TBB, or the Pthreads library—tend to be as generic and universal as possible, to guarantee the portability of the application across different platforms. Execution models, in contrast, depend on the specific hardware and software environments of the target platform. For portable code, the same programming model must be mapped to different execution contexts. Here is the place where the compiler optimization options play a fundamental role in performance.

Figure 1.2 in Chapter 1 shows the *shared memory programming model* that applies to multithreaded applications. This is the simple and straightforward vision a programmer has of a multithreaded application: a number of virtual processing units—*virtual CPUs*—allocated to the process, having access to the totality of the memory owned by it. Different virtual CPUs are of course running different threads. When this simple programming model is mapped to an executing platform, ideally each virtual CPU should be mapped to a unique core. But this need not be the case: it is possible to have in an application more threads than cores allocated to the process.

When a multithreaded application is executed in a computing platform, two extreme cases can be distinguished:

- *Parallel execution:* the different threads are executed by different cores in a multicore system.
- *Concurrent execution:* the different threads are executed by only one core, or by a number of cores smaller than the number of threads.

The benefit of parallel execution in enhancing performance is evident. A process runs with optimal performance if it disposes of as many cores as active threads. But this is not necessary, because the operating system can schedule M threads on N cores ($M > N$) in a fair way, by allocating to each thread successive *time slices* on the available CPUs. It is therefore possible to engage more threads than CPUs in an application. This is a very common situation, for example, in the case of interactive applications, as will be shown later on. In particular, N may be equal to 1, and a correctly crafted code with M threads must run equally well (with much less performance, of course) and deliver the correct results. Testing a multithreaded code on a single CPU is a useful first step in the development of multithreaded applications.

One may, however, have doubts about the interest of over-committing the number of threads, in particular for an application that will run on a single processor system: a single execution stream looks, in principle, more natural and efficient. Nevertheless, because of the way the life cycle of a thread is conceived, concurrent programming with overcommitted cores can in many circumstances contribute to improve the performance or the efficiency of an application.

2.3.1 **THREAD LIFE CYCLES**

Figure 2.7 is a diagram showing the thread life cycle in an application. It represents all possible states of a thread from the moment it is created:

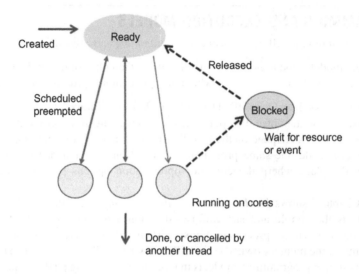

FIGURE 2.7

Life cycle of a thread.

- *Ready:* the thread is a ready pool that contains the set of threads that are waiting to be scheduled on a core.
- *Running on cores:* the thread is in progress. Two things can happen to a running thread:
  - If threads are over-committed, it will at some point be preempted by the operating system and placed back in the ready pool, in order to give other threads the opportunity to run. The operating system *does not preempts* threads if there are as many CPUs available as active threads.
  - It may be moved to a *blocked state*, releasing the core, waiting for an event. At some point, another thread will produce the expected event and release the waiting thread, which goes back to the ready pool to be rescheduled. This is an *event synchronization mechanism*, controlled by the programmer, and discussed in Chapter 6.
  - *Termination* occurs when the thread is done, or when it is canceled by other threads.

One important observation is that *the transition to a blocked state can be controlled by the programmer.* In all the native or basic libraries there are logical constructs that allow a programmer to put a thread out of the way for some time, until, for example, some data item takes a predefined value. This is called *waiting on a condition*, and plays a fundamental role in the synchronization of threads.

2.4 BENEFITS OF CONCURRENT PROGRAMMING

Figure 2.7 is a diagram showing the possible states in the life cycle of a thread. The existence of a blocked state sheds some ligth on the benefits of concurrent programming. We insist on the fact that *a thread in a blocked state is not using CPU resources*, simply because it is not scheduled. CPU resources are fully available to the remaining running threads.

Overlapping computation and IO.

Let us assume that a process does a lot of computation and I/O. The process may be running concurrently with other processes in a multitasking environment, and the I/O devices it needs are not immediately available. In such a situation, *the whole process is blocked*. If, instead, the process is multithreaded and the I/O operation is handled by one specific thread, then only the I/O thread is blocked. The other threads can continue to run, for as long as the treatment they perform is independent of the outcome of the I/O operation. Overlapping computation and I/O in this way boosts the application performance—even in a single core system—when shared resources are over-committed (Figure 2.8).

Multithreaded servers.

Another example of concurrent programming can be found in the context of client—server software architectures. Let us assume that a heavyweight server has to deal with a large crowd of different clients, accessing the server to request specific services. A server that is not multithreaded will be providing undivided attention to the first client that starts a transaction. Any other client that comes later on will be obliged to wait in face of a dumb server, until it becomes available again for a new client.

One way out of this unacceptable situation is to have a multithreaded server that dispatches one thread per client to handle the requests, and returns immediately to listen to eventual new requests. If the server runs on a platform with a large number of processors, every client will get immediate optimum service. If the number of concurrent clients is much bigger than the CPU resources available, transactions will take roughly the same amount of time as the number of active clients, but at least every client will have the illusion of being immediately served. Performance is not boosted, but the response time of the server is acceptable. This example shows that concurrent programming allows for better interactive interfaces

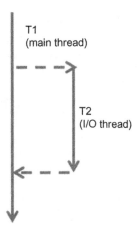

FIGURE 2.8

Overlapping computation and I/O.

Graphical interfaces.

Exactly the same argumentation applies to graphical interfaces (GUIs). Any application disposing of a GUI for interactive access will have from the start at least another thread, called the *event thread*, in addition to the main thread. The event thread is created by the system, and it is not directly seen by the programmer. But the programmer knows that this is the thread that will execute whatever functions he writes for the following operations:

- Handling external events, like mouse clicks or keyboard hits. These events are put by the system in a queue—called the *event queue*—and serviced by the event thread on a first come, first served basis.
- Partially or totally repainting and upgrading the GUI window. The repaint requests are queued with the external events, and serviced in the same way.

We conclude, as before, that concurrent programming is a necessary software technology for efficient interactive interfaces. This is the reason why the Windows operating system and the Java programming language—strongly oriented from the start toward graphical interfaces—have intrinsic multithreading services, instead of an external library.

CREATING AND RUNNING THREADS

3.1 INTRODUCTION

In high-level programming environments—like OpenMP or TBB—threads are implicit, and the basic thread management operations discussed in the first part of this chapter are silently performed by the runtime library. Most of the examples in this book, indeed, use OpenMP, TBB, or the high-level utilities of the vath library. Nevertheless, understanding the way basic libraries set up a multithreaded environment is useful knowledge, which definitely contributes to the main purpose of this book: learning to think about threads. It may be useful, in a specific parallel context, to launch one or more threads to manage a special issue, like a long network connection, and it is good to know how this can be done.

The rest of the chapter is organized as follows:

- First, an overview is proposed of the Pthreads, Windows, and C++11 interfaces for the creation of a team of worker threads, in order to perform some parallel treatment. A few simple examples are given in each case.
- Next, a C++ class from the vath library is introduced that provides a direct and user friendly way of encapsulating the native libraries' programming interfaces. A number of simple examples are presented.
- Then, anticipating the discussion of Chapter 10, a first look is taken at OpenMP, focusing on those basic features needed to implement an OpenMP version of the previous examples. Our purpose is to underline the universality of concepts and similarities between different approaches.
- Finally, to justify the interest in understanding different programming environments, an example of an application emulating a database search is proposed. This example is easily implemented using features from the basic libraries that were not available in OpenMP before the recent 4.0 release.

3.2 OVERVIEW OF BASIC LIBRARIES

Based on their functionality, the utility functions proposed by the basic libraries can be classified as follows:

- Thread management functions, dealing with the issues related to thread creation, termination, and return. They are discussed in this chapter.

- Thread synchronization functions, a critical set of library functions dealing with the basic synchronization mechanisms for threads. They are discussed in Chapters 5 and 6.
- Miscellaneous services, specialized services, often useful in application programming:
  - Function calls dealing with thread identities, and with initialization issues in library routines, useful when the number of threads engaged in its execution is not known at compile time. This subject is introduced in this chapter.
  - Thread-local storage, providing a mechanism for allowing threads to keep a private copy of dynamically allocated local data. This feature is extensively discussed in Chapter 4.
  - Thread cancel functions. Used for enabling a thread to terminate (kill) another thread. This delicate feature is rarely used in application programming. It is sketched in the final example of this chapter.
- Thread scheduling functions allowing the programmer to determine the priority level of a new thread. By default, threads are democratically scheduled with equal priorities, and this option is very rarely modified in application programming. This feature, used mainly in system programming, is far too advanced to be discussed in this book.
- Signal handling functions. They deal with the interaction of threads and signals in inter-process communications. Again, this subject is beyond the scope of this book.

Various aspects of Pthreads, Windows, and C++11 programming are therefore discussed in this and the next chapters, concerning the basic issues of thread management and synchronization, and providing a number of examples as well as portable application codes.

3.3 OVERVIEW OF BASIC THREAD MANAGEMENT

Most basic concepts and features are common to all basic libraries. They all make extensive use of a number of specific data items to create, manage, and synchronize threads. Several new *data types* are therefore introduced. They may have a slightly different look and feel in Pthreads, Windows (C libraries), and in C++11, but their behavior is very similar. In Pthreads and Windows, they are opaque structures whose inner content is not directly relevant to the programmer. In C++11, they are, naturally, C++ objects. These data types represent the threads themselves, as well as other objects whose purpose is to implement the different basic mechanisms for thread synchronization.

In order to create a thread a *thread function* must be specified, which is the function to be executed by the new thread during its lifetime. Different native libraries adopt different signatures for the thread function. The library function called to create the thread receives as one of its arguments, a pointer to the thread function to be executed by the new thread.

Moreover *thread attributes* must be specified, defining the way in which the new thread is asked to behave under certain circumstances. The most relevant thread attributes, common to all native libraries because they correspond to generic properties of threads, are:

- The size of the stack attached to the thread.
- The way the thread behaves when the thread function it executes terminates. *Detached threads* just disappear after restoring their resources—like the stack—to the system. *Joinable threads* wait to

be contacted (joined) by another thread to which they may eventually transfer a thread function return value.
- The way a thread reacts when killed by another thread: either it stops immediately or it defers cancellation until it reaches a predefined place in the instruction flow.
- The scheduling properties, which, as explained above, allow the programmer to determine the priority level of the new thread.

This information must be passed to the function call that creates the thread. Pthreads packs all the different thread attributes in a unique thread attribute data item, which is then passed to the thread creation function. Windows does not pack thread attributes; they are all passed as distinct arguments to the thread creation function. In C++11, thread attributes are private data items in the C++ object that represents the thread. All thread creation functions accept reasonable default values for the thread attributes, if they are not specified in the thread creation function call. We will focus in the rest of this book on the first two attributes, which are the most relevant ones for applications programming, and ignore the others.

Stack size.
The default stack size may need to be increased if the thread function and/or the functions it calls create too many local variables, thereby producing a stack overflow. But remember that the default stack size is platform dependent, and therefore not portable. It may happen that a stack overflow that occurs in some systems does not occur in others.

Joining threads.
As explained above, when a thread finishes executing its instruction flow, there are two possibilities. Either the thread is detached, in which case it terminates and restores its proprietary resource (the stack) to the system, or it is joinable and does not disappear before being contacted by another thread. Obviously, this is in all cases a synchronization event: because the joining thread knows, when the time comes, that the joined thread has terminated, it can rely on this information to proceed accordingly (for example, using results provided by the joined thread). In Pthreads, the detached or joinable status of a thread is a permanent attribute established when the thread is created. We will see later on that C++11 and Windows do not rely on thread attributes to handle this feature.

Comments on error handling
Library functions report errors if something goes wrong. But internal errors coming from an incorrect operation of the library itself are extremely unlikely, and if they happen the only reasonable thing to be done is to abort the program. Most of the time, library errors are generated because library functions access corrupted data, like for example accessing objects that have previously been destroyed.

In multithreading programming the most dreadful errors are those arising from an incorrect control of thread synchronization. These kinds of errors are called *race conditions* because the program outcome depends on the non-reproducible order on which asynchronous threads access a given data item. These programming errors are not reported by the library functions, and the best possible protection is to make sure they do not happen, following the protocols and best practices discussed in the forthcoming chapters. Some programming environments propose auxiliary tools that are capable of detecting race conditions. Avoiding race conditions is the subject of Chapter 5.

3.4 USING POSIX THREADS

The Pthreads library has been available since the early days of the Unix operating system, and there is a large number of bibliographical references, mainly on the Internet. Two classic books on this subject are "Programming with Posix Threads" by D. Butenhof [11], and "Pthreads Programming" by B. Nichols, D. Buttlar, and J. P. Farrel [12]. A good support is also provided by the Unix-Linux man pages, and a good starting point to browse the manual documentation is to run man pthreads.

3.4.1 PTHREADS ERROR REPORTING

Traditional Unix and C language conventions on error status reporting rely on library functions returning an integer value. A function call that succeeds returns a non negative integer. Programmers can then use positive return values to return some useful additional information, or return zero if all is needed is to report a successful function return. On failure, ordinary library functions return the special value (-1) and set the global value errno to whatever error code needs to be reported. Users must therefore monitor the function return value and take special action—like checking the value of **errno**—if the return value is (-1).

Checking the value of a global variable in a multithreaded environment is not at all appropriate. If a thread detects a (-1) as a return value and decides to check errno, there is no way to know if the errno value is the relevant one, or if it has been subsequently modified by another thread since the initial error condition occurred. Therefore, the Pthreads library adopts another convention for error reporting that does not rely on testing a global variable:

- Pthreads functions *always return the value 0 on success*.
- If the function call is not successful, then the *positive* error codes defined in errno.h are transferred to the caller via the function return value.
- Pthreads library functions never return directly any useful information other than error reporting. Another kind of information is returned via pointer types passed as function arguments.
- If one wants nevertheless to transfer useful information to the caller through return values, *negative integers* can be used. A negative return value *cannot* be an error code. We will use this option in our later discussion of synchronization objects.

Conventions adopted.

In principle, for each library function call one should check the return value. However, in case of error there is little that can be done other than aborting the program. In order to avoid exceedingly verbose listings, error checking is suppressed in the listings copied in the text of this book, ignoring the return values. The code below shows how a function call looks in the source code:

```
//Pthread function call in text:
// - - - - - - - - - - - - - - - -
pthread_XXXX(arguments);

//Pthreads function call in sources
// - - - - - - - - - - - - - - - -
int status = pthread_XXXX(arguments)
if(status)
    {
    fprintf(stdout, "Error in pthread_XXXX");
    exit(0);
    }
```

LISTING 3.1

Conventions on error checking

3.4.2 PTHREADS DATA TYPES

Pthreads introduces a number of new data types. They are named following the generic form identifier_t: some characteristic name that unambiguously describes the type and the role of the variable, followed by the underscore appending a t at the end. This convention is traditionally adopted in C to introduce user-defined data types.

> Pthreads data types are OPAQUE data objects. They can be seen as C structures whose internal implementation is hidden to the programmer. These opaque structured are accessed via library functions. Their addresses are passed to the library functions that operate on them. Programmers writing portable code should make no assumption about their precise representation.

For example, pthread_t is a thread identifier, a kind of identity card that uniquely identifies a thread during its lifetime. This identifier is initialized by the function pthread_create() that creates the thread. Other data types are, for example, pthread_mutex_t, a data structure used to control concurrent access to shared data, and pthread_cond_t, a data structure used to implement event synchronization of threads. They are discussed in Chapters 5 and 6.

Some Pthreads data types identify thread specific objects—like threads, mutexes, or condition variables. Other Pthread data types define *attributes* of these objects—like pthreads_attr_t—which encapsulate a set of specific thread attributes defining their behavior under certain circumstances. They are set by the programmer before the thread is created, and the attribute variable address is passed to pthreads_create(). Attribute data types are introduced with the purposing of adding new functionality to the library without changing the existing API.

Even if a data item of type pthread_t is, in most systems, an unsigned integer, well-crafted code should not rely on this fact. The precise content of a given data type depends on the specific Pthreads implementation, and this is, naturally, a highly non-portable issue. However, the Pthreads library includes a number of accessory functions providing a portable interface to the inner content of the opaque objects. Data types values should therefore be initialized and modified by following the Pthreads specifications. This means using library provided interface functions for reading or modifying attribute values, and, in some cases, using predefined values provided by the library for their initialization. The examples developed later on will clarify the manipulation of attribute data types.

3.4.3 THREAD FUNCTION

The thread launching a new thread calls the pthread_create() library function and passes to it, among other things, *a pointer to the function that the new thread must execute*. This thread function is required in Pthreads to have a well defined signature:

(void *) th_fct(void *P);   (function name is arbitrary)

It is therefore necessary to provide a function that receives a void* and returns a void*. The Pthreads library adopts this signature to allow data to be passed from the parent thread to the children threads at start-up, and from the worker thread back to a joining thread at termination, as will be discussed next. Indeed, a void* is a universal container in C: the address of *any* data structure can be cast to a *void** and passed to the thread function. This function will, when the time comes, recast it to a pointer to the original data type, before using it. In the same way, the thread function can allocate any data structure and return its address as a void* to the joining thread.

One should be aware that passing data back and forth to a new thread in this way is not really mandatory. Indeed, global variables are shared by all threads in the process, and threads can communicate by writing and reading them. However, since threads are asynchronous, this requires explicit synchronization in order to make sure the writes and reads occur in the expected order. Therefore, this simple, built-in way of passing information to a new thread without explicit synchronization is useful, and this feature will sometimes be used in the rest of the book. C++11 does not support this feature: its thread functions return void. C++11, however, introduces an additional synchronization mechanism enabling the programmer to retrieve a return value from a terminating thread, which will be described in Chapter 6. Chapter 9 proposes a portable utility that enables the safe transfer of data values among threads.

3.4.4 BASIC THREAD MANAGEMENT INTERFACE

Here is the signature of the functions used for basic thread management in Pthreads:

```
int pthread_create(
      pthread_t              *thread,
      pthread_attr_t         *attr,
      (void *) (*thread_fct) (void *),
      void                   *arg);

int pthread_join(
      pthread_t            *thread,
      void                 **value_ptr);
```

LISTING 3.2

The basic Pthreads thread management functions

Consider first the pthread_create() function, which seems to have a rather complicated signature. Four arguments are passed to this function:

- A pointer to a thread identifier. This is an *output* parameter: the function receives the address of an uninitialized data item and, when it returns, the thread identifier has been initialized and henceforth identifies the thread just created.
- A pointer to a thread attribute variable. This is an *input* parameter. This thread attribute has been previously initialized to whatever attributes are required for the new thread. If the NULL value is passed, the library adopts the set of default attributes for the thread.
- A pointer to a function thread_fct(), i.e., the thread function. This is the function the thread will execute during it lifetime. It must, of course, be declared and defined somewhere else in the code, and its address is passed here. Remember that, in C-C++, the address of a function is just its name.
- A void pointer arg that is precisely the argument to be passed to the thread function thread_fct().

Notice that, when this function is called, the thread function is not called directly. This function simply passes to the Pthreads library the information needed to create the new thread. The thread function will be called by the Pthreads library after the execution environment of the new thread (in particular, the new stack) has been created and installed in the application.

3.4.5 DETACHMENT STATE: JOINING THREADS

It was stated before that a thread created as *detached* just disappears when the thread function terminates and the eventual return value of the thread function is ignored. But a *joinable* thread needs to make contact with another thread to really terminate its life cycle.

When a thread is created, the Pthreads library returns a unique thread identifier of t type pthread_t. Any other thread that knows the identifier ID of the target thread whose termination needs to be verified can make the following call:

```
void *P;
...
pthread_join(ID, &P);    // wait until thread ID terminates
```
LISTING 3.3

Joining a terminating thread

When this call is made by a thread joining another target thread, the following things happen:

- If the target thread has terminated, the join operation takes place immediately: the joining thread eventually recovers the return value, and the target thread finishes its life cycle.
- Otherwise, the runtime code moves the joining thread to a blocked state, *not using CPU resources*. When the target thread terminates, the runtime code wakes up the joining thread, which is then rescheduled, and the join operation takes place.

The above described mechanism is a special case of a generic *event synchronization* mechanism, which will be discussed in detail in Chapter 6 (the event in this case being the termination of the target thread). The target thread void* return value is recovered at the address pointed by P, passed as second argument. Passing NULL as second argument means the joining thread is not interested in the return value, which is ignored. *We emphasize again that this is really a synchronization point among two threads.*

Some miscellaneous issues

There are a few useful Pthreads library functions that propose some miscellaneous services:

- void pthread_exit(). Normally, a thread terminates when its thread function terminates. But a call to this function in some place of the thread function—or in functions called by it—immediately terminates the running thread.
- pthread_t pthread_self(). This function returns the thread identity of the caller thread.
- int pthread_equal(pthread_t t1, pthread_t t2). This function compares two thread identities, and returns 0 if they are different or 1 if they are identical. As stated before, thread identities are opaque objects that cannot be compared directly. An example will be provided showing the utility of these last two library functions.

3.4.6 SIMPLE EXAMPLES OF THREAD MANAGEMENT

A few simple examples of the Pthreads protocol to create a team of worker threads follow. The sources are well commented, and will not be completely reproduced here.

Example 1: Hello1_P.C

Listing 3.4—source in file Hello1_P.C—shows how to create a set of threads that print a message to the screen. Threads are then joined one at a time by the main thread.

```
#include <stdio.h>
#include <pthread.h>

#define NTHREADS  4

/*- - - - - - - - - - - - - - - - - - - - - - - - -
 * Declare an array of thread identifiers. This array
 * will be initialized by pthread_create()
 *- - - - - - - - - - - - - - - - - - - - - - - */
pthread_t hello_id[NTHREADS];

/*- - - - - - - - - - - - - - - - - - - - - - - -
 * This is the thread function executed by each thread.
 * Thread functions receive and return a (void *), but
 * here the argument and return value are ignored
 *- - - - - - - - - - - - - - - - - - - - - - - - - */
void *hello_world (void *arg)
   {
   printf ("Hello, world \n");
   return NULL;
   }

int main (int argc, char *argv[])
```

```
{
int i, status;

/*- - - - - - - - - - - - - - - - - - - - - - - - - - - - -
 * Create threads. The first NULL means that the new thread
 * picks the default attributes. The second NULL is the void
 * pointer passed as argument to the thread function
 *- - - - - - - - - - - - - - - - - - - - - - - - - - - - */
for(i=0; i<NTHREADS; i++)
     pthread_create (&hello_id[i], NULL, hello_world, NULL);

/*- - - - - - - - - - - - - - - - - - - - - - - - - - - - -
 * Join the threads in the same order they have been created.
 * The NULL argument means that we do not want to receive the
 * thread return value in the join operation.
 *- - - - - - - - - - - - - - - - - - - - - - - - - - - - */
for(i=0; i<NTHREADS; i++)
   pthread_join (hello_id[i], NULL);

printf("\n From main : threads have been joined\n");
return 0;
}
```

LISTING 3.4

Creating threads: Hello1_P.c

Example 1: Hello1_P.C

To compile, run make hello1p. The number of threads is 4.

Example 2: Hello2_P.c

In this example, a new feature is added to the code described above. The possibility of passing an argument to the thread function is used to communicate to each worker thread an integer value (its rank). The rank values start from 1, and they correspond to the order in which threads are created. A worker thread can then use its rank value to select the work to be performed through conditional statements. In the present case, each thread prints a message reporting its rank.

This code introduces a global array holding the integer rank values, and passes to each thread the address of the corresponding array element, cast as a void pointer. Listing 3.5 indicates the modifications made to Hello1_P.c

```
int th_ranks[NTHREADS+1];    /* array of integers */

/*- - - - - - - - - - - - - - - - - - - - - - - - - - - - -
 * This is the new thread function executed by the threads.
```

Continued

```
 * It now receives an argument, and prints its value.
 *- - - - - - - - - - - - - - - - - - - - - - - - - - - */
void *hello_world (void *arg)
   {
   int rank;
   rank = *(int *)arg;    // read integer value
   printf ("Hello IDRIS from thread %d \n", rank);
   return NULL;
   }

int main (int argc, char *argv[])
   {
   int n, status;

   // Initialize the ranks array
   for(n=1; n<=NTHREADS; n++) th_ranks[n] = n;

   /*- - - - - - - - - - - - - - - - - - - - - - - - - - - -
    * Create threads. adopting default attributes. The last
    * argument is the rank argument  passed to the thread function.
    *- - - - - - - - - - - - - - - - - - - - - - - - - - - - */

   for(n=1; n<=NTHREADS; n++)
      pthread_create (&hello_id[n], NULL, hello_world,
                      &th_ranks[n]);

   // The rest of the code is unchanged
   ...
   }
```

LISTING 3.5

Creating threads: Hello2_P.C

Example 2: Hello2_P.C

To compile, run make hello2p. The number of threads is 4.

Example 3: Hello3_P.C

This example does exactly the same as the preceding one, in a way that superficially looks correct but which in fact is not. Rather than using a global array holding the integer rank values, we may try to make things simpler by just passing to each thread the address of the loop counter n incremented by the main thread.

```
int main (int argc, char *argv[])
   {
   int n, status;
```

```
/*  — — — — — — — — — — — — — — — — — — — — — — — — —
 * Create threads. The code passes to each new thread the
 * address of the loop counter n. This looks correct, but it
 * is not.
 *— — — — — — — — — — — — — — — — — — — — — — — — — — */
for(n=0; n<NTHREADS; n++)
    pthread_create (&hello_id[n], NULL, hello_world, (void*)&n);

// The rest of the code is unchanged
...
}
```

LISTING 3.6

Creating threads: Hello3_P.C

Example 3: Hello3_P.C

To compile, run make hello3p. The number of threads is 4.

The first thing to be observed is that the loop counter n—whose address is passed to the thread functions executed by the new threads—is a *local variable* sitting in the stack of the main thread. The new threads will be reading its value via the pointer they receive. This is then one of the first examples of a thread publishing its private data and allowing other threads to read it, as discussed in Chapter 2, which is, technically, a legitimate operation.

However, this code is incorrect, because the implicit assumption has been made that the thread just created is immediately scheduled, and that it immediately reads the loop counter value n *before main() has increased it to launch the next thread*. This is just not true: threads are asynchronous, and no reasonable assumptions can be made on the way they are scheduled. When this code is executed, the rank values reported are not predictable. Some rank values may be missing because they were not read before the loop counter is increased, and others may be repeated because they were read more than once.

This is the first example of a *race condition* in which the results of the execution of a code are not deterministic, because they are sensitive to the way threads are scheduled. As we will see, explicit synchronizations are required to avoid race conditions.

Example 4: Intrinsic rank of a thread

In the two preceding examples, a team of worker threads was created by passing explicitly an integer value, corresponding to the order in which threads are created. Notice that this integer rank is also the index of the thread identifier in the global identifier array, called hello_id[] in the examples above.

In the vath utility we will soon discuss, this integer rank is extensively used to identify a thread, and we would like to install a context in which functions called by the primordial thread function can also know the rank of the running thread. The GetRank() function listed below solves this problem.

```
// thread identity array
// - - - - - - - - - - - -
pthread_t hello_id[NTHREADS+1];

// Auxiliary function that returns the caller
// thread rank
// - - - - - - - - - - - - - - - - - - - - - -
int GetRank()
    {
    pthread_t my_id;
    int n, my_rank, status;

    my_id = pthread_self();    // who  am I?
    n = 0;
    do
        {
        n++;
        status = pthread_equal(my_id, hello_id[n]);
        } while(status==0 && n < NTHREADS);

    if(status) my_rank=n;      // OK, return rank
    else my_rank = (-1);       // else, return error
    return my_rank;
    }
```

LISTING 3.7

Computing a running thread rank: Hello4_P.C

The basic idea is simple. The function calls pthread_self() to get the identity of the running thread. Then it scans the hello_id[array, comparing the running thread identity with the stored thread identities, until there is a fit. It returns the running thread array index, or (-1) if the caller thread is not a member of the workers team.

The full example is in source file Hello4_P.C. Notice that in this case we no longer need to pass explicitly the integer rank to each worker thread. We have presented this function in the way it is used in the vath library, where thread ranks are in the range $[1, N]$. For this reason, a hello_id[] array of dimension NTHREADS+1 is introduced, and the first slot is not used.

Example 4: Hello4_P.C

To compile, run make hello4p. The number of threads is 4.

Example 5: Retstring_P.C

This example shows how the pthread_join() function can be used by a worker thread to transfer a return value to the joining master thread. The main thread launches one worker thread, which allocates memory, creates a string, and returns its address to the main thread. This example is proposed to illustrate how the return value mechanism works, but this feature will not be used in the rest of the book.

Example 5: Retstring_P.C

To compile, run make retstring. There is a master thread and a worker thread that returns a string to the master.

3.5 USING WINDOWS THREADS

The multithreading support of the Windows operating system has today the same conceptual structure as the support provided by POSIX threads. Library function names may be different, but the basic functionalities are very close. In the early days of Windows NT there was an area—event synchronization of threads—where the protocols and best practices were very different. However, since Windows Vista a number of new features have been introduced in the Windows API that, to a large extent, filled the gap with the POSIX threads programming interfaces.

Today, migrating code to and from Pthreads is much easier. The whole Windows API is accessed through an upper software layer called the CRT (C Runtime Library), which benefits from an excellent online documentation, to which we will systematically refer in this book. In the Windows API home page [13], the most relevant entries for our purposes are in the System services -> Threads and System services->Synchronization links. But we will be more precise in each particular case.

Windows thread data types

As stated before, thread support in Windows is part of the operating system. Thread objects, as well as other synchronization objects, are therefore managed by the Windows kernel. They are identified in Windows by a data type called HANDLE, which is in fact un unsigned long integer. Client code asks the kernel to create a specific object—a thread, a mutex, etc.—and the kernel returns a HANDLE to the object. This handle can be seen as an index in some internal array where the kernel allocates and ranges the corresponding objects. Client code must pass the handle to the kernel when requesting services involving the target object. However, all handles are of the same kind, so it is the programmer's responsibility to keep track of the kind of object that corresponds to a given handle.

3.5.1 CREATING WINDOWS THREADS

The most basic way of creating a thread is a call to the CreateThread() function, which takes several parameters including a reference to the thread function, and returns directly the thread handle. This is not, however, the recommended way of creating a Windows thread, partly because there is no guarantee the thread will already be scheduled when the function returns. This may, in some complex contexts, raise some problems.

Windows has two other high-level C functions that can be called to create a thread: _beginthread() and _beginthreadex(). Their signatures, as well as the signatures of the thread functions they require, are given in Listing 3.8:

```
// Thread function for _beginthread():
// – – – – – – – – – – – – – – – – – –
void th_fct1(void *data);

unsigned int _beginthread(
        void      (*th_fct1) (void *),        // thread fct
        unsigned stack_size,                   // stack size
        void      *data);                      // arg of thread fct


// Thread function for _beginthreadex()
// – – – – – – – – – – – – – – – – – – –
unsigned int __stdcall th_fct2(void *data)

unsigned int _beginthreadex(
        void      *sec_attr,                   // security attribut
        unsigned (*th_fct2) (void *),          // thread fct
        unsigned stack_size,                   // stack size
        void      *data,                       // arg of thread fct
        unsigned flag,                         // state flag
        unsigned *thID);                       // thread ID
```

LISTING 3.8

Creating Windows threads

In both cases, the thread function takes, as in Pthreads, a void* as argument. But the first one (for _beginthread()) has no return value, while the second (for _beginthreadex() returns an unsigned int. We will soon see that there is some logic to this, given the way both functions operate. Let us first examine the function arguments. There are many of them, because Windows does not pack thread attributes in a unique attribute data item. But passing in most cases the value 0 (for integers) or NULL (for pointers) selects reasonable default values.

- Return value: Both thread creation functions return the thread handle in the form of an unsigned int. When this handle is passed to library functions that act on the thread, it must be explicitly recast to a HANDLE, as we will see in the examples that follow.
- Arguments:
  - A pointer to the thread function, as well as a void pointer to its data argument, as was the case in Pthreads.
  - A stack size, if the default value needs to be modified. Otherwise, passing 0 picks the default stack size.
  - A void* to a security attribute of the threads. We will always accept the default value. The Windows API documentation can be consulted for further details.
  - A flag (unsigned int) that decides whether the thread starts running immediately or is created in a suspended (blocked) state. In the second case, the new thread starts running when the function ResumeThread() is called, with the corresponding thread handle as argument. Passing the value 0 for this flag creates a thread that starts running immediately.

   – A pointer to an unsigned integer, called thID in the listing above, which is an *output* parameter where the kernel returns another integer identifier of the new thread, *different form the thread handle*. Its possible usefulness is discussed below.

Why are there two different thread creation functions?

These two functions are not members of the basic Windows API; they belong to un upper software layer called the CRT (C Runtime Library). The initial purpose of _beginthread() was to have a simple and direct way of creating a thread. This function was extended later because the additional arguments incorporated in _beginthreadex() were needed in many cases. However, besides passing more detailed information, a fundamental difference was introduced in the way these two functions manage the handles of the threads they create. When a thread created with _beginthread() terminates, the kernel will immediately close (release) its handle. This very same handle can eventually be attributed to another thread created later. In this case, the programmer has no control whatsoever on the lifetime of the thread handle. For terminating threads created with _beginthreadex(), the handle must be explicitly closed by the programmer by calling the CloseHandle() function, typically after joining the target thread.

   Therefore, in spite of the fact that _beginthread() looks simpler, it has to be used with care. Let us imagine that a thread is created and its handle stored in h1. Later on, a second thread is created and its handle stored in h2. It may happen that, in the meantime, the first thread has terminated, and the kernel has reused the first handle to create the second thread. In this case, h1==h2 refers to the *second* thread, not the first which has already terminated. The usage of _beginthreadex() is recommended, even if threads are not joined, to prevent reusage of handles by the kernel.

   Another way of looking at this issue is to say that _beginthread() is safer when dealing with detached threads whose termination is not tracked and, from this point of view, it is natural that its associated thread function has no return value. On the other hand, _beginthreadex() is more naturally related to the creation of joinable threads.

   Terminating threads: In the same way that pthreads_exit() terminates a POSIX thread when called by a thread function (or a function directly or indirectly called by the thread function), Windows has two other CRL functions, _endthread() and _endthreadex(unsigned n), that terminate threads created with _beginthread() or _beginthreadex(), respectively.

   Sleeping. Windows has a very handy utility: the Sleep(msecs) function, which puts the caller thread in a blocked state for a duration of msecs milliseconds. This utility will be used extensively in our examples.

3.5.2 JOINING WINDOWS THREADS

The Windows API has two functions a thread can call to wait for the termination of a thread, of for the termination of a worker team, whose signatures are given in Listing 3.9.

```
DWORD WaitForSingleObject(
        HANDLE hd1,                  // target thread handle
        DWORD  dwMillisecs);         // duration of wait

DWORD WaitForMultipleObject(
```

Continued

```
        DWORD  count              // size of Hdl array
        HANDLE *Hdl,              // array of thread handles
        BOOL   waitAll,           // flag that defines action
        DWORD  dwMillisecs);      // duration of wait

// Getting return values
// - - - - - - - - - - -
DWORD  dwRetval;        // return value recovered here
HANDLE h;               // target thread handle
...
GetExitCodeThread(h, &dwRetval);
```

LISTING 3.9

Joining Windows threads

- In this context, DWORD is equivalent to uint.
- WaitForSingleObject():
  - The caller thread waits for the termination of the thread whose handle is passed as an argument.
  - This is a *timed wait*. The caller thread waits up to dwMillisecs milliseconds. It returns the symbolic constants WAIT_TIMEOUT if the wait interval is exhausted, or WAIT_OBJECT_0 if the function returns because the target thread terminated before.
  - In order to have an indefinite wait, the symbolic constant INFINITE is passed as a second argument.
- WaitForMultipleObject:
  - Hdl is an array of thread handles, of size count.
  - This function waits for the termination of one or all the threads identified in the handle array Hdl.
  - If waitAll is true, it waits for the termination of all the threads. Otherwise, waits for the termination of the first.
  - The timed wait works as in the previous case.
  - Return values are the same as in the previous case if the function waits for all the threads (the only usage we will make). For the more general case, look at the Windows API documentation.

These wait functions have a broader scope than waiting for thread termination. It was observed before that joining a thread can be seen as a special case of event synchronization: the joining thread waits for an event, the event being the termination of the joined thread. Windows considers thread termination as a synchronization event triggered by the terminating thread. Other Windows synchronization objects also trigger synchronization events, and a thread can wait for them by calling the same functions, but passing the appropriate handles to the other objects. Notice also that, contrary to the join() function in Pthreads, these functions have no reference whatsoever to the thread function return value. In order to recover the return value of a thread created by _baginthreadex(), the third function listed above, GetExitCodeThread(), must be called. It behaves as follows:

- The first argument is the target thread handle, and the second argument is an output parameter where the thread function return value is recovered.
- The return value is the symbolic constant STILL_ACTIVE if the thread is still running when the function is called, in which case the value returned in the second argument is not relevant. Otherwise, the value recovered can be trusted.

It follows that the correct protocol to join a worker thread is first, wait for termination, then get the return value, and finally close the thread handle.

3.5.3 WINDOWS EXAMPLES OF THREAD MANAGEMENT

Example 6: Hello1_W.C

Here is the listing of our first Windows example, Hello1_W.C. A thread is created, using _beginthreadex(), to print a hello message to the screen. Notice that the process.h header must be included when the _beginthreadex() function is used. This example has been tailored to show some of the features and issues discussed above.

```
#include <windows.h>
#include <process.h>
#include <iostream>

using namespace std;

unsigned __stdcall threadFunc(void *p)
    {
    unsigned n = reinterpret_cast<int>(p);
    Sleep(200);
    if(n<0) _endthreadex(0);
    return n;
    }

int main()
    {
    unsigned long th;
    unsigned ID;
    int      retval;
    cout << "\n Enter return value (int) : " << endl;
    cin >> retval;

    th = _beginthreadex(NULL, 0, threadFunc, (void*)retval, 0, &ID);
    if(th==0)
        {
        cout << "\n beginthreadex failed" << endl;
        return -1;
        }
    cout << "\n Thread running " << endl;
```

Continued

```
for(;;)
  {
  DWORD dwExit;

  GetExitCodeThread(reinterpret_cast<HANDLE>(th), &dwExit);
  if(dwExit==STILL_ACTIVE) cout << "\nThread still running" << endl;
  else
    {
    cout << "\n Thread exit code was " << dwExit << endl;
    break;
    }
  }
// tell system that we are finished with this thread
CloseHandle((HANDLE)th);
return 0;
}
```

LISTING 3.10

Creating a Windows thread

First, notice the simplicity of the thread function: it just returns the integer received as the argument. However, this thread function terminates normally only if the received argument is positive, in which case it corresponds to an unsigned integer. Otherwise, the thread function terminates with a call to _endthreadex(). The thread function sleeps for 200 ms before terminating, in order to have a reasonable duration for its life span.

The main() function first reads from stdin the user-selected thread return value (so that one can pass either positive or negative values to check the way the program works). Then, the new thread is created. In this example, default values are adopted for the security attribute, the stack size, and the suspended flag. And the integer value read from stdin is passed to the new thread. This value is printed in the hello message.

After creating the new thread, main() waits for its termination in a peculiar way: it enters into a loop that keeps trying to read the return value for as long as the thread is still active. The loop breaks when the thread is no longer active, and the return value is read and printed. Because the target thread has been put to sleep for 200 ms, there are lots of "thread still running" messages. Once the return value is recovered, main() closes the target thread handle.

This way of waiting for the target thread is wasteful for long waits, because the main thread keeps using CPU cycles in the for loop. When, instead, the main thread calls WaitForSingleObject(), it waits in a blocked state not using CPU cycles. This is the correct wait strategy that will henceforth be adopted.

Example 6: Hello1_W.C

To compile, run make hello1_w.

Example 7: Hello2_W.C

This example is the Windows version of the example previously developed in Pthreads: creating a team of worker threads that prints a message indicating their intrinsic rank, and joining the team. The auxiliary function GetRank()—that computes the intrinsic rank of the caller thread—demonstrates the utility of the thread identity returned by _beginthreadex(), different from the thread handle. Indeed, the only way a thread has of knowing its own identity is by calling the GetCurrentThreadId() function, which returns the thread identity as an unsigned integer. Therefore, in order to identify the rank of a running thread this return value must be compared to the thread identities returned when the thread was created. The GetRank() function in Listing 3.11 is identical to the similar functions encountered before in the Pthreads environment.

```cpp
using namespace std;

unsigned        *ID;    // array of thread identities
int             nTh;    // number of threads

int GetRank()           // auxiliary function
   {
   unsigned my_id;
   int n, my_rank, status;

   my_id = GetCurrentThreadId();      // determine who I am
   n = 0; status = 0;
   do
      {
      n++;
      if(my_id == ID[n]) status=1;
      } while(status==0 && n < nTh);
   if(status) my_rank=n;    // OK, return rank
   else my_rank = (-1);     // else, return error
   return my_rank;
   }

unsigned __stdcall threadFunc(void *p)    // thread function
   {
   int rank = GetRank();
   Sleep(500*rank);
   cout << "\n Hello world from thread  " << rank << endl;
   Sleep(500*rank);
   return 0;
   }

int main(int argc, char **argv)
```

Continued

```
{
int n;
unsigned long *th;
HANDLE        *hThread;

if(argc==2) nTh = atoi(argv[1]);  // get nTh from command line
else nTh = 4;

th = new unsigned long[nTh+1];    // allocate arrays
hThread = new HANDLE[nTh+1];

ID = new unsigned[nTh+1];
for(n=1; n<=nTh; n++)             // create threads
    {
    th[n] = _beginthreadex(NULL, 0, threadFunc, NULL, 0, &ID[n]);
    hThread[n] = (HANDLE)th[n];
    }

// Wait for threads to exit
DWORD rc = WaitForMultipleObjects(nTh, hThread+1, TRUE, INFINITE);

for(n=1; n<=nTh; n++) CloseHandle(hThread[n]);
cout << "\n Main thread exiting" << endl;
delete [] ID;
delete [] hThread;
delete [] th;
return 0;
}
```

LISTING 3.11

Creating a worker team

Notice that there are three thread related arrays in this example (we keep using offset 1 arrays, always allocating one extra unused slot):

- th[ ]: this is the array of thread handles returned by _beginthreadex() as unsigned long.
- hThread[ ]: this is the previous array recast to the HANDLE type, needed for waiting for threads or for closing the handles. This array is superfluous, because the th array elements can always be recast as handles on the fly, but we found the code is clearer in this way.
- ID[ ], an array that stores the thread identities returned by _begintreadex(). In the code above, this array is global because it is accessed both by main() and the GetRank() functions. The other arrays do not need to be global, because they are accessed only by main().

The main function reads the number of threads from the command line (four threads is the default) and then allocates the three thread related arrays. Then, the worker threads are created in a loop where the three arrays are initialized. Finally, all the worker threads are joined by a call to WaitForMultipleObjects(), with the following arguments:

- nTh, the number of threads, is the size of the hThread array.
- hThread+1 is the starting point of the relevant, size nTh, thread handle array. We are jumping on the first, unused hThread array element.
- TRUE means we are waiting for the termination of all the threads.
- INFINITE means the wait is unlimited.

Once the worker threads have been joined, their handles are canceled. The thread function just gets the thread rank and prints a message. The worker thread lifetimes have been stretched by putting the threads to sleep for durations depending on their ranks.

Example 7: Hello2_W.C

To compile, run hello2_w.

3.6 C++11 THREAD LIBRARY

The C++11 standard has incorporated a complete set of multithreading facilities into the C++ standard library. This evolution is a significant step in software engineering: the possibility of disposing of a portable, low-level programming environment providing practically all the services and features of the native libraries. Developers can use C++11 threads to implement sophisticated system programming with full portability as an extra bonus.

3.6.1 C++11 THREAD HEADERS

When programming in Pthreads, the only header file required to be included is pthread.h. Likewise, Windows only requires windows.h and sometimes process.h, as explained in the previous section. The C++11 thread library, instead, requires a number of specific header files corresponding to the different proposed services, listed below. All the C++11 classes are naturally defined in the std namespace.

- <thread>: facilities for managing and identifying threads, or for putting a thread to sleep for a predetermined time duration.
- <mutex>: facilities implementing mutual exclusion, in order to enforce thread safety in shared data accesses by different threads. This subject is discussed, for all programming environments, in Chapter 5.
- <condition variable>: basic level synchronization mechanism allowing a thread to block until notified that some condition is true or a timeout is elapsed. This subject is discussed, for all programming environments, in Chapter 6.
- <future>: C++11 specific facilities for handling asynchronous results from operations performed by another threads, discussed in Chapter 6.
- <atomic>: Classes for atomic types and operations. Discussed, for all programming environments, in Chapters 5 and 8.
- <chrono>: classes that represent points in time, durations, and clocks. Very complete date-time programming environment, used in this book only to measure execution times.
- <ratic>: compile-time rational arithmetic, not directly used in this book. This facility is needed for the chrono services.

A very complete and detailed discussion of the C++11 threads standard is developed in the book, "C++ concurrency in action" [14]. This book is a basic reference on the subject. Its Appendix D proposes a detailed reference of all the library components.

A few words about implementations. Most widely adopted compilers are today fully—or almost—C++11 compliant. GNU 5.0 or higher compiles all the examples proposed in this book. Visual Studio 2013 has some minor limitations in what coincerns the chapter 4 examples. The GNU compiler C++11 status can be found on the GCC compiler website [15]. Two broadly used programming environments implement the C++11 thread library:

- Boost is fully compliant with the C++11 multithreading standard library. In most cases it is sufficient to replace the std:: namespace qualifier by the boost:: namespace qualifier to match the C++11 standard. Some facilities have different names: the std::chrono header must be replaced by boost::date-time, and the programming interfaces are not exactly the same. In the rest of the book we will adopt the strict C++11 standard and comment about Boost whenever appropriate.
- The TBB library has integrated, as a standalone utility not necessarily linked to the TBB programming environment, a partial implementation of the C++11 standard dealing with thread management and synchronization: the services proposed in the <thread> and <condition_variable> headers.

One should also be aware that both Boost and TBB propose very useful extended facilities that have not been incorporated into the C++11 standard, like the reader-writer locks discussed in Chapter 8.

3.6.2 C++11 ERROR REPORTING

C++11 thread library functions do not return error codes. Return values, if any, only return relevant information resulting from the function operation. As a C++ library, C++11 threads throw exceptions in the case of failure. Remember that exceptions can be looked at as non-local return values, not aimed only to the direct caller. When an exception is thrown, there is a normal function returned to the caller. But if the caller has not explicitly set up a try-catch block to catch it, the exception is returned to its caller, and so on and so forth. The exception keeps climbing the hierarchy of nested function calls until somebody has set up the try-catch safety net that catches it. In the absence of any safety net, the exception writes a message when it arrives at the main function, and terminates the program.

The C++11 standard is very explicit on the exceptions thrown by the different library functions. Catching exceptions is often employed by library writers, but in the applications programming we will be developing in this book there is hardly the need of explicitly catching them. After all, even if we do catch them, what else can we do other than abort the program?

3.6.3 C++11 DATA TYPES

In C++11, the new data types for multithreading are, naturally, C++ classes defined in the std namespace. Library functions are most often—but not always—*public member functions* of these classes. We will soon discuss how they operate.

Rather than explicitly passing the address of an object, as is the case in Pthreads and Windows, the standard C++ semantics is employed: member functions are called on an object (whose address, remember, is implicitly passed to the function by the C++ compiler, via the this pointer).

3.6.4 CREATING AND RUNNING C++11 THREADS

C++11 thread creation and management is implemented in the std::thread class, representing a thread. Its role is very clear: *when an object instance of this class is created, a new thread is launched.* This std::thread object can be seen as representing the new thread's identity, in the same way a pthread_t object represents a thread identity in Pthreads.

A new thread is therefore started by constructing an instance of std::thread and passing a pointer to a thread function in the constructor of the object. The C++ standard is less strict than Pthreads/Windows in what concerns the signature of the thread function: the thread function can be any function that returns void, with an arbitrary number of arbitrary arguments. Listing 3.12 shows the C++11 protocol for thread creation:

```
void thread_fct(arg1, arg2, ...);        // definition of thread function
...
std::thread T(thread_fct, arg1, arg2);   // launch the thread T
```

LISTING 3.12

Creating a C++11 thread

Several important points are worth noting:

- The new thread is created and starts running as soon as the std::thread object T is created. The new thread immediately starts executing the thread function passed as argument.
- As stated above, *the thread function can take an arbitrary number of arguments of practically any type.* In fact, it can take arguments of any *copyable* type, namely, a type that disposes of a copy constructor.
- The thread constructor exhibited in Listing 3.8 above *copies* the thread function address and arguments to some internal working place, where they will be read once the thread environment is created and the thread function is called. This is fine, as long as the thread function arguments are passed by value. However, it may happen that the thread function expects *a reference* to some external variable to return a result. In this case, special care is needed. This issue is discussed in detail in the examples that follow.
- The C++ library *does not* directly manage return values from the thread function as Pthreads/Windows do. The function used to launch a new thread always returns void. However, C++11 proposes an independent mechanism, the future facility, that allows a thread to recover asynchronous data values generated by another thread.

Remember also that in C++ it is possible insert a function object—namely, an object that acts also as a function—anywhere a pointer to a function is expected. Function objects are a powerful C++ feature. They are heavily used in the STL, or in other multithreading libraries like TBB and Boost. For this reason, a discussion of their properties is proposed in Annex B, in particular explaining how function objects can replace pointers to functions, with extended capabilities.

In a function object, *the name of the object can be used as a function name*, and the member function called in this way is the operator() member function, whose signature—arguments and return values—can be adapted to the application requirements. Here is the way a function object is defined and passed to the std::thread constructor:

```
class mytask       // define function object class "task"
   {
   // private data
   // private member functions

   public:
    ... // Constructor, destructor
    ... // other member functions

    void operator()(arg1, arg2, ...)  // this makes task a function object
       {
       // code for operator(...) function
       }
    ...
   };

...
mytask tk;                             // define function object tk
std::thread T(tk, arg1, arg2, ...):   // launch thread
```

LISTING 3.13

Creating a C++11 thread with a function object

Notice the flexibility of this approach. The function object constructor can also be used to pass data values that may be required for the operation of the member functions. We will see this in detail in one of the examples that follow.

Comments on threads as objects

The fact that C++11 threads are associated with objects may initially induce some confusion. Normally, C++ objects are seen as black boxes that encapsulate data and provide services to client code via their public member functions. Threads, on the other hand, are just asynchronous execution streams. So how are these two views linked together?

We know that the std::thread object T represents the identity of the new execution stream launched when the object is created (Figure 3.1). However, as an object, the thread T is an instance of a class, with a number of member functions that can be called by client code. Therefore, the natural question that comes up is: where do the client codes requesting the services of T come from? The answer is that *they come from other threads in the application*. Indeed, other threads can access the T member functions to produce some action on the thread it represents. Notice that when this happen the called member function acting on T runs in the caller thread environment, not in the target thread represented by T.

The C++11 thread termination interfaces implement the same concepts as Pthreads/Windows: threads can be joined or detached. There are, however, a few subtleties that programmers should be aware of. In C++11, join() and detach() are member functions of the std::thread class, corresponding to operations that need to be performed on a thread.

- Any created thread must be either joined or detached *before the thread object that represents the thread is destroyed*. If that is not the case, the whole process terminates when the thread object is destroyed.
- A thread that wants to join another thread T calls T.join(). When this happens, the caller thread moves to a blocked state and waits, until the execution stream associated to T terminates. After a thread is joined, its execution stream no longer exists. The associated T object represents, until it is destroyed, a special object called not-a-thread.
- On the other hand, a thread can be detached by calling T.detach(), to let the thread represented by T fade away and disappear gracefully after termination. After detachment, its execution stream continues naturally to execute until the thread function terminates, but the associated object T becomes invalid and, again, it represents a not-a-thread object. After detachment, a thread can no longer be acted upon by other threads.

```
...
void task_fct(...);
std::thread T(task_fct):    // launch new thread T
...
T.join();                // caller thread waits for T to terminate
...
T.detach();              // Function returns immediately,
                         // T is no longer related to the detached thread
```

LISTING 3.14

Joining or detaching threads

The stack size.
The C++11 standard does not propose any explicit way of modifying the default thread stack size. Boost has a special class attrib whose only role is to fix the stack size of the caller thread.

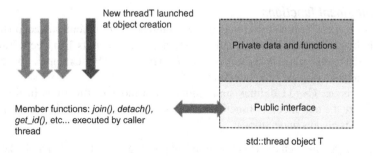

FIGURE 3.1

std::thread object T.

Scope of C++11 thread objects

An important issue is where and how std::thread objects should be created: as global objects or as objects local to the thread that creates the new thread? The scope of the thread objects depends on the way they will be accessed. A thread object can be created as a local object to the parent thread, instantiated at the appropriate place where the new thread needs to start running. However, in this case, only the parent thread will be able to join or detach it. This may be sufficient in many applications.

If a more general context is needed in which any running thread needs to access other thread objects, they should be declared with global scope. But in this case their constructor will be called before main() starts, and we may end up with new threads running too early, before the main() function has set up the stage of the application. In order to avoid this, a *lazy initialization* strategy is required, by declaring *global pointers* to std::thread objects. Later on, main() or any other thread will create the new, global thread objects at the right place with a call to the new operator that initializes the global pointers. The next section provides one explicit example of this approach.

Useful member functions of std::thread

The C++11 documentation can be consulted for a complete description of the std::thread class. Here, we quote two member functions frequently used in the applications, in particular in the vath library. In the functions and data names below, the std:: namespace is understood.

- thread::sleep_for(duration d). This function call puts the target thread in a blocked state for time interval d. It is useful to simulate some amount of work done, by slowing down for a given elapsed time interval the thread progression. In the function signature given above, *duration* is a type defined in the <chrono> header, and the Annex at the end of this chapter describes the way this data type operates. The examples in the next section show how the sleep_for() member function is used in practice.
- thread::thread_id thread::get_id(). C++11 defines a data item thread_id for each thread object, and the function get_id() returns its value. Now, since the thread object itself identifies a thread, why do we need another thread identifier? The point is that very often thread identities need to be compared—we have seen an example in the GetRank() functions in Pthreads and Windows—and C++11 overloads the comparison operators ==, != for thread_id objects. C++11 also overloads the output operator << for a thread_id object, so the thread identities can easily be printed.

std::this_thread global functions

As explained before, member functions run in the caller thread environment, and act on the target thread object on which they are called. If main() calls T.sleep(d), then main puts T to sleep. But what happens if we want an action to take place *in the caller thread environment*? For example, how can a thread put itself to sleep for a given elapsed time interval?

To handle this issue, C++11 defines some global, non-member functions in the std::this_thread namespace. Here are the non-member function versions of the two member functions discussed before (the std namespace is always understood):

- this_thread::sleep_for(duration d). This function call puts the caller thread in a blocked state for time interval d.
- thread::thread_id this_thread::get_id(). Returns the thread_id of the caller thread.

3.6.5 EXAMPLES OF C++11 THREAD MANAGEMENT

A few examples of C++11 thread operation are presented next, to illustrate and complete the previously introduced concepts.

Launching worker threads

Example 8. In the first example, a worker thread waits in a blocked state for a given number of seconds to simulate a long computation or I/O operation. The main thread launches the worker thread and waits for its termination by calling its join() member function.

The thread function executed by the worker thread is given in Listing 3.15. For clarity, the initial and final messages the worker thread sends to stdout have been suppressed, and only the real code is kept: two lines of code that put the thread to sleep for a number of milliseconds passed as argument. The first line creates a milliseconds duration object defined in the <chronos> header. In this way, the mSecs integer passed as argument is interpreted as a number of milliseconds. For a duration coded in seconds, a std::chrono::seconds object should be constructed. The second line passes this duration object to the sleep_for() function in the this_thread namespace, as discussed in the previous section. The thread then sleeps for the duration is passed as an argument.

The main() function constructs the std::thread object T by passing to the constructor the address of the thread function (which is its function name) and the value of the integer argument to be passed to it. In our case, the worker thread waits for 3 s. Then, main() joins the worker thread, waiting for its termination.

```
#include <iostream>
#include <thread>
#include <chrono>

void ThreadFunc(unsigned mSecs)
    {
    std::chrono::milliseconds workTime(mSecs);  // create duration
    std::this_thread::sleep_for(workTime);      // sleep
    }


int main(int argc, char* argv[])
    {
    std::thread T(ThreadFunc, 3000);    // thread created
    std::cout << "main: waiting for thread " << std::endl;
    T.join();
    std::cout << "main: done" << std::endl;
    return 0;
    }
```

LISTING 3.15

Launching a worker thread

Example 8: Cpp1_S.C

To compile, run make cpp1s.

Example 9. This example modifies the way the thread in the previous example is created. The thread function is always the same. In Example 8, the std::thread object T is created as a local object inside the main() function, in the main thread stack. Consequently, this thread object can only be accessed and acted upon by the main thread.

To create a thread with global scope, the *lazy initialization* strategy discussed above is adopted: rather than declaring a global thread object, a *global pointer* to a thread object is declared. This global pointer is, when the time comes, initialized by main() by a call to the new operator, and it is at this point that the new thread starts running because it is at this point that its constructor is called. This approach is shown in Listing 3.16.

```
std::thread *Wth;     // global data

int main(int argc, char* argv[])
    {
    std::cout << "main: startup" << std::endl;
    Wth = new std::thread(ThreadFunc, 3000);  // thread created
    std::cout << "main: waiting for thread " << std::endl;
    Wth->join();
    std::cout << "main: done" << std::endl;
    delete Wth;
    return 0;
    }
```

LISTING 3.16

Launching a worker thread

Notice that, after the join() function returns, Wth is still a valid pointer, pointing to a not-a-thread object still sitting in the heap. Deleting this pointer at the end of main() restores the memory allocated in the heap.

Example 9: Cpp2_S.C

To compile, run make cpp2s.

Example 10. Next, a thread is created using a function object. Listing 3.17 defines a class used to compute the square root of a number using the iterative Newton's method. This is an ordinary class, with an operator() member function. This class requires three pieces of information: the target number whose square root is to be computed, a guess for the square root value used a starting point of the iterations, and an upper limit to the accepted number of iterations in the calculation.

To demonstrate the flexibility of the function object approach, this information is passed in two different ways: the target value and the initial guess are passed as arguments to the operator() function, but the upper limit to the number of iterations is passed via the function object constructor, as shown in Listing 3.17.

```cpp
class Worker          // This is the function object
   {
   private:
    unsigned Niters;

   public:
    Worker(unsigned N) : Niters(N) {}

    void operator()(double target, double guess)
       {
       std::cout << "Worker: computing sqrt(" << target
               << "), iterations = " << Niters << std::endl;

       // use Newton's method
       // - - - - - - - - - -
       double x;
       double x1 = guess;
       for(unsigned i=0; i<Niters; i++)
          {
          x = x1 - (x1*x1 - target) / (2 * x1);
          if(fabs(x-x1) < 0.0000001) break;
          x1 = x;
          std::cout << "Iter " << i << " - " << x << std::endl;
          }
       std::cout << "Worker: answer = " << x << std::endl;
       }
   };

int main(int argc, char* argv[])
   {
   Worker w(612);             // object w is constructed
   std::thread T(w, 25, 4);   // thread function is w(25, 4)

   std::cout << "main: waiting for thread " << std::endl;
   T.join();
   std::cout << "main: done" << std::endl;
   return 0;
   }
```

LISTING 3.17

Using a function object

The main() function code exhibits the operation of the function object used to create the thread. The thread function the new thread executes is the operator() member function of the Worker class. First, a Worker object w is created (the name is arbitrary). Once the object is created, the operator() member function can be called by using the object name; namely, by invoking w(25, 4) to compute the square root of 25 starting from a guess of 4. The thread constructor is therefore invoked, as before, by passing as arguments the function object name and the arguments to be passed to the operator() function.

Example 10: Cpp3_S.C
To compile, run make cpp3s.

Notice that in this example the result of the computation is printed to the screen, but it is not returned to the main thread. Given the flexibility of function objects, we could imagine returning the result to the main thread by defining an additional public double result field in the Worker class, where the final result is stored before the operator() function completes. Then, the main thread would read the result from the function object w after the worker thread is joined.

The idea is good, but it does not work as such, because of the *copy semantics* used by the thread constructor mentioned before: the function object arguments are passed by value, and the function object itself is copied to another object used internally by the library. Therefore, the return value will not be stored in the original function object w known to main(), but in the internal working copy used by the library. To make this idea work, *the object w known by main() must be passed by reference*, in the way we discuss next.

Passing values by reference
Example 11. Consider first a simple example: a thread function whose only purpose is to update an external variable passed by reference, as shown in Listing 3.18. The thread function adds 10 to the integer passed by reference.

```
void ThreadFunc(int& N)  // a simple thread function
   { N += 10; }

int main(int argc, char* argv[])
   {
   int N = 10;
   std::cout << "\n Initial value of N = " << N << std::endl;
   // - - - - - - - - - - - - - - - - - - - - - - - - - - - -
   std::thread T1(ThreadFunc, N);
   T1.join();
   std::cout << "First value of N = " << N << std::endl;
   // - - - - - - - - - - - - - - - - - - - - - - - - - - - -
   std::thread T2(ThreadFunc, std::ref(N));
   T2.join();
   std::cout << "Second value of N = " << N << std::endl;
   // - - - - - - - - - - - - - - - - - - - - - - - - - - - -
```

```
    return 0;
    }
```

LISTING 3.18

Passing arguments by reference

The main function launches successively two threads. In the first thread T1, the target integer N is passed by value to the constructor, and it is a reference to this value internally stored by the runtime system that will be passed to the thread function. The update will take place, but its target is the internal copy of N, and not the value that main() knows. The program execution shows that our known value of N is not updated.

Next, a second thread T2 is launched, but now N is passed to the constructor using the std::ref(N) qualifier. The program execution shows that now N is correctly updated.

Example 11: Cpp4_S.C

To compile, run make cpp4s.

Example 12. Next, Example 10 is reconsidered, in order to show how to implement the previous idea for returning the result of the computation to the main thread. The Worker function object class is modified by adding a public field double result, where the operator() function stores the result. Then, the std::ref(w) qualifier is used in the constructor to pass the function object itself by reference. In this way, it is the function object known to us and not an internal copy that holds the result at the end of the computation.

```
class Worker
    {
    private:
     unsigned Niters;

    public:
     double result;
     ...
     // the rest is the same
    };

int main(int argc, char* argv[])
    {
    Worker w(500);
    std::thread T(std::ref(w), 25, 7);   // w passed by reference
    T.join();
    std::cout << "main: result obtained is " << w.result << std::endl;
    return 0;
    }
```

LISTING 3.19

Passing a function object by reference

Example 12: Cpp5_S.C

To compile, run make cpp5s.

Transferring thread ownership

It is clearly understood that a std::thread T object represents a thread, which is a unique resource. If a thread object could be copied, we could end up with several objects representing the same unique resource, which is not acceptable. Therefore, *std::thread objects are not copyable*. The copy constructor and the assignment operator are by design deleted in the std::thread class. Threads, however, can be moved from one thread object to another. A thread linked to a thread object T1 can be transferred to another empty object T2, which becomes its identifier, and the initial object T1 becomes a not-a-thread after the move.

Example 13. Listing 3.20 shows how this ownership transfer is performed. A thread T1 that sleeps for 5 s is run. The whole point is to have the thread active long enough so that the transfer operation can be safely performed. When the thread T1 is launched and its thread_id is immediately printed, the code execution reports a positive integer value.

Next, a new thread object T2 is created calling std::move(T1), and the new T1 identity is printed. The reported value is 0, the code for not-a-thread. On the other hand, the reported identity value for T2 is the same as the original T1 identity.

```
void ThreadFunc()
   {
   std::chrono::seconds workTime(5);
   std::this_thread::sleep_for(workTime);  // sleep
   }

int main(int argc, char* argv[])
   {
   std::thread T1(ThreadFunc);      // launch thread  T1
   std::cout << "T1 identity = " << T1.get_id() << std::endl;
   std::thread T2 = std::move(T1);  // transfers thread ownership
   std::cout << "New T1 identity = " << T1.get_id() << std::endl;
   std::cout << "T2 identity    = " << T2.get_id() << std::endl;
   T2.join();
   return 0;
   }
```

LISTING 3.20

Transferring thread ownership

We will come back to the ownership transfer issue in the last example in this section.

Example 13: ThMove_S.C

To compile, run make thmoves.

Launching a worker team

Example 14. This example is the CPP11 version of the Hello4_P.C Pthreads example in which a set of N threads is created. Each worker thread will be identified by an integer rank in [1, N]. Worker threads print a hello message, indicating their rank. The interesting part of this example is the C++11 version of the GetRank() function previously discussed, as well as the procedure adopted for the allocation of N worker threads in the heap.

```cpp
std::thread    **Wth;     // array of thread pointers
int            nTh;      // number of threads

int GetRank()            // auxiliary function
   {
   std::thread::id my_id, target_id;
   int n, my_rank;

   my_id = std::this_thread::get_id();
   n = 0;
   do
      {
      n++;
      target_id = Wth[n]->get_id();
      } while(my_id != target_id && n < nTh);

   if(n<=nTh) my_rank = n;  // if rank OK, return
   else my_rank = (-1);     // else, return error
   return my_rank;
   }


void helloFunc()             // thread function
   {
   std::chrono::milliseconds delay1(500);
   std::this_thread::sleep_for(delay1);   // first delay
   int rank = GetRank();
   // - - - - - - - - - - - - - - - -
   std::chrono::seconds delay2(rank);
   std::this_thread::sleep_for(delay2);   // second delay
   std::cout << "Hello from thread number " << rank
             << std::endl;
   }

int main(int argc, char* argv[])
{

   if(argc==2) nTh = atoi(argv[1]);
```

Continued

```
   else nTh = 4;

   Wth   = new std::thread*[nTh+1];      // allocate thread array
   for(int n=1; n<=nTh; ++n)             // create threads
      Wth[n] = new std::thread(helloFunc);

   for(int n=1; n<=nTh; ++n) Wth[n]->join(); // Join threads
   std::cout << "main: done" << std::endl;

   for(int n=1; n<=nTh; ++n) delete Wth[n]; // delete threads
   delete [] Wth;                        // delete array
   return 0;
   }
```

LISTING 3.21

RunTeam1_S.C

An array Wth[n], n=1, ... N of std::thread* pointers is allocated. Then, each one of these pointers is initialized with a new std::thread object. The global object Wth declared outside main() is a pointer to an array of std::thread objects. This array has size (N+1), because we want to manipulate an *offset 1* vector of thread identities. Therefore, the first slot Wth[0] is not used, and thread objects are allocated starting from Wth[1]. The main function launches and then joins the worker threads.

A few comments about the thread function are in order. When created, the worker threads are first delayed for 500 ms. The reason is that they all call GetRank() to know their rank, and that this function scans the global array Wth. Therefore, the purpose of this initial delay is to ensure the array is completely initialized when accessed. Then, there is a second delay in which each thread sleeps for an interval in seconds equal to their rank. The purpose of this delay is to separate the messages written to stdout.

Example 14: RunTeam1_S.C

To compile, run make runt1s.

Example 15. Finally, this last example shows how to do the same thing (allocating and running a set of nTh worker threads) in a way that shows again the ownership transfer in operation. We will launch nTh threads and stock them in a STL vector container of threads.

The thread function is very simple: it gets a rank integer as argument, sleeps for a duration equal to its rank in seconds, and prints a message to stdout, reporting its rank.

```
#include <iostream>
#include <thread>
#include <chrono>
#include <vector>

void helloFunc(unsigned rank)
```

```
    {
    std::chrono::seconds workTime(rank);
    std::this_thread::sleep_for(workTime);   // sleep
    std::cout << "Hello from thread number " << rank
            << std::endl;
    }

int main(int argc, char* argv[])
    {
    unsigned n, nTh;
    if(argc==2) nTh = atoi(argv[1]);
    else nTh = 4;

    std::vector<std::thread> workers;
    for (n=0; n<nTh; ++n)
        workers.push_back(std::thread(helloFunc, n));

    for(auto &th : workers) th.join();
    std::cout << "Main: done" << std::endl;
    return 0;
    }
```

LISTING 3.22

RunTeam2_S.C

Let us now look at the main function, where there is a lot of action going on in a couple of lines. First of all, a STL vector container of std:: thread objects, called workers, is declared. It is initially an empty vector. Next, threads are created and inserted in this container. Notice that the explicitly created threads are temporary objects that are bound to be destroyed at the end of the loop iteration. These temporary objects are inserted into the vector container, but we know they cannot be copied. Rather, they are moved, which means the thread ownership is transferred to the thread object created inside the container. At this point, the initial temporary thread object becomes a not-a-thread object, and can safely be destroyed at the end of the loop iteration.

Example 15: RunTeam2_S.C

To compile, run make runt2s.

3.7 SPool UTILITY

Several of the previous examples implemented a *fork-join* pattern in order to perform a given parallel treatment. A team of worker threads was created with an explicit assignment coded in the thread function, and then the worker threads were joined by the client thread. In our simple previous examples, all the worker threads were doing the same job (printing a message to *stdout*). A very common pattern in more realistic parallel applications occurs when the worker threads are asked to performing the same action on different sub-sectors of the data set. This very common work sharing construct is called a

SPMD (Single Program, Multiple Data) parallel pattern. It only requires the forking and joining of a set of worker threads, all executing the same thread function on different sectors of the data set.

The SPool utility, included in the vath library, provides a simple interface for implementing a fork-join parallel pattern. As all the classes in this library, SPool is portable in the sense that it has a Pthreads, Windows, and C++11 implementation. This C++ class encapsulates the previously discussed basic libraries thread management interfaces, and it also provides a few useful additional utilities. Its public interfaces are very close in spirit to the way OpenMP implements a fork-join parallel pattern (to be discussed later in this chapter). However, as we will see, there are some differences in design and programming style.

We will henceforth speak of *creating a parallel region* when forking and joining a set of worker threads to perform a parallel treatment. In all the examples that follow, this happens only once in the application, and one can then imagine creating the new worker threads if and when they are needed, and joining them when they terminate and disappear from the scene. However, in many real applications like the ones we will meet in later chapters the creation of a parallel region occurs more than once, often inside a loop that is executed a huge number of times. When this happens, creating new threads every time they are needed and destroying them when they finish introduces too much thread management overhead. Remember that, among other things, every time a new thread is created or destroyed, the stack memory buffer that goes with it must be allocated or released.

In this case, it is more efficient to create the worker team only once, and put them in a blocked state (as indicated in Chapter 2) until some other thread needs their services to run a parallel region. This is efficient because, when sleeping in a blocked state, the worker threads do not use CPU resources and therefore they do not compete for resources with the remaining threads in the application. This is the strategy the SPool adopts, as well as any other high-level management utility like OpenMP or TBB. Later on, we will give some hints on the way this software architecture is implemented

A set of threads available for usage in the way described above is called a *thread pool*. The SPool utility is in fact a thread pool limited to the execution of SMPD parallel jobs, which explains its name.

Role of the client thread

We call the *client thread* the thread that creates the parallel region. Typically, the client thread is the main thread that starts with the process, but this is not required. Thread environments are democratic, and any thread can launch a new worker thread team. Our main design choice is that the client thread *does not join the workers team, and does not participate in the execution of the parallel job*. After activating the workers team, the master thread may continue to do something else and, at some point, it waits for the termination of the activity of the worker threads.

This is slightly different from OpenMP. We will soon see that, in OpenMP, a master thread that reaches a parallel section and launches a team of worker threads suspends whatever task is executing and becomes a *de facto* member of the worker team. The master thread resumes execution of the suspended initial task when the parallel treatment is finished. It would look as if this design choice enables a better usage of CPU resources, if the parallel section engages as many threads as available cores. However, in our case, a master thread waiting to join other threads performs an idle wait and moves to a blocked state *not using CPU resources*. Therefore, if the master thread has nothing to do, all the executing cores are fully available to the worker threads. To sum up: our design choice adds some flexibility to the parallel code because:

- It allows a client thread to continue to do some useful concurrent work after launching the worker team. But if there is no useful work available, CPU resources are not wasted.
- It allows a master thread to create several totally independent worker teams, and execute several independent parallel routines in parallel. This parallel pattern, not easy to implement in OpenMP, will be discussed in detail in Chapter 12.

Here is the public interface of the SPool class:

THE SPOOL PUBLIC INTERFACE

1—Constructing a Spool Object

SPool(int nTh, double stksize=0.0)

- Constructor of the team of nTh worker threads.
- Second argument is, in Pthreads, a scale factor that multiplies the default stack size.
- Second argument is, in Windows, a new value for the stack size.
- If the second argument is zero (default), the stack size is not modified.
- Called by client (master) threads.

2—Forking and joining threads

void Dispatch(void (*fct)(void *), void *arg

- Wakes up and activates the worker threads, executing the task function passed as argument
- Returns immediately after activating the worker thread set.
- Worker threads are identified by an integer rank in [1, N].
- The rank can be used to select the work to be done by each thread.
- Called by client threads.

void WaitForIdle()

- The caller thread moves to a blocked state until all the worker threads complete their previous assignment.
- Called by client threads.

3—Utilities, called by worker threads

int GetRank()

- Returns the rank of the caller worker thread.

void ThreadRange(int& beg, int& end)

- Work sharing utility function.
- Distributes indices in an global integer range across worker threads.
- beg and end are input-output parameters.
- On input, [beg, end) is the global index range.
- On output, [beg, end) is the index sub-range allocated to the caller thread.

void CancelTeam()

- Called by a worker thread to cancel and stop the activity of all the worker team.
- The caller threads informs all other workers that they must terminate.
- This call also terminates the ongoing job.

void SetCancellationPoint()

- Called by a worker thread, to check for cancellation request.
- If cancellation is requested, the current task function terminates.

This public interface is simple: it involves the constructor and destructor of the thread set, as well as member functions to launch a parallel job and wait for its termination. There are also three other utilities useful for some specific applications. Each worker thread in the set is uniquely identified by an integer value called rank in the range $[1, N]$. Any worker thread in the team can learn about its rank by calling the member function GetRank().

Creating SPool objects

The constructor of a SPool object takes two arguments:

- The number N of threads in the set.
- The second argument—a double—corresponds in the Pthreads implementation to a scale factor for the stack size: the default stack size provided by the operating system is multiplied by this scale factor. In the Windows implementation, this value, recast as a long, becomes the new stack size that replaces the default size. In the C++11 implementation, this argument is ignored. If the scale factor passed to the constructor is 0 (the default value), the default stack size is not modified.

These different ways of handling the stack size (something that in any case is rarely needed) are motivated from the fact that in the Pthreads implementation it is possible to inquire about the current stack size value and multiply it by the scale factor. In other environments, instead, there is no direct way of knowing the current stack size value. Therefore, one needs to try a new, absolute value of the stack size and pass it to the constructor.

Running the thread team

The Dispatch() member function activates the N worker to execute the function passed as argument. This function returns immediately after activating the N worker threads. As discussed above, the client thread that calls Dispatch() has the choice of continuing to do some other useful work in parallel with the work done by the thread team, before waiting to join the worker threads.

The master thread at some point calls the member function WaitForIdle(). This function operates *as if* the master thread waited for the termination and joins one by one all the worker threads. Listing 3.23 shows how the SPool objects are used in practice

Creating and using SPool objects

A workers team is created by constructing a SPool object, and the point is: where and how should this object be constructed?

If all we plan to do is fork-join the workers team with the Dispatch–WaitForIdle function calls, then only the client thread needs to access the SPool object, and in this case there is no harm in declaring it as a local object to the client (master) thread. However, most of the time the worker threads need to be able to access the SPool object in order to call some of the utility functions. In this case, the SPool object must be declared with global scope (outside main()), so that it can be seen and accessed by all the threads in the application. From now on, we will most of the time declare SPool objects with global scope.

There are still two possible options to create this global SPool object. If the number of worker threads is hardwired in the application and known at compile time, then it is possible to directly create a global object, initialized by the runtime system before main() starts. Notice that in this utility there is no problem in creating the worker team too early, for reasons that will soon be clear. If, instead, the number of threads is obtained from the command line or from an input file, we are lacking information to create the object in this way. In this case, *a global pointer* to a SPool object is declared. The pointer is initialized later on by main() with a call to the new operator. Listing 3.23 shows how this option proceeds.

```
void th_fct(void *P);
SPool *TS;               // SPool pointer

int main (int argc, char *argv[])
    {
    int nTh;             // read from command line
    TS = new SPool(nTh);  // default values for 2nd arg
    TS->Dispatch(thfct, NULL);
    // – – – – – – – – – – – –
    // Here, main can do other work
    // – – – – – – – – – – – –
    TS->WaitForIdle();            // main joins all worker threads
    delete TS;
    }
```

LISTING 3.23

Using SPool objects

ThreadRange() utility

This function is called by worker threads in a work sharing context where the purpose is to parallelize a loop. In this case, a set of contiguous vector indices must be distributed among the worker threads, to select the sectors of the data set on which each thread will act. This function determines the optimal sub-range of indices for a given worker thread, resulting from a fair work distribution among workers. This is possible because each thread knows the number of threads in the team, as well as its own rank value and the global index range, so that it can compute the optimal sub-range of indices it must handle. See the details of the operation of this function in the example that follows dealing with the addition of two vectors.

CancelTeam() utility

This is the only sophisticated piece of programming in this class. A worker thread calling this function forces the immediate cancellation of the ongoing parallel job. There are some mild implementation differences:

• In Pthreads, this utility relies on a very efficient, native thread cancellation service. The worker threads terminate their lifetime. After cancellation, the thread pool is no longer active, and cannot be reused for another parallel job. But it is always possible to construct on the fly another pool if needed.

- In Windows and C++11, this utility relies on an advanced synchronization tools described in Chapters 8 and 9. In this case, *the parallel job is cancelled*, and the worker threads remain active to perform another job if needed.

3.7.1 UNDER THE SPOOL HOOD

It is instructive to understand the way the SPool objects operate, by creating a pool of threads and putting it in a blocked state waiting to be activated by client threads. Figure 3.2 shows the pool operation:

- Threads are created and launched by the SPool constructor. They execute a thread function defined internally in the class, which implements the behavior that follows.
- As soon as the threads are created, they go to sleep in a blocked state.
- A client thread that dispatches a job initializes an internal pointer to the function to be executed and releases the blocked threads.
- At wake up, the worker threads call the task function via the internal function pointer, and goes back to a blocked state when they complete its execution.
- And so on, and so forth. The worker threads keep executing this infinite loop as new job requests are dispatched.
- When the SPool destructor is called, the worker threads are released, they exit the infinite loop, and are joined by the external master thread that called the destructor.

Notice that the task function passed to the Dispatch() member function is not a thread function in the usual sense, it is a function called by the already existing threads. For this reason, this function does not need to adopt the imposed thread function signature in Pthreads, and it returns void instead of void*.

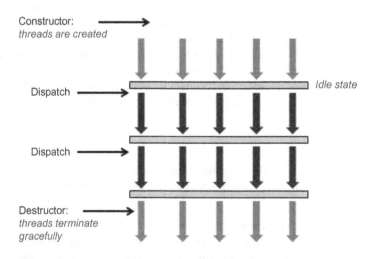

FIGURE 3.2

Operation of the SPool thread worker team.

The source code for the SPool class is simple and compact because it relies on a high-level synchronization utility—a blocking barrier—discussed in Chapter 9. An example is included in Chapter 9 that illustrates the inner behavior of the SPool class.

3.8 SPool EXAMPLES

Let us now take a look at a few simple examples based on the SPool utility, illustrating some common issues in applications programming. These examples use some general-purpose utility classes from the vath library. Their usage is simple and evident:

- **Class Rand**. Objects of this class generate uniformly distributed random doubles in [0, 1].
    - An object R is declared as Rand R(int n), where n is a seed that initializes the generator.
    - Random doubles d are obtained by d = R.draw().
- **Class CpuTimer**. Objects of this class are used to measure execution times of selected code blocks contained between calls to the member functions Start() and Stop().
    - Execution times are reported by a call to Report().
    - This function prints both the *user time*, which is the total execution time of all the threads in the application (equal to the sequential execution time), and the *wall time*, which is the real time elapsed.
    - Obviously, the parallel speedup is the ratio of user to wall time. On a dual-core laptop, for example, the optimal performance is a wall time equal to half the user time.

Given the simplicity of the examples, there is no point in using too many threads to exhibit the speedup resulting from the parallel computation. Two worker threads are often hard wired in the source codes.

3.8.1 ADDITION OF TWO LONG VECTORS

This is a very simple *embarrassingly parallel* problem. The initial sequential source code is in file add_vectors.C. The relevant part of the sequential code is listed below:

```
double A[VECSIZE], B[VECSIZE], C[VECSIZE];

int main (int argc, char *argv[])
    {
    int i, j, nsamples;

    // Get nsamples from the command line
    // - - - - - - - - - - - - - - - - -
    for(int j=0; j<nsamples; n++)
        {
        for(n=0; n<VECSIZE; n++) C[n] = A[n] + B[n];
        }
    ...
    }
```

LISTING 3.24

Adding two vectors : add_vectors.C

The vector addition is repeated nsamples times to be able to measure reasonable execution times. The parallel code is in file AddVectors.C. The main thread launches two worker threads, and each one computes the sum of the first or the second half of the vectors. This application is qualified as *embarrassingly parallel* because no communication whatsoever is required between the worker threads or between the worker threads and the main thread.

Details of the thread function are shown below, because it uses the ThreadRange() work sharing utility. This function receives *a reference to two integers* called beg and end in Listing 3.25, which are *input-output parameters*. On input, these integers are initialized with the values of the global vector index range. This member function knows the rank of the caller thread as well as the number of threads. Therefore, it can compute the index range appropriate to the caller thread. When the function returns, the function arguments contain the caller thread index sub-range.

Notice that we have adopted in this book the C++ STL conventions for index ranges. They are defined by the first and the one past the end values, so ranges are described by the half open interval [*beg, end*).

```
SPool TH(2);          // two worker threads.

void *thread_fct(void *P)
   {
   int beg = 0;                  // initialize [beg, end) to global range
   int end = VECSIZE;
   TH.ThreadRange(beg, end);   // now, [beg, end) is the index range for
                               // this thread
   for(int j=0; j<nsamples; j++)   // compute nsample tiles the sum
      {
      for(int n=beg; n<end; n++) C[n] = A[n] + B[n];
      }
   }
```

LISTING 3.25

Thread function in AddVectors.C

Executing the sequential and the parallel codes for a very large number of samples shows without surprise a speedup of 2.

Example 16: AddVectors.C

To compile, run make addvec. The number of threads is 2. The number of samples is passed from the command line (the default is 1000000).

3.8.2 MONTE CARLO COMPUTATION OF π

The algorithm for the Monte Carlo computation of π is very simple. Look at the Figure 3.3, where a box of side 1 is shown, containing a quarter of a disk of radius 1. The ration of the area of the disk to the area of the box is, naturally, $\pi/4$.

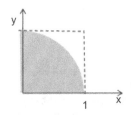

```
double ComputePi()
    {
    double x, y, retval
    long n, count=0;

    for(n=0; n<SAMPLE; n++)
        {
        x = R.draw();
        y = R.draw();
        if( (x*x+y*y) <= 1.0) count++;
        }
    retval = 4.0 * count / SAMPLE;
    return retval;
    }

R provides uniform random numbers
in [0, 1].
```

FIGURE 3.3

Algorithm for the Monte Carlo computation of π.

Suppose that a number SAMPLE of random points of coordinates (x, y) are generated inside the box, by using for x and y uniformly distributed random numbers in $[0, 1]$. These points will uniformly fill the box. Let count be the number of these random points that fall inside the disk. Obviously, the ratio count/SAMPLE will approach the ratio of areas—i.e., $\pi/4$—when SAMPLE is very large. This ratio therefore determines π. The figure also shows the code of a function that computes π.

A parallel version of this code can be written as follows:

- The main thread launches two worker threads. They will share the computational work by executing the code indicated above using SAMPLE events per thread.
- Each worker thread determines its own number count1 or count2 of accepted events. Then, they communicate this number to the main thread, which puts everything together and computes the final value of π as $\pi = 2.0(count1 + count2)/SAMPLE$.

The sequential code for this problem is in source file calcpi.C. Here is the parallel code, contained in the source file CalcPi.C:

```
#include <stdlib.h>
#include <CpuTimer.h>
#include <iostream>
```

Continued

```
#include <Rand.h>
#include <SPool.h>

using namespace std;

SPool TH(2);                    // two worker threads
unsigned long count[3];         // storage of partial results
long nsamples;                  // initialized by command line
Rand R(999);                    // random number generator

void task_fct(void *P)
   {
   unsigned long ct;
   double x, y;
   int rank = TH.GetRank();     // get thread rank in [1, nTh]
   ct = 0;
   for(int n=0; n<nsamples; n++)
      {
      x = R->draw();
      y = R->draw();
      if((x*x+y*y) <= 1.0 ) ct++;
      }
   count[rank] = ct;            // store partial result in global array
   }


int main(int argc, char **argv)
   {
   CpuTimer TR;
   double x, y, pi;

   if(argc==2) nsamples = atoi(argv[1]);
   else nsamples = 1000000;

   TR.Start();
   TH.Dispatch(task_fct, NULL);
   TH.WaitForIdle();
   pi = 4.0 * (double)(count[1]+count[2]) / (2*nsamples);
   TR.Stop();
   TR.Report();

   cout << "\n Value of PI = " << pi << endl;
   }
```

LISTING 3.26

CalcPI.C code

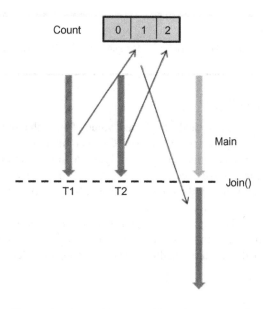

FIGURE 3.4

Worker threads communicating partial results to main().

Here we see for the first time the necessity of communicating partial results obtained by each worker thread, to the master thread. This can be done by introducing a global integer array, count[ ]. The worker thread of rank k writes its partial result at the array element count[k]. Then, the main thread uses these partial results to complete the computation, but *only after returning from the wait that guarantees that all the worker threads have completed their assignment*, to make absolutely sure the count array contains the correct data (a complete explanation of the fact that, after the wait operation, the master thread will read the correct data values from the global array, will be presented in Chapter 7). This looks rather obvious, as illustrated in Figure 3.4.

Notice also that in this computation of π we are just accumulating partial results provided by each thread. This kind of operation, called a *reduction operation*, is very common in applications programming. The partial results can be directly accumulated in a global variable, but, as discussed in Chapter 5, this requires special care. The next chapters will describe general ways of performing reduction operations in multithreaded environments.

The number of threads in CalcPi.C is hardwired to 2. With a reasonably large number of samples, you should be able to see a speedup of 2 for the parallel code, using the O3 compiler option. This speedup is also verified on a dual-core laptop, in spite of the fact that we are using *three threads*: the main thread plus the two worker threads that do the job. This confirms what has often been stated before: while waiting to join the worker threads, the main thread is not using CPU resources. The two cores are therefore fully available for the worker threads.

Example 17: CalcPi.C

To compile, run make calcpi. The number of threads is 2. The number of samples is passed from the command line (the default is 1000000).

3.8.3 THREAD SAFETY ISSUE

When the CalcPi1 code is executed, it yields the correct value of π, with a precision that increases with the number N of samples. More precisely, in a Monte Carlo computation, the precision increases like $\sqrt{N}$: in order to improve the precision by one decimal figure, N must be multiplied by a factor of 100. One can also observe that consecutive executions of the *same code, with the same number of samples* do not return exactly the same value all the time. Results will be slightly different, within the precision of the calculation. This is not very important in this case, because the result is known in advance and can be trusted. In other cases, having an application that provides non-reproducible results may be disturbing. The code we are discussing is not entirely *thread safe*, in the sense that it exhibits some mild dependence on the way threads are scheduled. The next chapter is devoted to a discussion of this issue.

3.9 FIRST LOOK AT OpenMP

A complete discussion of OpenMP is presented in Chapter 10, but it is quite instructive to now take a first look at the way in which the previous SPool based examples can be formulated in OpenMP. The main issue is the replacement of the SPool driven fork-join mechanism by the equivalent fork-join mechanism in OpenMP, based on the parallel directive.

Thread management in OpenMP is implemented with *directives*, followed by a code block to which the directive applies. A directive together with its associated code block is called an OpenMP *construct*.

```
int main(int argc, char **argv)
    {
    ...
    #pragma omp parallel nthreads=2
        {
        // code to be executed by the
        // worker threads
        }
    ...
    }
```

LISTING 3.27

Parallel directive in OpenMP

The listing above shows the parallel construct. When the main thread reaches the parallel construct, it suspends its ongoing task joins the worker team and all together executes the code inside the block. On exit from the block, when all workers have finished, the main thread resumes the suspended execution. Notice that OpenMP does not require a clean cut, well-defined task function inside the code block. The task function will be constructed by the compiler, as long as it is able to understand the programmer intentions. And, in order to make these intentions clear, OpenMP provides a number of *clauses* added to the directive that inform the compiler how a parallel task must be constructed from the code block that follows. The statement nthreads=2 is a clause used to select the number of worker threads (including the master thread). Other clauses have to do with the nature of the data items in the code block (shared? local to a thread?...) All these issues are examined in detail in Chapter 10.

In our examples, we have started thinking parallel from the start, clearly identifying the global variables, and the variables local to the main and the worker threads. In all cases, explicit task functions to be executed by the worker threads are provided. In this context, the migration to OpenMP is straightforward. Here below is the OpenMP version of the CalcPi code, in the source file, CalcPiOmp.C. The code that follows is very close to the SPool code we discussed before, with only three modifications that are explicitly underlined in Listing 3.28.

```
#include <stdlib.h>
#include <TimeReport.h>
#include <iostream>
#include <Rand.h>

// — — — — new OPENMP — — ——
#include <omp.h>
// — — — — — — — — — — — ——

using namespace std;
unsigned long count[2];        // storage of partial results
long nsamples;                 // initialized by command line
Rand R(999);                   // random number generator

void task_fct()                // task executed by each OpenMP thread
   {
   unsigned long ct;
   double x, y;

   // — — — — — — new OPENMP — — ——
   int rank = omp_get_thread_num();  // get thread rank in [0, nTh—1]
   // — — — — — — — — — — — — — — ——

   ct = 0;
   for(int n=0; n<nsamples; n++)
      {
      x = R—>draw();
      y = R—>draw();
      if((x*x+y*y) <= 1.0 ) ct++;
      }
```

Continued

```
    count[rank] = ct;              // store partial result un global array
    }

int main(int argc, char **argv)
    {
    TimeReport TR;
    double x, y, pi;

    if(argc==2) nsamples = atoi(argv[1]);
    else nsamples = 1000000;
    TR.StartTiming();

    // – – – – – – new OPENMP – – – – –
    #pragma omp parallel nthreads=2
        {
        task_fct();
        }
    // – – – – – – – – – – – – – – – – –

    pi = 4.0 * (double)(count[0]+count[1]) / (2*nsamples);
    TR.StopTiming();
    TR.ReportTimes();

    cout << "\n Value of PI = " << pi << endl;
    }
```

LISTING 3.28

OpenMP version, CalcPIOmp.C

Here are the modifications introduced in the code:

- The header file omp.h is included, instead of SPool.h.
- In the task function task_fct(), the call to GetRank() is replaced by a call to the OpenMP library function omp_get_thread_num, which returns the thread rank. However, keep in mind that in OpenMP ranks are in the range [0, Nth-1]. The master thread that gets involved in the worker team always carries the rank 0.
- The parallel section is created with the parallel directive. Since all the work of creating the thread function is already done, the parallel code block reduces to a call to task_fct().
- Finally, the size of the count array has been adapted to the fact that now thread ranks are 0 or 1 (instead of 1 and 2 as in the SPool case).

Example 18: CalcPiOmp.C

To compile, run make calcpiomp. The number of threads is 2. The number of samples is passed from the command line (the default is 1000000).

When running this code, a perfect speedup of 2 is observed. There is no difference in performance with respect to the SPool based code.

3.9.1 EXAMPLE: COMPUTING THE AREA UNDER A CURVE

Our next example is another computation of π based on the following result:

$$\int_0^1 \frac{4}{1+x^2}\, dx = \pi$$

This integral is computed by launching N threads. Using a domain decomposition strategy, each worker thread computes the integral in different subdomains of the initial domain $[0, 1]$. As in the previous example, a reduction needs to be performed, to collect the partial results coming from each thread. This problem is handled for the time being in the same way as before: worker threads deposit their results in a global array of doubles, and the main thread completes the computation after the workers team is again idle.

The source code is in the file AreaPi1.C. In order to introduce some new features, we have chosen to leave the number of worker threads open. The main thread gets the number of threads from the command line, with a default value if there is no input from the user. The main differences with the previous example are:

- The size of the global array that will hold the partial results provided by the worker threads is not known. This array is dynamically allocated by the main thread once the number of worker threads is known.
- All threads call a global function—taken from *Numerical Recipes in C*, [16]—that computes the integral of an arbitrary function $f(x)$ in an arbitrary interval $[a, b]$ with given precision. As discussed in the next chapter, this function is thread safe because it has no persistent internal state, and its return values depend only on the argument list.
- Each worker thread determines the limits of its integration domain from the knowledge of the number of threads nTh and its own rank.

Here is a partial listing showing the thread function.

```
// Global data
// – – – – – –
double *result;    // this array stores partial results

// Thread function
// – – – – – – – – –
void thread_fct()
   {
```

Continued

```
    double size = 1.0/nTh;
    int rank    = omp_get_thread_num();
    double a    = rank*size;
    double b    = (rank+1)*size;
    retval = Area(a, b, my_fct, 0.0000001);   // NRC routine
    result[rank] = retval;
    }
```

LISTING 3.29

Another computation of π

Example 19: AreaPi.C

To compile, run make areapi. The number of threads is read from the command line (the default is 4).

A Spool version of this example is also available. Again, both versions are very close and the differences are easy to understand.

Example 20: AreaPiOmp.C

To compile, run make areapiomp. The number of threads is read from the command line (the default is 4).

3.10 DATABASE SEARCH EXAMPLE

In the programming style adopted up to now, the similarities between the SPool and OpenMP versions of our examples are so evident that one may legitimately wonder about the interest of looking at alternatives to OpenMP. This is indeed the case because the examples examined up to now have a very simple fork-join parallel pattern. The SPool utility will be reconsidered in Chapter 12, including a detailed discussion of what specific parallel contexts may benefit from the innocent looking difference with OpenMP (client threads not getting involved in the parallel job execution). One of the reasons for looking at basic libraries is that OpenMP does not always give programmers direct access to all their possible services, mainly because most of the time they are not needed in applications programming. However, occasionally, some low-level services may help to solve efficiently a given computational problem, as we will have the opportunity of observing in later chapters. One of the reasons for implementing the Spool utility was the necessity of properly canceling a parallel treatment. This is possible in OpenMP only since the latest 4.0 release.

The SPool tools to needed cancel a parallel job are the CancelTeam() and SetCancellationPoint() member functions, used to solve the following problem. Imagine that N worker threads are performing a search in a database. Each thread is performing the same search on independent data sectors. Obviously, once a thread finds the requested data, the parallel search must be stopped. Now, it is possible to formulate this problem by synchronizing the worker threads in such a way that at each step in the search they all know what all the others are doing, and can stop when one of them completes the search. But this approach introduces a substantial synchronization overhead that spoils the parallel performance. It is in fact much more efficient to let all the threads go ahead without any kind of synchronization. The first thread that completes the search calls the CancelTeam() function before terminating. This function smoothly terminates the operation of the worker threads.

The program listed below simulates a database search by launching a number of worker threads that keep retrieving a random number in [0,1] from a random number generator R, until they get a number equal to a given target, called target in Listing 3.30, within a given precision EPS. Each worker thread has its own, local, random number generator, initialized with a unique seed depending on the thread rank. Therefore, each thread retrieves a personalized random number suite, so that there is only one thread that completes the random search first.

The thread function is straightforward: threads enter an infinite loop retrieving random numbers. The purpose of the call to SetCancellationPoint() is to check if a cancellation request has been posted, and if that is the case this function call terminates the ongoing task. The thread that finds the requested target writes the target found as well as its rank in a global structure, and calls CancelTeam(), which terminates the job. The master thread, after the job termination, reads the result of the search from the global structure.

```
struct Data      // data passed to main thread
   {
   double d;
   int    rank;
   };

SPool *TS;
const double EPS = 0.000000001;
const double target = 0.58248921;
Data D;

// The workers thread function
// – – – – – – – – – – – – – – –
void th_fct(void *arg)
   {
   double d;
   int rank = TS–>GetRank();
   Rand R(999*rank);

   for(;;)
      {
      TS–>SetCancellationPoint();
      d = R.draw();
      if(fabs(d–target)<EPS)
         {
         D.d = d;
         D.rank = rank;
         TS–>CancelTeam();
```

Continued

```
                 }

             }
         }

  int main(int argc, char **argv)
      {
      int nTh;
      if(argc==2) nTh = atoi(argv[1]);
      else nTh = 2;

      TS = new SPool(nTh);          // create workers
      TS->Dispatch(th_fct, NULL);   // launch job
      TS->WaitForIdle();

      std::cout << "\n Received value " << D.d << " from thread "
                << D.rank << std::endl;
      delete TS;
      return 0;
      }
```

LISTING 3.30

DbSearch.C: simulating a database search

The main function is also simple. The number of threads is read from the command line (the default is 2). Increasing the precision (by decreasing EPS) increases the work to be done to find the result. The source file is DbSearch.C.

Example 21: DbSearch.C

To compile, run make dbsearch. The number of threads is read from the command line (the default is 4).

Executing the codes, for the Pthreads version the result comes out in about 1 second. This service uses a native thread cancellation service. Trying to implement this code using standard synchronization tools like barriers, in which each thread checks at each loop iteration what all others are doing, results in unacceptable performances (more than 20 s). The OpenMP 4.0 implementation using the parallel section cancellation service—discussed in Chapter 10—is as efficient as the SPool version proposed here.

3.11 CONCLUSIONS

The simple examples discussed in this chapter have introduced some relevant issues common in multithreaded applications programming. This was first done by using a simple C++ class that encapsulates the basic library protocols for thread creation and termination. However, as shown in the OpenMP versions of the examples, the programming issues are very general and relevant for any programming environment.

We have been able to cope with the communication problems raised in our examples by waiting for worker thread termination before using their partial results. But this is too restrictive. More powerful synchronization tools will be introduced in Chapter 9 that will allow us, among other things, to easily handle data transfers among threads.

3.12 ANNEX: CODING C++11 TIME DURATIONS

The <chrono> header is rather sophisticated, and it proposes a variety of ways of describing *time durations*—intervals of time relative to an initial date, typically the moment at which a function is called—as well as absolute dates in the future. We will meet, as we proceed, a variety of functions that execute *timed waits*, called either wait until(), in which an absolute date for the end of the wait is given, or wait_for() in which the thread waits for a given duration. Absolute dates will never be used in this book, so we restrict ourselves to the description of time durations.

The std::chrono::duration class is defined as follows:

```
template <typename Rep, typename Period>
std::chrono::duration<Rep, Period> const& time_duration;
```

LISTING 3.31

Declaration of the duration class

There are therefore two template parameters that select two types needed to define a duration. The idea is simple: a duration object, called time_duration in the listing above, stores a number of clock ticks:

- The second template parameter is a type that defines the time period between successive ticks, expressed as a fraction of a second. This is achieved by an instance of the std::ration<N, D> class that defines the rational number N/D:
    - std::ratio< 1, 50> is one fiftieth of a second.
    - std::ratio<1, 1000> is one millisecond.
    - std::ratio<60, 1> is one minute.
- The first template parameter is the integer type of the data item that stores the number of ticks (time_duration above): short, int, long, long long.
    - std::chrono::duration<short, std::ratio<1, 50>> count stores in a short the number of one fiftieths of a second.
    - std::chrono::duration<long, std::ratio<60, 1>> stores in a long the number of minutes.

This is the most general way of defining a duration. There are also template specialization that simplify programming, like std::chrono::milliseconds and std::chrono::seconds, that declare integers representing milliseconds and seconds, respectively. They have been used in our previous examples.

THREAD-SAFE PROGRAMMING

4.1 **INTRODUCTION**

We learned in Chapter 2 that it is perfectly legitimate to have several threads concurrently calling the same library function. A few subtle issues arise, however, in this context. A function is said to be *thread safe* if its behavior, when called by client code in a multithreaded environment, is in conformity with its service specifications. This is, however, not always the case, and this chapter explores different ways of restoring thread safety when this happens.

The concept of thread safety also applies to data sets. It is by no means obvious that a data set—a vector container, for example—will behave according to expectations when concurrently accessed by several threads. The STL containers, in fact, are not thread safe: they do not operate as expected when used directly in a multithreaded environment, and special precautions must be taken. Thread safety for data sets is discussed in-depth in the next chapter.

4.1.1 **FIRST EXAMPLE: THE MONTE CARLO π CODE**

The CalcPi Monte Carlo code yields the correct value of π, with a precision that increases with the number of samples N. However, it was observed that consecutive executions of the *same code, with the same number of samples* do not return *exactly* the same value all the time. Results are slightly different, within the precision of the calculation. This is not very important in this case. But in other cases, having an application returning non-reproducible results may be disturbing. Are we facing a feature, or a bug?

The behavior of the CalcPi.C code is easily understood: it arises from the fact that *the two worker threads are accessing the same, global, random number generator*. Indeed, the random number generator R is declared with global scope, and its draw() function is called by both threads, which is a legitimate action. The problem results from the nature of the random number generator itself.

There is in fact nothing random in a random number generator. The generator returns a *deterministic* suite of numbers *that look random*. The suite is cyclic: after a usually very long period, it repeats itself. Initializing the generator just chooses the starting point of the cyclic suite. In fact, the generator maintains a persistent internal state between successive calls that determines the outcome of the next call. For the particular generator used in the CalcPi code, this persistent internal state is carried by the integer variable called seed. When the generator is called, the current value of seed determines both the returned random number and the new value of seed to be used in the next call.

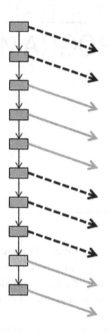

FIGURE 4.1

Two threads calling a global random number generator.

Consider now two threads—a black thread and a gray thread, calling a global generator as shown in Figure 4.1. The generator is represented by the gray box. After returning a value its internal state is changed, and this new internal state determines the next return value. As the figure shows, the generator correctly does its job and delivers to the two threads a unique and deterministic suite of pseudo-random numbers. But the way in which these numbers are distributed among the two threads is not reproducible, because it depends on the particular way in which the threads are scheduled at each run. Since the random numbers received by each thread are not strictly the same at each run, there will be small differences in the acceptance results for each one of them, and this will reflect in small differences in the final result for π.

This is the first example of a *thread safety* issue: the sensitivity of an application to the inner workings of the thread scheduler. Even if in this example the problem can be ignored, this is something that one should definitely be able to control. There are of course clean solutions to this issue, which are the subject of this chapter.

4.2 SOME LIBRARY FUNCTIONS ARE NOT THREAD SAFE

It should be obvious by now that stateless library functions, limited to the manipulation of the argument values passed to the function and local variables sitting in the stack, are thread safe. The stack mechanism for function calls guarantees thread safety in this case. On the other hand, *functions that maintain a persistent internal state between calls*, which records the history of previous calls

str $\longrightarrow$

FIGURE 4.2

Parsing a string.

to determine the outcome of the next one, *are not thread safe*. They should not be used as such in multithreaded codes, because they cannot be shared among threads. Functions maintaining an internal state can only be used in a *function per thread* basis.

A classical example taken from the C standard library is the strtok function, used to parse a string and to extract tokens from it (which are like the words in a phrase), after defining the characters that separate tokens (like the whitespace in Figure 4.2). The signature of this function is given below.

```
#include <string.h>

char* strtok(char *str,          // the target string
             const char *delim);  // token delimiter chars
```

LISTING 4.1

strtok() function

This function parses a string into a sequence of tokens as follows:

- On the first call to strtok(), the string to be parsed is specified in str. In subsequent calls to parse the same string, the str argument must be NULL.
- The delim argument specifies a set of characters that delimit the tokens in the parsed string.
- Each call to strtok() returns a pointer to a null-terminated string containing the next token. The returned string does not include the delimiting character.
- If no more tokens are found, the function returns a NULL pointer.
- Obviously, strtok() maintains an internal state that records the parsing position in the initial string. *If the function is called again with a non-null* str *pointer, the function forgets about its previous internal state and starts parsing the new string.*

Let us now imagine that thread T1 starts parsing the string str1 and that, before the parsing is finished, thread T2 starts parsing another string str2. When T1 calls strtok() again, it will receive a token from str2, not from str1!. The situation in this case is totally different from the previous Monte Carlo example, where the lack of thread safety was producing slightly different results in the application. Here, the results will be totally wrong.

The C standard library provides *reentrant versions* of many functions that are not thread safe. Reentrant means the functions are thread safe, and can be safely used in a multithreaded environment. The function we have been discussing has a reentrant version called strtok_r(), but with a different signature. Take a look at the man pages (man strtok).

Reentrant library functions are a great help to programmers, but in many cases we have to provide our own reentrant routines. This is the subject we will discuss next.

4.3 DEALING WITH RANDOM NUMBER GENERATORS

Random number generators—widely used in many areas of computational sciences—will be used to discuss in detail the different options for implementing thread safety when dealing with functions with persistent internal state. The objective is the generation of distinct and reproducible sequences of random numbers for each thread participating in the parallel treatment. There are three different ways of attaining this goal, and they will be illustrated with the Monte Carlo computation of π discussed in the previous chapter.

How can a function maintain a persistent state?

In order to understand how functions with persistent internal state operate, let us go back to the very simple generator that produces uniform deviates in [0, 1], used in the Monte Carlo computation of π. We will often use in this book the *Park-Miller minimal standard generator* described in Chapter 7 of [16]. Here is the definition of the generator (for details about the constant values, review the Rand.h include file)

```
double Rand()
    {
    static int seed = 999;
    seed = (seed * IMUL + IADD) & MASK;
    return (seed * SCALE);
    }
```

LISTING 4.2

Simple random number generator

In this function, the persistent internal state is the integer seed. It looks superficially as if it was a local variable, but it is not. Local variables, allocated in the executing thread stack, are destroyed when the function returns. The whole point is the static qualifier of seed , which makes all the difference: the compiler manages in this case to preserve this variable across function calls. Static variables are secretly allocated by the compiler on the heap, and they are accessed through a pointer the compiler stores in some place where it can be recovered every time the function is called. This is what is really happening under the hood, even if the programmer thinks he is manipulating just a special local variable. Another point to be observed is that the initialization statement of the static variable is only executed the first time the function is called. When this generator is accessed by different threads, all the threads share the same seed. This is what makes this function thread unsafe.

Three different strategies can be adopted to restore thread safety for functions with internal persistent state:

- Adopt the standard C library strategy and write a new, stateless reentrant function by changing the signature of the generator in the way discussed in the following.
- Rather than using a global library function accessed by all threads, C++ objects can be used to generate random numbers. It is then possible to allocate a *local* random number generator to each thread. We dispose in this way an independent generator allocated to each parallel task engaged in the computation.
- *Thread local storage* services—proposed by all programming environments—can be used to implement reentrant versions of global, stateful library functions, *without changing their signature*.

This is achieved by modifying the behavior of static variables. They are no longer shared, because these utilities introduce *one static variable per thread*.

The relative merits of all these options will be assessed after discussing the way they operate.

4.3.1 USING STATELESS GENERATORS

In this case, the internal state is taken away from the internal data set of the generator. Instead, it is passed as a new argument in the function call. Each thread allocates its own, proprietary, internal state in a local structure, and passes a pointer to this structure as an argument to the generator, who can then access, use, and modify it. Now, the generator has no memory and no history. It reads and modifies the state received as argument and returns the corresponding random number. If, in addition, each thread performs a personalized initialization of the internal state, each thread will dispose of a personalized and reproducible random number sequence.

A partial listing of the source file McSafe.C is shown below, where the Monte Carlo computation of π is reformulated using a reentrant generator. The listing shows the modified version of the Rand() library function: the signature has changed, and a pointer to the seed to be used is passed as an argument. In the thread function, each thread initializes its local integer seed in a particular way. Different threads have different seeds, multiples of 999 (remember that SPool ranks start at 1). When the code is executed, results are perfectly reproducible.

```
double Rand(int *seed)     // reentrant generator
   {
   *seed = (*seed * IMUL + IADD) & MASK;
   return (*seed * SCALE);
   }

void task_fct(void *P)     // task function
   {
   double x, y;
   long count;

   int seed, rank;
   rank = TH.GetRank();
   seed =999*rank;

   count = 0;
   for(size_t n=0; n<nsamples; n++)
      {
      x = Rand(&seed);
      y = Rand(&seed);
      if((x*x+y*y) <= 1.0 ) count++;
      }
   accepted[rank] = count;
   }
```

LISTING 4.3

Partial listing of McSafe.C—stateless generator

Example 1: McSafe.C

To compile, run make mcsafe. The number of threads is 2. The number of samples is read from the command line (the default is 1000000).

4.3.2 USING LOCAL C++ OBJECTS

C++ provides a simple way of handling the problem of disposing of one independent generator per thread. Rather than defining a function with internal state, a class with private data can be defined as follows:

```
class Rand
    {
    private:
     long seed;

    public:
     Rand(long S) : seed(S) {}

     double Draw()
        {
        seed = (seed * IMUL + IADD) & MASK;
        return (seed * SCALE);
        }
    };

...
SPool TH(2);            // global SPool, 2 threads
...

void task_fct(void *P)
    {
    double x, y;
    long count;
    int rank;

    rank = TH.GetRank();
    Rand R(999*(rank+1));
    count = 0;
    for(size_t n=0; n<nsamples; n++)
       {
       x = R.Draw();
       y = R.Draw();
       if((x*x+y*y) <= 1.0 ) count++;
       }
    accepted[rank] = count;
    }
```

LISTING 4.4

Generating random numbers with C++ objects

It is now possible to have in the application as many independent objects instances of the class as we want, each with its own private internal data encapsulating the internal state of the generator. The member function Draw() implements the algorithm that, acting on the private data, returns the random sequence.

If only one global Rand object is used to provide random numbers—as it was done in the previous chapter—then we are in the same trouble as before. But the point now is to create one *local* Rand object per thread, as shown in Listing 4.4. Notice that the internal state is initialized by the constructor of the Rand objects in a thread specific way, using as before the thread rank to define the initial seed of the uniform deviate. This procedure is similar to the previous one, except that now the bookkeeping of passing the internal state to the generator function is implicitly managed by the compiler.

Example 2: McObj.C

To compile, run make mcobj. The number of threads is 2. The number of samples is read from the command line (default is 1000000).

4.4 THREAD LOCAL STORAGE SERVICES

All multithreaded programming environments provide a *thread local storage* feature—henceforth called TLS—that generalizes static variables to a multithreaded environment. Static variables can now be allocated on a per thread basis, and a function accessed by several threads can dispose of *one independent static variable per thread*. This section presents the way TLS is implemented in the various programming environments.

TLS facilities are not restricted to the enforcement of thread safety in function calls. Chapter 9 will show how TLS utilities, combined with the atomic utilities discussed in Chapter 8, can be used to implement a custom barrier synchronization utility that outperforms the native Pthreads barriers, as demonstrated by the full applications discussed in Chapters 13–15.

TLS utilities operate as follows:

- Thread local variables maintain their value between function calls.
- If the function is called by several threads, the library runtime system *maintains in the heap a copy of one data element per thread* between function calls, with a well-established ownership. A thread always recovers its proprietary data value at all subsequent function calls. This is true no matter how many threads are calling the function.

Before discussing how this feature is implemented in the different programming environments, it is useful to understand how such a mechanism, sketched in Figure 4.3, can operate under the hood. Let us imagine that a given function needs to benefit from thread local storage for a generic data item T (an integer seed, for example, as in our previous examples):

- The application code first requests the creation of a *global container* where T* pointers—integer pointers in our case—will be stored by different threads between successive function calls. This global pointer container is called a key in Pthreads.

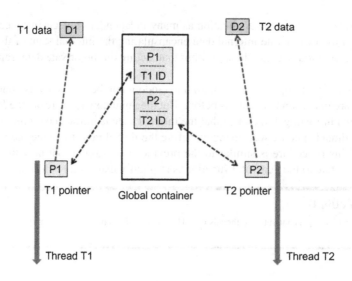

FIGURE 4.3

Thread local storage mechanism.

- There is a first initialization phase where each thread allocates on the heap and initializes its own copy of the persistent data item. In Figure 4.3, thread T1—or T2—allocates an integer D1—or D2—at the address P1—or P2. Once this is done, each thread stores this pointer in the global pointer container.
- At each function call, the thread safe function recovers first the relevant pointer from the container. The container keeps track of pointer ownership, by establishing a map between the stored pointers and the caller thread identity. Each thread executing the function receives in return its proprietary pointer. The function can then read or modify the value of thread the local persistent data item.
- If an application has several different data items requiring TLS, an independent pointer container per data item is required.

The thread local storage interfaces in Pthreads and Windows follow very closely the description given above. In C++11, OpenMP, and TBB the pointer manipulation is hidden to the programmer and the initialization of thread local variables is simpler. We discuss next the specific thread local storage interfaces proposed by the different programming environments.

4.4.1 C++11 THREAD_LOCAL KEYWORD

C++11 has a simple and efficient implementation of thread local storage, based on the thread_local keyword, which declares a variable for which an instance per thread is constructed in the application.

In C++11, thread_local variables can have different scopes:

- Namespace scope (global scope),
- Static data members of classes,
- local variables inside functions. In this case, they act as a static local variable per thread.

In the first two cases, they are constructed before first use. Local thread_local variables inside a function are initialized the first time as the flow control passes through their declaration in a given thread. Destructors are called when the owner thread returns or calls std::exit().

Thread local variables have, as discussed before, different addresses in different threads. C++11 allows programmers to publish them: a normal pointer to a thread_local variable can be obtained by one thread and passed to another thread. Listing 4.5 shows how the global Rand() generator is rendered thread safe, in the CalcPi.C code:

```
SPool *TH;        // global thread pool

double Rand()
    {
    thread_local int my_seed = 999 * TH->GetRank();
    int retval = (my_seed * IMUL + IADD) & MASK;
    my_seed = retval;
    return (retval * SCALE);
    }

// Task function and main function are the same as in
// CalcPi.C.
```

LISTING 4.5

McSafe_S.C (partial listing)

Look at the declaration and initialization of the thread_local my_seed in the Rand() function. There is a substantial amount of intelligence in this unique statement: it is executed *the first time that a new thread calls the function*. Moreover, a thread specific initialization of my_seed, proportional to the rank of the caller thread, is implemented. In the Monte Carlo computation that follows, each thread receives a personalized, reproducible suite of uniform deviates.

Example 3: McSafe_S.C

To compile, run make mcsafe_s. The number of threads is 2. The number of samples is read from the command line (the default is 1000000).

4.4.2 OpenMP THREADPRIVATE DIRECTIVE

OpenMP also introduces another elegant programming interface for TLS: a threadprivate directive that promotes a static local variable to a TLS status. Again, here are the very simple modifications that need to be introduced in the unsafe random number generator Rand() to make the CalcPiOmp.C example (Listing 3.28 in Chapter 3) thread safe. The source code is McSafeOmp.C:

```
double Rand()
    {
    static int seed = 999 * omp_get_thread_num();
    #pragma omp threadprivate(seed)
```

Continued

```
        seed = (seed * IMUL + IADD) & MASK;
        return (seed * SCALE);
        }
```

LISTING 4.6

Partial listing of McSafeOmp.C

All that has happened here is that a directive has been added to the unsafe version of the Rand()
function, which promotes the previously declared static variables seed to a threadprivate status.

Example 4: McSafeOmp.C

To compile, run make mcsafeomp. The number of threads is 2. The number of samples is read from the command line (the
default is 1000000).

4.4.3 WINDOWS TLS SERVICES

Windows has a simple TLS service, with programming interfaces that closely follow the description
shown in Figure 4.3. For each local variable that requires TLS, a container of pointers is requested
to the operating system, which returns an index identifying the container. Then, each thread uses this
index to store or retrieve the pointer referring to the thread local instance of the variable, *cast as void
pointers*. Here is the Windows TLS programming interface, as described in the Windows API online
documentation [13]:

- DWORD TlsAlloc(). This function call returns an index that identifies the global pointer container,
  seen by all threads. Any thread in the process can subsequently use this index to store and retrieve
  its proprietary pointer.
- BOOL TlsSetValue(DWORD index, LPVOID ptr): Stores the pointer value ptr in the container
  referenced by index. Threads make this call to store their local pointer value when the local
  variable is first allocated. Returns false in case of failure.
- LPVOID TlsGetValue(DWORD index): Threads call this function to retrieve their pointer value at each
  function call.
- BOOL TlsFree(DWORD index): Releases the pointer container when the service is no longer needed.

Listing 4.7 shows how the above programming interface is used in the computation pf π. The
main difference with the C++11 or OpenMP environments is that there is no automatic initialization of
thread local variables the first time the generator is accessed. Allocation, initialization, and storage of
proprietary pointers must be done explicitly. In the program below, tlsIndex is the index returned by the
kernel, identifying the pointer container. This index is initialized by main() when the program starts.

The InitPointer() function listed below is an initialization task performed by all threads, which
allocate and initialize their individual seeds, and store the corresponding pointers in the global pointer
container. The only modification to the Rand() function is the first statement in the function body, in
which the proprietary pointer is retrieved from the pointer container. The task function computing π is
not modified. Finally, notice that the main() function *launches two parallel jobs*: the pointer initialization
job and the actual computation.

```
// Global variables
// - - - - - - - -
SPool *TH;
...
DWORD tlsIndex;    // Windows TLS container
...
void InitPointer(void *P)   // Initialization parallel job
   {
   int *seedptr;
   int rank = TH->GetRank();

   // Allocate seed in the heap, and store pointer in
   // tlsIndex
   // - - - - - - - - - - - - - - - - - - - - - - - - -
   seedptr = new int(999*rank);
   TlsSetValue( tlsIndex, static_cast<void*>(seedptr));
   }


double Rand()  // modified generator
   {
   int *my_seed = static_cast<int*>(TlsGetValue(tlsIndex));
   int retval = (*my_seed * IMUL + IADD) & MASK;
   *my_seed = retval;
   return (retval * SCALE);
   }


// The main function
// - - - - - - - - -

int main(int argc, char **argv)
   {
   long C;
   ...
   tlsIndex = TlsAlloc();    // initialize global container
   ...
   // Initialize thread specific pointers
   // - - - - - - - - - - - - - - - - - -
   TH->Dispatch(InitPointer, NULL);
   TH->WaitForIdle();

   // Perform the computation
   // - - - - - - - - - - - -
   TH->Dispatch(task_fct, NULL);
   TH->WaitForIdle();

   C = 0;
   for(int n=1; n<=nTh; ++n) C += accepted[n];
   double pi = 4.0 * (double)C / (nsamples*nTh);
   cout << "\n Value of PI = " << pi << endl;
   }
```

LISTING 4.7

Partial listing of McSafe_W.C

Example 5: McSafe_W.C

To compile, run nmake mcsafe_w. The number of threads is 2. The number of samples is read from the command line (the default is 1000000).

4.4.4 THREAD LOCAL CLASSES IN TBB

TBB implements TLS by following the same strategy described before, but the programming interfaces are slightly different: an explicit initialization of thread local variables is not needed, and there are no explicit pointer manipulations. The TBB documentation on this subject can be found in the "Thread Local Storage" topic [17].

TBB has two different implementations of TLS in two class templates, the template parameter T being the type of the thread local data variable to be stored. Object instances of these classes are the global containers that store the different T* pointers. Both TBB classes implement TLS, but they differ in the nature of some additional services they provide. The two classes are:

- combinable<T>. This class is useful when a reduction of the different instances of the thread local variable needs to be performed.
- enumerable_thread_specific<T>. This class enables access to the global container holding the different instances of the thread local variable, as an STL container, with iterators, in order to perform more sophisticated operations on this data set.

Rather than discussing the classes in detail, the simple example discussed in the previous sections is reexamined, and one of the TBB classes is used as a standalone utility, to make the Rand() generator thread safe. The rest of the code is the same as in CalcPi.C. With this example in mind, it is easy to understand the TBB documentation to get more information if needed [18].

The code source is McSafeTbb.C, partially listed below. Allocations and initializations of the thread local variables are done implicitly by the library—as it was the case in C++11 and OpenMP. All that is required here is the definition of a function taking no arguments and returning a T object—an integer in our case—that is used by the library to initialize each new instance of the thread local variable. This function is called finit() in Listing 4.8. The library knows about it because a pointer to this function is passed via the constructor of the global pointer container.

```
#include <SPool.h>
#include <tbb/enumerable_thread_specific.h>
...
int finit();              // forward declaration
...
SPool   TH(2);            // global variables
long    nSamples;
tbb::enumerable_thread_specific<int> seed(finit);

int finit()               // auxiliary initialization function
```

```
    {
    int retval;
    retval = 999 * TH.GetRank();
    return retval;
    }

// The random number generator
// - - - - - - - - - - - - - - --
double Rand()
    {
    tbb::enumerable_thread_specific<int>::reference my_seed = seed.local();
    int retval = (my_seed * IMUL + IADD) & MASK;
    my_seed = retval;
    return (retval * SCALE);
    }
```

LISTING 4.8

Partial listing of McSafeTbb.C

There are a number of subtleties in this code that need careful discussion. First, the header file enumerable_thread_specific.h needs to be included. Notice that:

- A seed object of type enumerable_thread_specific <int> needs to be declared with global scope. This global seed object is in fact the container that stores the different instances of the thread local integer variable.
- The object constructor receives as argument the pointer to a function—called finit() in the code above—that TBB will use to initialize the different instances of the seed for each thread, if and when they will be created. If no argument is passed to this constructor, a default initialization is used.
- At this point, the seed container is empty. The main() function has not yet started, and the worker threads are not yet created.
- The real action is in the first code line in the body of the Rand() function, which declares the my_seed object. This object is a reference to the local instance of the seed, returned by the local() member function of the class.
- The TBB documentation specifies that the thread local instance of seed stored in the container *is created and initialized the first time the* local() *member function is called by each thread*. This is similar to the way C++11 and OpenMP work.
- At this point, we dispose of my_seed, which is a *reference*—i.e., an alias—of the thread local variable stored in the container. Changes in my_seed automatically change the values of the stored thread local variable.

The initialization function finit() performs the same initialization used before in other versions of this example: the initial generator seed is 999 times the rank of the caller thread, which, in this case, is always bigger or equal to 1.

Example 6: McSafeTbb.C

To compile, run make mcsafetbb. The number of threads is 2. The number of samples is read from the command line (the default is 1000000).

Executing this code returns exactly the same results for the variance as the previous thread safe versions of this example. Notice that this example is portable, since it only depends on TBB and the vath library. It can then be run as such on any Linux or Windows environment.

4.4.5 THREAD LOCAL STORAGE IN PTHREADS

The Pthreads library proposes the keys service as a very general way of generating and managing thread specific data items. This service closely parallels the general description above, with the key object playing the role of the global pointer container.

Some people consider this service clumsy and inefficient. The point is that, written in C, Pthreads utilities are often rather verbose, and programmers must perform explicitly some actions—initializations, or explicit pointer manipulations—that are implicit in all the other programming environments we have just discussed.

If you absolutely need to understand the Pthreads keys service, take look at the McSafe_P.C source code, and look at the way the Rand() function is rendered thread safe. For more details on the keys service, look at the Pthreads documentation. Another interesting alternative for Pthreads programmers is to use the standalone TBB thread local class in a Pthreads environment.

Example 7: McSafe_P.C

To compile, run make mcsafe_p. The number of threads is 2. The number of samples is read from the command line (the default is 1000000).

4.5 SECOND EXAMPLE: A GAUSSIAN RANDOM GENERATOR

The internal persistent state engaged in the previous example is very simple: just an integer variable. In order to make it clear how to manage a more complex situation, another example is included, in which the internal persistent state is composed of three variables of different types.

This application is simple: testing the behavior of a generator of Gaussian deviates with variance 1. A Gaussian generator returns a double on the real axis. The probability of getting a return value in the tiny interval $(x, d + dx)$ is

$$P(x)\, dx = \frac{1}{\sqrt{(\pi)}} \exp -x^2\, dx$$

Obviously, the probability of getting *any* value on the real axis is 1:

$$\int_{-\infty}^{\infty} P(x)\, dx = 1$$

Let us assume that we keep getting Gaussian deviates from the generator and marking their values on the real axis. The density of points so obtained follows the Gaussian law indicated above: it is mainly concentrated around the origin, with a characteristic width. A rough idea of the width of the Gaussian distribution is provided by the mean value of x^2. This is done by getting N samples of x from the generator and computing the mean value mv as

$$mv = \frac{1}{N} \sum_{i=1}^{N} x_i^2$$

The computation is done using two threads, each one computing the above mean value for N/2 samples. The main() function recovers the partial results from each thread, and averages them. This is the final result, which should be equal to one.

Box-Muller algorithm

The Box-Muller algorithm for generating Gaussian deviates consists of a mapping that transform two uniform deviates in [0, 1] into two Gaussian deviates. Gaussian deviates are therefore generated by pairs. A function GRand() producing Gaussian deviates is shown in Listing 4.9.

```
double Grand()
   {
   static double ransave = 0.0;    // internal state variable
   static int flag = 0;            // internal state variable
   double x1, x2, scratch;

   if(flag)
      {
      flag = 0;
      return ransave;
      }
   else
      {
      x1 = Rand();
      x2 = Rand();
      scratch = sqrt(-2*log(x1));
      x1 = cos(2 * PI * x2);
      x2 = sin(2 * PI * x2);
      ransave = scratch * x2;
      flag = 1;
      return(scratch * x1);
      }
   }
```

LISTING 4.9

Box-Muller algorithm

This Gaussian generator maintains a persistent internal state for two reasons:

- It uses internally the very simple uniform generator in [0, 1] used before, and it needs an integer seed for it. This seed is the persistent internal state that controls the operation of the uniform generator.
- Gaussian deviates are therefore generated by pairs. One value is returned to the caller and the other is reserved for the next call. Besides the seed, the internal state is therefore defined by:
    - a double randsave, which stores the possible return value for the next call,
    - an integer flag, which indicates if a precomputed return value is available in ransave.
- If a return value is available, the generator returns it. Otherwise, two values are produced; one is returned and the other is stored for the next call.

Gaussian examples

Here is a list of the different versions of the Gaussian generator examples. In all cases, the number of threads is hardwired to 2, and the number of samples used in the computation can be passed by the command line (the default value is 10000000).

- GrUnsafe.C: the straightforward, thread unsafe version of the example. To compile, run *make grunsafe*.
- GrSafe.C: the reentrant, stateless version of the generator. To compile, run *make grsafe*.
- GrObj.C: the version based on a local C++ class. To compile, run *make grobj*.
- GrWin.C: the version based on the Windows TLS service. To compile, run *nmake grwin*.
- GrOmp.C: the version using OpenMP the threadprivate directive. To compile, run *make gromp*.
- GrTbb.C: the version based on the TBB thread local storage facility. To compile, run *make grtbb*.

4.6 COMMENTS ON THREAD LOCAL STORAGE

Thread local storage provides an elegant and efficient way of implementing thread safety for functions with internal state. This looks like the perfect solution to the initial problem of providing one stateful function per thread. This is a robust solution *as long as one has a well-identified, distinct parallel task per thread*.

This has indeed been the case in all the examples discussed so far. OpenMP parallel sections and our SPool utility establish a one-to-one mapping between the parallel tasks that are using the random number generators, and the worker threads that execute them. But this does not need to be the case in general. Starting from Chapter 10, more general parallel constructs will be discussed in which it is possible to have more independent tasks than active threads. In this case, the task to thread mapping is not one to one. Threads take over new tasks when they are ready, according to well-established scheduling strategies. Threads can also suspend ongoing tasks to serve other tasks waiting for execution. In TBB and OpenMP, the task to thread mapping has a high level of sophistication. It is an *unfair* mapping, in the sense that it does not necessarily operate on a first come, first served basis.

If the task to thread mapping is not one to one, the thread local storage mechanism does not guarantee thread safety. *Thread safety requires one independent stateful function per task, not per thread*. If more than one task is executed by the same thread, thread safety is broken because several stateful functions are sharing the same thread local internal state in a non-reproducible way.

The only robust strategy that works in all cases is implementing one stateful function *per task*, which is exactly what was done in the first two options. In these cases, persistent internal state is owned by a task, not by a thread. The most efficient and universal solution to the problem discussed in this chapter is then using task local C++ objects with internal state, or its poor man version provided by the first option discussed above.

4.7 **CONCLUSION**

This chapter has proposed a thorough discussion of thread safety in the context of function calls. This is not the end of it, there are very critical thread safety issues related to the access of global data structures in a multithreaded environment. This is the subject of the next chapters.

CONCURRENT ACCESS TO SHARED DATA

5

5.1 FIRST COMMENTS ON THREAD SYNCHRONIZATION

The examples in previous chapters have shown that, even in the simplest parallel contexts, some degree of synchronization among the running threads is in general required. This is a very general issue: in most parallel applications, the underlying algorithms require that the threads execution be correlated at some points. Embarrassing parallel applications, where the tasks executed by threads are totally independent, are rare. Furthermore, it will be shown in Chapter 7 that synchronizations are required to ensure memory consistency: a thread reading a data value in memory must be guaranteed that the related write operations have already taken place, and that it is reading the correct values because all the expected previous writes have been correctly registered into the main memory.

This chapter and the next one develop a discussion of the most basic thread synchronization issues. Parallel languages and multithreading libraries provide direct support for a few *synchronization primitives*, which are basic mechanisms from which more elaborate synchronization tools can be built, better adapted to the high-level concurrency patterns that occur in real applications. Besides the natural synchronization mechanisms occurring at thread creation and termination discussed in Chapter 3, *there are essentially two basic synchronization mechanisms for threads:*

Mutual exclusion, in which threads are forced to execute a code block one at a time, and **event synchronization**, in which threads are forced to wait until some event occurs (an event being, for example, a data item reaching a specific value).

Indeed, *any* parallel synchronization pattern can be handled with these two basic synchronization primitives. They are, of course, explicitly or implicitly present in all multithreading programming environments. But they present different levels of programming difficulty for application programmers. Mutual exclusion is rather high level and easy to use. Event synchronization is a wait-notify mechanism in which a thread decides to wait until another thread notifies the occurrence of an expected event, and this is, instead, a rather low-level primitive. An application programmer equipped with only these tools will have a substantial amount of work to do to cope with the specific high-level concurrency patterns that appear in applications. Over the years, however, native libraries like Pthreads and Windows have been extended to incorporate a number of additional high-level synchronization tools based on these primitives.

The good news is that the basic synchronization concepts are universal, and the programming interfaces are similar in all multithreading libraries. When high-level tools are developed, it is not difficult to migrate them to a different programming environment. The utility classes in the vath library, providing high-level synchronization services, are implemented in Pthreads, Windows, and C++11.

The fact that any synchronization context can be implemented using mutual exclusion and event synchronization does not mean that these basic primitives provide the most efficient solution in all cases. The applications examples presented in Chapters 13, 14, and 15 indicate that high-level utilities constructed with these basic primitives do not always provide the best possible performance in contexts with very significant synchronization overhead. In those cases, custom synchronization interfaces constructed with the atomic utilities improve in general the code performance.

The rest of this chapter deals with the different ways of implementing mutual exclusion among threads. Besides the basic mutual exclusion primitives, all programming environments—except Pthreads—also implement the atomic variable concept. Atomic variables can efficiently replace the basic mutual exclusion protocols in some specific contexts. They also provide tools to set up efficient custom synchronization utilities, and a few examples in Chapters 7 and 8 illustrate their relevance.

5.2 NEED FOR MUTUAL EXCLUSION AMONG THREADS

Let us consider a multithreaded application where all worker threads occasionally increment a shared counter. The thread function executed by all worker threads would look like this:

```
int counter;
void *thread_function(void *arg)
    {
    ...
    counter++;
    ...
    }
```

LISTING 5.1

Threads incrementing a global counter

This increment operation looks very innocent, but in fact it is not. Current microprocessors implement *load/store architectures*, where direct memory operations are not supported. To increment the counter, the processor *reads* its value from memory to an internal register, increments it, and finally *writes* the new value back to memory. The increment operation is therefore not *atomic*, in the sense that it involves several successive complex operations. Nothing prevents two threads running on two different cores from reading the same value at almost the same time, before the first reader had time to increment the counter and write it back to memory. In this case, both threads will increment the same initial value. The final value of the counter is increased by 1, in spite of the fact that it has been incremented twice.

Things can also go wrong even if the two threads are sharing cycles on the same core. Indeed, nothing prevents thread A from being preempted by the operating system precisely in the middle of the increment operation, after the read and before the write. Then thread B is scheduled and increments the counter, after reading the same, old value not yet updated by thread A. When thread A is rescheduled, it will complete its ongoing update. The end result is the same as before: the counter is increased by one, in spite of the fact that two threads have increased it.

This is a classical example of a *race condition*: the outcome of the computation depends on the way threads are scheduled by the operating system.

A RACE CONDITION occurs when several asynchronous threads are operating on the same shared global data item, and the result of the operations depends on the way the threads have been scheduled.

In concurrent or in parallel programming, threads require a mechanism that locks the access to shared global variables, allowing them to safely complete some operations, avoiding race conditions. A mutual exclusion mechanism is needed, in which a well-identified code block cannot be executed by more than one thread at the same time.

A CRITICAL SECTION is a code block that must be executed by one thread at a time. A thread cannot enter a critical section if another thread is inside. This mechanism is used to exclude possible race conditions.

The way to implement critical sections is indeed very simple. Threads entering a critical section are forced to acquire ownership of a shared global resource that can only be owned by one thread at a time. Such a resource is called a *mutex*, a short name for *mutual exclusion*. Before entering the critical section, a thread acquires ownership of a mutex by *locking* it. When the mutex is locked, other threads that reach the critical section code are forced to wait for it to be released. A thread exiting the critical section unlocks the protecting mutex. If there are other threads waiting for it, the operating system reschedules one of them, which then locks and takes ownership of the mutex.

This mechanism preventing race conditions in parallel programming also operates correctly when threads are over-committed. If the operating system preempts a thread in the middle of a critical section, the thread moves to the ready queue waiting to be rescheduled, *keeping the mutex ownership*. It is therefore impossible for other threads to enter the mutex protected code block. They have to wait until the owner thread is rescheduled, completes the critical section treatment, and releases the mutex.

Critical sections are required whenever thread safety needs to be enforced when accessing shared variables. Imagine, for example, the case of several threads adding elements at the tail of a shared vector container. They do so by retrieving a pointer to the end of the array, storing the new value and increasing the pointer. However, if two threads retrieve the same pointer value—which may occasionally happen if the code is not protected by a critical section—they will end up storing two values at the same place. The data set is corrupted: it does not contain the data elements it is supposed to.

5.3 DIFFERENT KINDS OF MUTEX FLAVORS

All multithreading libraries provide a basic mutex service implementing the mutual exclusion protocol enabling the creation of a critical section. Mutexes can be locked and unlocked and, when locked, they are owned by only one thread. Then, all libraries broaden the service scope by introducing mutexes of different types, having extended capabilities that can be used by the programmer to fine-tune the application performance.

Private versus public mutexes:

A mutex is in general private to a process, in which case it is only accessed by the process threads. This is the standard case. In Windows, however, mutex and other synchronization objects are handled by the kernel and are public in the sense that they can also be shared by different *processes*. In this case, the mutex is allocated in a shared memory block, and used to protect access to shared memory data. Pthreads also provides public mutexes that can be shared by several processes. The public mutex can be locked by the threads in the different processes that are accessing a shared memory block.

Public mutexes are designed to be used in inter-process communications via shared memory. Only the native Pthreads and Windows libraries support them. This mechanism, not directly related to multithreading, is outside the scope of this book.

Standard versus spin mutexes:

When a thread calls the function that locks and acquires a mutex, the function does not return until the mutex is locked. This is typical for event synchronization: a thread waiting for an event, namely, the fact that it has acquired mutex ownership. There are two ways in which this can happen:

- An *idle wait*: the thread waiting to lock the mutex is blocked in a wait state as explained in Chapter 2. It releases the CPU, which can then be used to run another thread. When the mutex becomes available, the runtime system wakes up and reschedules the waiting thread, which can then lock the now available mutex.
- A *busy wait*, also called a *spin wait*, in which a thread waiting to lock the mutex *does not release the CPU*. It remains scheduled, executing some trivial do nothing instruction until the mutex is released.

Standard mutexes normally subscribe to the first strategy, and perform an idle wait. But some libraries also provide mutexes that subscribe to the spin wait strategy. The best one depends on the application context. For very short waits spinning in user space is more efficient because putting a thread to sleep in a blocked state takes cycles. But for long waits, a sleeping thread releases its CPU making cycles available to other threads.

Fair versus unfair mutexes:

When a mutex is released and there are several threads waiting to lock it again, the operating system selects the next thread that takes ownership. A fair mutex lets threads acquire the mutex in the order they requested the lock. This strategy avoids starving threads, because each one of them will get in due time its turn. Unfair mutexes do not respect the order in which the mutex lock is requested. They can be faster, because they allow threads that are ready to run to jump over the waiting queue and take ownership of the mutex if the thread that is next in line to acquire it is in a blocked state for other reasons.

Recursive mutexes:

When a thread owning an ordinary mutex tries to lock it again, the result is undefined and the lock call returns an error code. *Recursive mutexes* allow *the owner thread* to lock them recursively several times. A recursive mutex has internally a counter that counts the number of nested locks. It will only be released after being unlocked by its owner thread as many times as it was locked.

Recursive mutexes are needed, as you can guess, in recursive algorithms. Imagine a library function that internally manipulates complex data structures that need exclusive access for thread safety. The function will then lock and unlock an internal mutex to protect access to the data structure. However, if the function is recursive and needs to call itself, the mutex that protects the internal data structure must be a recursive mutex.

Another context that sometimes requires recursive mutexes are C++ classes with internal private data that, for thread safety reasons, require exclusive access. In this case, a mutex is defined inside the object to protect the private internal data. This mutex will be locked and unlocked by the member functions of the class to manipulate the critical internal private data. Imagine now that a derived class is defined with member functions that, again, need to lock the internal mutex. If, in addition, these member functions call member functions of the parent class that also lock the mutex, then the mutex needs to be recursive. This pattern is very common in Java.

Try_lock() functions:

All libraries propose, besides the lock() and unlock() functions to lock and unlock a mutex, a trylock() function that enables a thread to *try to lock a mutex*. This function *never waits*. If the mutex is available, it returns 1 after locking the mutex. Otherwise, it returns 0 meaning *mutex not available*. The intention is to allow programmers to optimize code by testing the mutex availability. If the mutex is not available, the caller thread can proceed to do something else and come back later on to try again.

Timed mutexes:

Some libraries also propose mutexes supporting a *timed trylock* feature. In this case the lock function does not return immediately, and performs a timed wait for a number of milliseconds passed as argument in the function call. Then, it proceeds as before: it returns 1 (or 0) if it succeeds (or fails) in locking the mutex.

Shared mutexes:

A shared mutex has two lock modes: shared and exclusive. In shared mode, several threads can take simultaneous ownership. This feature, introduced for optimization purposes, seems to contradict the very nature of the mutex operation. But the point is that, when several threads are accessing a data set, the operations performed can be classified as *write operations*, which modify the data set, and *read operations*, which don't. It is true that write operations need exclusive access to the data set. Read operations, instead, only need the guarantee that the data set will not be modified while they are reading, so they need to exclude simultaneous writes. But they do not need to exclude simultaneous reads, and can share the mutex with other readers.

This is a feature introduced to optimize performance in some specific cases. Obviously, critical sections conspire against parallel performance—we will see this happening in some examples in this chapter—and the motivation is to reduce excessive mutual exclusion contention. Shared mutexes are also called read-write mutexes. This is a subtle subject, and a detailed discussion is postponed to Chapter 9.

Table 5.1 shows the mutex flavors proposed by the different libraries. It is interesting to observe that TBB and C++11 expand the basic mutual exclusion service in different directions. TBB adds options

Table 5.1 Mutex Flavors in Different Programming Environments

	Mutex Flavors				
	Pthreads	**Windows**	**C++11**	**OpenMP**	**TBB**
mutex	X	X	X	X	X
recursive	X		X	X	X
timed	X	X	X		
timed recursive			X		
spin fair	X				X
spin unfair					X
shared	X	X			X

for fair and unfair spin locks, which, as we will see, aims at enhancing mutual exclusion performance. C++11, instead, proposes a refined locking strategy by incorporating timed standard and recursive mutexes.

NOTE: As indicated in Table 5.1, C++11 does not propose a ready-to-use spin mutex. However, we will see in Chapter 8 that the std::atomic class provides the tools needed to construct a spin lock.

The mutual exclusion programming interfaces of the different environments are discussed next, paying particular attention to the basic mutual exclusion services. The trylock() (return immediately if the mutex is locked) or the timed lock (wait to lock for a fixed amount of time) options will not be discussed in detail. In practically all the examples developed in this book, every time a mutex needs to be locked, there is nothing else that can be done in the meantime if the mutex is not immediately available. However, keeping in mind that these options are useful when occasionally meeting a context in which they may help to improve the code.

5.4 PTHREADS MUTUAL EXCLUSION

Pthreads introduces two types of mutexes, distinguished by the wait policy (idle or spin) when threads are trying to lock them:

- A standard mutex type pthread_mutex_t. Threads using these mutex objects perform an idle wait. This mutex is, by default, an ordinary mutex: private, fair, and non-recursive.
  - This mutex is accompanied by an associated attribute variable of type pthread_mutexattr_t that can be used to modify its properties.
  - With the help of this attribute variable, this mutex can in principle be made public or recursive. In application programming, changing to a recursive mutex is the only interesting option. This feature may depend on the particular Pthreads implementation. Readers are advised to consult the man pthread_mutex_init manual page.

- The attribute variable that modifies the mutex properties is passed as an argument to the initialization function (see below). If the attribute variable is NULL, the default initialization is adopted.
- This mutex also admits a default static initialization when the object is declared (see Listing 5.2).

- A spin lock of type pthread_spinlock_t. Threads using these mutex objects perform a spin wait. *There is no attribute data type associated to this mutex.* The spin lock is never recursive, and the only attribute a programmer can choose is its process scope. This is done directly, without an attribute data type.

5.4.1 MUTEX-SPIN-LOCK PROGRAMMING INTERFACE

Listing 5.2 shows how to declare a mutex or a spin-lock, as well as a mutex attribute. It also shows how to perform a default initialization at the moment the mutex object is declared, and how to use mutex attributes to make a recursive mutex.

```
pthread_mutex_t      my_mutex;     // declare mutex
pthread_mutexattr_t  attr;         // declare mutex attribute

pthread_spinlock_t      my_splock;  // declare spinlock

// Default mutex initialization
// - - - - - - - - - - - - - -
pthread_mutex_t  my_mutex = PTHREAD_MUTEX_INITIALIZER;

// Explicit mutex initialization
// - - - - - - - - - - - - - -
pthread_mutex_init(&my_mutex, NULL);

// spin_lock initialization
// - - - - - - - - - - - - -
pthread_spin_init(&my_splock, PTHREAD_PROCESS_PRIVATE);

// Initializing "my_mutex" as a recursive mutex
// - - - - - - - - - - - - - - - - - - - - - - -
pthread_mutexattr_init(&attr);     // initialize attribut
pthread_mutexattr_settype(&attr, PTHREAD_MUTEX_RECURSIVE);
pthread_mutex_init(&my_mutex, &attr);
```

LISTING 5.2

Mutex and spin-lock declarations

As indicated in Listing 5.2, it is possible to initialize a mutex when it is declared by using a symbolic constant defined in pthread.h. In this case, the mutex takes the default attributes: private to the process, and *not recursive*. For spin locks, there is no static initialization.

PTHREADS MUTEX-SPIN-LOCK INTERFACE

int pthread_mutex_init(&my_mutex, &attr
int pthread_spin_init(&my_splock, PTHREAD_PROCESS_PRIVATE)

- Mutex and spin-lock initialization.
- If attr=NULL, mutex takes default private attributes.
- An explicit attribute variable is needed to construct a recursive mutex.
- Spin locks are always fair and non-recursive.

int pthread_mutex_destroy(&my_mutex)
int pthread_spin_destroy(&my_splock)

- Destroys the mutex or spinlock whose address is passed as argument.

int pthread_mutex_lock(&my_mutex)
int pthread_spin_lock(&my_splock)

- Locks the mutex or spin lock whose address is passed as argument.
- If the mutex is already locked, this function blocks until the caller thread succeeds in locking the mutex.

int pthread_mutex_unlock(&my_mutex)
int pthread_spin_unlock(&my_splock)

- Unlocks the mutex or spin lock whose address is passed as argument.
- Called by the thread that owns the mutex.

int pthread_mutex_trylock(&my_mutex)
int pthread_spin_trylock(&my_splock)

- Tries to lock the mutex or spin lock whose address is passed as argument.
- This function always returns immediately. It never waits.
- If the mutex is available, it lock the mutex and returns 1.
- If the mutex is not available, it returns 0.

Pthreads also disposes of the pthread_mutex_timedlock() function, in order to limit the wait for the mutex availability. This requires using the Unix time structures defined in the <time.h> header. Look at the pthread_mutex_timedlock manual page for details.

For spin locks, there is no default initialization and no usage of attribute variables. The spin-lock initialization is always done by a call to pthread_spin_init() by passing a symbolic constant that defines its process scope. Public spin locks across processes will never be used. The behavior of the remaining Pthread functions is exactly the same as in the mutex case. Some examples later in this chapter as well as in Chapter 13 provide comparisons of the relative performances of mutexes and spin locks.

5.4.2 SIMPLE EXAMPLE: SCALAR PRODUCT OF TWO VECTORS

A first simple example of mutex usage is provided by the computation of the scalar product of two long vectors. The number of worker threads is hardwired to 2. The partial results obtained by each thread are directly accumulated in a mutex protected shared global variable. This first example is very inefficient, and it is proposed only for pedagogical reasons, in order to have a measure of the negative impact of excessive mutual exclusion contention. A more efficient way of handling this issue follows next.

5.4.3 FIRST, VERY INEFFICIENT VERSION

Here is the listing of the first version of this example, in source file ScaProd1.C.

```
#define VECSIZE  10000000
double A[VECSIZE];          // Global variables
double B[VECSIZE];
double dotprod;
pthread_mutex_t mymutex = PTHREAD_MUTEX_INITIALIZER;
SPool TH(2);      // two worker threads

void *thread_fct(void *P)
   {
   double d;
   int beg, end;
   beg = 0;                         // initialize [beg, end) to global range
   end = VECSIZE;
   TH.ThreadRange(beg, end);   // now [beg, end) is the sub-range for
                               // this thread
   for(int n=beg; n<end; n++)
      {
      d = A[n]*B[n];
      pthread_mutex_lock(&mymutex);
      dotprod += d;
      pthread_mutex_unlock(&mymutex);
      }
   }


int main(int argc, char **argv)
   {
   CpuTimer TR;       // object to measure execution times
   Rand R(999);       // random generator used to initialize vectors

   dotprod = 0.0;
   for(int n=0; n<VECSIZE; n++)
      {
      A[n] = -1.0 + 2.0 * R.draw();       // value in [-1, 1]
      B[n] = -1.0 + 2.0 * R.draw();       // value in [-1, 1]
      }

   TR.Start();
   TH.Dispatch(thread_fct, NULL);
   TH.WaitForIdle();
   TR.Stop();

   std::cout << "\n Scalar product is = " << dotprod << std::endl;
   TR.Report();
   }
```

LISTING 5.3

Scaprod1.C

The code listed above is a straightforward extension of the dot product algorithm to a shared memory parallel programming environment. The full range of vector indices is divided into subranges allocated to each worker thread. Notice in particular the following features of this example:

- The purpose of the mymutex mutex is to protect the global variable dotprod where the worker threads accumulate their partial results. This mutex is initialized to default attributes with a symbolic constant, defined in pthread.h.
- The main() function initializes dotprod to zero, initializes the A and B vector components to random values in $[-1, 1]$ to keep the scalar product reasonably bounded, and runs the threads in the usual way.
- The worker threads accumulate partial results directly in the global variable dotprod. All updates of this variable are protected with the locked mutex.
- In this approach, the mutex is locked and unlocked a very large number of times (as many times as vector components). This is highly inefficient, and can easily be avoided.

Example 1: ScaProd1_P.C

To compile, run make scp1_p. The number of threads is 2. The number of times the scalar product is computed is read from the command line (the default is 1000000).

When the code is executed on two cores, practically no parallel speedup is observed: the wall and user times are practically the same (about 0.9 s each) and, even worst, there is a huge system time of about 0.7 s. The code spends a huge amount of time in the operating system kernel moving the threads back and forth to a blocked state every time they wait for a locked mutex.

5.4.4 ANOTHER INEFFICIENT VERSION USING SPIN LOCKS

In the next example, file Scaprod1S.C, the code is exactly the same, except that now a spin lock is used, instead of an ordinary mutex. In this case the application profile is different. The system time is zero, and the wall time (0.6 s) is half the user time (1.2 s). This shows very clearly that the two threads are active all the time, sharing the application workload, and that the spin lock is a better choice when there is a lot of mutual exclusion and threads can keep running without releasing its CPU. Nevertheless, the last word has not yet been said: there is still a much better way of handling this issue.

Example 2: ScaProd2_P.C

To compile, run make scp2_p. The number of threads is 2. The number of times the scalar product is computed is read from the command line (the default is 1000000).

5.4.5 CORRECT APPROACH

It should by now be obvious what is wrong with the previous examples: there is excessive mutual exclusion among the worker threads. Mutual exclusion *serializes* the access to a shared variable, and in so doing it conspires against the parallel performance searched for when introducing threads.

Excessive mutual exclusion spoils parallel performance. Mutual exclusion must be restricted to the strict minimum required to preserve the integrity of the algorithms.

There is in our case an obvious way to proceed to avoid excessive mutual exclusion. Each thread can accumulate its partial results *in a local variable*. Then, before termination, each thread accumulates only once its computed contribution to the scalar product in the global variable scalarprod. In this way, the mutex is only locked a number of times equal to the number of threads (2 in our case). A more efficient version of the code is given in the source file Scaprod2.C; the only difference is in the thread function, listed below (the auxiliary local variable is d).

```
void *thread_fct(void *P)
    {
    double d = 0.0;
    int beg, end;
    beg = 0;                       // initialize [beg, end) to global range
    end = VECSIZE;
    TH.ThreadRange(beg, end);   // [beg, end) is the range for this thread

    for(int n=beg; n<end; n++) d += A[n]*B[n];

    pthread_mutex_lock(&mymutex);
    scalarprod += d;
    pthread_mutex_unlock(&mymutex);
    }
```

LISTING 5.4

Thread function in Scaprod2.C

Example 3: ScaProd3_P.C

To compile, run make scp3_p. The number of threads is 2. The number of times the scalar product is computed is read from the command line (the default is 1000000).

Running the program, one can observe that the performances are much superior to the previous versions, and that the system time is practically absent. In the first version, there was excessive overhead generated by excessive mutual exclusion. In the spin-lock version, threads are never blocked, but they spend a large amount of time turning around doing nothing, waiting for the mutex. The technique of introducing auxiliary local variables to reduce mutual exclusion is so obvious that it is used implicitly in programming environments with automatic parallelization capabilities, like the data-sharing directives of OpenMP that will be discussed in Chapter 10.

5.5 OTHER SIMPLE EXAMPLES

Mutexes are always associated with a shared variable—or a set of shared variables—they protect, and it is good programming practice to declare them together in order to improve the source code clarity.

In C++, it is possible to do better by *encapsulating* shared variables together with the protecting mutex inside an object that provides thread-safe services to its clients. Here are a couple of simple examples:

5.5.1 REDUCTION<T> UTILITY

Reduction operations of the kind performed in most of the previous examples, where partial results coming from different threads are accumulated in some global variable, are so common in application programming that we have set up a simple template class called Reduction<T>, where T represents a generic type for which the addition operation is defined. This class encapsulates a variable of generic type T and the mutex that guards the increment operations performed on this variable. It is used to easily perform mutex-protected reduction operations on variables of this generic type.

Remember that template library utilities are *text libraries*. The compiler cannot produce code until the user specifies what the generic data type T is. Then, all one has to do is to include the source files in the client code, and the library code is compiled with the application. No specific libraries need to be specified to the linker.

The source file Reduction.h is very simple. The constructor initializes the internal mutex, and the destructor of the class destroys it. Listing 5.5 shows how the class is used.

```
#include <Reduction.h>
...
Reduction<double> RD;    // creates object to perform reductions on a double
...
RD.Accumulate(d)         // accumulates double d inside RD. Called by workers
double d = RD.Data()     // returns the internal data to caller
RD.Reset();              // resets to zero the internal data, so that RD can be
                         // used to perform a new reduction.
```

LISTING 5.5

Interface of the Reduction<T> template class

The source code ScaProd4_P.C uses a Reduction<double> object to accumulate the partial results of threads. This reduction facility will often be used in the forthcoming examples. This class, as all the classes in the vath library is portable. There are also a Windows and C++11 implementations using the mutual exclusion interfaces discussed next.

Example 4: ScaProd4_P.C

To compile, run make scp4_p. The number of threads is 2. The number of times the scalar product is computed is read from the command line (the default is 1000000).

5.5.2 SAFECOUT: ORDERING MULTITHREADED OUTPUT TO STDOUT

The following chapters propose lots of examples in which several threads are created which, among other things, write messages to stdout. Since threads are asynchronous, these messages are most often all mixed up if written directly to stdout. The solution to this problem is to use a mutex to provide to each thread exclusive access to stdout. A very simple class that encapsulates the protecting mutex and implements this idea is discussed next.

In order to reduce mutual exclusion to the strict minimum, it is important to separate the construction of the complete output message—which is done locally by each thread—from the actual flushing of the message to stdout, done with a locked mutex. To construct the message, a local std::ostringstream object is used, which, instead of writing to stdout, employs a C++ strings as output device. When using the standard operators for formatted IO to write to an ostringstream object, a string is constructed. Then, the whole message, when ready, is sent to stdout using a SafeCout object.

The very simple source code is in file SafeCout.h. This class has a unique member function Flush(ostringstream& os) that does three things:

- Extracts the string from os.
- Locks the mutex, writes the string to stdout *appending an end of line*, and unlocks the mutex.
- Finally, it resets os with an internal null string, so that the client thread function can use it again to prepare the next message.

Listing 5.6 shows the simple usage of the SafeCout class:

```
#include <SafeCout.h>
#include <sstring>
using namespace std;
...
SafeCout  SC;          // creates global object, flushes strings to stdout
...
void *thread_function(void *P)
   {
   ostreamstring os,
   int rank;
   ...
   // Here, thread wants to write to stdout.
   // Write instead to os
   // – – – – – – – – – – – – – – – – – – – –
   os << "This is the output message from thread " << rank;

   // Now, make a mutex protected flush to stdout
   SC.Flush(os);
   ..
   }
```

LISTING 5.6

Using the SafeCout class

The two classes discussed above are portable. Besides the Pthreads implementation, there are also Windows and C++11 implementations using the mutual exclusion interfaces discussed below.

5.6 WINDOWS MUTUAL EXCLUSION

Multithreading interfaces in Windows are an integral part of the operating system. Besides threads, Windows has a mutex and a few other kernel objects whose usage parallel the thread creation protocol. The creation of an specific object is demanded, and a HANDLE is returned that allows the client code to access the object. The Windows mutex is therefore a public mutex that can be used to protect access to memory shared between processes. The Windows mutex also supports timed waits for the mutex availability.

For ordinary, private mutual exclusion operations Windows has introduced another lightweight interface more efficient than the mutex object, because kernel participation is restricted to the strict minimum: the CRITICAL_SECTION object, used to construct a critical section in the same way the ordinary Pthreads mutex was used before. An object is declared, and its address is passed to specific functions for initialization, lock, unlock, and destruction of the object. These objects do not support timed waits, but we will never perform timed waits in locking a mutex anyway. Here is the CRITICAL_SECTION programming interface:

WINDOWS CRITICAL SECTION INTERFACE

CRITICAL_SECTION CS

– Declares a CRITICAL_SECTION object, called CS (the name is arbitrary).

void InitCriticalSection(&CS)

– Initializes the CriticalSection object CS.

void EnterCriticalSection (&CS)

– Locks the associated mutex.

void LeaveCriticalSection (&CS)

– Unlocks the associated mutex.

void DeleteCriticalSection (&CS)

– Destroys the CRITICAL_SECTION object CS.

Migrating the previous Pthreads codes to Windows is straightforward. Take a look for example at the Windows implementations of the SafeCout and Reduction<T> classes, as well as the Windows version of the scalar product of two vectors:

Example 5: ScaProd2_W.C

To compile, run make scp2_w. This example migrates ScaProd2.C to Windows by using the Windows critical sections in the thread functions.

5.7 OpenMP MUTUAL EXCLUSION

Critical sections can be constructed in OpenMP in two ways: by locking a mutex with library function calls, or by using the critical directive. The first option, which closely parallels the Pthreads and Windows interfaces, is described here. The critical directive (which in fact encapsulates a mutex lock) is discussed in Chapter 10, devoted to OpenMP.

The header file omp.h, which must be included in any code using OpenMP, defines two types of mutexes:

- An ordinary mutex of type omp_lock_t
- A recursive mutex of type omp_nest_lock_t

No attribute variables are needed, because the mutex behavior is fully specified by its type. All mutexes are private; OpenMP is not concerned with interprocess communications. All mutexes are fair. Finally, OpenMP does not explicitly discriminate between idle and spin waits for threads waiting to lock a mutex. But the OpenMP standard introduces an environment variable that allows programmers to select the wait strategy for the whole application, discussed in Chapter 10. It is not clear that all OpenMP versions actually implement this feature. Listing 5.7 indicates how to declare OpenMP mutexes:

```
omp_lock_t         my_lock;    // object declaration
omp_nested_lock_t  my_nlock;   // object declaration
```

LISTING 5.7

Declaration of OpenMP mutexes

The OpenMP library functions for mutex initialization, locking, unlocking, and destruction are given below. They behave exactly like the corresponding Pthread functions, with minor differences: mutexes must be initialized explicitly before usage with a function call (there is no default initialization) and mutex attributes are not needed in OpenMP.

....

OpenMP MUTEX INTERFACE

void omp_init_lock(&my_lock)
void omp_init_nest_lock(&my_nlock)

– Mutex initialization

void omp_set_lock(&my_lock)
void omp_set_nest_lock(&my_nlock)

– Locks the mutex whose address is passed as argument
– If the mutex is already locked, this function blocks until the caller thread succeeds in locking the mutex

void omp_unset_lock(&my_lock)
void omp_unset_nest_lock(&my_nlock)

– Unlocks the mutex whose address is passed as argument
– Called by the thread that owns the mutex

int omp_test_lock(&my_lock)
int omp_test_nest_lock(&my_nlock)

– Tries to lock the mutex whose address is passed as argument.
– This function always returns immediately. It never waits.
– If the mutex is available, it lock the mutex and returns 1.
– If the mutex is not available, it returns 0.

void omp_destroy_lock(&my_lock)
void omp_destroy_nest_lock(&my_nlock)

– Destroys the mutex whose address is passed as argument.

Notice that all functions return void except the test functions, which are the OpenMP version of trylock, that return an integer. Here are some further comments on this mutex interface:

- The init functions must be called to create the mutex. After creation, the mutex is of course in an unlocked state.
- For nested locks, the test function returns the new nesting count if the lock is available or already owned by the caller thread. This function returns 0 is the lock is not currently owned by the caller thread.

Example 6: ScaProd_Omp.C

To compile, run make scap_omp. This example migrates ScaProd2.C to OpenMP by using the OpenMP locks in the thread functions and the parallel directive inside the main thread to create the parallel section where the scalar product is computed.

5.8 C++11 MUTUAL EXCLUSION

The C++11 thread library defines four different classes corresponding to four mutex types. As is the case for all objects with exclusive ownership, mutex objects cannot be copied or assigned. But they can be moved.

- The std::mutex class, a normal, non-recursive mutex.
- The std::recursive_mutex class, a recursive mutex.
- The std::timed_mutex class, a normal, non-recursive mutex that allows for timeouts on the lock functions.
- The std::recursive_timed_mutex class, a recursive mutex that allows for timeouts on the lock functions.

In C++11, there is no option related to the wait strategy. There is, however, a finer control of the wait duration in lock functions that is not present in the other programming environments (except Pthreads). An example in Chapter 8 shows how a spin mutex class can be constructed using the std::atomic class.

All four mutex classes have a standard, default no-argument constructor, as well as three basic member functions for locking and unlocking: lock(), unlock() that returns void, and try_lock() that returns true when returning with a locked the mutex, and false otherwise. The timed mutex classes have two additional member functions for timed mutex waits:

- try_lock_for(delay) that will try to lock the mutex for a given duration delay.
- try_lock_until(date) that will try to lock the mutex until the absolute date passed as argument.
- Both functions return true if they return with a locked mutex, or false if they have been timed out and the mutex is not locked.

5.8.1 SCOPED LOCK CLASS TEMPLATES

C++11—as well as other C++ libraries like TBB and Boost—also implements an alternative method for locking mutexes: the *scoped locking method*. The basic idea is that, rather than locking the mutex with a member function call, a different class is used for this purpose, for reasons that will soon be clear. In C++11—and Boost—there are two classes whose role is to lock and unlock mutexes: the lock_guard<T> and the unique_lock<T> classes. The purpose of the first one is discussed next. Later on, we will explain why the second one is also needed.

- Different mutex types have different features, and locking-unlocking requires different functions. Remember the OpenMP or Pthreads interfaces: there are different functions for different mutex types.
- In C++11, the std::lock_guard<T> template argument T defines the mutex type on which the class operates. This template argument is one of the four mutex classes. This is the way the mutex type to be locked is selected.
- The std::lock_guard<T> constructor receives a mutex of the corresponding type as argument. When the object is created, *a reference to this mutex is stored, and the mutex is automatically locked.*
- The std::lock_guard<T> destructor unlocks the stored mutex.

Listing 5.8 shows how to construct a critical section with a mutex and a lock_guard object:

```
std::mutex  MyMutex;      // declare mutex
...
   {
   std::lock_guard<mutex>  MyLock(MyMutex);    // construct and lock
   // — — — — — — — — — — —
   //  critical section code
   // — — — — — — — — — — —
   }    // here, the destructor of Mylock is implicitly called
```

LISTING 5.8

Critical section with scoped locking

The braces delimiting the mutex protected code block are critical, because they define the scope of the critical section. The mutex is locked when MyLock is created on an entry in the code block. On exit of the code block, the MyLock object goes out of scope and its destructor is called, unlocking the mutex. There are two advantages in this critical section programming style:

- There is no risk of forgetting to unlock the mutex, in which case the code would deadlock because other threads will wait forever to acquire it.
- The code block is *exception safe*: the mutex is automatically unlocked even if the code returns because an exception is thrown inside the critical section. Indeed, when an exception is thrown a normal function return follows that destroys all the function local objects. Even if it is very rare to explicitly throw exceptions inside a critical region, library functions called at these places may eventually throw them.

This scoped lock mechanism is just a special case of a very common C++ idiom called RAII (Resource Allocation Is Initialization) where, instead of directly allocating a resource (pointer, file) a new object is introduced to perform the allocation in its constructor and the deallocation in its destructor. This is, for example, the case of smart pointers. This strategy guarantees that resources will in all cases be correctly restored to the system. When a smart pointer is destroyed, the referenced memory block is automatically deleted, so there in no risk of memory leaks in the application.

Why is another scoped locking class needed?

The std::lock_guard<T> class only provides strict scoped lock-unlock services for simple or recursive mutexes. Let us be more precise. A lock_guard object can be used when the locking needs are just a simple lock at the beginning of the critical section, terminating unconditionally by an unlock at the end. A lock_guard locks the target mutex when created, and never releases the lock during its lifetime. There is no way of interrupting the mutex lock and then locking it again. This lock_guard class can only be used as shown in Listing 5.8.

There are, however, programming contexts in which this direct and straightforward critical section protocol is not sufficient. Consider a context in which a function is called inside the critical section. This function needs to relax momentarily the mutual exclusion constraint in order to give other threads the chance of operating on the data items protected by the mutex. This scenario cannot be implemented if the critical section is constructed with a lock_guard object. C++11 introduces another more sophisticated class, std::unique_lock<T>, to cope with this context.

The std::unique_lock<T> class implements the additional amount of flexibility required by the programming context described above. It allows for deferred locking: it is possible to construct the lock, telling him that the mutex will be locked later on. It is also possible to unlock the mutex before the lock object is destroyed. Obviously, this class is tailored to be used with the timed mutexes. However, if the unique_lock is used to construct the critical section, it can then be passed as argument to a function that needs to unlock the mutex, so that other threads can operate on the data, and lock the mutex again before returning, so as to continue the normal execution of the critical section. This concurrency pattern—which may look weird at first sight—will play a fundamental role when discussing event synchronization. The event synchronization primitive is built on a construct of this kind.

The only usage of the unique_lock that we will make in this book is in the event synchronization protocol discussed in Chapter 6. Examples of simple mutex locking in C++11 are provided by the C++11 implementations of the SafeCout and Reduction<T> classes, in which mutex locking proceeds as indicated in Listing 5.8, using the std::lock_guard<std::mutex> class. There are also the C++11 versions of the scalar product examples developed initially in the Pthreads environment.

5.9 TBB MUTUAL EXCLUSION

The TBB mutual exclusion interfaces are designed with an special care for simplicity and performance. As in C++11, mutex objects of different types are instances of different TBB classes, and all these mutex types share a similar locking-unlocking programming interface. Mutual exclusion performance is fine tuned simply by selecting different mutex types. The TBB documentation on the mutex interfaces can be found in the "Synchronization" topic in the Reference Guide [17].

5.9.1 MUTEX CLASSES

TBB introduces six classes to declare mutex objects, each one having its own characteristics:

- The mutex class. Objects of this class are non-recursive, and perform an idle wait. The include file is tbb/mutex.h.
- The recursive_mutex class. Objects of this class are recursive, and perform an idle wait. The include file is tbb/recursive_mutex.h.

- The spin_mutex class. Objects of this class perform a spin wait. They are very fast for short waits, but they are not fair or scalable (a discussion of scalability follows next). The include file is tbb/spin_mutex.h.
- The queuing_mutex class. Objects of this class also perform a spin wait, but they are fair and scalable. The include file is tbb/queuing_mutex.h.
- The spin_rw_mutex class. A shared (read-write) spin_mutex. The include file is tbb/spin_rw_mutex.h.
- The queuing_rw_mutex class. A shared (read-write) queuing_mutex. The include file is tbb/queuing_rw_mutex.h.

As indicated in the TBB documentation, the first two mutex types—the normal mutex and the recursive mutexes—are just wrappers on top of the mutexes provided by the native operating system libraries. In Unix-Linux systems, they are therefore implemented on top of the Pthreads mutex. Then, TBB adds two kinds of mutexes—spin and queuing mutexes—where threads wait for mutex availability by spinning in user space. Finally, there are the read-write spin and queuing mutexes that will be discussed in more detail in Chapter 9.

Spin and queuing mutexes have different scalability properties. The concept of *scalability* for a mutex may at first sight seem odd, because mutual exclusion serializes the thread's execution and in all cases conspires against parallel performance. In the TBB mutex context, scalability means that, in serializing code execution, the mutex will never do worst than restoring single thread performance. Now, we may wonder how performance could possibly be worst, since, after all, all mutexes are supposed to do is to serialize code execution. The point is that, when spin waiting, threads are continuously monitoring some memory location for a value change. This adds workload to the initial application, as well as network contention. Important mutual exclusion overhead may induce a global workload significantly bigger than the initial, sequential workload. In this case, we say that the mutex is non-scalable.

The two flavors of TBB spin mutexes are complementary. The spin_ mutex is supposed to be very fast in lightly contended situations, but it is not scalable. Moreover, it is unfair, probably because the next thread in line waiting for the lock will not get immediate ownership if for some reason it has been preempted by the operating system. On the other hand, the queuing_mutex is not as fast as the previous one in lightly contended contexts, but it is scalable and fair.

Selecting the correct mutex flavor may help to optimize a multithreaded code. However, no matter what kind of mutex is used, mutual exclusion is to be limited as much as possible. If an application requires excessive contention on a mutex, the best strategy is to reconsider the algorithms, as was done with the scalar product example, where the naive excessive contention was disposed of by the introduction of new local variables in the thread function.

5.9.2 SCOPED_LOCK INTERNAL CLASSES

As C++11, TBB also implements the scoped lock pattern for mutex locking and unlocking. There are three major differences between the TBB and C++11 approaches:

- TBB does not have timed mutexes. The different mutex flavors are designed to optimize the performance of unlimited waits when locking a mutex. C++11, instead, focuses on timed mutexes.
- TBB has a unique class, scoped_lock to lock mutexes, whose functionalities parallel those of the unique_lock in C++11.

- C++11 mutexes can be locked directly. This is not the case in TBB. Mutex objects cannot be locked or unlocked directly. All the locking-unlocking goes through the scoped_lock interface.

Rather than using class templates to select the mutex type, TBB provides six different implementations of a unique tbb::scoped_lock class, by making this class *an internal class* inside each one of the six mutex classes. The name of the internal class as well as the names of their member functions are the same, but they are implemented differently inside each mutex class. In fact, they are really *different* classes, because the internal class name must in all cases be qualified with the name of the container class.

tbb::MX::scoped_lock is the name of the TBB scoped lock inner classes, where MX is one of the mutex classes mutex, recursive_mutex, spin_mutex, queuing_mutex, spin_rw_mutex, queuing_rw_mutex.

Besides two different constructors, these classes have two member functions:

- acquire(mutex_name), that locks mutex_name
- release(), that unlocks a previously locked mutex

Listing 5.9 shows how the TBB mutual exclusion interface is used.

```
using namespace tbb;

MX    MyMutex;        // MX is a mutex class

// – – – – – – – – – – – – – – – – – – – – – – – – – –
MX::scoped_lock  Slock;      // first constructor
                             // no mutex referenced
Slock.acquire(MyMutex);      // lock MyMutex
SLock.release();             // unlocks MyMutex
// – – – – – – – – – – – – – – – – – – – – – – – – –

MX::scoped_lock  MLock(MyMutex);   // scoped locking
                                   // MyMutex is locked
```

LISTING 5.9

TBB critical section interface

Listing 5.9 shows how to create mutexes and the corresponding locks that act on them. The scoped_lock objects can be used to lock mutexes in the usual way, by calling the acquire() and release() member functions, or in the scoped lock way by passing a mutex to the constructor.

The TBB scoped_lock objects allow the mutex they own to be unlocked and locked again during their lifetime. Consider again the case of a function called inside the critical section, that needs to relax momentarily the mutual exclusion constraint in order to allow other threads operate on the data items protected by the mutex. As shown in Listing 5.10, the scoped_lockobject is passed as argument to the function, which can use it to unlock and then lock again the mutex before returning.

```
using namespace tbb;

mutex  MyMutex;      // declare mutex
```

```
...
   {
   tbb::mutex::scoped_lock  Slock(MyMutex);    // construct and lock
   // – – – – – – – – – – – – – –
   //  Critical section code
   //  Call here a function that needs to access the data
   //  protected by MyMutex. Pass the scoped lock to the
   //  function:
   Fct(Slock);
   // – – – – – – – – – – – – – –
   }    // here; destructor of Slock is implicitly called
```

LISTING 5.10

Construction of a critical section with a scoped lock

Example 7: ScaProd_Tbb.C

To compile, run make scap_tbb. This example is identical to ScaProd2.C in which threads are run using the SPool utility, except that the critical section is now constructed using a TBB mutex, following the strategy described in Listing 5.10. This is an example of interoperability of different programming environments.

TBB provides also more general Reader-Writer locks. They will be discussed with synchronization tools in Chapter 9.

5.10 FIRST LOOK AT ATOMIC OPERATIONS

Mutexes are not the only way of implementing thread safety in concurrent accesses to shared variables. A useful and fast alternative to locked mutex access to simple shared variables is provided by a limited set of *atomic operations*, which are guaranteed to be performed in an indivisible way, as if they were a unique machine instruction. Any atomic operation executed by a thread is seen as an *instantaneous* operation by the other active threads. We have already seen that increasing or updating a counter is a complex operation that involves several steps: load, increment, and store. If the counter is implemented by an atomic data type, its update is guaranteed to be seen as a compact operation in which a memory value is instantaneously replaced by a new memory value.

Atomic operations are very efficient because they are implemented by low-level hardware and/or operating system instructions specially designed to support thread synchronizations. The TBB, Boost, and C++ thread libraries provide C++ classes defining *atomic data types*, on which a limited set of atomic operations are defined. Besides implementing an alternative to mutex locking, these classes also provide tools for implementing custom synchronization protocols, as will be shown in Chapter 8. OpenMP does not have specific atomic data types, but enables a variety of atomic operations via the atomic directive. Windows does not have an explicit atomic data type either, but there are a substantial number of library functions that provide an equivalent service.

However, atomic operations have limitations and cannot replace mutexes in all cases. They cannot, for example, be used to create a critical section involving a complex code block. In OpenMP, atomic operations are defined for fairly small data sizes, the largest size being the size of the largest scalar, typically a double-precision floating-point number. TBB restricts explicit atomic operations to integer or pointer types. C++11 deals with bool, integer, and pointer types, and partially extends direct atomic operations to any *suitable* generic type T (we will clarify later on what suitable means).

To sum up, the status of atomic operations in the programming environments discussed in this book is the following:

- Pthreads does not support atomic operations.
- OpenMP supports atomic operations for basic data types via an atomic directive.
- TBB support atomic operations for integer and pointer types.
- C++11 standard—and Boost—support atomic operations for integer, boolean, enum, pointer, and in addition generic types satisfying specific conditions.

5.10.1 ATOMIC OPERATIONS IN OPENMP

There are no new atomic data types in OpenMP. The atomic keyword is used to qualify an operation. This keyword is used in a directive that specifies: *the operation that follows in the following line must be performed atomically*. Here is the general form of the OpenMP atomic construct:

```
#pragma omp atomic { read | write | update | capture } [seq_cst]
    expression
```

LISTING 5.11

OpenMP atomic construct

The atomic directive is qualified with one of the four clauses listed above, which describe the nature of the atomic operation. There is an additional seq_cst clause whose meaning is explained below. The qualifying clauses operate as follows:

- The atomic construct with the read clause performs an atomic read of the memory location designated by x, regardless of the native machine word size.
- The atomic construct with the write clause performs an atomic write of the memory location designated by x, regardless of the native machine word size.
- The atomic construct with the update clause performs an atomic update of the memory location designated by x, using the designated operator.
- The atomic construct with the capture clause performs an atomic update of the memory location designated by x, using the designated operator. In addition, the initial or final value of x is stored in the memory location y, according to the form of the statement following the directive (see Table 5.2). Notice, however, that only the read or write of x are performed atomically. Neither the evaluation of expr nor the write to y need to be atomic with respect to the read or write of x.
- *The seq_cst clause, which means sequential consistency is an OpenMP 4.0 extension.* When inserted, the atomic operation is forced to include an implicit memory fence, i.e., an implicit flush operation without a list.

Table 5.2 lists the expressions that correspond to each one of the four qualifying clauses. The conventions adopted are the following:

- x and y are scalar data types.

Table 5.2 Directive Clauses and Related Atomic Operations

Atomic Directive Qualifying Clauses	
read	y=x;
write	x = expr;
update	x++;
	++x;
	x–;
	–x;
	x binop= expr;
	x = x binop expr;
	x = expr binop x;
capture	y = x++;
	y = ++x;
	y = x–;
	y = –x;
	y = x binop expr;
	y = x = x binop expr;
	y = x = expr binop x;

- expr is an expression with scalar type that does not reference x or y. Notice also that expr *is not computed atomically.*
- binop is one of the following binary operations: +, *, -, /, &, ; |, <<, or >>.
- Notice that the last two update and capture expressions are OpenMP 4.0 extensions.

AtomicTest.C example in OpenMP
Listing 5.12 shows how to replace the mutex locked increment of a shared variable by an equivalent atomic update of a long counter.

```
#include <omp.h>
...
long nsamples;          // number of MonteCarlo events per thread
long C;                 // used to accumulate acceptances

void *thread_fct(void *P)
   {
   double x, y;
   int rank;

   rank = TH.GetRank();
   Rand R(rank*999);
   for(int n=0; n<nsamples; n++)
      {
```

Continued

```
x = R.draw();
y = R.draw();
if((x*x+y*y) <= 1.0 )
    // – – – – – – – – – – – – – – – – – –
    #pragma omp atomic update
        ++C;  // atomically accumulate in  C
    // – – – – – – – – – – – – – – – – – –
    }
}
```

LISTING 5.12

AtomicTestOmp.C (partial listing)

Besides the replacement of the SPool utility by the OpenMP parallel section, we observe minor differences in the task function. The variable C used to accumulate acceptances is now an ordinary long, and its increment in the task function is preceded by the qualified atomic directive.

Example 8: AtomicTestOmp.C

To compile, run make atestomp. The number of threads is hardwired to 2.

5.11 CONTAINER THREAD SAFETY

Containers are commonly used data structures in applications programming. They store and manage collection of objects of the same type. Different types of containers store elements in different ways, providing different levels of performance for various insertion, traversal, and extraction operations. Programmers can therefore select the type of container most adapted to the problem at hand. The C++ Standard Template Library provides a number of very efficient containers: vectors, queues, linked lists, sets, and maps. All of them support, of course, a number of insertion or deletion operations that modify the data set.

STL containers, however, are not thread-safe. Consider, for example, an insertion operation of a new vector element at the tail of a STL std::vector<T> container, where elements are stored in consecutive positions in memory. The vector container maintains internally a pointer to the vector end. A thread that invokes the insert_last() operation on the container launches an operation in which the end pointer is read, the new vector element is copied to this memory address, and the pointer is incremented to point to the new vector end. Obviously, this operation is not thread-safe: a new thread can start the same operation *before* the end pointer is updated, and the two threads end up storing the vector element in the same place. The final result is that two or more threads stored data, but there is only one new data value in the container. The STL containers must therefore be used with care in a multithreaded context.

When using non-thread-safe containers, the only option for programmers is to use mutual exclusion and perform the container operations that are open to data races inside a critical section. However, container operations are complex in general, and the critical sections that protect them may end up implicitly involving reasonable big code blocks, with a potential degradation of parallel performance in case of significant contention in the containers access.

5.11.1 **CONCURRENT CONTAINERS**

A better option is to use if possible *concurrent containers*, i.e., thread-safe containers that encapsulate internally whatever is required to control race conditions. Concurrent containers use two basic techniques to enforce thread safety:

- *Restricted locking*. Critical sections are used internally to protect only the sensitive parts of the code, and mutex locking is restricted to a strict minimum. We will meet in Chapter 9 a thread-safe queue class—ThQueue<T>—that build upon the STL queue to make it thread safe.
- *Lock-free algorithms*, in which race conditions are controlled without serializing the thread operation. The basic concepts behind lock-free algorithms are discussed in Chapter 8.

5.11.2 **TBB CONCURRENT CONTAINER CLASSES**

TBB is a powerful programming environment for multithreaded processes. Besides the thread management services, based on an implicit thread pool, which will be discussed in Chapters 11 and 16, TBB also incorporates a large number of standalone utilities that can profitably be used in *any* programming environment, like the concurrent containers classes. As a general rule, these classes support concurrent insertion and traversal, but not concurrent erasure. According to the TBB documentation—"Containers Overview" topic in [17]—thread safety is implemented using both fine locking—involving highly optimized internal critical sections—and lock-free algorithms of the kind discussed in Chapter 8.

- **Sequential containers**:
    - concurrent_vector:
    - concurrent_queue:
    - concurrent_bounded_queue:
    - concurrent_priority_queue:
- **Associative container**:
    - concurrent_hash_map:
- **Unordered containers**:
    - concurrent_unordered_set:
    - concurrent_unordered_map:

These classes can be considered as thread-safe versions of many of the STL container classes. The main difference is that in TBB there is a unique template parameter T, which is the type of the objects stored in the container, while the STL containers have a second optional template parameter that allows the user to specify a memory allocator class. But this STL feature—overriding the default STL memory allocator—is rarely used in practice.

Sequential containers are containers in which the position of an element depends on the order in which it has been inserted, not on its value. The STL has vectors, queues, and priority queues, but it does not have a bounded queue. Bounded queues have a finite capacity and many features that come with it: producers wait if the queue if full, consumers wait if the queue is empty. The ThQueue<T> class discussed in Chapter 9 is a bounded queue, and TBB's bounded queue is very close in essence to this class.

Associative containers are ordered in the sense that the position of an element depends on its value. They are often implemented as a binary tree. The STL has two kinds of associative containers: maps and sets. They are very efficient for search operations, but there is a rather expensive prize to pay for insertions and deletions, which enforce a reorganization of the container. The concurrent_hash_map container is a thread-safe version of the STL map. Recently, the STL has introduced unordered sets and maps: search operations are less efficient, but they have better performance for insertions and deletions. The TBB classes for unordered containers are thread-safe versions of the corresponding STL classes.

An example involving the usage of TBB's bounded queue will be presented in Chapter 15. Readers are referred to the TBB reference guide [18] for the concurrent containers whose usage is accessible to anybody having minimal experience with STL containers.

5.12 COMMENTS ON MUTUAL EXCLUSION BEST PRACTICES

This chapter has presented a broad description of mutual exclusion programming interfaces. Different programming environments exhibit slightly different interfaces and functionalities, but the basic concepts and strategies are strictly the same. Locks are the fundamental tools for implementing mutual exclusion to prevent race conditions. Atomic operations, as will be shown in Chapter 8, are powerful tools for implementing custom synchronization utilities, but they can replace mutex locking only in some specific cases.

Restricted scope of atomic operations

The OpenMP example shows that atomic operations are very efficient for guarding an integer variable or a pointer. But they cannot replace mutex locking in more complex circumstances. Indeed, *a code block composed of a suite of atomic operations is not atomic*. Therefore, it is not possible to construct a critical region just by piling up atomic operations. Very often, maintaining a locked mutex for the duration of the compound action cannot be avoided.

How many different mutexes do we need?

Consider an application written in C style, with all the shared variables accessible to all threads defined as global variables. Let us also imagine that two critical sections need to be introduced in the code, and call them A and B. The question is: how many mutexes are needed? One or two?

The answer is: it depends. If both critical sections are modifying the *same* data, then obviously *the same* mutex must be used in critical sections A and B. Indeed, having a thread executing critical section A and another thread executing critical section B at the same time is not thread safe, because the two threads are accessing the same data. Mutual exclusion requires the same mutex in A and B. If, instead, the two critical sections are uncorrelated in the sense that different data items are modified, then *two different mutexes are more efficient*, because in this case two different threads can safely execute the two critical sections simultaneously. If only one mutex is used, the application is still thread-safe, but suffers from unnecessary additional contention. *Increasing the number of mutexes decreases the contention.*

The conclusion is: *each state variable should be guarded with a dedicated mutex*. By *state variable* we mean either a unique data item or a complex data set that as a whole specifies some specific state of the application.

Encapsulation helps in controlling complexity

Rather than using the C programming style, encapsulating data in C++ objects makes it more practical to manage thread safety. An object can encapsulate a lot of internal data, and shared objects can of course be accessed by many different threads. If an object is *immutable*, in the sense that its internal state is not changed by member functions, then it is thread-safe. If an object is mutable, then the simplest thing to do is to incorporate a mutex inside the object, guarding the object state. If the member functions lock and unlock the mutex whenever appropriate, the object will be thread-safe. If a lot of objects are created, there will be of course one mutex per object: there is no mutual exclusion contention among different objects. Mutexes are initialized in the object constructor, and destroyed in the object destructor.

This strategy is so efficient that Java automatically includes a hidden mutex in each object. Programmers do not need to declare it.

Compound thread-safe operations are not thread-safe

Operations of type *check and act*, where if something is true an action is taken, are very common in any kind of programming. Let us consider an example: a vector container class with thread-safe member functions. Consider two of them: contains(T), which returns true if *T* is a vector element and false otherwise, and add(T), which inserts *T* somewhere in the container. Even if each member function is thread-safe, the following check and act construct is not, and a mutex lock is required for thread safety:

```
vector V;
...
if(!V.contains(d)) V.add(d);
```

LISTING 5.13

Compound thread-safe operations

This observation is the same made before about atomic operations: a compound operation made of atomic operations is not atomic.

Encapsulation helps in controlling complexity

Concurrent data structures are not thread-safe

EVENT SYNCHRONIZATION

6.1 IDLE WAITS VERSUS SPIN WAITS

It often happens in concurrent or parallel programming that a given thread reaches a point in which nothing useful can be done before other threads have completed some part of their workload providing the information required to pursue the ongoing task. The fact that expected information has become available is considered as an *event*. The initial thread needs eventually to wait for the occurrence of this event before pursuing its execution stream. The event synchronization mechanisms discussed next allows threads to wait for expected events.

When discussing mutexes, it was observed that a thread waiting to lock a mutex could wait for the mutex availability in two ways: moving to a blocked state and liberating the executing CPU (*idle wait*), or keeping ownership of the CPU by executing a do-nothing instruction while waiting (*busy wait*). This is a particular case of event synchronization, the event being in this case the mutex availability. These two options apply to *any* kind of event synchronization, and we proceed to describe them in a more precise way.

The synchronization mechanisms discussed here are universal in the sense that, barring minor semantic differences, they operate the same way in all basic libraries: Pthreads, Windows, and the C++11 standard. We start by proposing a precise definition of an event:

An event is described by any boolean expression, called *predicate*, that switches values passing from *false* to true or vice-versa. The event occurs when the predicate is toggled.

Idle wait, also called system wait

The idle wait mechanism *is a native library synchronization primitive*, operating in the following way:

- When thread A needs to wait for the value true of a global predicate, it calls a function that puts A in a blocked state if predicate==false, waiting for the expected event to happen. The function blocks, and returns only when the wait is terminated and A is rescheduled.
- When the time comes, another thread B toggles the predicate to predicate=true and wakes up thread A in a way to be described next.
- This mechanism is robust. While waiting, thread A yields the executing core, which becomes available to run other threads. Thread A is not rescheduled to run until it wakes up. When this happens, A is moved to the ready pool, and is rescheduled when a core becomes available.

- This protocol requires the participation of a communication agent triggered by thread B to wake up thread A. Such a communication agent is called a *condition variable*.

Busy wait, also called spin wait
The busy wait *is not* a native synchronization primitive. It must be explicitly programmed, as it will be shown later on. It operates in the following way:

- Thread A, that needs to wait for an event, executes a do-nothing loop of the kind while(!predicate), for as long as the predicate is false.
- This avoids system calls, but the waiting thread remains scheduled using CPU resources for the whole duration of the wait.
- This looks simple and straightforward, but the mechanism is delicate, because the waiting thread keeps reading a predicate value in memory waiting for an update coming from another thread, and the fundamental memory consistency issue—*when does a memory value written by a thread become visible to other threads?*—cannot be avoided.
- The do-nothing loop does not work as such. Memory consistency requires further synchronizations in order to have a spin wait working correctly. Without them, thread A may never seen the update made by another thread B. Chapter 7 discusses how to program a spin wait, after exploring in more detail the memory consistency issue.
- Notice that, since the waiting thread remains active, no wake up notification agent is needed. Threads communication operates directly through the monitoring of a shared predicate.

Plan for the rest of the chapter
First, a careful discussion of how the first mechanism operates in Pthreads, Windows, and C++11 is presented. OpenMP, which focuses on high-level, easy-to-use synchronization constructs, does not provide a programming interface for idle waits. TBB did not initially propose this basic synchronization primitive either because, as discussed in detail later on, its direct usage is unsafe in the TBB thread management environment. But recently TBB has incorporated an implementation of C++11 synchronization as a standalone utility that naturally includes the idle wait synchronization primitive.

The idle wait discussion that follows focuses on understanding *why this synchronization primitive is designed in this way*. But this basic idle wait mechanism will rarely be used directly. It will, most of the time, be encapsulated in high-level, easy-to-use objects implementing complex synchronization patterns, like barriers, thread pools, pipelines, etc., allowing the programmer to focus on *what to do*, not *how to do it*.

Nevertheless, going through this discussion is in my opinion a good pedagogical exercise that enhances the understanding of concurrent programming. The programming idioms discussed in this section, as well as the specific examples that follow, are rather simple, and they are the same in all libraries and programming environments. They will first be introduced using Pthreads, and then their Windows and C++11 implementations will follow.

At the end of this chapter, some useful utilities introduced by C++11 to implement event synchronization—*futures* and *promises*—are discussed. They have a more restricted scope than condition variables, but they are portable and easy to use in application programming.

6.2 **CONDITION VARIABLES IN IDLE WAITS**

Condition variables are, like mutexes, opaque data structures in Pthreads—their type is pthread_cond_t—or Windows—their type is CONDITION_VARIABLE. In C++11, they are object instances of the std::condition_variable class. Pthreads also introduces (very rarely used) condition variables attributes, of type pthread_condattr_t, which are initialized by calling functions that specify their properties, exactly as was the case for threads and mutexes. We will never need in this book to go beyond condition variables with default attributes, whose initialization is very simple. In Windows and C++11, condition variables attributes are not needed.

The role of condition variables is simply to establish a link between cooperating threads that need to communicate on the basis of an event. Condition variables behave like wake-up clocks: they ring when an event happens under the action of a thread that signals an event, but they know nothing about the *nature* of the event or the threads they are waking up.

Condition variables are agents that signal that something has happened. They are associated to a contract between cooperating threads, but they know nothing about the nature of the contract or the threads to which their signal is addressed.

- When a thread decides to wait, it calls a library function to which it passes a condition variable. This means: *I am getting out of the way until this condition rings and wakes me up.* The library function clearly does not return until the calling thread is active again.
- When a thread decides to wake up sleeping threads, it calls a library function to which it passes a condition variable. This means: *wake up one—or all—the threads currently waiting on this condition.*
- That is all there is. The precise event that is triggering these actions does not directly show up in these transactions.

The fact that a condition variable has no direct knowledge of the nature of the expected event may seem at first sight somewhat strange. Obviously, condition variables and event predicates are related to each other, but *maintaining this relationship is the programmer's responsibility.* This feature adds in fact a substantial amount of flexibility to this event synchronization primitive, as the examples at the end of the chapter will show.

Three data elements are therefore intimately related in any event synchronization mechanism:

- A shared data item, the predicate, whose change of value determines the occurrence of the synchronizing event.
- A mutex that guards the access to the boolean predicate.
- A condition variable used for signaling the synchronizing event.

It is good programming practice to declare these variables together, whenever possible. Before getting involved with the basic libraries condition variables programming interfaces, let us take a look at some declarations of global synchronization variables.

```
bool  predicate;

pthread_mutex_t mymutex = PTHREAD_MUTEX_INITIALIZER;    // Pthreads
pthread_cond_t  mycond  = PTHREAD_COND_INITIALIZER;
```

Continued

```
CRITICAL_SECTION    CS;              // Windows
CONDITION_VARIABLE  CV;

std::mutex              mymutex;   // C++11
std::condition_variable mycond;
```
LISTING 6.1

Declaring event synchronization objects.

In all cases, a mutex that protects a predicate is declared, as well as a condition variable related to the predicate. In Pthreads, a static initialization is used, that adopts the default attributes for these variables. This will be largely sufficient for our purposes in this book. In Windows, the condition variable must be initialized with a function call given below. The C++11 declarations do not require further initializations, because they just call the no argument constructor of the corresponding classes. Notice also that the predicate related to the expected event does not need to be an explicit boolean variable. It can also be a boolean expression (namely, an expression that evaluates to true of false) involving arbitrary data types.

6.3 IDLE WAITS IN PTHREADS

This section deals with the idle wait implementation in Phreads: first the programming interfaces, and then the details of the wait protocol. *Keep in mind that the wait protocol discussed in a Pthreads context operates in exactly the same way in all other basic libraries.* After considering Pthreads in detail, the implementation of these same concepts in Windows and C++11 is discussed.

PTHREADS CONDITION VARIABLE INTERFACE

int pthread_cond_destroy(*cond)

– Destroys the condition variable whose address is passed as argument.

int pthread_cond_wait (*cond, *mutex)

– Puts the thread to wait on the condition passed as argument.
– The wait is unlimited. If the condition is not signaled, the thread waits forever.
– This function blocks until the waiting thread wakes up and is rescheduled. The mutex whose address is passed is the mutex that guards the predicate.

int pthread_cond_wait(*cond, *mutex, *date)

– Puts the thread on a *timed wait* on the condition passed as argument.
– If the condition is not signaled before the date passed as third argument, the wait is timed out, thread wakes up, and this function returns 1.
– Otherwise, the thread wakes up when the condition variable is signaled, and the function returns 0.
– struct date is a particular date data item defined in sts/times.h.

int pthread_cond_signal(*cond)

– Signals the condition variable passed as argument.
– Wakes up *one* of the threads waiting on the condition.

int pthread_cond_broadcast(*cond)

– Signals the condition variable passed as argument.
– Wakes up *all* the threads waiting on the condition.

6.3.1 **WAITING ON A CONDITION VARIABLE**

There are two functions a thread may call to wait on a condition variable. The first one is the simplest, in which the thread waits forever until the event is signaled. The second one performs a *timed wait*: by passing a time interval: the thread goes to sleep for a number of milliseconds, and wakes up if it has not been waken up before by the signaling of the condition variable. This timed wait for an event—a feature in all basic libraries—is a very powerful service. It is seating under the hood of useful high-level utilities introduced in Chapter 9.

It may be surprising to see *the mutex that protects the predicate involved in the wait on condition call*. This is not obvious, and it is in fact related to a subtle issue in the wait protocol discussed next.

6.3.2 **WAIT PROTOCOL**

How is a thread put to wait on a condition? Imagine that the predicate variable is an integer count, and that the purpose is to synchronize threads on the condition count==0. This is the protocol *that must be used in all cases.*

```
int        count;
pthread_mutex_t r_mutex = PTHREAD_MUTEX_INITIALIZER;
pthread_cond_t    cond = PTHREAD_COND_INITIALIZER;

void *thread_function(void *s)
   {
   ...
   pthread_mutex_lock(&r_mutex);
   while(count != 0) pthread_cond_wait(&cond, &r_mutex);
   pthread_mutex_unlock(&r_mutex);
   ...
   }
```

LISTING 6.2

Wait protocol

There are several relevant issues in this apparently innocent piece of code. The top of Listing 6.2 shows the default static initialization of the mutex and the condition variable linked to the predicate count. Furthermore, notice that, in the body of the function:

- The mutex is first locked because the predicate count must be accessed for testing its value.
- The code enters a while() loop and calls pthread_cond_wait(), if the predicate is not true. *This function does not returns immediately*. It enters a wait *with a locked mutex*, and returns—again *with a locked mutex*—when the thread is rescheduled after wake up.
- Because the mutex is always locked on return, the code can execute a new iteration of the while loop and check again the predicate. If it is true, the thread breaks away from the while loop and unlocks the mutex. Otherwise, the thread calls again pthread_cond_wait() and starts a new wait.

Now, one may wonder how is it possible, if the mutex has been locked all the time, that some other thread had toggled the predicate? Figure 6.1 describes what happens *inside* the pthread_cond_wait() function:

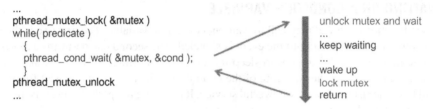

FIGURE 6.1

Wait on condition mechanism.

- This function starts by *atomically* unlocking the mutex passed as argument and setting the thread in a wait state. Then it waits peacefully until the condition is notified.
- The mutex is therefore unlocked while the thread is waiting. Otherwise, nobody else would ever be able to access and modify the predicate. However, *before returning, the wait function locks again the mutex passed as argument.*
- Now we can understand why the mutex must be passed to the function that executes the wait on condition: she is in charge of unlocking the mutex during the wait, and locking it again after the thread wakes up.

Why should the predicate be checked again on return?

Another subtle point to be observed is that this protocol is tailored to force a new check of the predicate after return from the wait. A while{} loop is mandatory for this to happen; using a conditional if() statement will not force the check of the predicate after return from the wait.

This check is imposed by thread safety, to prevent a subtle race condition from happening. Indeed, the above described wait protocol leaves a tiny window open for a race condition. It is not impossible that, between the condition variable notification that wakes up the sleeping thread and the mutex re-lock, another thread comes in and changes again the predicate. If this is the case, when the function returns and the predicate is checked, the thread goes back to a wait as it should. Therefore, the while() loop is mandatory for thread safety.

Why an atomic mutex lock and wait?

The just described wait protocol raises another interesting question. Why are the lock-unlock mutex actions delegated to the pthread_cond_wait() function itself? The reason is that the two actions—unlocking the mutex and moving the thread to a blocked state—must be done atomically, which means this compound operation must look instantaneous to other threads. Otherwise, there is the risk of missing a condition variable notification. Indeed, consider the following scenario:

- The active thread that, finding the predicate not true, has decided to wait, is preempted *right after unlocking the mutex, but before it had time to register as a waiting thread.*
- One could argue that there is, in principle, no problem. This thread—henceforth called thread A—should be able to register and go to wait later on, when it is next scheduled.
- However, it may happen that other threads that are scheduled in the meantime have set the predicate to true. If this happens, one of them has notified the condition on which thread A should be waiting.

- But thread A *is not waiting*, precisely because it has not yet registered as a waiting thread. Therefore, thread A misses this notification and, when it is scheduled again, it waits on a condition that has already been notified, *with the wrong value of the predicate*.

This kind of behavior is obviously incorrect, and the only way to prevent it is *to have an atomic mutex unlock and wait*: these two actions are tied together in such a way that threads just cannot not be preempted in the way described above. This is exactly what is guaranteed by the wait on condition function calls. The need to cope with this problem forces the scheme adopted by all the basic libraries (Pthreads, Windows, C++11).

6.3.3 WAKING UP WAITING THREADS

The Pthreads library uses two notification mechanisms for waking up waiting threads: one is called *signal* and the other is called *broadcast*. The reason is that there may be more than one thread waiting on a given condition variable cond.

A SIGNAL wakes up only ONE thread waiting on the condition variable. A BROADCAST wakes up ALL threads waiting on the condition variable.

The pthread_cond_signal() function wakes up only one thread waiting on the condition cond. Which one is actually waken up is not controlled by the programmer, it is decided by the scheduler. The function pthread_cond_broadcast() wakes up all threads waiting on the condition cond.

Which one of this two functions is required depends then on the context. In a barrier synchronization, for example, threads go to sleep as they reach the barrier synchronization point, and the last thread that reaches the barrier wakes up all other threads. In this case, a broadcast is mandatory.

6.4 WINDOWS CONDITION VARIABLES

The initial versions of the Windows operating system did not provide support for condition variables. Windows has a global strategy for waiting for things to happen: threads to terminate, mutexes to be unlocked, events to occur. In all cases the relevant object is created, a HANDLE is returned and used by client code to query the target object or to request services from it. The Windows kernel objects, like the condition variables met before, signal events but their programming interfaces do not follow the condition variable wait protocol presented before, because the associated wait functions are not tailored to receive a predicate guarding mutex as argument.

Fortunately, Windows Vista introduced condition variables in the Windows API, which operate in exactly the same way as the condition variables in the other basic libraries, making code migration a very simple affair. Here is the Windows condition variable programming interface. Full details are available in the Window API online documentation [13].

WINDOWS CONDITION VARIABLE INTERFACE

CONDITION_VARIABLE CV

– Declares a CONDITION_VARIABLE object, called CV (the name is arbitrary).

– This object must be associated to a CRITICAL_SECTION object that guards the predicate.

void InitializeCoditionVariable(&CV)

– Initializes the CONDITION_VARIABLE object CV.

bool SleepConditionvariable(&CS, &CV, DWORD msecs)

– Sleeps on the condition variable CV.
– This is in general a timed wait, for a duration of msecs milliseconds.
– For an unlimited wait, the symbolic constant INFINITE must be passed as third argument.
– Return value is true if thread has been effectively waken up by the condition variable.
– Return value is false if wait interval has expired, or other error occurred.
– See discussion below for the way to handle a false return.

void WakeConditionVariable (&CV)

– Wakes up *one* thread waiting on the condition variable.

void WakeAllConditionVariable (&CV)

– Wakes up *all* threads waiting on the condition variable.

Handling timed waits.

When the return value of the Sleep ConditionVariableCS() function is false, it must be decided whether the wait has been timed out or whether another error has occurred. This is achieved by calling the function GetLastError(DWORD *error) that returns in the output parameter error an error code. If the error code returned equals the symbolic constant ERROR_TIMEOUT, we have a normal return resulting from a timed out wait. This approach is used in our Windows implementation of the BLock utility to be discussed in Chapter 9.

Why does the name in the Sleep...() function ends with a "CS"? The reason is that this function requires a condition variable associated with a critical section object to guard the predicate. There is another wait function call SleepConditionVariableSWR(), in which the condition variable is associated with a *slim read-write lock*, also introduced by Windows Vista, which will be discussed in Chapter 9. Again, this feature is introduced to optimize certain parallel contexts, and it will never be used it in this book.

Listing 6.3 summarizes the Window condition variable wait protocol for an unlimited wait. As you can appreciate, it is identical to the Pthreads protocol in Listing 6.2.

```
bool predicate;
CRITICAL_SECTION CD;
CONDITION_VARIABLE CV;

void *thread_function(void *s)
   {
   ...
   EnterCriticalSection(&CS);
   while(!predicate)
      SleepConditionVariableCS(&CS, &CV, INFINITE);
   LeaveCriticalSection(&CS);
   ...
   }
```

LISTING 6.3

Windows wait protocol

6.5 C++11 CONDITION_VARIABLE CLASS

Idle waits for an event are also implemented in C++11 using condition variables. The C++11 standard defines two condition variable classes as well as an enumeration class that defines return values for timed waits.

```
namespace std
    {
    enum class cv_status{timeout, no_timeout};

    class condition_variable;
    class condition_varyable_any;
    }
```

LISTING 6.4

C++11 condition variable classes

Consider first the std::condition_variable class. Besides a simple no argument constructor, this class provides the member functions listed below, which operate in the same way as the previous C interfaces in Pthreads and Windows. Naturally, there is a slight difference in the fact that these C++ member functions are called on a std::condition_variable object, whose address is implicitly passed by the compiler via the this pointer.

....

: **C++11 CONDITION VARIABLE INTERFACE**

: void notify_one()

: – Wakes up *one* thread waiting on the caller condition variable object.

: void notify_all()

: – Wakes up *all* threads waiting on the caller condition variable object.

: void wait(std::unique_lock<std:: mutex>& lock)

: – Performs an unconditional wait on the caller condition variable object.
: – Using a std::unique_lock<std::mutex> for locking in the code block in which the wait is performed is
:   mandatory. See the comments below.

: template< typename R, typename P>
: cv_status wait_for(unique_lock<mutex>& lock, **const std::chrono::duration<R, P> time_interval**)

: – The two template parameters are the types needed to define a duration object, to represent a time interval.
: – Performs a timed wait on the caller condition variable object.
: – If the condition is not notified during the elapsed time interval passed as second argument, this function
:   returns timeout.
: – If, instead, the condition is notified the function returns no_timeout.
: – See the comments below, and the duration discussion in the Annex of Chapter 3.

There is another version of the timed wait, wait_until(), which involves an absolute time date for the end of the wait, instead of a time duration. It is not listed above because it will never be used in this book. The usage of duration data items has already been discussed in Chapter 3, when examining the way a thread puts itself to wait for a predefined time interval. Examples of timed waits are given below.

The wait() functions described above implement the same protocol previously discussed in Pthreads and Windows. It is easy to understand why a std::unique_lock locking a std::mutex is needed in the C++11 implementation. As we know, the wait() function needs to internally unlock the mutex during the wait and lock it again it before the return, and this is not possible with a lock_guard scoped lock. The extended flexibility of the unique_lock is required in this function call.

The other class, std::condition_variable_any, works with any kind of scoped locks and mutexes. This class has internally a more sophisticated implementation. As far as we are concerned, the features provided by the simpler std::condition_variable class are largely sufficient for our purposes.

Listing 6.5 summarizes the C++11 condition variable wait protocol for an unlimited wait. It is of course identical to the Pthreads and Windows protocols discussed before.

```
bool predicate;
std::mutex my_mutex
std::condition_variable cv;

void *thread_function(void *s)
   {
   ...
      {
      std::unique_lock<std::mutex> my_lock(my_mutex);
      while(!predicate)
        cv.wait(my_lock);
      }
   ...
   }
```

LISTING 6.5

C++11 unlimited wait protocol

NOTE: a portable utility is proposed in Chapter 9, encapsulating in a easy-to-use programming interface the Pthreads, Windows, and C++11 event synchronization protocols with unconditional or timed waits.

Another form of the wait() functions

C++11 proposes another version of the idle wait functions, which incorporates the predicate in the function call and avoids the need for using the while() loop to check for spurious wakeups. In this case, an additional argument must be passed to the wait() functions: a pointer to a function—or a function object—that takes no arguments and returns the value of the predicate. Here are the function declarations, taken from the C++11 documentation [14]. They will be clarified with an explicit example.

```
template< typename Pred>
void wait(unique_lock<mutex>& lock, Pred pred)
```

- Performs an unconditional wait on the caller condition variable object.
- This function performs internally the while loop that checks again the predicate.
- The function only returns if the predicate is true.

```
template< typename R, typename P, typename Pred>
bool wait_for(unique_lock<mutex>& lock, const
```
std::chrono::duration<R, P> time_interval, Pred pr)

- Performs a timed wait on the caller condition variable object.
- Returns false if the condition is not notified during the elapsed time interval passed as second argument.
- Returns true if the condition is notified and the predicate is true.

6.6 **EXAMPLES OF IDLE WAIT**

We propose next a couple of examples that exhibit the way the idle wait primitive works in practice. Since these codes are not portable because they target explicitly the basic libraries, there are separate Pthreads, Windows, and C++11 versions of each example. The Pthreads version is used below to exhibit the way the codes are organized, but the Windows and C++11 versions are identical, barring the mild semantic differences just discussed.

6.6.1 **SYNCHRONIZING WITH AN IO THREAD**

Let us assume that the main thread dispatches a worker thread to perform a lengthy I/O operation, and at some point later on it needs to wait for its completion. There is a trivial way of handling this problem: the main thread just joins the worker I/O thread. However, it may happen that the worker thread is not joinable, or that it must stay alive to continue to do something else after completing the I/O operation. In this case, the way to proceed is to put the main thread to wait on a condition, and let the worker thread signal the condition when the I/O operation is completed.

To simulate a lengthy I/O operation, this example uses a utility to be discussed in Chapter 9: a Timer object. Timer objects are local to a thread. When the owner thread calls its Wait() member function, the thread goes to sleep for the number of milliseconds passed as argument. We have seen before that this is easily done in C++11 and Windows. The Pthreads implementation, however, involves some sophisticated programming. The Timer utility encapsulates the three implementations in a common interface. A Timer will be used to stop the worker thread for 2 s.

The Pthreads source code for this example is in file IoTask_P.C. Here is the listing.

```
bool  flag;
pthread_mutex_t flock = PTHREAD_MUTEX_INITIALIZER;
pthread_cond_t fcond  = PTHREAD_COND_INITIALIZER;
SPool TS(1);                 // one worker thread

void io_thread(void *idp)    // worker thread code
```

Continued

```
{
Timer T;
T.Wait(2000);      // perform IO
std::cout << "\n IO task done. Signaling" << std::endl;

pthread_mutex_lock(&flock);     // toggle predicate
flag = false;
pthread_mutex_unlock(&flock);
pthread_cond_signal(&fcond);    // signal change
return(NULL);
}

int main(int argc, char **argv)
{
flag = true;
TS.Dispatch(io_thread, NULL);

// – – – – wait for false – – – – – –
pthread_mutex_lock(&flock);
while(flag==true)
    pthread_cond_wait(&fcond, &flock);
pthread_mutex_unlock(&flock);
// – – – – – – – – – – – – – – – – –

std::cout << "\n From main: IO operation completed "
         << std::endl;
TS.WaitForIdle();
return 0;
}
```

LISTING 6.6

loTask_P.C

In this code flag is the boolean variable used as predicate, flock is the mutex protecting flag, and fcond is the condition variable used to signal that flag has been toggled. The main() function initializes flag to true, launches a worker thread, and waits for false. The worker thread is first blocked for 2 s (this is the I/O operation). Then, it toggles the predicate *with a locked mutex* and signals the event.

Examples 1: loTask_P.C, loTask_S.C, loTask_W.C

To compile, run make iotask_p, iotask_s or iotask_w. This example exhibits event synchronization between the master and a worker thread.

6.6.2 TIMED WAIT IN C++11

Since the C++11 interfaces discussed above for timed waits are not self-evident, an example follows clarifying their meaning. The idea is simple. A worker thread is launched to perform a lengthy I/O operation, emulated by sleeping for 5 s. The main() function, rather than performing an indefinite wait for the event, only waits for a succession of 1-second intervals until the expected event occurs. Running the example, it is observed that the wait is timed out four times, as expected, before the event occurs.

The wait_for() version that incorporates the predicate will be used to implement the timed wait, because this makes life much simpler. Indeed, when dealing with a timed wait there are *two* things to be checked:

- Has the function returned because the wait has been timed out, or because the event has been signaled?
- In the last case, is it a real or an spurious wakeup? This is the reason behind the while loop that checks the predicate again.

The wait_for() version that incorporates the predicate merges internally these two checks and returns a unique answer: true if the event has been signaled *and the predicate is true*, and false in case of timeout. An auxiliary function must be provided, which returns the value of the predicate. This function is called MyPred() in Listing 6.7.

```
using namespace std;

condition_variable CV;
mutex my_mutex;
bool predicate = false;

bool MyPred()
    {
    // This function is always called with the lock owned by the
    // waiting thread locked, according to C++11 documentation
    // - - - - - - - - - - - - - - -
    bool retval = predicate;
    return retval;
    }

void worker_thread()
    {
    chrono::duration<int, milli> delay(5000);
    this_thread::sleep_for(delay);
        {
        unique_lock<mutex> lock(my_mutex);
        predicate = true;
        }
    CV.notify_one();
    cout << "\n I/O operation terminated " << endl;
    }

int main(int argc, char **argv)
    {
```

Continued

```
bool retval;
chrono::duration<int, milli> delay(1000);
thread T(worker_thread);
T.detach();
do
    {
    unique_lock<std::mutex> my_lock(my_mutex);
    retval = CV.wait_for<int, milli>(my_lock, delay, MyPred);
    if(!retval) cout << "\n Timed out after 1 second" << endl;
    }while(!retval);
cout << "\n Wait terminated " << endl;
    }
```

LISTING 6.7

TimedWait_S.C

The worker thread sleeps for 5 s, sets the predicate to true, and notifies the change. The main thread enters a do loop; each loop iteration waits for 1 second and continues if the wait return value indicates a timeout. One interesting point in this code is the MyPred function, which reads the predicate and returns its value. One could imagine that reading the predicate should be done with the locked mutex. This is not, however, needed. The C++11 documentation explicitly indicates that the predicate function to wait_for() *is always called internally with a locked mutex*. See the C++11 documentation annex in [14].

Example 2: TimedWait_S.C

To compile, run make twait_s. This example exhibits event synchronization between the master and a worker thread.

6.6.3 BARRIER SYNCHRONIZATION

Barrier synchronization is probably one of the most commonly used synchronization tools in application programming, particularly in codes implementing a data parallel context in which different threads are performing the same operations on different subsets of a global data set. The computation of a scalar product of two vectors performed in Chapter 5 is a simple example of a data parallel program.

There are many iterative data parallel algorithms in which the same computational workload must be repeatedly applied to the global data set until convergence is achieved. When this happens, it is necessary to make sure that all threads sharing the computational workload are always working at the same iteration level. The original algorithm will not be respected if a thread starts manipulating global data at the (N+1)st iteration while some other threads have not yet completed the Nth one. This requires a *barrier synchronization* at the end of each iteration. At this point, all cooperating threads must wait for those that are not yet finished, before continuing with the next iteration. Chapters 13–15 will show several barrier synchronizations of this kind in action.

Barrier synchronization can be implemented in a simple way. The main idea is to introduce a shared counter whose initial value is the number of cooperating threads. When a thread reaches the synchronization point, it decreases the counter and waits on a condition variable if the counter has not reached zero. The synchronizing event happens when the last thread finally decreases the shared counter to zero. At this point, this thread does not wait: it notifies the other waiting threads that the event they are waiting for has taken place, and that they can all resume execution.

The Pthreads and Windows libraries do have a barrier primitive, and OpenMP has a barrier directive. The simple example that follows demonstrates how a barrier synchronization code operates. A set of Nth threads is launched: All threads write a "before" message, wait on the barrier, write an "after" message, and exit. The code works properly if, no matter how many threads, all "before" messages precede the "after" messages.

```c
#include <stdio.h>
#include <stdlib.h>
#include <pthread.h>
#include <SPool.h>

int      count, Nth;
pthread_mutex_t count_lock = PTHREAD_MUTEX_INITIALIZER;
pthread_cond_t count_cond  = PTHREAD_COND_INITIALIZER;
SPool *TS;

// Auxiliary function called by worker threads
// - - - - - - - - - - - -
void BarrierWait()
    {
    // - - - - - - - - - - - - - - -
    // Acquire mutex and decrease count. If count>0, wait on
    // condition. If count==0, print ID and broadcast wake up.
    // - - - - - - - - - - - - - - -
    pthread_mutex_lock(&count_lock);                    // LOCK
    count--;
    if(count)
        {
        while(count)
            pthread_cond_wait(&count_cond, &count_lock);
        pthread_mutex_unlock(&count_lock);              // UNLOCK
        }
    else
        {
        printf("\n Broadcast sent by last thread \n\n");
        pthread_cond_broadcast(&count_cond);
        pthread_mutex_unlock(&count_lock);              // UNLOCK
        }
    }

// Worker threads code
// - - - - - - -
void worker_thread(void *idp)
```

Continued

```
    {
    int my_rank = TS->GetRank();
    printf("Thread %d before barrier\n", my_rank);
    BarrierWait();
    printf("Thread %d after barrier\n", my_rank);
    }
 int main(int argc, char **argv)
    {
    if(argc==2) Nth = atoi(argv[1]);
    else Nth = 2;
    count = Nth;

    TS = new SPool(Nth);
    TS->Dispatch(worker_thread, NULL);
    TS->WaitForIdle();
    return 0;
    }
```

LISTING 6.8

Simple barrier code, Pthreads version

In the code above, the main thread does nothing beyond initializing data, and launching the parallel job. It does not participate in the barrier synchronization, an affair involving only the worker threads. The number of worker threads is obtained from the command line (the default is 2), and main initializes the thread pool SPool object with the required number of threads. The main thread also sets initially the counter integer, which is the predicate in the barrier wait, to the number of threads.

In the thread function listed above, each worker thread prints a message before and after calling the BarrierWait() function, which encapsulates the whole barrier synchronization pattern between the worker threads. Listing 6.8 shows how the BarrierWait() function implements the algorithm previously described:

- When the function is called, it starts by locking the mutex and decreasing the counter.
- If the counter is not zero, the thread goes to wait *with the locked mutex*, according to the wait protocol.
- If the counter is zero, the thread does not wait. It prints a broadcast message, then it broadcasts the condition that will wake up all the waiting threads, unlocks the mutex, and returns.

Examples 3: Barrier_1_P.C, Barrier_1_S.C, Barrier_W.C

To compile, run make barr1_p, barr1_s or barr1_w. The number of worker threads is read from the command line (the default is 2).

When running the code one observes that, no matter how many worker threads are launched, there are first the "before" messages of all threads, then the broadcast message of the last thread, and finally the "after" messages of all threads.

Problem: this barrier cannot be reused

This code is admittedly very simple. In fact, it is too simple to be useful in general. The reason is that we have constructed a one-shot, disposable barrier. There is no way to call the same BarrierWait() function later on in the same code, simply because the worker threads have no way of resetting the counter flag to its initial value Nth when the threads are released.

Indeed, one could imagine that the thread that arrives last and decreases the counter to zero, could instead reinitialize it to the initial value. But this does not work, because the wait protocol forces threads to check again the predicate counter==0 when they wake up, before breaking away from the while() loop. If they find at wake up a non-zero counter, they go back to sleep. Threads never emerge from the barrier, and the code deadlocks.

Solution: a reusable barrier

The BarrierWait() function can be modified, so as to make it reusable. I first learnt the elegant solution to this problem in D. Butenhof's book, *Programming with POSIX Threads* [11]. It exhibits the flexibility induced by the fact that the condition variable knows nothing about the event to which it is associated, and that programmers are free to choose the predicate describing an event in the most convenient way.

The basic idea is therefore to replace the counter predicate by a more convenient way of describing the event. Any boolean expression that toggles between false and true qualifies as a predicate. This program is therefore modified by adding a new boolean variable called bflag, coupled to the counter in the following way:

- When counter reaches zero, the last thread resets counter to Nth *and toggles the boolean* bflag.
- On successive barriers, bflag will be toggled from true to false to true and so on. *The predicate for the condition variable wait is not the actual value of* bflag, *but the fact that* bflag *has been toggled.*

Now, a thread that has called BarrierWait() can test for the change in bflag in a simple way: it copies the initial value of bflag to a local variable my_flag, and enters a wait with the predicate my_flag==bflag. When it wakes up, it checks if this is still true. Listing 6.9 shows the new, modified, reusable BarrierWait() function. In the client code, the threads execute two consecutive barriers, and everything works correctly. No matter how many threads cooperate in the barrier, the messages they send to stdout are well separated.

```
#include <mutex>
#include <condition_variable>
#include <SPool.h>

int     count, Nth;
bool    bflag;
SPool   *TS;
std::mutex count_mutex;
std::condition_variable count_cond;

// Auxiliary function called by worker threads
// - - - - - - - - - - - - - - - - - - - - - -
void BarrierWait(int R)
```

Continued

```
   {
   std::unique_lock<std::mutex> lock(count_mutex);
   bool my_flag = bflag;
   count - ;
   if(count)
      {
      while(my_flag == bflag)
         count_cond.wait(lock);
      }
   else
      {
      predicate = !predicate;
      count = Nth;
      printf("\n Broadcast sent by thread %d\n\n", R);
      count_cond.notify_all();
      }
   }


// - - - - - - - - - -
// Worker threads code
// - - - - - - - - - -
void worker_thread(void *idp)
   {
   int my_rank = TS->GetRank();
   printf("Thread %d before first barrier\n", my_rank);
   BarrierWait(my_rank);
   printf("Thread %d before second barrier\n", my_rank);
   BarrierWait(my_rank);
   printf("Thread %d after all barriers\n", my_rank);
   }


// - - - - - - - - - - - - - - - - - -
// Main, same as in previous listing...
// - - - - - - - - - - - - - - - - - -
```

LISTING 6.9

Reusable barrier code, C++11 version

Example 4: Barrier2_P.C, Barrier2_S.C, Barrier2_W.C

To compile, run make barr2_p, barr2_s or barr2_w. The number of worker threads is read from the command line (the default is 2).

Comments

In programming with threads, it is good practice to plan for the worst even if the worst is very unlikely. Therefore, let us imagine that there is a large number of worker threads and two very close barriers, as in Listing 6.9. Consider what may happen soon after the threads in the first barrier are released. They are released one after the other, and it is possible that the first released threads reach the second barrier and call again BarrierWait() *before* other threads have emerged from the first wait and checked again their predicate in the first barrier call. Therefore, *the same predicate that allows the threads to emerge from the wait in the first barrier must be able to put them to wait in the next barrier call.* You should convince yourself that this is indeed the case, and that the above barrier wait algorithm is robust.

In Chapter 9, C++ classes will be introduced that encapsulate the barrier code discussed above, as well as other alternative barrier algorithms. Object instances of these classes are easy to use high-level barriers. Remember that Pthreads and Windows have already easy to use barrier utilities, but this is not the case in C++11 or TBB. OpenMP disposes of a barrier directive that will be discussed in Chapter 10.

6.7 C++11 FUTURES AND PROMISES

The C++11 thread standard introduces some additional event synchronization utilities that are very useful in application programming. Somewhat more restricted than condition variables, they are easier to use and very efficient in some specific contexts. These utilities are defined in the <future > header.

6.7.1 STD::FUTURE<T> CLASS

Instances of this class are used to represent *one-off* events, i.e., unique events that will happen only once in the future. This is the restriction with respect to condition variables. Indeed, the reusable barrier example has shown that a unique condition variable can serve to synchronize an unlimited number of future events. Futures, instead, cannot be reused. On the other side, the interesting point is that future objects, besides implementing the synchronization with the one-off event, can be directly used to recover data values returned by it. Future objects transfer data values across threads, and the template parameter T is the related data type. This template parameter must be set to void if the object is used only for synchronization.

An immediate application of this utility is the recovery of a return value from an asynchronous task executed by another thread. When discussing thread function signatures, we observed in Chapter 3 that, contrary to Pthreads and Windows, C++11 thread functions do not return a value. The future class solves this problem, as shown in the example below.

```
include <iostream>
#include <chrono>

int MyFct(int n)
    { return (42+n); }

int main()
    {
    // asynchronous function call:
    // - - - - - - - - - - - - - -
    std::future<int> retval =
        std::async(std::launch::asynch, MyFct, 2);
```

Continued

```
    std::chrono::milliseconds ms(3000);
    std::this_thread::sleep_for(ms);    // wait 3 seconds
    std::cout << "\nThe value returned is "<<retval.get() << std::endl;
    }
```

LISTING 6.10

ExFuture_S.C

A simple function MyFct is defined, taking an integer argument and returning another integer value. In this example, the future event is the asynchronous execution and termination of this function. The future object retval is initialized by the return value of the std::asynch() function, discussed below. This function, which received as arguments a pointer to the function to be executed, as well as the argument to be passed to it, returns immediately *before* the function is executed. Then, main() waits for 3 s before recovering the return value by a call to the get() member function of the future object.

Example 5: ExFuture_S.C

To compile, run make exfuture.

std::asynch() function

This template function is one of the three possible ways of associating a task with a future.

- It operates exactly like the std::thread constructor. Besides the first argument discussed next, it receives the function pointer and as many other arguments as needed to call the function. The function pointer and the arguments that follow are copied to some internal storage before the function is called, and arguments are then passed by value. If arguments must be passed by address, the std::ref() qualifier must be used, as was the case of the thread constructor in Chapter 3.
- The first argument is a *policy* argument. The std::asynch function may either launch a new thread to run the function, or run it in the current thread and defer the function call to a later time, when the future return value is requested. The argument passed in the example above forces the asynchronous execution in a new thread. Passing std:: launch::deferred, the function call is deferred in the current thread. This first argument can also be ignored, in which case the function behavior is implementation dependent: one of the two policies is applied.

Basic std::future member functions

Very much like the std::thread objects discussed in Chapter 3, std::future objects are not copyable. Like thread objects, a future object can be moved to another one, transferring ownership of the expected event. The moved object becomes invalid, no longer associated with an asynchronous result.

Here are the most relevant member functions of the future<T> class:

BASIC FUTURE<T> INTERFACES

std::future<T> F;

- Default constructor.
- Defines a future not yet associated to an explicit task.

bool valid()

- Checks if the future is associated with an asynchronous result.
- Returns true if this is the case, false otherwise.

void wait()

- If the associated state contains a deferred function, invokes the deferred function and stores the return value.
- Otherwise, it blocks until the asynchronous result associated with *this is ready.

template <typename Rep, typename Period>
future_status wait_for(std::chrono::duration<Rep, Period> const& delay)

- Waits until asynchronous result is ready, or until the time delay is elapsed.
- Returns std::future_status_ready in the first case.
- Returns std::future_status_timeout in the second case.
- Returns immediately if a deferred function call has not yet started execution.
- Return value in this last case is std::future_status_deferred.

T get()

- If the associated state contains a deferred function, invokes the function and returns the return value.
- Otherwise, it blocks until the asynchronous result associated with *this is ready, and then returns the value.

To provide another simple example, the way a thread can wait for a I/O operation is examined next, using futures instead of condition variables. The worker thread executing the asynchronous operation will just wait for 4 s, to simulate a long I/O operation, writing appropriate messages before and after the wait. The main() function uses a std::future<void> object to wait for the event.

```
void io_thread()      // worker thread
   {
   std::chrono::milliseconds ms(4000);
   std::cout << "\n IO thread waiting for four seconds" << std::endl;
   std::this_thread::sleep_for(ms);
   std::cout << "\n IO operation done" << std::endl;
   }

int main(int argc, char **argv)
   {
   std::future<void> FT = std::async(io_thread);   // dispatch async fct
   FT.wait();                                      // wait for event
   std::cout << "\n Main terminates" << std::endl;
   }
```

LISTING 6.11

lo1_S.C

In the next example, the asynchronous operation is the same, but the main() function, rather than performing an indefinite wait for the event, only waits for a succession of one second intervals until the expected event occurs. Running the example, one observes that the wait is timed out four times, as expected, before the event occurs. Notice how much easier it is to program this example with futures than with condition variables.

```
void io_thread()
   { // as in previous listing }

int main(int argc, char **argv)
   {
```

Continued

```
      std::chrono::milliseconds ms(1000);
      std::future<void> FT = std::async(io_thread);  // dispatch

      std::future_status status;
      do
         {
         std::cout << "\n Main waits for 1 second" << std::endl;
         status = FT.wait_for(ms);
         } while (status == std::future_status::timeout);
      std::cout << "\n Main terminates" << std::endl;
      }
```

LISTING 6.12

Io2_S.C

There are a few other std::future features worth keeping in mind. There are naturally wait_until() member functions using absolute dates rather than time durations. It is also possible to associate several threads to a "one-off" event. This cannot be done with the original std::future class, which models unique ownership of the asynchronous result. C++11 introduces the std::shared_future class, which is now copyable, so that ownership can be shared. Several threads can have each a proprietary copy of a shared future object, all associated to the same event. A return value can in this way be broadcasted to several threads waiting for the result.

Examples 6 and 7: Io1_S.C, Io2_S.C

To compile, run make io1_s and io2_s.

6.7.2 STD::PROMISE<T> CLASS

Dispatching an asynchronous task with the std::async() function is not the only way of associating a future object with an asynchronous result. There are two others: promises and packaged_tasks. We discuss next the way a std::promise<T> object sets a data item—of type T—which can later on be read with an associated std::future<T> object. The pair promise-future works as follows:

- First of all, a global std::promise<T> object is declared.
- The client thread that wants to recover later on the data item will do two things:
  - Construct the appropriate future object, initialized by a call to the get_future() member function of the promise object. Indeed, it is the promise object that provides the related future object.
  - Call, when the time comes, the get() function of the future object to receive the expected result.
- The worker thread that computes the expected data value sets, when the time comes, the value of the promise by calling the set_value() member function. In so doing, the future becomes *ready* and can retrieve the stored value.

This mechanism is shown in Listing 6.13, where the client thread performs an unlimited wait for an emulated I/O operation. Since the transfer of a data value is needed to implement the client-worker synchronization, a constant integer value is exchanged among the two threads. In this approach, the worker thread that executes the asynchronous task is launched in the usual way. The worker thread is detached because there is no need to join it to observe the end of the I/O task.

```
std::promise<int> P;

void io_thread()
    {
    std::chrono::milliseconds ms(4000);
    std::cout << "\n IO thread waiting for four seconds" << std::endl;
    std::this_thread::sleep_for(ms);
    std::cout << "\n IO operation done" << std::endl;
    P.set_value(13);         // this makes the associated future ready
    }

int main(int argc, char **argv)
    {
    std::future<int> FT = P.get_future();    // get future from promise

    std::thread T(io_thread);    // launch worker thread
    T.detach();

    int retval = FT.get();       // wait for future event
    std::cout << "\n Main terminates with value " << retval << std::endl;
    }
```

LISTING 6.13

Pio1_S.C

Finally, the previous example is reconsidered: now, main() performs successive 1-second timed waits for the end of a 4-second I/O operation, to show the flexibility of this approach. Getting the data value—which is not relevant in this case—is not really needed. The client thread can perform timed waits as before on the future object, and the waited event is the fact that the future is marked as ready when the data value is stored in the promise.

```
std::promise<int> P;

void io_thread()
    { // as in previous listing }

int main(int argc, char **argv)
    {
    std::future<int> FT = P.get_future();    // get future from promise

    std::thread T(io_thread);        // launch worker thread
    T.detach();
```

Continued

```
    std::chrono::milliseconds ms(1000);
```

```
std::future_status status;
do
    {
    std::cout << "\n Main waits for 1 second" << std::endl;
    status = FT.wait_for(ms);
    } while (status == std::future_status::timeout);

std::cout << "\n Main terminates " << std::endl;
    }
```

LISTING 6.14

Pio2_S.C

Examples 8 and 9: Pio1_S.C, Pio2_S.C
To compile, run make pio1_s and pio2_s.

Hopefully, this discussion is sufficient to convince C++ programmers of the substantial interest of the extended C++11 synchronization utilities. There are many interesting subjects not discussed here. If, for example, a promise is not fulfilled because the promise object is destroyed without setting the data value, an exception is stored instead. The client thread may in this way be informed that something is not correct. C++11 has a very efficient way of transferring exceptions among threads. All these subjects are discussed extensively in [14].

CACHE COHERENCY AND MEMORY CONSISTENCY

7.1 INTRODUCTION

Writing robust and efficient multithreaded programs requires a precise understanding of the behavior of memory system with respect to read and write operations from multiple processors. In a sequential program, it can be taken for granted that a read operation on a memory location will read the last value previously written at the same location. Indeed, in sequential codes the concept of *last write operation* is precisely defined by *program order*, namely, the order in which the read-write operations appear in the program. In a multiprocessor system threads are asynchronous, and read and write operations executed by different threads are not naturally related by program order. Therefore, the question of *when* a data value written to a memory location by one thread is read by a read operation executed by another thread is open to discussion, and requires a deeper understanding of the behavior of the memory system. Arguing about the correctness of a multithreaded code is clearly impossible without a precise answer to this question.

This is a complex issue because it is strongly coupled to—and often in conflict with—the large variety of hardware and software optimizations implemented in current computing architectures to beat what in Chapter 1 was called the *memory wall*. It is not the purpose of this chapter to get involved in a in-depth discussion of this subject, only needed by low-level libraries or compiler writers. Rather, we intend to develop a very qualitative description of what the major issues are—so that readers understand the motivation of the final conclusions of this chapter—trying to conform to A. Einstein's recommendation: *make things as simple as possible, but not simpler*.

The issues to be discussed are of course central for shared memory programming. They have naturally received a lot of attention in the past, and have made some people uneasy towards the implementation of multithreading with libraries on top of thread unaware compilers [19]. Fortunately, barring some pathological cases, applications programmers can safely live with the final conclusions of this chapter.

I strongly recommend readers consult an excellent review paper by S. Adve and H-J. Boenm, *Memory Models: A Case for Rethinking Parallel Languages and Hardware* [20, 21]. Another slightly more advanced but still quite readable discussion can be found in [22].

7.2 CACHE COHERENCY ISSUE

Let us take a detailed look at the cache coherency mechanism. Figure 7.1 shows a SMP platform made of dual-core sockets, with a shared L2 cache memory in each socket.

Let us now imagine that two threads, T1 and T2, running on different sockets have read the A or B data items, and that they both have a corresponding cache line in their L2 caches. Imagine next that one of them, say T1, modifies the value of A. The T1 thread has no problem, because its L2 cache now has the new correct data value. But thread T2 still has the old incorrect value in its L2 cache, so there is a *cache coherency* problem. In order to restore cache coherency, thread T1 that modified A must send a message to all other sockets participating in the process indicating that the cache line that contains A is no longer reliable and must be invalidated. In this way, other threads needing to read A will fetch again the value from the main memory, where hopefully the new updated value is stored.

This cache coherency mechanism requires therefore a persistent communication context among sockets in a SMP platform, and this is the main reason SMP architectures can hardly be extended into the massive parallel domain. It is just too expensive and unrealistic to try to enforce cache coherency among thousands of SMP nodes. Notice also that the mechanism that guarantees cache coherency may have a significant impact on performance that programmers must be aware of. Let us imagine that several threads in a process keep repeatedly updating a shared data item A (a counter, for example). Each time A is updated all cache lines holding A are invalidated, and each subsequent access to A costs the full main memory latency. In this context cache memories are useless, and the performance application may be significantly slowed down.

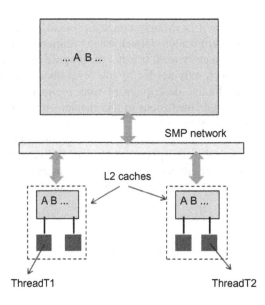

FIGURE 7.1

Illustrating the cache coherency issue.

7.2.1 **FALSE SHARING PROBLEM**

The cache coherency mechanism may sometimes slow down the application performance even if different threads keep updating different variables. Imagine next—see Figure 7.1—that thread T1 keeps updating A and thread T2 keeps updating B. These are now different variables but, *if they are nearby data items sitting on the same cache line*, everything happens as before, as if shared variable was accessed. Any update of A or B invalidates both A and B. Cache lines are repeatedly invalidated, with the subsequent performance degradation if memory accesses are too frequent. This is the *false sharing* problem, to be discussed in more detail later on.

7.2.2 **MEMORY CONSISTENCY ISSUE**

The cache coherency mechanism just described provides two benefits to application programmers:

- It guarantees a thread will not read an obsolete value of a data item from its L2 cache, if this data item has been updated by another thread.
- It promises that the new, updated value of the data item will at some point be available in the main memory for a read by another thread.

Cache coherency is therefore a critical part of the memory system, but *it does not settle the memory consistency issue*. It is simply a mechanism that propagates a newly written value in a memory location to its cached copies, by invalidating the cache lines where the copies reside, thereby forcing the associated cores to retrieve the modified value from main memory. There is naturally a time delay in completing a write: the cached copies must be invalidated, and the new value must reside in memory. The cache coherency protocol does not guarantee *when* the write operation completes, and it *does not* answer the following fundamental question:

When a data value updated by one thread is visible in main memory to another threads?

Obviously, a clear answer to this question is needed to be able to discuss the correctness of multithreaded programs. This answer is provided by the *memory consistency model of the programming environment*. This is a rather subtle question because memory consistency is also a hardware issue closely related to the tricks deployed to reduce the negative impact of the large main memory latencies. Different hardware platforms may handle memory consistency in different ways, and compiler writers need to do whatever is needed to adapt the software memory coherency model to the underlying hardware infrastructure.

7.3 **WHAT IS A MEMORY CONSISTENCY MODEL?**

A memory consistency model of a shared memory multicore architecture provides a formal specification of how the multicore memory system behaves, so that the outcome of a memory read operation is uniquely defined in spite of the asynchronous operation of the different threads. One could imagine enforcing each core to know at every instant what every other core in the system is doing. But this is very expensive in terms of performance and invalidates whatever performance bonus can be expected from the asynchronous execution of several concurrent execution streams. Moreover, most of the time this information is not needed. Therefore, a memory consistency model is the result of a trade-off between memory consistency guarantees that make programming easier, and performance. A memory consistency model tells programmers what guarantees they can expect from the memory system when accessing shared memory locations. It also provides a few low-level instructions allowing programmers to enforce whatever additional memory co-ordinations are required by the underlying algorithms and not guaranteed by the programming environment. These low-level instructions are called *memory fences*.

7.3.1 SEQUENTIAL CONSISTENCY

The simplest memory consistency model is *sequential consistency*. This model has been formally defined by Lamport [23] as follows:

> A multiprocessor is **sequentially consistent** if the result of any execution is the same if the operations of all the processors were executed one at a time in some sequential order, and the operations of each individual processor appear in this sequence in the same order specified by its program.

In other words: take two threads, and imagine that the operations of each one are represented by a deck of cards, a red and a blue deck. Now push the two decks against each other to interleave the cards. In the final deck, the red as well as the blue cards maintain their initial program order, but the interleaving is totally arbitrary. This arbitrary interleaving is just a manifestation of the asynchronous nature of the threads operation. Nevertheless, there is a precise ordering of the operations of different threads. It is implicitly assumed here that memory writes and reads are instantaneous operations that take immediate effect.

This is a very clear cut memory model. However, serializing the execution of the different instructions streams cannot be the way a parallel code executes in real life. This is why the definition of sequential consistency requires that the result of any execution should come out *as if* the code was executed in the way described above.

In order to see the implications of the sequential consistency requirement, we look at a classic example taken from Chapter 8 in the classic reference on computer architectures [24]. Listing 7.1 shows side by side two code segments executed by threads T1 and T2:

```
int X=0; int Y=0;     // shared variables

Thread T1              Thread T2
- - - - - - - -        - - - - - - - - -
...                    ...
X = 1;                 Y = 1;
if(Y==0)               if(X==0)
  { ... }                { ... }
```

LISTING 7.1

Implications of sequential consistency

In this case X and Y are shared variables initialized to 0. Threads T1 and T2 write to X and Y, respectively, and then read the other variable. If, as it is assumed in the sequential consistency statement, writes always take immediate effect and are immediately seen by other processors, then it is impossible for both if() statements to evaluate to true. Indeed, reaching the statement means that either A or B have been assigned the value 1. If, instead, the write operations are for some reason delayed (and indeed they are, as discussed in the next section), then it is possible that:

- Thread T1 runs ahead of thread T2, so it sets X=1 and reads Y=0.
- Thread T2 is late but not too late, and by the time it reads X the write operation from T1 has not yet completed, in which case it reads X=0.
- Now, both if() statements evaluate to true.

The conclusion is that when the code above is executed, sometimes only one and sometimes both of the two if() statements is executed. Now, one may ask if this behavior should be tolerated, and the answer depends on the programmer's intentions. If the underlying algorithm can leave with both alternatives, then there is no problem. If, instead, the algorithm requires one of the two if() statements to be true, this behavior cannot be tolerated, and sequential consistency must be enforced.

Enforcing sequential consistency leads to the installation of additional constraints between the memory operations in which the same data is being written and read by different threads. The read of T2 must be delayed until the write of T1 is completed. Likewise, the read of T1 must be delayed until the write of T2 is completed. This amounts to establishing "happens before" synchronization operations between the activities of different threads. Chapter 8 will show in detail how "happens before" relations are enforced in the different programming environments.

7.3.2 PROBLEMS WITH SEQUENTIAL CONSISTENCY

There are two major issues to be considered when thinking about sequential consistency.

Memory accesses are not atomic

The simple sequential consistency model above assumes that memory accesses are instantaneous (atomic) and that they complete in the order in which they are issued. This is absolutely not the case. Figure 7.2 sketches the standard hierarchical memory model. At some point, a thread updates a variable sitting in its L2 cache. The cache coherency protocol invalidates the cache lines where the copies reside, thereby forcing the associated cores to retrieve from main memory the modified value. There is naturally a time delay in completing a write: the cached copies must be invalidated, and the new value must reside in memory, in order to be seen by other threads.

Indeed, *writes to main memory can be delayed*. To understand why, remember the expression given in Chapter 1 for the time required to transfer N bytes from processor to memory or vice versa:

$$T = L + \frac{N}{B}$$

where L, the latency, is a characteristic of the memory device, and B, the bandwidth, is a quality factor of the network interconnect. As discussed in Chapter 1, the bandwidth can be improved by enhancing the network quality, but the latency of mass memory chips is of a few hundreds of processor cycles, and we are forced to live with that. It is therefore obvious that one way to improve memory access performance is collecting as much data as possible in a memory block before moving it. In this way, the big latency is paid only once, and not several times. This is the reason why modern processors often

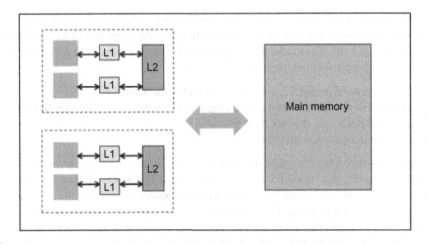

FIGURE 7.2

Hierarchical memory system: read-writes from L2 to main memory are not atomic.

dispose of *write buffers* where data is deposited when, after a write to the L2 cache, new data values must be moved to memory. This introduces a further delay in the completion of the write operation. Likewise, *reads from main memory may be advanced*. The compiler may issue them earlier than needed in order, again, to optimize memory activity. Because of these hardware optimizations, it is not easy to give a precise meaning to *program order* in a multicore system.

Conflicts with sequential compiler optimizations

When the compiler produces the object code in a sequential program, it breaks down the original code into a sequence of low-level machine instructions, and tries to execute them in the most efficient way by exploiting the *instruction level parallelism*. The compiler only guarantees that *the result is consistent with program order execution*. The real code executed is not in program order because of the various optimizations performed by the compiler or the hardware to optimize performance. Many compiler optimizations—such as code motion or loop transformations—or hardware optimizations—like pipelining or multiple issue—lead to overlapping or reorder of memory operations. But for sequential execution streams the compiler can manage to implement the illusion of program order. It is sufficient to respect data and control dependencies among basic instructions. Two memory operations are forced to respect the program order when they are to the same memory location, or when one controls the execution of the other. As long as these data and control dependencies are respected, the compiler and the hardware can freely reorder operations to different memory locations.

In a multicore platform, things become more complex, because:

- The compiler has all the information and the capability of reordering memory accesses and yet guaranteeing sequential consistency *only when dealing with a single, sequential instruction stream*.
- Extending this capability to multiple, simultaneous execution streams is only possible by giving up most of the code optimizations that are at the base of single core performance.

Before discussing the compromises adopted to manage this conflicting context, we take a look at a simple example that shows how the same code, executed in systems with different memory consistency models, can behave in a completely different way. We will, of course, come up later on with the steps that need to be taken to have consistent, portable code.

An amusing example

The example discussed next is the programming of a simple busy wait. The code listed below is supposed to behave as follows:

- There is a shared integer variable, synch, initialized to 0.
- The main thread launches another thread whose only activity is to wait until this shared variable becomes 1. Disregard for the time being the message indicating that it has been released, commented away.
- After launching the waiting thread, the main thread increases synch to 1, and joins the terminating thread. We know that the waiting thread has been released because the join function call returns. If the waiting thread is not released, this function call does not return and the code deadlocks.

The source file Test.C is listed below. We use the SPool utility to manage the waiting thread.

```
int synch;
SPool TS(1);
pthread_mutex_t mutex = PTHREAD_MUTEX_INITIALIZER;

void ThreadFct(void *P)
   {
   while(synch != 1);
   // printf("\n Thread released\n");
   }

int main(int argc, char **argv)
   {
   synch = 0;

   TS.Dispatch(ThreadFct, NULL);    // launch thread
   // – – – – – – – – – – – – – – – – – – – – – – – – – –
   pthread_mutex_lock(&mutex);      // increase synch
   synch ++;
   pthread_mutex_unlock(&mutex);
   // – – – – – – – – – – – – – – – – – – – – – – – – – –
   TS.WaitForIdle();                // join
   return 0;
   }
```

LISTING 7.2

Programming a busy wait

Notice that precautions have been taken concerning shared variables: the increment of the integer synch variable is performed with a locked mutex. This may look like overkill, because in this example nobody else is modifying this variable, but we will see later on that this mutex is in any case needed here for memory consistency reasons. Notice also that *we did not bother to read this variable with a locked mutex*. After all, why should we? A read does not changes the value of synch. We will also see later on that *locking for the read the same mutex used for the write is needed for memory consistency reasons*. This will be the fundamental conclusion of this chapter.

If this code is executed in any Intel x86 architecture (32 or 64 bits), everything is fine and the waiting thread is released. This architecture has a very strict memory consistency model, and the best practices we will discuss in the next sections are not really needed. However, if the code is executed on an IBM Power6 system running AIX the code deadlocks because the waiting thread is not released.

Let me first tell you what I think is going on in the Power6 system. The memory coherency model is more relaxed, and allows some optimizations that would normally not be allowed in more strict models. The compiler, when writing the simple code for the waiting thread, starts by reading synch, whose value is loaded into a register. Since, from the point of view of the waiting thread, nobody else is accessing this variable, the compiler does not bother to read it again from main memory and keeps testing the register value. This is why it will never see the new value written to memory. This clearly shows that a thread can maintain a temporary (or permanent, as in this case) view of memory that is not consistent with the state of the main memory.

How can I guess that this is what is going on? It turns out that, shooting in the dark, I added the print statement initially commented away in the waiting thread function, *and, in doing so, the thread was released*. Now, the print statement has absolutely nothing to do with memory consistency. But an educated guess is that, in order to execute this function call, the compiler needed to use the register holding the *synch* value. Then, when the printf function returns, a new value is read from main memory.

Obviously, programmers cannot live with this erratic, non-portable code with platform-dependent behavior. The basic issues required to ensure memory consistency for robust and portable codes are discussed next.

7.4 WEAK-ORDERING MEMORY MODELS

Strict sequential consistency constrains many hardware and compiler optimizations, and the commonly adopted way out of this conflict is to relax those constraints, while providing at the same time safenets directly or indirectly controlled by the programmer. They are used to restore memory consistency if and when memory operations performed by different threads need to be ordered to guarantee algorithmic integrity.

It is beyond the scope of this book to review the different relaxed memory consistency models implemented by the existing computing platforms. We will only refer to the so-called *weak ordering models*, because they are the ones most commonly adopted in libraries and programming environments. These models classify memory operations into two categories: *data operations*, which are the ordinary reads and writes, and *synchronization operations*, providing the safenets needed to partially restore memory consistency. These models are based on the observation that, typically, memory operations can be reordered within a data region, between synchronization operations, without affecting the correctness of the program. Threads are allowed to maintain a temporary view of memory different from the real state of the memory system. Synchronization operations restore the memory consistency.

7.4.1 MEMORY FENCES

The simplest synchronization memory operation is a *memory fence* instruction. Informally speaking, when such an instruction is issued by a running instruction stream, *no new memory operation is started until this instruction returns, and this happens when all the ongoing memory operations are completed.* At this point, the consistency between the threads view of memory and the real content of the memory system is restored. The result of all the memory operations prior to the memory fence are seen by all threads. It is clear that the presence of a memory fence instruction imposes severe memory-ordering constraints to the compiler, who can no longer reorder preceding (or succeeding) memory accesses beyond (or before) the fence operation point.

In fact, real life is slightly more subtle. Weak-ordering memory models distinguish two types of memory synchronization operations, whose purpose is to reduce as much as possible the constraints they impose, by adapting the operation to the context:

- **Acquire operations**: The memory order constraint is that succeeding operations are not reordered before the fence instruction, but no constraint is imposed on preceding memory operations.
- **Release operations**: The memory order constraint is that preceding operations are not reordered beyond the fence instruction, but no constraint is imposed on succeeding memory operations.

Obviously, the fence operation described first as an acquire-release fence. But it is easy to imagine contexts in which looser memory ordering constraints are useful. Locking a mutex, or reading the value of an atomic variable (discussed in the next chapter), are acquire operations: the thread acquires the right to read a value. Unlocking the mutex, or storing a new value in an atomic variable, are release operations, because they may release a potentially blocked thread. The mutex case is discussed in more detail in the next section. A more precise discussion of these concepts is developed in Chapter 8, when discussing how atomic utilities are used to trigger synchronizations that enforce a precise order between memory operations performed by different threads.

Native libraries or high-level programming environments do not always provide explicit memory fence instructions for programmers. Memory fence instructions are implicit, and they are inserted at the appropriate places in some basic synchronization or management primitives. Then, the end user is instructed about the best practices required to ensure memory consistency. Many programming environments—C++11, Windows, OpenMP, TBB—provide explicit instructions for memory ordering control, in general through their atomic services, discussed in Chapter 8.

7.4.2 CASE OF A MUTEX

The mutex lock-unlock operations are typical places where memory fences are inserted. As shown in Figure 7.3, a memory fence instruction is issued just before the mutex lock function call returns, and just before the mutex unlock function call releases the mutex. Notice that this applies to any kind of mutex. Why are these memory fences needed?

- The fact that the mutex is locked is indicated by a flag inside the mutex object. The first memory fence is needed in order to make absolutely sure that any other thread trying to lock the mutex will see that it is locked. *Mutex locking is an acquired memory operation.* Memory operations testing the mutex state will never be moved up on top of the acquire fence.

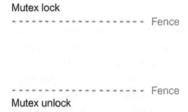

Mutex lock

- - - - - - - - - - - - - - - - - - - Fence

- - - - - - - - - - - - - - - - - - - Fence

Mutex unlock

FIGURE 7.3

Memory fences in mutex locking-unlocking operations.

- The second memory fence instruction is also needed to make sure that, when the mutex is unlocked, all the other threads in the system will see the result of all the memory operations performed inside the critical section.
- *Mutex unlocking is an release operation*. Memory operations updating the mutex protected variable will never be moved down below the release fence.

Now, let us try to read the last written value of a shared variable. *This is guaranteed if the read is performed by locking the same mutex used for the write.* The reason for this is that the release fence following the write synchronizes with the acquire fence before the read, establishing a "happens before" relation between the write and the read. This is, admittedly, a somewhat vague explanation. A more precise discussion followed by examples is developed in Chapter 8. Mutex locking, initially introduced to implement mutual exclusion when writing a shared variable, is also needed for reads to guarantee memory consistency.

Mutex locking is not just about mutual exclusion. Mutex locking is also needed to guarantee memory visibility when accessing shared variables.

7.4.3 PROGRAMMING A BUSY WAIT

On the base of this observation, the busy wait code of Listing 7.2 can be re-examined, to make it portable. The main function—which writes to the shared synch variable with a locked mutex—is unchanged. The waiting thread function, instead, must read this variable with a locked mutex. Listing 7.3 gives the correct version of this thread function.

```
int synch;
pthread_mutex_t mutex = PTHREAD_MUTEX_INITIALIZER;
...
void *ThreadFct(void *P)
   {
   int my_synch;
   do
      {
```

```
pthread_mutex_lock(&mutex);
my_synch = synch;
pthread_mutex_unlock(&mutex);
}while(my_synch != 1);
}
```

LISTING 7.3

Correct thread function for busy wait

A do loop keeps reading memory. We know that the mutex must be locked when the shared variable synch is read. A first idea would be to lock and unlock the mutex outside of the do loop. But this is wrong, because in this case the do loop keeps reading the old value of synch without ever releasing the mutex, and no other thread will ever be able to change its value. The code deadlocks. The correct way of programming the spin wait is given above. The thread function declares a *local* flag (called my_flag in the code). Then, the waiting thread enters a do loop in which:

- The mutex is locked-unlocked just to copy the predicate value to the local flag my_flag.
- Then, the value of my_flag is tested to decide if another iteration is required.
- Since the mutex is unlocked at each iteration, other threads have a chance of acquiring it.

Example: Waiting for the IO task using a spin wait

As an example of the utilization of spin waits, the previous IoTask.C example in Chapter 6 is re-examined. The main thread waits for the completion of a long IO operation delegated to a worker thread. OpenMP threads are used in this example.

```
bool      flag;              // predicate
omp_lock_t mylock;           // mutex (guards predicate)

// Code for workers tasks
// - - - - - - - - - - - - - - - - - - - - -
void io_task()
   {
   Timer T;
   T.Wait(2000);  // perform IO operation
   std::cout << "\n IO operation done. Signaling" << std::endl;

   // change flag value
   omp_set_lock(&mylock);
   flag = false;
   omp_unset_lock(&mylock);
   }

void main_task()
   {
   bool my_flag;
   do
     {
```

Continued

```
    omp_set_lock(&mylock);
    my_flag = flag;
    omp_unset_lock(&mylock);
    }while(my_flag==true);
   std::cout << "\n Main task released" << std::endl;
   }

void TaskFct()
   {
   int rank = omp_get_thread_num();
   if(rank==0) main_task();
   else io_task();
   }

int main(int argc, char **argv)
   {
   flag = true;
   omp_set_num_threads(2);
   #pragma omp parallel
      { TaskFct(); }
   return 0;
   }
```

LISTING 7.4

IoTaskOmp.C

In this code:

- main() initializes the predicate to true, sets the number of threads to 2, and launches an OpenMP parallel section where all tasks execute the function TaskFct().
- TaskFct() gets the rank of the executing thread, and calls main_task() if rank==0, or io_task() if rank==1.
- The IO task is identical to the one discussed before: when the Timer returns after 2 s, this task toggles the value of the predicate to false.
- The main task executes a spin wait as long as the predicate is true, and prints a message when the thread is released.

7.5 PTHREADS MEMORY CONSISTENCY

Here are the memory consistency engagements of the Pthreads library, which result from the existence of implicit memory fences in different library functions:

- Thread creation: memory values a thread can see when it calls pthreads_create() can also be seen by the new thread. Any data written to memory after the call may not be seen by the new thread.

- Mutex unlock: whatever memory values a thread can see when it unlocks a mutex—directly, or waiting on a condition variable—can also be seen by another thread that later locks the same mutex.
- Condition signal or broadcast: whatever memory values a thread can see when it signals or broadcasts a condition variable, can also be seen by a thread that is awakened by that signal or broadcast.
- Thread join: whatever memory values a thread can see when it terminates can also be seen by the thread that joins with it by calling pthread_join().

Memory consistency safenets are therefore installed whenever threads are created or joined, and at the two basic synchronization primitives. Looking back at the simple fork-join examples presented in previous chapters, you can verify that these memory consistency rules have been implicitly applied in those cases.

7.6 OpenMP MEMORY CONSISTENCY

OpenMP puts implicit memory fences in the following synchronization contexts:

- At a barrier synchronization point
- On entry and exit of parallel and critical regions
- At omp_set_lock and omp_unset_lock regions
- At omp_set_nest_lock and omp_unset_nest_lock regions
- At omp_test_lock and omp_test_nest_lock regions, if the call succeeds and the region causes the lock to be set or unset
- Immediately before and after every task scheduling point

Again, the basic idea is the same: memory consistency safenets installed in fork-join sections, and in the basic synchronization primitives used by Open MP: mutex locks and barriers. We will see in Chapter 10 what a task synchronization point is.

7.6.1 FLUSH DIRECTIVE

OpenMP has, in addition, a flush directive that plays the role of an *explicit* memory fence. There general form of the directive is:

```
#pragma omp flush(a, b, ...)
```

LISTING 7.5

Correct thread function for busy wait

and, in this case, memory consistency is restored for variables (a, b ...). There is also a no argument form that acts exactly like a memory fence, restoring memory consistency for all shared variables in memory. Using this explicit memory fence instruction is delicate, and the official OpenMP documentation takes a lot of precautions in presenting its potential usefulness. One of the subtle points is that the flush directive itself can be reordered by the compiler, and therefore this directive cannot be manipulated with shaky hands. Users are encouraged to rely as much as possible on the implicit memory fences already incorporated in the synchronization primitives.

The flush directive has clearly been incorporated in OpenMP to facilitate some low-level optimizations, but, as with the atomic classes discussed in Chapter 8, it falls in the area of advanced low-level optimization tools whose usage is often useful, but never mandatory. Any memory consistency context can always be correctly implemented with mutex locking, as discussed before. It is nevertheless useful to dispose of a qualitative idea of the way other slightly more refined approaches operate, based on atomic utilities. This is the subject of next chapter. The memory consistency mechanisms discussed before will be clarified by discussing the std::atomic<T> class proposed by the C++11 thread standard.

ATOMIC TYPES AND OPERATIONS

8

8.1 INTRODUCTION

Atomic operations were introduced in Chapter 5 as a useful and fast alternative for implementing mutual exclusion among basic shared variables. They are guaranteed to be performed in an indivisible way, as if they were a unique machine instruction. This is, in fact, the way they are used in OpenMP. In other programming environments—Windows, TBB, C++11—atomic operations have a broader role: they enable programmers to enforce the ordering of memory operations of different threads and to construct in this way custom synchronization patterns. This is the subject of this chapter. The memory consistency concepts discussed in the previous chapter are essential for the discussion that follows.

The TBB and C++11 libraries provide C++ classes defining *atomic data types*, on which a set of atomic operations are defined. Windows does not have explicit atomic data types, but a number of C library functions provide an equivalent service. These atomic utilities are powerful weapons in skilled hands, opening the way to the design of efficient custom synchronization utilities enhancing multithreading performance.

As stated in Chapter 5 any synchronization context can always be managed with the two basic synchronization primitives: mutual exclusion and event synchronization. Nevertheless, a qualitative understanding of the way atomic utilities operate is useful knowledge. It is possible in this way to understand the basic ideas behind the so-called lock-free algorithms, whose purpose is to control race conditions in shared data accesses without blocking the participating threads. Later chapters explore also the possibility of substantially enhancing the performance of some realistic applications with the help of simple utilities based on atomic variables.

This chapter covers the basic atomic concepts and ideas, together with a few examples. The atomic classes proposed by the C++11 thread library and by TBB are discussed first. Then, the Windows atomic utilities are discussed. A very complete and exhaustive discussion of the C++11 atomic standard can be found in A. Williams book, *C++ concurrency in action* [14].

8.2 C++11 STD::ATOMIC<T> CLASS

The C++11 standard defines the std::atomic<T> class. The template argument T is a generic type: bool, integer, or pointer type, another basic type—like a double, for example—or a user-defined type fulfilling certain criteria. Explicit atomic operations can then be programmed in a simple way. However, not all the operations defined by the class member functions can be applied to all types: there are indeed a few specializations for specific types. In what concerns user-defined types, they must not have any virtual function or virtual base classes, and they have to be simple enough so as to use the default, compiler-generated copy and assignment operators.

8.2.1 MEMBER FUNCTIONS

In the discussion that follows, X and Y are type T atomic data items, and x, y, are type T ordinary data items. The member functions discussed below show an optional last argument M that corresponds to a *memory-ordering option*, related to memory consistency requirements that will be specified in detail later on. A default value is adopted if this optional argument is omitted.

STD::ATOMIC<T> INTERFACES

std::atomic<T> X

– Constructor.
– Creates an atomic variable X of type T.

bool X.is_lock_free()

– Returns true if the internal implementation of the atomic variable of type T is not emulated by mutex locking.
– Returns false if the atomic variable of type T is emulated by using mutex locking.

x = X.load(M)

– Reads in x the internal value of X.

void X.store(x, M)

– Initializes the internal value of X to x.

x = X.exchange(y, M)

– Sets the internal value of X to y.
– Returns the old value of X in x.

bool X.compare_exchange_strong(T& e, T x, M)

– Atomically compares the expected value e to the value stored in X, and stores x in X if equal.
– Returns true if exchange succeeds, false otherwise.

x = X.fetch_add(y, M)

– Atomically adds y to the value stored in X.
– Returns the old value stored in X.
– Alternative notation: X+= y;

x = X.fetch_sub(y, M)

– Atomically subtracts y to the value stored in X.
– Returns the old value stored in X.
– Alternative notation: X -= y;

x = X.fetch_or(y, M)

– Atomically ors the value stored in X with y.
– Returns the old value stored in X.
– Alternative notation: X |= y;

x = X.fetch_and(y, M)

– Atomically ands the value stored in X with y.
– Returns the old value stored in X.
– Alternative notation: X &= y;

x = X.fetch_xor(y, M)

- – Atomically xors the value stored in X with y.
- – Returns the old value stored in X.
- – Alternative notation: X ≙y;

X++; X−−;

- – Atomically increments or decrements the value stored in X.

The compare_exchange_strong() member function quoted above has another version with the same signature, called compare_exchange_weak. Notice that many "read and modify" atomic operations return the old value of X. The reason is that when these basic operations are used to build higher level synchronization constructs, the initial value of X is sometimes needed, as some of the examples that follow later on in the chapter will show (Table 8.1).

A few more comments concerning the properties of this class:

- The atomic<T> class, like the basic data types, has no explicit constructor. The only way to create an atomic variable is to declare it in the way indicated above. The C++ initialization rules for classes without constructors apply here. The atomic data item is initialized to 0 (if integer) or NULL (if pointer) when declared as a global variable with file scope, as static data item inside a function, or as a data member in a class.
- When pointers are used, the arithmetic operations comply with the *pointer arithmetic* specifications. The ++ operation, for example, increments an atomic T* of sizeof(T).
- Likewise, when an integer n is added to an atomic pointer T*, the pointer value is incremented by n.sizeof(T)

Example 1: Monte-Carlo computation of π

As a first simple example, let us go back to the Monte-Carlo computation of π discussed in previous chapters. Remember that two threads were counting the number of accepted events, and that the main issue was to communicate the partial acceptances to the main thread. The simplest thing to do now is

Table 8.1 Available Operations for the Different Atomic Types

Operation	bool	integer	pointer	basic or user
		Atomic Operations		
is_lock_free	X	X	X	X
load	X	X	X	X
store	X	X	X	X
exchange	X	X	X	X
comp_exch	X	X	X	X
fetch_add, +=		X	X	
fetch_sub, -=		X	X	
fetch_or, |=			X	
fetch_and, &=			X	
fetch_xor, ≙			X	
++, −−		X	X	

to define a atomic<long> global counter, incremented by each thread each time an accepted event is registered. Then, the main thread just uses the final value of this counter. The new version of this code is in the source file McAtomic_S.C. Listing 8.1 displays the new thread function.

```
#include <SPool.h>
#include <atomic>
SPool TH(2);              // set of two threads
long nsamples;           // number of MonteCarlo events per thread
std::atomic<long> C;     // atomic<long> to accumulate acceptances

void *thread_fct(void *P)
   {
   double x, y;
   int rank;

   rank = TH.GetRank();
   Rand R(rank*999);
   for(int n=0; n<nsamples; n++)
      {
      x = R.draw();
      y = R.draw();
      if((x*x+y*y) <= 1.0 ) ++C;  // accumulate in atomic C
      }
   }
```

LISTING 8.1

McAtomic_S.C (partial listing)

After joining the threads, main() uses the C value to compute π. A substantial amount of contention has deliberately been introduced in this example: the atomic counter is incremented a huge number of times. We know that a much better strategy would be to have each thread increment a private local counter, and then accumulate only once each final private count in the atomic counter. Nevertheless, the performance of this program is quite acceptable when compared to the CalcPi.C performance, where partial results are accumulated in local variables.

The excessive contention on the atomic integer is much less harmful than the excessive contention in mutex locking. The reason is that atomic operations are implemented using very low-level hardware and operating system facilities specially designed to implement thread synchronizations. This can be easily verified in this example: if an arbitrary additional input is added to the command line, the program accumulates acceptances in a mutex protected long instead. The atomic version runs several times faster than the locked mutex version.

Example 1: McAtomic_S.C

To compile, run make atest. The number of threads is hardwired to 2. Adding any arbitrary input to the command line, mutex locking replaces the atomic operation.

8.3 LOCK-FREE ALGORITHMS

Atomic classes make can be used to perform a thread-safe update of a shared data set without introducing critical sections, by implementing lock free algorithms, where threads may possibly perform redundant work, *but they are never blocked, waiting for a mutex availability.* Performing additional redundant work may in many cases be a better trade-off than the serialization enforced by the critical sections. The difference in both approaches is the following:

- Mutual exclusion is a *pessimistic* approach, planning for the worst. In acting on the data set, the programmer strategy is: *a race condition could possibly happen here, so we make sure that it never happens.*
- Lock-free algorithms implement an *optimistic* approach, planning for the best. In acting on the data set, the programmer strategy is *we go ahead, and if a race occurs we start all over again.* Of course, the whole point is having the right tool to detect that a race condition has indeed occurred.

The lock-free logic is discussed next. This is not really application programming, but the very instructive programming idiom that follows will certainly improve your understanding of multithreaded programming. This discussion demonstrates the power of the atomic<T> classes.

8.3.1 UPDATING AN ARBITRARY, GLOBAL DATA ITEM

Consider the update of a basic or user-defined type T. The fundamental tool for detecting race conditions is the compare_and_exchange member function, usually called CAS, for *Compare and Swap*. This is the basic tool enabling the implementation of lock-free algorithms. In most systems it is directly supported by hardware. The x86 and Intel 64 instruction sets have a unique CAS instruction that works naturally for integers and pointers. In PowerPC processors, the CAS operation is implemented by two instructions. The atomic<T> compare_and_exchange member functions clearly rely on these low-level hardware primitives, at least for integers and pointers. In C++11, the CAS operation is extended to arbitrary types, but this is not the case for Windows and TBB, where it remains restricted to integer or pointer types.

Figure 8.1 shows the lock-free algorithm for the update. Let old_value be the initial value of a data item, allocated in the heap and referenced by an atomic pointer P.

- In step 1, the initial content of P is copied to a local variable x.
- In step 2, another local variable y is allocated in the heap, referenced by an ordinary pointer Q. This variable is initialized to the new value that needs to be loaded in P.
- In step 3, a complex operation involving a comparison and an exchange is performed atomically: P is compared to its initial value, and if there has been no changes, P and Q are exchanged.
- At the end of this process, P references the updated new value.

In this algorithm, it is the CAS operation that detects possible race conditions. A race condition occurs if, in the lapse of time in which the active thread saves the initial value and allocates the new value, another thread—concurrently updating P—is faster and completes its own update. In this case, P has been modified, the comparison fails, and the update does not take place. Indeed, a race condition has occurred, and knowing that the race is lost the update is aborted and eventually started again from

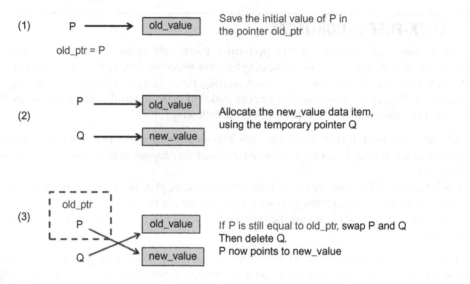

(1)   P ⟶ old_value   Save the initial value of P in the pointer old_ptr

old_ptr = P

(2)   P ⟶ old_value   Allocate the new_value data item, using the temporary pointer Q

Q ⟶ new_value

(3)   old_ptr P   old_value   If P is still equal to old_ptr, swap P and Q Then delete Q. P now points to new_value

Q   new_value

FIGURE 8.1

Lock-free algorithm for updating an arbitrary data item.

scratch. If the comparison succeeds and the exchange takes place, the atomic nature of this combined operation prevents it from being corrupted by another competing thread.

8.3.2 AREDUCTION CLASS

The AReduction class—for *Atomic Reduction*—has exactly the same public interfaces as the Reduction class introduced in Chapter 5, with a different implementation: a lock-free algorithm instead of mutex locking. This new class encapsulates an *atomic pointer* T* to an arbitrary data type, allocated in the heap.

```
#include <atomic>
template<typename T>
class AReduction
    {
    private:
     std::atomic<T*> P;

    public:
     AReduction() { P = new T(); }

     ~AReduction() { delete P; }

     T Data() { return *P; }

     void Reset()
        {
```

```
        T value  = *P;
        *P -= value;
        }

    void Update(T d)
        {
        T *oldptr, *newptr;
        do
            {
            oldptr = P;
            newptr = new T(*P+d);
            }while(P.compare_exchange_strong(oldptr, newptr)==false);
        }
    };
```

LISTING 8.2

AReduction class—Atomic, lock-free accumulator

Notice the simplicity of the Update(T d) member function: it executes a do loop that keeps iterating as long as the CAS operation fails because a race condition is detected. Notice also how the return value of compare_exchange() plays a critical role in the algorithm. The member function Data() returns the value of the data referenced by P, and the Reset() member function reinitializes the internal data to 0, so that a new reduction operation can be started.

This class operates exactly like Reduction.h. It accumulates values, and returns the result of the reduction via the Data() function call. Pointer manipulations are hidden to the user. The source code can be consulted in the file AReduction.h. The class is tested in ScaProd_S.C.

```
SPool TH(2);                   // set of two threads
AReduction<double> D;          // lock free double accumulator
double A[VECSIZE];
double B[VECSIZE];

void *thread_fct(void *P)
    {
    double d;
    int beg, end;
    beg = 0;                       // initialize [beg, end) to global range
    end = VECSIZE;
    TH.ThreadRange(beg, end);   // [beg, end) is now range for this thread
    for(int n=beg; n<end; n++)
        {
        d = A[n]*B[n];
        D.Update(d);
        }
    }
```

LISTING 8.3

Partial listing of ScaProd_S.C

Example 2: ScaProd_S.C

To compile, run make scaprod_s. The number of threads is hardwired to 2.

In running the example, you will observe that this code exactly reproduces the results of all the previous thread-safe versions of this calculation. Once again, unnecessary contention is deliberately introduced, but this code has better performance than the previous, mutex-based inefficient version, DotProd1.C.

8.4 SYNCHRONIZING THREAD OPERATIONS

Our interest moves next to the way atomic operations are used to implement synchronization patterns, by enforcing some degree of ordering among memory operations performed by different threads. The discussion that follows focuses on the C++11 library, but all the ideas and concepts developed here apply also, with minor modifications, to the TBB atomic class and to the Windows atomic utilities.

Let us imagine that a thread T1, updating some data structure, needs to enforce the fact that another thread T2 only accesses the same data structure after the update is completed. In other words, a *happens before* relationship must be established between the activities of threads T1 and T2.

This "happens before" relationship can be implemented as follows. A shared atomic<bool> X is introduced, with an initial false value. When T1 finishes its update, it stores the value true. T2 keeps loading the atomic flag until the value true is retrieved. At this point, T2 accesses the data structure. This is shown in Listing 8.4.

```
std::atomic<bool> X;

void ThreadFct1()        // thread T1
   {
   ...
   Operation A;
   X.store(true);
   ...
   }

void ThreadFct2()        // thread T2
   {
   ...
   while(X.load()==false);
   Operation B;
   ...
```

LISTING 8.4

"Happens before" relation between A and B

The reason why this code works is that *the store operation in thread T1 synchronizes with the load operation in thread T2 that reads the same stored value in the atomic variable.* The synchronization therefore occurs when T2 reads true. One can imagine that at this point a memory fence among the two threads is established, preventing operations in T1 before the store to be moved beyond the fence, and operations in T2 after the load to be moved before it. This mechanism establishes a "happens before" relation between operations A and B in the two threads.

Inside a given thread, there is a natural "happens before" relation among successive operations, provided by program order. Moreover, "happens before" relations are transitive. Therefore, the code above implements a "happens before" relation between any operation before the store in T1 and any other operation after the load in T2.

Atomic operations induce in this way synchronization relations that enforce some degree of memory consistency, with a refined control provided by the optional second argument M in the member functions, called a *memory order option*. In the example above, the default value of this option—which is sequential consistency—is used; it constitutes the strongest possible enforcement of memory consistency. Other explicit options can be used to reduce this level of enforcement, with the purpose of avoiding the cost of additional synchronizations that are not strictly needed in a particular context. The discussion that follows clarifies these issues.

8.4.1 MEMORY MODELS AND MEMORY ORDERING OPTIONS

Three memory models proposed by C++11, which, together with the memory ordering options that can be used in each one of them, are described next. Memory order options are symbolic constants passed as second argument to the atomic class member functions. As stated before, the same memory models are implemented in TBB and Windows, with minor implementation differences.

- **Sequential consistency**: This memory model imposes the strongest memory order constraints. In fact, there is more to sequential consistency than the happens before relation exhibited in Listing 8.2. Broader global synchronizations are implemented, forcing all threads to see all the sequential consistent synchronizations in the program happening in the same order. There is, in a given program, a unique global order of sequentially consistent atomic operations, seen by all the threads in the process.
  - memory_order_seq_cst: This ordering enforces sequential consistency, preventing preceding (or succeeding) memory operations to be reordered beyond (or before) this point. But there are also subsidiary global synchronizations as discussed above. An example will be given next. *This is the default value for the second argument in member functions.*
- **Acquire-release**: In this model, stores and loads still synchronize as described above, but there is no global order. Different threads may see different synchronizations happening in different orders. Memory order options are:
  - memory_order_release Prevents preceding memory operations from being reordered past this point.
  - memory_order_acquire Prevents succeeding memory operations from being reordered before this point.
  - memory_order_consume A weaker form of the acquire option: memory order constraints only apply to succeeding operations that are computationally dependent on the value retrieved (loaded) by the atomic variable.

Table 8.2 Memory Order Options for Atomic Operations

Options for Atomic Operations	
Operation	Memory Options
Store	memory_order_seq_cst
	memory_order_release
	memory_order_relaxed
Load	memory_order_seq_cst
	memory_order_acquire
	memory_order_consume
	memory_order_relaxed
Read-modify-write	all available options

- memory_order_acq_rel. Combines both release and acquire memory order constraints: a full memory fence is in operation.
- **Relaxed**: In this model, the basic store-load synchronization described above does not occur, and no "happens before" relations across threads are established.
    - memory_order_relaxed. There is no ordering constraint. Following operations may be reordered before, and preceding operations may be reordered after the atomic operation.

Finally, it is important to observe that not all memory ordering options are adapted to all member functions. Atomic operations are of three kinds: *load, store*—the load() and store() member functions—and *read_modify_write*—all the other member functions. Table 8.2 lists the memory ordering options available to each type of atomic operation.

The rest of this section provides a very qualitative discussion of the differences between the different memory ordering options, so that readers can feel more or less at ease when dealing with references on this subject. A couple of examples will also be examined. There are, in this subject, a substantial number of subtleties that are beyond the scope of this book. Readers willing to go deeper into this subject should consult the exhaustive discussion presented in [14].

8.4.2 USING THE RELAXED MODEL

Relaxed memory ordering options can be used when the atomic operation is not involved in a synchronization activity, and all that is expected from them is mutual exclusion. In the first example—Listing 8.1—where an atomic counter is incremented in the Monte Carlo computation of π, different threads increment the counter, but the order in which this happens is totally irrelevant.

The relaxed model is not easy to use in complex situations. The C++ atomic services also provide programmers with the ability to introduce explicit memory fences, and a relaxed model with explicit fences may help library writers perform refined optimizations. Explicit C++11 fence interfaces will not be discussed any further. Again, a very exhaustive discussion of all these issues is developed in [14].

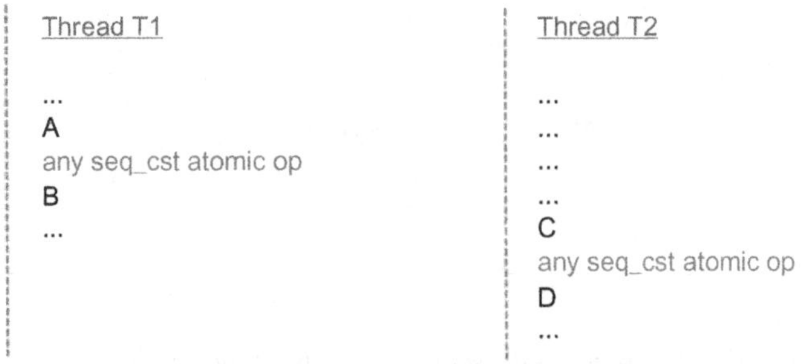

Thread T1	Thread T2
...	...
A	...
any seq_cst atomic op	...
B	...
...	C
	any seq_cst atomic op
	D
	...

FIGURE 8.2

Global order among sequentially consistent operations.

8.4.3 GLOBAL ORDER IN SEQUENTIAL CONSISTENCY

All sequentially consistent atomic operations are executed in a global order that is seen by all the threads in the process. Figure 8.2—inspired by an example proposed in the Boost documentation—shows two threads executing sequentially consistent operations. They do not need to be using the same atomic variable; different variables will do as well. When the program is executed, an absolute order is established, which means that *either A happens before D—the order in the figure—or C happens before B.*

Sequential consistency establishes therefore "happens before" relations between remote operations—with eventual performance penalties—that may or may not be needed in each particular application to preserve the algorithm integrity.

8.4.4 COMPARING SEQUENTIAL CONSISTENCY AND ACQUIRE-RELEASE

The same synchronization relation exposed in Listing 8.3, leading to a "happens before" relation between operations A and B, can be implemented by enforcing release memory order in the store and acquire memory order in the load, as shown in Listing 8.5. If all the program requires is the establishment of this local "happens before" relation between A and B, then the acquire-release model is largely sufficient to preserve the algorithm integrity.

```
#include <atomic>

std::atomic<bool> B;

void ThreadFct1()          // thread T1
   {
   ...
   Operation A;
   B.store(true, memory_order_release);
   ...
   }
```

Continued

```
void ThreadFct2()          // thread T2
   {
      ..
   while(B.load()==false, memory_order_acquire);
   Operation B;
   ...
```

LISTING 8.5

"Happens before" with acquire-release

The only way to see the difference with sequential consistency is to examine the additional side effects when more than one synchronization is programmed. Figure 8.3—inspired from an example in [14]—shows two independent load-store synchronizations: threads T1-T2 establish a "happen before" relation between A and B, and threads T3-T4 establish an independent "happens before" relation between C and D.

If the acquire-release model is used, this is the end of the story: there is no global order established among the two synchronization operations. If, instead, the sequential consistency model is used, all four threads must see the two synchronization operations happening in the same order, and this leads to additional constraints on the way the threads operate.

In order to see this point, threads T2 and T4 are asked, after the synchronizations take place, to load the values of Y and X, respectively. Let us assume that T2 reads the value false. At this point, T2 knows that the T3-T4 synchronization comes after the T1-T2 one, and that the store in X happened before the store in Y. But this order must be seen by all threads, including T4, which means that, when T4 loads X, *it must necessarily read the value true*, because the store in X happened before D. To sum up:

- In the sequential consistency model, threads T2 and T4 cannot both read the value false.
- In the acquire-release model, the two synchronizations are totally independent, and threads T2 and T4 can read any value.

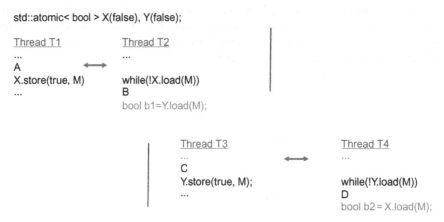

FIGURE 8.3

Two independent "happens before" relations.

8.4.5 CONSUME INSTEAD OF ACQUIRE SEMANTICS

The consume option is an optimized version of the acquire. When an atomic load operation takes place:

- If acquire semantics is used, no memory operation following the load can be moved before it.
- If consume semantics is used, the previous memory order constraint only applies to operations following the load *that have computational dependence on the value read by the load*. This more relaxed requirement reduces the constraints imposed on the compiler, who can now reorder memory operations he could not reorder before, which may result in enhanced performance.

The consume semantics is typically used with atomic pointers. Listing 8.6 shows an example in which a thread transfers to another thread the value of a shared double.

```
#include <atomic>

std::atomic<double*> P;      // initialized to NULL
double               d;

void ThreadFct1()            // thread T1
   {
   ...
   d = 5.25;
   P.store(&d, memory_order_release);  // store pointer to d
   ...
   }

void ThreadFct2()            // thread T2
   {
     ..
   double *p;
   do
      {
      p = P.load(memory_order_consume);
      }while(p==NULL);
   // other operations
   double x = *p;       // use the loaded pointer
   ...
   }
```

LISTING 8.6

"Happens before" with consume-release

In this case, the only "happens before" relation that holds is the one between the initialization of d in thread 1, and the retrieval of is value by the load operation on P in thread 2.

8.4.6 USEFULNESS OF MEMORY_ORDER_ACQ_REL

The memory_order_acq_rel option can be useful to simplify transitive "happen before" relations. Let us consider the following scenario involving three threads:

- Thread T1 executes an operation A followed by a release operation on an atomic variable S1.
- Thread T2 executes a acquire operation on S1, followed later on by another release operation an atomic variable S2.
- Finally, thread T3 executes an acquire operation on S2, followed by an operation B.

Then, operation A in T1 "happens before" operation B in T3. This synchronization pattern can be simplified, using the acquire-release memory order option. First, only one atomic variable S is needed. Then,

- Thread T1 executes an operation A followed by a release operation on S.
- Thread T2 executes any read_and_modify operation on S, with acq_rel semantics.
- Finally, thread T3 executes an acquire operation on S, followed by an operation B.

8.5 EXAMPLES OF ATOMIC SYNCHRONIZATIONS

Some examples of high-level synchronization utilities are proposed next, to be used in later chapters. They illustrate the way atomic operations implement custom synchronization patterns. These examples are proposed for pedagogical purposes, in order to add some real content to the previous discussion.

8.5.1 SPINLOCK CLASS

When discussing mutual exclusion, we observed that Pthreads proposed a special kind of mutex, called spinlock, in which threads keep executing a busy wait in user space when waiting to lock the mutex, instead of moving away to a blocked state waiting to be waken up.

It was also observed that there is no native spin lock in C++11, but it is now very easy to build one. Here is a SpinLock class taken from an example proposed in the Boost documentation, providing the traditional Lock() and Unlock() member functions.

```
class SpinLock
   {
   private:
    std::atomic<bool> _state;

   public:
    SpinLock() :
       {
       _state.load(false, memory_order_acquire);
       }

    void Lock()
       {
       while(_state.exchange(true, memory_order_acquire) == true)
       }

    void Unlock()
       {
       _state.store(false, memory_order_release);
```

```
        }
    };
```

LISTING 8.7

SpinLock class

Let us examine in detail the way this streamlined code operates:

- The internal state of a shared SpinLock object used to enforce mutual exclusion is an atomic bool having two values: true when locked and false when unlocked.
- The Lock() member function calls bool exchange(true, M), which changes the internal state of the atomic variable to true and returns the old value.
- This all happens inside a while loop, which in fact executes a busy wait: it keeps replacing the internal state by the true value, and this loop keeps executing as long as there is no effective replacement because the old value was already true. The while loop breaks when it finds a false state because another thread has released the mutex.
- The exchange operation adopts an acquire semantics, needed to catch a change of state previously executed by another thread.
- The Unlock() member function just stores the false value in the atomic variable state. It adopts the release memory order, so that any atomic variable access that comes after can see the new state value.

This is a very simple and elegant implementation of a spin lock. It correctly enforces mutual exclusion *as long as all threads respect the lock-unlock protocol*. In the code above, there is no notion of lock ownership: nothing prevents a thread from unlocking a spin-lock it has not previously locked, in which case mutual exclusion is corrupted. The spin-lock class in the vath library prevents this from happening by incorporating thread identities in the internal state (see the SpinLock.h source file). This class is used in Chapter 9 to implement a spin barrier. Further examples are also found in this chapter.

This class is fully portable. It is implemented in C++11 and Windows using the atomic services, as explained above. In Pthreads, lacking atomic services, this class is just a wrapper for the native spinlock_t mutex discussed in Chapter 5.

Example: TSpinLock.C

An example follows in which this class is tested in a context of very high mutual exclusion contention: the database search emulation example discussed at the end of Chapter 3. Worker threads keep calling a random number generator until they get a value close to a target value. When this happens, a global flag is toggled to inform the other threads that the result is available, and all infinite loops stop. If all the threads keep checking the global flag at each iteration, performance is extremely poor. The TSpinLock.C alleviates this performance issue while keeping a high amount of mutual exclusion contention by checking the global flag only every 10 iterations. This raises, of course, another problem, because now it is possible for two or more threads to find simultaneously a value close to the target. It is a good exercise to understand how this issue is resolved: another mutex is introduced to catch the first value available. The source file explains in detail the programming strategy.

Example 3: TSpinLock.C

The database search case. Two worker threads are used. To compile, run make tsplock.

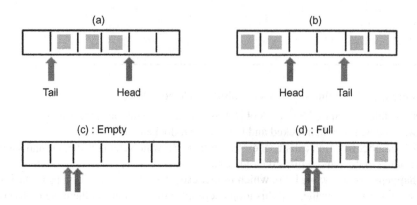

FIGURE 8.4

Circular buffer.

When the code is executed with the configuration given in the example, the Pthreads version take about 3 s, while the versions using the atomic implementations take about 2 s.

8.5.2 CIRCULAR BUFFER CLASS

The next example is a simple, but rather subtle, exercise in atomic synchronizations: Readers are strongly encouraged to take a look at it.

A circular buffer is a utility used to transfer successive data values from a producer thread to a consumer thread, who retrieves the data in FIFO (first in first out) order. This kind of data structure will be used when pipelining threads, a subject discussed in detail in Chapter 15. A producer thread performs some partial operation on a data set (think of one row of a matrix) and stores it in the buffer as a data identifier (think of the row index) to inform the consumer thread that it can go ahead and complete its part of the operation. The circular buffer discussed next assumes that there is one producer and one consumer thread. This is sufficient to implement the pipeline concurrency pattern.

The circular buffer, implemented by a template RingBuffer class, is shown in Figure 8.4. A RingBuffer object stores an array of type T data items, T being the template parameter of the class. The buffer size Size is also passed as a template parameter. Another private data members are head and tail, the array indices where the next insertion—or extraction—take place. The circular nature of the array means that head and tail grow modulo Size: the next value to Size-1 is 0. Figure 8.4 shows some typical configurations: (a) and (b) show a partially filled buffer, (c) shows an empty buffer, and (d) shows a filled buffer.

Circular buffers are useful for two reasons. First of all, this is the only practical way of handling a context in which the buffer size cannot be guessed "a priori": there may be an enormous number of insertions and extractions. The second, most important, reason is that the circular buffer helps to regulate the workflow between the producer and the consumer activities:

- The producer thread calls, to insert a new value, a Push() function that operates as follows:
    - Reads the current value of head.
    - If the buffer is full, returns false.

- − Stores the input data in the buffer at the head position, stores in head its next value, and returns true.
- The consumer thread calls, to extract a new value, a Pop() function that operates as follows:
  - − Reads the current value of tail.
  - − If the buffer is empty, returns false.
  - − Reads the requested data in the buffer at the tail position, stores in tail its next value, and returns true.

The finite buffer size prevents therefore the producer thread from running too much ahead of the consumer thread: insertions are refused when the buffer is full because the consumer is late in extracting data. It is understood that Push() and Pop() need to check if the buffer is full or empty; Figure 8.4 shows that in both cases head==tail. In order to distinguish both configurations, another atomic integer C is introduced, to be increased—or decreased—whenever head—or tail—start a new round. When the buffer is empty, head and tail have performed the same number of rounds, and C=0. When the buffer is full, head is one round ahead, and C=1. The counter C is atomic only for mutual exclusion reasons: both threads are modifying it.

Need for synchronization

The next point is to understand when and how memory operations must be synchronized. In ordinary configurations, with a partially filled buffer, synchronizations are hardly needed: Push() and Pop() operations are acting on *different* array elements. Problems arise when the buffer is empty or full, because in this case both operations may end up acting on the same array element.

The discussion that follows assumes there is only one producer and one consumer thread. This class is not designed to be used in other cases, when more than one thread is executing the Push() or Pop() functions.

The C++11 implementation of the RingBuffer class is defined in Listing 8.8. Consider the Pop() operation: if the buffer is empty, the operation fails, and that is the end of it. However, the Extract() member function keeps popping until the operation no longer fails, because an element has just been inserted at the target place. At this point, it is necessary to make sure the write to the buffer element by Push() *happens before* the read of the same buffer element by Pop(). Likewise, when the buffer is full, the read of the buffer element by Pop() must *happens before* the write to the same buffer element by Push().

```
template <typename T, int Size>
class RingBuffer
    {
    private:
    T buffer[Size];
    std::atomic<int> head, tail;
    std::atomic<int> C;

    int NextHead( int n)
```

Continued

```
       { if(n==(Size-1)) C++; return (n+1)%Size; }

   int NextTail( int n)
       { if(n==(Size-1)) C--; return (n+1)%Size; }
  public:
  RingBuffer() : head(0), tail(0) {}

  bool Push(const T& value)
     {
     int H = head.load(memory_order_relaxed);
     if(H == tail.load(memory_order_acquire)              // <=== T
           && C.load(memory_order_relaxed)) return false;
     buffer[H] = value;
     head.store(NextHead(H), memory_order_release);   // <=== H
     return true;
     }

  bool Pop(T& value)
     {
     int T = tail.load(memory_order_relaxed);
     if(T == head.load(memory_order_acquire)              // <=== H
           && !C.load(memory_order_relaxed)) return false;
     value = buffer[T];
     tail.store(NextTail(T), memory_order_release);   // <=== T
     return true;
     }

  void Insert(const T& value)
     { while(Push(value)==false); }

  void Extract(T& value)
     { while(Pop(value)==false); }
  };
```

LISTING 8.8

RingBuffer class

The Push() and Pop() functions are listed above. Imagine, for example, that the buffer is full, and that Push() is trying unsuccessfully to insert a new element, because it reads that head=tail and C!=0. Then, the consumer thread pops a value, and stores the next value of tail with release semantics at the place tagged <=== T in Listing 8.8. The thread executing Push() reads, again at the place tagged <=== T, the new value of tail with acquire semantics, which indicates that the buffer is no longer full. At this point, the load-store of the same value of tail with acquire-release semantics establishes the required "happen before" relation between the read of buffer[n] preceding the store and the write of buffer[n] following the load. This implements the correct synchronization for a concurrent operation on a full buffer.

It is easy to check that the correct synchronization for an empty buffer is enforced by the stores and loads of head at the places tagged as <=== H in Listing 8.8. In this case, the write of buffer[n] "happens before" the read of buffer[n]. All the other atomic operations—initial reads of head and tail, reads and writes on C—are not involved in synchronizations, and are executed with relaxed semantics.

Example: TRBuff.C

The C++11 implementation of the RingBuffer class is tested by compiling the TRBuff.C with the CPP11_ENV=1 environment variable. Indeed, this portable class is also implemented in Windows— using the Windows atomic facilities discussed in Section 8.6—and in Pthreads—using the basic synchronization utilities due to the lack of atomic support. The producer thread inserts successive positive integer values in the buffer, followed by a negative value to inform the consumer that the game is over. The consumer keeps calling Extract() and printing the value until it extracts a negative value.

Example 4: TRBuff.C

Using a circular buffer to implement a producer-consumer pattern between two threads. To compile, run make trbuff.

8.6 TBB ATOMIC<T> CLASS

The tbb::atomic<T> class is similar to the std::atomic<T> class just examined, and the official documentation can be found in the "Synchronization" topic in the Reference Guide [17]. There are, however, a few differences.

In the tbb::atomic<T> class the template argument T is restricted to either an integer type (signed or unsigned integers or longs), to a pointer type, or to an enumeration type. Explicit atomic operations on integer types can be therefore programmed in a simple way, and atomic pointers can be used to implement thread-safe operations for other basic or user-defined data types, as the previous example has shown.

Listing 8.9 shows the properties of the tbb::atomic<T> class. The same conventions are used: capital letters—like X, Y—are type T atomic data items, while lowercase letters—like x, y—are ordinary type T data items.

```
// Variable declarations
// – – – – – – – – – – –
tbb::atomic<T> X;            // default constructor
tbb::atomic<T> X(T value);   // not atomic, see comments below

T  x, y;                     // x, y are ordinary integers or pointers

// Three basic member functions, that all return the
// old value of X:
// – – – – – – – – – – – – – – – – – – – – – – – – – –
x = X.fetch_and_store(y)     // Execute X=y
x = X.fetch_and_add(y)       // Execute X+=y
```

Continued

```
x = X.compare_and_swap(y, z)   // If X equals z, execute X=y.
// Overloaded operators on atomic variables,
// Special cases of fetch_and_store, fetch_and_add
// – – – – – – – – – – – – – – – – – – – – – – – – –
x = X;           // read in x value of X – This is a load
X = x;           // write to X the value x – This is a store

X++;             // increment atomic variable
X––;             // decrements atomic variable
X+=x;            // add x to X
X–=x;            // subtract x from X
```

LISTING 8.9

Atomic operations in tbb::atomic<T>

This class provides basically the same services as the C++11 atomic types:

- There are no explicit load() and store() member functions, but these operations can be performed with X=x and x=X.
- Another way to perform a load, to be used later on, is using x = X.fetch_and_add(0), which does not modify X and returns its value.
- fetch_and_store() corresponds to exchange() in C++11.
- compare_and_swap() corresponds to compare_and_exchange() in C++11.
- fetch_and_add() implements the basic arithmetic operations on integers and pointers. As in C++11, atomic operations on pointers implement pointer arithmetic.
- There are no logical atomic operations.

The basic constructor is a default constructor, provided by the compiler. The C++ initialization rules for classes without explicit constructors apply here. The atomic data item is initialized to 0 (if integer) or NULL (if pointer) when declared as a global variable with file scope, as static data item inside a function, or as a data member in a class. There are some reasons for this, which are discussed in the documentation annex of [14]. The second constructor exposed in Listing 8.9, providing an explicit initialization value to the atomic variable, *is not atomic*. An alternative is to construct first the atomic variable with the default constructor and then load its value.

8.6.1 MEMORY ORDERING OPTIONS

TBB has a simpler scheme for memory ordering options, while maintaining the essential features of C++11. A memory_semantics enumeration is defined, providing the basic options for the acquire-release memory model. Memory semantic options *are not* passed as arguments to the member functions. Rather, template versions of the member functions are defined as having the memory_semantics values as template parameters, as shown in Listing 8.10.

```
namespece tbb
   {
   enum memory_semantics
       { acquire, release };
   }
```

```
// Enforcing acquire semantics on a store
// – – – – – – – – – – – – – – – – – – – – –
x = X.fetch\_and\_store<acquire>(y);
```
LISTING 8.10

TBB memory ordering options

The complete pattern is the following:

- All the member functions in Listing 8.9 have a sequential consistency memory order semantics.
- If the memory semantics have to be downgraded to acquire or release, the template version of the member function is used, as shown in Listing 8.10.
- The overloaded operators in Listing 8.9 all have an intrinsic memory semantics choice:
  - The store operation X=x uses *release* semantics.
  - The load operation x=X uses *acquire* semantics.
  - The three other basic functions use *sequential consistent* semantics.

A comment is useful at this point. It was observed before that there are no explicit load or store operations, which these can be implemented with x=X (with acquire semantics) or X=x (with release semantics). If, instead, sequential consistent semantics is required for a load or a store, the fetch_and_store(x) function can be used for a store, and x = fetch_and_add(0) can be used for a load.

Example: TRBuff_T.C

The C++ classes and examples discussed before can easily be ported to the tbb::atomic<T> class. Notice, in particular:

- The class RingBuff_T implements the RingBuffer class using the TBB atomic class. The class is defined in the header file RBuff_T.hh.
- This class is tested in the TRBuff_T.C code.

Example 5: TRBuff_T.C

Producer-consumer pattern between two threads, TBB implementation. To compile, run make trbuff_t.

8.7 WINDOWS ATOMIC SERVICES

The Windows API, being a C library, does not defines atomic types. But Windows proposes a large number of functions—called Interlocked functions—implementing the mutual exclusion or synchronization services discussed before, including the memory order options. They are well documented in [13].

Windows API -> System services -> Synchronization -> Interlocked functions

This reference shows a long list of functions, with a brief description of their action. Clicking on the function name, another web page is reached with a more detailed description of the function signature and a number of comments on their correct usage. All the interlocked functions follow a number of rules concerning the function names and signatures:

- Atomic operations act on char, integer, or void pointer types.
- The atomic operation, the target data type, and the memory order option are all coded *in the function name*. This is the reason there is an impressive number of interlocked functions.
- Function names are of the form:
    - Interlocked(Operation)(Data size)(Memory option)
    - (Data size) and (Memory option) are optional. Default values are for target data a 32 bit long, and for memory option sequential consistency.
    - Explicit data sizes are 8 for char, 16 for short int, and 64 for long long int.
    - Explicit memory options can be Acquire, Release to implement the acquire-release memory model, and NoFence, which obviously corresponds to the relaxed model discussed before for C++11.
- Function arguments are in all cases the target data item—an in-out argument passed by address—and additional data items needed for the operation, passed by value.
- The return value is in all cases either the previous or the last value of the target data.

We have stated that the default memory order option is sequentially consistent. In fact, the Windows documentation guarantees that this default option implements a strong acquire-release memory fence. Notice that atomic operations only act on void pointers: the address of the target data item is passed cast as a void*. Indeed, this is the only way of manipulating in C a generic address. Another piece of information to keep in mind is that some interlocked functions—like CompareExchange—require that target data items be 32- or 64-bit aligned, otherwise they may behave in an unpredictable way on multicore x86 platforms or any other non-x86 platform.

Porting std::atomic code to Windows native code is perhaps a bit tedious but not difficult, since the basic concepts and ideas are the same. In order to illustrate the usage of the interlocked functions, the Windows implementation of the RingBuffer class is listed below.

```
template <typename T, int Size>
class RingBuffer
    {
    private:
     T buffer[Size];
     long head, tail, C;

     int NextHead( int n)
        {
        if(n==(Size-1)) InterlockedIncrementNoFence(&C);
        return (n+1)%Size;
        }

     int NextTail( int n)
        {
        if(n==(Size-1)) InterlockedDecrementNoFence(&C);
```

```
        return (n+1)%Size;
        }

    public:
     RingBuffer() : head(0), tail(0), C(0) {}

    bool Push(const T& value)
       {
       int H = head;
       if(H == InterlockedAddRelease(&tail, 0) && (C>0)) return false;
       buffer[H] = value;
       InterlockedExchangeAcquire(&head, NextHead(H));
       return true;
       }

    bool Pop(T& value)
       {
       int T = tail;
       if(T == InterlockedAddRelease(\head, 0) && (C==0)) return false;
       value = buffer[T];
       InterlockedExchangeAcquire(&tail, NextTail(T));
       return true;
       }

    // Insert() and Extract() do not change
    };
```

LISTING 8.11

Windows implementation of the RingBuffer class

The head and tail indices, as well as the counter C, are now ordinary long integers. To atomically increment the C counter the InterlockedIncrementNoFence() function is used, with a relaxed memory option because this atomic operation is not involved in a synchronization pattern. The same applies to the atomic decrements of C.

In the Push() and Pop() head and tail are stored with acquire semantics and loaded with release semantics. The stores are straightforward: the store operation is performed by InterlockedExchange(), which atomically replaces the value of the first argument by the value provided by the second argument. Incidentally, to check the consistency with previous discussions it is possible to verify that there is no InterlockedExchangeRelease() function: store operations accept only acquire semantics.

The load operation is slightly more subtle. There is no explicit load atomic operation, like in C++11, because the target is a standard data item that can be read directly. But an atomic operation returning the target value with release semantics is needed, to implement the acquire-release synchronization. The InterlockedAdd(&target, data) function adds data to the target and returns the new value. Then, just adding 0 atomically returns the data value. This is what is done in Listing 8.11, by choosing the function with release semantics.

The circular buffer implementation provided by this class operates correctly, as shown by the same test code shown before in Example 4, TRBuff.C, but compiled in the Windows environment.

Example 5bis: TRBuff.C

Using a Windows native circular buffer to connect two threads, when compiled in the Windows environment. To compile, run nmake trbuff.

It is also useful to look at the SpinLock.h source where the Windows implementation of this class is defined.

8.8 SUMMARY

Atomic services have been used in this chapter to implement synchronization utilities—lock-free reduction services, spin locks, and ring buffers—incorporated in the vath library with the standard portable strategy: the same programming interfaces in all programming environments. Their status is summarized below:

- **SpinLock**: Programming interface as in Listing 8.7.
    - Implemented in C++11 and Windows using the corresponding atomic services.
    - In Pthreads, there are no atomic services. This class just encapsulates the native spinlock mutex proposed by Pthreads.
- **AReduction**: Same programming interface as Reduction.h, described in Chapter 5.
    - Implemented in C++11 and Windows using the corresponding atomic services.
    - No Pthreads implementation.
- **RingBuffer**: Programming interface as in Listing 8.8.
    - Implemented in C++11 and Windows using the corresponding atomic services.
    - Implemented in Pthreads using the basic synchronization primitives.
- **RingBuff_T**: Programming interface as in Listing 8.8. A TBB implementation of RingBuffer.

HIGH-LEVEL SYNCHRONIZATION TOOLS

9.1 INTRODUCTION AND OVERVIEW

This chapter examines several high-level concurrency patterns common in applications programming, and the C++ utility classes contained in the vath library proposed to manage them. Our pedagogical purpose is to discuss a variety of examples illustrating various ways of synchronizing threads. The vath utility classes sometimes simply encapsulate basic synchronization primitives in portable interfaces, and often propose other services that are not directly available in the basic multithreading libraries discussed in this book.

The implementation of the vath synchronization utilities is not discussed in detail. References to implementations are made only when a relevant pedagogical issue deserves particular attention. Interested readers can consult the vath source code, which is well documented. Most of the C++ synchronization classes are rather simple, relying on aspects of the basic libraries discussed in this or in the previous chapters. Effort has been made to have sources as simple and readable as possible. Readers willing to develop a deeper understanding of these subjects can also consult several books that present the state of the art in developing of custom synchronization utilities. A rigorous and advanced discussion is contained in *The Art of Multiprocessor Programming*, by M. Herlijy and N. Shavit [25]. Advanced material in the C++11 environment is available in [14].

The vath services are discussed in detail, for several reasons:

Extended portability
This simple library has a Pthreads, Windows, and C++11 implementation, with common programming interfaces. It can be used as such in any Unix-Linux or Windows system.

Interoperability with OpenMP
This library proposes optional thread management interfaces (thread pools). But the synchronization utilities can be used, for example, in an OpenMP environment, as is the case for several examples in the following chapters.

Pure OpenMP utilities
Some of the utilities dealing with synchronizations among individual threads have a fourth implementation (besides Pthreads, Windows, and C++11) using pure OpenMP code. This option has been included for OpenMP developers willing to avoid interoperability concerns.

The vath library deals with thread management and synchronization. This chapter is devoted to thread synchronization. A lightweight thread management utility—the SPool class—has already been introduced in Chapter 3. A more sophisticated thread management utility called NPool, exhibiting many of the OpenMP and TBB features, is discussed in detail in Chapter 12. After discussing the vath thread synchronization utilities, this chapter concludes with a general overview of thread pools as high-level thread management utilities.

9.2 GENERAL COMMENTS ON HIGH-LEVEL SYNCHRONIZATION TOOLS

As stated in Chapter 2, threads are introduced to run concurrent tasks, implementing mandatory parallelism. In all the examples examined so far, a worker thread was launched for each parallel task in the application, thereby establishing a one-to-one mapping between tasks and threads. This strategy will henceforth be referred to as a *thread centric* programming paradigm.

This is not, however, the only way in which multithreaded environments like OpenMP or TBB are structured today. Starting in the next chapter, *thread pools* will be introduced as high-level thread management environments, where threads are created first, wait silently in a blocked state if they are not needed, and are woken up and activated to perform tasks if and when their participation is required. In this environment, it is always possible to activate one thread for each specific task in the application, but it is also possible to run applications involving more parallel tasks than threads in the worker team. A *task-centric* execution model can be implemented, in which tasks are queued and executed when worker threads become available. Even better, they are not necessarily executed in the order in which they were submitted: the task scheduler may be unfair, for very good reasons that will be discussed later. In this context, the task to thread mapping is not necessarily one-to-one. Parallel computations may engage a number of parallel tasks substantially bigger than the number of worker threads.

Figure 9.1 shows the most general parallel execution context: tasks are executed by threads, and threads run on cores. The ideal context is clearly the one in which there is a one-to-one mapping

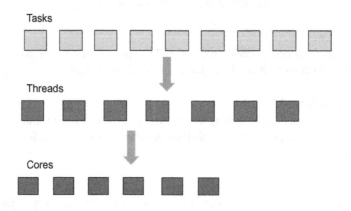

FIGURE 9.1

Tasks are executed by threads, and threads run on cores.

between tasks, threads, and cores. However, this is often not the case. It may happen that the total number of tasks is not hardwired in a computation, because tasks launch internally new tasks. It may also happen that the number of executing cores is less than the number of active threads in the application.

The purpose of this chapter is the synchronization of threads. The synchronization algorithms are programmed in the tasks executed by the threads. However, it is important to keep in mind that:

Synchronization tools synchronize threads, not tasks. Using synchronization tools without clear control of how tasks are mapped to threads can sometimes deadlock the code or deliver incorrect results. This issue will be frequently reexamined in the following chapters.

A simple example helps to clarify this observation. Let us assume a program involving a parallel computation on N tasks, with a barrier synchronization among them. The barrier utility is naturally initialized to N participants. The code deadlocks when run on M threads (M<N), because at the barrier synchronization point it will keep waiting for threads that will never come. Another example was given at the end of Chapter 4, concerning thread local storage. Thread safety is guaranteed only if the tasks that access thread private variables are assigned to different, well-identified threads.

Also keep in mind that only the mapping of task to threads is delicate, the mapping of threads to cores is not. If a number of correctly synchronized threads is running on a smaller number of cores, threads will be preempted and rescheduled by the operating system, but the synchronizations will in all cases operate correctly, and the application should run flawlessly, with lower performance.

9.3 OVERVIEW OF THE VATH SYNCHRONIZATION UTILITIES

There are several synchronization utilities discussed in this chapter:

- **Timers**, objects that put a thread in an idle wait state for a predefined amount of time.
- **Boolean locks**, objects that encapsulates the basic idle or spin waits for an event, discussed in Chapters 7 and 8.
- **Synchronization points**, a rendezvous point for two or more threads that synchronizes a write and one or several reads of a memory location. This is a safe and robust way of exchanging data between a producer thread (the one that writes to memory) and one or more consumer threads that read data values from memory.
- **Barriers**, synchronization tools that establish a rendezvous point for a predefined number of threads, discussed in Chapter 7.
- **Blocking barriers**, barriers in which the waiting threads are not released by the last thread reaching the barrier point. They are released by an external client thread.
- **Thread safe queue**, a first-in, first-out *thread safe* queue container implementing the producer-consumer paradigm. Consumer threads wait for data if the queue is empty, and producer threads wait if they attempt to insert data in a full queue. The queue capacity is chosen by the programmer.

- **Pipelines**, tools that encapsulate the synchronization of pipelined threads, thereby simplifying the programming of applications requiring this specific concurrency pattern. Pipeline classes are discussed in Chapter 15, entirely devoted to this issue.
- **Reader-Writer locks**, generalized locks that enforce mutual exclusion for some operations only (writes), while other operations (reads) may proceed concurrently in a standard way.

The discussions of these utilities describe their purpose and their user interface, followed by examples. Occasionally, qualitative indications about the implementation are given, when useful for a better understanding of their operation.

9.3.1 CODE ORGANIZATION

The vath utilities are C++ classes, providing services to C-C++ client code. They only require from the user some very limited basic knowledge on *programming with objects*. The C++ source code relies, of course, on the Standard Template Library (STL), but this is hidden to the end user. Sometimes, the *generic programming* C++ features are used, with the purpose of writing generic code—template functions and classes—in which one or several data types are kept as parameters to be specified by the client code later on, at compilation time. For example, class templates are used in utilities where data is exchanged between threads, leaving as a template parameter the exchanged data type.

With the only exception of Timers (which concern only one thread) all synchronization objects must naturally be shared by several threads. Therefore, they have to be declared with global scope, and there are in this case the two options we already discussed for the SPool utility in Chapter 3. If the parameters needed by the object constructor are known at compile time, synchronization objects can be declared directly as global objects. Otherwise, a delayed construction of the object must be adopted: a global pointer to the object is declared, initialized later on by a call to new.

```
thread_function(void *P)
   {
   Timer T;
   ...
   T.wait(200);     // wait for 200 milliseconds
   ...
   }
```

LISTING 9.1

Using a proprietary Timer.

9.4 TIMERS

The Timer utility puts the caller thread to wait in a blocked state for a predefined duration time interval (coded in milliseconds). It was indicated in Chapter 3 that C++11 already has a Timer provided by the function std::this_thread::sleep_for(), and that Windows also provides a built-in Timer through the Sleep() function. In Pthreads, however, programming a Timer is substantially more involved. This class was introduced mainly to be able to write portable application code.

The interest of Timer objects is the capability of delaying for a given time interval the execution flow of a thread. The first example given in Chapter 3 simulated a lengthy I/O operation by getting a thread out of the way for a few seconds. When testing synchronization constructs in several examples in the chapters that follow, different threads are delayed for very different time intervals in order to more efficiently track the way the synchronization pattern operates.

9.4.1 USING A TIMER

The Timer class is declared in Timer.h. Here is the public interface of the class:

TIMER PUBLIC INTERFACE

Timer()

– Constructor.
– Creates a Timer object.

Timer()

– Destructor.
– Destroys the Timer object.

int Wait(long ms)

– Caller threads waits for ms milliseconds.
– Returns 0 on success, or positive number on failure.

9.4.2 COMMENT ON IMPLEMENTATION

In Windows and C++11, this class just encapsulates the native timer service. In Pthreads, a thread calling this function performs a *timed wait* for a predetermined time interval, on a condition variable totally hidden from any other thread in the process, and that consequently will never be signaled. *The timed wait will therefore be necessarily timed out after the requested wait interval.* It is therefore important to avoid sharing Timers between threads.

9.5 BOOLEAN LOCKS

BLock (Boolean Lock) objects are synchronization objects that encapsulate in a portable and user friendly way the basic *idle wait on condition* event synchronization mechanism, discussed in Chapter 6, or the *spin wait protocol* discussed in Chapter 7. A Boolean lock can be seen as a black box containing internally a Boolean state variable (a predicate) taking the values (true, false), as well as a guarding mutex and—for idle waits only—a condition variable signaling the changes of state. The expected synchronization event corresponds to the fact that the state variable is toggled.

Client treads can do three different things with the Boolean lock:

• They may read or reset the value of the internal state variable.
• They may reset the state variable and notify waiting threads that it has been changed. For spin waits, this notification is not needed, because waiting threads keep reading the state variable and can detect its change.

- They may wait until some other thread changes the state variable. Idle waits can be *timed waits* for a fixed numbers of milliseconds, or indefinite waits until the state change occurs. Spin waits are, naturally, indefinite waits.

9.5.1 USING THE BLock CLASS

The BLock class is the general-purpose utility that encapsulates the idle wait protocol discussed in Chapter 6. A typical *use case* for the Boolean lock is the IO example discussed in Chapters 3 and 6. When a thread is launched to perform an assignment—like a computation, an important data transfer on the network or a lengthy I/O operation to a file—this utility enables the main thread or other threads to check every now and then, using timed waits, if the operation has been completed, or simply wait indefinitely until it is done. The synchronization pattern proceeds as follows:

- The main thread sets the Boolean lock to false before launching the worker thread.
- The worker thread does its job and, when it is finished, sets the Boolean lock to true and notifies the change.
- The main thread, at some point, waits for the Boolean lock to switch to the true state.

    Here is the description of the BLock public interface:

....

BLock INTERFACES

BLock()

– Constructor.
– Creates a Boolean Lock with the default internal state (false).

BLock(bool b)

– Constructor.
– Creates a Boolean Lock with an internal state equal to b.

bool GetState()

– Returns the value of the internal state.

void SetState(bool b)

– Sets the internal state to the value b.

int Wait_Until(true/false, long timeout)

– Caller thread waits until the internal state becomes true or false for *timeout* milliseconds.
– If *timeout=0*, this becomes an unconditional wait, and the caller thread waits forever until the true state is notified.
– Return value: 0 if the function returns because true has been notified, and 1 if the function returns because the wait has been timed out.

void Set_And_Notify(bool new_state)

– Sets the internal state to new_state and signals the change.
– Only one waiting thread is woken up.

void Set_And_Notify_All(bool new_state)

– Sets the internal state to new_state and broadcasts the change.
– All waiting thread are waken up.

We insist on the fact that the client code that puts a thread to wait may choose between an *unconditional wait*—until the condition is notified—or a *timed wait*, in which case threads do not wait forever: the wait on condition returns after a predetermined time interval if the condition is not notified. The client thread can return to do some other useful work before waiting again.

In this class, idle waits are timed for a specified number of milliseconds passed as argument in the function call. For an unconditional wait, until the event is signaled, the timewait argument must be 0 milliseconds.

9.5.2 BLock EXAMPLES

The IO example discussed in Chapter 6, showing the way condition variables operate, are re-examined next. The synchronization pattern is the following:

- The master thread sets the private BLock predicate to false and launches the IO thread.
- The IO thread waits for a long time interval (5 s), toggles the private predicate to true, and notifies the event.
- After launching the worker thread, the main thread starts a do loop in which it keeps waiting for the true state for only 1 second. If the wait is timed out, the master thread prints a message, starts a new loop iteration, and waits again. The loop breaks when finally the timed wait ends not because it has been timed out, but because the change of state has been notified.

Here is the listing of the source file TBlock.C.

```
SPool TH(1);        // set of one worker thread
BLock *B;

void th_fct(void *arq)
    {
    Timer T;
    T.Wait(5000);
    B->SetAndNotify(true);
    std::cout << "\n Boolean flag set and notified" << std::endl;
    }

int main(int argc, char **argv)
    {
    int status;
    B = new BLock(false);    // create and initialize BLock object
    TH.Dispatch(th_fct, NULL);    // launch worker thread
    do
        {
        status = B->Wait_Until(true, 1000);
        std::cout << "\n Got return value = " << status
                << std::endl;
        } while(status==0);
```

Continued

```
TH.WaitForIdle();
delete B;                // delete BLock object
return 0;
}
```

LISTING 9.2

TBlock.C code.

Example 1: TBlock.C

To compile, run make tblock. Running the program with the parameters in Listing 9.2 shows that the main thread prints 4-5 timeout messages, as expected, before detecting the change of state.

There is a second example, in source file TBlockOmp.C, which shows OpenMP interoperability. The code is the same as in the previous case, except that the parallel directive in an OpenMP environment is used, instead of the SPool utility, to run the worker threads. Incidentally, keep in mind that this is the *only* way of implementing timed waits in an OpenMP context.

Example 2: TBlockOmp.C

To compile, run make tblockomp. The same output as in the previous example.

9.5.3 BOOLEAN LOCKS IMPLEMENTING SPIN WAITS

The Boolean Lock utility just discussed is a general-purpose utility with very acceptable efficiency in most cases. There are, however, computational contexts with high synchronization overhead where Boolean locks are intensively used for very short unconditional waits, and in these cases the fact that waiting threads are systematically preempted and rescheduled may have a negative impact on performance. In these contexts, spin waits are more efficient. There are two spin wait Boolean lock classes provided by the vath library. They are portable, and can be used "as such" in any programming context.

- **SpBlock**: Implements the spin wait protocol discussed in Chapter 7, where waiting threads keep reading a shared state variable, protected by the SpinLock object discussed in Chapter 8. Implementations in Pthreads and Windows-C++11 are very different:
  - In Pthreads, the SpinLock encapsulates the native spinlock mutex.
  - In C++11-Windows, the SpinLock is constructed using atomic services, as discussed in Chapter 8.
- **OBlock**: The spin wait protocol is implemented using OpenMP locks to protect the state variable. This is OpenMP code; this class is proposed for users that prefer to avoid interoperability issues.

It goes without saying that, in cases of very high synchronization contention, the atomic implementations of SpBlock are the most efficient ones, as the examples in Chapter 14 will show. *These classes have all the same public interfaces*, which is the same as the BLock interface, with only two differences:

- There are no timed waits, and the Wait_Until(true/false) member function does do not receive a timeout argument. They wait forever until the expected change of state occurs.
- There are no Set_And_Notify() or Set_And_NotifyAll() functions. Indeed, waiting threads are always active, constantly checking the state variable, and they will read the new value as soon as it becomes visible to them.

Example. The previous example is now coded using the OBLock class, except that, since there is no timed wait available, the master thread just waits for the predicate to be toggled. The source file is TOmpBlock.C.

Example 3: TOmpBlock.C

To compile, run make tompblock. Pure OpenMP code.

9.6 SynchP< T > TEMPLATE CLASS

SynchP objects are special-purpose Boolean locks used to order a write and one or several reads of a generic data item by different threads.

Consider the case where thread A (henceforth, called the producer thread) needs to communicate some data value to threads B, C (henceforth, called the consumer threads). The producer thread can, of course, write the data to some global data buffer, and the consumer threads can read from it, but it is obvious that a synchronization is required to make sure the write took place before the reads, *and that the reading threads are reading the last value written to the data item, as discussed in Chapter 7.*

To handle this pattern, an object is constructed, analogous to a Boolean lock, but also incorporating the exchanged data item as an internal private variable. Since the data type that will be accessed is not known in advance, the *generic programming* capability of C++ is used to keep it as a *template parameter* to be specified by the client code later on.

9.6.1 USING SynchP<T> OBJECTS

The SynchP.h file contains the SynchP<T> template class, where T is the symbol for an abstract data type that is exchanged between the producer and consumer threads. Remember that template classes are declared *and defined* in the included *.h file. There is no separate object file incorporated in the library, simply because the compiler cannot generate object code before the client code defines what the data type T is.

The programming interface is very simple. Besides the constructor and the destructor, there are only two methods, Post() called by the producer thread, and Get() called by the consumer threads.

....

SYNCHP<T> PUBLIC INTERFACE

SynchP<T>()

- Constructor.
- Creates a SynchPoint<T> object with the default internal state (false).

void Post(T& elem, int nReaders)

- Posts the T data item of value *elem*.
- *nReaders* is the number of threads that will read the data.
- Function call waits eventually for the object to be ready.
- Called by the producer thread.

T Get(T)

- Reads and returns the previously posted T data item of value *elem*.
- Function call may wait if producer is late.
- Called by the consumer thread.

The synchronization pattern implemented by this interface, illustrated in Figure 9.2, proceeds as follows:

- The initial state of the Boolean state variable is false. When the state on the SynchP object is false, the object is either brand new, or it is available to be reused again because any previous data transfer has already been completed by all the planned reader threads.
- The producer thread calls the Put() function to write the data by indicating also how many readers are expected. If this function finds a true state, it concludes that the SynchP object is still busy with the previous transfer and waits for false before proceeding. As soon as the state is false, the producer thread writes the data, toggles the state to true (because the object is now busy again!), notifies the change to consumer threads that may be waiting for data, and returns.
- Notice that the producer thread is only blocked if the SynchP object is not ready. Otherwise, *the producer thread is not blocked*.
- Consumer threads eventually wait for true if the producer thread is late. Then they read the data and decrease an internal counter that keeps track of the number of reads. When the read counter reaches 0, the state is changed to false (object is now available for reuse) and the change is signaled.

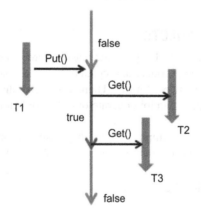

FIGURE 9.2

SynchP operation: one writer and two readers.

- *Notice that consumer threads are only blocked if the producer is late.* Otherwise, they are never blocked.

9.6.2 COMMENTS

This is a flexible synchronization mechanism in which threads are forced to wait only if it is absolutely necessary. Think of what happens if the only available synchronization mechanism is a barrier, as is the case in pure OpenMP. The OpenMP barrier synchronizes *all* the threads—the producer, the consumers, and all the remaining worker threads—at the barrier synchronization point. Then, it is sufficient to put the write of the producer and the reads of the consumers before and after the barrier call, respectively. However, if the operation needs to be repeated, a new barrier call is required *before* the next write to make sure all the previous reads are finished. Therefore, we have to count *two barrier calls*, each one blocking all threads, for each point-to-point data transfer operation. The synchronization provided by the SynchP class is much more efficient. When running 248 threads in a Intel Xeon Phi, it is totally wasteful to block the whole team just to exchange data between a few of them.

The template code for the SynchP class listed above is very general, because it applies to *any* data type (and not only to the primitive data types like double, integer, etc.), provided that the class defining the data type T: satisfies some requirements.

- The class has a no parameter constructor—so that the compiler can implement the instruction T retval = T().
- The class has an assignment operator, so that the compiler can implement the instruction retval = element.

9.6.3 SynchP<T> EXAMPLES

The example that follows proposes code in which one thread repeatedly posts a double to two other threads (see Figure 9.2). The source file is TSynch.C. The master thread proceeds as follows:.

- First, it launches the two consumer threads, and waits for 3 s.
- Next, it posts a double value to two consumer threads. A new double value is posted next, by reusing the synchronization object.
- Finally, it joins the consumer threads.

As far as the consumer threads are concerned, they wait twice for 500 ms and try to read the next value coming from the master thread. Obviously, they will have to wait. Here is the code source listing.

```
SPool *TH;
SynchP<double> B;

void *th_fct(void *arg)
    {
    double d;
    int rank = TH->GetRank();
    Timer X;
```

Continued

```
        for(int n=0; n<2; n++)
            {
            X.Wait(500);
            d = B.Get();
            std::cout << "\nWorker thread " << rank << " got value " << d
                      << std::endl;
            }
        }

int main(int argc, char **argv)
    {
    int nTh;
    Timer Tm;

    if (argc==2) nTh = atoi(argv[1]);
    else nTh = 2;
    TH = new SPool(nTh);

    // launch worker threads
    // - - - - - - - - - - -
    TH->Dispatch(th_fct, NULL);

    // Main thread code
    // - - - - - - - - -
    Tm.Wait(3000);
    double d = 1.3546;
    for(int n=0; n<2; n++)
        {
        d += 1.0;
        B.Post(d, nTh);
        std::cout << "\n Main : value posted" << std::endl;
        }

    TH->WaitForIdle();
    std::cout << "\n Main :  worker threads joined" << std::endl;
    return 0;
    }
```

LISTING 9.3

TSynch.C

This example also shows how to instantiate the SynchP<T> class for a specific data type (in this case a double): it is sufficient to declare a global SynchP<double> object. From there on, the compiler generates code that is a specialization of the template code to the particular data type required in this application.

Example 4: TSynch.C

To compile, run make tsynch. By modifying the Timer calls the order in which events happen can be inverted in order to check that the synchronization pattern works in all cases.

There is also in this case a second example, in source file TSynchOmp.C, with the worker threads managed in an OpenMP environment, to validate the interoperability with OpenMP.

Example 5: TSynchOmp.C

To compile, run make tsynchomp.

9.6.4 OpenMP VERSION: THE OSynchP< *T* > CLASS

This class is yet another *pure OpenMP utility* that performs exactly like the SynchP<T> class by using OpenMP busy waits. The public interfaces are exactly the same.

Example 6: TOmpSync.C

To compile, run make tompsynch.

9.7 IDLE AND SPIN BARRIERS

Barrier synchronization is probably one of the most commonly used synchronization patterns in application programming, particularly in scientific codes. At a barrier synchronization point, members of a set of N cooperating threads wait until all the members are present. A full discussion is given in Chapter 6 concerning the way this utility operates, as well as the subtleties involved in programming a reusable barrier object. To the extent that the barrier algorithm is based on condition variables, the threads waiting in a barrier call are executing an *idle wait*.

The vath library proposes four barrier synchronization classes:

- The Barrier class, implemented as discussed in Chapter 6, by having the waiting threads performing an idle wait. This Barrier class is to some extent redundant because Pthreads and Windows have today a barrier utility. We use it in the examples in order to have portable codes.
- The SpBarrier class, which is a *spin barrier* where the waiting threads keep spinning in user space without releasing the CPU. Its implementation relies on the SpinLock mutex class discussed in Chapter 8.
- The ABarrier class, which is, again, a *spin barrier*, but using a highly efficient barrier algorithm based on an atomic predicate and, curiously, the usage of thread local storage, taken from [25]. Its implementation in C++11 and Windows relies on the native support for atomic variables and thread local storage. *There is no Pthreads implementation, due to the absence of atomic support*.
- The TBarrier class, identical to ABarrier, but using TBB atomic and thread local storage utilities. This redundancy is introduced because the ABarrier class does not run in Pthreads (due to the

absence of atomic support). The TBB implementation is fully portable, and can also be used in a Pthreads environment.

9.7.1 USING THE BARRIER CLASSES

The public interfaces are the same for all kinds of barrier objects, so that it is quite easy to substitute them in an application, with one minor exception for the ABarrier case, discussed in the next subsection:

BARRIER PUBLIC INTERFACE

Barrier(int N)

– Constructor.
– N is the number of worker threads synchronized by the barrier.

int Wait()

– Calling threads wait until the group of cooperating threads is released by the last thread arriving at the synchronization point.
– Returns a positive number if the call fails. If the call is successful, all cooperating threads return 0 except the last one, which returns (-1).

Why should the last thread reaching the barrier point return (-1) instead of 0? There is nothing special about the last thread; this is just an easy way of selecting one of the partner threads after the barrier call. Often a barrier is used to move from a *parallel region* where all the threads share some specific assignment to a *sequential region* where a treatment is trusted to only one thread. The barrier return value is a handy way of selecting with an if statement one specific active thread, in particular in cases where the worker threads do not have a built-in rank value identifier.

As far as performance is concerned, it is difficult to see the difference between the different barrier implementations in codes with small or moderate barrier contention. But in Chapter 13 an application where there is a substantial amount of barrier contention will be considered, and in this case the atomic spin barrier code exhibits much better performance than the code using the idle wait barriers.

9.7.2 ABarrier IMPLEMENTATION

The case of the ABarrier utility illustrates how custom synchronization utilities, constructed using services provided by the basic libraries, often help to significantly improve the performance of applications exhibiting substantial synchronization overhead. Chapter 14 is partly devoted to an application dealing with the solution of two-dimensional differential equations. When examining the scaling behavior of this application, it was found that the vath implementation using the SPool environment and the standard Barrier class discussed above was very deceptive: starting from four threads, the wall execution time started to increase with the number of threads!

It soon became clear, after a few tests, that the SPool environment itself was not to blame, so the next step was to look for improved barrier algorithms. Scalable barrier algorithms have received sustained attention because of the necessity of efficiently synchronizing thousands or tens of thousands of MPI processes in large-scale distributed memory applications.

The ABarrier algorithm that follows is taken from Chapter 10 in *The Art of Multiprocessor Programming* [25]. It is shown in Figure 9.3. There are no condition variables, because this is a spin

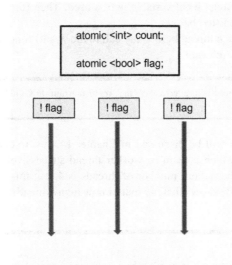

FIGURE 9.3

ABarrier algorithm.

barrier: waiting threads keep reading the predicate to detect the change. There is no mutex locking, because atomic variables are used. Besides std::atomic, the C++11-Windows implementations rely on the thread local storage services discussed in Chapter 4, because each thread keeps a thread private bool that preserves its value across successive Wait() function calls. This feature is needed to make the barrier algorithm reusable (remember the barrier discussion in Chapter 7).

The ABarrier object has two private atomic data items: an integer count that is initialized to the number of participating threads, and decreased every time a new thread starts a wait. There is also an atomic bool flag, a predicate that is toggled to release the waiting threads, initialized to an arbitrary value, say, false. The participating threads start initially with a thread private flag opposite to the predicate. Now, the algorithm operates as follows:

- A thread that calls Wait() decreases the counter and starts a spin wait comparing its private flag to the predicate, until they are equal.
- The last thread to call Wait() resets the counter to the number of threads, and toggles the predicate. This releases the remaining waiting threads.
- Before returning from the Wait() call, *all threads toggle their private flag*, so the initial condition is restored (private flags opposite to the predicate) and the barrier can be used again.

The source code is in ABarrier.h. This class in implemented in C++11 and Windows, and a small modification is introduced in the user interface to dispose of a portable utility. The point is that, as discussed in Chapter 4, the thread local storage services in C++ and Windows have some differences. All threads must initialize their thread local variables, and in C++11 this is automatic the first time each thread calls the function using them. But in Windows the initialization is not automatic, and must be done explicitly before the thread local variable is first used. Therefore, an initialization function is added to the member functions listed below:

void InitTLS() is called by each thread before any call to the Wait() function. In C++11, this function does nothing. In Windows, it is relevant.

---

void InitTLS() is called by each thread before any call to the Wait() function. In C++11, this function does nothing. In Windows, it is relevant.

A real-life test of this class will be discussed in Chapter 14. Just to check that it works, a simple example is proposed next in which a team or worker thread successively prints messages to stdout and performs a barrier call. The default number of threads is 4, but this can be overridden from the command line. Running the code shows that, no matter how many threads, the successive messages are correctly ordered.

Example 7: TABarrier.C

To compile, run make tabarrier. The number of threads (4 by default) can be changed from the command line.

Look in particular at the initialization issue in this example. Before launching the real parallel job, a preliminary parallel job is executed in which each thread calls the initialization function.

9.8 BLOCKING BARRIERS

In the standard Barrier utility, the participating threads are blocked at the barrier synchronization point, and they are released by the last thread performing the Wait() call. This is a tool for internal synchronization of a team of N working threads.

A blocking barrier implements a similar synchronization pattern, except that the participant threads *are not released* by the last one that arrives to the synchronization point: they remain blocked. They are all released when an external client thread calls the ReleaseThreads() member function, as sketched in Figure 9.4. In fact, this utility introduces a synchronization between a team of worker threads performing a parallel computation and a client master thread that is driving the whole process. This utility is useful when the worker threads need new results injected from the client thread to proceed beyond the barrier synchronization point, or when the client thread needs to recover some partial result at some intermediate point in the execution of a parallel job by the worker threads.

9.8.1 USING A BLOCKING BARRIER

A blocking barrier is a barrier, so they share with the barrier classes the same constructor and the same Wait() function called by the worker threads engaged in the barrier synchronization point. There are, however, three new member functions dealing with the synchronization with the master thread. These new member functions, called naturally by the master threads, behave as follows:

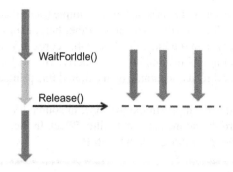

FIGURE 9.4

Blocking barrier operation.

ADDITIONAL BkBarrier PUBLIC INTERFACES

void WaitForIdle()

– Called by client threads.
– This function returns when all the participant threads have reached the barrier point.

void ReleaseThreads()

– Called by client threads, after a call to WaitForIdle().
– The participant threads are released.

bool State()

– Called by client threads.
– Returns true if all threads have reached the barrier point, 0 otherwise.

9.8.2 FIRST SIMPLE EXAMPLE

This section develops two examples. The first one is in source file TBkBarrier.C, a simple test of the BkBarrier class implementing the following scenario:

- The main thread launches a number of worker threads (read from the command line; the default is 2 threads).
- All the worker threads execute the same code:
    - they enter a loop in which they first wait for a random time interval,
    - then they print an identification message,
    - and finally they wait on a blocking barrier.
    - This loop is executed 4 times.
- The main thread enters a loop in which:
    - it first waits for the worker threads to be idle (so that they have all written their messages),
    - then it prints a line and releases the threads, so that they can continue their planned execution flow.
    - This loop is also executed 4 times.
- Finally, the main thread joins the worker threads.

The code is simple and compact, and it uses one or two simple tricks that are well documented in the source file. For this reason, it will not be discussed any further here. I suggest executing the code with a large number of threads (larger than the number of available cores in your system) to verify that the complex synchronizations used in this example work properly. You will see the lists of identification messages emitted by the worker threads, separated by the dotted line printed by main() at each blocking barrier synchronization point.

There are two versions of this example. In the first one, in source file TBkBarrier.C, worker threads are managed using our standard thread management utility SPool. In the second version, in source file TBkBarrierOmp.C, worker threads are managed by OpenMP.

Example 8: TBkBarrier.C

To compile, run make tbkb. The number of threads is read from the command line (the default is 2).

Example 9: TBkBarrierOmp.C

To compile, run make tbkbomp. This is the OpenMP version of the previous example.

9.8.3 PROGRAMMING A SIMPLE SPMD THREAD POOL

The next example presents another interesting application of the blocking barrier synchronization pattern: running and driving a simple SPMD thread pool. A SPMP (Single Program, Multiple Data) thread pool is a team of worker threads that operate exactly like our well-known SPool utility. In fact, this example exhibits some of the inner workings of the SPool pool. It will certainly contribute to sharpening your understanding of thread synchronization. Here is the global organization of this example:

- First, a set of worker threads is launched. They wait on a blocking barrier, and are next released *after being told what task to execute next.*
- After completing their task assignment, the worker threads are again blocked at the blocking barrier, waiting for their next assignment.
- When the time comes, the main thread releases again the worker threads from the blocking barrier synchronization point, *after informing them of the task to execute next.*

For the sake of clarity, some selected critical parts of the code are discussed in detail.

How the worker threads are launched

Let us first consider how to launch a set of working threads that wait to be told what to do next. Here is the code for the thread function executed by the worker threads when they are created.

```
BkBarrier *BB;              // global blocking barrier
void (*task)();             // a global pointer to a task function
...
void *ThFunction(void *P)
  {
```

```
// Enter an infinite loop.
for(;;)
   {
   BB->Wait();     // Here worker threads sleep
   (*(task))();    // call the function pointed by task
   }
}
```

LISTING 9.4

SimplePool.C (partial listing).

In Listing 9.4:

- BB is a global pointer to a blocking barrier, initialized by main() when the number of worker threads is known.
- task *is a pointer to a task function that has no arguments and no return value.* In due time, main() will initialize this pointer with the address of a specific task function having the same signature.

The thread function enters an infinite loop where it waits at the blocking barrier, and when released it calls the task function referenced by task. I hope readers appreciate how the BkBarrier class.contributes to the simplicity and elegance of this code.

A task is described in this example with a function that takes no argument and returns void. This is totally arbitrary, and any another convenient signature for the task function could have been used. The only function signature that must be respected is the signature of the thread function passed to the basic libraries. But the task function is just a function called by the real thread function once the thread is running, and its signature is our own personal choice. Return values are not needed in general, but the task function could have taken an arbitrary number of arbitrary arguments.

How main() drives the worker thread activity

Every time main() needs the services of the worker threads, it dispatches a new task by a call to the following function.

```
void Dispatch(void (*TSK)())
   {
   BB->WaitForIdle();
   pthread_mutex_lock(&mytask);
   task = TSK;
   pthread_mutex_unlock(&mytask);
   BB->ReleaseThreads();
   }
```

LISTING 9.5

SimplePool.C (partial listing).

This function receives as argument the address of an explicit task function defined somewhere else in the code (remember, in C-C++ the address of a function is just its name). The main thread:

- waits until the worker threads have finished their previous assignment,
- then it re-initializes the task pointer with the new task function address and
- finally it releases the worker threads.

The global mutex mytask guards access to the global shared pointer task. Notice, again, how the BkBarrier interfaces make this code very simple and elegant.

How worker threads terminate

The worker threads are executing an infinite loop. How can they break away and terminate? This is easy: when the main function no longer needs the services of the worker threads, it submits a specific termination task that calls the thread termination library functions—like pthread_exit() in Pthreads or _endthreadex() in Windows. This forces the normal termination of the worker threads, which can then be joined by the master thread.

Full example

The full example is in source file SimplePool.C. It produces exactly the same output as the first example discussed before, but it is programmed in a more flexible way. Two task functions are defined:

- A NormalTask() task function that executes the same code as in the first example: a timed wait to delay the execution, followed by an identification message in stdout. Notice that this task function just describes the work performed by the thread: all the BkBarrier synchronizations have been factored away.
- An ExitTask() task function that forces the worker thread termination by a call to the appropriate thread termination library function.

As far as the main thread is concerned, it dispatches several times the normal task followed by the WaitForIdle() call and then dispatches the exit task to terminate the operation of the worker threads.

Notice that there are two mutexes in this program. One of them guards naturally the task pointer that is accessed by all threads. The other mutex is used to order the output to stdout (the SafeCout utility could have been used instead). If the threads do not have exclusive access to the screen, their identification messages are very often mixed up.

Example 10: SimplePool_P.C, SimliPool_S.C

To compile, run make spool_p or spool_s. The number of threads is read from the command line (the default is 2). The output of this program is the same as the output of the first example.

The programming strategy and idioms deployed in this example are used in the implementation of the SPool thread pool utility.

9.9 ThQueue<T> CLASS

The synchronization utility discussed in this section—a thread-safe queue—is useful when implementing pipelined software architectures connecting producer and consumer threads. A queue is a FIFO (first in, first out) container where data is extracted in the same order in which it is stored. Data is inserted by producer threads and retrieved by consumer threads. A queue can be implemented as an array where data is inserted at its tail and extracted from its head. Objects of this type are also needed in the implementation of other utilities (thread pools and pipelines).

FIGURE 9.5

Thread-safe ThQueue queue.

The C++ STL library has a queue< *T* > template container, where *T* is an arbitrary data type. The STL queue is unbounded, in the sense that if producers are more active than consumers, the queue size can grow indefinitely because data insertions are never blocked. The ThQueue<T> class, sketched in Figure 9.5, extends the STL queue to a more intelligent, thread-safe *bounded* container with a finite capacity where insertions can be blocked, providing more controlled data flow control between producer and consumer threads, as the examples that follow will show.

TBB also proposes bounded and unbounded concurrent queue utilities. The class discussed here is very close to the TBB concurrent_bounded_queue class, with a few extra features providing refined control of the termination of the queue operation.

Design requirements

The design of this utility implements the following features:

- The queue has a finite capacity, fixed when the object is constructed. This finite capacity is useful to provide some degree of load balance by preventing producer threads from running too much ahead of consumer threads.
- Producer threads wanting to insert data in a full queue perform an idle wait until the queue is no longer full (because consumer threads have removed data).
- Consumer threads wanting to extract data from an empty queue perform an idle wait until the queue is no longer empty (because producer threads have inserted data).
- The queue pipeline can be stopped in a clean and efficient way. When some client thread declares the queue as closed, producer threads are no longer able to insert data. Consumer threads are provided by the queue with all the information required to correctly drain a closed pipeline by servicing pending data, and stopping gracefully when no further data is available.

9.9.1 USING THE ThQueue<T> Queue

....

THE THQUEUE PUBLIC INTERFACE

ThQueue<T> Q(int N)

- Constructor.
- Creates a ThQueue Q of capacity N, holding data items of type T.

Q.GetSize()

– Returns the capacity of Q.

int Q.Add(const T& elem)

– Adds elem to the ThQueue Q. Called by producer threads.
– Returns 0 if the insertion failed because the queue is closed, 1 otherwise.
– If the queue is full, this function does not return. It executes an idle wait until the insertion becomes possible.
– When inserting to an empty queue, this function notifies the *queue not empty* condition that wakes up possible waiting consumer threads.

T Q.Remove(bool& flag)

– Returns the next data item in the queue. Called by consumer threads.
– flag is an *output parameter*.
– If flag is true, Q is active and T comes from the queue.
– If flag is false, Q is closed and T is a fake data item.
– If the queue is empty, this function does not return. It executes an idle wait until the removal becomes possible.
– When removing from a full queue, this function signals the *queue not full* condition that wakes up possible waiting producer threads.

void Q.CloseQueue()

– Closes the ThQueue.
– After this call, insertions are not possible and removals behave in the way discussed above, which enables the correct draining of the queue.
– If the queue is full, this function does not return. It executes an idle wait until the insertion becomes possible.

In order to better understand why the member functions behave in the way just described, the issue of correctly stopping a producer-consumer pipeline must be examined. In an application in which some master thread has a global view of the operation and the client code can control whether there is as much data retrieved as data inserted, there is no problem. However, it may also happen that this is not the case, and that the code executed by the consumer threads has no direct knowledge of the producer's activity. In this case, the information that there is no more data coming along the queue must be conveyed by the queue itself.

If there is only one producer and one consumer thread, it is possible to agree on a specific data value to signal the end of the queue operation. The producer thread queues the value, and the consumer thread knows that no more data is available when this value is dequeued. In this case, the RingBuffer class introduced in Chapter 8 can directly be used. If, however, there are several producer and/or consumer threads, the issue of terminating the producer-consumer connection is more subtle. To cope with this issue, the ThQueue class has internally a flag called active that controls the behavior of the Add() and Remove() member functions. When the queue is created, the active flag is always true. When the ClosePool() function is called by some thread that decides the game is over, the flag is toggled to false and, at this point, the producer and consumer threads behave differently:

- **Producer threads**: If they try to insert data after the queue is closed, the Add() function does not perform the insertion. It returns immediately with an error code. This solves the problem for producer threads.
- **Consumer threads**: After the queue is closed, there may remain some residual data in the queue that must be dequeued and processed. This is why the Remove() function returns a data item, but it

also returns an output Boolean variable flag *that qualifies the accompanying data item returned*, as follows:

- if flag==true, the accompanying data item is valid, because it has been extracted from the queue. The consumer thread knows that it can go ahead with its standard processing.
- if flag==false, the accompanying data item is a fake, invalid data value not taken from the queue because *the queue is closed and empty*. When this happens, the consumer thread knows that it must disregard the returned value and stop removing data from the queue.

In all applications of this utility, client threads must therefore continue to retrieve data items from the queue while checking the Boolean flag returned also by the Remove() function, until they retrieve a data item flagged as false.

9.9.2 COMMENTS ON THE PRODUCER-CONSUMER PARADIGM

The producer-consumer paradigm sustained by this utility is a common parallel construct. It is used internally in other higher level utilities, like the pipeline classes discussed in Chapter 15 or the thread pool NPool utility discussed in Chapter 12. This paradigm, however, must be used with care. Producer threads produce data sets on which consumer threads have to act next. However, if the data sets are important it is totally inefficient to put them in the queue. This forces copying the data set at least two times, for insertion and for removal from the queue, thereby introducing a significant and totally unnecessary memory access overhead, because producer and consumer threads can share global data after all. This is indeed the whole point in multithreading programming. When implementing the producer-consumer paradigm, the queue is in general used to propagate *control information*: indices or pointers to shared data sets, not the data sets themselves.

Queuing data sets forces copying the data because the ThQueue class uses internally a STL queue class, and the STL containers implement *copy semantics*: objects inserted or read from the containers are copied. This is different from the Java containers, which use *reference semantics*: objects are not copied into the containers, which only store a reference to them.

The ThQueue utility is used—in a way transparent to the user—when implementing thread pools. A task corresponds to a C++ object—containing among other things information about the task function to be executed as well as the arguments to be passed to it. Task objects can have arbitrary size, and they are transferred from the thread submitting the parallel job to the thread executing the task. However, only *a pointer to a task object* is queued, with very limited impact on performance.

9.9.3 EXAMPLES: STOPPING THE PRODUCER-CONSUMER OPERATION

Two simple examples follow that demonstrate the mechanism implemented by ThQueue to stop the queue operation. The first one deals with several producers and one consumer, the second one with several consumers and one producer.

Several Producers: TQueue1.C

This example introduces three producer threads and one consumer thread. All producers keep inserting integers until one of them closes the queue. The example shows that the remaining producers stop inserting, and that the consumer thread correctly drains the queue extracting all the residual integers inserted in the queue.

A pool of three producer threads is created. The main thread, rather than waiting in a blocked state, plays the consumer role, extracting integer values and printing them in the screen. The integer values queued depend on the producer threads, so it is easy to know which one of the producers inserted each value printed by main:

- Producer 1 inserts 100 integers, starting from 1. Then, it closes the queue.
- Producer 2 inserts consecutive integers starting from 1000, until the insertion is rejected because the queue is closed.
- Idem for producer 3, with values starting at 100000.

Listing 9.6 shows the implementation of this producer strategy. Running the code, it is verified that producer 1 has inserted the 100 values, and that producers 2 and 3 have at some point stopped inserting. On the other hand, main correctly drains the queue and stops. With the default queue capacity (40 integers) it is observed that producers 2 and 3 have queues substantially with fewer integer values than producer 1, and that the last values inserted change across different runs. This was to be expected, given the limited queue capacity and the fact that producers are blocked when the queue is full. Increasing the queue capacity relaxes the insertion constraints on the producers, and it is observed that the number of items queued by producers 2 and 3 grows.

```
int C;              // queue capacity
SPool  TS(3);       // three producer worker threads
ThQueue<int> *THQ;  // reference to thread safe queue

void ThFct(void *arg)      // Thread function
   {
   int n, start_index, retval;
   int rank = TS.GetRank();

   if(rank==1)     // Producer 1 code
      {
      for(n=1; n<=100; n++) THQ->Add(n);
      THQ->CloseQueue();
      }
   else            // Producers 2 and 3
      {
      if(rank==2) start_index = 1000;
      else start_index = 100000;
      n = 1;
      do
         {
         retval = THQ->Add(start_index+n);
         n++;
         }while(retval);
      }
   }

int main(int argc, char **argv)
   {
```

```
    bool read_flag;
    int  read_value;

    if(argc==2) C = atoi(argv[1]);
    else C = 40;
    THQ = new ThQueue<int>(C);

    TS.Dispatch(ThFct, NULL);     // run threads
    // – – – – – – – – – – – – – – – – – – – –
    // This main thread dequeues and print values
    // as long as they are relevant
    // – – – – – – – – – – – – – – – – – – – –
    for(;;)
        {
        read_value = THQ->Remove(read_flag);
        if(read_flag == false) break;
        else std::cout << read_value << std::endl;
        }
    TS.WaitForIdle();    // synchronize with workers
    delete THQ;
    }
```

LISTING 9.6

Several producers: TQueue1.C.

Several Consumers: TQueue2.C

In the second example, main() acts as producer and queues 200 consecutive integer values. A pool of three consumers is constructed; each consumer dequeues values and prints them to stdout for as long as the value is a valid one. The correct termination is verified. This is the pattern used internally in the thread pool utility discussed in Chapter 12.

Examples 11 and 12: TQueue1.C and TQueue2.C

To compile, run make tqueue1/tqueue2. The queue capacity can be overridden from the command line (the default is 40).

9.10 **READER-WRITER LOCKS**

Consider an application where several threads are recurrently performing two different operations on a given data set: an operation called generically a **write** operation that modifies the data set and changes its internal state, and another operation called generically a **read** operation that extracts information without modifying the data set or changing its state. An obvious example that comes to mind is a team of threads accessing an ordinary, thread-unsafe, shared STL container. But these generic write and read operations are not necessarily memory operations; they may also be operations in which a shared resource—a shared file, for example—is accessed.

The traditional mutual exclusion mechanism—allowing access of one thread at a time to the data set—may introduce unnecessary synchronization overhead. The write operation must obviously be exclusive, but there is in general no harm in letting several threads perform the read operation concurrently. The read operation only needs the guarantee that the data set is not modified by a write during the read. If the number of threads is important and the reads are much more frequent than the writes, the ordinary mutual exclusion mechanism may induce a severe performance penalty.

Reader-Writer locks—also called shared locks—are optimization utilities designed to safely relax some of the constraints of the strict mutual exclusion mechanism, thereby allowing several threads to perform read operations concurrently. This problem is not as trivial as it may look at first sight. Just locking a mutex for writes but not for reads is not sufficient, because *a write operation must exclude any other write or read*. Moreover, in the particular case of memory operations, memory consistency, as discussed in Chapter 7, enforces a mutex lock for the reads.

Reader-Writer locks are proposed by all programming environments, except OpenMP and C++11. Figure 9.6 shows their operation. Exclusive write sections (black threads) are well separated from concurrent read sections (gray threads). A point that requires careful discussion is the way the transitions from exclusive to concurrent regions (and viceversa) are managed. Indeed, reader-writer locks are particularly efficient in the presence of lots of readers and a few writers. However, if writers are forced to wait for as long as there are ongoing readers, they can eventually starve (never get the lock) in the presence of too many readers. The way of guaranteeing the absence of starvation is discussed later on.

9.10.1 PTHREADS RWMUTEX

In Pthreads, a reader/writer locks works like an ordinary mutex, the only difference being that there are two different functions for locking in read or in write mode. The unlock function is the same in both cases. The programming interface is as follows:

- pthread_rwmutex_t lock declares a reader/writer lock.
- Its address is passed to pthread_rwmutex_init() for initialization. There are no attributes for this type of mutex. Destruction works in the same way.
- pthread_rwmutex_rdlock(&lock) locks lock in read mode.

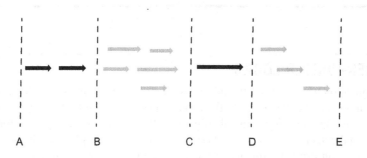

A	B	C	D	E

FIGURE 9.6

Operation of a reader-writer lock. Black threads are writers, and gray threads are readers.

- pthread_rwmutex_wrlock(&lock) locks lock in write mode.
- pthread_rwmutex_unlock(&lock) unlocks lock in any mode.

The man pages provide additional information (look, for example, at man pthread_rwlock_init).

9.10.2 WINDOWS SLIM READER-WRITER LOCKS

Reader-writer locks in Windows were introduced by Windows Vista. The programming interface is described below. As for Pthreads, I have not found in the documentation any reference to the ordering policy for write-read transitions. An educated guess is that starvation is guaranteed not to occur, using policies of the kind described later on.

Windows introduces a new synchronization object, SWRLOCK, that must be declared with global scope, and its address passed to the initialization, acquire, and release functions. Here is a summary of the programming interface, taken from the Windows API online documentation [13]:

SWRlock member functions

- SWRLOCK lock declares a SWRlock.
- InitializeSWRLock(&lock) initializes the reader-writer lock.
- Locking in shared mode. Called by read operations.
    - void AcquireSWRLockShared(&lock).
    - int TryAcquireSWRLockShared(&lock). Does not wait. Returns 0 if mutex is unlocked, or 1 if mutex is locked.
    - void ReleaseSWRLockShared(&lock).
- Locking in exclusive mode. Called by write operations.
    - void AcquireSWRLockExclusive(&lock).
    - int TryAcquireSWRLockExclusive(&lock). Does not wait. Returns 0 if mutex is unlocked, or 1 if mutex is locked.
    - void ReleaseSWRLockExlusive(&lock).

Notice that the TryAcquire....() functions listed above have only been supported since Windows 7.

9.10.3 TBB READER-WRITER LOCKS

TBB introduces two reader-writer mutex classes, spin_rw_mutex and queuing_rw_mutex. They have exactly the same design profiles as the standard spin_mutex an queuing_mutex classes discussed in Chapter 5, and they operate in the same way, with a few minor modifications:

- These reader-writer mutexes are always locked using the internal scoped_lock classes.
- TBB introduces an extra Boolean parameter called write that is passed to the scoped_lock functions. If writer is true(false) the mutex is locked in exclusive(shared) mode.
- There are two additional member functions allowing the programmer to upgrade a reader mutex to writer or downgrade a writer mutex to reader, but we do not have simple examples to propose to illustrate their relevance.

Listing 9.7 shows two ways of locking a spin_rw_mutex in exclusive (writer) mode. To lock in shared (reader) mode, change the write parameter to false.

```
using namespace tbb;

spin_rw_mutex    RWmutex;    //  create RWmutex

// Explicit locking:
spin_rw_mutex::scoped_lock  Slock;         // construct scoped lock
Slock.acquire(RWMutex, bool write=true); // lock RWmutex
...
SLock.release();                           // unlock RWmutex

// Scoped locking:
    {
    spin_rw_mutex::scoped_lock  MLock(RWmutex, bool write=true);
                                        // RWmutex is locked

    ...
    }
```

LISTING 9.7

Locking TBB reader-writer mutexes.

The TBB documentation indicates that the reader/writer locks have write priority. This means the reader-writer lock is fair and read requests are blocked when there is a pending write request, as will be discussed in the next section.

9.11 RWlock CLASS

The RWLock class is a simple wrapper of the native Pthreads and Windows reader-writer utilities. The member functions are listed below. *This class does not have a C++11 implementation*, because there are no native reader-writer lock services in C++11. One option in this environment is to use the TBB or Boost shared mutex classes.

RWLOCK INTERFACES

RWLock()

– RWLock constructor.
– Creates a reader-writer lock.

int Lock(bool mode)

– When mode is true-false, locks in write-read mode. .
– Returns error code in Pthreads.
– Return value is not relevant in Windows.

int TryLock(bool mode)

– When mode is true-false, tries to lock in write-read mode.
– This function never waits.

- Returns 1 if lock is acquired, 0 otherwise.

int Unlock(bool mode)

- Unlocks a reader-writer lock in the mode it was locked.
- Returns an error code in Pthreads.
- Return value is not relevant in Windows.

9.11.1 EXAMPLE: EMULATING A DATABASE SEARCH

A first example, well adapted to the functionality of a reader-writer lock, is the database search example developed in Section 3.10. In Chapter 3, a built-in feature of the SPool utility, enabling the cancellation of a parallel job, was used. Here, the cancellation of the parallel region is implemented by reading and writing a shared flag. The worker threads keep reading the flag—initially false, called interrupt in Listing 9.8—to check if cancellation is requested. The thread that requests the cancellation toggles the flag to true. There are therefore a huge number of reads, and only one write: an ideal use case for testing the reader-writer lock performance.

The RWLock class is used in this example. The partial listing of the source file DbSearch_P.C that follows is very close to Listing 3.30 in Chapter 3. The main() function is the same. In the thread function the check for cancellation is performed by reading the flag with the lock in read mode, and the write to cancel the process is made with the lock in write mode.

```
SPool *TS;
const double EPS = 0.000000001;
const double target = 0.58248921;
Data D;

bool    interrupt;    // NEW, initially false
RWLock rw_lock;       // NEW, protects flag

// The workers thread function
// - - - - - - - - - - - - - -
void th_fct(void *arg)
    {
    double d;
    int rank = TS->GetRank();
    Rand R(999*rank);

    for(;;)
        {
        // - - - - - - - - - - - - - - - - - - - - - - - - -
        // check the interrupt flag and eventually break
        // - - - - - - - - - - - - - - - - - - - - - - - - -
        rw_lock.Lock(false);
        my_flag = interrupt;
        rw_lock.Unlock(false);
```

Continued

```
         if(my_flag) break;
         // - - - - - - - - - - - - - - - - - - - - - - -

         d = R.draw();
         if(fabs(d-target)<EPS)
            {
            D.d = d;
            D.rank = rank;
            // - - - - - - - - - - - - - - - - - -
            // Request interruption and break
            // - - - - - - - - - - - - - - - - - -
            rw_lock.Lock(true);
            interrupt = true;
            rw_lock.Unlock(true);
            break;
            // - - - - - - - - - - - - - - -
            }
         }
      }
```

LISTING 9.8

DbSearch_P.C: simulating a database search. The windows version DbSearch_W.C is similar.

Example 11: DbSearch_PW.C

To compile, run make dbs_pw. The number of threads is 4 by default. It can be overridden from the command line.

The observed performance is not as good as in the Chapter 3 example using the SPool built-in job cancellation service, based on the native Pthreads thread cancellation utilities. But it is better than the standard mutex-locking performances.

9.11.2 EXAMPLE: ACCESSING A SHARED CONTAINER

An example is provided in the file VAccess.C. The target data set whose thread safety is enforced is an STL integer vector container std::vector<int>. This container is repeatedly accessed by a set of reader and writer threads. The initialization code reads the number nTh of threads from a data file, *and creates two different thread pools of* nTh *threads each*: one for reader and the other for writer threads. The code organization is described below using the RWLock interfaces.

Writer threads
- The integer values each writer thread inserts in the vector container depend on its rank. A thread of rank k starts inserting at the integer value v = 10 k, and continues from there on.
- Each writer thread performs the following steps five times:
    - It waits for a random time interval in the range [0, 2000] milliseconds.
    - It increments v and calls Lock(true).
    - It inserts v at the end of the container, and calls Unlock(true).

- After operating five times, the thread terminates.

The write operations occur randomly, but the container values are related to the thread ranks as described above. When looking at the container content, one knows from which thread each inserted item comes from.

Reader threads

The reader threads repeatedly access the container to read and print its content to stdout. They execute a read loop until the main thread signals the end of the operation. At each iteration of the read loop:

- Reader threads wait for 250 ms, in order to slow down the read operations.
- They call Lock(false), and print the container to stdout, using an utility function provided by the vath library.
- Finally, they call Unlock(false) to close the read operation.

The main thread interrupts the read operations after a time interval (in milliseconds) read from the data file. Once the read operation is interrupted, the main thread joins the reader and the writer teams.

Example 12: VAccess.C

To compile, run make vaccs. The number of writer and reader threads, as well as the duration of the reads, are read from the data file vaccs.dat.

The code output shows several times the content of the container on stdout (as many times as read operations took place), and also shows how the container grows as interleaved write operations take place.

This example shows how having two (or more) independent thread pools in the same application may simplify the programming of some parallel contexts. A more elaborate example is developed in Chapter 12.

A TBB version.

The previous code, using RWLockVA, is portable. A TBB version is proposed in VAccessTbb.C, in order to provide an example of the usage of the TBB shared mutex class.

Example 12: VAccessTbb.C

To compile, run make vaccstbb. The number of writer and reader threads, as well as the duration of the reads, are read from the data file vaccs.dat.

9.11.3 COMMENT ON MEMORY OPERATIONS

The previous example involves *memory operations*, and it seems to contradict the conclusions of Chapter 7 concerning memory coherency: exclusive writes are naturally protected by a mutex, but read operations must lock the same mutex to make sure they capture the last written value to the memory location involved. Looking back to Figure 9.6, it is clear that read operations are not locking anything:

otherwise, they could not act concurrently. Therefore, we may ask: *how do we know that memory consistency is guaranteed for memory operations?*

The answer is that the write and the read sectors in Figure 9.6 are separated by memory fences located at boundary points A, B, C, D, and E, provided by an internal mutex. This guarantees that memory will be coherent every time the read operations start.

9.12 GENERAL OVERVIEW OF THREAD POOLS

It should be clear by now that a parallel job is composed of a collection of logical, weakly coupled units of sequential computation: the tasks. Parallelism is implemented by mapping tasks to threads for parallel execution, with occasional synchronizations required by the algorithm integrity. All the examples and applications discussed until now exhibit a simple fork-join parallel context in which the N tasks of a parallel job are uniquely mapped to a set of N distinct worker threads. This is indeed the basic operational model of the simple SPool utility and the OpenMP parallel directive that has been used all along.

More complex applications may require more than a simple fork-join parallel pattern. An application may need to repeatedly activate a varying number of worker threads in order to perform a substantial number of different parallel tasks. A network server may need to request the services of a new thread to treat the connection established by a new client. Rather than creating and destroying the worker threads as they are needed, it is much more efficient to dispose of a stock of blocked threads sleeping in an idle wait state, and wake them up to execute new tasks when needed. An example was given early in this chapter, using a blocking barrier to manage the worker threads. Indeed, waking up sleeping threads is more efficient than creating them from scratch every time they are needed (which involves, among other things, creating a new stack buffer for each new thread). It may also happen that the number of tasks to be executed by a parallel job is not known in advance. This is indeed the case of recursive *divide and conquer* algorithms, where tasks recurrently split in two or more smaller tasks as long as the computational workloads are bigger than some predefined granularity.

This leads to the introduction of *thread pool* environments to implement efficient task management. A thread pool is a collection of worker threads, by default sitting silently in the background executing an idle wait, waiting to be woken up to perform a task. Worker threads go back to an idle wait when no new tasks requests are available. Their presence in an application does not reduce the available CPU resources when the pool is not active.

A parallel treatment is a collection of tasks, not threads. The precise implementation of the task concept depends of course on the particular thread pool programming environment, but in all cases it incorporates precise information about the function that describes the computation to be performed. In the simple thread pools involved in the SPool utility of the OpenMP parallel region, there is a one-to-one mapping of tasks to threads, and tasks start running as soon as the parallel treatment is launched. However, we will see in the following chapters this is not the most general case, and programming environments are designed to cope with contexts in which the number of tasks submitted for execution is bigger than the number of worker threads in the pool. As tasks are submitted, they are queued in some way until the worker threads finish or suspend previous assignments and become available to service new tasks.

The way tasks are mapped to threads depends on the particular programming environment. In some cases, task scheduling is fair and tasks are served on a first come, first served basis. In other cases, sophisticated unfair strategies may be deployed to decide which task is executed next. This is the case in OpenMP and TBB.

Three different thread pools are considered in the following chapters:

- **A—OpenMP**, a well-established, widely adopted programming environment, available in FORTRAN and C-C++. OpenMP played a leading role in enabling the adoption of shared memory programming in SPMD platforms. A complete coverage of OpenMP, including the most recent 4.0 release, is presented in Chapter 10.
- **B—TBB** A C++ library proposing a substantial number of standalone utilities for multithreading, and a task-centric thread pool programming environment using sophisticated strategies to optimize the mapping of tasks to threads. TBB is discussed in Chapters 11 and 16.
- **C.—NPool class**, a C++ utility for the management of a team of worker threads, implementing many of the OpenMP and TBB features. The scheduling strategies for managing parallel tasks are less ambitious than in these environments. Nevertheless, the interest of this utility is that it implements a slightly different programming style that simplifies the deployment of some specific parallel contexts. This utility is discussed in Chapter 12.

Clearly, different design choices induce some differences in user interfaces and programming styles. Nevertheless, a substantial number of pitfalls and best practices are common to all of them. Insight into multithreading is considerably enhanced by comparing the different ways in which they are resolved, and by keeping in mind the different development strategies they enable.

OpenMP

Overview

OpenMP is a mature, standard API for writing shared memory parallel applications in C, C++, and FORTRAN. When SMP architectures with shared memory nodes emerged in the computing market in the mid-1990s, all leading software and hardware vendors quickly agreed on a standard aimed at easing the task of developing multithreaded applications. At that time, native multithreading libraries— widely used in system programming—lacked high-level, easy-to-use interfaces for thread management and synchronization. The advent of OpenMP encouraged application programmers to quickly take advantage of the availability of a few CPUs to boost the performance of their sequential applications. Indeed, the OpenMP strategy is based on directives inserted in sequential codes, guiding the compiler in producing multithreaded code. Clearly, starting from a sequential code and quickly boosting its performance by adding a few directives is indeed a very attractive option, and it played a major role in driving the adoption of shared memory application programming in the early days. The examples in previous chapters adopted instead a parallel focus from the start, and organized the application code accordingly: OpenMP is indeed a very flexible programming environment, also well adapted to this programming style.

The include file for the OpenMP API is omp.h, which consists of:

- *Directives* used to manage and synchronize threads.
- *Environment variables* used to set the main configuration options of OpenMP.
- *Runtime routines*: There are three kinds:
    - Lock routines that provide fine control of mutual exclusion (already discussed in Chapter 6).
    - Execution environment routines that provide useful information and allow the programmer to set up configuration options of an OpenMP program at runtime.
    - Portable timing routines.

The core of the OpenMP API is the management of an *implicit thread pool*, present in any OpenMP code. By implicit we mean that the thread pool is already created by the runtime system when the main() function starts. All the user has to do is activate the worker threads with the parallel directive, as shown by several examples in the previous chapters. OpenMP has many other features required to implement sophisticated parallel applications (nested parallel jobs, dynamically generated tasks, etc.). In addition, OpenMP proposes *work-sharing* directives that perform an automatic parallelization of loops. This

OpenMP feature is used mainly in a microtasking programming style, where the code remains most of the time in sequential mode, and individual loops are parallelized as they are encountered.

Given the substantial length of this chapter, it is probably useful to start by explaining how its content is organized:

- Overview of the basic OpenMP execution model, and the programming interfaces for configuring OpenMP:

  - Section 10.1 extends the discussion of the basic OpenMP execution model, initiated in previous chapters.
  - Section 10.2 discusses the various ways of configuring OpenMP to adapt the execution environment to the requirements of specific applications.

- OpenMP directives for thread management and synchronization:

  - Section 10.3 describes the OpenMP directives for managing a team of worker threads and sharing the computational workload among them, as well as the accompanying clauses that adapt the directive operation to a specific parallel context.
  - Section 10.4 deals with the OpenMP synchronization directives.
  - Section 10.5 proposes several examples of thread management, work-sharing, and thread synchronization. All these examples refer to the basic OpenMP programming model dealing with regular parallel contexts, where the work-sharing patterns are easily controlled by the programmer. More complex examples along the same lines are found in the three chapters (Chapters 13–15) devoted to specific applications.

- Extended, task-centric, OpenMP execution model. In-depth discussion of the task API, including new OpenMP 4.0 features:

  - Section 10.6 describes the task API—introduced in OpenMP 3.0, 3.1, and further extended in OpenMP 4.0—as an extended execution model tailored to deal with irregular or recursive parallel patterns. The way in which the task API is articulated with the basic programming model is carefully discussed.
  - Section 10.7 proposes several examples of irregular or recursive problems where the task API plays a central role, including all the new task API features incorporate by OpenMP 4.0.
  - Section 10.8 discusses a few best practices to keep in mind when using the task API.

- Further OpenMP 4.0 features:

  - Section 10.9 introduces a new OpenMP 4.0 feature: the cancellation of parallel regions or task groups. An example simulating a database search illustrates the relevance of this feature.
  - Section 10.10 describes the OpenMP 4.0 new programming interfaces for heterogeneous computing: offloading code blocks to accelerators. The basic ideas are exposed, but at the time of the preparation of this manuscript this feature was not fully implemented in the available compilers. Examples will be in due time incorporated to the accompanying software.
  - Section 10.11 deals with the new OpenMP 4.0 programming interfaces implementing thread affinity.
  - Section 10.12 presents the new OpenMP 4.0 programming interfaces implementing vectorization, as a way of enhancing single-core performance. Again, at the time of the

preparation of the manuscript this feature was not fully implemented in the available compilers. But vectorization has already been available for some time in the Intel compilers, and examples of vectorization are proposed in the three chapters (Chapters 13–15) dealing with specific applications.

Some of the sections quoted above—in particular Sections 10.2 and 10.3—deal with a substantial amount of material. We have tried very hard to make them adaptable both to a first reading, providing a global overview of the subject, and to subsequent readings searching for specific information.

OpenMP RESOURCES

Given the OpenMP status—a widely adopted programming standard—there are naturally a huge amount of bibliographic references, in particular articles and tutorials on the Internet that can be easily consulted. We make below a few comments on this subject:

- The classical OpenMP reference is the book by Barbara Chapman, Gabrielle Yost, and Ruud van der Paas, *"Using OpenMP"* [26], which, given its high pedagogical standards, remains a very useful tool for programmers.
- The official OpenMP Architecture Review Board (ARB) site [27] has a wealth of information, in particular:
  - The official OpenMP Application Programming Interface [28]
  - The official OpenMP4.0 examples document [29]
  - Pointers to articles and tutorials, at the /resources link
- Among the tutorials, I particularly appreciate the SC14 tutorial "Advanced OpenMP: Performance and OpenMP4.0 Features," by B.R. de Supisnki et al. [30]. The material proposed in this tutorial provides additional insight and examples on many of the subjects discussed in this chapter. A useful OpenMP SC14 video can be found in [31].

10.1 BASIC EXECUTION MODEL

The basic OpenMP execution model, in its simplest form, was already introduced in Chapter 3. OpenMP implements a *fork-join* execution model in which at some point of its lifetime a thread meets a *parallel directive* that activates a team of N threads to perform some parallel treatment (how the team size N is fixed is discussed later on). This model is a *thread-centric* model, in the sense that, as shown in Figure 10.1(a), each active thread in the team has a well-defined task assignment when a parallel region is entered. Barring a very mild exception to this statement that will be discussed later on, it is fair to say that the programmer knows at any time what every thread in the worker team is doing. This corresponds to the traditional view implemented in the basic multithreading libraries, in which a thread is identified with the task it runs.

OpenMP creates a unique task pool for the whole application, but this thread pool is dynamic in the sense that the number of worker threads in the OpenMP pool *is not fixed; it can be enlarged dynamically*. If more parallelism is needed, more threads are added to the pool. Indeed, OpenMP supports nested parallel regions. As indicated in Figure 10.1(b), a thread in a parallel team can in

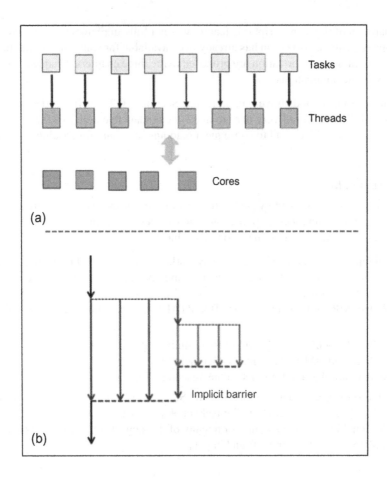

FIGURE 10.1

OpenMP execution model.

turn create a new parallel region and become the master thread of the new worker team. When this happens, OpenMP incorporates the new threads required to run it in such a way that each active implicit task is mapped to a thread. The encountering thread can fix the number of threads required by setting the number of threads for the next parallel regions. Then the execution of the nested parallel region proceeds as follows:

- The current task being executed by the black thread is suspended.
- (N-1) new threads are activated. Whether the new threads are created on demand or simply activated from a dock of previously created sleeping threads is an implementation-dependent issue.
- Including the initial thread triggering the nested parallel region, *which becomes the master thread of the new team*, the N worker threads start immediate execution of a set of *implicit tasks* that have been prepared by the programmer, in the code block that follows the parallel directive.

- Threads in the team have ranks in [0, N-1] that can be obtained by an OpenMP library function call. Rank 0 corresponds to the master thread. As usual, the thread rank (which is called the *thread number* in OpenMP) can be used to select the particular job to be done by the thread, using conditional statements.
- When the nested parallel region completes its treatment, the master thread resumes the execution of the interrupted task.

In spite of the fact that one task in the external parallel region was suspended when the inner parallel region was encountered, the mapping of implicit tasks to threads is very precise. We know at any time what every thread in the team is doing. Do not be confused by the *implicit* qualification given above to the tasks executed at the start of a parallel region; this simply means they are completely defined when the parallel region is encountered.

OpenMP 3.0 introduced a new task directive, used to dynamically incorporate an additional workload in an already running parallel region, with a fixed numbers of worker threads. Tasks created in this way are called *explicit tasks*. There is no conceptual difference between explicit and implicit tasks; they are in all cases units of sequential computation assigned to the worker threads. But the addition of explicit tasks is a major extension of the basic execution model that requires careful discussion, because in this case potential parallelism (more concurrent tasks) is incorporated in the application without increasing the number of threads in the pool. Section 10.6 discusses at length the way this new, extended execution model is interfaced with the basic historical OpenMP execution model described above.

Notice that there is no notion of "job submission" in OpenMP. The master thread that encounters a parallel region suspends whatever it is doing and joins the new worker team to contribute to the execution of the new predefined tasks. Rather than a "job submission," there is a temporary transition to a new parallel context. At the end of the parallel region, an implicit barrier synchronization operates, and then the master thread resumes the execution of the initially suspended task.

Notice also that the thread number (the rank of a thread) depends on the context. The thread that creates the nested parallel region in Figure 10.1(b) is not the master thread, so its thread number is initially different from 0. However, inside the nested parallel region, this thread becomes the master thread of the new inner team and acquires the thread number 0. This will be shown explicitly in one of the examples in Section 10.5.

The basic, traditional OpenMP execution model is largely sufficient for regular problems in which programmers can easily grasp the way of distributing the parallel workload among the worker threads. However, this execution model is not optimal for addressing irregular, unstructured, or recursive problems for reasons that will be discussed in Section 10.6. The task extension started in the 3.0 release and vigorously continued in the last 4.0 release is motivated by this fact.

10.2 **CONFIGURING OpenMP**

OpenMP is a very flexible programming environment. It relies on a set of internal control variables (ICVs) to configure the behavior of a program. ICVs are *conceptual variables*. Indeed, the OpenMP standard fixes the way OpenMP behaves, not the way it is implemented. It establishes that OpenMP must behave *as if* its behavior was determined by the values of a set of configuration variables with given names. But this does not necessarily mean that they exist as such in each specific implementation of the standard.

As programmers, we are concerned by the logical behavior of OpenMP, not by its implementation. ICVs must therefore be used as they are described in the standard. ICVs store information such as the number of threads to activate in future parallel regions, whether nested parallelism are enabled or not, the size of the threads stack, and so on. Their values can be queried with runtime library functions, and set with environment variables, runtime library functions, and sometimes with directive clauses.

Different ICVs can have different scope:

- *Global scope*: they are fixed once and for all and apply to the whole program.
- *Device scope*: OpenMP 4.0 introduces the possibility of deploying an application on heterogeneous platforms mixing different kinds of computing architectures. The *device* concept is introduced to distinguish standard CPUs, co-processors, or GPU accelerators. It is obvious that teams of worker threads running on different devices should be allowed to have different attributes. Therefore, many previously global ICVs now have device scope: there can be one copy per device. In addition, a new ICV called default_device_var has been introduced, to identify the device on which the current code is executed by default.
- *Task scope*: Finally, most ICVs—like the number of threads to be activated the future parallel sections—have a local *task scope*. This means that each OpenMP task keeps its own value of these ICVs. When new tasks are created at parallel and task directives, they inherit the ICV values of the parent task. When a task modifies some ICVs, the modification is valid during its lifetime, but ancestor values are not modified. In this way, dynamic modifications of the OpenMP operational environment have a hierarchical structure: they do not propagate upward in the hierarchy of nested parallel regions or recursive task creations.

Initial values of ICVs can be set with environment variables. These initial values can in some cases be modified at runtime with library function calls or with directive clauses. In order to offer an overall view of the configuration options available in OpenMP, we list in Table 10.1 all the available ICVs, including the new ones introduced by OpenMP 4.0). This table lists the scope of each ICV, the name of the associated environment variable, and the capability offered to the programmer for retrieving its value or for modifying it at runtime. The get qualifier in the function call column means there is a library function of the form omp_get_xxxxx() that retrieves its value. The set qualifier means there is a library function of the form omp_set_xxxxx() that can be called to override previous values.

There are three types of actions performed by IVCs: controlling some global aspects of the program execution, controlling the behavior of parallel regions, and controlling the way the directive for automatic parallelization of loops shares the loop workload across the different worker threads. A qualitative discussion of their role is proposed next. *The OpenMP Reference document has a very precise description of every environment variable, as well as the library accessory functions* [28].

Controlling program execution

- *stack-size-var*: Controls the stack size for the OpenMP threads. Note that there is no way of knowing or modifying the implementation defined default stack size at runtime. In the case of stack overflow error, the program must be run with a hopefully bigger stack size by setting OMP_STACKSIZE to an integer equal to the requested size in bytes.

Table 10.1 Internal Control Variables			
ICV	**Scope**	**Environment**	**fct Calls**
dyn-var	Task	OMP_DYNAMIC	Get, set
nest-var	Task	OMP_NESTED	Get, set
nthreads-var	Task	OMP_NUM_THREADS	Get, set
run-sched-var	Device	OMP_SCHEDULE	Get, set
def-sched-var	Device	None	None
stacksize-var	Device	OMP_STACKSIZE	None
wait-policy-var	Device	OMP_WAIT_POLICY	None
thread-limit-var	Task	OMP_THREAD_LIMIT	Get
max-active-var	Device	OMP_MAX_ACTIVE_LEVELS	Get, set
active-levels-var	Task	None	Get
bind-var	Task	OMP_PROC_BIND	Get
place-partition-var	Task	OMP_PLACES	None
cancel-var	Global	OMP_CANCELLATION	Get
default-device-var	Task	OMP_DEFAULT_DEVICE	Get, set

Note: the last four ICVs listed above are specific to OpenMP 4.0

- *wait-policy-var*: Controls the preferred behavior of waiting threads: spin or idle wait. The default value is implementation dependent. Possible values for OMP_WAIT_POLICY are active for spin wait and passive for idle wait.
- *thread-limit-var*: Defines the maximum number of threads that can be activated in an OpenMP program. Its initial default value is implementation dependent. The value of OMP_THREAD_LIMIT must be equal to a positive integer. The behavior of the program is implementation dependent if this value is bigger than the number of threads the implementation can support.
- *cancel-var*: Enables the cancellation of parallel regions or other parallel constructs. The values of OMP_CANCELLATION must be true (cancellation enabled) or false (cancellation disabled). Cancellation is disabled by default. A full discussion of this issue is given in Section 10.9.
- *bind-var*: Controls the binding of threads to places (cores). When binding is requested, the runtime system is asked to bind each thread to a specific core. Values of OMP_PROC_BIND can be false (binding not requested), true (binding requested), or a string specifying the binding policy. All these details are discussed in Section 10.11 on thread affinity.
- *place_partition_var*: OpenMP 4.0 introduced a way of describing the places (cores, sockets) where the threads can be allocated and run. This ICV describes the places available for allocating threads, in order to implement thread affinity. Section 10.11 offers a detailed discussion of the different ways of setting the associated OMP_PLACES environment variable.
- *default-device-var*: Defines the default target device, where code is executed by default. Its value is set by the OMP_DEFAULT_DEVICE environment variable, and modified by a call to the omp_set_default_device() function at runtime.

Controlling parallel regions

- *nthreads-var*: Fixes the number of threads requested for the next encountered parallel region. Its default initial value is implementation dependent. An initial value is specified by setting OMP_NUM_THREADS. Values can be retrieved at runtime by calling omp_get_num_threads(), or modified by calling omp_set_num_threads(int n).
- *nest-var*: Controls whether nested parallelism is enabled for encountered parallel regions. Its values can be false (0) in which case OpenMP ignores the nested parallel directive and produces sequential code, or true (1). Its default initial value is implementation dependent. Values assigned to OMP_NESTED are true of false. Values retrieved by omp_get_nested()—or passed to omp_set_nested()—are 0 or 1.
- *max-active-levels-var*: Controls how deep one can go in nesting parallel regions. The initial default value depends on the implementation.
- *active-levels-var*: The only role of this variable is to retrieve, at runtime, by a call to the omp_get_active_level() function, an integer that informs how deep the executing code is placed in the nested parallel sections hierarchy.
- *dyn-var*: Controls whether the dynamic adjustment of the number of threads is enabled for encountered parallel regions. The comments that follow clarify the relevance of this ICV.

Note that, in many implementations, nested parallel regions are by default disabled, so the first thing to do in a program with nested parallelism is to call omp_set_nested(1) to enable this functionality. Otherwise, OpenMP will ignore nested parallel regions: only the encountering (master) thread is allocated to the nested parallel region, and this is the only thread that executes the related tasks. In other words, we end up with sequential code.

Setting the number of threads for the next parallel section when nested parallelism is enabled is also very helpful. When encountering a nested parallel regions, OpenMP adds the number of threads needed to comply with the new request. The number of threads in the pool is in this way adapted to the application requirements, as long as it does not exceed the maximum number of threads authorized to participate in the OpenMP program, determined by the thread-limit ICV. Or, as long as it is authorized by the nesting level control, which we discuss next.

Setting the global ICV, called max-active-levels-var, is also important in programs with substantial nested parallelism. If the level of nested parallelism goes beyond this limit, OpenMP again ignores the parallel directives and generates sequential code. The existence of this limit is to a large extent required by OpenMP execution model we just described. Having lots of threads in a parallel region, each one encountering a nested parallel region, each one encountering in turn a nested parallel region, and so on, may produce an explosive growth of the number of threads in the applications, leading to an overwhelming over-subscription of CPU and memory resources (remember, each time a new thread is created a new stack memory buffer is allocated). This ICV is therefore a safe-net preventing this from happening.

Next, we come to the meaning of the *dynamic adjustment of threads* ICV. As the number of threads in the pool increases, it may happen that, when the number of threads requested for the next parallel region is added to the current team, the maximum number of threads in the application is exceeded. If this ICV is enabled, OpenMP allocates fewer threads than requested, to fit the thread limit. This is the dynamical adjustment of the number of threads. If this ICV is disabled, OpenMP ignores the parallel directive and generates sequential code. In most implementations, the default thread limit is enormous (several millions for the Linux GNU compiler). Therefore, unless one is dealing with a very peculiar application, this ICV can safely be maintained at its default value (false).

Controlling the automatic parallelization of loops

OpenMP has a work-sharing parallel for directive that acts on the for loop that follows by sharing the execution of the loop iterations across the worker threads in the parallel region. There are several ways of scheduling the loop workload among the worker threads, which are selected by the value attributed to the *run-sched-var* ICV. The *def-sched-var* ICV determines the scheduling policy to be used by default, in the absence of an explicit choice. These issues are reviewed in more detail in Section 10.3.4, when discussing the work-sharing directives.

10.3 THREAD MANAGEMENT AND WORK-SHARING DIRECTIVES

OpenMP is today a very rich programming environment. The parallel behavior of an application is created and structured with directives. There are three kinds of basic, traditional directives: thread management and work sharing—directly related to the activation and scheduling of parallel jobs—and directives that synchronize the worker threads activity. OpenMP 4.0 has incorporated a number of additional directives for task synchronizations, vectorization, cancellation of parallel constructs, and code offloading to external devices. We will first concentrate on the basic directives used to activate and structure a parallel treatment, including their OpenMP 4.0 extensions. New features introduced by OpenMP 4.0 are discussed at the end of the chapter.

In C-C++, the OpenMP directives take the following form:

```
...
#pragma omp directive (optional clauses)
    {
    // code block (present in some directives)
    }
...
```

LISTING 10.1

General form of an OpenMP directive

Directives apply to the code block that follows. Note, however, that most synchronization directives—like the barrier or taskwait directives—induce a local synchronization action, and do not act on a code block. The optional clauses—that apply mainly to thread management and work-sharing directives—provide the compiler with additional information about the way the required parallel treatment should be organized. These optional clauses are of course needed to make the programmer intentions clear. Otherwise, they can be ignored.

10.3.1 PARALLEL DIRECTIVE

The parallel directive, which creates a team of N worker threads, is the fundamental parallel construct in OpenMP. Any other management, work-sharing, or synchronization directive operates inside the parallel context so established. The parallel directive together with the code block that follows will be referred to as a *parallel construct*.

The parallel directive operates in the way described in detail in Section 10.1, summarized as follows:

#pragma omp parallel
- Constructs a parallel region with N worker threads.
- Drives a single program, multiple data (SPMD)-like job: the N threads execute the same task function.
- There are therefore as many identical implicit tasks as threads in the team.
- The common task function is constructed by the compiler from the code block that follows.
- There is an implicit barrier at the end of the code block.
- Several clauses are accepted.

There are two types of clauses:

1. *Functional clauses* that define some details of the operation of the directive.
2. *Data-sharing attributes clauses* that are required to clarify the scope of data items, and help the compiler construct the task function to be executed by the worker threads.

The parallel code block contains the input needed by the compiler to construct the task function to be executed by each worker thread. OpenMP is a very flexible programming environment, supporting a large variety of programming styles as long as the programmer's intentions are clear to the compiler. The parallel code block can be a set of explicit statements, including possible calls to auxiliary functions, taken directly from the sequential version of the code. In this case, the directive has to be completed with clauses—called data-sharing clauses—that make it very clear to the compiler the scope of the different variables in the code, and enables the construction of an unambiguous task function.

```
...
int n, m;
float a, b;
#pragma omp parallel (optional clauses)
    {
    // the variables n, m, a, b are referenced in this
    // code block
    }

...
```

LISTING 10.2

General structure of a parallel directive code block

Remember that one of the initial objectives of OpenMP enables the parallelization of sequential codes by inserting directives. Therefore, the scope of data items when the transition from sequential to parallel execution (and vice versa) takes place, often needs to be clarified. Variables declared as global from the start are shared by all threads no matter how many threads and parallel regions are introduced in the code. But what happens to the variables that are local to the thread encountering the parallel region, like the variables n, m, a, b in Listing 10.2 above? Should they become shared by all the threads in the new parallel region, or should they be made private, each thread in the team having its own local copy? And, if each thread has its own copy, how should their initial values be captured? These are the issues resolved by the data-sharing clauses. The detailed description of the data-sharing clauses is postponed to Section 10.3.6, because they are common to other management or work-sharing directives not yet introduced.

Functional parallel clauses:

Here is the list of parallel directive clauses not related to data-sharing attributes:

- if(*scalar-expression*): This clause is evaluated before the creation of the parallel region. If the scalar expression evaluates to true the parallel region is created. If it evaluates to false, the directive is ignored and the compiler produces sequential code.
- num_threads(*integer-expression*): Again, this clause is evaluated before the parallel region is created. The number of threads activated when a parallel directive is encountered is fixed by the OMP_NUM_THREADS environment variable, or by a call to the omp_set_num_threads(N) library function—which overrides the environment variable value if it exists. If this clause is used, it overrides both the environment variable and the function call values if they exist.
- proc_bind(master I close I spread): Specifies the mapping of OpenMP threads to places (cores), within the places listed in the *place-partition-var* ICV. This is a new OpenMP 4.0 feature, discussed in Section 10.11 on thread affinity.

10.3.2 MASTER AND SINGLE DIRECTIVES

The master and single directives—to be used inside a parallel construct—encapsulate code to be executed by only one worker thread. Considered as synchronization directives by OpenMP, they are very useful in structuring OpenMP code. They are introduced when, in the middle of a parallel region, some specific computational activity must be performed by only one thread, like increasing a global counter, opening a file, or initializing a global variable. Here is a description of their mode of operation, shown in Figure 10.2:

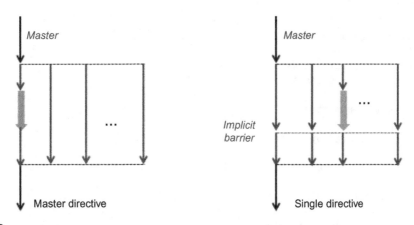

FIGURE 10.2

Operation of the master and single directives.

#pragma omp master
  - *To be used inside the a parallel construct.*
  - The code block that follows is only executed by the master thread.
  - There is no implicit barrier at the end of the master code block.
  - The remaining worker do not wait for the termination of the code block.
  - No clauses required.

#pragma omp single
  - *To be used inside a parallel construct.*
  - The code block that follows is only executed by one of the threads of the team.
  - There is an implicit barrier at the end of the single code block.
  - The remaining worker threads wait for the termination of the code block.
  - The implicit barrier can be overridden with the nowait clause.

The listing below shows a program where the main() thread creates a parallel section, and master and a single directives are encountered inside the parallel code block.

- When the master directive is encountered, the code block that follows is executed only by the master thread, and there is no implicit barrier at the end. If the other threads need to wait for the master thread, an explicit barrier directive is required.
- When the single directive is encountered, the code block that follows is executed by only one thread, but now there is an implicit barrier at the end that forces all other worker threads to wait for the completion of the single code block. This barrier can be disabled with the nowait clause in the directive.
- Waiting or not waiting for the sequential code block depends on the context. If all one needs is to have one of the threads of the team write a report message to stdout, for example, then the remaining threads do not need to wait. If, instead, a file is opened and the remaining threads will access it, then the implicit or explicit barrier synchronization is needed.

```
int main()
  {
  ...
 #pragma omp parallel [clause] ... [clause]
     {
     // -  implicit tasks code block ---
     // all threads are active here
     ...
     #pragma omp master
        {
        // executed by master
        }
     // all threads active again
     ...
     #pragma omp single (nowait?)
        {
        // executed by single thread
        ..
        } // implicit barrier here
```

```
    // all threads active again
    ...
    }
// task encountering the parallel directive resumes here
...
}
```

LISTING 10.3

Parallel region encountering master and single directives

Many of the examples that follow later in the chapter show the relevance of these directives. The single directive will be repeatedly used in Section 10.7, dealing with the task API examples, in order to implement a parallel environment in which a team of N worker threads is created by a parallel directive, but only one thread is initially activated to perform a task. The remaining threads are activated when further explicit tasks are created and submitted for execution by this initial implicit task. This pattern is shown in the listing below:

```
int main()
{
...
#pragma omp parallel [clause] ... [clause]
    {
    #pragma omp single
        {
        // this task will create further tasks, which in
        // turn may create further tasks...
        }
    }
...
}
```

10.3.3 SECTIONS AND SECTION WORK-SHARING DIRECTIVES

It was previously stated that in the basic OpenMP execution model—being a task-centric environment—there is a one-to-one mapping between implicit tasks and thread, *barring one minor exception*. These directives implement the exception we referred to. They are used, once a parallel region has been established, to establish a work-sharing pattern different from the default one (one unique task function, with all workers executing the same task). Inserted as subdirectives inside a parallel construct, they specify one-by-one a set of different individual tasks to be executed by the worker threads.

#pragma omp sections
   – *To be used inside a parallel construct.*
   – The code block that follows provides a precise list of individual tasks for execution.
   – Each task is defined by the *section* directive that follows.
   – The number of tasks may be different from the number of threads.
   – This mechanism can be seen as the submission of a number of individual tasks to a pool of N worker threads.
   – Several clauses are accepted.

- *#pragma omp section*
  - – To be used in the code block of a sections directive.
  - – The code block that follows is an individual task to be executed by a thread in the team.
  - – No clauses required.

The sections directive corresponds therefore to a context in which N different tasks are submitted for execution to the pool. If this is all that happens in the enclosing parallel region, the sections directive can be merged with the enclosing parallel directive, as shown in Listing 10.4. Tasks are defined by N successive section directives in the code block, also shown in the listing below. The number of worker threads in the team is chosen in the usual way *and is in general different from the number of submitted tasks.*

```
...
...
#pragma omp parallel sections (optional clauses)
    {
    #pragma omp section
        {  task1();  }
    #pragma omp section
        {  task2();  }
    ...
    #pragma omp section
        {  taskN();  }
    }                      // implicit barrier here
...
```

LISTING 10.4

General form of the parallel sections directive

OpenMP always activates the requested number of threads Nth. If N>Nth, some tasks will be postponed, as in any ordinary thread pool. If, instead, N<Nth, some threads will do nothing initially. But they can be activated later on to execute new tasks dynamically created with the task directive, discussed in Section 10.6. Explicit examples will be proposed later on. Finally, there is always an implicit barrier at the end of the parallel sections code block, so that the master thread exits the parallel section when all submitted tasks have been executed.

As in the previous cases, the code blocks following the section directive that define each individual task can consist of a task function like in the listing above, or a list of instructions and arbitrary function calls. In this case, *keep in mind that the clauses used to guide the compiler are global to all tasks* and must be introduced at the top level of the parallel sections directive, since the inner section directives do not admit clauses. In other words: data-sharing instructions provided to the compiler must be common to all tasks. Obviously, when lots of tasks doing very different things need to be run, this programming style can become error prone and confusing. For this particular construct, it seems more adequate to encapsulate the different task functions, avoiding clauses as much as possible. This is what is done in the examples that follow later on.

10.3.4 **FOR WORK SHARING DIRECTIVE**

This directive requests the automatic parallelization of the (nested, in general) loops that follows. The work distribution across threads is performed by OpenMP. This directive is well adapted to a microtasking programming style, where the code remains mainly in sequential mode and loops are parallelized as they are encountered. When the parallel construct is created with the only intention of parallelizing a loop, and contains no other statement, the parallel for shortcut directive can be used before the loop.

#pragma omp for
- The work performed by the for loops that follows is distributed among the worker threads.
- One specific schedule clause provides a fine control on the way the loop range is split into chunks and distributed across threads.
- Default is equal size chunks, one chunk per worker thread in the team.
- There is an implicit barrier at the end of the loop region unless the nowait clause is specified.

Besides the data-sharing clauses discussed in the next section, this directive admits a few functional directives:

- schedule specifies how iterations of the associated loops are grouped into contiguous nonempty subsets, called chunks, and how these chunks are distributed among the worker threads.
  - schedule(static, *chunk-size*): Iterations are divided into chunks of size *chunk-size*, and chunks are assigned to the worker threads in a round-robin fashion in the order of the thread number.
  - schedule(dynamic, *chunk-size*): Chunks are assigned to worker threads as they request them. Each thread executes a chunk and then requests another one, until no chunks are left.
  - schedule(guided, *chunk-size*): Similar to dynamic, with a minor difference in the way chunks are prepared. See the OpenMP documentation [28].
  - schedule(auto): The scheduling decision is relegated to the compiler and runtime system.
  - schedule(runtime): The scheduling decision is deferred until runtime, and the schedule policy and chunk size are taken from the *run-sched-var* ICV.
- collapse(n) indicates to the compiler that *loop fusion* must be performed. The n nested for loops that follow the directive are merged in a larger, unique iteration space, which is next distributed among the worker threads following the policy selected by the schedule clause. The order of iterations in the merged iteration space is determined by the natural order implied by the sequential execution of the nested loops.

An example of the operation of the different schedule strategies is proposed in Section 10.6.1, when comparing the performance of the parallel for construct against the task construct in the context of an irregular problem. Examples of the schedule and collapse clauses are found in the applications discussed in Chapters 13–15.

10.3.5 **TASK DIRECTIVE**

Once the number of active threads in a parallel region has been launched and the parallel job starts execution, OpenMP can depart from the initial *one task per thread* mode of operation, and implement some way of queuing tasks and scheduling their execution. We have already seen that the number of tasks defined under a parallel sections directive may be bigger than the number of active worker threads in the team. On the other hand, the task directive enables the *on-the-fly creation of new, explicit tasks inside a parallel region*, to be executed by the current worker team. Even in an SPMD context where there are initially as many tasks as active threads, the number of tasks can therefore be dynamically increased by the task directive.

The task directive, introduced by OpenMP 3.0, constitutes a major evolution of OpenMP programming model. We postpone to Section 10.6 the detailed discussion of the task programming interfaces, as well as the motivations for their adoption in the OpenMP programming model.

10.3.6 DATA-SHARING ATTRIBUTES CLAUSES

In the simple examples proposed in previous chapters, a parallel focus was adopted from the start, by declaring all variables with the correct scope (global or local), and explicitly writing the task function that encapsulates the parallel block code. In this case, data-sharing clauses were not needed, because the task function was already unambiguously constructed. In OpenMP, the signature of the task function is open, as long as the compiler understands the programmer intentions: it is possible to pass data values, and even recover return values from it, as the examples that follow will show.

Table 10.2 lists all optional accompanying clauses that come with OpenMP thread management directives that require them: parallel, parallel sections, for, task, and single, as well as the new OpenMP 4.0 directives simd and teams. The clauses listed in blue are the so-called data-sharing attribute directives, needed to explain the compiler the role and fate of different data items when the task code is not totally encapsulated in a task function. The examples that follow show how they operate.

The necessity of the data-sharing attribute clauses can be easily understood. Variables declared outside main are unambiguously shared, and seen by all threads. Variables declared *inside* a code block are unambiguously local variables. The point is how to interpret variables that are referenced both inside and outside a parallel code block, in the enclosing environment corresponding to the task that triggers the parallel region. Should they be shared by all parallel tasks, or should each task have its own local copy? In addition, when entering a parallel region, we may want local variables to be initialized

Table 10.2 Directive Clauses							
	Parallel	**Sections**	**Task**	**Single**	**for**	**simd**	**Teams**
private	X	X	X	X	X	X	X
shared	X		X				X
default	X		X				X
firstprivate	X	X	X	X	X		X
lastprivate		X			X	X	
copyin	X						
copyprivate				X			
reduction	X	X			X	X	X
nowait		X		X	X		

Notes: The first five clauses listed above are data sharing attributes. Notice also that "sind" and "teams" are new OpenMP 4.0 constructs.

with their previous immediate value in the enclosing environment, and when exiting the parallel region we may want to recover the last value they received inside some specific parallel construct (sections or loop regions). Then, the following clauses are available:

- *private* (list of variables): Declares that the variables in the list are private to each task. They will be implemented as local variables to each task function.
- *shared* (list of variables): Declares that the variables in the list are shared by all tasks. They will behave as global variables for the duration of the construct. But this does not means they are reallocated as global variables: *as explained below, this is a mechanism for passing data by reference* from the parent task encountering the parallel construct to the tasks executed by the worker threads.
- *default* (shared/none): Determines the default data-sharing attribute of variables referenced in a parallel or task construct.
- *firstprivate* (list of variables): Declares that the variables in the list are private to each task, and initializes their value inside the tasks with the value of the original data item when the parallel construct is encountered. *This is a mechanism for passing data by value* from the parent task encountering the parallel construct to the tasks executed by the worker threads.
- *lastprivate* (list of variables): Declares that the variables in the list are private, and causes the corresponding original list items to be updated *after the end of the* sections *or* for *constructs* with its value in the lexically last section construct, or its value in the sequentially last iteration of the associated loop. This directive is only relevant for work-sharing constructs. See the OpenMP documentation for further details.
- *copyin* (list of variables): Copies the values of the master thread's private variables in the list, to the corresponding private variables of all the other members of the team. This copy is done after the team is formed, but prior to the start of execution of the parallel construct.
- *copyprivate* (list of variables): This clause only applies to the single directive. It provides a mechanism for broadcasting a result from the thread executing the single implicit task to the other implicit tasks in the parallel region. This occurs after the execution of the block associated to the single construct, but before any of the threads in the team have left the implicit barrier. In this way, all the remaining tasks capture a result computed by the single implicit task.
- *reduction* (reduction-symbol: list): The *reduction-symbol* corresponds to an associative operation. Each variable in the list is treated as firstprivate: local instances are initialized with its value before the parallel construct. On exit from the construct, its original value is replaced by the result of the reduction operation applied to all local instances. We have often used reductions based on the addition operation to collect partial results produced by the worker threads.

Default Scope

Default scope for variables not referenced in data-sharing clauses. For the parallel directive, they are shared by default in C-C++. For the task directive, they are firstprivate by default in all programming languages.

Comments on data-sharing clauses

Consider first the shared clause: as stated above variables tagged as shared *behave as global variables* for the duration of the construct. It looks as if OpenMP was promoting a private local variable in the parent task to a global status. In fact, this is not really needed, because shared does not necessarily means *global*: shared only means that all worker threads have been granted access the original local variable sitting in the parent thread stack. For this to happen, it is sufficient that the parent thread publishes its local data by passing to other threads a pointer to it. Therefore, when a shared variable occurs in a task code block, the compiler is really implementing a pointer or a reference to the parent task local data. This explains a statement often found in the literature: local data items in the parent task tagged as firstprivate are captured by value, and those tagged shared are captured by reference.

Consider next the reduction clause. Listing 10.5 shows how it operates. Let us assume that partial results computed by the worker threads need to be accumulated. This was often done this in the past by asking the worker threads to accumulate their partial results in a mutex-protected global variable. OpenMP can perform the required reduction directly, as shown.

```
...
int n, m;
float a, b;

a = 0.0;    // initialize a
#pragma omp parallel reduction(+:a)
   {
    ...
    // each implicit task computes its value of a
    ...
   }

// Here, a is the sum of all the partial results computed
// by the implicit tasks
...
```

LISTING 10.5

Reduction operation

- Before the parallel section, a is a local variable in the main function or in the encountering thread. This variable is initialized before the parallel region is entered.
- The a variable declared in the reduction clause is treated as firstprivate: each worker thread gets an initialized copy.
- Before exiting the parallel section, the values of these private copies are collected together by the reduction operation indicated in the clause, and the result is affected by the initial local main variable a.
- After the parallel section, a contains the result of the reduction operation performed by the worker threads.

OpenMP has a reduction operation implemented for the most relevant arithmetic and logical associative operations. OpenMP 4.0 has introduced the possibility of incorporating user-defined reductions. For more details on this feature, look at the declare reduction clause in the OpenMP documentation [28].

10.4 SYNCHRONIZATION DIRECTIVES

We already covered the master and single directives, considered by OpenMP as synchronization directives, which is not unreasonable: they establish a privileged role for one of the threads in the team, and in addition the single directive adds a barrier synchronization (see below) at the end of its code block.

OpenMP proposes two directives for mutual exclusion:

#pragma omp critical name
 - Implements mutual exclusion in the code block that follows.
 - Critical sections can be named.
 - Critical sections with the same name share the same mutex.
 - All unnamed critical sections share also a unique *no name* mutex.

#pragma omp atomic
 - The instruction that follows must be executed atomically.
 - Mainly used to atomically update a variable.
 - See Chapter 5 for a detailed description of this directive.

The critical directive is discussed below, in order to show how it relates to the mutual exclusion interfaces based on library function calls, discussed in Chapter 6.

#pragma omp barrier
 - Establishes a barrier synchronization point.
 - The barrier engages all the worker threads in the current parallel section.

This is probably the most widely used synchronization directive in OpenMP. It is important to keep always in mind that *this directive synchronizes all the threads of the worker team.* Remember that the barrier interfaces proposed by the basic and vath libraries require an initialization specifying the number of threads expected at the synchronization point, which may be different from the number of worker threads in the pool. This is not the case in OpenMP. We will come back to this point when discussing in Section 10.6 the three-task synchronization directives that follow. Their relation to the barrier synchronization mechanism is original and subtle, and requires careful explanation.

#pragma omp taskwait
 - To be used inside a task code block.
 - Implements task synchronization.
 - The current task waits for completion of all its direct descendant child tasks.

#pragma omp taskyield
 - To be used inside a task code block.
 - Establishes a user-defined task synchronization point.
 - This means that, at this point, the current task can be suspended to allow the executing thread service another task.
 - This directive helps the runtime system to optimize task scheduling.

#pragma omp taskgroup (OpenMP 4.0)
 - To be used inside a task code block.
 - New parallel construct, implementing task synchronization.

- Directive is followed by a code block.
- The current task waits at the end of the code block for completion of all its descendant tasks: (children, children of children, etc.).

Task synchronizations are discussed in full detail in Section 10.6, devoted to the task API. Finally, there are two miscellaneous directives. The first one is useful, for example, when all the worker threads are asynchronously writing to stdout, and we want to order the output. The second one re-establishes memory consistency in specific contexts.

#pragma omp ordered
- Orders the execution of code block inside a loop region.
- The ordering is established according to the loop iterations.
- The thread executing the first iterations enters the ordered block without waiting.
- Threads executing subsequent iterations wait until all ordered blocks of previous iterations are completed.

#pragma omp flush(list)
- Restored memory consistency for all the variables in the list.
- Very low level directive, to be used with extreme care.
- There are restrictions on its placement. See the OpenMP documentation.

There is indeed in OpenMP a rather limited number of high-level synchronization directives. OpenMP does not offer any other high-level synchronization tools of the kind discussed in Chapter 9. This is quite understandable, given the initial motivation for OpenMP: the directive-based approach to the parallelization of existing sequential codes. When directives are inserted in a sequential code to make it multithreaded, it is not possible to pinpoint individual threads to establish synchronization patterns among them. The best we can do is a collective synchronization (barrier directive) or isolate individual threads (master and single directives). However, this synchronization context is sufficient to cope with any concurrency pattern in the traditional OpenMP context not involving explicit tasks. In any case, we have already insisted on the fact that the supplementary synchronization utilities discussed in Chapter 9 can also be used in an OpenMP environment.

10.4.1 CRITICAL DIRECTIVE

All the OpenMP run-time library functions managing mutual exclusion were presented in Chapter 6. This API is as rich and complete as those proposed in other programming environments, including ordinary locks, recursive locks, and the *testlock* functions, which try to lock a mutex and return if the mutex is not immediately available. This section examines the alternative, directive-based tools for mutual exclusion.

The purpose of the critical directive is to implement mutual exclusion in a code block. Does this mean we can forget about the lock routines API? The answer is clearly no if a refined implementation of mutual exclusion involving recursive locks or the testlock functions is required. The critical directive is at best a substitute to ordinary mutex locks. Understanding its relation with mutex locks is important, in order to make the correct strategic decisions in developing applications.

Critical sections can be named

The critical directive can be followed by an arbitrary name. *This name names a specific hidden mutex.* All critical directives with the same name in the code, lock the same hidden mutex. This means there is contention among them. Therefore, giving different names to different critical sections is a way of reducing the contention among different blocks of code for which mutual exclusion is not required, by locking different hidden mutexes.

The critical directive can also be used *as such*, with no name. In this case, OpenMP allocates a mutex to the *no name* critical construct, and again, it is always the same mutex that will be locked, so that there is contention among all the *no name* critical constructs. Programmers must keep these observations in mind in order to avoid introducing unnecessary mutual exclusion contention in a code.

Named critical sections versus mutex locking

Since a named critical section is equivalent to locking a specific mutex, can we conclude that named critical sections can replace mutex locking in all cases? The answer is no, as the following example shows. Imagine that, in a C++ class implementing some service, thread safety requires exclusive access by client code to some internal private variables in the class. Two options are available:

- A mutex is explicitly declared as a class member and used to guard the access to the critical variables, members of the class.
- Rather than declaring a class member mutex, member functions access the critical variables inside *a named critical section.*

This looks the same, but it is not. Imagine that the client code instantiates 15 objects of this class. In the first case, we end up with 15 different mutexes, and there is no contention among them. Threads cannot access simultaneously *the same object*, but they can freely access simultaneously different objects, which is what we want. In the second case, there is a unique mutex—linked to the critical section name—that protects all 15 objects, which creates unnecessary contention, and this is most likely not what we want.

10.5 EXAMPLES OF PARALLEL AND WORK-SHARING CONSTRUCTS

This section develops eight simple examples, with the purpose of illustrating the thread management and work-sharing concepts discussed so far. The first three examples reconsider the Monte-Carlo computation of π discussed in Chapter 3, illustrating the OpenMP flexibility in adapting to different programming styles for parallel sections, including the parallel for directive. Next, two examples illustrate the usage of the master and single directives inside a parallel section, as well as the generation of nested parallel regions. The values of some ICVs are checked, and the way the different implicit tasks are mapped to threads is exhibited. Finally, three simple examples deal with the parallel sections construct.

10.5.1 DIFFERENT STYLES OF PARALLEL CONSTRUCTS

In the simple examples proposed in previous chapters, a parallel focus was adopted from the start. All variables were declared with the correct scope (global or local), a task function encapsulating the parallel block was explicitly written, and reductions were computed by accumulating partial results in mutex-protected global variables. Data-sharing attribute clauses were not needed in this context, because OpenMP was already provided with an unambiguously constructed task function.

An OpenMP version of the Monte-Carlo computation of π using this programming style was discussed in Section 4.1. It is instructive to see how the same problem can be handled by using directives to directly modify the original sequential code, listed below:

```
// Initial sequential code:
// .....................
int main(int argc, char **argv)
   {
   long nsamples;
   Rand R(999);
   double x, y, pi;
   unsigned long count;

   // get nsamples from command line
   count = 0;
   for(size_t n=0; n<nsamples; n++)
      {
      x = R.draw();
      y = R.draw();
      if((x*x+y*y) <= 1.0 ) count++;
      }
   pi = 4.0 * (double)(count) / nsamples;
   cout << "\n Value of PI = " << pi << endl;
   }
```

LISTING 10.6

Sequential Monte-Carlo computation of π

Remember that objects of the class Rand generate uniformly distributed random doubles in the interval [0, 1]. The code listed above generate nsamples of uniformly distributed points inside a box of side 1, and counts how many of them are inside the unit circle. The ration count/nsamples determines the value of π.

Adding directives to the listing above

In constructing the parallel version, the purpose is to dispose of several threads sharing the work of producing samples and counting how many of them are accepted. Two threads are activated, each one examining nsamples/2 samples. The listing below shows the modified, parallel code. The only modification needed to implement the parallel version is the introduction of the parallel directive with a few relevant clauses, and in particular the reduction clause. Another important modification—using local random number generators—is needed in this case to make the code thread-safe, as discussed in Chapter 4. All this can be accomplished by adding a few OpenMP statements and directives to the sequential code.

```
int main(int argc, char **argv)
  {
  long nsamples;
  double pi;
  unsigned long count;

  // get nsamples from command line
  count = 0;
  omp_set_num_threads(2);

  #pragma omp parallel firstprivate(nsamples) \
                       reduction(+:count)
    {
    // task function ......................
    double x, y;
    int rank = omp_get_thread_num()+1;
    Rand R(999*rank);
    for(size_t n=0; n<nsamples/2; n++)
      {
      x = R.draw();
      y = R.draw();
      if((x*x+y*y) <= 1.0 ) count++;
      }
    // end of task function ...............
    }
  pi = 4.0 * (double)(count) / nsamples;
  cout << "\n Value of PI = " << pi << endl;
  }
```

LISTING 10.7

Parallel Monte-Carlo computation of π

The modifications introduced to the sequential code are the following:

- The number of threads in the next parallel section is fixed by a call to omp_set_num_threads(2) just before the parallel directive.
- The scratch variables x, y are declared in the body of the task function, and they are unambiguously local variables in each thread.
- Consider next nsamples, a local variable initialized by main(). By declaring it firstprivate, each thread gets a local copy with the value the local main variable had on entry to the parallel section. Note that nsamples could have been declared initially with global scope, in which case this clause is not needed.
- Finally, there is the reduction clause that performs the reduction operation needed to accumulate the acceptance count computed by each worker thread.

This example shows how clauses serve to transfer information to tasks. The firstprivate clause transfers local variable values from the encountering master thread to all the other workers. The reduction clause collects local results from the worker threads and transfers the result of the reduction operation to the master thread that resumes the task in execution when the parallel region was encountered.

Example 1: CalcPi1.C

To compile, run make calcpi1. The number of threads is 2. The number of Monte-Carlo events is read from the command line (default is 10000000).

A version using parallel for

The next example is the construction of a parallel version using the parallel for work-sharing directive. The main computational work in this code takes place after all in a for loop. This will be done, again, by adding directives to the sequential code, but the structure of the code is different from the previous example. The purpose in that case was to help the compiler to construct a thread function, and we were able to refer to the rank of the executing thread, and to introduce local random number generators. Moreover, the work distribution among threads was done by hand: each one of the two threads was managing nsamples/2 samples.

Nothing like that is possible when the parallel work sharing is totally implicit. The parallel for directive acts only on the for loop that follows. This means that it is not possible to define local random number generators with thread-specific initialization, and we have to rely on a global function Rand(), with thread safety being ensured by using thread local storage, as discussed in Chapter 4. Here is the listing of the main() function.

```
int main(int argc, char **argv)
   {
   long nsamples;
   double pi;
   double x, y;
   unsigned long count;

   // get nsamples from command line
   count = 0;
   omp_set_num_threads(2);
   #pragma omp parallel for firstprivate(nsamples) private(x, y) \
                     reduction(+:count)
    for(size_t n=0; n<nsamples; n++)
       {
       x = Rand();
       y = Rand();
       if((x*x+y*y) <= 1.0 ) count++;
       }

   pi = 4.0 * (double)(count) / nsamples;
   cout << "\n Value of PI = " << pi << endl;
   }
```

LISTING 10.8

Parallel Monte-Carlo computation of π

The reduction operated on the count variable works as in the previous example. The code uses the thread-safe Rand() generator function discussed in Chapter 4, in which a thread-specific initialization is implemented.

Example 2: CalcPi2.C

To compile, run make calcpi2. Uses the for work-sharing directive. The number of threads is 2. The number of Monte-Carlo events is read from the command line (default is 10000000).

Yet another version of the Monte-Carlo code

Leaving aside the previous version using the parallel for directive, we have seen so far two different versions of the Monte-Carlo computation of π: a fully encapsulated task function with no directives in Chapter 3, and the version above constructed by adding directives to the sequential code. To show the OpenMP flexibility, yet another version is proposed next in which the task function is only partially encapsulated in an auxiliary function.

```
unsigned long Get Acceptance(long NS)
    {
    double x, y;
    unsigned long my count;

    int rank = omp_get_thread_num()+1;
    Rand R(999*rank);
    for(size_t n=0; n<NS/2; n++)
       {
       x = R.draw();
       y = R.draw();
       if((x*x+y*y) <= 1.0 ) my count++;
       }
    return my count;
    }

int main(int argc, char **argv)
    {
    long nsamples;
    double pi;
    unsigned long count;

    // get nsamples from command line
    count = 0;
    omp_set_num_threads(2);

    #pragma omp parallel firstprivate(nsamples) \
                     reduction(+:count)
```

Continued

```
    { count = Get Acceptance(nsamples); }

pi = 4.0 * (double)(count) / nsamples;
cout << "\n Value of PI = " << pi << endl;
}
```

LISTING 10.9

Yet another parallel Monte-Carlo computation of π

The computation is now organized in a different way:

- The auxiliary function Get Acceptance, *executed by each thread*, receives as argument the number of samples and returns the computed acceptance. This auxiliary function uses internally a local random number generator with thread-dependent initialization: the thread rank is used to select the initial seed of the generator (it is increased by one unit to avoid the value 0 for the seed).
- The parallel code block just calls this function, receives the return value in count, and performs the reduction of count as in the previous examples.
- The variable nsamples must again be declared firstprivate. Indeed, each task function needs its value in order to pass it to the auxiliary function. Again, this clause could be avoided if nsamples was declared with global scope.

Example 3: CalcPi3.C

To compile, run make calcpi3. The number of threads is 2. The number of Monte-Carlo events is read from the command line (default is 10000000).

10.5.2 CHECKING ICVs AND TRACKING THREAD ACTIVITY

Checking ICVs

The example that follows demonstrates the usage of the single directive inside a parallel section, checks some global ICV values, and shows how the ICVs can be modified in nested parallel regions. The program creates first a parallel section with two threads, and then each one of these threads creates in turn a nested parallel region of three threads, as shown in Figure 10.3.

When main() starts, some default values of global ICVs are checked, and in particular the maximum number of threads accepted in the application. Then, a parallel region of two threads is created (region 1 in Figure 10.3). Each one of the two threads in region 1 creates in turn a three-thread parallel region (region 2 in Figure 10.3). A barrier is placed after the nested parallel regions, so that the two initial master threads are synchronized when they enter region 3 in the external parallel region. The purpose of the program is to check and print some ICV values in all the parallel regions in the program: the two nested parallel construct—in region 2—and the external parallel construct—in region 3. However, our intention is to print one message per team, not one message per thread, and for this reason the single directive is used. Here is a sketch of the code organization, starting from the first (external) parallel region encountered:

```
int main(int argc, char **argv)
   {
   ..
   omp_set_num_threads(2);
```

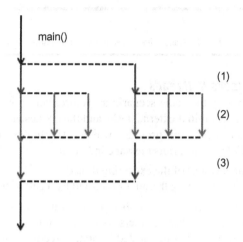

FIGURE 10.3

Nested parallel sections implemented in Examples 4 and 5.

```
#pragma omp parallel          // external, with 2 threads
   {
   ...                        // executing region 1
   omp_set_num_threads(3);
   // - - - - - - - - - - - - - - - - - - - - - - - - - - -
   #pragma omp parallel       // entering region 2 in Fig 10.3
      {
      #pragma omp single
         {
         // checks of ICVs and messages
         }
      }                       // exiting region 2
   // - - - - - - - - - - - - - - - - - - - - - - - - - - -
   #pragma omp barrier        // synchronizes the 2 threads when
   ...                        // entering region 3
   #pragma omp single
      {
      // checks of ICVs and messages
      }
   }                          // end of external
}
```

LISTING 10.10

Layout of the code related to Figure 10.3

This code is a useful exercise to understand how the single directive works. Its role in the listing above is to have only one thread in each team checking IVCs and writing to stdout. The other threads in each team are idle. The role of the barrier after the nested parallel regions is to synchronize the two external threads and make sure the region (3) message is not printed before they both emerged from the nested parallel region.

Example 4: Icv1.C

To compile, run make icv1. The number of threads is hardwired to the configuration shown in Figure 10.3.

Tracking the mapping of tasks to threads

This example implements exactly the same scenario as before, but now our intention is to check in detail how the eight tasks (the two initial external tasks and the six nested tasks) are distributed among the total number of threads allocated to this program, which is six. In this example, every single task in the external and nested parallel regions prints message indicating:

- The OpenMP thread number (rank) of the executing thread.
- The pthread_t identity of the executing thread, as returned by a call to the pthread_self() function.

The point here is that the OpenMP thread number depends on the context. When the second thread in the first parallel region (thread number 1) enters its nested parallel region, it becomes master and takes the thread number 0. After exiting the nested region, it recovers the thread number 1. On the other hand, the pthread_t identity of a thread is an absolute identifier controlled by the system, with no reference to OpenMP. Following the output of this program we can follow what each one of the six different threads is doing.

How can we output a pthread_t value? We know that, strictly speaking, this is an opaque data item with unknown structure. However, it turns out that, in Linux, the C++ instruction cout << pthread_self() works correctly because the pthread_t data type returned by pthread_self() is in fact implemented as a long integer.

Example 5: Icv2.C

To compile, run make icv2. The number of threads is hardwired to the configuration shown in Figure 10.3.

10.5.3 PARALLEL SECTION EXAMPLES

Behavior of the barrier directive

Contrarily to the barrier function calls in the Pthreads or vath libraries—in which the barrier utility is always initialized with the number of threads participating in the synchronization—the barrier directive in OpenMP does not requires any initialization: it adapts automatically to the number of worker threads in the parallel region where the directive is used. This is perfectly consistent with the parallel region execution model: all worker threads executing the same task function. There are therefore N worker threads and N barrier calls.

One may, however, ask what happens in an OpenMP parallel sections environment involving Nth worker threads, in which there are N implicit tasks with an internal barrier directive, submitted for execution. The barrier directive appears then in a number of implicit tasks different from the number of worker threads. How does the code behave? The situation is ambiguous because OpenMP only sees independent tasks since the notion of "parallel job" is absent. If N>Nth, should the execution context be interpreted as one big job involving all the tasks, or as consecutive jobs involving a lower number of tasks each?

The example developed in the source file Sections.C—listed below, some irrelevant details have been left aside—submits six identical tasks with an internal barrier directive, and *before* and *after* messages on both sides of the barrier. The number of threads is read from the command line, with a default of six (the same as the number of tasks).

```
void Barrier_Task()
   {
   int rank = omp_get_thread_num();
   ...
   std::cout << "\n Thread  " << rank <<  " before barrier "
               << std::endl;
   #pragma omp barrier
   std::cout << "\n Thread  " << rank <<  " after barrier "
               << std::endl;
   }

int main(int argc, char **argv)
   {
   int nth;
   // read nth from command line
   ...
   #pragma omp parallel sections thunderheads(nth)
      {
      #pragma omp section { Barrier_Task();}   //
      #pragma omp section { Barrier_Task();}
      #pragma omp section { Barrier_Task();}
      #pragma omp section { Barrier_Task();}
      #pragma omp section { Barrier_Task();}
      #pragma omp section { Barrier_Task();}
      }
   return 0;
   }
```

LISTING 10.11

Barrier behavior, Sections.C

When the code is executed with the default values, or with more threads than tasks, the output corresponds to our expectations: all the *before* messages precede the after messages. With fewer threads than tasks, *the code does not deadlock*, but I suspect that the resulting behavior may be implementation dependent. In the case of the GNU compiler with, for example, three threads, OpenMP adapts the barrier behavior to the number of threads. Three tasks are executed first, correctly synchronized at the barrier point, and three other tasks are executed next, again correctly synchronized at the barrier point. We obtain three *before* messages followed by three *after* messages, and then the same pattern repeats when the three threads execute the remaining three tasks. Try running four threads, and see what happens.

Example 6: Sections1.C

To compile, run make sect1. The number of tasks is 6. The number of threads is read from the command line (the default is 6).

Dispatching a I/O operation

The code used to test Boolean locks in Chapter 9, where one extra thread is dispatched to perform a lengthy I/O operation, is re-examined. The I/O task simulates the operation by putting the executing thread to wait for 5 s. The other task checks every second if the I/O operation is finished. The synchronization of both threads is implemented with a Boolean lock.

The source code is in file Sections2.C. Here is the listing of the main() function:

```
int main(int argc, char **argv)
    {
    int status;
    B = new BLock(false);

    #pragma omp parallel sections num_threads(2)
        {
        #pragma omp section
            MainTask();
        #pragma omp section
            TaskIO();
        }
    delete B;
    return 0;
    }
```

LISTING 10.12

Main() function for Example 6

The main thread initializes the global Boolean lock to false, and launches the parallel job. There is no more OpenMP in this code. The two task functions: TaskIO() that waits for 5 s before toggling the Boolean lock to true, and MainTask() that checks every second if the toggling has taken place, are the same functions we used in the previous versions of this code.

Example 7: Sections2.C

To compile, run make sect2. The number of threads is hardwired to 2.

Data transfers among tasks

Finally, the example proposed in Chapter 9 to test the Synch<T> is also re-examined. Remember that this utility synchronizes the writing of a type T data item by one thread with the reading of the new value by other threads, and that the number of expected readers is fixed when the writer thread posts the new value.

This example constructs a three-thread parallel region, in which there is one writer thread that passes the value of a double data item to two reader threads, which is done three consecutive times. Reader threads print the received values, so there will be altogether six reader messages.

This is a pure OpenMP example. The code uses a global OSynch<double> object to synchronize the threads. This class is the pure OpenMP version of the Synch<T> class introduced in Chapter 9, and the public interfaces are the same. The writer and readers task functions are therefore practically the same functions used before. The driver code in the main function is very simple:

```
int main(int argc, char **argv)
    {
    #pragma omp parallel sections num_threads(3)
      {
      #pragma omp section
          WriteTaskFunction();
      #pragma omp section
          ReadTaskFunction();
      #pragma omp section
          ReadTaskFunction();
      }
    }
```

LISTING 10.13

Partial listing of Sections3.C

Example 8: Sections3.C

To compile, run make sect3. The number of threads is hardwired to 3.

10.6 TASK API

Prior to the introduction of the task directive in OpenMP 3.0, the thread-centric OpenMP execution model was based on the fact that the only tasks that could be executed in a parallel region were the implicit tasks initially declared when the parallel region was encountered. The basic principle was a default one-to-one mapping of implicit tasks to threads, with the exception of the single construct—that activates only one thread—and the parallel sections construct that enable the execution of a number of implicit tasks different from the number of threads in the team. However, in all cases, the tasks executed in the parallel construct were there from the start. The introduction of explicit tasks triggered *inside* a parallel region, for reasons that are discussed next, corresponds to a significant extension of the original execution model.

10.6.1 MOTIVATIONS FOR A TASK-CENTRIC EXECUTION MODEL

When parallel regions are nested to incorporate a finer structure into the parallel treatment, OpenMP adds the additional threads required to cope with the enhanced parallel activity, maintaining a kind of one-to-one mapping between implicit tasks and threads. Nested parallel regions enable programmers to cope with, for example, irregular or highly recursive patterns. But this approach is not totally satisfactory.

The reasons are simple to understand. The fact that nested parallel regions keep adding the additional worker threads that are needed to run the new, nested implicit tasks may substantially increase the number of over-committed threads running on the fixed number of cores allocated to the application. As discussed in Chapter 2, this is not by itself a problem: the operating system will distribute time slices of the available CPU resources to give all threads a chance to run. However, preempting and rescheduling threads is a *system* activity that, if excessive, may negatively impact the parallel performance of the application. Moreover, every time a new thread is created, a new stack memory buffer is attributed to the new thread: excessive thread creation may lead to exhaustion of memory resources.

This is probably the reason why OpenMP has always allowed programmers to control the level of nesting in an application. Beyond the level L of nesting set by the set_nested(L) library call, nested parallel regions are ignored and replaced by sequential code.

The different ways of scheduling a large number of tasks on a fixed number of threads has attracted substantial attention from computer scientists. The problem is complex, because, if the main target is obtaining the maximum possible performance, there are several parameters to consider, like memory usage, cache memory re-usage optimization, and a few others. There is a clear consensus that over-committing a large number of tasks on a *fixed* number of threads—equal, ideally, to the number of cores allocated to the application—is much more efficient than over-committing a large number of threads on a fixed number of cores. One important reason is that task rescheduling is much more efficient and can be implemented in user space. This execution model is shown in Figure 10.4. Cilk [3] was the first programming environment to implement this approach, based on a *task stealing scheduling strategy* that will be described in Chapter 15, when discussing TBB. Cilk strongly influenced the OpenMP tasking extension started in the 3.0 release, as well as the TBB multithreading environment.

The task directive incorporates a task-centric scheduling strategy into the original OpenMP execution model, which is extended, not abandoned. This directive enables the inclusion of new explicit

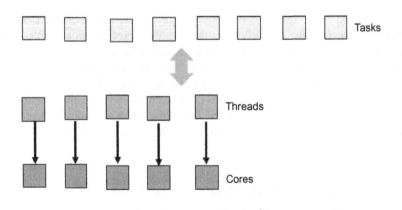

FIGURE 10.4

Task-centric execution model.

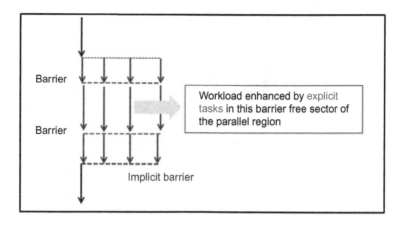

FIGURE 10.5

Task-centric implementation in OpenMP.

tasks inside a running parallel region, with a fixed number of threads. The number of worker threads is not changed, but the number of tasks submitted for execution is allowed to grow dynamically. Tasks are therefore executed by the threads of the team, and their data environment is constructed at creation time. Once created, task execution may be delayed or suspended. These features add enormous flexibility to the management of irregular problems or recursive parallel patterns.

Figure 10.5 shows the way the task-centric scheduling strategy is incorporated into the OpenMP execution model. *In a barrier-free sector inside a running parallel region*, the computational workload can be extended with additional explicit tasks. The initial implicit tasks can spawn new tasks, which in turn can spawn new tasks, and so on and so forth. The important point to keep in mind is that all the parallel activity (initial implicit tasks plus additional explicit tasks) will be completed by the time the worker threads reach the following (implicit or explicit) barrier. In other words, explicit tasks have a lifetime limited by the next barrier in the enclosing parallel region.

This fact is easy to understand. Barriers synchronize *threads*, not *tasks*. Barriers only know that at some point they have to release the threads reaching the synchronization point. Explicit tasks before the barrier, which only increase the workload of the worker threads, are totally unknown to the barrier. The task scheduler will make sure that threads reach the barrier only after having exhausted all the workload provided by the implicit and explicit tasks.

10.6.2 EVENT SYNCHRONIZATIONS AND EXPLICIT TASKS

An important observation is in order at this point: care must be exercised when synchronizing explicit tasks generated in a parallel region. It was often stated before that Chapter 9 synchronization utilities constructed with basic libraries tools could be used in a OpenMP environment, and several examples were presented in previous chapters. However, this is true only in parallel regions without explicit tasks, where the thread-centric execution model applies. As stated before, synchronization tools synchronize threads, not tasks. In the absence of a precise mapping of tasks to threads, event synchronization tools are unsafe, as shown below.

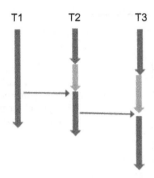

FIGURE 10.6

Parallel context that may deadlock on two threads.

To summarize, the synchronization rules in a task-centric region are the following:

- *Mutual exclusion* is safe, and critical sections, mutex locking or atomic operations coexist peacefully with the unfair synchronization policies for tasks.
- *Event synchronizations* like spin or idle wait barriers, Boolean locks, or any other low- or high-level event synchronization tools are not safe, and cannot be used to synchronize explicit tasks.

Figure 10.6 shows a simple parallel context that may or may not deadlock when tasks are over-committed, according to the way they are scheduled. Task T3 performs a spin or idle wait, and is released by task T2. Task T2, in turn, performs also a spin or idle wait and is released by T1, before releasing T2. When the tasks are run by two threads, they execute correctly if T1 and T2 are executed first. However, if T2 and T3 are executed first, the code deadlocks because the two threads executing T2 and T3 are blocked, and there is no thread available to execute T1 and release them.

However, the question can be asked, what are we supposed to do if, nevertheless, we need to synchronize tasks? The answer is that tasks must be synchronized by the task scheduler itself. This is accomplished by introducing hierarchical relations among tasks that guide the way the scheduler executes them. TBB introduced from the start a powerful environment that implements this strategy, to be discussed in detail in Chapter 16. OpenMP 4.0 introduced a depend clause that establishes hierarchical relations among sibling tasks. Section 10.7.5 shows in detail how to implement a barrier for tasks by using this clause.

10.6.3 TASK DIRECTIVE AND CLAUSES

We call an *explicit task* a task created by the task directive. An explicit task will always be a child of an initial implicit task, or the child of another explicit task previously created by the same directive. Therefore, the task directive only appears inside a task function code. Here is the form of the directive:

```
int main()
{
...
#pragma omp parallel
```

```
      {
        ...
        #pragma omp task [clause] ... [clause]
            {
              // -  task code block - --
            }
      }
  }
```

LISTING 10.14

General form of the task directive

#pragma omp task
- *To be used inside a task region.*
- The code block that follows is a new task submitted to the pool.
- This new task joins the ongoing parallel job in the current parallel region.
- The task will ultimately be executed by a thread in the team where it is created. No additional threads are added to the worker team.
- Several clauses are accepted.

A task created in this way will be scheduled according to the worker threads' availability. It may start immediate execution, it may be delayed, and when scheduled it may be suspended and resumed later if needed. We will see later on that task suspension is critical to avoid deadlocks when tasks are over-committed in a thread pool. Here are the clauses associated with this directive:

- Four basic data-sharing clauses are listed in Table 10.2: private, shared, default, and firstprivate.
- *if(expression)*: If the Boolean expression evaluates to false, the encountering thread does not submit the task to the pool. Instead, it suspends the execution of its current task and starts immediate execution of the new task. Execution of the suspended task is resumed later. In this case, the new task creation reduces for all practical purposes to a simple function call. The purpose of this clause is to put some limits on the creation of too many explicit asynchronous tasks.
- *untied*: Tasks—implicit in a parallel region or explicitly created by the task directive—are tied to a thread by default. This means the thread that starts executing them keeps the ownership of the task for all its lifetime. If for some reason the task is suspended, its execution will be resumed by the same thread. Declaring a task untied means the initial executing thread does not keep ownership, and that any other thread can resume execution. This gives the runtime system more flexibility for rescheduling suspended tasks and may provide better performance. However, allowing suspended tasks to migrate across threads may introduce other potential pitfalls that programmers should be aware of. This issue is discussed in Section 10.8.
- *final (Boolean expression)*: If the Boolean expression is true, this clause declares the task as final. A final task forces all its children to become *included* tasks. An *included* task is a task whose execution is sequentially included in the current task region. This means the task is undeterred, and immediately executed by the encountering threads.
- *mergeable*: Declares that the task can be merged into an ordinary function call.
- *depend (dependence-type: list)*: Establishes dependencies among sibling tasks, that is, among tasks that have been directly spawned by a common ancestor. The dependencies so established are used to order the way in which the tasks are scheduled: a task will only be executed after all tasks it

depends are terminated. The way this directive operates is discussed in one of the examples that follow.

Note the difference between the if() and final() clauses. When the Boolean expression is true, the if() clause replaces the task itself by a function call, and the final() clause forces the encountering thread to execute the task immediately instead of submitting it to a ready pool for later scheduling. Note also that OpenMP is the only programming environment that allows migration of suspended tasks. This is not the case in TBB and in the NPool utility discussed in the following chapters.

The *depend* clause is a new OpenMP 4.0 feature. Introducing hierarchical dependencies among tasks is a very powerful evolution. Explicit hierarchical dependencies among tasks are a major feature of the Intel TBB environment. Task dependencies are needed to implement *synchronization patterns among tasks*, not among threads. A forthcoming example shows in detail how the depend clause can be used to implement a barrier synchronization among an arbitrary number of tasks running in a parallel section with a fixed number of threads.

10.6.4 TASK SYNCHRONIZATION

The next question that needs to be asked is: once new explicit tasks are dynamically created, how can the parent tasks that launched them know they are finished? OpenMP has a powerful and clever synchronization model for explicit tasks, as shown in Figure 10.7. It can be summarized as follows:

- *barrier synchronization*: All possible explicit tasks created in a parallel section (children, children of children, etc.) terminate at the next barrier directive (implicit or explicit).
- *taskwait synchronization*: A task can wait for termination of its *direct children tasks* at a taskwait directive in its task function code. Note that children of children are not catched by this directive.

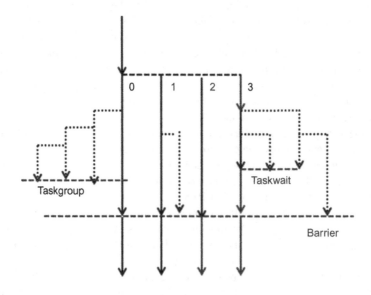

FIGURE 10.7

Task synchronizations at barrier, taskwait, and taskgroup directives.

- *taskgroup synchronization, in OpenMP 4.0*: At the end of a code block associated to a taskgroup directive inserted in its task function code, a task waits for termination of *all, direct, or indirect descendants* generated inside the code block.

The four blue tasks in Figure 10.7 are the initial implicit tasks associated with the parallel region. The explicit tasks created with the task directive are marked in red. The figure shows several recursive patterns of explicit task generation. For some of the explicit tasks, their terminations are synchronized with their ancestors via the taskwait or taskgroup directives Other explicit tasks terminate directly. However, in all cases, the scope of the explicit tasks is bounded by the next barrier directive. The initial implicit tasks are not released from the barrier synchronization point until all the explicit tasks generated before the barrier are terminated.

The two other thread pool environments to be discussed in the next two chapters—TBB and NPool—are also task-centric environments proposing also taskwait and taskgroup utilities with features very similar to the ones discussed above for OpenMP.

10.6.5 OpenMP 4.0 TASKGROUP PARALLEL CONSTRUCT

The taskgroup directive was introduced above as a new task synchronization feature in OpenMP 4.0. In fact, it is much more than that: it is a new parallel construct that enhances the expressive power of OpenMP, for applications requiring dynamical task generation. We may think of a traditional parallel region as a construct encapsulating a parallel job in a thread-centric environment. In the same way, it is possible to think of the taskgroup construct as a construct encapsulating a parallel job executed by explicit tasks.

The taskgroup construct enables implementing a programming style in which a task launches a complex recursive parallel treatment, continues to do something else and, when the time comes, waits for the job termination. This style of code organization is shown in the listing below. The significant added value provided by the taskgroup construct will be demonstrated later on, first by looking at a divide and conquer algorithm used before for the computation of the area under a curve, and then discussing an unbalanced, unstructured, recursive algorithm that cannot possibly be parallelized without the taskgroup construct.

```
int main()
  {
  ...
  #pragma omp parallel
     {
     #pragma omp single
        {
        ...
        #pragma omp taskgroup
           {
           // - - - - - - - - - - -
           // implicit task continues here
```

Continued

```
          ...
          // task spawns as many explicit tasks as
          // needed, which in turn can spawn more
          // tasks, and so on
          ...
          // implicit task continues here, doing other things
          ..
          // The implicit task waits, before exiting the taskgroup
          // code block for the termination of all its direct or
          // indirect descendants
          }
      // The implicit task continues here
      ...
      }     // end of single task
    }       // end of parallel region
  ...
  }
```

LISTING 10.15

General structure of a taskgroup construct

In the listing above, the main thread opens a parallel region with the intention of activating a set of worker threads. Inside the parallel region, there is a unique implicit task executed, defined inside the single code block. This task can be considered as the continuation of the execution stream suspended when the parallel region was encountered. This unique implicit task continues execution, and at some point decides to launch a parallel job. To do so, it opens a taskgroup code block, spawns all the tasks of the parallel job (which in turn can spawn other tasks), and continues the execution of its own workload. When the task reaches the end of the code block, it waits for the termination of all its direct or indirect descendants, that is, the termination of the submitted job. Then, it continues execution, using the outcome of the job. The task terminates at the end of the single code block, and at the end of the parallel region the worker threads are decommissioned and the initial execution stream resumed.

10.7 TASK EXAMPLES

The examples that are developed in this section have been designed to illustrate the operation of OpenMP tasks.

10.7.1 PARALLEL OPERATION ON THE ELEMENTS OF A CONTAINER

The purpose of this example is to demonstrate the efficiency of tasks in handling a strongly unbalanced parallel pattern. Unbalanced means the amount of work performed by each task is highly erratic, so it is difficult if not impossible, with the standard methods, to achieve a balanced workload distribution among the worker threads.

A map operation is performed on all the elements V[n] of a vector of doubles of size N. A map operation changes the initial value of the vector element by another value:

```
for(int n=0; n<N; n++) V[n] = f(V[n]);
```

and the task function $f(x)$ is such that the amount of computation it generates is highly irregular as we move along the container. It can be described as follows:

- Each container element is first initialized with a private uniform random value in [0, 1], by calling a global random number generator.
- The task acting on a given container element repeatedly calls a uniform random generator until it gets a value that is close to the initial value within a given tolerance, for example, 0.0001, called precision in the code.
- The initial container element value is replaced by the new close value so obtained.
- Obviously, increasing (or decreasing) the precision increases (or decreases) the average computational work done on container elements.
- In our example, we take a vector size N = 100000, and the precision is decreased by four orders of magnitude from an initial value of 0.0000001, as we move along the container. This produces the workload pattern shown in Figure 10.8.

Using OpenMP tasks to do this operation is not really mandatory. The operation described above is a map operation, and it is sufficient to write a single loop and share the loop operation among several threads. However, a straightforward application of the parallel for directive is inefficient in this unbalanced problem. With N threads, this directive splits the loop iteration space in N chunks, one for each thread. It is, however, obvious that the first chunk workload is much bigger than the last one, and the code performance will be very far from exhibiting a speedup equal to the number of threads. The situation can be improved by using the schedule clause to reduce the chunk size. Nevertheless, we will show that in this case the task scheduling strategy implements a better load balance for the operation of the underlying thread pool, which outperforms the parallel for construct.

The complete listing is in source file Foreach1.C. Let us first look at the global variables in the code, and to the task function executed by each task:

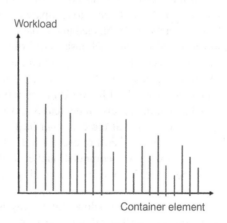

FIGURE 10.8

Computational workload for vector elements.

```
// Global variables
// - - - - - - - -
int  nTh;
int  N;
double p_initial, p_final;
std::vector<double> V;
SafeCounter SC;

double precision(int n)
    {
    double a = (p_final - p_initial)/N;
    return (a*n+p_initial);
    }

void Replace(int n)
    {
    Rand R(999 * SC.Next());
    double x;
    double eps = precision(n);
    double d = V[n];
    do
        {
        x = R.draw();
        }while( fabs(x-d)>eps );
    V[n] = x;
    }
```

LISTING 10.16

Task function in this example

The target of the map operation is the vector V, initialized by main() in the way described above. The task function uses internally a random number generator to compare its output with the initial value of the target element. Following the best practices established in Chapter 4, each task owns its own, local, random number generator. However, we also want each task to dispose of a distinct and personalized random suite. For this reason, the initial seed of each local generator is chosen in a task-specific way. Tasks get a unique, integer rank from a global SafeCounter object. This class has been designed to increase and return an integer counter at each call of its Next() member function, in a thread-safe way.

The second point to be observed is that the precision decreases as we move along the container: it interpolates between an initial precision p_initial at the container head and a final precision p_final at the container tail. True enough, the computational cost of each task is random, but if the precision was constant along the container we would expect the computational cost of each subrange computation in a parallel for loop to be roughly the same. Decreasing the precision along the container adds load imbalance to the problem.

Let us next consider the main() function, listed below. After array initialization and a sequential computation, two parallel computations are performed, the first using a parallel for construct and the second by launching N explicit tasks.

```
int main(int argc, char **argv)
   {
   int n;
   CpuTimer T;
   Rand rd(777);

   // Set parameter values
   // Initialize vector target
   // Perform sequential computation

   omp_set_nested(1);
   omp_set_num_threads(2);

   // parallel for computation
   // - - - - - - - - - - -
   T.Start();
   #pragma omp parallel for schedule(static, N/24)
      for(n=0; n<N; ++n) Replace(n);
   T.Stop();
   T.Report();

   // task computation
   // - - - - - - - -
   T.Start();
   #pragma omp parallel
      {
      #pragma omp single
         {
         n = 0;
         while(n < N)
            {
            #pragma omp task untied
              { Replace(n); }
            n++;
            }
         }
      #pragma omp barrier
      }
   T.Stop();
   T.Report();
   // print V[0], V[N/2], V[N-1]
   }
```

LISTING 10.17

Main() function in the present example

First, look at the parallel for computation. With the default scheduling for the work distribution—as many chunks as threads, four in this case—the parallel computation is totally unbalanced. Smaller chunks and different scheduling strategies can be used to better distribute the workload among threads: chunks of sizes N/24 and N/48, and the static and dynamic scheduling options, as discussed below.

Consider the task computation. Note that, because of the single directive, *there is only one initial implicit task executed by one of the worker threads*, whose role is to generate all the remaining explicit tasks that operate on the container. As the extra tasks are generated, all the worker threads in the team participate in their execution as soon as they are available. This, as we shall see, is confirmed by the observed speedup of the program execution. After the sequential and parallel computations, the code prints some selected container elements to verify that they have indeed been modified.

This example also shows the OpenMP flexibility in the definition of task functions. Let us take a closer look at the code in order to understand the scope of the different variables, as well as how and why the correct information is conveyed to the ultimate explicit tasks. Here is the scenario implemented by OpenMP:

- The loop variable n is initially a local variable to main().
- As the parallel section and then the single directive are entered, n is by default private. Therefore, inside the single code block where the loop over n operates, it is just a local variable to the task generating thread.
- As the task code block is entered, *local variables in the parent task are treated as firstprivate by default*, so a new variable n is created *and initialized with the parent task value*.
- Finally, inside each explicit task, this variable is passed as argument to the Replace() function. This is the reason why the loop index n is correctly transferred to the explicit tasks.

Example 9: Foreach1.C

To compile, run make feach1. The number of threads is hardwired to 4. The vector size is N = 1000000, the default initial precision is 0.0000001, and the default final precision is 1000 times smaller. The initial and final precisions can be overridden from the command line. Look at the code source.

The performance measurements for the configuration described in the box above are given in Table 10.3. These results speak for themselves. It was known from the start that the parallel for

Table 10.3 Four Worker Threads: Execution Times in Seconds			
Performance of Foreach1.C			
Algorithm	**Wall**	**User**	**System**
sequential	9.25	9.25	0
for: auto	7.37	9.42	0
for: static, N/24	5.68	9.42	0
for: static, N/48	5.14	9.55	0
for: dynamic, N/24	5.02	9.51	0
for: dynamic, N/48	4.25	9.72	0
task	2.54	10.13	0.02

computation with automatic scheduling would strongly suffer from load unbalance. Using chunks of sizes N/24 an N/48 improve the performance, but we are far from obtaining the expected speedup for four threads. The task computation is flawless, in spite of the fact that we have generated one million tasks! The speedup is close to 4, with small system overhead and very limited user overhead (total user time of 10.13 s instead of the sequential user time of 9.25 s).

10.7.2 TRAVERSING A DIRECTED ACYCLIC GRAPH

The example proposed in this section deals with a parallel context that cannot be parallelized with a traditional thread-centric approach. The parallel context is unstructured (there is no predefined pattern establishing the order in which tasks are scheduled) and unbalanced (the amount of computational work performed by each task is unpredictable). The parallel context is also recursive, and the critical role played by the taskgroup construct will be shown.

This section incorporates excerpts of the Intel Threading Building Blocks documentation. The example discussed here is an OpenMP version of the parallel do preorder_traversal example available in the TBB release, in directory //examples//parallel_do. Most of the source files are directly taken from this example, with Intel's permission.

Description of the parallel context

We will consider a collection of Cell objects, instances of a class defined in the header file Cell.h. Cell objects have internally, among other members, a data item updated by a member function, if and when the input data required by the operation is available.

In a directed acyclic graph, cell objects are hierarchically organized as shown in Figure 10.9. *This hierarchical organization is not known at compile time, it is randomly initialized at runtime. Cells may have 0, 1, or 2 ancestors. Ancestors provide the input data for the cell update, and this operation depends naturally on the number of ancestors in a way to be described next. It is clear that a cell will*

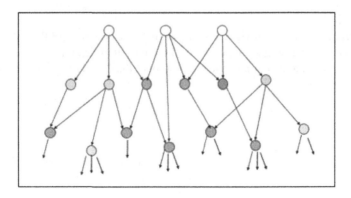

FIGURE 10.9

Directed acyclic graph. White, gray and black cells have 0, 1 or 2 ancestors, respectively.

be updated only when all its ancestors are updated. The purpose of the parallel code is to update the complete graph.

The only modification introduced in the TBB example is in the nature of the data items contained in the cells and their update operations, which has absolutely no impact on the real issue—parallel update of the graph—addressed by the example. In the original TBB code, cells contain 24 × 24 matrices, and update operations are matrix operations involving the matrices in ancestor cells. The only objective is to provide some relevant work to do to the parallel tasks. In our case, we adopted our traditional trick for providing unbalanced work for a task: cells contain a double target value, and update operations repeatedly call a random number generator until they get a value, close within a given precision, to a target to be specified below. The task workload is not uniform, and the amount of work can be increased by increasing the precision.

Updating the cells

The update operation itself is not critical for the discussion that follows. The real issue here is a sophisticated task synchronization pattern to implement a parallel graph traversal. The purpose of the update operation is to introduce some reasonable amount of computation in each task, in order to test the parallel efficiency of the parallel algorithm. This is the only place in which the original Intel code is modified. In the original TBB code, cells contain 24 × 24 matrices, and update operations are matrix operations involving the matrices in ancestor cells. Here, we adopted our traditional trick for providing unbalanced work for a task: cells contain a double target value, and update operations repeatedly call a random number generator until they get a value, close within a given precision to a target specified below. The task workload is not uniform, and the amount of work can be increased by increasing the precision.

- Each task in the parallel code will dispose of a private random number generator in [0, 1].
- Cells with no ancestors are initialized by a simple call to the generator.
- Cells with one ancestor: let a be the value of the ancestor data item. Tasks keep calling the generator until a number close to (1-a) is obtained, with a given precision ϵ.
- Cells with two ancestors: let a1 and a2 be the values of the ancestor data items. Tasks keep calling the generator until a number close to (a1+a2)/2 is obtained, with a given precision ϵ.
- The precision ϵ can be used to control the average computational workload of the tasks.

Cell and graph classes

The source file Graph.h contains the original Intel code with the definition of the Cell and Graph classes. File VGraph.h, used in this example, incorporates the minor modifications related to the replacement of matrix data items by random doubles. The declaration of the Cell class is given below:

```
class Cell
    {
    public:

    double  value;          // cell data
    int ref_count;          // number of ancestors not yet ready
    int n_ancestors;        // number of ancestors

    Cell*   input[2];       // ancestors of this cell
```

```
std::vector<Cell*> successor;   // set of successors

void update();                  // cell update function
};
```

LISTING 10.18

Cell class

Some comments on Cell class members:

- ref_count is an integer that counts initially the number of ancestors. This integer is decreased every time an ancestor is updated. When it reaches zero, the Cell object knows that its update() function can be called.
- ancestors also registers the number of ancestors. It used by update() to select the update operation to be performed. Indeed, ref_count cannot be used for this purpose, because this integer value is decreased during the computation, as explained above.
- input[2] is an array that store pointers to ancestor cells.
- successor is a dynamical vector of pointers to successor cells. As we will see below, the number of successors—that can take any value—is determined when the graph is constructed.

Constructing the directed acyclic graph

Figure 10.10 shows the construction of the directed acyclic graph, which proceeds as follows:

- The constructor Graph G creates a graph. It defines internally an empty STL vector of cells.
- The member function G.create_random_dag(N) starts by allocating an STL vector of cells of size N. Then, successive vector elements are visited. For each vector element, the number of ancestors is randomly selected. If there are ancestors, they are again randomly chosen among the preceding vector elements. Then, the cell is initialized (ref_count, input pointers) and, in the ancestor cells, a pointer to the current cell is added to the successors vector. At this point, the graph is constructed. It follows from this procedure that the number of ancestors is limited to 2, but the number of successors is arbitrary.
- G.get_root_set(std::vector<Cell*>& root_set) is another useful function. It receives as argument a reference to an empty STL vector of cell pointers. It fills this vector with the addresses of the root cells, namely, cells that have no ancestors. Obviously, cells with no ancestors are the starting point of the graph traversal algorithm.

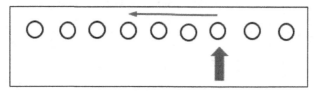

FIGURE 10.10

Constructing a directed acyclic graph.

Graph traversal code

The parallel code for this example is in source file PreorderOmp.C. The listing below shows the function that used to generate the tasks that perform the cells updates, as well as a high-level function that drives the whole graph traversal.

```
int  nTh;              //
Graph G;

void  UpdateCell(Cell *C)
    {
    C->update();

    #pragma omp atomic write     // restore reference count
    C->ref_count = C->ancestors;

    // Visit successors, and decrease their ref_count.
    // If ref_count reaches 0, launch an UpdateCell task
    // – – – – – – – – – – – – – – – – – – – – – – – – – –
    for(size_t k=0; k<C->successor.size(); ++k)
        {
        Cell *successor = C->successor[k];
        #pragma omp atomic update          // atomic update
        – –(successor->ref_count);

        if( 0 == (successor->ref_count) )
            {
            #pragma omp task
                { UpdateCell(successor); }
            }
        }
    }


// Auxiliary function that does the job
// – – – – – – – – – – – – – – – – – –
void ParallelPreorderTraversal(std::vector<Cell*>& root_set)
    {
    std::vector<Cell*>::iterator pos;
    #pragma omp taskgroup
        {
        for(pos=root_set.begin(); pos!=root_set.end(); pos++)
            {
            Cell *ptr = *pos;
            #pragma omp task
                { UpdateCell(ptr);}
            }
        }
    }
```

LISTING 10.19

PreorderOmp.C (partial listing)

Let us first examine the UpdateCell(Cell *C) function, which is the function executed by the parallel tasks that updates C. This function is called when the ref_count of C reaches zero. In the first place, the data update is performed. Then, the initial value of ref_count, equal to the number of ancestors, is restored, to return to the initial state in case the graph is traversed again.

Next, this function visits all the successor cells and atomically decreases their reference count, to inform them that one ancestor has been updated. If the successor ref_count reaches zero, a new OpenMP task is launched recursively to update it. The whole graph traversal is triggered by explicitly calling UpdateCell() on the root cells, with no ancestor. The remaining cells will be updated recursively. The fundamental task synchronization mechanism in this problem is the atomic update of the successors ref_count.

The ParallelPreorderTraversal() function that drives the whole graph traversal procedure takes as argument a reference to an STL vector containing the pointers to the root cells. All this function does is execute a for loop updating the root cells. However, root cells are approximately one-third of the total number of cells, and all the others are updated recursively as explained above. In order to make sure the function returns when the whole traversal is completed, the for loop must be inserted in a taskgroup code block. On exit from the code block, all the recursive tasks are terminated.

```
int nTh;            //
Graph G;
...
int main(int argc, char **argv)
  {
  int nTh, nCells, nSwaps;
  CpuTimer T;
  ...
  ...                            // initializations
  G.create_random_dag(nNodes);   // set the acyclic graph
  std::vector<Cell*> root_set;
  G.get_root_set(root_set);

  omp_set_num_threads(nTh);      // do the traversal
  T.Start();
  // - - - - - - - - - - - - - - - - - - - - - - -
  for(unsigned int trial=0; trial<nSwaps; ++trial)
    {
    #pragma omp parallel
      {
      #pragma omp single
        { ParallelPreorderTraversal(root_set); }
      }
    }
  // - - - - - - - - - - - - - - - - - - - - - - -
  T.Stop();
  // Report results
  }
```

LISTING 10.20

PreorderOmp.C: the main function

Table 10.4 Graph With 4000 Nodes and 30 Successive Traversals (GNU 4.9.0 Compiler)

Graph Traversal Performances			
n_threads	Wall	User	System
1	58.1	58.1	0.0
2	29.16	58.16	0.0
4	14.77	58.92	0.0
8	7.65	60.94	0.0
16	4.13	66.53	0.1

The main() function is listed above. The number of threads nTh, the total number of cells in the graph nCells, and the number of successive traversals nSwaps are read from the command line. The default values are (4, 1000, and 5). The graph is traversed several times in order to achieve reasonable execution times with a small graph. Once the graph G is constructed, a parallel section is created to dispose of a team of worker threads, and a unique implicit task is created under a single directive to execute the loop on the root cells.

Table 10.4 shows the wall user and system times as the number of threads is doubled at each step. We observe the very high quality of the results for this highly unstructured, recursive problem. Perfect scaling starts to weaken between 8 and 16 threads, but the performance is still quite acceptable. Notice the absence of system activity, as well as the very modest amount of synchronization overhead, as reported by the user execution time. We have, for 16 threads, a small 10% increase of total CPU time.

Example 10: PreorderOmp.C

To compile, run make ompreorder. To execute, run ompreorder *nTh, nCells, nSwaps*. The default parameter values are 4, 1000, and 5.

10.7.3 TRACKING HOW TASKS ARE SCHEDULED

This example demonstrates that a new explicit task can be executed by another threads if available, or by the parent thread itself if nobody else is immediately available. The scenario, as shown in Figure 10.11, is described.

- A two-thread parallel region is created.
- The rank 1 thread waits for 1 s, creates a new task (in red in the figure), and continues by writing an identification message.
- The rank 0 thread is kept out of the way for a lapse of time T, by using a timer.
    - If T is much longer than 1 s, the rank 0 thread is not available to execute the new task. In this case, the scenario "b" is chosen: the rank 1 thread suspends its ongoing task, executes the new one, and finally resumes its original task.

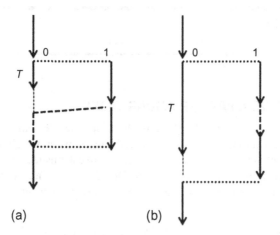

FIGURE 10.11

Example 11: scheduling of the red explicit task.

- If T is much smaller than 1 s, the rank 0 thread is available and executes the new task, according to scenario "a."

Tasks print messages indicating which thread is in charge of its execution. These scenarios are validated by the example code.

Example 11: Task2.C

To compile, run make task2. The number of threads is hardwired to 2. The time interval T is 500 ms by default. This can be overridden from the command line, by passing an integer value in milliseconds.

10.7.4 BARRIER AND TASKWAIT SYNCHRONIZATION

The following example shows that explicit tasks are terminated at the next (implicit or explicit) barrier. The scenario is very simple: a parallel region with N worker threads is launched. All but one immediately hit a barrier. The remaining thread spawns a long level 1 explicit task, before hitting the barrier. This child task in turn spawns another even longer level 2 explicit task. The example verifies that the N threads are released only after all the explicit tasks launched before the barrier are completed.

Example 12: Task3.C

To compile, run make task3. The number of threads is hardwired to 2.

The next example demonstrates task synchronization. In the previous example, the level 1 task, shorter than the level 2 one, terminated before. A taskwait directive is now added in the level 1 task, forcing it to wait for its level 2 child. The code execution verifies that this task terminates later. The source file is Task4.C.

Example 13: Task4.C

To compile, run make task4. The number of threads is hardwired to 2.

10.7.5 IMPLEMENTING A BARRIER AMONG TASKS

This example shows the way OpenMP 4.0 establishes dependencies among tasks, with the depend clause involving a *dependence type* and a list of shared data items on which the task depends. In Intel TBB, tasks are C++ objects and hierarchical dependencies are established when they are allocated (they can, e.g., store a pointer to another parent task). In OpenMP, tasks are implemented as code blocks attached to the task directive, and shared variables are used to establish dependencies among them. The depend clause operates as follows:

- depend(*dependence-type, list of data items*). Dependencies are derived from the information conveyed by the dependence type and the list of data items.
- Dependence types can be in, out, or inout:
    - in dependence-type: the generated task depends on all previously generated sibling tasks that reference at least one of the items in an out or inout dependence-type list.
    - out and inout dependence-types: the generated task depends on all previously generated sibling tasks that reference at least one of the items in an in, out, or inout dependence-type list.

These rules are indeed very flexible. They allow programmers to establish flow dependencies (some tasks executing after others have terminated), anti-dependencies (some tasks executing before other tasks are scheduled to run), or more complex dependencies in which tasks that need the results of other tasks are ordered in order to guarantee the integrity of the underlying algorithms.

We start with a simple example of flow dependency. Let us go back to the computation of the area under a curve, but this time the computation is not recursive: the integration domain is split by hand in Ntk equal subdomains, and an explicit task is spawned for each subdomain. Partial results coming from the computing tasks are collected in a mutex-protected global variable.

A parallel region with Nth threads is first created. As discussed in Chapter 3, the area could be easily computed in the SPMD way, by assigning one parallel task to each thread. However, for the purposes of this example, a number of parallel tasks different from Nth will be used. Again, this is easily done: using the single directive, only one implicit task is activated, which spawns the Ntk computing tasks and waits for their termination with a taskwait directive. After that, a global variable where partial results have been accumulated holds the final value of the computation.

In the example that follows, a small change is introduced in this scenario by imagining that, after the area is computed, something must be done with the area result *before* the parallel job terminates, that is, before the initial implicit task takes over after the taskwait directive. An extra task is therefore launched in the parallel job, and dependencies are used to make sure it is scheduled after the parallel area computation terminates. *This extra task is in fact establishing a barrier among the computing tasks.*

Here is the listing of the example, in source file Depend.C. The function integrated is the good old function $4.0/(1.0 + x^2)$, whose area in the interval [0, 1] is π. The subsidiary task that executes after the parallel computation just prints some information to stdout.

```
#define EPSILON   0.0000001

using namespace std;

double result;     // global variable
int    synch;      // used for synchronization

// The function to be integrated
// – – – – – – – – – – – – – – – – – –
double my_fct(double a)
   {
   double retval;
   retval = 4.0 / (1.0+a*a);
   return retval;
   }

// Generic, sequential integration routine
// Integrates func(x) in [a, b] with precision eps
// – – – – – – – – – – – – – – – – – – – – – – – – –*/
double Area(double a, double b, double (*func)(double),
            double eps=EPSILON);

// The main function
// – – – – – – – – – –
int main (int argc, char *argv[])
   {
   int nTh = 2;          // default value, number of threads
   int nTk = 4;          // default value, number of tasks
   result = 0.0;
   synch  = 0;

   // override from command line
   // – – – – – – – – – – – – – –
   if(argc==2) nTh = atof(argv[1]);
   if(argc==3)
      {
      nTh = atof(argv[1]);
      nTk = atof(argv[2]);
      }

   // Set the number of threads
   // – – – – – – – – – – – – – –
   omp_set_num_threads(nTh);

   // – – – – – – – – – – – – – – – – – – – – – – – – –
   // Create the parallel region, and activate only
```

Continued

```
      // one implicit task.
      // – – – – – – – – – – – – – – – – – – – – –
      #pragma omp parallel
         {
         #pragma omp single
            {
            // Here starts the implicit task
            // Spawn the nTk computing tasks
            // – – – – – – – – – – – – – –
            for(int n=0; n<nTk; ++n)
               {
               #pragma omp task depend(in: synch)
                  {
                  double a = n/nTk;    // global range is [0, 1]
                  double b = (n+1)/nTk;
                  double res = Area(a, b, my_fct, EPSILON);
                  synch++
                  #pragma omp critical
                     result += res;
                  }
               }
            // Next, spawn the printing task
            // – – – – – – – – – – – – – – –
            #pragma omp task depend(out: synch)
               {
               synch++;
               cout << "\n Area result from inner task is " << result;
                  << "\n Value of synch is " << synch << endl;
               }
            #pragma omp taskwait
            }
         }
      return 0;
      }
```

LISTING 10.21

Depend.C

The variable result is used to accumulate partial results, and the variable synch is used to establish the dependencies among tasks. The code establishes some default values for Nth and Ntk, and reads eventual new values from the command line. Then, the parallel section is created, and the single implicit task launches first the Ntk computing tasks, followed by the additional printing task. Note that:

- The first Ntk computing tasks have an in dependence on synch. Since there is no previous sibling task with out or inout dependency on synch, these tasks are totally independent and can execute concurrently.
- The printing task has an out dependency on synch. It is therefore dependent on all the previous computing tasks and will execute after them.
- The printing task prints the result for the area. If everything executed as expected, the result must be π.

- All tasks increase the value of sinch (this is not really needed, as we discuss next). The value printed by the printing task must be Ntk+1.

A few further comments are in order. First, notice that referencing the synchronization variable inside the tasks is not required. The correct dependencies are established if synch is referenced only in the depend clauses. This can easily be checked by suppressing the synch++ instruction in the dynamic tasks. Second, ordinary variables can also be used to establish dependencies. In the example above, the synch variable can be completely disposed of and result can be used instead in the dependency clauses. Third, a task can have more than one depend clause with different dependence types for different variables. I strongly recommend looking at the matrix multiplication example proposed in the official OpenMP examples document [29].

Example 14: Depend.C
To compile, run make depend. The number of threads is hardwired to 2.

10.7.6 EXAMPLES INVOLVING RECURSIVE ALGORITHMS

We turn next to the discussion of the OpenMP version of two recursive examples: computation of the area under a curve and the parallel version of the quicksort algorithm.

Consider first the recursive computation of the area under a curve. The algorithm is implemented as follows: if the range of integration is bigger than a given granularity, a task splits the domain into two halves and launches two child tasks for each subdomain. Otherwise, when the integration range is finally smaller than the granularity, the task computes the area and returns in some way the partial result. Two programming styles are possible:

- Blocking on children. Tasks spawning two children wait for their return value. This is the natural implementation in OpenMP 3.1, using the taskwait directive.
- Nonblocking style. Tasks that split the domain do not wait for return values, they terminate immediately after spawning the two child tasks. Final tasks that do the real computational work accumulate partial results in a mutex-protected global variable. This style is only possible with the OpenMP 4.0 taskgroup construct.

The next two sections develop in detail these two programming options.

Area under a curve, blocking style
The basic computational tool in this example is a library function Area(a, b, fct, eps)—taken from Numerical Recipes in C [16]—that computes the area under the function fct(x) in the interval [a, b] with precision eps. Then, a recursive task function is constructed for the problem at hand. If the integration domain [a, b] is larger than a given granularity G, the task splits it into two halves and launches two identical recursive tasks for each subdomain. When the domain size is finally smaller than the granularity, the area is computed and the results are returned to the parent tasks in the following way.

Figure 10.12 shows the code organization in this example. A team of N worker threads is created in a parallel region, but only one initial implicit task A is activated, under the single directive. This task recursively generates all the other tasks in the problem. In Figure 10.12, an initial domain of integration of size 1 and a granularity of 0.25 are assumed. Task A spawns tasks B1 and B2, which operate on domains of size 0.5, and blocks on a taskwait directive, waiting for their return values. Tasks B,

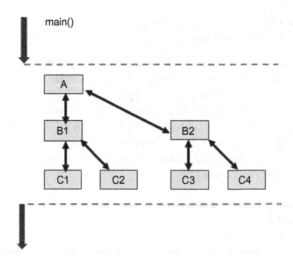

FIGURE 10.12

Area computation, blocking style.

in turn, spawn the four-level C tasks and wait for their return. Tasks at level C stop the recursive domain decomposition, compute the partial results, and return their values to the parent tasks. Here is the listing of the recursive task function:

```
double AreaRec(double a, double b, double L,
          double (*func)(double), double eps=EPSILON)
   {
   double x, y, medval, retval;
   // identification messages here

   if( fabs(b-a) > L)
      {
      medval = 0.5*(b-a);

      #pragma omp task untied shared(x)
         { x = AreaRec( a, a+medval, L, func); }
      #pragma omp task untied shared(y)
         { y = AreaRec( a+medval, b, L, func); }

      #pragma omp taskwait
      retval = x+y;
      }
   else retval = Area(a, b, func, eps);
   return retval;
   }
```

LISTING 10.22

Recursive task function for the area computation

This code deserves a careful discussion to illustrate, once again, how clauses are used to transfer information between parent and child tasks. Note that *the recursive area function returns to its parent task the value of the area for the subdomain passed as argument*. If the task is a final compute task in the task tree hierarchy that *does not* spawns other child tasks, the situation is clear: the task function just returns its computed value. The point that needs further discussion is, what happens when the executing task needs to recover return values from its two child tasks?

In the code above, there are several data items in the enclosing environment of the parent task, a, b, L, medval, func, that are needed in the child tasks. They are by default firstprivate, and they are captured by value by the child task functions, which is what we want.

The parent task function declares in addition two local variables x, y, which will receive the return values of the two subdomain areas if the problem is split into two halves. These variables, being declared shared, are passed by reference to the child tasks. When the child tasks terminate, they hold the expected return values.

Finally, the parent task returns to its parent (x+y), after the taskwait directive, needed to ensure that all children have terminated and that x and y hold the correct return values.

The complete example code, in file AreaOmp.C, includes an identification message every time the AreaRec() function is entered, so that the task generation and execution process can be followed in the output. The listing below shows the way the parallel execution is triggered in the function main():

```
int main (int argc, char *argv[])
    {
    int n, nTh;
    double result;
    double A = 0.0;
    double B = 1.0;
    double G = (B-A)/5;

    // get nTh from command line
    omp_set_num_threads(nTh);
    #pragma omp parallel
        {
        #pragma omp single
            {
            result = AreaRec(A, B, G, my_fct);
            }
        }

    cout << "\n result = " << result << endl;
    return 0;
    }
```

LISTING 10.23

Driver for the recursive area computation

There are in this code local variables in the main() function like result, A, B, and G that are referenced in the parallel region and in the task code block. This code works "as such" because, for the parallel directive, variables are shared by default in C-C++. We do not need to specify their scope. Arguments are passed to AreaRec by address, and this is the reason the local variable result will ultimately hold the correct return value at the end of the parallel section. Try adding the private(result) clause to the parallel directive, verify that in this case the result is 0, and convince yourself that this is what you should expect.

Example 15: AreaOmp.C

To compile, run make areaomp. Computational parameters are hardwired in the code (see the listing above). The number of threads is read from the command line (the default is 2).

Area under a curve, nonblocking style

This example shows an alternative strategy for performing the recursive area computation, based on the OpenMP 4.0 taskgroup directive. Figure 10.13 shows the code organization in this example. Again, an N worker threads team is created in a parallel section, and only one initial implicit task A is activated under the single directive. Again, this task recursively generates all the other tasks in the problem. But now, there are no return values to parent tasks. If a task gets an assignment on a domain bigger than the granularity, *it spawns two child tasks for each half subdomain, and terminates.* At the bottom of the task tree, the C tasks compute their partial results and accumulate them in a mutex-protected global double variable.

Here is the listing of the modified recursive task function:

```
double AreaRec(double a, double b, double L,
          double (*func)(double), double eps=EPSILON)
```

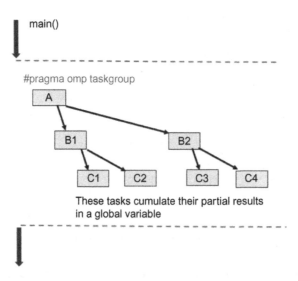

FIGURE 10.13

Area computation, nonblocking style.

```
    {
    medval, retval;
    // identification messages here

    if( fabs(b—a) > L)
        {
        // spawn two tasks and terminate
        // — — — — — — — — — — — — — —
        medval = 0.5*(b—a);

        #pragma omp task untied shared(x)
            { AreaRec( a, a+medval, L, func); }
        #pragma omp task untied shared(y)
            { AreaRec( a+medval, b, L, func); }
        }
    else
        {
        Timer T;
        T.Wait(1500);
        retval = Area(a, b, func, eps);
        RD.Accumulate(retval);    // global Reduction<double>
        }
    }
```

LISTING 10.24

Modified recursive task function for the area computation

In this listing, RD is a global Reduction<double> object used to accumulate the partial results provided by the worker threads. A timer is used to delay the worker threads performing the partial area computations, to explicitly show that the task A effectively waits for all its descendants under a taskgroup construct. Now let us look at the taskgroup construct by examining the main()function code:

```
Reduction<double> RD;
...
int main (int argc, char *argv[])
    {
    // same as before
    // ...
    #pragma omp parallel
        {
        #pragma omp single
            {
            // Here starts task A
            // — — — — — — — —
            #pragma omp taskgroup
```

Continued

```
          {
          AreaRec(A, B, G, my_fct);
          // This task A could do, if needed, other things here,
          // before waiting for descendants at the end of this
          // code block.
          }
        }
      }

    cout << "\n result = " << RD.Data() << endl;
    return 0;
    }
```

LISTING 10.25

Driver for the nonblocking area computation

As before, only one implicit task A is activated in the parallel region. Inside this task, a taskgroup construct is inserted, before calling the recursive task function, that returns immediately after launching the recursive child task generation process. At this point, task A could do other useful things if needed before waiting for the termination of all its descendants at the end of the taskgroup region. Note the difference with the taskwait directive, which blocks the tasks at the place where the directive is inserted.

Example 16: AreaOmpBis.C

To compile, run make areabis. Computational parameters are hardwired in the code (see the listing above). The number of threads is read from the command line (the default is 2).

10.7.7 PARALLEL QUICKSORT ALGORITHM

Quicksort is a recursive algorithm that operates on containers of any type for which the LessThan operation is defined. The container is sorted in increasing order. The recursive sort algorithm is well adapted for recursive task parallelism. The sequential version is reviewed first, focusing on the type of integer array. The algorithm, however, manipulates pointers and works for arrays of any type equipped with the < operation.

A function qsort is defined next that sorts an integer array in the range [*beg, end*) where *beg* is an integer pointer to the first element of the array, and *end* is a past the end pointer that points to the memory position where a new integer could be inserted. These are the standard STL conventions for describing container ranges. Remember that C-C++ accepts past the end pointers as long as they are only used in pointer arithmetic and never referenced (because they are not pointing to a valid container element). The function qsort() listed below will be called by recursive tasks whenever they have real work to perform, as was the case for the Area() function in the previous example. When examining the qsort() code, keep Figure 10.14 in mind.

```
void qsort(int *beg, int *end)
  {
  if(beg != end)
```

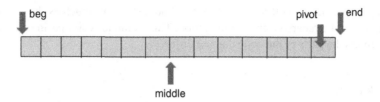

FIGURE 10.14

Operation of the quicksort algorithm.

```
    {
    - end;
    int pivot = *end;
    int *middle = partition(beg, end, LessThan(pivot));
    swap(*end, *middle);
    qsort(beg, middle);
    qsort(++middle, ++end);
    }
}
```

LISTING 10.26

Sequential quicksort algorithm

Here is how way this code operates:

- If beg != end, this means, with our range conventions, the container is not empty and we can proceed.
- The last container element is then read by decreasing the end pointer and referencing it. Now end has been moved one step to the left and points to the last array element, whose value is pivot.
- Our intention next is to reorganize the container by placing the last integer in the array, pivot, in its final position. This is done by the partition STL algorithm. Given a range and condition, this algorithm reorders the container, putting at its head all the elements that satisfy the condition. The algorithm then returns a pointer middle to the position of the first element that *does not* satisfy the condition.
- In our case, the condition is LessThan(pivot). This is a function object defined in the source file that will be used by the algorithm to compare all the integers in the array to pivot. When the partition algorithm returns, all the integers less than pivot are stored before the position pointed by middle.
- It is now obvious that middle is the final position of pivot. The integer sitting at this position, that is, *middle, is swapped with pivot, which is sitting at *end.
- Next, the same quicksort algorithm is recursively applied to the array to the left of middle, with range [beg, middle), and to the array right of middle, with range [middle + +, end + +). In this second case, middle is incremented to jump over pivot, which is already at its place, and end is increased to place it as the past the end pointer.

Note that middle is not necessarily at the middle of the initial container. The sizes of the two leftover containers can be anything, which leads us to slightly modify the recursion strategy of the previous example. The container ranges will be passed to the child tasks, very much as the integration domain ranges were passed in the recursive area computation. This example is similar in spirit to the previous one, and only reports the parts of the code that are different.

Recursive task function

A recursive task function is now constructed to be used in the OpenMP parallel version. This function receives as arguments the range pointers of the domain to be sorted. The task function starts developing the quicksort algorithm until pivot is at the right place. Then, it enters the recursive part and successively examines the two domains to the left and to the right of pivot. If the subarray size is smaller than the granularity G the task function calls directly qsort to complete the sorting of the subdomain. Otherwise, it spawns a recursive task to sort the subdomain. In our example code, there is a message printed to the screen every time a child task is spawned.

```cpp
void Pqsort(int *a, int *b)
  {
  cout << "\n Inside Pqsort" << endl;
  - - b;
  int pivot = *b;
  int *middle = partition(a, b, LessThan(pivot));
  swap(*b, *middle);

  if( (middle—a) < G) qsort(a, middle);
  else
      {
    #pragma omp task untied
        {
        cout << "Child task 1 submitted " << endl;
        Pqsort(a, middle);
        }
      }

  ++middle;
  ++b;
  if( (b—middle) < G) qsort(middle, b);
  else
      {
    #pragma omp task untied
        {
        cout << "Child task 2 submitted " << endl;
        Pqsort(middle, b);
        }
      }
  }
```

LISTING 10.27

Parallel quicksort task function

This function starts by placing at its final position the last element of the container. Then the function repeats itself for the two subranges before and after this element. If the residual container sizes are larger than the granularity, a new recursive task is launched. Otherwise, there is a direct call to the sequential qsort() function.

This algorithm performs an *in place* modification of the container, and no return values need to be recovered. Notice that different threads are simultaneously accessing and modifying a shared container, a situation that in general requires mutual exclusion. However, it is not difficult to convince oneself that in this algorithm different tasks—possibly executed by different threads—are modifying in place *nonoverlapping subranges of the container*. Therefore, this algorithm does not require mutual exclusion for thread safety.

Another detail to be observed: a and middle are integer pointers so, according to the pointer arithmetic, (middle-a) with a pointing to the first element and middle as past the end is the number of elements in the left container. The same applies to the right container.

```
int main(int argc, char* argv[])
    {
    int n = 100000;
    G = 20000;
    if(argc>1) n=atoi(argv[1]);

    int *a = new int[n];
    for(int i=0; i<n; i++) a[i]=i;
    random_shuffle(a, a+n);

    #pragma omp parallel num_threads(2)
        {
        #pragma omp single
            Pqsort(a, a+n);
        }

    CheckSort(a, n);
    return 0;
    }
```

LISTING 10.28

Parallel quicksort driver

As far as the main() function is concerned, all steps are by now standard: data input, pool initialization, and submission of a single task parallel job, which triggers the recursive operation. Finally, main() checks if the final array is properly ordered.

Example 17: QsortOmp.C

To compile, run make pqsort. The number of threads is read from the command line (the default is 2).

With the initial data n=100000, G=20000, and C=20, the code runs smoothly.

10.8 TASK BEST PRACTICES

It is useful to draw attention to some pitfalls that may eventually occur in a task-centric environment. They arise from the use of thread-specific utilities in an environment in which threads may be servicing different tasks.

10.8.1 LOCKS AND UNTIED TASKS

As was stated before mutual exclusion can be safely used in a task-centric environment. This is in general true, but OpenMP has a special feature that may, in some particular contexts that are admittedly very rare, require particular care.

In general, the mapping of tasks to threads in a task-centric environment is *nonpreemptive*. This means a thread that starts executing a task will keep ownership of the task until its termination. The running thread may suspend the task execution to serve other tasks, but the task execution will always be resumed by the same owner thread. This is the case of the thread pools discussed in the next chapters: the TBB programming environment and the NPool class. OpenMP, instead, supports *untied* tasks; namely, tasks that, when suspended, can be resumed by another thread. This feature is obviously introduced to optimize task scheduling.

In the presence of untied tasks, mutex locks require special care. When a mutex is locked in a task, it is the executing thread that takes ownership of the mutex. Let us now imagine a scenario in which an untied task creates a critical section and spawns another task *from inside the critical section* (a highly unusual but legitimate thing to do). Now, OpenMP allows a task to be suspended at certain places called task synchronization points, and task spawn is one of them. Therefore, the parent task may be suspended and, being untied, resumed later in the middle of the critical section by another thread. At the end of the critical secretion, *the new thread will try to unlock a mutex that it does not owns*, and the code deadlocks.

This scenario is very unlikely but possible. It may also occur by accident when using a programming style that does not encapsulate tasks and keeps nesting directives and code blocks. The lesson here is that care should be exercised with critical sections and locks when using explicit untied tasks.

10.8.2 THREADPRIVATE STORAGE AND TASKS

As discussed in Chapter 4 threadprivate variables are static variables—they live across function calls—that are stored on a *per thread* basis. A function accessing a threadprivate variable recovers at each function call the value belonging to the executing thread. Threadprivate variables were used in Chapter 4 to enforce thread safety when using a global random number generator accessed by several threads.

Let us now imagine that explicit tasks are used to run a parallel Monte-Carlo calculation similar to the computation of π discussed in Chapters 3 and 4. The basic idea is to have *each task* participating in the parallel treatment accessing a totally independent random number generator. In Chapter 4, a thread-safe, global generator function was used, incorporating a threadprivate seed initialized in a thread-dependent way. This code organization implements consistent, independent random suites *for each thread*. Now, in the absence of a one-to-one mapping of tasks to threads, thread safety is not so obvious.

Indeed, let us now imagine that N tasks are sharing the work of this Monte-Carlo computation. Three cases are possible:

- There are at least as many worker threads in the pool as tasks, and tasks are tied. In this case, nothing is wrong, each task is uniquely mapped to a thread, and the code is thread-safe. Results are reproducible.
- Tasks are tied, but there are fewer worker threads than tasks. There is therefore no unique mapping between threads and tasks, as some threads will execute more than one single task. In this case, *different tasks will be accessing the same threadprivate variable*. Thread safety is broken, because the results will depend on the particular way in which tasks are scheduled.
- Tasks are untied. Even if there are more threads than tasks, thread safety cannot be guaranteed if there is other activity in the parallel region that may force the suspension of tasks.

In all these cases, the code will always run, but thread safety is broken. Therefore, we come to the same conclusion as before: threadprivate storage should be used with care in the presence of explicit tasks. For the particular problem discussed here, the solution of using local C++ objects as random number generators is better and fully thread-safe in all cases, because a consistent random number generator is available *per task, not per thread* and there is no thread-safety problem.

Notice that this discussion applies to any thread local storage utility, in any programming environment.

10.9 CANCELLATION OF PARALLEL CONSTRUCTS

OpenMP 4.0 incorporates a new service enabling the cancellation of parallel constructs. This is a very useful extension of OpenMP. An example was proposed in Chapter 3, simulating a database search, which demonstrated the interest of canceling thread activities using a thread cancellation service incorporated in the SPool utility. In this example, a team of worker threads is launched to concurrently explore different sectors of a data set, and the first one that finds the target data terminates gracefully after forcing the termination of the other members of the team. The same strategy can be used, for example, to cancel a parallel job if an error occurs.

OpenMP 4.0 introduces a new feature, focused on the cancellation of a parallel treatment. This service, easy to use, is based on two directives: one to request the cancellation, and the other to insert checks to detect if a cancellation has been requested.

10.9.1 CANCEL DIRECTIVE

This is a standalone directive, with the following form:

```
...
#pragma omp cancel [construct-type] [if(expression)]
...
```

LISTING 10.29

Cancel directive

This directive must specify the type of parallel construct (parallel, sections, for, taskgroup) whose cancellation is requested. When this directive is encountered, the cancellation of the innermost enclosing region of the type requested is activated. An optional if(scalar-expression) clause is possible, in which case the cancellation request is ignored if the scalar expression evaluates to false.

The cancel directive is operational only if the *cancel-var* ICV is true, otherwise it is ignored. This ICV is set by the OMP_CANCELLATION environment variable, and a call to the omp_get_cancellation() library function returns its value. However, there is no way to modify it at runtime. Therefore, codes activating the cancellation service must necessarily run with OMP_CANCELLATION set to true.

When a thread hits a cancel directive, it signals to the runtime system that the cancellation request must be implemented on the other tasks involved in the target parallel construct and terminates the current task.

10.9.2 CHECKING FOR CANCELLATION REQUESTS

This is, again, a standalone directive, with the following form:

```
...
#pragma omp cancellation point [construct-type]
...
```

LISTING 10.30

Cancel directive

When cancellation is enabled, threads check in all cases for cancellation requests at all implicit or explicit barriers. This directive introduces additional user-defined points where cancellation requests are checked. When a thread encounters one of these points, it checks for eventual cancellation activation by a cancel request. If this is the case, the thread continues execution at the end of the canceled parallel construct in the way we discuss next.

It is interesting to observe that in the OpenMP cancellation mechanism it is the parallel tasks, not the running threads, that are canceled. Consider, for example, the cancellation of a taskgroup, where a task driving this construct waits for the termination of all its descendants. The task that encounters the "cancel taskgroup" construct jumps to its termination point. Any other task that would normally run to completion, runs until a cancellation point is reached and then it jumps to the end of its taskgroup region (i.e., it terminates). Finally, any task that has not begun execution is discarded, which implies its completion. An example of taskgroup cancellation will soon follow.

When a parallel construct is canceled, the master thread resumes execution at the end of the canceled region after a cancellation point is encountered. Any explicit tasks that may have been created by a task construct and their descendants are canceled according to the taskgroup semantics discussed above.

In the OpenMP environment, programmers are responsible for the correct management of the resources allocated to the parallel tasks. If a task is canceled while holding a locked mutex, the mutex will remain locked and nobody else will be able to lock it again. In C++, it is possible to make use of the scoped locking utilities proposed by C++11 or TBB to avoid this problem, because a canceled task terminates normally, and the mutex is automatically released. The Pthreads thread cancellation service has special interfaces to enforce automatic restitution of resources to the system in the C language context.

The examples that follow reconsider the database search example of Chapter 3 in the OpenMP 4.0 context. The first one, in source file DbOmp4-A.C, is exactly the example already discussed in Chapter 3, but now using the parallel region cancellation mechanism. In the second example, in source file DbOmp4-B.C, the same code is reorganized by using a taskgroup construct instead of a parallel region, and the cancellation of the taskgroup construct is demonstrated.

10.9.3 CANCELING A PARALLEL REGION

As in Chapter 3, a parallel region is launched where tasks keep calling a local random number generator trying to get a value equal to a given target value, with a precision EPS. The first task that hits the target cancels the parallel region. Here is the listing of the task function executed by the worker threads:

```
const double EPS = 0.00000001;
const double target = 0.58248921;
Data D;

// The workers thread function
// - - - - - - - - - - - - - --
void worker_fct()
    {
    double d;
    int rank = omp_get_thread_num();
    Rand R(999*(rank+1));
    std::cout << "\n Thread " << rank << " starts" << std::endl;

    while(1)        // infinite loop
       {
       #pragma omp cancellation point parallel    // check for cancellation
       d = R.draw();
       if(fabs(d-target)<EPS)
          {
          D.d = d;
          D.rank = rank;
          #pragma omp cancel parallel
          }
       }
    }
```

LISTING 10.31

DbOmp4-A.C

Tasks enter an infinite loop in which they first check if a cancellation has been requested. Then, they get a random number from the generator. If the target is found, the task writes the search result in a global structure D and cancels the parallel region.

Example 18.A: DbOmp4-A.C

To compile, run make dbomp4-a. The number of threads is read from the command line (the default is 2).

10.9.4 CANCELING A TASKGROUP REGION

Next, the previous computation is reformulated by using explicit, dynamically generated tasks rather than the implicit tasks associated with a parallel region. The basic idea is to recursively generate a set of tasks that perform the database search. One initial task is launched inside a parallel region that spawns two child tasks and terminates. The child tasks will in turn spawn two children each and terminate, and so on, until the recursive task generation process comes to an end. The final tasks execute the database search code. To control the task generation process, an integer deepness is read from the command line, which determines the number of recursive task generation steps performed before the actual computation starts. Here is the listing of the recursive task function used in this example:

```cpp
const double EPS = 0.00000001;
const double target = 0.58248921;
Data D;
SafeCounter SC;
int    deepness;

void task_fct(int deep)
    {
    int rank;
    double d;
    rank = SC.Next();
    std::cout << "\n Task " << rank << " starts" << std::endl;

    if(deep < deepness)
        {
        // launch two child tasks
        #pragma omp task
        task_fct(deep+1);
        #pragma omp task
        task_fct(deep+1);
        }
    else
        {
        Rand R(999*rank);
        // perform the search
        while(1)
            {
            #pragma omp cancellation point
            d = R.draw();
            if(fabs(d-target)<EPS)
                {
                D.d = d;
```

```
            D.rank = rank;
            #pragma omp cancel taskgroup
            }
        }
    }
}
```

LISTING 10.32

DbOmp4-B.C: the task function

Note the following issues in the task function above:

- The task function receives as argument an integer deep.
- If deep<deepness, the task terminates after spawning two child tasks with argument (deep+1).
- If deep==deepness, the search is performed, after creating a local random number generator with a task-dependent initial seed based on the task rank.
- Since we need to identify *tasks, not threads*, a unique rank value for each task is obtained from our SafeCounter utility.
- The while loop that performs the search is identical to the one used before in a parallel region, except that the cancellation protocol refers now to a taskgroup.

The listing below shows the way the parallel computation is launched from the main() function:

```
int main(int argc, char **argv)
    {
    int nTh;

    // get number of threads and deepness from command line:
    // - - - - - - - - - - - - - - - - - - - - - - - - - - -
    nTh = 2;
    deepness = 2;
    if(argc==2) nTh = atoi(argv[1]);
    if(argc==3)
        {
        nTh = atoi(argv[1]);
        deepness = atoi(argv[2]);
        }

    omp_set_num_threads(nTh);
    #pragma omp parallel
        {
        #pragma omp single
            {
            #pragma omp taskgroup
                {
                #pragma omp task
                task_fct(0);
```

Continued

```
                }
            }
        }

    std::cout << "\n Thread " << D.rank << " found value "
              << D.d << std::endl;
    return 0;
    }
```

LISTING 10.33

DbOmp4-B.C: the main function

First, default values for the number of threads and the deepness are defined. They can be overridden from the command line, by passing either the number of threads or the number of threads and the deepness. Then, a parallel region is established with the given number of threads in order to set up a pool of worker threads to execute the dynamically generated tasks that will follow.

Because of the single directive that follows, the parallel region activates only one initial implicit task, which executes the single block code. This initial implicit task immediately encounters a taskgroup code block. Inside the taskgroup region, it then launches an initial explicit task with deep argument equal to 0, and waits at the end of the taskgroup region for the termination of all the generated descendant tasks.

Example 18.B: DbOmp4-B.C

To compile, run make dbomp4-b. The number of threads as well as the deepness can be modified from the command line (the default is 2 threads and deepness 2). By increasing the deepness, the number of active tasks is increased.

10.10 OFFLOADING CODE BLOCKS TO ACCELERATORS

One of the major evolutions in OpenMP 4.0 is support for heterogeneous computing platforms involving different computational devices: standard CPUs, associated with GPU accelerators or co-processors like the Intel Xeon Phi platform. The OpenMP code is compiled and launched in a host device, and a set of device directives can be used to offload code blocks for execution in partner accelerator devices. These directives manage both the offloading of executable code blocks as well as the necessary data movements between the host and external devices. Given the current impact of accelerator devices in high-performance computing, this is a major evolutionary step taken by OpenMP.

At the time of writing this utility is not yet fully implemented in the available 4.0 compliant compilers (like GNU 4.9). The code is correctly compiled, but the directives are ignored and the code blocks are executed in the host device. The discussion that follows describes the basic code offloading protocols adopted by OpenMP 4.0, which are simple, compact, and easy to understand. Their impact will be determined by the quality of the implementations, when they do become available.

10.10.1 TARGET CONSTRUCT

The fundamental offloading tool in OpenMP 4.0 is the target directive that specifies that the following code block must be executed in a target device characterized by an integer identifier.

```
pragma omp target device(int) map(map-type : list) if(scalar expression)
    {
    // structured block, executed in
    // target device
    }
```

LISTING 10.34

Target directive

This directive accepts three optional clauses: device, map, if, and it operates as follows:

- The executable code block is executed in the device identified by the device clause. If the clause is absent and there are no available devices, the executable code block is executed in the host.
- Note that *there is no concurrent activity between host and target devices*: the encountering task in the host *waits* for the device to complete the target region. This is likely to evolve in future OpenMP releases.
- If the scalar expression passed in the if clause evaluates to false, the executable code block is executed in the host device. This clause operates as all the similar if clauses in OpenMP: a logical test that maintains or invalidates the directive.
- The map clause controls the way data is moved between host and target device. This clause is useful to reduce to a strict minimum the data transfers between target and host. It involves a type of map action and a list of associated data items that are to be mapped according to the declared map type. Map types are:
  - *alloc*: on entry to the target region each list item has an undefined initial value. In other words, they can be directly allocated in the target device.
  - *to*: each list element is initialized in the target device with the original item value in the host. Data is copied from host to target.
    from: on exit from the target device, list item values are assigned to the original items in the host. Data is copied from target to host.
  - *tofrom*: data is copied from host to target on entry, and from target to host on exit. This is the default behavior in the absence of a map directive: any variable referenced in a target construct that is not declared in the construct is implicitly treated as if it had appeared in a map clause with a tofrom map type.

It may happen that, in a target section, different data items need to be mapped with different map types. In this case, several different map directives may be used in the target construct. The official examples document [29] proposes a few clear examples for mapping arrays.

10.10.2 TARGET DATA CONSTRUCT

In the target construct previously discussed, a map strategy must be specified every time a computational kernel is offloaded for execution in a given target device. Always focused on minimizing as much as possible data transfers between host and target device, OpenMP offers the possibility of mapping data in a way that can be useful to several successive computational kernel offloads. This is the purpose of the target data directive, which only defines a map action without an accompanying executable code offload.

```
pragma omp target data device(int) map(map—type : list) if(scalar expr)
   {
   // structured block starts execution in host
   ...
   #pragma omp target [clauses]
      {
      // offloaded to target
      }
   // back to host
   ..
   #pragma omp target [clauses]
      {
      // offloaded to target
      }
   ...
   }
```

LISTING 10.35

Target data directive

As shown in the listing above, all the target data directive does is prepare a data environment in the target device. Then, the encountering task continues execution of the code block that follows in the host, until different target directives that force an offload are encountered. These directives benefit from the target data environment set up by the enclosing target data region. They may include additional map clauses referencing data items not included in the enclosing target data directive. Again, the official examples document proposes a few clear examples of the target data construct [29].

10.10.3 TEAMS AND DISTRIBUTE CONSTRUCTS

Another new feature of OpenMP 4.0 is the teams construct, which launches several independent teams of worker threads. This is a kind of super-parallel directive encapsulating several parallel directives executing autonomous parallel treatments. The operation of the teams directive activating four teams of three threads each is shown in Figure 10.15, and the code is given in the listing below.

```
...
#pragma omp teams num_teams(4) thread_limit(3)
   {
   // code here is executed only by the master threads of each team
   ...
   ...
   #pragma omp parallel
      {
      // code here is executed by the full team
      ..
      }
   }
...
```

LISTING 10.36

Operation of the teams directive

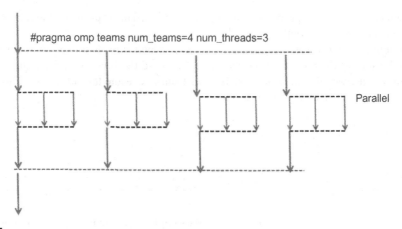

#pragma omp teams num_teams=4 num_threads=3

Parallel

FIGURE 10.15

Operation of the teams construct.

Other clauses used to establish parallel regions—default, private, firstprivate, shared, reduction—are also accepted. This is natural, because the teams directive can be seen as establishing a parallel region for the master threads of each team. The number of teams can be selected by the nteams clause, or by library function calls, as was the case for the number of threads. The official documentation states that the number of threads in each team is implementation defined, but in all cases it is less or equal to the value specified in the thread_limit clause. Threads now have two identifiers: the team number (starting from 0) and the traditional thread number, which identifies the threads inside a team. When the code enters the teams region, all the teams are ready, *but only the master threads of each team (thread number 0) start the execution of the encountered code.* The remaining threads in each team are activated only when the team encounters a parallel region.

A few comments are in order here. First, observe that the teams construct in not very different from the operation of nested parallel regions, apart from the fact that the number of threads in each team is not strictly enforced. The main advantage is that the number of nested parallel regions that are activated is dynamic in the sense that it is not hard-coded, but determined by a clause or a library function call. This provides an additional flexibility that is welcomed in the context in which this construct is expected to be used.

The second observation is that the teams construct is only accepted in offloaded code. Indeed, it is rejected by the compiler if it is not inside a target region. And, if the target code is executed in the host, the teams construct is ignored. This will probably evolve in future OpenMP releases, but, for the time being, the teams construct is only a way of adapting a given parallel treatment to the memory hierarchy of accelerator devices.

Accelerator devices dispose of hundreds of cores, with a hierarchical organization. Cores are grouped in medium-sized SMP blocks sharing a common memory for the block. Then, there is an overall global memory shared by all blocks. Memory accesses are more efficient if they are restricted to the innermost shared block memory. Adjusting the thread activity and the data placement to this memory organization is the real purpose of the teams construct. This is probably the reason the number of threads in each team is not strictly enforced.

Finally, OpenMP 4.0 also has the distribute directive, which spreads the iterations of one or more loops across the master threads of all the teams that execute the binding teams region. The master threads can in turn activate the intrinsic tasks of their team to execute the subset of iterations they are in charge of. Here is the syntax of the construct:

```
...
#pragma omp distribute [clauses]
for-loops
...
```

LISTING 10.37

Distribute directive

Here follows an example, taken from the official examples document [29], showing how the computation of the scalar product of two vectors is offloaded to an accelerator device using all the directives discussed so far. The function dotprod() receives as arguments the pointers B and C to the vector arrays, the vector size N, the size block_size of the vector chunks that will be distributed across the different teams, the number of teams, and the number of threads per team.

```
double dotprod(double *B, double *C, int N, int block_size,
               int n_teams, int block_threads)
   {
   double sum = 0;
   int i, i0;

   #pragma omp target map(to; B[0,N], C[0,N])
      {
      #pragma omp teams num_teams(nteams) thread_limit(block_threads)  \
                   reduction(+:sum)
         {
         // - - - - - - - - - - - - - - - - - - - - - -
         // This is the master threads code; sum is now
         // a private variable inside each master thread.
         // - - - - - - - - - - - - - - - - - - - - - - -
         #pragma omp distribute
         for(i0=0; i0<N; i0 += block_size)
            {
            // - - - - - - - - - - - - - - -
            // launch the parallel sections
            // - - - - - - - - - - - - - - -
            #pragma omp parallel for reduction(+=:sum)
            for(i=i0; i<min(i0+block_size, N); i++)
              sum += B[i]*C[i];
            }
```

```
        }        // teams terminate here
    }            // end of offloaded code
  return sum;
  }
```

LISTING 10.38

Scalar product of two vectors

Let us carefully examine this code:

- The function enters a target region in which the target vectors are mapped to the target device. The variable sum has, by default, a map tofrom: its final result will be recovered on the host at the end of the target region.
- Inside the target region, teams of worker threads are created, and the master threads are activated. The variable sum becomes by default a private variable inside each master thread. The reduction clause in the teams directive performs the reduction of the local values of src in each master thread.
- Next, in the master threads code, there is an external for loop with a block_size stride. If there was no distribute directive, all the master threads would execute the complete loop. However, because of the distribute directive, successive iterations of the loop are executed by successive master threads in round-robin order.
- Finally, each master thread activates the partner worker threads in the team with a parallel for directive. Again, the sum variable becomes a private variable for each worker thread, and the inner reduction clause accumulates the workers' partial results into the sum variable of the corresponding master thread.
- On exit from the target region, the final value of sum is mapped to the host.

The previous discussion summarizes the basic concepts in OpenMP 4.0 dealing with the offloading of code blocks to target accelerator devices. The devices API also proposed several ways of merging directives (e.g., target and teams can be merged in target teams).

10.11 THREAD AFFINITY

Thread affinity issues deal with the mapping of threads to cores as a means of optimizing access to a hierarchical memory system. If, for example, two threads are systematically accessing the same shared data, obviously it pays in memory performance to have them running in two cores that share the same L2 cache. Likewise, we know that accesses to the main memory are not uniform, because a given core may have different access times for different main memory banks. Performance benefits can be obtained if some kind of *togetherness* can be established between the core executing a thread and the data set the thread is acting upon, by placing the data in memory banks close to the executing core.

How is this togetherness with main memory data implemented by the operating system? Let us consider the memory allocation of a long vector. The fact that the whole vector is a unique consecutive array in logical memory does not necessarily mean it is a unique, consecutive array in physical memory.

The virtual memory systems of current computing platforms map blocks of contiguous logical memory addresses (called *memory pages*) to physical memory pages in different banks. And the way this mapping distributes consecutive pages in different banks can be decided by the operating system at execution time, using the traditional first touch policy. In the case of the long vector mentioned earlier, the operating system will try to map the page that contains the vector to a memory bank close to the core that first accesses it for initialization. If the vector spreads over several logical pages, and different cores initialize different sections of the vector, the operating system will do its best to establish a map from logical to physical memory addresses in such a way that different subarrays sit as close as possible to the cores that first initialized them. In this way, data can be distributed in main memory so as to optimize the nonuniform access times.

Notice, however, that paying attention to data placement in memory or to optimized usage of shared L2 caches is useless if threads can migrate across cores, which is in fact a very common event. When threads are preempted and moved to a blocked state, either because they are over-committed sharing CPU cycles or because an idle wait has been requested by the programmer, there is absolutely no guarantee that, when rescheduled, they will be run by the same core. *By default, threads are not tied to cores.*

> The OpenMP thread affinity interface guides the placement of specific threads on specific cores. Threads remain tied to the core they are placed on the whole duration of their lifetime.

This guidance is implemented by:

- An environment variable, OMP_PLACES, describing the hardware configuration on which the threads must be placed, and providing the value for the place_partition_var ICV. This description is performed once at the start of the code execution, and there is no way of retrieving the place_partition_var value, or of modifying it.
- When a parallel region starts, a description is provided of the placement policy requested for the worker threads. This placement strategy is defined by the OMP_PROC_BIND environment variable, which sets the value of the bind_var ICV. Its values can be retrieved by a library function call. However, the default thread affinity strategy established by the bind_var ICV can be overridden in a particular parallel region by the proc_bind clause associated with the parallel directive that defines the placement policy for the threads activated in the corresponding parallel region.
- The proc_bind() clause receives one policy placement argument that can be either scatter, close, or master.
- Placement policies applies to *threads* executing the initial implicit tasks in the parallel section. This means we know where the initial implicit tasks are executed. But there is absolutely no placement policy for the eventual explicit tasks generated in the parallel region, other than the fact that they will be executed by the placed threads in the worker team.

Figure 10.16 shows an SMP node made out of two quadricore sockets allocated to the application, which we will use to illustrate the thread placement policies. There are in this case eight cores available altogether. We assume that hyperthreading is enabled in the architecture, and that each core runs two hardware threads (a common situation today). In this context, parallel sections will be launched with different numbers of threads and different placement policies. The first step is to set the environment variable that describes the hardware configuration. This is done as follows:

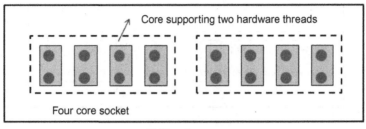

FIGURE 10.16

SMP node based on two quadricore sockets.

- We start by numbering—from 0 to 15—the hardware threads that can be run in the configuration.
- Cores are described by a sequence of integers corresponding to the associated hardware threads, enclosed in braces. For example, successive cores in the configuration of Figure 10.9 can be described as {0,1}, {2,3}, ..., {14, 15}.
- An initial_index : length : stride notation can also be used to describe sequences of integers. If the stride is omitted, it is 1 by default. Therefore, the cores in the configuration of Figure 10.9 can also be described as {0:2}, {2:2}, {4:2}, ..., {14:2}, the stride being 1 by default in this case.
- The initial_value : length : stride notation can also be extended to describe sequences of cores: the initial value is a core rather than an integer, and we add the number of cores that follow and the stride for the first hardware thread in each core. Therefore, the whole sequence of cores in Figure 10.9 can be described as {0:2}:8:2. This means the initial core repeats 8 times, with the initial hardware thread label jumping with stride 2.

With these conventions, the OMP_PLACES environment variable is defined by a string that describes the hardware configuration in the way described above. Here are three equivalent ways of setting OMP_PLACES for the example of Figure 10.9:

```
export OMP_PLACES = "{0,1},{2,3},{4,5},{6,7},{8,9},{10,11},{12,13},{14,15}"
export OMP_PLACES = "{0:2},{2:2},{4:2},{6:2},{8:2},{10:2},{12:2},{14:2}"
export OMP_PLACES = "{0:2}:8:2"
```

LISTING 10.39

Setting OMP_PLACES

It is important to keep in mind that for OpenMP places are cores. There are therefore eight places in the example above. Hyperthreading, if enabled, will be activated when more than one thread is placed in a core. When several threads are placed in the same core, the system will use time slicing to run them.

10.11.1 SPREAD POLICY

Let us consider that the spread policy is applied to T threads on P places, and that T<=P. The runtime system constructs P'=P/T subpartitions and places a thread in each one of them. Figure 10.17

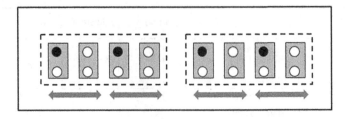

➤ : Subpartitions associated to the placed (black) threads

FIGURE 10.17

Scatter policy for four (black) threads.

shows how four threads are spread on the eight places corresponding to the configuration shown in Figure 10.16.

It is very important to keep in mind that the four subpartitions have a real role in the operation of the system, besides defining the placement of the threads. Indeed, these subpartitions correspond to the places available if the threads launch in turn a nested parallel region. In other words: for the placed threads, the subpartition becomes the new value of the placement description environment variable.

Placement policies are chosen to fit the application profile. If we are running an SPMD computation in which each thread acts mainly on its own data subset, with limited access to nonproprietary data items, then the spread policy is appropriate. Leaving four unused places in each subpartition may be very useful if, later on, the initial tasks launch a nested parallel section that access the parent data set, because they will be sharing the L2 cache.

You can easily guess what happens in some special cases. If we have five threads rather than four in our example, the size P' of the subpartitions is reduced to only one core. There will be five threads placed in consecutive cores, and eventual nested parallel regions will be run in the core of the master thread. If we have more threads than cores—let us say, ten threads—then the partition size is by default 1, threads are placed in consecutive cores and then wrap around eight, so that two cores will run two threads.

10.11.2 CLOSE POLICY

Let us first consider the case T<=P. When the number of threads does not exceed the number of cores, threads are placed in successive cores. But there is a difference with the spread policy: in this case, there are no subpartitions. The threads in the team will inherit the same, initial value of the place-partition ICV.

When T>P, the first T/P threads of the team (including the master thread) execute on the parent's place. The next T/P threads execute in the next place in the place partition, and so on, with wraparound. Let us go back to our example: consider that we are placing 16 threads, and that the parent thread that launches the parallel section is running on the place 2. Threads 0 and 1 run at place 3, threads 2 and 3 run at place 3, and so on. After the wraparound, threads 13 and 14 run at place 0 and threads 15 and 16 run at the place 1.

The close strategy is optimal if the eight threads are all acting on the *same data set*. In this case, because of their placement inside a unique socket, the share the L2 cache and access to shared data is optimized.

10.11.3 MASTER POLICY

In the master strategy, all threads in the parallel region execute at the place of the parent thread. Note that this will activate hyperthreading if enabled, but in our example time slicing will operate if more than two threads are placed according to this policy. The master policy may be useful if the parallel region launches occasionally subsidiary explicit tasks that must share data with the master thread.

10.11.4 HOW TO ACTIVATE HYPERTHREADING

In the example discussed above, you will notice that hyperthreading is activated, in the spread or close policies, only if threads are over-committed. In general-purpose computing platforms, hyperthreading helps to optimize CPU resources, but it is not a major performance factor. However, in highly specialized computing platforms (like IBM Blue Gene of Intel Xeon Phi) hyperthreading is mandatory to achieve optimal core performance.

Let us go back to our example, with four threads running on the hardware architecture of Figure 10.9. The question is, how can we force the placement of two threads per core? The solution is in the definition of the OMP_PLACES environment variable: we are not obliged to initialize it with all the places available in the hardware configuration. We just define a place partition of only two cores:

```
export OMP_PLACES = "{0:2}:2:2"
```

LISTING 10.40

Restricted number of cores

This solves the problem of enforcing hyperthreading for our four threads. Notice, however, that this place partition remains valid for the whole code, and cannot be changed.

10.12 VECTORIZATION

A very important extension of OpenMP 4.0 is the SIMD construct, which enforces vectorization of loops. As discussed in Chapter 1, vectorization is a parallelization technique designed to boost *single core performance* by implementing a single instruction, multiple data (SIMD) paradigm in which basic arithmetic instructions operate on vector chunks rather than on individual operands. Vectorization comes after multithreading in the parallelization hierarchy. The parallel for directive distributes different loop subranges across different worker threads. Inside each parallel task, the simd directive instructs the compiler to use native SIMD instructions to compute the assigned loop. Modern architectures rely on vectorization to deliver a substantial fraction of the full core performance.

10.12.1 SIMD DIRECTIVE

The simd directive has the following form.

```
...
#pragma omp simd [clauses]
for-loops
...
```

LISTING 10.41

Simd directive

In the vector addition example discussed in Chapter 3, the simd directive can be applied as follows:

```
...
double A[VECIZE], B[VECSIZE], C[VECSIZE];
...
#pragma omp parallel for
  #pragma omp simd
    for(int n=0; n<VECSIZE; n++) C[n] = A[n] + B[n];
...
```

LISTING 10.42

Adding two vectors

In this case, the parallel for directive will first split the vector operation in subranges allocated to different threads, and then every worker thread will compute its vector addition using the native SIMD instructions that concurrently add small chunks of vectors, the chunk size depending on the number of SIMD lanes available in the underlying hardware. In this case, one should observe a double speedup, coming from multithreading and vectorization. In an ideal case, this speedup is the number of threads times the number of SIMD lanes.

Simd clauses

Here are the clauses accepted by the simd directive:

- private, lastprivate, and reduction operate in the same way as in the multithreaded parallel constructs.
- collapse(n) also operates in the same way. The n nested for loops that follow the directive are merged in a larger, unique iteration space, which is next computed using native SIMD instructions. The order of iterations in the merged iteration space is determined by the natural order implied by the sequential execution of the loops.
- safelen(n): This clause indicates that two iterations executed concurrently cannot have a distance larger than n in the logical iteration space. Each concurrent iteration is executed by a different SIMD lane. In other words, the optimal value of n is the number of SIMD lanes available in the underlying hardware.
- linear(*argument list: constant linear step*): This is a modified form of the firstprivate clause used in other parallel constructs (and not available here). Logical iterations of the SIMD loop are numbered $(0, \ldots, N)$. Variables in the argument list are initialized to a value depending on the loop iteration, equal to the value when the simd directive is encountered, plus the iteration number times the linear step.

- aligned(*argument list: alignment*): The argument list contains arrays or pointers to arrays in C-C++. Variables in the argument list are aligned to the number of bytes expressed in the alignment parameter. This parameter is optional, and its default value is implementation dependent.

Notice that OpenMP 4.0 accepts pointers to arrays by default, leaving to the programmer the responsibility of guaranteeing the absence of *aliasing*, that is, the fact that the pointers involved in the vectorized algorithm are pointing to nonoverlapping memory blocks. Aliasing is a traditional problem with pointers and vectorization. Consider the following vector computation of A += B:

```
...
double A[VECIZE];
double *B;
...
// initialize B: this is aliasing
B = A-1;
...
#pragma omp simd
for(int n=1; n<VECSIZE; n++) A[n] += B[n];
...
```

LISTING 10.43

Aliasing issue

The simple appearance of the for loop above is deceptive: this loop cannot be vectorized. Because B[n]=A[n-1], there is a *data dependency* among consecutive iterations. To compute an iteration, we need the result of the previous one. If we insist in vectorizing the loop, we get a result that is not what we want. In OpenMP 4.0, it is the programmer's responsibility to make sure this does not happen. Intel compilers, instead, will not vectorize a loop involving pointers if it is not totally clear that there is no aliasing. Programmers dispose of directives to tell the compiler that vector dependencies can be safely ignored. We will come back to this point in Chapters 13 and 14.

10.12.2 DECLARE SIMD DIRECTIVE

Let us assume we want to vectorize the following loop corresponding to a map parallel pattern, where the same operation is applied to all the elements of a collection:

```
...
double *B;
double *A;
...
#pragma omp simd
for(int n=0; n<VECSIZE; n++) A[n] = f(B[n]);
...
```

LISTING 10.44

Need for SIMD functions

where $f(x)$ if a function that takes, in this example, a double argument, and returns a double. The declare simd directive enables the creation of SIMD versions of a given function the compiler can use to process multiple arguments—sitting on different SIMD lanes—with a single invocation. There are no restrictions on the signature of the function, which can take several arguments.

```
...
#pragma omp declare simd [clauses]
function declaration or definition

...
// In example above:
// - - - - - - - -
#pragma omp declare simd
double f(double x);
```

LISTING 10.45

Declare simd directive

Declare simd clauses
Here are the clauses accepted by the declare simd directive. They provide information about the nature of the function arguments and the way they have to be initialized, as well as information on the way the function is intended to be used.

- simdlen(n): number of concurrent arguments in the function.
- uniform(argument list): the data items in the list have an invariant value for all concurrent executions of the SIMD loop.
- linear(argument list: linear step): the data items in the argument list must be initialized, when the function is invoked, in the way already discussed for the simd directive.
- aligned(argument list: alignment): operates as in the simd directive.
- inbranch: the function will always be called from inside a conditional statement.
- notinbranch: the function will never be called from inside a conditional statement.

Further discussion of the usage of vectorization directives will be developed in Chapters 13 and 14.

10.13 ANNEX: SafeCounter UTILITY CLASS

In a thread-centric environment, worker threads have an intrinsic integer identifier, that is, *rank*. In a task-centric environment, it is often useful to have similar integer identifier *for tasks*. This can be handled by passing a rank value to each task when they are created. But another useful alternative is to dispose of a thread-safe global counter returning successive integer values to tasks asking for the next integer. In this way, each task disposes of a unique integer identifier. This is the purpose of the SafeCounter class, which obviously encapsulates a mutex-protected integer counter. Here is its public interface:

SafeCounter PUBLIC INTERFACE

SafeCounter()

- Constructor.
- Creates a SafeCounter object. Internal integer is 0.

- ˜ SafeCounter()

  - Destructor.
  - Destroys the SafeCounter object.

  int Next()

  - Returns the next integer.
  - The first returned integer is 1.

  void Reset()

  - Resets the internal counter for a new use.

CHAPTER

INTEL THREADING BUILDING BLOCKS

11

11.1 OVERVIEW

The Intel Threading Building Blocks (TBB) library has been available in the public domain as open source software for several years. Easily installed and configured (see Annex A), this library outfits C++ for multicore parallelism. It comprises complete documentation and a substantial number of code examples illustrating its most important and subtle aspects:

- The documentation accompanying the release is accessed from /docs/index.hmtl in the TBB installation directory. It contains complete information on all the library components.
- The examples accompanying the release are in the /examples directory.
- The online documentation at the website. Three links are particularly important: the Reference Manual [17], the tutorial TBB Getting Started [32], and the User Guide [33]. All contain detailed discussions and examples of the TBB operation, with the Reference Manual including complete information on all library components.
- James Reinders book, *Intel Threading Building Blocks*, develops a complete and pedagogical presentation the TBB parallel programming environment [34].
- The *Structured Parallel Programming* book by M. McCool, A. D. Robison and J. Reinders [35] discusses in detail the way TBB—as well as OpenMP and Cilk Plus [1]—cope with a large variety of parallel contexts. This book, an advanced tutorial in parallel programming, contains detailed and useful information on the way these three programming environments operate.

The core of the library is a task-centric programming and execution environment, implementing, as it is also the case of OpenMP and Cilk Plus, refined strategies for task scheduling. The TBB shared memory programming API operates at three levels of abstraction:

- At the highest level, TBB provides powerful STL-like algorithms, implemented as C++ template functions or classes, that drive parallel processing while hiding from the programmer the underlying operation of the thread-pool scheduler. Many of these high-level algorithms adopt a fork-join strategy at the task level, designed to optimize load balance and cache memory efficiency. They can be seen as automatic parallelization engines that extend in several directions the functionality provided by the parallel for directive in OpenMP.
- At the next level, TBB enables limited direct access to the task scheduler. A simple and elegant task scheduler API is provided by the task_group class, enabling immediate access to the most basic scheduler services. To put it in a nutshell, this programming interface is a simplified handle

to a set of features integrating the taskwait (tasks waiting for direct children) and taskgroup (tasks waiting for all descendants) synchronization constructs, as well as the task group cancellation features, discussed in the previous chapter on OpenMP.

- Finally, there is the complete task scheduler API, providing access to several additional features, the most important being the establishment of hierarchical relations among tasks to drive the operation of the task scheduler. A preview of this feature was given when discussing the depend task clause in OpenMP. Indeed, OpenMP 4.0 has recently incorporated hierarchical task dependency features. In TBB, the hierarchical relations among tasks are at the core of the scheduler architecture.

The first two levels of abstraction: high-level STL like parallel algorithms and the simplified access to the task scheduler are the subject of this chapter. More advanced use of the TBB task scheduler is discussed in Chapter 16.

TBB is at the core of Intel's Parallel Suite. Intel also proposes a C++ extension called Cilk Plus [1] with an underlying execution model close to TBB. By just adding three new keywords to C++, Cilk Plus provides a simple way of expressing potential parallelism. However, Cilk Plus requires compiler support, while TBB runs as a standalone library. We will come back to this point later in this chapter.

11.2 TBB CONTENT

In addition to the task management algorithms and APIs, TBB proposes several other standalone utilities worth keeping in mind, even if other environments (OpenMP, native threads) are adopted to manage threads. In fact, the TBB documentation underlines the fact that TBB has been designed to interoperate with OpenMP and the native threads libraries. A few interoperability examples have already been given in previous chapters, and a few others will come in the following ones.

Here is a summary of the additional utilities provided by the TBB programming environment:

- Concurrent containers with built-in thread safety (discussed in Chapter 5).
- Mutual exclusion tools: several types of mutex and scoped locks, discussed in Chapter 5, as well as the tbb::atomic<T> class, discussed in Chapter 8.
- Improved memory allocation tools that replace the standard memory allocation routines (malloc-free, new-delete) by more efficient and scalable allocators that enhance memory allocation performance in a multithreaded environment.
- Thread local storage: TBB proposes two classes to implement thread local storage:

    - combinable
    - enumerable_thread_specific (discussed in Chapter 4)

- TBB also proposes an implementation of an important subset of the C++11 multithreading library, basically, the thread management features in the <std::thread> header, and the event synchronization features in the <condition_variable> header.

A few comments on the status of these utilities may be useful at this point. Remember that the TBB programming model is a *task-centric* model, where the mapping of tasks to threads is not one-to-one. Some of these standalone utilities (concurrent containers, mutual exclusion, memory allocation routines) can safely be used in the TBB task-centric environment, but others (thread local storage, C++11 event synchronization) must be handled with care. It has already been emphasized in previous chapters that thread local storage *does not* guarantee thread safety if the task to thread mapping is not one-to-one, and that synchronization constructs based on condition variables synchronize threads, not tasks. In a task-centric environment, event synchronization must be implemented directly on tasks by using the depend clause in OpenMP or the hierarchical relations among TBB tasks to be discussed in Chapter 16.

In fact, TBB introduced from the start its own mutual exclusion tools, however, *no explicit tools for event synchronization were available for a long time* simply because they are not compatible with the task-centric programming model. Thread-centric utilities (thread local storage, C++11 synchronization) were added later to enlarge the programmer's toolbox, and they are, indeed, useful. An example is given in Chapter 14, in which an application with a substantial amount of barrier contention exhibits very poor parallel scalability when Pthreads barriers are used. An alternative, more efficient barrier algorithm is available, involving atomic variables and thread local storage [25]. However, Pthreads not having atomic utilities, the algorithm is implemented in the TBarrier class—discussed in Chapter 9— using tbb::atomic<T> and one of the TBB thread local storage classes. When this new barrier class is used, the performance of the application significantly improves.

The rest of this chapter reviews in detail the high-level TBB parallel algorithms. Simple examples of their operation are presented, and Chapters 13–15 discuss the TBB implementation of several complete parallel applications. Chapter 16 explores the details of the TBB scheduler. Our intention is to enable readers to develop clear insights on the code development options that TBB provides, and on its complementary role with respect to other programming environments.

11.2.1 HIGH-LEVEL ALGORITHMS

Here is a list of the high-level parallel algorithms proposed by TBB. They are all referenced in the "Algorithms" topic in the Reference Guide [17].

Parallel_for: The parallel_for algorithm is used to implement a map operation, in which a specific action described by a function object is applied to a collection of elements in a container. This algorithm implements a *divide and conquer* strategy that performs a recursive domain decomposition of the data set.

Parallel_reduce: When, in addition, reductions must be performed in order to collect partial results from each parallel task—as was the case in most the data parallel examples we discussed— the parallel_reduce algorithm is required. Again, this algorithm automatically performs the domain decomposition of the data set, setting up an elegant way of performing internally the reduction operations.

Parallel_scan: This algorithm is more subtle. Its relevance can be usefully illustrated with a simple example. Consider the computation of the following loop:

```
int X[N];
...
for(int n=1; n<N, ++n)
    X[n] += X[n-1];
```

LISTING 11.1

Using the parallel_scan algorithm.

in which the value of each vector component X[n] is replaced by the accumulated sum of all the previous components. This scan operation for the addition operation exhibits a data dependency that blocks its immediate parallel computation. However, *if the operation is associative*, it is possible to organize the computation by performing two passes over the data set. In this case, the amount of computational work is increased, but the work can be done in parallel. The TBB tutorial has a very clear description of the way this algorithm operates. The parallel scan concept can be extended to any associative operation that has an identity element (like the 0 for addition).

Parallel_for_each: A simpler version of parallel_for, which avoids the weaponry required to automatically perform a recursive domain decomposition.

Parallel_do: This algorithm performs, like parallel_for, a parallel iteration over a range, with an additional feature: the possibility of optionally adding more work at each iteration, with the help of the auxiliary class parallel_do_feeder.

Parallel_invoke. Receives as arguments pointers to functions (up to 10 functions) that are invoked in parallel.

Parallel_sort: Parallel generalization of the sort algorithms proposed by the STL, discussed in Chapter 10.

Pipeline This algorithm is a class template. A producer-consumer synchronization is implemented via a data item (a token) that runs along the pipeline. It is discussed in detail in Chapter 15.

There is substantial added value provided by the TBB parallel algorithms. The implicit work-sharing strategies are somewhat more diversified than the ones proposed in OpenMP.

11.3 TBB INITIALIZATION

All the TBB software components are defined in the tbb namespace. As usual in C++, this namespace may be directly accessible as if it was the global namespace with the traditional using namespace tbb declaration, and we will assume in what follows that this is always the case. Otherwise, the tbb:: scope must be explicitly used in all TBB components in the program. The TBB documentation on this topic is in the "Task Scheduler" topic in the Reference Guide [17].

The initialization of the library requires the creation of a tbb::task_scheduler_init object in the application. The constructor of this object performs the required initialization, and the destructor shuts down the task scheduler. Moreover, the switch -ltbb—in Linux—or /link tbb.lib—in Windows—must be included in the linker in order to access the runtime TBB library.

The task scheduler constructor accepts three possible arguments that specify the number of threads managed by the scheduler:

- task_scheduler_init::automatic. In this case the number of threads in the application is equal to the number of cores available in the computer platform running the program.
- A *positive integer* defining the number of threads to use.
- task_scheduler_init::deferred. In this case, the task scheduler is created but the number of threads is not defined. It is specified later on with a call to task_scheduler_init::initialize (nThreads).

The very simple example TbbInit.C exhibits these initialization options by getting them from the command line and printing a message indicating the initialization strategy adopted. With no command line arguments, the initialization is automatic. Otherwise, the number of threads is read from the command line. If the value 0 is passed, the initialization is deferred and the code prompts the user later to specify a positive number for the number of worker threads. Listing 11.2 illustrates how the task scheduler object TS—the object name is obviously arbitrary—is created following these rules.

```
#include <tbb/task\_scheduler\_init.h>
...
using namespace tbb;
...
int main(int argc, char **argv)
   {
   int nTh;
   ...
   if(argc==1)
      task_scheduler_init TS(
          task_scheduler_init:: automatic);
   else if(argc==2)
      {
      nTh = strtol(argv[1], 0, 0);
      if(nTh==0)
        task_scheduler_init TS(
            task_scheduler_init:: deferred);
      else   task_scheduler_init TS(nTh);
      }
   ...
   return 0;
   }
```

LISTING 11.2

TbbInit.C source code.

The task scheduler TS does not need to be explicitly destroyed because the destructor is implicitly called when the object goes out of scope, in this case at the end of main(). Explicit destruction in the middle of the program is also possible [34].

Example 1: TbbInit.C

To compile, run make tbbinit. The initialization option is passed from the command line (see text above).

The automatic initialization is quite interesting. One of the purposes of TBB is to simplify as much as possible the deployment and operation of multicore applications. With this initialization, the application adapts automatically to the number of cores available in the computing platform. This means that an application that has been running on a dual-core laptop will immediately run *as such, with no change and no recompilation*, on a four-core laptop. However, when running applications on large shared memory multicore servers accessed by many users, one may not want to run on all the available cores in the SMP platform.

11.4 OPERATION OF THE HIGH-LEVEL ALGORITHMS

TBB relies on C++ semantics to propose an elegant way of handling domain decomposition and work-sharing utilities in a multithreaded environment. In the OpenMP parallel for directive, work sharing is controlled by the number of threads available in the parallel region. In some of the TBB algorithms, work-sharing is not directly related to the number of threads in the pool. Rather, it is handled recursively. The initial workload submitted to the pool is repeatedly split until a predefined minimal workload—called granularity—is reached. Another difference with OpenMP is that the work sharing algorithms are not restricted to loops. In fact, the abstractions involved in these algorithms enable at least parallel_for and parallel_reduce to handle contexts in which the domain decomposition is applied to a data set *of any kind*, as long as it is splittable. Some examples will soon follow.

Here is the declaration of the parallel_for template function. The declarations of the two other functions are identical to this one:

```
template<typename Range, typename Body>
void parallel_for(const Range& R, const Body& T);
```

LISTING 11.3

Parallel_for signature.

The template parameters Range and Body (names are arbitrary) refer to two different types—C++ classes—that are required to have very precise interfaces—i.e., specific public member functions—internally used by the algorithms:

- A Range type models an *iteration space*, namely, a data set that defines the iteration range of a loop, or, more generally, the space in which the algorithm operates. A fundamental requirement for this data type is that *it must be splittable*. The split operation on an object of type Range divides the object into two equal parts: one assigned to the original object (that shrinks to half its initial size) and the remaining one assigned to a new object.
- A Body type that encapsulates the algorithm operation on a Range object. This is, in fact, a function object class that defines the task function to be executed by threads on an arbitrary range that ultimately results from successive splittings of the original range passed to the function.

These two data types are defined by their behavior, namely, by the public member functions they implement. They may be considered as the answer to *callbacks* coming from the template function, who is asking the client code for the additional information needed to adapt its operation to the problem at hand. The same situation is encountered when a C library function asks for a pointer to a function to specify behavior. In fact, the Body class is really a function object, which is the C++ generalization of a pointer to a function (see more details on function objects in Annex B).

11.4.1 INTEGER RANGE EXAMPLE

Listing 11.4—from source file IntRange.h—is an example of a Range type that models an integer range employed in a standard for loop. This example is presented only for pedagogical purposes; TBB has built-in template range classes for integer ranges. The member functions defined in this example are the ones required by the algorithms using it. In modeling a range, additional functions may be defined if needed for code clarity and efficiency, but the ones defined here must in all cases be implemented.

```cpp
#include <tbb/tbb_stddef.h>

class IntRange
    {
    private:
     int Beg;
     int End;
     int granularity;

    public:
     IntRange( int b, int e, int g)
        {
        Beg = b;
        End = e;
        if(b>e)
           {
           Beg = e;
           End = b;
           }
        granularity = (End-Beg)/g;
        }

    IntRange(IntRange\& R, tbb::split)
        {
        int middle = (R.End+R.Beg)/2;
        End = middle;
        Beg = R.Beg;
        granularity = R.granularity;
        R.Beg = middle;
        }

    bool empty() const
        { return (End == Beg); }

    bool is_divisible() const
        { return (End >(Beg+granularity+1)); }

    int begin() const
```

Continued

```
        { return Beg; }

    int end() const
        { return End; }
    };
```

LISTING 11.4

IntRange Range class.

This class describes the half-open integer range [Beg, End) using the STL conventions: Beg is the first index in the range, and End is the next after last index, not in the range. Remember that this STL convention is motivated by a convenient way of writing loops.

Besides Beg and End, the IntRange class incorporates another private data member, granularity. The range object will be split into two equal parts if its size is bigger than the granularity. When a range object is first constructed, its granularity is determined by an integer value n, as a fraction (End-Beg)/n of the initial size. The constructor of IntRange objects take three arguments: the limits of the initial range and the integer n that determines the requested granularity.

Other functions called by the algorithm are:

- empty(), which returns true if the range is empty.
- is_divisible(), which returns true if the range size is bigger than the granularity.
- begin() and end(), which return the limits of the range object.

Notice the const qualifier in the definition of these functions. This means they are read-only and do not modify the private data in the object. Never forget these qualifiers; C++ is very touchy when it comes to type checking, and const qualifiers are part of the data or member function types. The TBB library will not accept the range class if they are omitted.

The only subtle point in this class is the *split constructor* IntRange(IntRange& R, tbb::split) listed above, which receives as arguments a reference to an existing IntRange object, as well as a split data item, defined in the include file tbb/tbb_stddef.h. The introduction of this split data item—which is in fact an empty object—is just a trick that serves no other purpose than allowing the compiler to distinguish the split constructor from the standard copy constructor. Indeed, any C++ class has a copy constructor, either explicit provided by the programmer or implicitly defined by the compiler, that constructs a clone of the initial object passed as argument. In our case, the copy constructor has signature IntRange(IntRange& R), and it is present even if there is no explicit definition. Therefore, a spurious extra argument is needed in order to distinguish the split constructor—which also takes a reference to a target object—from the copy constructor.

The action of the split constructor is shown in Figure 11.1. It constructs a new range object with half of the target object range, and then it shrinks the target object range to the other half, so that we end up with two half-range objects. Notice that the split data item is ignored in the function body.

11.4.2 BUILT-IN TBB RANGE CLASSES

The class IntRange listed above is meant as an example to show the content of the Range concept; it will be used it in the examples that follow to show that it effectively works. TBB has two built-in template classes for integer-like ranges that are more sophisticated than the example above and

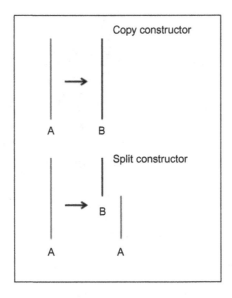

FIGURE 11.1

Difference between the copy and split constructors.

that should be adopted in real applications (see the "Algorithms->Range Concept" in the Reference Guide [17]).

- blocked_range<T> is a half-open range of elements of type T that can be recursively split. The type T must satisfy some requirements that include integer types, pointers, and STL random access iterators.
- blocked_range2d<T> is a two-dimensional extension of the previous class.

These classes follow the strategy outlined in the example, but they have several additional features. They trigger error-checking assertions when the debug version of the TBB library is used. Furthermore, the granularity argument in the constructor can be avoided when working with versions of the algorithms in which the granularity is dynamically determined from the task scheduler operation.

11.4.3 **FORK-JOIN PARALLEL PATTERN**

The basic task-scheduling mechanism implemented by the TBB divide and conquer algorithms for managing the recursive splitting of the initial range is the fork-join construct shown in Figure 11.2: an initial task 1 spawns a child task 2 and the control flow continues in the parent task 3. The parent task that triggers the fork will be referred to as the *continuation* task. At some point, tasks 2 and 3 are synchronized: the parent (continuation) task waits for its child. Then, the parent task continues execution as task 4. This process is recursive: child or continuation tasks can in turn trigger new, nested fork-join constructs.

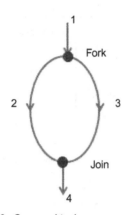

3 : Spawned task
2 : Continuation task

FIGURE 11.2

Fork-join construct.

The *Structured Parallel Programming* book [35] has a full chapter devoted to the fork-join parallel pattern, with a detailed discussion of its implementation not only in TBB but also in Cilk Plus [1]—based on new keywords added to the language—or in OpenMP—based on task spawn and wait. In all cases, *task stealing* is the mechanism that transforms the potential parallelism—expressed by the task spawn operation—into a mandatory parallel processing where other worker threads take over the task execution. The operation of the TBB scheduler will be described in detail in Chapter 16. For the time being, it is sufficient to know that.:

- Waiting tasks are queued waiting for execution. Each thread has its own, proprietary queue.
- A spawned task is queued in the proprietary queue of the thread executing the parent task.
- When a thread is idle and looks for a next task to execute, the first place it looks at is its proprietary queue.
- When a thread is idle and its proprietary queue is empty, *it steals a task from another, non-proprietary, queue* (Figure 11.3).

In this approach, real parallel processing is activated by task stealing, when an idle thread having no input from its own queue chooses a victim task from another queue. It is interesting to observe that TBB and Cilk Plus have different behavior in what concerns task stealing, due to different design options. In TBB, it is the child task that is queued and eventually stolen if there is a sufficient number of worker threads, and the parent task continues normal execution by its executing thread. In Cilk Plus, it is the *continuation* task that is queued and eventually stolen, and the thread that was initially executing the parent task starts executing the spawned task. To understand the difference, imagine that there is only one worker thread. In this case, the Cilk Plus choice corresponds to standard sequential execution of a function call: the spawned task is executed first, and the parent task suspends execution until the function returns. In TBB, it is the other way around: the spawned task will be dequeued and executed only when the continuation task reaches the join synchronization point. There are, of course,

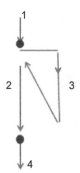
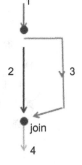

No task stealing:
running thread executes 3 and
then 2, no join operation

Available thread steals
and executes task 2. A join
operation is performed.

FIGURE 11.3

Modes of execution of the fork-join pattern.

different pros and cons for these different choices. The Cilk++ strategy is more difficult to implement, and requires compiler support. The TBB library, instead, works with any compiler.

Chapter 8 of the *Structured Parallel Programming* book [35] has a very detailed discussion of the fork-join pattern and of many of its implications in specific parallel contexts: the fact that task stealing in Cilk Plus and TBB effectively balance the fork-join workload, or the major impact on stack space usage of the different strategies: *continuation stealing* in Clik Plus, *child stealing* in TBB. It turns out that the Cilk Plus strategy can guarantee a more efficient stack space usage.

The fork-join strategy using the Body and Range types is also used in the parallel_reduce and parallel_scan algorithms. The Range classes are all the same, but the Body classes have specific requirements for each algorithm.

11.5 SIMPLE PARALLEL_FOR EXAMPLE

The parallel_for algorithm can be used when the parallel treatment involves the activation of a number of embarrassingly parallel tasks with no communications among them. In the example that follows, the initial range will be successively split into a series of nested fork-join constructs until sub-ranges reaches the limits tolerated by the given granularity, as sketched in Figure 11.4. Ultimately, we are left with a number N of equal size sub-ranges, so that N tasks are executed by the thread pool. Notice that N is in all cases a power of 2. It is obvious that if N is bigger than the number of threads in the pool, task stealing will be rare and in most cases the same thread will take care of different sub-ranges. As expected, too small a granularity induces excessive fork-join overhead and conspires again overall performance.

FIGURE 11.4

Nested fork-join patterns in the parallel-for algorithm.

A simple example of a Body class is provided by the parallel computation of the following loop:

```
double *X, *Y;
// X and Y, size N, are initialized to random values
for(int n=0; n!=N; ++n) X[n] += Y[n];
```

LISTING 11.5

Simple parallel loop.

i.e., adding vector Y to vector X. The range class in this example is the IntRange class defined above. Here is the Body function object class for this problem:

```
class AddVectorBody
   {
   private:
    double *X, *Y;

   public:
    AddVectorBody(double *x, double *y) : X(x), Y(y) {}
    void operator() (const IntRange& R) const
       {
       for(size_t n=R.begin(); n!=R.end(); ++n)
          X[n] += Y[n];
       }
   };
```

LISTING 11.6

Body class for the parallel loop.

This class has, as private internal data, the addresses of the vectors to be added. The constructor just initializes the two vector pointers. As in any C++ class, there is also in this case an (implicit) copy constructor that constructs a new object by copying the object data, i.e., the vector pointers.

This class is a *function object class*, because it overloads as a member function the function call operator operator(). This allows the client code using the class to instantiate an object with an arbitrary name, and use this object name as a function name, as shown in Listing 11.7.

```
double *X, *Y;
IntRange(0, 1000, 4);          // construct range
AddVectorBody my_name1(X, Y);  // define function object
...
my_name1(R);                   // calls operator()(R)
...
```

LISTING 11.7

Using function objects.

Given the importance of function objects and the extensive usage made by TBB, Annex B summarizes their properties and discusses their interest and relevance. A very important point to keep in mind is that function objects are objects, and that consequently they can be copied. As explained in Annex B, they generalize the concept of function pointer, enabling additional features that pointers to functions do not have.

The body of the operator() function defines the task to be performed by the executing worker thread on an arbitrary range, ultimately resulting from successive splittings of the initial range. *Notice the* const *specifier in the definition of this function*: this means the private function object data cannot be modified by this member function. This const specifier is required by the library, and in the present case it just guarantees it is not possible for the operator() function to modify the vector pointers. The reason is easy to understand: the algorithm will use the copy constructor to produce copies of this function object to handle them to different threads, and it is necessary to guarantee that they all refer to the same vectors. This, however, does not prevent each operator() function from modifying *the data the pointers point to*, as it is the case of the vector X, whose components are indeed updated by this function.

11.5.1 PARALLEL_FOR OPERATION

The parallel_for algorithm implements the fork-join strategy discussed above. Obviously, the worker threads that receive a task to execute start by taking a look at the range. If it is splittable, the executing thread splits it into two halves, spawns a child task dealing with one half of the range, and continues the execution of the continuation task dealing with the other half. If the range is not splittable, the initial task is executed.

Let us go back to Figure 11.3 that shows the two options available to the scheduler to execute a fork-join pattern. When the range is splittable, the following actions take place:

- The executing thread puts *the child task* in its own task queue and starts executing the continuation task.
- The child task can eventually be stolen by another idle thread in the pool.
- If no other idle thread in the pool steals the queued child task, the current thread dequeues and executes it when the continuation task terminates.
- If another available thread steals the child task, *it gets a copy of the parent thread task function object* and uses it to concurrently execute the task. The copy of the function object is obtained, naturally, from the copy constructor.

- A synchronization between parent and child operates at the joining point. Notice the thread that continues with the execution of task 4 is in all cases the same as the one executing initially task 1. We will come back to this point in Chapter 16.

11.5.2 FULL ADDVECTOR.C EXAMPLE

The full example is in file AddVector.C. The code reads the input data from the addvec.dat file: vector size N, number of threads nTh and granularity Gr. It initializes the vector components to uniform random values in [0, 1]. Then it applies the parallel_for algorithm as described below:

```
int main(int argc, char **argv)
    {
    double *X, *Y;

    // allocate and initialize X, Y
    // read from file N, nTh, Gr
    // print X[0], X[N/2], Y[0], Y[N/2]

    task_scheduler_init init(nTh);
    IntRange R(0, N, Gr);
    AddVectorBody B(X, Y);
    parallel_for(R, B);

    // print again X[0] and X[N/2], to check
    return 0;
    }
```

LISTING 11.8

AddVec.C main function.

Example 2: AddVec.C

To compile, run make addvec. Input data is read from file addvec.dat.

11.6 PARALLEL REDUCE OPERATION AND EXAMPLES

Embarrassingly parallel contexts are rare because most of the time some kind of information must be passed or shared among tasks. Common concurrency contexts require, for example, the accumulation or the comparison of partial results provided by each task. This is the kind of concurrency pattern handled by the parallel_reduce algorithm.

The parallel_reduce algorithm also accepts Range and Body types as template parameters. The Range classes model range values and do not require any further modification. The Body classes, however, *are not* the same as the classes for parallel_for algorithm. Indeed, the necessity of performing a reduction operation requires a more refined implementation of the fork-join pattern, and some modifications are introduced to the way the body classes operate.

11.6.1 FIRST EXAMPLE: RECURSIVE AREA COMPUTATION

In order to exhibit the flexibility of the TBB basic algorithms, a first example of the usage of the parallel_reduce algorithm is proposed next, adapted to a problem *not dealing with a parallel loop*, namely, the parallel computation of the area under a curve already discussed several times in previous chapters.

The first issue is to define a new Range class on which the algorithm operates. This is done in the include file RealRange.h. This class models a splittable interval on the real axis. It has exactly the same member functions described in the listing of IntRange.h, but with very mild modifications adapting it to a real interval rather than a succession of integer values.

The structure of the body class, defined in Listing 11.9, has a few modifications required by the necessity of managing the partial results computed by each task. This class refers to the auxiliary library function area() discussed in previous chapters that receives as arguments the limits of integration and a pointer to the function to be integrated, and returns the area with a given precision.

```
double area(double a, double b, double(*func)(double));

class AreaBody
    {
    private:
     double (*fct)(double x);

    public:
     double partial_area;

     AreaBody(double (*F)(double)) : fct(F),
                    partial_area(0.0) {}

     AreaBody(AreaBody& A, split) : fct(A.fct),
                    partial_area(0.0) {}

     void operator() (const RealRange& R)
        {
        partial_area += area(R.begin(), R.end(), fct);
        // print debug message
        }

     void join(const AreaBody& A)
        {
        partial_area += A.partial_area;
        }
    };
```

LISTING 11.9

Body class for the area computation.

New, public data items

This class stores a private pointer to the function to be integrated, and a public double partial_area that is used to store partial results. The ordinary constructor initializes the function pointer to the passed argument value, and also initializes partial_area to 0. Each task function object constructed and used by the algorithm carries internally this information. Notice that in this class the member operator() function no longer has the const qualifier, because this function updates the partial_area value. Notice also that partial_area is public, simply because ultimately it will be read by the client code in order to retrieve the final result of the reduction.

Additional, "split" constructor

The body class listed above has the standard constructor that initializes the function pointer, as well as the initial value of partial_area. There is also the implicit copy constructor built by the compiler that copies to a new object the values of all the private and public data items stored in the target object.

A new, additional constructor, different from the copy constructor, is needed by the algorithm. The split argument is, again, just a trick to distinguish it from the copy constructor. However, in this case, the "split" constructor does not split anything: it just constructs a new function object from a reference to another target function object. The main point is that the new object is not an exact clone of the original one: the split constructor *does not copy* the value stored in partial_area; rather, it reinitializes this data item to the original value 0.

This new constructor is needed for a correct management of partial results. If there is no task stealing and the same thread is handling different ranges, the partial area results keep accumulating in the partial_area value, which is what we want. However, when there is task stealing, the new stealing thread gets a copy of the function object of the parent task. But it may happen that the parent task function object has *already* in its guts partial area results, because it has already explored other sub-ranges. If the normal copy constructor was used to provide a copy to the new thread, this new thread would inherit these values, and this is definitely not what the algorithm wants, because previous values are already taken into account in the parent thread that continues execution of the continuation task. The new thread must start with a brand new function object with no memory of previous partial results. This is exactly what the split constructor does: it creates a new function object where only the function pointer is copied from the target, the partial_area data item taking the standard initialization values. The split constructor therefore erases the memory of previous computations by other threads stored in partial_area, and starts a brand new strand of partial reductions.

The conclusion is: the split constructor is used every time there is task stealing, to create a brand new concurrent task executed by another thread. If there is no task stealing the split constructor is not called: it is the original parent thread that takes over the continuation task after executing the spawned task.

Performing the reduction

At this point, the new join() member function enters the game. It is called by the algorithm to close a fork-join construct with task stealing, to perform the reduction between partial results held by the spawned and continuation tasks. Obviously, calls to join() are paired to calls to the split constructor at a task stealing fork-point.

The caller task adds to its internal partial_area value the value provided by the target task. At the end of the algorithm operation, all the copies of the task function object are destroyed, and the initial task function object passed to the algorithm holds internally the final result of the reduction.

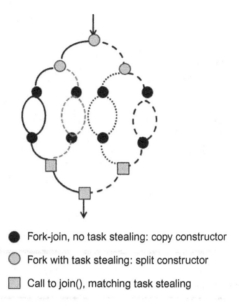

● Fork-join, no task stealing: copy constructor

○ Fork with task stealing: split constructor

▢ Call to join(), matching task stealing

FIGURE 11.5

Nested fork-join patterns in the parallel-reduce algorithm.

This mechanism is illustrated in Figure 11.5. Flow lines with different structure correspond to different threads (4 threads in the figure). Fork vertices with lines of different structure indicate that task stealing has taken place. These vertices are paired with join vertices where the join() function is called. Some conclusions:

- The reduction is performed partly by the operator() function, and partly by the join() function.
- The operator() function accumulates the sub-range result to whatever previous result is already stored in the partial_area data. This guarantees that the reduction is correctly performed in the case of sequential execution without task stealing. Finally, the join() function performs the reduction at a joining point of two threads.

The code for the main() function is given below. There is nothing new besides the occurrence of the new Range object.

```
// Function to be integrated
double FCT(double x)
    {
    return sin(x);
    }

// The main function
int main(int argc, char **argv)
    {
```

Continued

```
double a, b;
int nTh, Gr;
InputData();
task_scheduler_init init(nTh);

RealRange R(a, b, Gr);
AreaBody B(FCT);
parallel_reduce(R, B);
std::cout << "\nFinal result for area is : "
          << B.partial_area << std::endl;
return 0;
}
```

LISTING 11.10

PRarea.C main function.

Example 3: PRarea.C

To compile, run make prarea. Input data is read from file prarea.dat.

11.6.2 SECOND EXAMPLE: LOOKING FOR A MINIMUM VALUE

The next example elaborates on an advanced example proposed in the "Parallelizing simple loops" section of the TBB User Guide [33]: the parallel search of the minimum value of a vector, as well as its vector index (location). This example is interesting because it shows in a different way the flexibility of the parallel_reduce algorithm. Only some minor modifications have been added here, showing in detail the way the algorithm operates. A size N vector X of doubles is initialized with uniform random values in the interval [-100, 100]. The purpose of the example is to search for the value and location of the minimum value.

The range class used here is the IntRange class introduced before. The body class stores a private copy of the target vector address, and two public data items: a double minval to store minimum values and an int minindex to store the corresponding vector index. In this example, the operator() function scans the given range looking for the minimum value, but the values of minval and minindex are updated only if minval beats the stored value holding partial results from previous sub-ranges. And, as shown in Listing 11.11, the join() function only updates its minval and minindex values if minval is beaten by the value held by the target task.

```
class MinvalBody
   {
   private:
    double *V;

   public:
    double minval;
    int    minindex;
   ...
```

```
void join(const MinvalBody& A)
    {
    if(A.minval < minval)
        {
        minval = A.minval;
        minindex = A.minindex;
        }
    }
};
```

LISTING 11.11

Partial listing of body class for the minimum search.

Complete MinVal.C example

The source file for the example we are currently discussing is MinVal.C. To compile, run make minval. The main() function is listed below:

```
int main(int argc, char **argv)
    {
    int N, Gr, nTh;
    Rand Rd(999);

    InputData();
    V = new double[N];  // allocate and initialize
    for(int n=0; n<N; ++n)
        V[n] = 200.0 * Rd.draw() - 100.0;

    task_scheduler_init init(nTh);
    IntRange R(0, N, Gr);
    MinvalBody B(V);
    parallel_reduce(R, B);
    std::cout << "\nOverall minimum value is : "
              << B.minval << "  at index " << B.minindex
              << std::endl;
    return 0;
    }
```

LISTING 11.12

MinVal.C main function.

The InputData() is the same as the one of the previous example: it reads N, nTh, and Gr from the file minval.dat. Then, it allocates and initializes the target vector V.

Notice that B is the initial function object, which, when passed to the algorithm, will start exploring the initial full range R. As we will soon verify, this function object will be copied at a fork with stealing, and then the copies will be destroyed at the corresponding join() call. At the end of the day, when the function returns, the initial function object B holds the final values of minval and minindex, which are read and printed to stdout.

Example 4: MinVal.C

To compile, run make minval. The input data is read from file minval.dat.

In the real code, some debug features are introduced in the body class in order to track the operation of the algorithm. A MinVal function object has another private internal integer variable called body_id that identifies its different split copies. When the initial function object B is created, its identity is 1. Each time the split constructor builds a new function object, it increases *a thread-safe counter* and assigns the next integer value to the new object. A thread-safe counter is provided by a simple class defined in the include file SafeCounter.h. In this way, all the different "split" copies of the initial function object created by the algorithm are identified by a unique integer rank.

Each time the operator() function is called, a debug message is printed before exit. This message includes:

- The identity of the function body that called the function.
- The identity of the executing thread. This is done by inserting a call to the appropriate library function (see Chapter 3).
- The sub-range that was explored, and the final values of minval and minindex.

The code employs a global mutex to serialize access to stdout, in order to print clear messages from each thread. Here are some typical program outputs with N=10000 and nTh=2. First, let us consider a granularity Gr=2:

```
– – – – – – – – – – – – – – – – – – – – – – – – – – – –
Body ID : 1,  thread = 3077502720
Interval ( 5000, 10000 ), minval = −99.8998, at index 5184

Body ID : 2,  thread = 3076447040
Interval ( 0, 5000 ), minval = −99.9748, at index 4619

Overall minimum value is : −99.9748  at index 4619
– – – – – – – – – – – – – – – – – – – – – – – – – – – – – –
```

This is clearly a straightforward fork-join with task stealing: there are two different function bodies executed by two different threads. The function body 1 split the initial interval and started execution of the spawned task covering the half-range [500, 1000). A second thread with a new function body executes the continuation task covering the half-range [0, 500). If a granularity Gr=4 is chosen next, the nested fork-join constructs are organized as follows:

```
– – – – – – – – – – – – – – – – – – – – – – – – – – – –
Body ID : 1,  thread = 3078035200
Interval ( 7500, 10000 ), minval = −99.7154, at index 8499

Body ID : 2,  thread = 3076979520
Interval ( 2500, 5000 ), minval = −99.9748, at index 4619

Body ID : 1,  thread = 3078035200
Interval ( 5000, 7500 ), minval = −99.8998, at index 5184
```

```
Body ID : 2,  thread = 3076979520
Interval ( 0, 2500 ), minval = −99.9748, at index 4619

Overall minimum value is : −99.9748  at index 4619
- - - - - - - - - - - - - - - - - - - - - - - - - - - - - -
```

This output corresponds to the same initial fork-join with task stealing seen before, followed by a nested fork-join naturally without task stealing because there no other available idle threads. One thread uses body 1 to scan the interval [7500, 10000) followed by [5000, 7500), and the other thread uses body 2 to scan the interval [2500, 5000) followed by [0, 2500). Notice also that the second message sent by body 2 looks weird because it reports a minimum at an index 4519, which is not in the range being scanned. This is simply because body 2 has already found a minimum in another range—look at the previous message—and this value is still valid in the current sub-range. This is exactly the behavior we expect.

To be fair, I must admit that this execution mode is not exactly reproducible. It happens sometimes that there is no task stealing at all and that the execution is purely sequential with only one function body. Very occasionally you may find three function bodies resulting from two stealings, probably because one thread completed its two sectors very quickly and came back to steal the second sector of the other thread.

11.7 PARALLEL_FOR_EACH ALGORITHM

The parallel_for_each algorithm is a simplified version of the parallel_for algorithm, without the dynamic domain decomposition driven by a Range class. This algorithm is very useful when a specific action—a map operation—must be performed in consecutive elements stored in an arbitrary container. Its signature is given in Listing 11.13.

```
#include <tbb/parallel_fo_each.h>
...
template<typename Iter, typename Body>
void parallel_for_each(Iter first, Iter last, const Body& B);
```

LISTING 11.13

Parallel_for_each algorithm signature.

This algorithm operates as follows:

- Iter is an input iterator (iterator with reading capability) adapted to the target container.
- Body is a unary function object, which defines an operator() member function acting on container elements of type T, with the following signature:

    - void operator()(T& t) const

- The function object B defines an action on a container element. The template function above applies this action to all container elements in the half-open range [first, last).
- This action on the container range is done in parallel.
- The STL proposes an identical, sequential for_each() template function.

Notice that the Body class satisfies in this case the same requirements as the parallel_for body class, except that it acts on an individual container element, not on all elements in a range.

11.7.1 SIMPLE EXAMPLE: FOREACH.C

This example targets a STL std::vector<double> container, namely, a vector of doubles, of size 1000. The container elements are initialized to a uniform random number in [0, 1].

The action of the Body class is a map operation on the components of a vector of doubles, identical to the one used in the OpenMP example in Section 10.7: the Body function keeps calling a uniform random number generator and comparing with the element value, until the difference is smaller than a given precision. When this happens, the initial element value is replaced by the new, very close value. By increasing the precision, the amount of work done on each container element is increased.

As in the previous OpenMP example, there is a small subtlety in this code: the Body function object defines internally a local random number generator to perform its task. The parallel algorithm generates a different instance of the Body function object for each participating thread and, as in all the previous Monte Carlo examples, each task disposes of a *different* random number sequence. Therefore, different instances of the Body class must dispose of different initial seeds. Look at the sources to see how, as in the OpenMP example, this issue is handled using the SafeCounter auxiliary class.

Example 5: for_each.C

To compile, run make feach. This is the sequential code, using the STL for_each algorithm.

Example 6: ForEach.C

To compile, run make foreach. This is the parallel code, using the TBB parallel algorithm.

This example runs on two threads. For large precision (large amount of work done on each container element), the parallel speedup is quite acceptable.

11.8 PARALLEL_DO ALGORITHM

In its simplest form, this algorithm has the same signature as parallel_for_each in Listing 11.13: a function object Body class acts on all the elements of a container within the range defined by the two iterators. However, this algorithm is used when extra work must be optionally added. The TBB release has a complete example in the /examples/parallel_do directory—the parallel traversal of a directed acyclic graph—adapted to OpenMP and extensively discussed in Section 10.7.2.

Remember that in this example the starting point, after the construction of the graph, was the construction of a vector container including all the Cell pointers referring to root cells, with no ancestors. In the TBB implementation, the parallel_do algorithm starts by updating all the elements of this container. In updating a cell, reference counts of successors are decreased, and some may reach 0, in which case the successor is recursively updated. The capability of adding new work is used to handle this recursive update. Readers are encouraged to look at the TBB example, easily accessible after all the explanations of the code provided in Section 10.7.2.

11.9 PARALLEL_INVOKE ALGORITHM

This algorithm invokes simultaneously several functions, and runs them in parallel. When the parallel_invoke template function returns, all the functions have completed their operation. The algorithm incorporates a set of overloaded functions that run between two and ten functions in parallel. Here are the template functions signatures:

```
#include <tbb/parallel_invoke.h>
...
template<typename Func0, typename Func1>
void parallel\_invoke(const Func0& f0, const Func1& f1);
...
template<typename Func0, ... ,typename Func9>
void parallel\_invoke(const Func0& f0, ... const Func9& f9);
```

LISTING 11.14

Parallel_invoke algorithm signature.

Notice that:

- Func0, Func1, ...Func9 template arguments are function objects that define an operator function with the following signature:

   - void operator()() const;

- As in the STL, pointers to functions can be used instead of function objects.

If pointers to functions are used, they must point to functions that receive no argument. According to the documentation, possible return values are ignored.

11.9.1 SIMPLE EXAMPLE: INVOKE.C

This example re-examines the Monte Carlo computation of π that was encountered several times in the past. Here, the idea is simple: a function is written that implements the Monte Carlo algorithm for a given number N of events, and returns in a global variable the acceptance count. If this is done for several functions simultaneously, the main() function can obtain an improved value of π by using the total number of events and the total acceptance.

Look at the source file Invoke.C. Two threads are used in this example. A unique function object class is defined that implements the Monte Carlo algorithm. Then, two different instances of this class provide the two independent function to be passed to parallel_invoke.

One of the problems of this algorithm is the impossibility of passing or returning values from functions. Notice, however, how the function object approach shortcuts this limitation in an elegant way. Parameters needed for the function operation can be passed via the object constructor, and return values can be stored internally as *public* data items to be read at the end of the day by the client code.

This is yet another simple example of the fact that function objects are *smart pointers to functions* that enable the existence of several identical functions with personalized internal state.

This example shows the same subtlety discussed before. The function object operator() function declares a local random number generator, and we want different instances of this class to use different random number sequences. Once again, the SafeCounter auxiliary class is used for this purpose.

Example 7: Invoke.C

To compile, run make invoke. This version of the code uses function objects.

Running the example, a very correct parallel speedup is observed, comparable to the other versions of this code. We have provided, for comparison, another version of the code using ordinary functions, to emphasize the fact that in this case one two different functions need to be defined, doing the same thing.

Example 8: InvokeFct.C

To compile, run make invokefct. This version of the code uses ordinary functions.

11.10 HIGH-LEVEL SCHEDULER PROGRAMMING INTERFACE

TBB has recently introduced the task_group class that implements an elegant and easy-to-use programming interface to the task scheduler. The official documentation is in the "Task Group" link of the Reference Guide [17].

This class can be used to run a group of tasks—which can be dynamically enlarged with new tasks once running—as a single, encapsulated parallel job. It implements the two basic synchronization patterns discussed for OpenMP tasks: waiting for direct children and waiting for all descendants. It also implements a task group cancellation utility, very much like the one discussed in the OpenMP environment.

The task_group class has two basic member functions: the run() member function that allocates and spawns a task, and the wait() member function that waits for the termination of all tasks previously spawned by the task_group object. It is important to keep in mind that this member function waits for all descendants, not just direct children. This section shows how this happens in detail, on the basis of the same examples already proposed in the OpenMP chapter.

11.10.1 DEFINING TASKS IN THE TASK_GROUP ENVIRONMENT

Tasks are in general defined in TBB as instances of a class derived from the basic task class, in which the execute() virtual function is defined. The specific derived task class must be defined, and objects instances of this class must be constructed and submitted for execution to the scheduler. This is what we will be doing in Chapter 16, when discussing the low-level scheduler API based on the task class.

This protocol has been enormously simplified in the task_group environment. In the first place, a task function is directly defined by a function object Func, which must provide the member functions listed below:

- Func::Func(const Func&): a copy constructor. If all the copy of the function object requires is copying data items, then the default copy constructor provided by the compiler is adequate.
- Func::~Func(): a destructor. Same comment as before.
- void Func::operator()() const: Task function executed by the function object.

In practice, all that is required is the definition of the constructor of the function object, as well as the operator() member function. Notice that whatever local data items in the parent task need to be captured by the new task must be passed via the constructor either by value or by reference. The operator() function itself receives no argument and returns void.

Once the function object class is defined, instances of this class must be allocated, to define a specific task. But the nice thing is that all these steps can be bypassed: the *lambda function syntax* for function objects discussed in Annex B enables the definition and allocation of function objects on the fly, at the place where they are needed. This leads, once the lambda syntax is understood, to very elegant and compact code.

11.10.2 TASK_GROUP CLASS

Here is the listing of the task_group class, defined in the tbb namespace:

```
class task\_group
   {
   public:
     task\_group();
     ~task\_group();

     template<typename Func>
     void run(const Func& f);          // spawn

     template<typename Func>
     void run_and_wait(const Func& f);  // spawn and wait

     task_group_status wait();          // wait for all

     bool is_cancelling();   // check if cancellation requested
     void cancel();          // request cancellation
   };
```

LISTING 11.15

Task_group class.

- The function run() receives a reference to a task function object. But the functor constructor, or a lambda expression, can equally well be passed. The examples in the next section show in detail how this works.

- The wait() function returns task_group_status, which is an enumeration with three symbolic values:
  - not_complete: not canceled, not all tasks in the group have completed.
  - complete: not canceled, all tasks in the group have completed.
  - canceled: task group received cancellation request.
- The function run_and_wait() is equivalent to run(); wait(); but guarantees that the task is run on the current thread.
- Two member functions, cancel() and is_cancelled(), enable programmers to cancel the operation of a group of tasks, in the way discussed below.

A few examples already encountered in the OpenMP context are discussed in the next section to show in detail how the task_group class monitors the execution of a group of tasks. Two important features will in particular be exhibited: the dynamic operation of task_group objects—tasks can be added when the group is already running—as well as the cancellation of a group of tasks.

The two cancellation member functions are very similar to the two OpenMP cancellation directives: requesting cancellation and checking if cancellation has been requested. But they work in a different way. In TBB, a task group object can be canceled at any time. If the cancellation request arrives before the tasks have been scheduled, they are not submitted for execution to the pool. On the other hand, the function is_cancelled() checks for cancellation and returns true of false, *but it does not cancel anything*. It is the programmer responsibility to implement the program logic that terminates a task when cancellation is requested.

11.11 TASK_GROUP EXAMPLES

The four examples developed in this section show in detail how function objects and lambda expressions are used to run and group of tasks, as well as various ways of using task_group objects to synchronize or cancel a group of tasks.

11.11.1 AREA COMPUTATION, WITH A FIXED NUMBER OF TASKS

The first example computes again the area of the function $4.0/(1 + x * x)$ in the interval [0, 1], whose value is π. This is done by activating Nth threads in the pool, and launching Ntk parallel tasks. The interval [0,1] is divided in Ntk sub-ranges of size 1.0/Ntk. Parallel tasks compute the area of each sub-range, and accumulate their partial results in a mutex protected global variable called result.

An orthodox approach is adopted in this case: a function object class AreaTask is explicitly defined, and its constructor is passed to the run() member function whenever a task is submitted for execution. Here is the listing of the source code, in file Tg1.C

```
double result;    // accumulates partial results
mutex  m;         // protects "result"
int    nTk, nTh;  // number of tasks and threads

double my_fct(double a);
double Area(double a, double b, double (*func)(double),
            double eps=EPSILON);
```

```
// Function object defining the task function
// - - - - - - - - - - - - - - - - - - -
class AreaTask
    {
    private:
     int rank;

    public:
     AreaTask (int n) : rank(n) {}

     void operator() () const
        {
        double a, b, res;
        a = rank*(1.0/nTk);
        b = (rank+1)*(1.0/nTk);
        res = Area(a, b, my_fct, EPSILON);
          {
          mutex::scoped_lock slock(m);
          result += res;
          }
        }
    };

// - - - - - - - - -
// The main function
// - - - - - - - - -
int main (int argc, char *argv[])
    {
    nTh = 2;
    nTk = 4;
    // Override the number of threads and/or the number
    // of tasks from the command line.

    task_scheduler_init init(nTh);
    // - - - - - - - - - - - - - - - - - -
    task_group tg;
    for(n=0; n<nTk; ++n) tg.run(AreaTask(n));
    tg.wait();
    // - - - - - - - - - - - - - - - - - -
    std::cout << "\n Area result is : " << result
              << std::endl;
    }
```

LISTING 11.16

Area computation, fixed number of tasks.

In Listing 11.16, the AreaTask constructor takes an integer argument, which is the rank of the sub-interval whose area is computed. The task function just computes the area by using our traditional Area() library function, and accumulates the partial result in the mutex-protected global variable result.

The main() function code is straightforward. After initialization, a task_group object local to main() is created and used to submit the Ntk tasks and wait for their termination.

Example 9: Tg1.C

To compile, run make tg1. This example spawn four tasks running on two threads. The number of threads and the number of tasks can be overridden from the command line.

11.11.2 AREA COMPUTATION, TASKS WAIT FOR CHILDREN

The next example deals with the recursive area computation in which tasks either compute the area of a sub-range and return the result to the parent task (if the sub-range is smaller than the granularity G), or they split their integration domain into two sub-domains, launch two child tasks, and wait for their return value. In this recursive algorithm, the only task synchronization required is spawning two child tasks and waiting for their termination. Therefore, each task that needs to do so defines its own, local task_group object and uses it to run the two child tasks and wait for their completion.

If the standard procedure of writing explicitly a function object class to define the task function was adopted, an AreaTask class should be defined, whose constructor takes three arguments: the limits [a, b] of the target sub-range, and a double *s pointing to an address in the parent stack where child tasks deposits the return value. In other words: a and b are captured by value, but s is captured by reference.

This is not, however, what is done in this case. Rather, a recursive function is defined to compute the area of a given range, and a lambda expression is used whenever this function needs to be transformed into a function object. Here is the listing of the code source for this example, in file Tg2.C.

```
int     nTh;        // number of threads
double  G;          // granularity

// This is a recursive function, not a class
// - - - - - - - - - - - - - - - - - - - - --
double AreaTask(double a, double b)
   {
   double result;
   if(fabs(b-a)<G)
      result = Area(a, b, my_fct);
   else
      {
      double x, y;
      double midval = a+ 0.5*(b-a);
      task_group tg;
      tg.run([&]{x = AreaTask(a, midval);});
      tg.run([&]{y = AreaTask(midval, b);});
      tg.wait();
```

```
        result = x+y;
        }
    return result;
    }

// – – – – – – – – –
// The main function
// – – – – – – – – – –*/
int main (int argc, char *argv[])
    {
    nTh = 2;           // default values
    G = 0.4444;

    task_scheduler_init init(nTh);
    double result = AreaTask(0, 1);
    std::cout << "\n Area result is : " << result << std::endl;
    }
```

LISTING 11.17

Area computation, waiting for children.

Let us first examine the recursive AreaTask(a, b function. It returns the area of the range passed as argument. This function operates in the traditional way: if the sub-domain size is smaller than the granularity, it returns directly the area. Otherwise, it splits the range into two sub-ranges and computes the area recursively. In this case, this function defines two local variables x, y that recover the recursive results of the two sub-ranges, *and calls itself recursively*. Our intention, however, is to run child tasks to do this job. Therefore, the function:

- Defines a local task_group object, used to run and wait for the two child tasks.
- Runs the tasks. But now, the run() member function requires a function object as argument, not an ordinary function. Therefore, a lambda expression is used to transform the function into a function object. The lambda expression syntax is clear: the variables x, y that receive the return values are captured by reference, and the limits of integration are captured by value (see Annex B).
- The function, as usual, calls wait() before returning x+y.

Finally, look at the main() function: it calls directly the function AreaTask(0,1). Indeed, all the taskwait synchronizations in this problem are local and internal to each recursive task. This function does not return before all the recursive partial results have been correctly returned to the parent tasks. It is indeed possible to introduce yet another task_group local to main() to run AreaTask(0,1) as a task, but this is superfluous in this case (it will not be superfluous in the next example).

Example 10: Tg2.C

To compile, run make tg2. This example runs four threads, with G=0.24. The number of threads and the granularity can be overridden from the command line.

11.11.3 AREA COMPUTATION, NON-BLOCKING STYLE

Next, the traditional non-blocking style is implemented, in which tasks spawn child tasks and terminate. Tasks that finally compute areas of sub-ranges accumulate their partial results in a mutex protected global variable, and are called result in Listing 11.18.

In this example, only a unique, overall wait of the complete computation is needed. Therefore, a unique, global task_group tg is introduced. New tasks will be dynamically added to this already running task group, who will be accessed by all tasks, but only to run their children. The main() thread is the only one that waits on tg. Here is the listing of the source code, in file Tg3.C

```
int   nTh;
double G;
task_group tg;
mutex  m;          // protects result
double result;     // accumulates partial results

// This is a recursive function, not a class
// - - - - - - - - - - - - - - - - - - - - -
void AreaTask(double a, double b)
   {
   double res;
   if(fabs(b-a)<G)
      {
      res = Area(a, b, my_fct);
         {
         mutex::scoped_lock lock(m);
         result += res;
         }
      }
   else
      {
      double midval = a + 0.5*(b-a);
      tg.run([=]{AreaTask(a, midval);});
      tg.run([=]{AreaTask(midval, b);});
      }
   }

// - - - - - - - - -
// The main function
// - - - - - - - - - -*/
int main (int argc, char *argv[])
   {
   double res;

   nTh = 2;     // default values
   nTk = 4;
   G = 0.2;
```

```
task_scheduler_init init(nTh);

tg.run([=]{AreaTask(0, 1);});
tg.wait();
std::cout << "\n Area result is : " << result << std::endl;
}
```

LISTING 11.18

Area computation, non-blocking style.

The previous strategy has been maintained, of defining an AreaTask(a,b) function—which now returns void—and using a lambda expression to transform it into a function object when needed. Notice that, since there are no return values, all the variables in the lambda expression are now captured by value.

In this recursive computation, the global task_group tg is used to run new tasks, but nobody waits. Only the main thread that starts the recursion waits on tg, after running AreaTask(0,1) as a task, not as a function.

Example 11: Tg3.C

To compile, run make tg3. This example runs four threads, with G=0.24. The number of threads and the granularity can be overridden from the command line.

11.11.4 CANCELING A GROUP OF TASKS

Let us now look again at the database search emulation example: a set of Ntk tasks keeps calling a random number generator providing uniform deviates in [0, 1], until one of them gets a value close to a given target with a predefined precision. Each task disposes of a local generator delivering a personalized random suite.

A task function SearchTask(int n) is defined. This function will be, again, transformed into a function object by using a lambda expression. The integer argument is a rank assigned to each task, used to initialize its local random number generator. Here is the listing of the source code, in file DbTbb.C.

```
struct Data        // output passed to main thread
   {
   double d;
   int    rank;
   };

const double EPS = 0.00000001;
const double target = 0.58248921;
Data D;
```

Continued

```
task_group tg;    // global task_group

// The workers thread function
// – – – – – – – – – – – –
void SearchTask(int n)
    {
    double d;
    Rand R(999*(n+1));
    while(1)         // infinite loop
       {
       if(tg.is_canceling()) break;   // check for cancellation
       d = R.draw();
       if(fabs(d–target)<EPS)
          {
          D.d = d;
          D.rank = n;
          tg.cancel();                // request cancellation
          }
       }
    }

// – – – – – – – – – – – – – – – – – – – – – –
// The main function gets the number of threads
// from the command line.
// – – – – – – – – – – – – – – – – – – – – – –
int main(int argc, char **argv)
    {
    int nTh = 2;
    int nTk = 4;

    // override from command line

    task_scheduler_init init(nTh);
    for(int n=0; n<nTk; ++n) tg.run([=]{SearchTask(n);});
    tg.wait();

    // Print search result
    // – – – – – – – – – –
    std::cout << "\n Task " << D.rank << " found value "
           << D.d << std::endl;
    return 0;
    }
```

LISTING 11.19

Emulation of database search.

Notice that the task_group tg is global: it is used by main() to run the worker tasks, but each task must also access tg to check or to request cancellation. Remember that the TBB runtime system will directly cancel the task group if the tasks are not scheduled. Otherwise, the programmer must provide the termination code if a running task must be canceled. This is exactly what happens in the SearchTask(n) function: the task activity is an infinite while(1) loop that breaks if the group cancellation has been requested.

Example 12: DbTbb.C

To compile, run make dbtbb. This example runs four threads and four tasks.

11.12 CONCLUSIONS

This chapter has covered the high-level programming interfaces for running parallel applications in the TBB task-centric environment. It can be observed that, at this level, there is a strong correspondence between the OpenMP task API and the TBB taskgroup class features: waiting for direct children, waiting for all descendants, and canceling a parallel construct. What is left is the option or ordering the way tasks are executed by establishing hierarchical dependencies among them. In OpenMP this issue is controlled by the depend clause when a task is created. TBB is much more explicit, by exhibiting in more detail the inner workings its task scheduler, whose enlarged features are discussed in Chapter 16.

FURTHER THREAD POOLS

12.1 INTRODUCTION

This chapter focuses on two thread pool utilities provided by the vath library. First, the SPool class—already introduced in Chapter 3 and frequently used in the examples developed in previous chapters—is reviewed, in order to better understand its design requirements. Then, another thread pool class called NPool, with complementary capabilities, is introduced. In fact, the SPool implements a slightly different design for the OpenMP *thread-centric* execution model, and the NPool class does the same thing for the OpenMP and TBB *task-centric* execution models.

The development of these utilities was initially motivated by the interest in simplifying the programming of some specific parallel contexts. The intention was not to compete with professional, well-established programming environments, or to replace widely adopted standards. The thread pools discussed in this chapter operate correctly, but they do not have the very high level of sophistication of the professional standards. However, the slightly different software architecture adopted in these utilities may constitute an interesting option in some specific programming contexts, as is shown in two examples deployed at the end of the chapter.

12.2 SPooL REVIEWED

As observed in past examples the SPool class operates like an OpenMP parallel region. When a job is submitted for execution, a task function encapsulating the computational work to be performed is passed to the pool. All worker threads in the pool execute the same task function. This utility implements a strict thread-centric environment, in which all the worker threads have a precise preassigned task to perform. There are, however, two differences with OpenMP:

- The SPool pool is explicitly created by the client threads that require its services. The OpenMP pool is implicit: there is a unique worker thread pool in the application that can be stretched by adding new threads as discussed in Chapter 10. In our case, there can be several independent pools operating in an application. An example was provided in Section 11.11.4, when discussing a reader-writer lock example: two different pools were used to run the writer or reader threads accessing a shared vector container.
- Unlike OpenMP, the client thread that launches a parallel job is in all cases external to the pool. The client thread does not join the set of worker threads. Instead, it is correctly synchronized with

the pool activity. The client thread can continue to do other things and, when the time comes, wait for completion of the submitted job.

The SPool class implements practically all the thread-centric OpenMP features. Consider, for example, the nested parallel region structure shown; Chapter 10, Figure 12.1. Since client threads must necessarily be external to the pool, it is obvious that a worker thread participating in an ongoing job cannot submit a nested job *to the same pool*. However, pools are now explicit, and nothing prevents worker threads from creating on the fly a new temporary, local pool, submit a job to it, and, again, when the time comes, wait for the job termination and destroy the local pool. Remember that OpenMP dynamically adds new threads to its pool to fit the nested parallel region requirements. In our case, rather than stretching the existing pool, a new one can be created. An example of this mechanism will be proposed later on.

There are two specific parallel contexts in which this pool architecture may be helpful, as shown in Figure 12.1:

• *Decoupling MPI and multithreading*. This was the motivation for introducing the SPool class. In a hybrid application, in which each MPI process internally activates shared memory computations, the main thread handles the MPI communications and all the details of the large-scale distributed memory code. This MPI thread does not get involved in shared memory computations. Rather, it offloads to one or more pools the internal shared memory parallel tasks, continues to handle its MPI workload, and ultimately waits for the submitted internal jobs. This effectively decouples the MPI and shared memory environments. Of course, a precise synchronization between the client MPI thread and internal worker threads executing the shared memory subroutines is required, but this is precisely what is incorporated by the SPool utility. An explicit example of this programming style is proposed at the end of the chapter.

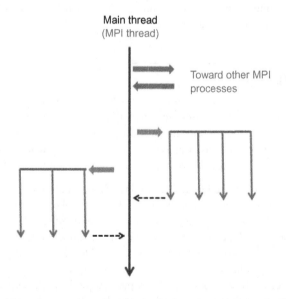

Main thread
(MPI thread)

Toward other MPI
processes

FIGURE 12.1

Typical usage of explicit pools in hybrid applications.

- *Running parallel subroutines in parallel.* Note that a client thread can simultaneously address several independent pools in the application. Indeed, as seen in Figure 12.1, the main thread has created two pools executing *two parallel tasks in parallel.* The asynchronous concurrent execution of parallel jobs is very easily implemented in the SPool environment. This feature first looked initially a bit far-fetched. Today, with the availability of Intel Xeon Phi architectures with 60 cores in a socket, running up to 240 threads, a programming style enabling the execution of several parallel jobs in parallel may be attractive in some cases, as it will be shown at the end of the chapter.

The SPool utility implements practically all the OpenMP thread-centric features. However, the OpenMP and TBB task-centric features discussed in the previous two chapters are missing. One option is to extend SPool, but it is much simpler to introduce another thread pool—called NPool— implementing a task-centric execution environment, while preserving the two basic features mentioned above: explicit pool construction, that is, client threads not members of the pool working team. The point is that, since pools are explicit, an application can simultaneously operate both kinds of pools. And a worker thread in a SPool—or NPool—can always construct a NPool—or SPool—on the fly to run a nested job that requires a different environment.

The rest of the chapter concentrates on the NPool class. We will be particularly clear on two specific points:

- The OpenMP and TBB features that *are not* implemented in NPool, as well as the possible performance impact of the simpler task scheduling strategies.
- The added value that the slightly different software architecture can eventually provide to some specific applications. A complete example that demonstrates how a significant performance boost can be obtained in a specific application by exploiting the possibility of running parallel subroutines in parallel—something not easily implemented in OpenMP and TBB—is discussed in Section 12.7 at the end of the chapter.

12.3 NPooL FEATURES

Besides the two basic features mentioned above—explicit pool, external client threads—a third one was adopted: making a parallel job an explicit, well-identified C++ object, with a well-defined identity returned to the client threads when the job is submitted for execution. There are two reasons for that; First, client threads must be to be able to query the pool about the job status. Second, client threads should be able to submit any number of different jobs *and wait for them in any order.*

The parallel job concept used in the NPool pool is close to the taskgroup concept implemented in OpenMP and TBB. There are, however, some differences that will show up as we go. The main building block for constructing a parallel job is, naturally, an object instance of a Task class that encapsulates, among other things, the specific function to be executed by the parallel task on the target data set. This class operates in the same way as the function object classes used by TBB in the task_group environment, to define specific tasks. It is also totally analogous to the TBB task class used by the full TBB task scheduler discussed in Chapter 16.

To define a parallel job, another simple class called TaskGroup (what else?) is introduced as a container of Task references. This class is used to pack the tasks that initially define the parallel job. This *must* be done because the parallel job must be submitted as a single entity, in one shot. Indeed,

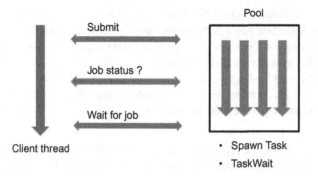

FIGURE 12.2

NPool job submission and management.

client threads get in return a job identifier that allows them to track the job execution or wait for its termination.

The submitted TaskGroup remains alive after submission, and it evolves dynamically. It helps to track the execution of the job, incorporating new tasks spawned by the worker threads, or destroying the terminating tasks. The basic job management features implemented by the NPool utility are summarized below. They are also shown in Figure 12.2:

- Submission of a task as an initially sequential job by a client thread. Nothing forbids this unique task from spawning further tasks when running.
- Submission of a TaskGroup object encapsulating a group of tasks as a unique parallel job, by a client thread.
- Job submission (initially sequential or parallel) returns a unique job identifier that can be used by client threads to inquire about job status or to wait for job termination.
- Jobs can grow dynamically. Tasks being run by the worker threads—either the initial tasks or their children—can spawn new child tasks. In all cases, tasks spawned by worker threads are automatically incorporated to the ongoing job to which the parent tasks belong.
- An *end of job* event is broadcasted to client threads when all the tasks, *including all the spawned tasks*, terminate.
- Spawning dynamical tasks and waiting for children operate in exactly the same way in OpenMP and TBB.
- Note that *only client threads can launch a new job*. Worker threads can only enlarge the ongoing job with new tasks.
- Nested parallelism is supported, in the same way as in the SPool utility. It follows from the statement above that *worker threads cannot submit a nested job to the pool they belong*. But they can legitimately be clients of *another* pool, and this is the way nested jobs are supported. It will be clear later on why NPool is tailored to work in this way.

Every time a job is submitted, an internal job manager object is created incorporating, among other data items, the initial TaskGroup and a Boolean lock in charge of the synchronization with the client tasks. There is one job manager per submitted job, and the job identifier returned to the client tasks targets the relevant job manager and Boolean lock.

It should be noted here that the mechanism of launching an arbitrary parallel job, getting a job identifier, and using it to wait for the job termination can also be implemented in TBB, using advanced programming techniques provided by the TBB scheduler API. A discussion of this feature will be presented in Chapter 16. The main difference with TBB is that in TBB, as in OpenMP, there is a unique, implicit TBB pool in an application.

After describing the basic NPool features, a more detailed discussion of this utility follows, organized as follows:

- A presentation of the user interface of the NPool class—simple and compact—for managing and running parallel jobs.
- A presentation of the Task and TaskGroup classes, needed to define, prepare, and submit a parallel job.
- Finally, a very qualitative discussion of the operation of the thread pool, and a comparison with OpenMP and TBB features.

12.4 NPool API

The NPool public interface is defined in the NPool.h file. The public member functions are simple—there are only seven of them—and intuitive. They are described in detail below, and shown in Figure 12.2.

NPOOL PUBLIC INTERFACE

1. Constructing an NPool Object

ThPool(int nTh)

- Constructor of the thread pool.
- Constructs a pool with nTh worker threads.
- Called by client threads.

2. Job Submission and Management

int SubmitJob(Task* T)
int SubmitJob(TaskGroup& TG)

- Submits a sequential or parallel job for execution by the thread pool.
- Returns 0 if the submission failed (submission by worker thread).
- Returns an integer bigger than 0 if the submission is successful.
- In this case, the integer so returned is a *job identifier*.
- Called by client threads.

bool JobStatus(int id)

- Returns the status of the job identified by id.
- If return value is true, job is running or waiting to run.
- If return value is false, job is terminated.
- Called by client threads.

void WaitForJob(int id)

- Waits until all the tasks in the job identified by id are finished.
- Prints message and aborts program if job identifier is invalid.

– Called by client threads.

void WaitForIdle()

– Wait until the whole pool is idle.
– Called by client threads.
– When this function returns, all the worker threads are idle.

3. Spawning and Waiting for Child Tasks

int SpawnTask(Task& T, bool iswaited=true)

– Spawns a child task for execution by the thread pool.
– Returns 0 if the submission failed.
– Returns 1 if the submission is successful.
– The second argument informs the runtime system if the parent task will wait for its child.
– If the parent task waits, there is no need to pass the second argument.
– If the parent task does not wait, the false value must be passed.
– Called by worker threads in the pool.

void TaskWait()

– Waits for the termination of all the child tasks previously spawned.
– Called by worker threads in the pool.
– Only *direct* child tasks are synchronized.

Notice that job management functions are always called by external client threads, and dynamic task spawning and taskwait synchronization functions are always called by worker threads in the team.

Client threads can call WaitForJob() to perform an idle wait until the job is finished, or they can call JobStatus() and return to some other activity if the job is still running. If these calls are made by a worker thread in the pool, the program is aborted with an error message.

The WaitforIdle() call means: wait until the pool is totally inactive, that is, there are no running jobs, or jobs waiting to run. This is a very handy utility when, for example, a large number of simple jobs has been submitted, and the client code only needs to know they are all finished. It is useful to keep in mind that this function call does not interfere with the tracking of individual jobs. It is possible to wait for some individual jobs, and at some point wait for all the remaining ones.

A WaitForIdle() call made by a worker thread is ignored, to avoid a deadlock. Indeed, a worker thread making this call goes to sleep while executing a task in a job. Therefore, the job will never be finished and the final result is a circular wait context.

The two functions for spawning and waiting for child tasks work exactly the same way as the task and taskwait directives in OpenMP, discussed in Chapter 10, or the similar TBB utilities discussed in Chapter 11. We underline once again the fact that *spawned tasks are incorporated into the parallel job of the parent task*.

12.5 BUILDING PARALLEL JOBS

Having a global overview of the NPool environment, a more detailed discussion follows concerning the construction of a parallel job. The methodology adopted is very close to the one implemented by the TBB task scheduler discussed in Chapter 16. This section paves the way for the construction of TBB tasks.

12.5.1 TASK CLASS

In C++, most natural implementation of the task concept is a C++ object instance of a task class. The advantages in implementing a task as a C++ function object have been underlined, when discussing the TBB task_group class. Here, rather than function objects, the more basic TBB approach is paralleled, in which explicit task classes as derived classes from a base Task class, defined in the include file Task.h as follows:

```
class Task
   {
   protected:
   // data items and member functions not accessible
   // to users, but accessible to derived classes
   ...
   public:
   ...
   Task();                       // constructor
   virtual ~Task();              // destructor
   virtual void ExecuteTask() = 0;   // interface
   };
```

LISTING 12.1

Task interface class.

This class contains private internal data items and member functions needed for task management and parent-child synchronization, but users of the utility are not concerned by them. Besides the constructor—which, among other things, initializes the private data items hidden to the user—and the destructor, there is the ExecuteTask() function, which is the task function to be called by the executing thread.

Note, however, that the ExecuteTask() function has been declared *virtual* and set equal to zero. This means this function will only be defined in derived classes. The Task class cannot be used as such to create task objects. This class is really just an interface that declares the existence of a service and provides a toolbox to implement it, once the precise task to be executed is specified in a derived class.

Therefore, in order to create real tasks, users must:

- Derive another task class from Task (the class name is arbitrary). This class naturally inherits all the protected member functions that are not visible to end users.
- Define the constructor and, if needed, the destructor of the derived class.
- Define the ExecuteTask() function for the derived class.

The derived class is only limited by the user's imagination. It may contain all the additional specific data items required by the task function, and eventually new auxiliary member functions if needed. The additional data items needed by the task to operate are, of course, initialized via the object constructor. The listing below displays a derived task class MyTask in which the task receives an integer rank as argument:

```
class MyTask: public Task
    {
    private:
     int rank;

    public:
     MyTask(int r): Task(), rank(r) {}

    void ExecuteTask()
       {
       // here comes the specific
       // task function code
       }
    };
```

LISTING 12.2

Derived task class.

As it is obvious from the example above, the derived class constructor can be adapted to the user's needs. Several different data arguments can be passed to the new task via the object constructor.

After a real Task class like MyTask is available, and the task is submitted to the pool for execution, the standard virtual function mechanism of object-oriented programming operates. The run-time code manipulates Task pointers. However, when a Task* has been initialized with the address of a MyTask object, it is the derived class ExecuteTask() function that is called.

This approach is the same as the one implemented in TBB, where there is a pure interface task class—more sophisticated than ours—with, again a task function as a virtual member function execute() returning a task*. The reason for returning a task* is that the TBB task management strategy is more sophisticated, as it allows a task to bypass the standard operation of the task scheduler, by returning the address of the task to be executed next. This issue is discussed in detail in Chapter 16.

12.5.2 TaskGroup CLASS

A TaskGroup is a container of Task* objects. In fact, this object is just an STL list of task pointers std::list<Task*>. A TaskGroup object encapsulates the initial set of tasks that defines a parallel job. It collects all the tasks that start with the job, and enables the submission of the parallel job as a single entity, related to a unique identifier. Here is the public interface:

TASKGROUP PUBLIC INTERFACE

TaskGroup()

– Constructor.
– Creates a empty TaskGroup object.

~ TaskGroup()

– Destructor.

– Destroys the TaskGroup object.

void Attach(Task *T)

– Inserts Task T in the TaskGroup container.

void Clear()

– Empties the TaskGroup container.

Users declare first an empty TaskGroup object, and then allocate each individual task and attach its address to it. In the listing below, MyTask1, MyTask2, and MyTask3 are three task classes, taking each an arbitrary number of arguments in their constructors. As was the case for tasks, TaskGroups are allocated in the heap, and the programming interface manipulates their addresses. This is the way to construct a group of these three tasks:

```
TaskGroup *TG = new TaskGroup()      // declare and initialize TG
MyTask1 *t1 = new MyTask1( args );   // construct task
TG->Attach(t1);                      // insert in container
MyTask2 *t2 = new MyTask2( args );   // construct task
TG->Attach(t2);                      // insert in container
MyTask3 *t1 = new MyTask3( args );   // construct task
TG->Attach(t3);                      // insert in container
```

LISTING 12.3

Constructing a TaskGroup.

When the task group pointer TG is submitted for execution, the pool returns, as stated before, a job identifier that can be used later on to inquire about the job status, or to put a client thread to wait until all the tasks in the group are finished.

Internally, the ThPool system associates a job manager object to each job. The job manager contains, among other objects, a Boolean lock. This job manager tracks the execution of the tasks in the job and uses the Boolean lock to signal to client threads that the job activity is completed. This establishes a powerful synchronization service between the client and worker threads.

Note that task groups are dynamic. When a sequential task is submitted directly to the NPool pool, the runtime code always constructs implicitly a one task TaskGroup, and returns its identifier. The reason is twofold:

- The Boolean lock associated with a TaskGroup is always needed to signal to the client code that the task is finished.
- Task groups are dynamic: A task in a parallel job can in turn submit child tasks, which joins the ongoing job and must therefore be incorporated into the parent task group.

12.5.3 MEMORY ALLOCATION BEST PRACTICES

A few basic facts concerning the allocation of tasks and task groups should be kept in mind, in order to avoid unexpected bugs and to make correct use of the NPool service.

Notice that the internal run-time code manipulates *pointers* to tasks and task groups. Therefore, tasks and task groups are created *on the heap* by initializing pointers with the new operator, as shown in the listing above.

The NPool code uses internally STL containers—lists, queues, maps—in several places, to store task or task group pointers, and *STL containers use copy semantics*: insertion operations copy the inserted object into the container. Then, when a task pointer object is attached to a TaskGroup object (as in the listing above), it is copied inside the internal linked list. Similarly, when Task* or TaskGroup* objects are submitted to the pool, they are copied inside the appropriate queues or placeholders.

This means that, after submission, the original Task* and TaskGroup* used to construct and submit a job are no longer needed. They can be destroyed or used again and reallocated by the client code, because the run-time code has already copied them at the right places. *However, they should never be deleted*, because this operation destroys objects that the pointers copied by the run-time code are pointing to. They become invalid, and the program crashes. The rule to keep in mind is the following:

Tasks and TaskGroups are allocated by client code submitting parallel jobs. These objects are deallocated by the internal run-time code, when the associated jobs are finished.

These observations justify the programming style that will be used in the examples. Very often, a parallel job is constructed where the tasks are identical, with possible differences in the values of the arguments passed to the constructor. Here is the way to construct and submit a parallel job composed of four identical MyTask tasks, passing a rank to each task and waiting for its completion:

```
ThPool *TP;
...
int main(int argc, char **argv)
  {
  ...
  // at this point, this task submits a job
  // and waits for termination
  TaskGroup *TG;
  for(int n=0; n<4; n++)
     {
     MyTask *t = new MyTask(n);
     TG->Attach(t);
     }                              // here, t destroyed
  int ID = TP->SubmitJob(TG);       // TG can be reused
  TP->WaitForJob(ID);
  }
```

LISTING 12.4

Submitting a parallel job with identical tasks.

The point to be observed in this listing is that, once the MyTask *t has been inserted into the TaskGroup container, it can be reused in the next loop iteration.

12.6 OPERATION OF THE NPooL

A qualitative understanding of a few details of the inner workings of the NPool utility is very useful to understand some of the pitfalls and best practices that will be discussed next. The management of

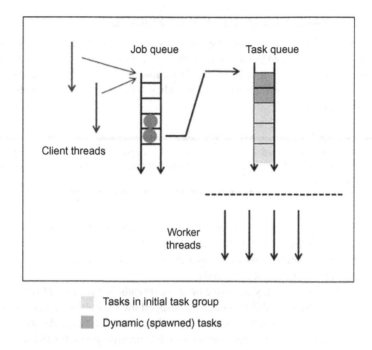

FIGURE 12.3

Schematic operation of the ThPool thread pool.

submitted jobs is in principle straightforward: tasks are queued in a task queue, and worker threads service them as they become available. If threads are sleeping because there was no work available, the queue wakes them up as soon as new tasks are ready to run.

In practice, the operation of the pool, as shown in Figure 12.3, is slightly more involved, for reasons that will soon be clear.

- There are in fact two queues: one in which the job requests (represented by a TaskGroup*) are queued, and a task queue, where the Task* involved in a specific parallel job are queued.
- Job requests are buffered in the TaskGroup* queue, and their tasks are flushed into the task queue on a job-per-job basis: only when a job is finished are the initial tasks of the next waiting job flushed to the task queue.
- Dynamic tasks spawned by worker threads during job execution are naturally queued in the task queue. Then, we have the situation represented in Figure 12.3: the initial tasks (in light gray in the figure) are the oldest tasks in the queue, and the dynamic tasks, if any (in dark gray in the figure) are at the back of the queue.
- Finally, the task queue is really a thread-safe *double-ended queue*. We will see that, in order to avoid deadlocks, tasks can be dequeued for execution from the head of the queue (oldest tasks) or from the tail (youngest tasks).

12.6.1 AVOIDING DEADLOCKS IN THE POOL OPERATION

The operational model of thread pools must implement ways of avoiding potential deadlocks related to dynamic task generation, which can occur when running parallel jobs. These potential deadlocks must be controlled by the operational design of the pool. We know that deadlocks can also occur when using event synchronizations in task-centric environments. They must be controlled by the programmer, as discussed in the next section.

> The pool deadlocks if *all the worker threads* are waiting for events that never happen, because they are triggered by tasks that are still queued and not executed, precisely because all the worker threads are waiting and there are no further threads available to dequeue and execute them.

The fact that the thread pool has a fixed number of worker threads may cause problems if the threads are over-committed. Look at the parallel pattern shown in Figure 12.4. The main thread launches a four-task parallel job. One of the parallel tasks spawns a child task and waits for it. Finally, all the tasks are synchronized at a barrier call, before the job ends.

This application will run smoothly with five or more threads in the pool. However, *in the absence of a task-suspension mechanism* enabling threads to suspend the execution of a task in order to service another tasks, this code deadlocks with less than five threads in the pool. At some point in the job execution, three threads are waiting at the barrier synchronization point for the arrival of the fourth thread (the one that submitted the child task). However, this thread keeps waiting for the completion of its child, which is never executed because there are no threads available in the pool to dequeue and execute the task.

A mechanism is therefore needed to allow threads to suspend the execution of a task and service another tasks.

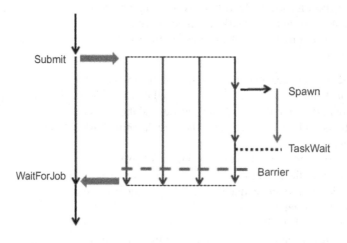

FIGURE 12.4

Spawning one child task.

Mapping tasks to threads

In this utility, the mapping of tasks to threads proceeds as follows:

- The mapping is *non-preemptive*: A task is tied to a specific worker thread for the whole duration of its lifetime. No matter what happens, the thread that initially removed the task from the ready pool and started execution is the one that will complete its execution if the initial execution is suspended.
- In addition, at one specific synchronization point—a TaskWait() function call—when a task decides to wait for all the child tasks it has previously spawned—the executing thread can suspend its execution and service another task in the way discussed next.

The mapping of tasks to threads just discussed is identical—and inspired from—the one adopted by TBB. OpenMP also allows a thread to suspend a task in some specific places, service other tasks, and resume later on the execution of the suspended task. In OpenMP, tasks are also tied to a thread by default. But as we have seen in Chapter 10 the user can declare them *untied*, allowing the suspended task to be resumed by another thread.

Running recursive tasks

When a task decides to wait for its children, the running thread checks if there are waiting tasks in the queue. If this is the case, then the worker threads are most likely over-committed. In this case, the running thread suspends —before waiting for children—the execution of the current task and *it dequeues for execution a task from the back of the queue*. In doing so, it picks the most recently spawned child task. It may even happen that it picks one of its own children, in which case the task submission operation is simply undone. This mechanism is coded inside the TaskWait() call. This function finally waits for children only when there are no further unscheduled tasks in the pool.

It is now clear why job requests are buffered, and only tasks belonging to a unique job are flushed into in the task queue. we know that in this way threads suspending the execution of a task will service child tasks *of the same job*. Indeed, servicing tasks of other jobs does not help prevent the deadlocks we are trying to dispose of.

Without a task suspension mechanism—which exists in all programming environments—it would be unsafe to run recursive parallel jobs where the number of tasks is not known from the start. Several of the examples proposed in the last two chapters show the robust execution of recursive applications with heavily over-committed worker threads resulting from important recursive task generation.

12.6.2 NESTED PARALLEL JOBS

As was stated before tasks executed by worker threads can only spawn new tasks attached to the ongoing job. The reason why worker threads cannot submit a completely different job to the pool they belong, and wait for its termination, results from the fact that job requests are buffered, as shown in Figure 12.5. The task group submitted by the worker thread will be queued in the task group queue and, at some point, the worker thread will start waiting for its termination. *However, at this point, the system deadlocks* because of a circular wait: the nested job will never be executed, because the ongoing job, waiting for its termination, will never complete.

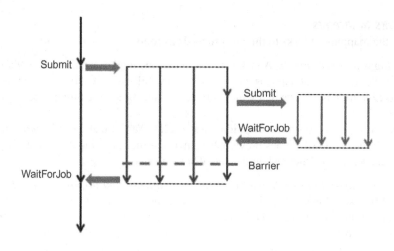

FIGURE 12.5

Nested parallel jobs.

Best practice for nested jobs: If a worker task wants to submit a nested job and dispose of all the synchronization benefits that come with a real parallel job encapsulating all its tasks, *it is always possible to create a new, local, short-lived* NPool *object, not known by other threads, and submit the job to it in the normal way*. See Section 12.6.3.

The subsidiary NPool object, being local to the submitting task, will be automatically destroyed when the task terminates. This is obviously very close to the OpenMP strategy of dynamically adapting the number of worker threads to the parallel context. This way of handling nested jobs is simple and robust, and specific examples will be presented in the following sections.

12.6.3 PASSING DATA TO TASKS

The interest and the necessity of passing to a child task data values that are local to the parent task has been discussed in previous chapters. In the NPool environment, passing data to child tasks follows the same protocols adopted by the TBB tasks in the task_group environment. The required data values are passed by value via the task constructor, which initializes the corresponding internal data items of the child task. To recover a return value from a child, data items are passed by address. A task allocates the local data item that will receive the value, and passes a pointer to its child. The child task will use this pointer, when the time comes, to write directly the return value to the target data item sitting in the parent task stack.

Remember, however, that *in order to recover the return value, the parent task must wait for its child* with a TaskWait call, because the target data item that receives the return value must still be alive when the child writes to it. If the parent task does not wait for its child, the task most likely terminates and, when the child task returns the value, the target data item has been destroyed from the running thread stack. Then, the pointer passed to the child task points to an invalid memory address, and the code crashes.

12.6.4 **ASSESSMENT OF THE NPooL ENVIRONMENT**

As stated before, the NPool environment operates correctly. With a few exceptions, all the task-centric OpenMP and TBB examples proposed in the previous chapters are correctly run by this utility. The vath library proposes a large number of tests to be executed after compilation that control the correct behavior of the utility. And, in addition, there are further examples that follow in this chapter.

The OpenMP and TBB features that *are not* incorporated in this utility are those related to the hierarchical relations among tasks used to implement event synchronization of tasks, not threads. An OpenMP example was proposed in Chapter 9, when discussing the OpenMP 4.0 depend clause. In TBB, hierarchical relations among tasks are accessible via the complete task scheduler API. They will be discussed in Chapter 16. Thread-affinity utilities are also missing, because they are just beginning to emerge in the basic libraries underlying vath.

Even if the NPool motivation is not to compete with OpenMP or TBB, it makes sense to ask how good this environment is, considered as an ordinary thread pool. The NPool scheduling strategies, tailored to track job execution, are less ambitious than the ones adopted in OpenMP and TBB based on the *task-stealing* approach described in Chapter 16. The adoption of a unique task queue with a first-last in, first-out operation certainly introduces a serialization point in the parallel operation, which, as it is well known, does not optimize—among other things—memory usage or cache reusage. The task-stealing strategy deploys one task queue per thread, and operates in such a way to optimize private cache reusage and load balance. This point has been strongly emphasized by the TBB architects.

These observations are of course quite correct. We would expect, however, to see a significant performance difference in irregular codes deploying a large amount of task generation. In all the examples, we have looked at, involving a moderate amount of recursive task generation, the NPool performances are comparable to OpenMP or TBB. The full applications deployed in the three chapters that follow will confirm this observation. Even the irregular, unbalanced, recursive example of a directed acyclic graph traversal discussed in Chapter 10—to be discussed later on, in Section 12.7.7—shows performance comparable to the OpenMP implementation, for the moderately small data set selected for the test.

It is our intention intend to modify in the future the NPool implementation by keeping the job buffering feature and adopting a task-stealing approach—as described in Chapter 16—for the execution of the job tasks.

12.7 **EXAMPLES**

There are several example codes provided with the library, for testing all the NPool features. We discuss first a few test codes that demonstrate all the features concerning task submission and management, nested parallel jobs, and child task spawning. Code listings will not be presented in full detail here; the sources are clear and well-documented. We just underline instead the few key points on which each example focuses.

Some of the examples described here have already been discussed in the OpenMP and TBB chapters, and minor modifications are needed to adapt them to the peculiarities of the NPool environment.

12.7.1 TESTING JOB SUBMISSIONS

The different features of the NPool class are tested: submitting a single task job, constructing and submitting a parallel job, waiting for an individual job, and waiting for all running jobs. In all cases, a task class defined in Listing 12.8 is used, consisting of:

- A start message printed to stdout, including a task identifier.
- A timed wait for a random time interval, simulating some significant job activity.
- A termination message printed to stdout, always including a task identifier.
- Tasks are identified by passing them an integer rank in the task class constructor.

```
RandInt  R(3000);   // produces random integers in [0, 3000]
NPool   *TP;        // reference to NPool

class TestTask: public Task
   {
   private:
    int rank;
    long timewait;
    Timer T;

   public:
   TestTask(int r): Task(), rank(r) {}

   void ExecuteTask()
      {
      cout << " TASK " << rank << " START" << endl;
      timewait = 2000 +(long) R.draw(); // random integer in [2000, 5000]
      T.Wait(timewait);
      cout << " TASK " << rank << " END" << endl;
      }
   };
```

LISTING 12.5

Simple task class.

The global variables in the listing above are:

- A reference to the NPool object, initialized by main() with the number of requested threads for the pool.
- A RandInt object R, whose member function R.draw() returns uniformly distributed random integers in the interval [0, N], N being passed as a constructor argument. This is an easy way to choose a random number of milliseconds in [0, N] for the timed wait.

The task function prints the start message, waits for a random time interval between 2 and 5 s, prints the termination message and returns. The messages output track how the submitted tasks have been executed.

Example 1: TNPool1.C

To compile, run make tp1. No command line arguments are required for the execution.

12.7.2 RUNNING UNBALANCED TASKS

The example discussed in Section 12.7.1 is reconsidered: a map operation on all the elements of a vector container, involving a very unbalanced action on each container element. Container elements are first initialized to a random double value in [0, 1]. Tasks acting on container elements keep calling a local random number generator until it retrieves a value close to the target value, within a given precision. The precision itself decreases as the map operation moves along the container.

This code is adapted to the NPool environment. In the OpenMP environment, a function Replace(int n) was used as a task function for the task acting on container element n. Here, a task class is needed, given in the listing below. The listing also shows the modifications made in the main() function.

```
class ReplaceTask : public Task
    {
    private:
    int n;

    public:
     ReplaceTask (int nn) : n(nn) {}

     void ExecuteTask()
        {
        Rand R(999 * SC.Next());
        double x;
        double eps = precision(n);
        double d = V[n];
        do
           {
           x = R.draw();
           }while( fabs(x-d)>eps );
        V[n] = x;
        }
    };


// The main function
// - - - - - - - - -
int main(int argc, char **argv)
   {
   ...
   // NPool computation. Construct first a huge
```

             Continued

```
// TaskGroup encapsulating the N tasks
// – – – – – – – – – – – – – – – – – – – –
TaskGroup TG;
for(int k=0; k<N; k++)
    {
    ReplaceTask *t = new ReplaceTask(k);
    TG.Attach(t);
    }

T.Start();
// – – – – – – – – – – – – – – – – – – – –
jobID = TP–>SubmitJob(TG);    // submit
TP–>WaitForJob(jobID);        // wait for job
// – – – – – – – – – – – – – – – – – – –
T.Stop();
...
// print results and exit
}
```

LISTING 12.6

Foreach.C (partial listing).

The number of threads and the number of tasks (i.e., the container size) are hard-coded to 4 and 100,000, respectively, as in the OpenMP example discussed in Chapter 10. Note that, in the listing above, a TaskGroup incorporating the 100,000 task pointers is constructed before submitting the job. The performance of this code as compared with the OpenMP implementation is shown in Table 12.1. There is clearly slightly more overhead but, given the huge number of unbalanced tasks, the results are satisfactory.

Example 2: Foreach.C

To compile, run make feach. There are 4 threads and 100000 tasks in the parallel job. The value of the precision can be over-ridden from the command line.

Table 12.1 100,000 Tasks, 4 Worker Threads: Execution Times in Seconds			
Performance of Foreach.C			
Environment	**Wall**	**User**	**System**
sequential	9.25	9.25	0
OpenMP	2.54	10.13	0.02
NPool	2.9	10.8	0.15

12.7.3 SUBMISSION OF A NESTED JOB

In this example, the main() thread launches a four-task parallel job, instances of the class OuterTask. One of the outer tasks launches, in turn, an inner, nested parallel job of, again, four tasks, instances of the class NestedTask. These inner tasks are identical to the outer ones: start message, timed wait, and termination message. The OuterTask class participating to the external job launched by main is listed below.

```
class OuterTask: public Task
    {
    private:
     int rank;

    public:
     OuterTask(int r): Task(), rank(r) {}
     void ExecuteTask()
        {
        cout <<  " START of Task " << rank << endl;
        if(rank==3)
           {
           // – – – – – – – – – – – – – – – – – – – – – – –
           // Creation of new task pool, job construction,
           // submission, wait for termination and implicit
           // destruction of the new task pool
           // – – – – – – – – – – – – – – – – – – – – – – –
           ThPool INPool(4);     // new, inner thread pool
           TaskGroup *TG;
           for(int n=0; n<4; n++)
              {
              NestedTask *t = new NestedTask(n);
              TG.Attach(t);
              }
           int ID = INPool.SubmitJob(TG);
           INPool.WaitForJob(ID);
           // – – – – – – – – – – – – – – – – – – – – – – –
           }
        B->Wait();
        cout << " END of task " << rank << endl;
        }
    };
```

LISTING 12.7

Modified OuterTask class.

This example demonstrates how to launch a nested parallel job: *the task that launches the nested parallel job does not submit it to its own thread pool.* Rather, it creates on the fly a new local thread pool to which the new job is submitted. This task pool has a limited lifetime and it is automatically destroyed when the task function returns. The listing below shows the new version of the OuterTask class.

Example 3: Nested.C

To compile, run make nt2. No command line arguments required. The inner nested job is correctly executed.

12.7.4 TASKGROUP OPERATION

The purpose of this example is to confirm the fact that child tasks are correctly incorporated into the ongoing job and tracked by the job manager. For this reason, a parent task will be spawning a bunch of child tasks *and not waiting for them*. The code workflow proceeds as follows:

- A one-task job is launched, and the main thread waits for its termination.
- The task in the submitted job spawns in turn four child tasks, which last between 3 and 5 s each, *and terminates, not waiting for its children*.

The code output shows clearly that the parent task terminates before its children. However, the job submitted by main() does not terminate because the child tasks are still active. The job termination message comes after the termination messages of the four child tasks.

Example 4: Spawn1.C

To compile, run make sp1. The number of threads in the pool can be chosen via the command line. The default is 4 (no command line argument).

12.7.5 PARENT-CHILDREN SYNCHRONIZATION

This example demonstrates parent-children synchronization via the TaskWait() function call. As in the previous example, a one-task job is launched, and the main thread waits for its termination. The task in the submitted job:

- Spawns five child tasks that last between 3 and 5 s each, and calls TaskWait() to wait for their termination.
- Spawns again two child tasks, and calls again TaskWait() to wait for their termination.
- Finally, it spawns again two tasks and returns, not waiting for them.

The code output shows the correct ordering of all the tasks. Again, the initial one task job terminates after the last two child tasks are finished.

Example 5: Spawn2.C

To compile, run make sp2. No command line arguments are required.

12.7.6 TASK SUSPENSION MECHANISM

This example demonstrates the task suspension mechanism. A two-task parallel job is launched. Each one of these two tasks spawns a child task and waits for its termination. There are therefore, at some point, two tasks are blocked waiting for their children, and the two child tasks to be executed. This code seems at first glance to require four threads.

In fact, even in the absence of task suspension, it only requires three threads to run properly, because the extra, nonblocked, worker thread can successively deque and execute the child tasks waiting in the task queue. In our case, since the two threads waiting for their child can suspend the ongoing task to run another task in the queue, the code runs properly with only two threads. It even runs correctly in sequential mode, with only one worker thread in the pool.

Example 6: Spawn3.C

To compile, run make sp3. The number of threads in the pool can be chosen via the command line. The default is 4 (no command line argument).

12.7.7 TRAVERSING A DIRECTED ACYCLIC GRAPH

The graph traversal example discussed in detail for the OpenMP environment in Section 12.7.1 is examined again in the NPool context. This is an irregular, unbalanced, and recursive example; that is, a good testing ground to check whether the NPool performance can sustain the comparison with the standard programming environment. The code sources are in file Preorder.C.

The code starts by constructing the graph G, and by extracting from a Graph member function a vector of pointers to the root cells, namely, the cells that have no ancestor and that consequently can be immediately updated. Then a recursive task function is defined such that, after updating a cell passed as an argument to the task, also recursively updates all the successor cells whose update has been enabled. The UpdateCell class that implements this task function is given in the listing below.

```
int  nTh;          // global variables
Graph G;
NPool *NP;

class UpdateCell : public Task
    {
    private:
      Cell *C;

    public:
     UpdateCell(Cell *c) : Task(), C(c) {}

     void ExecuteTask()
        {
        C->update();
        C->ref_count = C->op;     // reinitialize ref_count

        // Access successors and decrease their reference count.
        // - - - - - - - - - - - - - - - - - - - - - - - - - -
```

Continued

```
        for(size_t k=0; k<C->successor.size(); ++k)
          {
          Cell *successor = C->successor[k];
          if( 0 == -(successor->ref_count) )
            {
            UpdateCell *T = new UpdateCell(successor);
            NP->SpawnTask(T, false);
            }
          }
        }
    };


// Auxiliary function that does the job
// - - - - - - - - - - - - - - - - - -
void ParallelPreorderTraversal(std::vector<Cell*>& root_set)
    {
    int jobid;
    std::vector<Cell*>::iterator pos;

    TaskGroup TG;     // This TaskGroup contains the root cells
    for(pos=root_set.begin(); pos!=root_set.end(); pos++)
        {
        Cell *ptr = *pos;
        UpdateCell *T = new UpdateCell(ptr);
        TG.Attach(T);
        }

    jobid = NP->SubmitJob(TG);     // submit job and wait for it
    NP->WaitForJob(jobid);
    }
```

LISTING 12.8

Traversal task and auxiliary function.

The ExecuteTask() member function of the UpdateCell class follows the same logic than the OpenMP task function. Objects of this class receive a Cell* via the constructor. After updating the target cell, the successor cells are visited and their ref_count decreased. Then, when ref_count reaches zero, a new UpdateCell task is spawned. As was the case in the OpenMP version, we are using a tbb::atomic<int> to represent ref_count to enforce thread safety in its update. Note the second argument in the SpawnTask() function, which means the spawned task is not waited on by its ancestor.

Listing 12.12 also displays the auxiliary function that performs a graph traversal. In OpenMP, a parallel loop is run, by applying the update task function to the root cells, inside a taskgroup block. Here, a parallel job TG is constructed and submitted, whose initial tasks are the updates of all the root cells, the remaining cell updates following recursively.

The listing shows the main() function.

```
int main(int argc, char **argv)
   {
   int n, jobid;
   Centimeter T;
   int nTh, n Nodes, n Swaps;

   // Get command line input, initialize pool
   NP = new NPool(nTh);

   // Setup the acyclic graph
   // - - - - - - - - - --
   G.create_random_dag(nNodes);
   std::vector<Cell*> root_set;
   G.get_root_set(root_set);
   root_set_size = root_set.size();

   // Do the traversal
   // - - - - - - - -
   T.Start();
   for(unsigned int trial=0; trial<nSwaps; ++trial)
      {
      G.reset_counter();
      ParallelPreorderTraversal(root_set);
      }
   T.Stop();
   T.Report();
   }
```

LISTING 12.9

Main function for graph traversal.

The main function is practically identical to the one used in the OpenMP code. The code performance, for a configuration identical to the one used in Section 12.7.1 for OpenMP, is given in Table 12.2. Performance is comparable, within a few percent, to the performance of the OpenMP version.

Table 12.2 Graph With 4000 Nodes, and 30 Successive Traversals (GNU 4.9.0 Compiler)			
Graph Traversal Performances			
n_threads	**Wall**	**User**	**System**
1	58.3	58.3	0.0
2	29.3	58.9	0.06
4	14.9	59.2	0.18
8	7.92	61.8	0.45
16	4.53	66.53	0.8

Example 7: Preorder.C

To compile, run make preorder. The number of threads in the pool, the number of cells in the graph, and the number of traversals can be chosen via the command line. To run, execute preorder nTh nCells nSwaps. The default values are 4, 1000, and 5.

12.7.8 FURTHER RECURSIVE EXAMPLES

This section discusses the NPool versions of the recursive examples proposed in the OpenMP and TBB chapters. The recursive computation of the area under a curve will not be discussed in detail: barring some minor points, the codes are very close to the TBB task_group implementations in Chapter 11. Again, a programming style may be adopted in which tasks return a partial area return value, and they wait for children when the area range is split into two halves. Alternatively, since the job submission interface acts in fact like a task_group, a nonblocking style may be chosen in which tasks that generate children terminate immediately, and children accumulate partial results in a global variable.

In the nonblocking case, the recursive AreaTask class receives the integration range in the constructor parameters. Child tasks that compute partial results store their output in a global Reduction<double> object RD. Here is the listing of the main function driving the computation.

```
int main (int argc, char *argv[])
    {
    int n, jobID;
    double result;

    InputData();    // read Nth and G from file

    // Initialize the thread pool
    // – – – – – – – – – – – –
    TP = new NPool(Nth);

    // Submit task, and wait for idle
    // – – – – – – – – – – – – – – – –
    AreaTask *T = new AreaTask(0, 1);
    jobID = TP->SubmitJob(T);
    TP->WaitForJob(jobID);
    result = RD.Data();
    cout << "\n result = " <<  result << endl;
    return 0;
    }
```

LISTING 12.10

Main function, nonblocking style.

Example 8: AreaRec1.C

To compile, run make arec1. This code takes as input the number of threads in the pool Nth as well as the granularity G from the file arearec.dat.

In the blocking style case, the AreaTask recursive class constructor takes an extra parameter, the address of the data item where the area result must be returned. Here is the main function listing in this case.

```
int main (int argc, char *argv[])
    {
    int n, jobID;
    double result;

    InputData();    // read Nth and G from file

    // Initialize the thread pool
    // - - - - - - - - - - - - -
    TP = new NPool(Nth, 20);

    // Submit task, and wait for idle
    // - - - - - - - - - - - - - -
    AreaTask *T = new AreaTask(0, 1, &result);
    jobID = TP->SubmitJob(T);
    TP->WaitForJob(jobID);
    cout << "\n Result is = " <<  result << endl;
    return 0;
    }
```

LISTING 12.11

Main function, blocking style.

Example 9: AreaRec2.C

To compile, run make arec2. This code takes as input the number of threads in the pool Nth as well as the granularity G from the file arearec.dat.

Finally, the PQsort.C source file contains the NPool version of the parallel quicksort algorithm discussed in Chapter 9.

Example 10: PQsort.C

Qsort.C is a sequential version of this example. To compile, run make qsort. **PQsort.C** is the parallel version discussed above. To compile, run make pqsort.

12.8 RUNNING PARALLEL ROUTINES IN PARALLEL

This section focuses on the added value provided by the basic architecture of the vath thread pools—explicit pool, client threads external to the pool—when the parallel context can benefit from simultaneous access to different pools running several parallel routines inside an application.

This feature may be relevant in certain cases with the advent of SMP computing platforms—Intel Xeon Phi, IBM Power 8—disposing of hundreds of hardware threads.

The example developed next shows how it is possible to boost the performance of an application, bypassing the limitations imposed by its limited scalability as a function of the number of threads. The application is a computation that requires intensive access to a parallel utility that generates vectors of *correlated Gaussian fluctuations*. It is not important, for the time being, to have a precise idea of what this means; this point is clarified in the next chapter, in Section 13.2.1. The important point is that these vectors are generated by a Monte-Carlo algorithm that requires a significant amount of computation, and that this algorithm can be easily parallelized in an single program, multiple data (SPMD) style.

12.8.1 MAIN PARALLEL SUBROUTINE

The most important ingredient in the correlated generator algorithm can be rephrased as a molecular dynamics problem dealing with the computation of the trajectories of a set of N interacting particles moving in a line. The following chapter is entirely devoted to a thorough analysis of this molecular dynamics problem, and many of the statements that follow will be fully understood and justified. For the time being, we will consider that we dispose of a C++ class, called GaussVec, that acts as a provider of vectors of correlated Gaussian fluctuations, of size N. The listing below shows a partial listing of the class declaration, in GaussVec.h.

```
class GaussVec
    {
    private:
      double  **D;      // external matrix
      double   *V;      // external vector, return value
      ...
      SPool   *TP;
      Barrier *R;
      ...
      // several private member functions

    public:
      GaussVec(double **d, double *v, int vSize, int nThreads,
               double dt, double prob, long seed);
      ~GaussVec();
      void Print_Report();
      void Reset();

      void MCTask();
      void Request_Vector(int steps);
      void Wait_For_Request();
    };
```

LISTING 12.12

GaussVec class.

We should consider this class as a library routine; understanding its precise mode of operation is not necessary. However, a few comments are useful. This class incorporates internally a N×N matrix D, which defines the imposed correlations among the vector components, as well as a vector V where the return values are stored. Both data items are pointers passed by the client code via the class constructor. The class constructor also incorporates other external parameters, as well as the number of threads to be used in the parallel computation.

Note that this class includes an internal SPool reference, initialized by the constructor when the number of threads is known. In fact, a GaussVec object disposes of a private thread pool to run its parallel computation. There will be as many independent thread pools in the application as GaussVec objects. All these pools will be able to run asynchronously, providing independent correlated Gaussian vectors. An internal Spool utility is used here, rather than the NPool one, because the parallel algorithm is an SPMD computation perfectly adapted to a thread-centric environment. This particular point will be better understood in the next chapter.

There are a few public member functions:

- void McTask(): This function encapsulates the task function to be passed to the thread pool. It is never called by external clients, but it has to be public and not private. To understand why, look at the class implementation in GaussVec.C, where this issue is discussed.
- Request_Vector(int nsteps): This function call submits a new parallel job to the pool that computes a new correlated vector sample, stored in V. The integer argument controls how long the internal Monte-Carlo computation will be running to provide a new sample totally disconnected from the previous one.
- void Wait_For_Request() just calls the Wait_For_Job() SPool member function. This function returns when the previous vector request has completed.

12.8.2 CLIENT CODE

The full application is very simple: it is just a test of the quality of the correlated Gaussian vector generator. The main code requests correlated Gaussian vectors from a GaussVec provider and accumulates all the products Vi.Vj and their squares into two matrices M1 and M2. At the end of the run, an auxiliary routine uses the collected data to compute all the Vi.Vj mean values and their variances, compare with the requested mean values, and provide information about the generator quality, which turns out to be quite good for the specific parameters selected. External parameters are read from a data file cgauss.dat.

Clearly, the code performance is controlled by the GaussGen performance. The analysis developed in the next chapter shows that the algorithm involves parallel patterns of simple vector operations, either vector additions or matrix-vector multiplications, distributed across the worker thread team. This leads to a large succession of lightweight parallel sections separated by barrier synchronizations. For huge values of the vector size N and a reasonable number of threads, the thread computational workload dominates over the barrier synchronizations and the code exhibits good scaling properties. However, as the number of worker threads is increased, their computational workload decreases, synchronization overhead takes over, and the scalability limit is reached. The point to be kept in mind is that, for a given vector size, a scalability limit is reached at some point, such that it does not make sense to keep adding worker threads. In the example that follows, for vectors of size N = 900, this limit is reached for six threads.

Imagine, however, that there are lots of cores available in our computing platform. It is very easy, in this case, to boost the application performance *by using two or more asynchronous provider routines, each one in its scaling region*. In the code that follows, there are two GaussVec objects, GV1 and GV2, running asynchronously and acting as vector providers. The complete application is in file TwoGen.C.

```
int main (int argc, char *argv[])
    {
    ...
    GV1->Request_Vector(nSteps);
    for(sample=1; sample<=nS; sample++)
        {
        GV1->Wait_For_Request();
        GV2->Request_Vector(nSteps);
        // - - - - - - - - - - -
        // ...
        // Treat data provided by GV1
        // ...
        // - - - - - - - - - - - --
        GV1->Request_Vector(nSteps);
        GV2->Wait_For_Request();
        // - - - - - - - - - - - -
        // ...
        // Treat data provided by GV2
        // ...
        // - - - - - - - - - - - - -
        if( sample%50 == 0 )
           printf("\n sample %d done", 2*sample);
        }    // end of samples loop
    ...
    // post-treatment is performed here
    }
```

LISTING 12.13

Main function.

In the listing above, the main code runs a loop that generates two vector samples at each loop iteration, as follows:

- The main code waits for the request submitted to GV1, and then it submits a request to GV2, before treating the data received from GV1.
- When the data treatment is finished, the main code waits for the GV2 request, and then submits a new request to GV1 before treating the data produced by GV2.

For the vector size chosen in this example (N = 900) the GaussVec routine shows good scaling properties up to about six threads. From eight threads on, no further performance speedup is obtained. We have compared the performance of two codes using one or two generators—the source files are OneGen.C and TwoGen.C. The resulting performance is given in Table 12.3, and the results speak for themselves. For a few threads, there is no difference. However, there is a very significant performance difference when using two generators running on 6 threads each (in their scaling regions) instead of one generator running on 12 threads.

Table 12.3 Wall Execution Times in Seconds, 900 × 900 Matrix, 2000 Samples, With Intel C-C++ Compiler, Version 13.0.1

One vs Two Generators			
Threads	**Wall**	**User**	**System**
1	211		
1	211		
2	107.9	210.9	0.06
1+1	–	–	–
4	61.3	234	0.09
2+2	67.5	212.5	0.06
8	46.9	351	0.15
4+4	38.2	237	0.09
12	46.9	509	0.32
6+6	29.5	271.9	0.08

Example 11: OneGen.C and TwoGen.C

To compile, run make onegen or make twogen. Input data is taken from file cgauss.dat.

This example underlines the potential usefulness of running parallel routines in parallel when there is a sufficient number of cores available. And the important point to keep in mind is that this software architecture is very easily implemented with our explicit thread pools.

12.9 HYBRID MPI-THREADS EXAMPLE

This section reconsiders the same problem just discussed—the parallel generation of samples of correlated Gaussian vectors—by using MPI to implement a distributed memory software architecture. An MPI program involves a number of *processes* running concurrently, exchanging data values via explicit message passing. Each MPI process can, of course, internally activate threads, but they are a private affair: a process is not aware of the threads activated in other partner processes. The example in the previous section is reformulated by introducing N MPI processes: one master process that collects vector samples, and (N-1) slave processes that compute vector samples using the multithreaded GaussGen utility and then send them to the master process.

In the computationally intensive phase of the code, the master process just receives data packets from the slaves. The slaves, instead, have two things to do: compute the vector samples by running the GaussGen routine, and send them to the master. The main point of this example is to show how the design of the vath pools—keeping client threads outside of the workers teams—helps to overlap computations and communications in the slaves codes.

MPI has been designed to interoperate with multithreading libraries. The MPI library function calls used by processes to communicate are therefore thread-safe: there are no hidden internal states that determine the outcome of future calls. Any thread in a process can in principle send or receive messages from other processes, and this feature is often useful. But for a large number of applications it is sufficient to limit the MPI function calls to the main thread in each process, and this is indeed our case. Therefore, the main thread manages the MPI structure of the code, and offloads to SPool or NPool pools whatever shared memory parallel activity needs to be run in each MPI process. In MPI jargon, this is called *funneled multithreading support*, and it is good practice to request it explicitly in the MPI initialization steps, as discussed in detail in the example source MpiGauss.C.

MPI adopts a single program, multiple data style in which a unique main() function is executed by all the MPI processes. Each process receives an integer rank identity in $[0, N − 1]$. In our case, the rank 0 process will be the master. MPI processes need to allocate buffers for sending or receiving data. In our case, the master process allocates a vdata vector of doubles for receiving the vector samples from the slaves. The slaves, instead, allocate two vector buffers: a ivector buffer for retrieving the correlated Gaussian vectors computed by the GaussGen utility, and a ovector buffer for sending them to the master process. Two buffers are needed because these two operations overlap. At each step, these buffers are swapped, so a buffer that is retrieving data at one step will be used to send data to the master at the next step.

Listing 12.14 is a partial listing of the source for this example, MpiGauss.C. This file contains a number of additional comments that clarify some basic MPI issues, not reproduced here. Let us go directly to the computational part of the example, after all initializations.

- The master process executes a loop over the number of vector samples requested. For each sample iteration, it addresses to each slave a Mpi_Recv() call to get a vector sample, and accumulates the data needed for the final computation of mean value and variances.
- In the slave process, GV is the address of the GaussVec object providing the correlated Gaussian vector service. The slave process starts by filling the ivector buffer with a vector sample. Then, it enters a loop on the number of samples where, at each iteration it:
  - Swaps the *ivector and *ovector pointers. At this point, data to be sent to the master is in ovector.
  - Requests to GV the next data sample in ivector.
  - Before waiting for the return value, sends the data in ovector to the master process.
  - Waits for the GV return value.

```
// Global data
// - - - - --
double *vdata;          // owned by master
double *ivector;        // one per slave
double *ovector;        // one per slave

int main(int argc, char **argv)
   {
   MPI_Status stat;     // used by MPI
   int myid;            // this process rank
   int numprocs;        // number of MPI processes
```

```
int vsize;              // vector size
CpuTimer *T;            // only master will measure times
...
MPI_Init_thread(&argc, &argv, MPI_THREAD_FUNNELED, &thread_support);
MPI_Comm world = MPI_COMM_WORLD;
MPI_Comm_size(world, &numprocs);  // get numprocs
MPI_Comm_rank(world, &myid);      // get myid
int nSlaves = numprocs-1;         // number of slaves
int nSamples = 2000;              // number of samples per slave

// - - - - - - - - - - - - - - - - - - - - - - - - - - - --
// Initialization steps. See details and comments in MpiGauss.C
// - - - - - - - - - - - - - - - - - - - - - - - - - - - -
if(myid==master)
    { // master initialization }
else
    { // slave initialization }
MPI_Barrier(world);

// - - - - - - - --
// ENTER COMPUTATION
// - - - - - - - --

if(myid == 0)  // MASTER CODE
   {
   T->Start(); // master measures execution times
   for(int sample=0; sample<nSamples; sample++)
      {
      for(int sl=1; sl <=nSlaves; sl++)
         {
         MPI_Recv(vdata, vsize, MPI_DOUBLE, sl , MSG, world, &stat);

         // Collect data for for later analysis
         // - - - - - - - - - - - - - - - - - --
         for(int i=0; i<vsize; i++)
           for(int j=0; j<vsize; j++)
              {
              double scr = vdata[i]*vdata[j];
              MV[i][j] += scr;
              MV2[i][j] += scr * scr;
              }
         }

      if( sample%100 == 0 )    // report message
         std::cout << "\n sample " << sample << " done" << std::endl;
      }
```

Continued

```
      T->Stop();    // top measuring execution times
      }     // end of master code
  else
      {   // SLAVE CODE
      GV->Request_Vector(ivector, nSteps);
      GV->Wait_For_Request();
      for(int sample=0; sample<nSamples; sample++)
          {
          SwitchVectors();   // exchange ivector <-> ovector
          GV->Request_Vector(ivector, nSteps);

          // Before waiting, send previous vector to the master
          // - - - - - - - - - - - - - - - - - - - - - - - - -
          MPI_Send(ovector, vsize, MPI_DOUBLE, 0, MSG, world);
          GV->Wait_For_Request();
          }
      }  // end of slave code

  MPI_Barrier(world);    // a safe net

  // - - - - - - - - - - - - - - - - - - - - - - - - - - - - -
  // Master performs statistical analysis and reports results on
  // on the generator quality, comparing computed and exact values
  // - - - - - - - - - - - - - - - - - - - - - - - - - - - - -

  MPI_Finalize();
  return 0;
  }
```

LISTING 12.14

Partial listing of MpiGauss.C.

Inside each slave process, the computation of the next vector sample and the transfer to the master of the currently available vector sample run concurrently. In fact, all the complex shared memory computation is entirely encapsulated in the GV object which, as we know, has its own internal SPool for shared memory parallel processing.

In this code, the execution times of the master process are measured. Executing the code shows that the execution times (wall, user, system) are very close to the execution times of the OneGauss.C example of the previous section. This is to be expected: execution times are dominated by the cost of the shared memory vector samples computation, and each process is running one Gaussian generator.

Note that the total number of vector samples accumulated by the master process is equal to nSamples*nSlaves. By increasing the number of slaves, the amount of data produced for the final statistical analysis is increased, and it is observed that the execution times remain approximately constant. In fact, this code is a nice example of *weak scaling*: the problem size grows linearly with the number of MPI processes, and optimal parallel performance is traduced by a constant execution time. At some point, however, communication overhead will start to take over and weak scaling will be lost.

Example 11: MpiGauss.C

To compile, run make mpig. The makefile assumes the **mpich** library is adopted for MPI, but this can be easily modified to run with other libraries, like **openmpi**. Input data is taken from the file cgauss.dat.

MOLECULAR DYNAMICS EXAMPLE

13.1 INTRODUCTION

A few applications dealing with specific computational problems are discussed in this and the following two chapters. Our purpose is to examine in detail how they are structured and organized, understanding when, why, and how threads or tasks must be synchronized. Two major classical parallel patterns are addressed: *data parallelism*, where the same computational workload is concurrently executed by different threads on different sectors of the data set, and *control parallelism*, where worker threads overlap in time the execution of different successive tasks on the complete data set. Data parallelism is the subject of this and the following chapter. Control parallelism is discussed in Chapter 15.

This chapter focuses on a rather simple molecular dynamics application, involving the computation of the trajectories of a large number of interacting particles, which illustrates a number of basic multithreading issues. This example belongs to a class of problems where the amount of potential parallelism grows with the size of the data set (in this case, the number of interacting particles). Parallel work-sharing strategies are implemented by having different threads compute the trajectories of different groups of particles.

The example that follows is simple and compact, but its parallel implementation requires a number of synchronizations among the worker threads. It therefore provides a very adequate context for assessing the performance of some of the synchronization tools discussed in Chapter 9. This example will also be used to examine vectorization at the single-core level, capable of enhancing the initial performance boost induced by multithreading.

The computational problem to be solved is described first. Even if it looks simple at first sight, it is not, however, an artificial problem. In fact, this example is the most important component of the algorithm used by the GaussGen utility, introduced in the last example of Chapter 12 to generate vectors of correlated Gaussian random numbers.

13.2 MOLECULAR DYNAMICS PROBLEM

Consider a simple mechanical system made out of N point particles of equal mass (set equal to 1), *moving in one-dimension along the real axis* and subject to the action of forces that will soon be defined. Let

$$\vec{q} = (q_1, q_2, \ldots, q_N)$$

$$\vec{p} = (p_1, p_2, \ldots, p_N)$$

be the set of coordinates and the momenta—the velocities—of these N particles. We assume that the force acting on particle i is

$$F_i = -\sum_{i,j} D_{ij} q_j \tag{13.1}$$

where D is a real, symmetric, positive-definite $N \times N$ matrix. Positive-definite means the matrix has positive eigenvalues. The total energy of this mechanical system, equal to the sum of the kinetic and the potential energies, is given by

$$E = T + V = \frac{1}{2} \sum_i p_i^2 + \frac{1}{2} \sum_{i,j} q_i D_{ij} q_j \tag{13.2}$$

Readers with a physics background may have recognized that we are dealing with a collection of N coupled harmonic oscillators. The D matrix, being real and symmetric, can be brought to diagonal form by an orthogonal matrix O (a matrix whose inverse is just its transposed matrix):

$$ODO^T = Dd$$

where Dd is a diagonal matrix of the form

$$Dd_{ij} = \omega_i^2 \, \delta_{ij}$$

Since the eigenvalues of D are positive, they can be written as the square of a real quantity ω_i. Now, *knowing the matrix O*, it is possible to define a new set of coordinates and momenta:

$$P_i = \sum_{i,j} O_{ij} p_j$$

$$Q_i = \sum_{i,j} O_{ij} q_j$$

in terms of which the initial problem reduces to a set of *uncoupled, independent harmonic oscillators*. Each coordinate Q_i performs a harmonic oscillatory motion around the origin with frequency ω_i:

$$Q_i(t) = A_i \cos(\omega_i t + \phi_i)$$

The amplitudes A_i and phases ϕ_i are determined by the initial conditions for the coordinates and momenta. Therefore, the problem of the computation of the particle trajectories is solved if the D matrix is diagonalized, namely, if the matrix O and the eigenvalues ω_i are known.

Note that we are here in the presence of attractive restoring forces (they push the particles toward the origin of coordinates). Their strength grows as particles move away from the origin. The particle trajectories $q_i(t)$ will therefore remain bounded in a finite domain near the origin of coordinates, because they are linear combinations of the $Q_i(t)$ given by the equation above.

The diagonalization of the D matrix can be performed with well-known linear algebra algorithms, whose computational cost grows like N^3 with the matrix size. This is not by itself a major problem because, having paid this computational cost once, it is possible to compute as many trajectories as one wants or needs. The real problem is, however, that this mechanical system will be used in contexts in which the D matrix evolves with time, which forces repeated updates of the computation of its diagonal form. In this case, it is more efficient to perform directly a numerical integration of the initial system of coupled harmonic oscillators, using an algorithm whose computational cost grows like N^2. This is what will be done in the rest of the chapter.

13.2.1 RELEVANCE OF THE MECHANICAL MODEL

The simple mechanical model described in the previous section is the main component of an algorithm for generating vectors whose components are *correlated* Gaussian random numbers used in Chapter 12. Consider a vector of rank N, whose components are Gaussian random numbers produced by one of the standard generators used in previous chapters (e.g., Chapter 4).

$$\vec{\xi} = (\xi_1, \xi_2, \dots, \xi_N)$$

The vector components ξ_n are real (positive and negative) numbers, distributed following a Gaussian law. Loosely speaking, this means they represent independent events that know absolutely nothing of one another. The mathematical formulation of this idea is that *the mean value of the product of two different components is zero*. This is indeed very reasonable: vector components are positive or negative with equal probability, and in fact their mean value is zero. The product of two *different* components is not positive-definite. If they are indeed different and totally unrelated, the mean value of this product must also be zero. This can be checked by taking a large number of samples of the product of two different Gaussian random numbers. The fact that the components of our initial vector are uncorrelated can be expressed in a compact way as follows:

$$< \xi_i \xi_j > = \delta_{ij}$$

where δ_{ij} is just the identity matrix: $\delta_{ii} = 1$, and $\delta_{ij} = 0$ if $i \neq j$.

The problem we need to consider is the generation of vectors with *correlated* components. Individual vector components must be real numbers distributed around the origin. They are correlated in the sense that the mean value of the product of two components is now

$$< \xi_i \xi_j > = D_{ij} \tag{13.3}$$

where D is a predefined *positive-definite* matrix whose diagonal elements are still $D_{ii} = 1$, but the off diagonal elements are not zero $D_{ij} \neq 0$ if $i \neq j$. This statement, plus the requirement that an ordinary Gaussian generator is recovered when the correlations are switched off—namely, when $D_{ij} = \delta_{ij}$— define our problem. It turns out that a substantial part of a Monte-Carlo algorithm designed to generate the correlated Gaussian vectors can be reinterpreted in terms of the molecular dynamics problem formulated above. The D matrix that occurs in the potential energy of the mechanical system is the same D matrix that defines the required correlations in the equation above.

Correlated Gaussian fluctuations are needed, for example, in phenomenological models of protein folding. Macromolecules are represented by worm-like chains of beads connected by straight elastic segments with torsion. Beads represent molecular aggregates where some specific activity is located, and straight segments represent chains of DNA base pairs. These phenomenological models of super-coiled DNA need to take into account the interaction of the macro-molecule with the environment in which it evolves. Indeed, the macro-molecule is subject to collisions with the atoms or molecules present in its environment. This manifests itself in the form of a Brownian motion of the macro-molecule, namely, erratic movements that are superimposed to the displacements computed from the deterministic mechanical model itself. These Brownian motions of the worm-like chain are therefore simulated by additional random displacements in the positions of the beads. For an isolated bead—that is, a heavy molecule in an environment—the Brownian motion is well described by uncorrelated Gaussian fluctuations in the three directions of space, with a variance proportional to the temperature of the environment. This is called *white noise*. However, in our case, these displacements cannot be just a white noise: *because of the mechanical constraints operating on the beads, they are all correlated in a way dictated by the specific protein configuration*. A symmetric D matrix determining the way in which the Brownian displacements of the vertices are correlated is provided by the underlying mechanical model of the macro-molecule. This matrix is a function of the bead positions. Obviously, this correlation matrix changes as the macro-molecule configuration evolves.

13.3 INTEGRATION OF THE EQUATIONS OF MOTION

The numerical integration of Newton's equations of motion is performed in our case by using the *leapfrog method*. Time is discretized by introducing a finite time step δ.

Let $(q_i^{(n)}, p_i^{(n)})$ denote the coordinates at time $n\delta$ and the momenta at time $(n - 1/2)\delta$. Indeed, *in the leapfrog scheme, coordinates and momenta are not computed at equal times*: they are defined in two different inter-penetrating time grids. The integration procedure over one time step proceeds as follows (see Figure 13.1):

Step 1: When the coordinates $q_i^{(n)}$ are known, the accelerations $\overrightarrow{a}^{(n)}$ at the same time can be computed. Since the masses are 1, the acceleration is simply equal to the force as given by Equation (13.1):

$$a_i = -\sum_{j \neq i} D_{ij} q_j \qquad (13.4)$$

Step 2: Once the particle accelerations at time $n\delta$ are known, the velocities at time $(n + 1/2)\delta$ can be computed:

$$p_i^{(n+1)} = p_i^{(n)} + \delta\, a_i^{(n)}$$

Step 3: Once the velocities at time $(n + 1/2)\delta$ are known, the new positions at time $(n + 1)\delta$ can be computed:

$$q_i^{(n+1)} = q_i^{(n)} + \delta\, p_i^{(n+1)}$$

This completes the calculation of a leapfrog time step. Steps 2 and 3 involve simple vector operations, and the computational cost is therefore proportional to the vector size N. But the

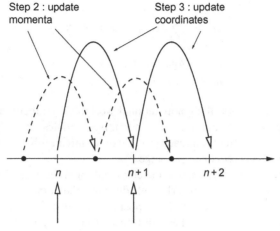

Step 2 : update
momenta

Step 3 : update
coordinates

n $n+1$ $n+2$

Step 1 : compute acceleration

FIGURE 13.1

Illustration of the leapfrog integration scheme.

computation of the acceleration for each particle requires a sum over all the others particles in the system. Therefore, the total computational cost of a leapfrog time step is N^2.

In this leapfrog scheme, the finite time step δ introduces systematic errors of order δ^3. We know the total energy is conserved in the system evolution. Energy conservation violations are therefore of the order δ^3. Monitoring the total energy values is a way of controlling *a posteriori* the precision of the trajectory computation.

Besides following the time evolution of our system, the total energy, given by Equation (13.2), needs to be computed from time to time. This equation involves coordinates and momenta *at the same time* t, and in the leapfrog method, if the coordinates are known at time t, the momenta are known at time $t - 0.5\delta$. Therefore, the values of the momenta at time t need to be computed as follows:

- Compute again the acceleration a_i at time t, using Equation (13.4).
- The momenta at time t are then given by $p_i + 0.5\delta\, a_i$.

The total energy is then:

$$E = \frac{1}{2} \sum_i (p_i + 0.5\delta\, a_i)^2 - \frac{1}{2} \sum_i a_i\, q_i \qquad (13.5)$$

13.3.1 PARALLEL NATURE OF THE ALGORITHM

The overall strategy for performing a parallel computation of the time evolution of our mechanical system is rather evident. Each leapfrog time step requires the following three operations, which are indeed vector operations on the particle indices:

$$a_i = -\sum_j D_{ij} q_j \quad i = 1, \ldots, N$$

$$pi \mathrel{+}= \delta\, a_i \quad i = 1, \ldots, N$$

$$qi \mathrel{+}= \delta\, p_i \quad i = 1, \ldots, N$$

In a shared memory framework, the computational workload can therefore be shared by several worker threads by assigning different sets of consecutive particles (namely, particles labeled by consecutive vector indices) to different threads. Each worker thread follows the trajectory of a set of particles whose indices are in a predefined subrange.

Most of the computational effort is spent in the computation of the acceleration of a given particle. Since the forces among particles grow linearly with distance, the computation of the acceleration a_i of the ith particle requires the knowledge of the positions of all the other particles in the system. A shared memory programming model, where all threads share the global data set, is ideally suited to this problem.

The same strategy could be implemented in a distributed memory environment, by distributing the workload in such a way that different sets of particles are followed by different MPI processes. However, each MPI process must have at each time step a copy of the whole position dataset in order to be able to compute the relevant accelerations. Once the positions of particles are updated, each MPI process must communicate to all others the new positions of its proprietary particles at each time step. This amounts to a large number of persistent messages equal to the square of the number of MPI processes. Parallel efficiency and scalability for this problem are very difficult to achieve in a distributed memory context.

13.4 Md.C SEQUENTIAL CODE

The Md.C application proposed next computes a very long molecular dynamics trajectory, given a time step δ, monitoring the values of the total and the kinetic energies of the system as the time evolution of the system proceeds. The computation proceeds as follows:

- A long trajectory involving nSteps time steps δ is computed.
- Then, the total and kinetic energies are computed and printed to stdout. Values of the total energy—a constant of the motion—validate the precision of the computation. Values of the kinetic energy are stored for future analysis.
- The trajectory computation continues, repeating the previous steps nSample times.
- At the end of the process, we dispose of nSample samples of the kinetic energy values. Their mean value and variance are computed and printed to stdout.

As stated before, this molecular dynamics code is really a part of a larger algorithm designed to compute correlated Gaussian fluctuations. There is, however, something that can be learned from this simplified computation. The kinetic energy is not by itself a constant of the motion, but it can be observed that its values are not wildly scattered. Instead, they appear concentrated inside a rather narrow range. Besides testing the scalability of the parallel algorithms involved in the application for solving the equations of motion, this code can be used to verify that, as the system size N grows, the kinetic energy fluctuations decrease (the variance gets smaller and smaller). In the thermodynamic limit $N \rightarrow \infty$, the mean value of the kinetic energy per particle is practically a constant, and it is this physical observable that defines the temperature of the system.

13.4.1 INPUT AND POSTPROCESSING

Besides the sequential version Md.C of this application, there are several other parallel versions using different programming environments and optimization options. All the details of the code not related to parallel processing (input, preprocessing, memory allocations) have been factored away in an independent module, MdAux.C, which must be linked with every one of the different code versions.

The listing below shows the common data set that is defined in MdAux.C.

```
// Global variables accessed in "MdAux.C" module
// - - - - - - - - - - - - - - - - - - - - - - -

int     Nb;              // input, number of beads
int     nTh;             // input, number of threads
int     nSteps;          // input, number of time steps in trajectory
int     nSamples;        // input, number of successive trajectories
float   delta;           // input, time step
float   dA, dB, dC;      // input, D matrix parameters

double  **D;             // correlation matrix
double  *q, *p, *a;      // position, momenta, acceleration
```

LISTING 13.1

Common data set in MdAux.C

The input parameters are read from the file md.dat. Besides the obvious parameters needed for the simulation, other parameters are needed to construct the correlation matrix D. Any symmetric, positive-definite matrix will do for the purposes of our computation here, but we have chosen a correlation matrix coming from a specific macro-molecule model. The three parameters, dA, dB, and dC, are used by an auxiliary function BuildMatrix() in the MdAux.C module to build the D matrix. This is also the reason the number of beads Nb is passed as input parameter, instead of the real matrix size N, which is N=3*Nb

The MdAux.C module defines two public functions that are called by main():

- **InitJob() function**
    - Reads the input data from file md.dat.
    - Allocates D, q, p, and a.
    - Constructs an initial state for the trajectory computation, by giving initial values to the q and p vectors. These initial values are provided by a Gaussian random generator.
    - Calls the BuildMatrix() function to construct D.
- **CloseJob() function**
    - Deallocates D, q, p, and a.

For postprocessing, the main() function uses the DMonitor class from the vath library to compute mean values and variances of a collection of doubles (in this case, the mean values and variances of the kinetic energy samples). This class is used as follows:

- DMonitor M declares the object M that provides the service.
- M.AccumData(x) increases an internal counter, and accumulates internally x—for the mean value computation—and x.x—for the variance computation.
- M.Reset() computes and stores the mean value and variance of the previously collected data, and resets the internal data to prepare for reuse in another computation. The previously computed results are retrieved by calling M.Average() and M.Variance().

13.4.2 SEQUENTIAL CODE, Md.C

Here is the sequential code listing.

```
// Auxiliary functions declarations
// – – – – – – – – – – – – – – – –
void   InitJob();      // in module MdAux.C
void   CloseJob();     // in module MdAux.C
void   ComputeTrajectory();

// Global variables in this module
// – – – – – – – – – – – – – – – –
double Ekin, Etot;       // kinetic and potential energies
DMonitor EK;             // to compute kinetic energy mean values
int N;

void ComputeTrajectory()
   {
   // – – – – – – – – – – – – – – – – – – – – – – – – – –
   // This function computes first the nStep time steps,
   // and then the kinetic and potential energies
   // – – – – – – – – – – – – – – – – – – – – – – – – – –
   int n, j, count;
   double scr;

   for(count=0; count < nSteps; ++count)
     {
     for(n=0; n<N; n++)      // computation of acceleration
        {
        a[n] = 0.0;
        for(j=0; j<N; j++) a[n] += D[n][j] * q[j];
        }

     for( n=0; n<N; n++)    //integration of equations of motion
        {
        p[n] -= (delta * a[n]);
        q[n] += (delta * p[n]);
```

```
            }
        }

    Ekin = 0.0;               // energy computations
    Etot = 0.0
    for(n=0; n<N; n++)
        {
        a[n] = 0.0;
        for(j=0; j<N; j++) a[n] += D[n][j] * q[j];
        scr = p[n] - 0.5 * a[n] * delta;
        Ekin += 0.5*scr*scr:
        Etot += 0.5*q[n]*a[n];
        }
    Etot += Ekin;
    }


// - - - - - - - - - -
// The main() function
// - - - - - - - - - -
int main(int argc, char **argv)
    {
    int sample;
    CpuTimer TR;

    InitJob();
    if(argc==2) nTh = atoi(argv[1]);
    N = 3*Nb;
    delta = 0.02;

    TR.Start();
    for(sample=1; sample<=nSamples; ++sample)
        {
    ComputeTrajectory();
        std::cout << "\n Ekin = " << Ekin << "        Etot = "
                << Etot << std::endl;
        EK.AccumData(Ekin);
    }
    TR.Stop();
    EK.Reset();
    std::cout << "\nAverage kinetic energy " << EK.Average()
            << "\nVariance:            " << EK.Variance();
    TR.ReportTimes();
    CloseJob();
    }
```

LISTING 13.2

Sequential Md.C code.

After performing all the required initializations, main() enters into the computation region and performs a loop over samples, calling the ComputeTrajectory() function that integrates the equations of motion for nSteps time steps, and returns the values of the total and kinetic energies in two global variables, Etot and Ekin.

The ComputeTrajectory() function executes the loop over the nSteps time steps, and then computes the total and kinetic energies. This function shows all the potential parallelism in this problem, and the main modifications in the parallel versions of the code will be performed here.

Example 1: Md.C

To compile, run make md. Sequential version. Input data is read from file md.dat. The number of threads, read initially from this file, can be changed from the command line.

13.5 PARALLEL IMPLEMENTATIONS OF Md.C

There are several different parallel implementations of the molecular dynamics application, discussed next.

13.5.1 GENERAL STRUCTURE OF DATA PARALLEL PROGRAMS

A typical data parallel code has the structure shown in Figure 13.2. The main() function starts and performs all the input, memory allocations, and initialization operations needed to set up the program context. Then, there is in general a series of parallel regions where the workload is distributed across a

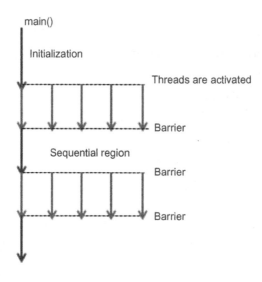

FIGURE 13.2

General structure of a data parallel code.

team of worker threads, followed by sequential sections where the workload is carried out by only one thread. Remember that in OpenMP the master thread suspends the ongoing task and joins the workers team, while in the case of the vath library pools the master thread is either doing something else or executing an idle wait.

There are several ways to organize the parallel treatment of Figure 13.2. In some simple cases, like in our molecular dynamics code, the parallel regions are restricted to loops that can be computed in parallel because the loop iterations are totally independent. In this case, a *microtasking* approach can be adopted. The OpenMP parallel for directive or the TBB parallel_for or parallel_reduce algorithms can be used to automatically distribute the loop workload across the worker threads. In this case, the code remains all the time in sequential mode with the exception of the work-sharing parallel sections related to the loops.

If the successive parallel regions in the code are all similar, in the sense that they involve the same number of threads acting on the same data sets, a *macrotasking* approach can be adopted. The complete parallel code consists of a unique parallel section executing a unique parallel task. The worker thread team is active all along, the code being by default in parallel mode. Eventual transitions to sequential regions are handled either by using the master or single directives in OpenMP, or by selecting only one active thread between two barriers (see the figure) with a conditional if(rank==n) statement.

13.5.2 DIFFERENT CODE VERSIONS

There are several different versions of the code that take the same input and produce the same output:

- *Md.C*: Sequential version.
- *MdOmp.C*. Parallel, OpenMp version using a macrotasking programming style (big parallel tasks with explicit synchronizations).
- *MdOmpF.C*: Parallel, OpenMP version using a microtasking programming style in which the loops involved in the leapfrog time step are parallelized using the parallel for directive.
- *MdTh.C*: Parallel version based on the NPool thread pool, using a macrotasking programming style. There are several barrier synchronization points in this application, and this version of the code allows us to select, using the preprocessor, either the standard Barrier class based on a idle wait, or the alternative SpBarrier class based on a busy wait, in order to compare their performance.
- *MdTbb.C*: Parallel TBB version using a microtasking style where the loops involved in the leapfrog time step are parallelized using the parallel_for algorithm.

These different code versions, corresponding to different multithreading environments and strategies, are portable as explained in Annex A. Additional optimization options, not directly related to multithreading, are also explored, such as vectorization or optimized memory accesses. This will been done at the end of the chapter for the OpenMP version of the code, using the capabilities of the Intel C-C++ compiler, because the OpenMP 4.0 simd vectorization directive was not yet implemented in the GNU compiler at the time of the preparation of this book. In well-adapted data parallel applications—and Md.C is one of them—the combination of multithreading and vectorization can provide significant performance enhancements.

13.5.3 OpenMP MICROTASKING IMPLEMENTATION, MdOmpF.C

This first OpenMP version of the code only requires a couple of minor changes to the sequential version:

- Add the parallel for directive in the loops involved in the leapfrog time step computation, as indicated in the listing below.
- Add also, in the code block where the parallel_for directive appears, a call to omp_set_num_threads() fixing the number of threads in the next parallel regions. Or, instead, add a num_threads clause in each parallel directive.
- Note that there is no change in the main function. Main just calls a function with internal, OpenMP-driven, parallel execution.

```
void ComputeTrajectory()
    {
    ...
    omp_set_num_threads(nTh);
    for(count=0; count < nSteps; ++count)
        {
        #pragma omp parallel for
        for(n=0; n<N; n++)      // computation of acceleration
            {
            a[n] = 0.0;
            for(j=0; j<N; j++) a[n] += D[n][j] * q[j];
            }

        #pragma omp parallel for
        for( n=0; n<N; n++)    //integration of equations of motion
            {
            p[n] -= (delta * a[n]);
            q[n] += (delta * p[n]);
            }
        }
    ...
```

LISTING 13.3

MdOmpF.C code (partial listing).

In the listing above, there is no collapse(2) clause in the parallel for directive acting on the double acceleration loop, asking for the fusion of the two nested loops into a huge single loop. In fact, the collapse clause here is refused by the compiler, politely explaining that because of the a[n]=0.0 initialization statement the two loops are not strictly nested. It is possible to separate in another previous loop the a[n] initialization, and this works, but the whole modification does not buy us substantial performance improvement. As will be discussed later on, *vectorizing the inner loop* is a much better option than using loop fusion.

The ComputeTrajectory() function includes also a loop involved in the energy computation that can also be the target of a parallel_for directive. This is not critical for performance, because energy computations are indeed very occasional. Nevertheless, the parallel for directive has been added in the energy computation loops in order to have the same level of parallel execution as in other implementations of the code.

Example 2: MdOmpF.C

To compile, run make mdompf. The input data is read from file md.dat. The number of threads, read initially from this file, can be changed from the command line.

13.5.4 OpenMP MACROTASKING IMPLEMENTATION, MdOmp.C

Here is the parallel OpenMP version of the code, in a macrotasking programming style. The most important changes are made in the ComputeTrajectory() function, which is transformed into a task function executed by the worker threads.

```
#include <ThreadRangeOmp.h>
...
// – – – – – – – – – – – – – – – – – – – – – – – – – –
// Task function for the computation of the molecular
// dynamics trajectory
// – – – – – – – – – – – – – – – – – – – – – – – – –
void ComputeTrajectory()
   {
   int n, j, count, rank;
   double ekin, epot, scr;
   int nl, nh;

   nl = 0;     // set thread range
   nh = N;
   ThreadRangeOmp(nl, nh);

   for(count=0; count < nSteps; ++count)
     {
     for(n=nl; n<nh; n++)      // computation of accelerations
     {
     a[n] = 0.0;
     for(j=0; j<SZ; j++) a[n] += D[n][j] * q[j];
     }

     #pragma omp barrier        // barrier 1

     for( n=nl; n<nh; n++)      // equations of motion
     {
     p[n] -= (delta * a[n]);
     q[n] += (delta * p[n]);
     }
     #pragma omp barrier       // barrier 2
     }
```

Continued

```
        // Trajectory done. Compute energies
        // - - - - - - - - - - - - - - -
        ekin = 0.0;
        epot = 0.0
        for(n=nl; n<nh; n++)
            {
            a[n] = 0.0;
            for(j=0; j<SZ; j++) a[n] += D[n][j] * q[j];
            // - - - - - - - - - - - - - - - - - - - - - -
            // Notice: we do not need a barrier here, because we are
            // not going to use the acceleration to update coordinates.
            // See the text below.
            // - - - - - - - - - - - - - - - - - - - - - -
            scr = p[n] - 0.5 * a[n] * delta;
            ekin += 0.5*scr*scr;
            epot += 0.5*q[n]*a[n];
            }

        #pragma omp critical      // accumulate in global variables
            {
            Ek += ekin;
            Et += (ekin+epot);
            }
        }


    // The main() function (partial listing)
    // - - - - - - - - - - - - - - - - -
    int main(int argc, char **argv)
        {
        ...

        TR.Start();
        for(sample=1; sample<=nSamples; ++sample)
            {
            Ek = 0.0; Et = 0.0;
            #pragma omp parallel
                {
                ComputeTrajectory();
                }
            // Print kinetic and total energies
            // - - - - - - - - - - - - - -
            std::cout << "\n Ekin = " << Ek << "        Etot = "
                    << Et << std::endl;
            M.AccumData(Ek);       // accumulate kinetic energy values
        }
        TR.Stop();
        ...
        }
```

LISTING 13.4

Partial listing of MdOmp.C code.

Work-sharing among threads

In order to implement the work distribution among threads by hand, an auxiliary function ThreadRange-Omp() has been introduced that operates in the same way as the ThreadRange() member function of the SPool utility. It receives as arguments two references to the global index range [0, N) and returns in these arguments the subrange appropriate for the caller thread. This function takes into account the fact that the OpenMP thread ranks are in [0, nThreads-1] instead of [1, nThreads] as is the case for the SPool utility. The function is defined in the include file ThreadRangeOmp.h.

After completing all the scheduled leapfrog time steps, each thread computes etot and ekin, their partial contributions to the total and kinetic energies. A critical section is then used to accumulate these partial results in the global variables Et and Ek, read by main().

Barrier synchronizations

The task function listed above involves two barrier synchronization points at each time step, and it is important to clearly understand the nature of the race conditions that enforce the presence of these two barriers. It is intuitively obvious that a barrier must be placed at points where worker threads must wait for results coming from other worker threads to proceed. But this is not all: worker threads must also avoid corrupting the work performed by the other partners.

Let us focus our attention on what a particular worker thread is doing. In examining the need of synchronization with other worker threads, two questions must be asked:

- *Criterium A*: How can my partner threads induce race conditions that invalidate my calculation?
- *Criterium B*: How can my computation induce race conditions that invalidate my partner's calculations?

Let us examine, on the basis of these two criteria, the role played by the two barriers encountered in the listing above:

- Barrier 1: forces a wait after the computation of the acceleration. Here, criterion B is at work. It may appear at first glance that, once the accelerations are known, each worker is free to go ahead and update the velocities and positions of the particles under its control. This looks very innocent, and one may conclude at first sight that no barrier is needed. However, it may happen that other threads are late in computing *their* accelerations, and they still need to read the current thread-owned coordinates at time step n, not at time step $n + 1$. Therefore, the current thread owned positions cannot be updated before all the other threads are finished computing their accelerations.
- Barrier 2: forces a wait at the end of a time step in the solution of the equations of motion, before starting a new loop iteration. Here, criterion A is at work: wait until all positions are updated before starting again with a new computation of the accelerations.

Example 2: MdOmp.C

To compile, run make mdomp. OpenMP version. Input data is read from file md.dat. The number of threads, read initially from this file, can be changed from the command line.

13.5.5 SPool IMPLEMENTATION, MdTh.C

Given the simplicity of the parallel algorithm, this version of the code uses the SPool thread pool utility. The thread function to be executed by each thread is very similar to the OpenMP function presented in the listing above. In the main function, the OpenMP parallel section is replaced by a job dispatching to the pool.

Idle-wait versus spin-wait barriers

The two barrier synchronization points that are repeatedly accessed inside a loop provide an excellent opportunity for testing the performance of the different barrier classes introduced in Chapter 9, corresponding to different wait strategies. The MdTh.C module uses the C preprocessor to select the different barrier interfaces: idle wait (Barrier class) or spin wait (SpBarrier class). In this version of the molecular dynamics code, B is a pointer to a barrier object, initialized as follows:

```
// In the global variable declarations:
// - - - - - - - - - - - - - - - - - -
#ifdef SPIN_BARRIER
SpBarrier *B;
#else
Barrier *B;
#endif

// In the main() initialization of B
// - - - - - - - - - - - - - - - - --
#ifdef SPIN_BARRIER
B = new SpBarrier(nTh);
#else
B = new Barrier(nTh);
#endif
```

LISTING 13.5

Selecting barrier type with preprocessor.

The rest of the code is unchanged, because both barrier classes have the same public interfaces.

Example 3: MdTh.C

To compile, run make mdth. SPool version. Input data is read from file md.dat. The number of threads, read initially from this file, can be changed from the command line.

Comparison of code performance does confirm that the spin-wait barriers moderately outperform the idle-wait barriers when the synchronization contention begins to be important. Consider first the tests performed running a medium-sized configuration in a four-core laptop. We take the case of Ns=660 beads (the vector size being therefore 1980), and 20 kinetic energy samples are computed, with 1000 trajectory time steps per sample. We are naturally using four threads. The other parameters in the run

Table 13.1 Wall Execution Times in Seconds, for 18,000 Particles, 10 Samples, 10 Time Steps per Sample (Using GNU 4.8 Compiler)

Idle vs Spin Barriers			
Barrier Type	**Wall (s)**	**User (s)**	**System (s)**
Idle	57	202.9	0.98
Spin	55.1	218.9	0.03
OpenMP	53.9	214.5	0.08

are the ones defined in the md.dat file that comes with the codes. Table 13.1 shows the measured wall, user and system times.

A data set of 1980 particles shared among four threads does not represent an enormous computational workload per thread, and we have in this configuration a total of 40,000 barrier calls per thread. Spin barriers systematically provide in this case a 3-4% better performance than idle-wait barriers. Performance improvements are expected to be more important when the number of worker threads (and the barrier contention) is increased. The barrier contention grows faster than linear with the number of threads.

The OpenMP performance reported in Table 13.1 does not change if the OpenMP spin-wait policy is forced by setting OMP_WAIT_POLICY to active. This probably means the OpenMP implementation is using a spin-wait policy by default.

13.5.6 TBB IMPLEMENTATION, MdTbb.C

The TBB implementation is again a microtasking style code, which remains in sequential mode. At each time step the main function just calls parallel_for twice, first to compute the accelerations, and next to update momenta and coordinates. Two very simple appropriate Body classes are then provided.

Occasionally, the code computes the total and kinetic energies, and it is not critical to perform this computation in parallel. However, for comparison with other implementations, a third Body class for the parallel energy computation using parallel_reduce is provided.

Example 10: MdTBB.C

To compile, run make mdtbb. Input data is read from file md.dat.

13.6 PARALLEL PERFORMANCE ISSUES

The performance of the different implementations of the molecular dynamics code are examined next, the target platform being a Linux SMP node composed of two Intel Sandy Bridge sockets, each socket integrating eight cores running two hardware threads each. In the Sandy Bridge socket, each core has its own, private L1 and L2 caches. This configuration can run up to 32 hardware threads, but hyper-threading has been excluded in our tests, and only one thread per core is run. In general-purpose Intel processors, hyper-threading is often useful, but it is not a *sine qua-non* condition for performance, as is the case for the Intel Xeon Phi co-processor.

A relatively large data set (18,000 particles) is chosen, and the runs are limited to short trajectories (10 time steps each) and only 10 energy samples. There are therefore only 100 time steps altogether. The motivation is to have short execution times, while giving each thread a large number of particles to work upon so as to maximize as much as possible the ratio of computation to synchronization overhead. Table 13.2 gives the execution times for the sequential code md and for the different parallel implementations, for 4, 8, 12, and 16 threads. In running the TBB implementation, the granularity in the parallel_for and parallel_reduce algorithms has been adjusted to fit the domain decomposition pattern to the number of worker threads. The Intel C-C++ compiler, version 13.0.1, has been used, because of its additional vectorization options, which will be discussed in the next section.

Two obvious comments follow from the results of Table 13.2:

1. *Comparable performance of all programming environments*, as well as the fact that the automatic work-sharing facility in OpenMP has the same performance as the macrotasking version with the work-sharing done "by hand." This is not, however, very surprising after all. The parallel pattern in this problem is rather trivial—a straightforward work-sharing data parallel pattern—and, given the limited number of time steps, there is a limited amount of synchronization overhead.
2. *Excellent scaling up to eight threads*. Up to eight threads, nice parallel behavior is observed, with a speedup proportional to the number of threads. Beyond eight threads, these nice scaling properties start to fade away. This is a rather common feature for memory bound applications running on general-purpose computational engines, not specially designed for high-performance computing. On-chip communications inside a socket are much more efficient than off-chip communications across sockets.

What features of this application contribute to the scalability limitations? First, there is the growing impact of synchronization overhead. In the macrotasking versions (SPool and OpenMP), there are

Table 13.2 Wall Execution Times in Seconds, for 18,000 Particles, 10 Samples, 10 Time Steps per Sample, With Intel C-C++ Compiler, Version 13.0.1

nb Threads	md	Performance			
		mdth	mdtbb	mdomp	mdompf
1	118.7				
4		27.3	27.2	27.2	27.3
8		14.4	13.9	14.3	14.1
12		10.3	9.9	9.9	9.9
16		8.27	7.94	8.2	8.2

two barriers per time step. In the microtasking versions (TBB and parallel for in OpenMP), there are no explicit barriers, but implicit barriers are present at the transition points from a parallel to a sequential region. Perfect scaling is only possible if synchronization costs are negligible with respect to computation. This is the case for a small number of threads. However, when profiling the mdth code execution for 16 threads, we can observe that barrier wait calls account for about 30% of the execution time. It is clear that, when the same fixed amount of work is shared among too many workers, they are forced to spend most of their time in synchronizing their activity.

Another issue worth thinking about is the efficiency of memory accesses. The hierarchical cache-based memory system is designed to take advantage of space and time locality: space locality, by moving a contiguous memory block to a cache line, and time locality, by keeping in the cache the most frequently accessed cache lines. When looking at the pattern of memory accesses to the $D[ij]$, $q[i]$, $p[i]$) arrays in our application, we observe that:

- The $D[ij]$ matrix is constructed in the initialization part of the code, and from there on it is only accessed in read mode, in the computation of the acceleration. Moreover, in this computation, *each thread repeatedly accesses the same exclusive set of contiguous rows*. This means these rows are likely to persist in the owner-thread L2 cache, if the cache is big enough. This memory access pattern is satisfactory.
- The same observation applies to the momentum vector $p[i]$. A given thread only accesses the contiguous momentum components corresponding to the particles under its control. Therefore, these momentum components are likely to persist in each thread L2 cache. It may happen, if subranges sizes are not an exact multiple of the cache line size, that threads A and B have a cache line with momentum values corresponding, for example, to the end of the thread A range and the start of the thread B range. In this case, the *false-sharing* phenomenon may occur: when A updates its momenta, the cache line is invalidated and thread B is forced to recover its momentum values from main memory in spite of the fact that they have not been updated (yet). However, for a big data set, this phenomenon is infrequent.
- The situation is completely different for the coordinates $q[i]$. In the acceleration calculation, all threads read the complete data set, and there is absolutely no locality of any kind in this case. Indeed, all threads upload the complete $q[i]$ vector into their L2 cache. Then, each one updates its exclusive part. This means all cache lines in all L2 caches are invalidated, and the complete data set must be recovered from main memory at the next time step.

The $q[i]$ memory accesses are not optimal, but they result from the nature of the problem at hand (long-range forces connecting all pairs of particles), and there is nothing we can do about it.

13.7 ACTIVATING VECTOR PROCESSING

Once a satisfactory multithreaded implementation of the application is obtained, additional performance improvement can be obtained if threads are executing loops that can be vectorized, which is true in our case. Vectorization, as explained in Chapter 1, is an SIMD (single instruction, multiple data) intrinsic parallel facility inside a core that enables the simultaneous execution of several loop iterations. The Sandy Bridge cores being used here have vector registers 256 bytes wide that can accommodate four SIMD lanes for doubles or eight for floats. In our case, where arrays of doubles are used, vectorization should provide a theoretical speedup of 4 if the code execution is strongly dominated by the execution of vectorizable loops.

Section 13.8 at the end of this chapter provides a short review of the Intel compiler vectorization programming interfaces. Readers are strongly encouraged to consult the official documentation [36]. Chapter 7 of J. Jeffers and J. Reinders book on Intel Xeon Phi programming [8] is also an excellent vectorization tutorial that applies to all Intel processors. Loop vectorization is the default behavior of the compiler, but its vectorization analysis is very conservative (as it should be), and in most cases it must be helped with directives to achieve a satisfactory vectorization. These basic directives are reviewed in Section 13.8 at the end of this chapter. We will concentrate on the OpenMP macrotasking mdomp implementation of our code, but vectorization is strictly a single-core optimization affair, having nothing to do with multithreading, and the same analysis can be implemented for vath of TBB implementations.

The MdOmpV.C file is the same as MdOmp.C, with added vectorization directives and a simple reformulations of the code needed to facilitate vectorization. The listing below shows the ComputeTrajetory() task function, where the vectorization directives are inserted.

```
void ComputeTrajectory()
   {
   int n, j, count, rank;
   double ekin, epot, scr;
   int nl, nh;

   double *V = D[0];      // new
   ...
   for(count=0; count < nSteps; ++count)
      {
      for(n=nl; n<nh; n++)       // computation of accelerations
         {
         scr = 0.0;
         #pragma ivdep
         for(j=0; j<SZ; j++) scr += V[n*N+j] * q[j];
         a[n] = scr;
         }

      #pragma omp barrier       // barrier 1

      #pragma ivdep
      for( n=nl; n<nh; n++)      // equations of motion
         {
         p[n] -= (delta * a[n]);
         q[n] += (delta * p[n]);
         }
      #pragma omp barrier       // barrier 2
      }
```

```
// Trajectory done. Compute energies
// Similar directives are applied in the loops
// that follow
// - - - - - - - - - - - - - - - - - - - - - -
...
}
```

LISTING 13.6

Vectorized trajectory computation (partial listing).

Vectorization is performed by using the mild #pragma ivdep, telling the compiler that the pointers that follow point to nonoverlapping regions in memory (see Section 13.8). The loops that update momenta and coordinates are directly vectorized with this directive. The double loop for the acceleration computation is slightly more subtle. The correct procedure in this case is to vectorize the huge inner loop that runs over the complete particle set. This part of the code has been rewritten in a way that helps the compiler better understand what is going on.

Indeed, when the strong #pragma simd directive was applied to force the vectorization of the initial version using the D[i][j] matrix elements, the vectorization failed with the *dereference too complex* error message (see Section 13.8). In fact, the compiler was reluctant to vectorize a construct with nested indirections, due to the way the D matrix was allocated. Section 13.7 later in this chapter shows the matrix allocation procedure: D is a pointer to an array of pointers to vectors of doubles. However, internally, D[0] is just a vector array of size NM where the D matrix rows are ranged one after the other, and this simpler data structure is better controlled by the vectorization tests performed by the compiler. The code was therefore reformulated to simplify the compiler job by using a vector array V=D[0] in the inner loop, instead of the D matrix elements themselves. With this modification, the loop was vectorized. Finally, the strong #pragma simd directive was replaced by the milder #pragma ivdep directive.

This episode shows that vectorization is not an affair that reduces to throwing the right directive at the right place. Compiler feedback is often needed for success. The #pragma omp simd directive introduced by OpenMP 4.0 has been discussed in Chapter 10. Having standard vectorization interfaces in OpenMP is a huge step forward, but keep in mind that the compiler feedback is not part of the standard, and that efficient usage of the OpenMP vectorization directive may require some familiarity with the specific implementation.

Another single-core optimization that can be explored is memory alignment. This code works with arrays of doubles coded over 64 bytes. In all platforms, L2 cache line sizes are a multiple of 64 bytes. The Sandy Bridge L2 cache lines, for example, are 512 bytes (8 doubles) wide. If the starting memory address of an array is 64 bytes aligned, namely, if this address is a multiple of 64 bytes, then array elements will never spread across a cache line boundary when array chunks are mapped to the cache memory. Memory alignment facilitates data transfers in the hierarchical memory system. As explained in Section 13.8, aligned memory allocation can be implemented by using an Intel replacement of malloc and free. Table 13.3 compares the performance of the mdomp code reported already in Table 13.2, with the vectorized version mdompv. The preprocessor has been used to select the memory alignment option. If the ALIGNED_MEM_ALLOC variable is defined (both in MdOmpV.C and MdAux.C), the Intel allocation routines are selected. Otherwise, the standard allocation with malloc() applies. In Table 13.3,

Table 13.3 Wall Execution Times in Seconds, for 18,000 Particles, 10 Samples, and 10 Time Steps per Sample			
Vectorization Performance			
nb Threads	mdomp	mdompv	mdompv(a)
4	27.2	10.5	11
8	14.3	8.5	8.6
12	9.9	8.3	8.4
16	8.2	8.2	8.25

the mdompv column corresponds to vectorization only, and mdompv_a to vectorization plus aligned memory allocation.

We can observe that, for four and eight threads, when the code has good scaling properties because computation dominates synchronization overhead, vectorization provides significant performance improvement: a speedup close to three for four threads and slightly above two for eight threads. We can also see that aligned memory allocation does not induce here a significant change in performance.

13.8 ANNEX: MATRIX ALLOCATIONS

Consider a M×N matrix D[m][n], where 0<=m<M and 0<=n<N. This corresponds to *matrix indices having offset 0*, as is customary in C-C++. This matrix will be allocated using *new* and *delete*, but the same thing can be done with *malloc* and *free*.

The allocation and deallocation procedures are as follows:

```
double **D;      //  is a pointer to an array of pointers to doubles

// Allocate an array of M pointers to (double *).

D = new (double *)[M];

// Allocate D[0] — the first usable pointer in the array above — as
// a huge array of doubles of size (N*M), where all the matrix
// elements go, one row after the other.

D[0] = new double[N*M];

// D[0][0] is pointing to the first element of the first row, and all
// the matrix elements follow. We will now initialize the pointers D[i]
// so that D[i][0] points to the first element of the ith row:

for(int n=1; n<N; n++) D[n] = D[n-1] + N;
```

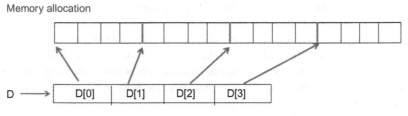

Memory allocation

D ⟶

D[0]   D[1]   D[2]   D[3]

Allocation of: double **D, as a 4×4 matrix

FIGURE 13.3

Matrix allocation procedure.

```
// Deallocation:
// – – – – – –
delete [] D[0];   // get rid of the data
delete [] D;      // get rid of the pointers
```

LISTING 13.7

Allocation of matrix of doubles.

Figure 13.3 shows clearly what happens for a 4*4 matrix, called D. Note that one of the advantages of this allocation procedure is being able to enable *loop fusion*: a double loop over rows and columns can be replaced by a single loop over $D[0][n]$ with $0 <= n < (N * M)$.

13.9 ANNEX: COMMENTS ON VECTORIZATION WITH INTEL COMPILERS

This section summarizes the compiler vectorization directives, as well as the Intel interfaces for aligned memory allocation [8, 36]. Automatic vectorization is enabled by default, and a typical command line for the compiler is (see the makefiles of this chapter):

icpc -O3 -vec-report=3 -omdomp MdOmp.C MdAux.C

The vec-report=3 switch demands a detailed report of the compiler vectorization activity. Every loop in the code is carefully examined, and the compiler produces a very detailed report for each one of them explaining why vectorization failed (the most common situation). The compiler has substantial built-in intelligence. It performs lots of checks and tests, and takes a very conservative attitude. At this point start the programmer efforts to help the compiler achieve an efficient vectorization of the critical loops that control the overall performance, by adding directives. These directives are hints to the compiler to remove certain restrictions it may be enforcing by default.

The Intel compiler allows programmers to guide the vectorizer activity at three different levels:

- *#pragma ivdep*: This means *ignore vector dependencies*. This directive instructs the compiler to ignore the checks concerning possible vector dependencies. A typical use case are loops with pointers to arrays: the compiler will refuse vectorization unless it is absolutely certain there is no aliasing; namely, that different pointers are not pointing to overlapping memory buffers. This directive provides the assurance that this is not the case. But the compiler remains very conservative on all other vectorization checks.

- *#pragma vector* [clauses]: This directive provides further hints for ignoring some other checks, but still leaves room for conservative behavior of the vectorizer. For example, #pragma vector always tells the compiler to ignore efficiency heuristics, but still only works if the loop can be vectorized. And #pragma vector aligned tells the compiler that all memory references in the loop are aligned on 64-byte boundaries.

- *#pragma simd* [clauses] is the most aggressive clause: It is a *vectorize or die* directive, asking the compiler to relax all requirements and make all possible efforts to vectorize the loop. This directive is roughly equivalent to #pragma vector always and #pragma ivdep, but more powerful because it does not perform any dependency analysis.

- The simd directive is very close to the same OpenMP directive. It accepts similar clauses: reduction, private, firstprivate, and lastprivate.

- There are, however, a number of restrictions for SIMD vectorization:
  - Loops must be countable: the number of iterations must be known before the loop starts to execute.
  - Some operations are not supported: the compiler produces an *operation not supported* error message.
  - Very complex array subscripts or pointer arithmetic may not be vectorized: the compiler produces a *dereference too complex* error message.
  - Loops with a very low number of iterations (low trip count) may not be vectorized: the compiler produces a *low trip count* error message.
  - Extremely large loop bodies (with many lines and symbols) may not be vectorized.
  - The SIMD directive cannot be applied to a loop containing exception handling code in C++.

For a more detailed discussion, the extensive Intel documentation on this subject can be consulted. We strongly recommend reading Chapter 4 of James Reinder's book on Intel Xeon Phi [8], which provides a clear and complete overview of all the programmer's vectorization options, as well as memory access optimizations like the data alignment issue discussed below.

13.9.1 DATA ALIGNMENT

Imposing data alignment on specific memory boundaries may help the runsystem to optimize memory accesses. The way to proceed is to align the data when memory is allocated, and then use directives in places where the data is used to inform the compiler that data arguments are aligned.

- Align the data.
- Use pragmas/directives in places where the data is used to tell the compiler that arguments are aligned.

Aligned dynamic memory allocation based on replacements of malloc() and free() provided by Intel C++ Composer XE. The malloc replacement, called _mm_malloc(), has the following signature:

```
void *_mm_malloc(int size, int base)
```

which is the malloc() signature with an extra argument base that defines the alignment. Pointers allocated in this way must be released with _mm_free(). The listing below shows some examples of aligned allocation of static and dynamic arrays.

```
// Aligned allocation of an static array
// – – – – – – – – – – – – – – – – – – – –
float A[1000] __attribute__((aligned(64))));

// Aligned declaration of pointers
// – – – – – – – – – – – – – – – –
_ _assume_aligned(ptr, 64); // ptr is 64B aligned

// Aligned dynamic allocation of an array of floats, starting on
// a 64 byte boundary
// – – – – – – – – – – – – – – – – – – – – – – – – – – – – – –
float *V = (float *)_mm_malloc(1000*sizeof(float), 64);
...
_mm_free(V);

// Informing the compiler of the alignment:
// – – – – – – – – – – – – – – – – – – – –
void myfunc(double p[])
   {
   __asume_aligned(p, 64);
   for(int n=0; n<N; n++) p[i]++;
   }

// Telling the compiler that ALL references are nicely aligned
// – – – – – – – – – – – – – – – – – – – – – – – – – – – – – – – –
#pragma vector aligned
for(n=0; n<N; n++)
   A[n] = B[n] + C[n];
```

LISTING 13.8

Data alignment examples.

FURTHER DATA PARALLEL EXAMPLES

14.1 INTRODUCTION

This chapter focuses on *stencil codes*, that is, parallel applications in which a map operation is performed on data values defined on a multidimensional grid. Data values updates are in general independent, and they can be performed in parallel, but they are updated in a way that depends on the near-neighbor values. A typical use case arises in image-filtering algorithms: pixel values defined on a two-dimensional grid are smoothed out by taking into account the neighbor pixel values. The set of near-neighbor data values that participate in the pixel update is called a stencil, and the whole image update process is a map operation in which each pixel is convoluted with its stencil. To the extent that pixel updates are totally independent, there is a huge amount of potential parallelism in this context.

Two examples concerning the solution of two-dimensional partial differential equations are developed. The first one is a straightforward map parallel pattern that can immediately benefit from multithreading and vectorization. The second example involves *data dependencies* that prevent a straightforward work-sharing pattern, and the way this issue can be handled is discussed in detail.

14.1.1 EXAMPLES IN THIS CHAPTER

The two examples proposed in this chapter involve solving the Laplace or Poisson equation in two dimensions. In the first case, the purpose is to determine the stationary temperature distribution $T(x, y)$ inside a rectangular metallic plate when the borders of the plate are maintained at some fixed temperature values. Under these conditions, the stationary temperature distribution is a solution of Laplace's equation:

$$\frac{\partial^2 T}{\partial x^2} + \frac{\partial^2 T}{\partial y^2} = 0$$

and the problem is to find the solution inside the plate with the given boundary conditions on the border.

The second example involves a two-dimensional rectangular domain bounded by metallic walls. Inside this rectangular domain, there is an electric charge with density $\rho(x, y)$ mainly concentrated in the center of the domain, and vanishing at the borders. The problem to be solved is the computation of the electric potential $U(x, y)$ inside the domain, which is a solution of Poisson's equation:

$$\frac{\partial^2 U}{\partial x^2} + \frac{\partial^2 U}{\partial y^2} = \rho(x, y)$$

with the boundary condition $U = 0$ on the four borders. Indeed, the electric potential must be constant on the conducting walls, and without loss of generality this constant can be set equal to zero.

14.1.2 FINITE-DIFFERENCE DISCRETIZATION

To obtain the numerical solutions of the above equations, the *finite-difference method* is adopted. The continuous (x, y) variables are discretized by introducing a two-dimensional grid, and by representing all continuous functions by their values at the discrete sets of points:

$$x_n = x_0 + n\Delta, \quad n = 0, \dots, (N-1)$$
$$y_n = y_0 + m\Delta, \quad m = 0, \dots, (M-1)$$

where Δ is the *grid spacing*. The point (x_0, y_0) corresponds to the lower-left corner of the rectangular domain. As shown in Figure 14.1, the whole rectangular domain, *including the borders*, is covered when the (m, n) indices swap the domains indicated in the equation above.

From now on, we will write $U_{m,n}$ for $U(x_n, y_m)$ and $\rho_{m,n}$ for $\rho(x_n, y_m)$. Now, $U_{m,n}$ is just a two-dimensional matrix with m as row index and n as column index, as shown in Figure 14.1. Using the standard finite-difference representation for the second derivative, the Poisson equation becomes

$$\frac{U_{m+1,n} + U_{m-1,n} - 2U_{m,n}}{\Delta^2} + \frac{U_{m,n+1} + U_{m,n-1} - 2U_{m,n}}{\Delta^2} = \rho_{m,n}$$

or equivalently

$$U_{m+1,n} + U_{m-1,n} + U_{m,n+1} + U_{m,n-1} - 4U_{m,n} = F_{m,n} \tag{14.1}$$

where $F_{m,n} = \Delta^2 \rho_{m,n}$. This is the discretized form of the original differential equations that will be used in what follows.

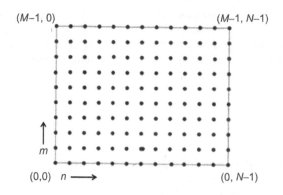

FIGURE 14.1

Discretization of the Laplace and Poisson problems.

14.2 **RELAXATION METHODS**

The different relaxation methods for solving Equation (14.1) start from an initial guess for $U_{m,n}$, a kind of approximate solution that fits the boundary condition. Then, an iterative procedure is applied, by successively updating all the values of this matrix, until convergence is achieved. The iteration procedure adopted by the different relaxation methods to be used next is easily described by rewriting Equation (14.1) as:

$$U_{m,n} = 0.25(U_{m+1,n} + U_{m-1,n} + U_{m,n+1} + U_{m,n-1}) - 0.25F_{m,n} \qquad (14.2)$$

The different iteration procedures swap all the grid points—except the boundaries where the $U_{m,n}$ values are fixed from the start—with a double loop, first over rows (loop on m) and next an inner loop on columns (loop on n), and replace the old value of $U_{m,n}$ by a new value given by the right-hand side of Equation (14.2). For the homogeneous Laplace equation, the source term is set to $F_{m,n} = 0$. The numerical solution we are searching for is a fixed point of this iteration procedure: old values are equal to new values. There are three iteration procedures to be considered:

- *Jacobi method*: The update Equation (14.1) uses *old values* in all sites during the grid swap. New, updated values of $U_{m,n}$ are copied to another matrix, but they are not used as they become available in the right-hand side of Equation (14.1). This means the updates of different grid points are totally independent and can be performed in parallel. This method can be easily parallelized, but its convergence is poor. The number of iterations needed is proportional to the problem size NM.
- *Gauss-Seidel method*: In this case, the new, updated values of $U_{m,n}$ *are used in the right-hand side of Equation (14.1) as soon as they become available.* Updated values are not copied to another matrix, because in this case $U_{m,n}$ is updated *in place*. However, there are now data dependencies because the update of a given grid site depends on the values of the previous updates, and parallel treatment is not straightforward. The convergence is better than in the Jacobi case, but still the number of iterations required for convergence is proportional to the problem size NM.
- *Over-relaxed Gauss-Seidel method*: Like Gauss-Seidel, except that the average of the four near-neighbor values in the right-hand side of Equation (14.1) is multiplied by an *over-relaxation parameter* ω in the range $1 \le \omega \le 2$. For $\omega = 1$, Gauss-Seidel is recovered. The case $\omega > 1$ corresponds to an overcorrection of the old result that accelerates the convergence. Indeed, for some optimal values of ω the number of iteration only grows like the square root of the problem size, $\sqrt{NM}$.

A good discussion of these relaxation methods applied to the problems discussed here can be found in Chapter 19 of *Numerical recipes in C* [16], where convergence issues are analyzed in detail. In the next examples, the grid swaps will be performed as follows. First, the difference $E_{m,n}$ between the old and new values of $U_{m,n}$ is computed at each site:

$$E_{m,n} = 4U_{m,n} - (U_{m+1,n} + U_{m-1,n} + U_{m,n+1} + U_{m,n-1}) - F_{m,n}$$

This quantity is a measure of the local error of the current approximate solution. Absolute values of $E_{m,n}$ are accumulated in a global variable E, which, at the end of the swap, measures the global error of the current approximate solution. The new values of $U_{m,n}$ are:

$$U_{m,n}^{\text{new}} = U_{m,n} + 0.25 \, \omega \, E_{m,n}$$

14.3 FIRST EXAMPLE: HEAT.C

The stationary temperature distribution in a rectangular plate, shown in Figure 14.1, is computed. The borders are maintained at a fixed temperature, as follows:

- The front border ($n = 0$) is a temperature $T = 1$.
- The back border ($n = N - 1$) is a temperature $T = 0$.
- On the upper and lower borders, there is a linear decrease of temperature from 1 to 0.

The obvious solution to this problem is a homogeneous temperature distribution in the vertical direction, with the same linear decrease in the horizontal direction imposed on the upper and lower rows in all the other rows of the two-dimensional domain:

$$T_{m,n} = -\frac{n}{(N-1)} + 1 \tag{14.3}$$

An approximate initial solution is adopted in this example, equal to the exact solution given above, plus a random value in each one of the inner grid points. Then, the Jacobi relaxation method is used to watch how this initial configuration relaxes to the correct stationary temperature distribution (Equation 14.3).

14.3.1 AUXILIARY FUNCTIONS IN HeatAux.C

As was done in the molecular dynamics example, a number of our auxiliary functions not directly related to multithreading, needed for pre and postprocessing, are factored out in the HeatAux.C file that must be linked with the different versions of the code discussed below. It is not necessary, for our purposes, to understand in detail how they operate. They are commented on in the code sources. These auxiliary functions are:

- void InputData(). Reads from an input file heat.dat the global variables needed to define the problem: the problem sizes N and M, and the values of three integer parameters: maxIts, the maximum number of iterations tolerated, nThreads, the number of threads (ignored by the sequential code), and stepReport, the number of iteration steps between two control messages sent to stdout.
- void InitJob(M, N). Allocates the two matrices U and V needed for the computation, following the procedure described in Section 13.8. Two matrices are needed because the matrix U is not updated *in place*: the result of its update is stored in matrix V. This function also sets the initial values of the temperature distribution $T_{m,n}$ in the way discussed above, and initializes the initial global error.
- PrintResult(). Prints the temperature distribution along x at mid-height to check that the correct solution has been obtained.

14.3.2 SEQUENTIAL HEAT.C CODE

The listing below shows the complete sequential code in source file Heat.C.

```
// Global data
/ - - - - - -
double **U, **V;
```

```
const double EPS = 1.0e-5;
double initial_error, curr_error;
int nIter;

// Data read from file "heat.dat"
// - - - - - - - - - - - - - - --
int N, M;
int maxIts, nThreads, stepReport;

// Auxiliary function: prepares next iteration, and decides
// if it must take place
// - - - - - - - - - - - - - - - - - - - - - - - - - - - - - -
bool NextIteration(double error)
   {
   double **swap = U;        // swap U and V matrices
   U = V;
   V = swap;

   nIter++;                  // increase counter, and print message
   if(nIter%stepCount==0)
      cout << "\n Iteration " << nIter << endl;
   // Decide if we keep iterating
   // - - - - - - - - - - - - --
   if( (error > EPS*initial_error) &&
            (nIter <= maxIts) ) return true;
   else return false;
   }


int main(int argc, char **argv)
   {
   int m, n;
   double global_error, error;
   bool isnext;

   // Initialize the run
   // - - - - - - - - - -
   InputData();
   InitJob(M, N);
   TimeReport TR;

   TR.StartTiming();
   do
      {
      global_error = 0.0;
      // Stencil operation for the update of the solution
```

Continued

```
// – – – – – – – – – – – – – – – – – – – – – – – –
for(m=1; m<(M−1); m++)
    {
    for(n=1; n<(N−1); n++)
        {
        error = U[m+1][n] + U[m−1][n] + U[m][n−1]
                + U[m][n+1] − 4 * U[m][n];
        global_error += fabs(error);
        V[m][n] = U[m][n] + 0.25 * error;
        }
    }
    moreCycles = NextIteration(global_error);
    }while(more Cycles)
TR.StopTiming();

// Output results, and exit job
}
```

LISTING 14.1

Sequential Heat.C code

There are a number of observations to be made about this code:

- The initial error, stored in the global variable initial_error, is initialized by InitJob().
- The computation is driven by a do loop that swaps the inner grid points and keeps updating the solution as long as the current error is bigger than a small factor EPS times the initial error, and as long as the number of iterations does not exceed the maximal accepted value provided as input to the program.
- Since, in the Jacobi method, $U_{m,n}$ is not updated in place, the current solution after an iteration is V, not U. Therefore, to always have U as the current solution the matrices must be swapped. Because of the way the matrices have been allocated, *it is sufficient to swap the pointers* U *and* V.
- The local error at each site is accumulated in a variable global_error initialized to 0 for each new swap of the grid. Then, at the end of the swap, this global error is copied to a global variable curr_error. This is redundant in this case, but will be needed in the parallel versions of this code.
- An auxiliary function NextIteration(double error) is defined, which prepares the next iteration and returns a bool that informs if it must take place, or if the iterative process must be stopped. This function swaps the matrices, increases the iteration counter, and performs the convergence test. A similar function will be used in all the parallel versions of the code.

Example 1: Heat.C

To compile, run make heat. The input data is read from file heat.dat. With the default parameters provided in this file, convergence is achieved after 56000 iterations.

14.4 PARALLEL IMPLEMENTATION OF HEAT.C

The natural and efficient way of distributing work among threads in this problem is to assign to each thread a set of contiguous matrix rows to update. It was shown in Section 13.7 in the previous chapter that the matrix rows are successively allocated in a large one-dimensional array of size NM. A subset of successive rows is therefore a compact one-dimensional vector array of contiguous elements in memory, on which a thread can efficiently operate. Once the external loop over rows has been distributed across threads, the inner loop over columns executed by each thread is an excellent candidate for vectorization. This standard approach—parallelize first, vectorize next—is natural because, as discussed in Chapter 2, vectorization is an internal, single-core affair. This procedure is adopted in all the parallel versions of the code.

As in the example in the previous chapter, there are several parallel versions of Heat.C:

- *HeatF.C*: OpenMP microtasking version using parallel for, with the collapse(2) clause to enforce loop fusion, possible in this case.
- *HeatOmp.C*: OpenMP macrotasking version, where the work distribution across tasks is done by hand.
- *HeatNP.C*: vath macrotasking version using the NPool thread pool.
- *HeatTbb.C*: TBB mictotasking version using the parallel_reduce algorithm.
- *HeatOmpV.C*: Previous HeatOmpV.C version, with a vectorized inner loop.

14.4.1 OPENMP MICROTASKING: HeatF.C

A first OpenMP parallel version of this code can be constructed simply by inserting the parallel for directive *before the outer loop on m* in the way indicated in the listing below.

```
...
global_error = 0.0;
#pragma omp parallel for collapse(2) reduction(+:global_error)
for(m=1; m<M-1; m++)
   {
   for(n=1; n<(N-1); n++)
      {
      error = U[m+1][n] + U[m-1][n] + U[m][n-1]
              + U[m][n+1] - 4 * U[m][n];
      global_error += fabs(error);
      V[m][n] = U[m][n] + 0.25 * error;
      }
   }
...
```

LISTING 14.2

Adding a directive in Heat.C.

The reduction clause is needed to accumulate the errors computed by each worker thread. When the outer for loop exits, global_error contains the full error of the Jacobi iteration. Besides the inclusion of omp.h, *the parallel for directive is the only modification introduced in the sequential version Heat.C. The collapse(2) clause enforcing loop fusion is critical. If it is omitted, parallel performance is very poor, as we will discuss in the next section.*

Example 2: HeatF.C

To compile, run make heatf. The input data is read from file heat.dat.

14.4.2 OPENMP MACROTASKING: HeatOmp.C

Let us look at the synchronization patterns that must be implemented in a macrotasking version. The listing below shows the task function that is called inside an OpenMP parallel region.

```
// Task function for OpenMP
// - - - - - - - - - - - - -
void TaskFunction()
    {
    int m, n;
    int beg, end;
    double global_error, error;

    // First, fix the thread loop range
    // - - - - - - - - - - - - - - - - -
    beg = 1;
    end = M-1;
    ThreadRangeOmp(beg, end);    // [beg, end) becomes thread range
    do
        {
        global_error = 0.0;
        for(m=beg; m<end; m++)  // thread loop range
            {
            for(n=1; n<(N-1); n++)
                {
                error = U[m+1][n] + U[m-1][n] + U[m][n-1] + U[m][n+1]
                        - 4 * U[m][n];
                global_error += fabs(error);
                V[m][n] = U[m][n] + 0.25 * error;
                }
            }
    #pragma omp critical
        { error_cumul += global_error; }

    #pragma omp barrier
    #pragma omp master
        { moreCycles = NextIteration(error_cumul); }
    #pragma omp barrier
```

```
        }while(moreCycles);
   }
```
LISTING 14.3

OpenMP task function.

This task function operates as follows:

- After determining its target subdomain (the external loop subrange), each thread enters the do loop that performs the successive updates of the matrix U.
- After the update, the thread error is accumulated in the global variable error_cumul, protected by a critical section.
- The code enters next a sequential region executed by the master thread. A barrier is needed to make sure all threads have completed the update before the sequential region is executed.
- In the sequential region, the possible next iteration is prepared. The function that returns the Boolean variable that decides if a new iteration is needed is the same as the one used in the sequential code except that, in addition, it re-initializes the global curr_error variable to 0, so that this variable can be used again at the next iteration—if any—to accumulate new partial error value results.
- Finally, all threads use the shared value moreCycles to decide if iterations must be pursued. Notice that, again, an explicit barrier is needed before the test, because there is no implicit barrier at the end of the master code block, and we need to make sure all threads will read the same value of moreCycles computed in the sequential region.
- The structure of the main() function is always the same: a parallel directive encapsulating a call to the task function listed above.

Example 3: HeatOmp.C

To compile, run make heatomp. The input data is read from file heat.dat.

14.4.3 NPOOL MACROTASKING: HeatNP.C

The source file HeatNP.C contains the parallel version based on the NPool thread management utility. As discussed in Chapter 11, parallel job submission requires the definition of a class defining the parallel tasks. The listing below shows the global variables used in this code, as well as the task class.

```
NPool            *TP;    // global variables
Barrier          *B;
Reduction<double> R;
bool             moreCycles;
...
class HeatTask : public Task
   {
   private:
    int rank;
```

Continued

```
public:
 HeatTask(int R) : rank(R) {}

 void ExecuteTask()
    {
    // — — — — — — — — — — — — — — — — — — — — —
    // Determine the range of rows allocated to
    // this task, from the number of threads and
    // the rank of this task
    // — — — — — — — — — — — — — — — — — — — —
    do
      {
      double error;
      // — — — — — — — — — — — — — — — — — — — —
      // Update matrix rows allocated to this task
      // rank, and compute the thread error value
      // — — — — — — — — — — — — — — — — — — — —
      R.Accumulate(error);
      B—>Wait();
      if(rank==1)
         {
         moreCycles = NextIteration(R.Data());
         R.Reset();
         }
      B—>Wait();
      }while(moreCycles);
    }
 };
```

LISTING 14.4

NPool task class.

Parallel task instances of this class receive as argument an integer rank. The global references to NPool and Barrier objects are initialized by the main function once the number of threads is known. The Reduction<double> object is used to accumulate partial errors. In the listing above, the task function follows exactly the same synchronization logic applied in the OpenMP code.

The main function gets the required number of threads from the input data file, and initializes the thread pool and barrier objects. Then, it follows the standard protocol for job submission: creation of a TaskGroup object, creation of the parallel tasks and insertion in the TaskGroup, submission of the TaskGroup, and wait for the job termination.

Example 4: HeatNP.C

To compile, run make heatnp. The input data is read from file heat.dat. This is the NPool parallel version.

These two macrotasking parallel versions are very close to each other, and they end up having comparable performance after the Barrier class listed above is replaced by a more efficient implementation of this synchronization utility, provided by the atomic-based ABarrier class. This interesting issue is discussed in more detail later on.

14.4.4 **TBB MICROTASKING: HeatTBB.C**

In the TBB environment, the parallel_reduce algorithm replaces the OpenMP parallel_for directive. As discussed in Chapter 11, two classes are needed: one class to describe the splittable integer range on which the algorithm operates—we use the blocked_range<int> class provided by the TBB library—and a "Body" class to describe the operation of the task function. This class is listed below.

```
// – – – – – – – – – – – – – – – – – – – – – – –
// The "Body" class used for the parallel_reduce
// TBB algorithm.
// – – – – – – – – – – – – – – – – – – – – – – –
bool moreCycles;
...
class DomainSwap
   {
   public:
   double error_norm;
   DomainSwap() : error_norm(0.0) {}
   DomainSwap(DomainSwap& dom, split toto) : error_norm(0.0) {}

   void operator() (const blocked_range<size_t>& rg)
      {
      for(size_t m=rg.begin(); m!=rg.end(); m++)
         {
         for(size_t n=1; n<(N-1); n++)
            {
            double resid = U[m+1][n] + U[m-1][n] + U[m][n-1]
                           + U[m][n+1] - 4 * U[m][n];
            error_norm += fabs(resid);
            V[m][n] = U[m][n] + 0.25 * resid;
            }
         }
      }

   void join(const DomainSwap& dom)
      { error_norm += dom.error_norm; }
   };

int main(int argc, char **argv)
   {
   // initialization
   ...
   task_scheduler_init init(nThreads);
```

Continued

```
tbb::tick_count t0 = tbb::tick_count::now();
do
   {
   DomainSwap DS;
   parallel_reduce(blocked_range<size_t>(1, M-1, M/nThreads), DS);
   moreCycles = NextIteration(DS.error_norm);
   }while( moreCycles );
tbb::tick_count t1 = tbb::tick_count::now();
// Output results and exit
   }
```

LISTING 14.5

TBB Body class.

The constructor of the TBB blocked_range class representing a splittable integer range requires a granularity argument that controls how deep the range splitting is carried out. The ideal situation is our case is to end up having as many final subranges as threads, and for this reason the granularity in the listing above has been chosen as M/nThreads. However, the number of final subranges is in all cases a power of 2, and some mild performance issues arise when the number of threads is not a power of 2. We will come back to this point in the next section.

Example 5: HeatTBB.C

To compile, run make heatbb. The input data is read from file heat.dat. This is the TBB parallel version.

14.5 HEAT PERFORMANCE ISSUES

Next, the performance of the different parallel implementations of the code are compared. However, the same word of caution given in the previous chapter applies here. Performance is strongly dependent on the code profiles and no general conclusion on the overall relative merits of the different programming environments should be formulated. The OpenMP and TBB task schedulers have lots of sophisticated features that are not tested in these relatively simple data parallel examples.

The first issue we have to face is the very poor scaling behavior of the NPool version of the code. This can easily be seen in a quick run performed in a four-core laptop, on a 400×400 matrix, comparing the macrotasking OpenMP and NPool versions. The results are shown in Table 14.1.

While the OpenMP scaling behavior is quite good, the NPool code heatnp has very poor scaling behavior for two threads, and it is imperative to understand why. The first suspicion is some unacceptable overhead coming from the NPool environment itself, but this is discarded when the same poor scaling is observed in a pure Pthreads version of the code, not depending on the NPool thread pool environment, and using in addition the native Pthreads barrier utility. At this point, we are led to explore alternative barrier algorithms, which end up with the adoption of the more efficient ABarrier atomic-based barrier utility discussed in Chapter 9, implementing a barrier algorithm taken from Chapter 8 in [25]. In practice, the equivalent TBarrier class is used, since Pthreads does not have an native atomic utility. Keeping the NPool environment, and just changing the standard barrier by the TBarrier, the results displayed in the heatnpa column are obtained, restoring an acceptable scaling behavior and matching the OpenMP performance.

Table 14.1 Wall Execution Times in Seconds, for M = 400 Rows and N = 400 Columns, With GNU 4.8 Linux Compiler

Heat Barrier Comparison			
Threads	heatomp	heatnp	heatnpa
1	60	64	57
2	29.7	40	28.4
4	14.7	29	15

Notes: The heatnp *code employs the standard* vath *barrier utility and* heatnp_1 *employs the TBB barrier.*

Table 14.2 Wall Execution Times in Seconds, for M=320 Rows and N=1200 Columns, With Intel C-C++ Compiler, Version 13.0.1

Heat Performance						
Threads	Heat	npool	omp	tbb	omp_f	omp_v
1	373					233
4		91.4	91.9	121.8	100.6	57.9
8		43.7	47.9	72	53.6	24.4
12		30.4	34.7	73	40.3	18.6
16		21.8	26.9	98	35.2	14.7

Note: The npool *version uses the TBB barrier.*

Incidentally, this is an example of the importance of keeping an eye on options provided by the basic libraries. They can, in some cases, provide excellent optimization improvements, as is the case here.

More significant performance tests can be performed on the same platform discussed in the previous chapter, an SMP node incorporating two Sandy Bridge sockets with eight cores each. The performance of the different implementations is given in Table 14.2.

A few comments are in order:

- A satisfactory scaling of the macrotasking codes, OpenMP and NPool with the TBB barrier, is observed.
- The microtasking versions (tbb and omp_f show slightly lower performance). The equality of the TBB wall times for 8 and 12 threads is due to the reasons discussed before: there are not 12 subranges that match the 12 TBB threads.
- The last column is the performance of the vectorized omp version. The only difference is just adding the Intel compiler #pragma simd directive before the inner loops. A performance increase close to 2 is obtained.

14.6 SECOND EXAMPLE: SOR.C

The next example deals with a two-dimensional rectangular domain bounded by metallic walls, in the presence of an internal electric charge density $\rho(x, y)$ mainly concentrated at the center of the domain, and vanishing at the borders. Our purpose is to solve Poisson's equation for computing the electric potential, using the Gauss-Seidel successive over-relaxation method. The interest of this example is the adoption of a method of solution having a much faster convergence rate, but at the price of introducing data dependencies that require more sophisticated parallelization strategies.

In the over-relaxed Gauss-Seidel method, updated values of the matrix U are used as soon as they become available, and in addition we have to use a value of the over-relaxation parameter ω in the range $0 \leq \omega \leq 2$. The implications of the immediate use of the updated values of U are as follows:

- As successive rows are swapped in the two-dimensional grid, the matrix U must be updated *in place*.
- The straightforward parallelism of the previous example is lost. The new value of $U_{m,n}$ depends on the updated values of $U_{m,n-1}$—the previous neighbor in the same row—and $U_{m-1,n}$—the nearest neighbor in the previous row. These data dependencies imply that:
  - A thread updating successive matrix elements in a row needs the updated values of the previous row. Row updates are no longer independent, and the thread work-sharing strategy used in the previous example does not apply here.
  - A thread updating a matrix elements in a row needs also the updated value of the predecessor in the same row. This kills the possibility of vectorizing the inner loops.

Data dependencies are very common in stencil codes, and there is a general methodology to cope with them, very well described in Chapter 7 of [35], entirely devoted to the optimization of stencil codes. One way to handle data dependencies is to find a plane—a line in our two-dimensional case—that cuts through the grid of intermediate results so that all references to previously computed values are on one side of this plane. In our case, this separating hyperplane would be descending diagonals on the two-dimensional grid. Then, operations on this separating hyperplane can be performed in parallel. We will say more on this approach at the end of the chapter.

An alternative way of handling this data dependency problem uses control parallelism instead of data parallelism by pipelining threads. This approach is discussed in detail in the next chapter. In the rest of this chapter, two other possible ways of handling the data dependencies in a data parallel approach are explored: the Gauss-Seidel method with white-black ordering—which is not generic and only works in our particular geometry— and the diagonal swapping of the grid, which partly reduces the data dependencies and enables a limited amount of potential parallelism.

14.6.1 GAUSS-SEIDEL WITH WHITE-BLACK ORDERING

One possible way of handling our data dependency problem is to consider the original rectangular two-dimensional grid of lattice spacing Δ, as two interpenetrating grids of lattice spacing 2Δ. The original grid points are labeled with a color attribute (the white or black grid points) to distinguish the two grids. This is shown in Figure 14.2.

It can be immediately observed that the updated U value on a white site depends only on the updated values of U at the neighboring black sites, and vice versa. In updating white (black) sites, only U values

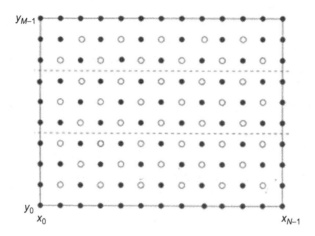

FIGURE 14.2

Gauss-Seidel with white-black ordering.

at black (white) sites are needed. Therefore, data dependencies are avoided if, starting with an initial configuration, with an approximate solution, white (or black) sites are updated first, and black (or white) sites are updated next. The matrix U can be then updated in place, and the updates of the white or black sites show the same amount of potential parallelism that was available in the previous example.

14.6.2 SEQUENTIAL CODE Sor.C

The sequential code for this example is similar to Heat.C, with a few differences:

- We are now solving the inhomogeneous Poisson equation. In updating $U_{m,n}$, the contribution of the source term $F_{m,n}$ must be included.
- The initial double loop that swaps the grid sites has to be changed to two successive double loops swapping the white and black grid sites.
- The over-relaxed Gauss-Seidel method is adopted, by introducing the over-relaxation parameter ω in the $U_{m,n}$ update, whose value is discussed below.

The organization of the code is the same as in the previous example. The listing below shows the part of the main() function that has been modified to include the two passes over white and black grid sited:

```
int main(int argc, char **argv)
    {
    int m, n;
    int nSh, mSh, pass;
    double error;
    ...
```

Continued

```
    do
        {
        error = 0.0;
        for(pass=1; pass<=2; pass++)      // passes loop
            {
            mSh = pass/2;
            for(m=1; m<M-1; m++)              // rows loop
                {
                nSh = (m+mSh)%2;
                for(n=nSh+1; n<N-1; n+=2)  // inner loop
                    {
                    error = U[m+1][n] + U[m-1][n] + U[m][n-1]
                            + U[m][n+1] - 4 * U[m][n];
                    error += fabs(error);
                    U[m][n] = U[m][n] + 0.25 * w * error;
                    }
                }
            }

        nIter++;
        if(nIter%1000==0)
            cout << "\n Iteration " << nIter << endl;
        }while( (error > EPS*initial_error) &&
                (nIter <= maxIts) );
    ...
    }
```

LISTING 14.6

Gauss-Seidel with white-black ordering.

The external loop over the two passes is not entirely obvious, and it took me some thinking to get it right. The problem is in principle very simple. For each pass, the external loop over rows m is executed in the standard way, and only the inner loop over n is modified. This inner loop has stride two and a starting offset that toggles between 0 and 1 as the index m moves from one row to the next one:

- For the first pass, the n initial offsets are 0, 1, 0, 1, … as m runs over 1, 2, 3, ….
- For the second pass, the n initial offsets are 1, 0, 1, 0, … as m runs over 1, 2, 3, ….

There is still, however, a mild data dependency among rows, because the offsets for each pass are determined by the starting value of the offset for the first row $m = 1$, and this is not known to threads other than the one in charge of the first subdomain. A way of determining the n loop offsets in an *absolute* way is needed, with no reference to the first row offset. This problem is solved by introducing the auxiliary variables mSh and nSh in the way indicated in the listing above. If the loop over m is restricted to a subdomain of consecutive rows, the two passes operate correctly and they are in fact swapping first the white grid and next the black grid in each subdomain.

Values of ω: What about the over-relaxation parameter ω? It can be shown—Chapter 19 in [16]— that the method is convergent only for $0 < \omega < 2$, and that, under certain mathematical restrictions satisfied by matrices arising from finite-difference discretizations, only the over-relaxation range ($1 < \omega < 2$) gives better convergence than the Gauss-Seidel method, which corresponds to $\omega = 1$. The question is: how better can the convergence be? We know that the number of iterations in Gauss-Seidel grows like the problem size NM. It can be shown that the over-relaxation method can converge after a number of iterations proportional to N, but only in a fairly narrow window of ω values around an optimal value. This optimal value can only be computed in some simple cases [16]; otherwise, it must be obtained empirically.

It turns out that, for the rectangular grid used in this problem, if $M \simeq N$, this optimal value is:

$$\omega \simeq \frac{2}{1 + \pi/N}$$

and this is therefore the value we use in the codes discussed here.

Example 6: Sor.C

To compile, run make sor. Sequential version. The input data is read from file sor.dat.

14.7 PARALLEL IMPLEMENTATIONS OF Sor.C

We very quickly show next the different parallel implementations. Apart from the presence of the two passes, the code organization is the same as in the Heat example.

14.7.1 OPENMP MICROTASKING: SorF.C

A first, quick OpenMP parallel version can be obtained by inserting the parallel for directive in each pass, just before the outer loop over rows. In this case, the compiler rejects the collapse(2) clause. Indeed, because of the nSh=(m+mSh)/2 statement between the outer and the inner loop, the two loops are not perfectly nested. Just inserting the parallel for directive produces correct parallel code, but with a very poor performance (an example will follow).

Trying to help the compiler to produce better code, the external loop over two passes was eliminated, and the two double loops for each pass were explicitly written. In this case, the performance is acceptable (again, an example will follow).

Example 7: SorF.C

To compile, run make sorf. Parallel version using parallel for. The input data is read from file sor.dat.

14.7.2 OpenMP AND NPool MACROTASKING

The macrotasking versions SorOmp.C and SorNP.C are, again, very close to the HeatOmp.C and HeatNP.C codes. The synchronization patterns are very close. The only difference to be underlined is the presence of an additional barrier, *because a barrier is required after each pass*. Indeed, when a thread is updating the boundary rows of its subdomain, it needs to use opposite color data coming from the neighboring subdomains, updated by other threads in a previous pass. Therefore, this additional barrier is needed to guarantee that all threads have finished the white updates before the black updates start, and vice versa.

Examples 8 and 9: SorOmp.C and SorNP.C

To compile, run make soromp or make sornp. The input data is read from file sor.dat.

14.7.3 TBB MICROTASKING: SorTBB

Again, the parallel_reduce algorithm is used for the matrix update. The Body class—called DomainSwap—is very similar to the one of the previous example. The only difference is that an additional private data item pass is added, corresponding to the pass value, passed as argument in the constructor. It is therefore clear that a different DomainSwap object must be allocated for each pass.

The listing below shows how these objects are used in the main() function.

```
int main(int argc, char **argv)
   {
   int n, status;

   InputData();
   InitJob(M, N);

   if(argc==2) nTh = atoi(argv[1]);   // initialization
   task_scheduler_init init(nTh);
   G = M/nTh;                         // granularity
   omega = 1.8;

   tbb::tick_count t0 = tbb::tick_count::now();
   // – – – – – – – – – – – – – – – – – – – – – – – – – – –
   do
      {
      DomainSwap DS1(1);            // pass 1
      parallel_reduce(blocked_range<size_t>(1, M-1, G), DS1);
      anorm = DS1.error_norm;
      DomainSwap DS2(2);            // pass 2
      parallel_reduce(blocked_range<size_t>(1, M-1, G), DS2);
      anorm += DS2.error_norm;

      nIter++;
      if(nIter%stepReport==0) printf("\n Iteration %d done", nIter);
      }while( (anorm > EPS*anormf) && (nIter <= maxIts) );
   // – – – – – – – – – – – – – – – – – – – – – – – – – – – –
```

```
tbb::tick_count t1 = tbb::tick_count::now();
// print results
}
```

LISTING 14.7

Partial listing of SorTBB

After each pass, the partial error is stored, as in the Heat example, in the error_norm field of the DomainSwap objects. They are read and accumulated in anorm, before the convergence test is performed.

Example 10: SorTBB.C

To compile, run make sortbb. The input data is read from file sor.dat.

14.8 SOR PERFORMANCE ISSUES

As in the previous example, a quick look at the code performance can be taken on a four-core Linux laptop. It should kept in mind that, because of the two passes, there are in this example more barriers than in the Heat code case. They are explicit (or implicit) in the macrotasking (or microtasking) versions. Table 14.3 shows the wall execution times for a 500 × 500 grid.

Scaling behaviors are satisfactory, except for the OpenMP microtasking sorf code and, again, the NPool code with the standard Pthreads-based barriers. This last issue is corrected as was done before, by using the ABarrier barrier class (last column in Table 14.3). The sorf issue has to do with the fact mentioned before, namely, inserting the parallel for directive inside the pass loop. The compiler does a better job if the pass loop is unrolled, as we will see below.

Next, performance was examined for a 800 × 800 configuration in a Linux SMP node incorporating two Sandy Bridge sockets with eight cores each. Wall execution times are listed in Table 14.4. The omp_f results are much better now, they correspond to unrolled pass loops. The npool scaling behavior—

Table 14.3 Wall Execution Times in Seconds, for M=500 Rows and N=500 Columns, With Linux GNU Compiler 4.8						
Sor Barrier Comparison						
Threads	**sor**	**soromp**	**sorf**	**sortbb**	**sornp_1**	**sornp_2**
1	25.8					
2		11.6	30	13.5	11.3	11.7
4		6.2	45	7.1	5.9	11
Notes: The sornp_1 *code employs the TBB barrier, and* sornp_2 *employs the standard* vath *barrier utility.*						

Table 14.4 Wall Execution Times in Seconds, for M=800 Rows and N=800 Columns, With Intel C-C++ Compiler, Version 13.0.1

				Sor Performances			
Threads	sor	omp	omp_f	tbb	np	np_tbb	omp_v
1	280						
4		71.7	79.3	76	69.3	62.9	48.1
8		37.3	45.8	44.3	85.5	32.8	25.2
12		26.1	33.6	45.6	78.9	24.2	18.8
16		28.8	38.3	41	104	27.7	20.4

column np—is very poor, but, as before, this is beautifully corrected by using the ABarrier utility—column np_tbb. The general trend that seems to emerge from the examples in this chapter is that the macrotasking versions are slightly more efficient.

Finally, the last column omp_v corresponds to the SorOmpV.C code, which is simply SorOmp.C with the vectorization pragma simd directive added before the inner loops in each pass. We can observe that, in the region where the code scales correctly, roughly below 12 threads, vectorization provides an additional speedup close to 2. Vectorization seems to be somewhat less efficient here than in the case of the Heat code, where the speedup was close to 3.

An educated guess to explain the reduced vector performance is to blame stride 2 in the vectorizable loops. Indeed, consider the case of the Sandy Bridge socked with four SIMD lanes for doubles. Vector registers are directly loaded with consecutive vector elements from the L2 cache, but the compiler masks the two elements that do not participate in the vector operation, and acts on the other two. There are therefore only two active SIMD lanes, and consequently only two operations per cycle, instead of four.

Example 11: SorOmpV.C

To compile, run make sorompv. This is simply SorOmp.C with vectorization directives added before the inner loops. The input data is read from file sor.dat.

14.9 ALTERNATIVE APPROACH TO DATA DEPENDENCIES

The red-black Gauss-Seidel method discussed in the previous sections is an efficient way of restoring potential parallelism in the presence of data dependencies. It is, however, obvious that this method is not generic: it works with our specific geometry and our simple near-neighbor stencil. Before closing the discussion of this chapter, it is interesting to look at more generic ways of restoring some amount of parallelism in the presence of data dependencies.

If the site update involves data dependencies from neighbor sites within a limited neighbor range, a general result [37] states that it is always possible to find a hyperplane slicing the grid in such a way that all the dependencies are on one side of the hyperplane. Under these conditions, the sites on the hyperplane can be updated in parallel. In the case of the Sor code, it is obvious that the slicing hyperplanes are the diagonals shown in Figure 14.3. Sites involved in the updating of diagonal sites, are all below the diagonal. If a lattice swap along successive diagonals is organized, sites on a diagonal can be updated in parallel.

Note that this approach is really generic, but the amount of parallelism generated is rather limited. On one hand, successive diagonals are not independent, and they have to be updated sequentially. On the other hand, this is really an irregular problem because the diagonal data set size changes from 1 to (N-2) and then back to 1 as the grid is swapped along the diagonals. Distributing a workload across several worker threads if the data set is too small is highly inefficient, as it only generates synchronization overhead.

At this point, we observe that the built-in domain decomposition strategy in the TBB parallel_reduce algorithm is very well suited for this context. A well-selected granularity can be used to control the number of parallel tasks generated by the algorithm, starting at 1 for the smaller diagonal sizes and growing to the number of worker threads for the largest diagonal sizes. This is probably the best possible parallel strategy for this generic approach.

Two versions of the Sor code based on the diagonal swap are available, generically called DSor:

- *DSor.C*: Sequential implementation of the diagonal swap. This code compares the diagonal swap to the direct, one-pass row swap of the grid.
- *DSorTbb.C*: Parallel version, using the TBB parallel_reduce algorithm as explained above.

Examples 12 and 13: DSor.C and DSorTbb.C

To compile, run make dsor//dsortbb. The input data is read from file sor.dat.

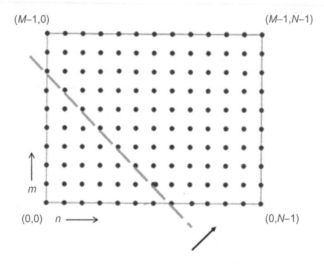

FIGURE 14.3

Diagonal swap to control data dependencies.

Running these examples, it is observed that they operate correctly, but that performance is not as good as in other cases. There are two reasons for that. First of all, it is clear that the amount of real parallelism is very limited: only the swapping of large diagonals provides significant parallel processing. The other point is that diagonal swapping systematically accesses nonconsecutive memory addresses, and that the locality advantages of the L2 caches is not very efficient here.

PIPELINING THREADS

15.1 PIPELINE CONCURRENCY PATTERN

In the traditional data parallel concurrency pattern, different threads perform simultaneously the same action on different subdomains of a data set. The *pipeline concurrency pattern* is an alternative organization of the worker threads operation. Worker threads act one after the other on the same data target, and parallelism occurs when their action on a collection of data targets is organized in an assembly line fashion, as discussed below. Rather than establishing a parallel pattern in space (memory) threads establish a parallel pattern in time. We speak, in this case, of *control parallelism*.

The pipeline concurrency pattern applies when:

- A large collection of identical data sets must be processed.
- The treatment to be performed on each member of the collection can be split in a set of N consecutive independent actions, called *stages*. This is shown in Figure 15.1(a).

The data samples (light gray boxes) shown in Figure 15.1 can be, for example, a collection of two-dimensional images generated by an application—our first example in this chapter—or the rows of a matrix—our second example. Figure 15.1(a) shows a single thread performing three successive operations (stages) on each data sample. As shown in Figure 15.1(b), parallel speedup can be generated if the different stages are executed by three different threads on three successive data samples. The team of worker threads is then organized as an *assembly line*, each worker thread acting on all the members of the data set, performing its assigned stage task. This parallel pattern requires, of course, a careful synchronization to make sure that a thread starts operating on a given member of the data set only after the thread executing the previous stage has completed its assignment. A thread that has just finished executing its partial task on a given sample must pass this information to its successor thread in the assembly line. This chapter discusses different ways of implementing this transfer of control information.

Worker threads overlap their operation in time, and if all the stages are of comparable complexity, involving sufficient computation so that the synchronization overhead is limited, then the optimal parallel speedup is equal to the number of stages. Otherwise, if the pipeline is not well balanced, the overall execution time per data element is the execution time of the longest stage (which also provides parallel speedup).

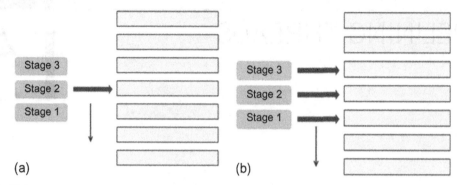

FIGURE 15.1

Pipeline concurrency pattern.

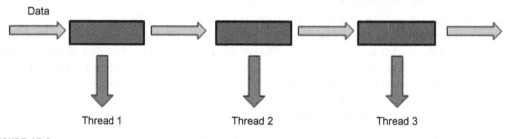

FIGURE 15.2

Another representation of the pipeline concurrency pattern.

The assembly line nature of the pipeline pattern can also be represented as shown in Figure 15.2. Rather than imagining the threads sweeping the elements of the data set collection, we can imagine these elements flowing along the pipeline and being acted upon by the successive stages. This image is fine, but it should not inspire the wrong idea concerning the applicability of the pipeline concurrency pattern:

Pipelines are efficient when the role of successive stages is to perform *in-place* modifications of the data set.

Indeed, the data samples on which the worker threads operate should be allocated in shared memory, avoiding copies from one stage to the next. Introducing lengthy memory operations along the pipeline completely spoils in most cases the benefits of concurrency. The only data that should really flow along the pipeline from one worker thread to the next is synchronization or control information, as the examples that follow illustrate.

15.2 EXAMPLE 1: TWO-DIMENSIONAL HEAT PROPAGATION

This first example focuses on an image production and treatment problem. A large number of two-dimensional data sets (images) are generated, and the nature of the problem requires performing a Fast Fourier Transform (FFT) on each one of them. Multithreading is relevant because the computation of each two-dimensional FFT can be pipelined as two successive one-dimensional FFTs. This example focuses therefore on the simplest possible pipeline, involving only two stages, but examining in detail the way in which the two threads are synchronized.

15.2.1 PHYSICAL PROBLEM

Consider a rectangular conducting plate, with sizes L_x and L_y in the x and y directions, initially heated at the center, as shown in Figure 15.3. This plate is not isolated: heat can flow in and out across the borders. Our intention is to watch how the heat initially concentrated at the center of the plate diffuses until the plate temperature $T(x, y)$ reaches ultimately a constant temperature configuration.

In order to allow heat to flow across the borders of the plate, *periodic boundary conditions* are imposed. This means we are really dealing with an infinite system that repeats itself an infinite number of times in the x and y directions. In such a system, the temperature distribution $T(x, y; t)$ is clearly a periodic function both in x and y, with periods L_x and L_y, respectively. The temperature distribution satisfies the heat conduction equation:

$$\frac{\partial T}{\partial t} = -\kappa \left(\frac{\partial^2 T}{\partial x^2} + \frac{\partial^2 T}{\partial y^2} \right)$$

where κ is the *heat diffusion coefficient*, whose physical dimensions are cm^2/s. Given an initial condition $T(x, y; 0)$ this equation determines the temperature distribution at a later time t. Our purpose is to compute the temperature distribution $T(x, y; t)$ at successive values of t until the temperature profile is completely flat. To simplify the output, the code shows the temperature profile at mid-height prints three temperature values at the front border, the center of the plate, and the back border along the x direction, as shown in Figure 15.3.

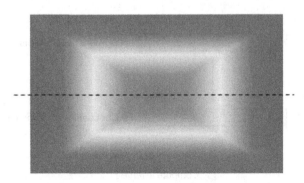

FIGURE 15.3

Heat diffusion in a rectangular plate.

15.2.2 **METHOD OF SOLUTION**

Section 15.9 summarizes the basic elements involved in the solution to this problem: finite-difference discretization of the heat diffusion equation, and the definition of the Fourier coefficients of the unknown solution. It is shown that the heat equation for the Fourier coefficients becomes a set of ordinary, uncoupled differential equations for each coefficient, immediately solved in terms of the known Fourier coefficients for the initial condition. The Fourier coefficients of the solutions as a function of time are therefore explicitly known, and given by Equation (15.8).

The procedure to solve our heat diffusion problem, shown in Figure 15.4, is straightforward:

- The Fourier coefficients of the initial temperature distribution are first computed and stored in a matrix D.
- Following Equation (15.8), the Fourier coefficients of the solution at time t are then obtained by multiplying each one of the t=0 Fourier coefficients stored in D, by the damping factors defined in Equation (15.7). The resulting Fourier coefficients at time t are stored in a matrix F.
- Finally, the inverse Fourier transform of F is computed, to obtain the temperature profile at time t.

We will be using in this example *complex* Fourier transforms, which are linear maps among complex matrices, because they are easier to work with. While the temperature distribution $T_{m,n}(t)$ is a real matrix, its Fourier transform $\tau_{i,j}(t)$ is a complex matrix. When the inverse Fourier transform is performed, the result is naturally a complex matrix whose imaginary part is a null matrix (all matrix elements equal to zero). At this point, a simple trick can be used to avoid wasting CPU cycles in computing a result that we know has to be zero. Since the Fourier transform is a linear map, it is possible to compute two temperature profiles at two successive times in one shot, by proceeding as follows:

- The Fourier transform of the temperature distribution at time t1 is computed from the matrix D. Results are stored in the matrix F.
- The Fourier transform of the temperature distribution at time t2 is computed from the matrix D. Results are stored in the matrix F2.
- The matrix iF2 is added to F1, and its inverse transform is computed. Then, the real part of the resulting F1 matrix is the temperature profile at time t1, and its imaginary part is the temperature profile at time t2.

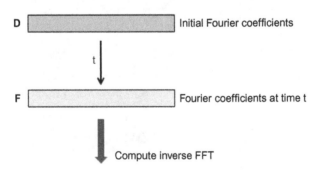

FIGURE 15.4

Data organization in sequential code.

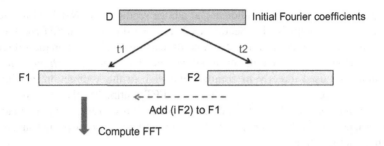

FIGURE 15.5

Data organization in sequential code.

Figure 15.5 shows the way the data structures are organized in the sequential version of the code. In the parallel version, all these preliminary steps are the same, the only difference being the fact that the final inverse FFT that provides the two temperature profiles at times t1 and t2 is pipelined over two threads.

One interesting observation following from Equation (15.8) is that it is possible to know at once the constant value T_∞ toward which the temperature will ultimately relax. Indeed, the coefficients $C_{j,k}$ are strictly positive, except for $j = k = 0$. Then, Equation (15.8) implies that, as t grows, all the Fourier coefficients tend to 0, except for $\tau_{0,0}(t)$, which remains equal to $\tau_{0,0}(0)$. Therefore, we know that:

$$T_\infty = \frac{1}{NM}\tau_{0,0}(0)$$

15.2.3 FFT ROUTINES

Section 15.10 at the end of the chapter contains a description of the FFT routines used in this example. The key routine is fft1, which computes the FFT of a one-dimensional complex vector of size N. The same routine computes the direct and inverse transforms. Since the FFT routines perform in-place modifications of the input data, the same vector that contains the initial input data contains its Fourier transform when the FFT routine terminates.

The listing below shows how the one-dimensional FFT routine operates. The vector size N must be a power of two (this is checked by the FFT routine).

```
std::complex<double> V[N];
...
fft1<double>(V, N, 1);  // direct FFT
//Here, V contains the Fourier coefficients of the initial vector
...
fft1<double>(V, N, -1); // inverse FFT
// The initial vector is now V/N
```

LISTING 15.1

Operation of fft1

Two-dimensional N×M matrices are allocated as a huge vector of size NM, holding the successive M rows, each one of size N, as explained in Section 13.7. The two-dimensional FFT routine fft2 computes the two-dimensional FFT as a succession of two one-dimensional FFTs, first in the *x* direction and then in the *y* direction. However, the one-dimensional routine fft1 *requires contiguous data* to operate. Therefore, it cannot be used directly to compute the FFT in the *y* direction, and an intermediate matrix transposition is necessary. The two-dimensional FFT routine fft2 therefore involves four steps: computing the one-dimensional FFT in the *x* direction for each row, transposing the matrix, computing again the one-dimensional FFT *in the new x direction*, and finally transposing again the matrix to recover the initial configuration.

It follows from this observation that the operation of fft2 is just the result of two successive, in-place, operations of a new routine called fft2h (half of fft2), which operates as follows:

- The one-dimensional FFT in the *x* direction is computed for each row.
- The matrix is transposed.

15.3 SEQUENTIAL CODE HEAT.C

Let us start by discussing the way the computational strategy just discussed is implemented. Input data is first read from a data file. Then, all the memory buffers are allocated, and the initial temperature distribution is defined, as indicated before, as a complex array D of size NM (with a null imaginary part). The first computational step passes this array to fft2, so that on return D contains, for the rest of the run, the Fourier coefficients of the initial condition.

The codes executes nSteps time steps, in which the initial time is incremented by a fixed amount δ at each step. The initial Fourier coefficients stored on D are propagated to time *t*, and the inverse FFT yields the corresponding temperature distribution. Two successive time steps are handled together—as discussed before—to avoid redundant computations. The resulting temperature distributions at mid-height are printed and compared with the (known) asymptotic value.

The listing below shows the set of global variables in the application.

```
std::complex<float> *D;      // holds FT of initial condition
std::complex<float> *F1;     // holds FT for time t1
std::complex<float> *F2;     // holds FT for time t2
float    *damp;              // array of damping factors, computed once.

// Data read from file fheat.dat
// - - - - - - - - - - - - - - - -
int      N, M;               // sizes of 2D array
int      nB;                 // number of working buffers F[]
int      steps;              // number of time steps
float    deltaT;             // time step
```

LISTING 15.2

Global data set in Heat.C

The codes adopt the same notation used in Figures 15.4 and 15.5. In the parallel versions, the working buffer F1 needs to be replaced by an array of working buffers of size nB. In the sequential code that follows, nB is ignored.

Template functions appear here and there because the std::complex<T> STL class can take, in our case, either float or double as the template argument. We work here with floats, but the code works equally well with doubles. A few auxiliary functions are defined to simplify the listings. They are next described in the order in which they appear in the code:

- InitJob() reads the input data from the fheat.dat file, allocates the memory buffers, and prints the input data values. CloseJob() releases the memory buffers.
- CInitialCondition(D, N, M, FCT1, FCT2, -a, -a, a, a) initializes the complex matrix D holding the initial temperature configuration:
  - FCT1 and FCT2 are pointers to two functions $f(x, y)$ that describe the real and imaginary parts of the initial temperature distribution. In our case, FCT2 is a function that returns 0 everywhere. The discretized values of the temperature in the two-dimensional domain are computed in such a way that the lower-left corner corresponds to (-a, -a) and the upper-right corner to (a,a) in physical space.
- PrintStatus(F1, N, M, t1, t2) prints the temperature distribution at mid-height for the two results (real and imaginary parts) encapsulated in F1. The real(imaginary) parts correspond to times t1(t2).
- The two functions quoted above, which receive as arguments the template data items D and F1, are themselves template functions. They work equally well for any choice of template argument in D and F1, and they are defined in the include file HeatUtility.h.

The listing that follows is the complete main() function of Heat.C.

```
int main(int argc, char **argv)
    {
    int Ntot;
    float a = 2.0;
    int k, count;
    float t1, t2;
    std::complex<float> _Im(0.0, 1.0);
    CpuTimer TR;

    InitJob();
    Ntot = N*M;
    deltaT = 3000;
    F1  = new std::complex<float>[Ntot+1];

    CInitialCondition(D, N, M, FCT1, FCT2, -a, a, -a, a);
    PrintStatus(D, N, M, 0.0, 0.0);

    fft2<float>(D, N, M, 1);          // FFT of initial condition

    TR.Start();
    t2 = 0.0;
    for(count=1; count<steps; count++)
        {
        t1 = t2 + deltaT;
```

Continued

```
            t2 = t1 + deltaT;

            for(k=0; k<Ntot; ++k)  // Copy D to F1 and F2
               {
               F1[k] = D[k];    // will be FT at time t1
               F2[k] = D[k];    // will be FT at time t2
               }

            // damp F1 to time t1, F2 to time t2
            // - - - - - - - - - - - - - - - --
            Damp(F1, M, N, t1);
            Damp(F2, M, N, t2);

            // Construct F1 + i * F2, and insert time information.
            // - - - - - - - - - - - - - - - - - - - - - - - - - -
            for(k=0; k<Ntot; ++k)
               F1[k] += _Im * F2[k];
            std::complex<float> c(t1, t2);
            F1[Ntot] = c;

            fft2h(F1, M, N, -1);            // first FFT half
            fft2h(F1, M, N, -1);            // second FFT half
            for(k=0; k<Ntot; ++k) F1[k] /= (N*M);
            PrintStatus(F1, N, M, F1[Ntot].real(), F1[Ntot].imag());
            }
      TR.Stop();
      TR.Report();
      CloseJob();
      }
```

LISTING 15.3
___
Main() function in Heat.C.

For each pair of successive time steps, the initial condition Fourier coefficients are copied to the F1 and F2 buffers, and then the Damp() function constructs the Fourier coefficients at times t1 and t2, using Equation (15.8). Then, iF2 is added to F1, before transforming back to physical space. Note that F1 is allocated with an extra slot at the end (which does not participate to the FFT operation) where time information is stored in the form (t1+i*t2). This is redundant in this case, but will be needed in the pipelined versions to inform the second stage of the time tags.

Example 1: Heat.C

To compile, run make heat. Sequential version. The input data is read from file fheat.dat.

The initial configuration is a Gaussian distribution concentrated at the center of the plate. Running the example, we can see how the temperature profile at mid-height along the plate progressively flattens until the known asymptotic value is reached.

15.4 PIPELINED VERSIONS

The parallel versions of the code deploy a two-stage pipeline, in which the first stage performs exactly the same steps discussed before but, once the final value of F1 is known, only the first half of the FFT is computed by using fft2h. Then, the second stage is released to complete the second half of the FFT computation and prints the two temperature profiles.

This computational strategy introduces two basic issues:

- Additional data buffers are needed, to enable the simultaneous operation of both threads. Obviously, more than one working buffer F1 is required if the two threads produce in-place modifications of two successive data samples.
- The two threads must be synchronized, so that the second stage acts on a given data buffer only after the first one has completed its operation.

15.4.1 USING A CIRCULAR ARRAY OF WORKING BUFFERS

To cope with the first issue, *an array of* nB *buffers* F1[k]—where the index k is in the range k=0,1,...,nB-1—is introduced, as shown in Figure 15.6. The optimal values of the number (nB) of working buffers depends on the way the worker threads are synchronized, and will be discussed later. The first pipeline stage stores the Fourier coefficients at times t and $t + \delta$ in F1[k], computes the first half of the two-dimensional FFT, and moves to the next buffer F1[k+1] to repeat the computation for times $t+2\delta, t+3\delta$, and so on. The second stage follows behind by completing the second half of the FFT computation, and by printing the two temperature profiles. This array of buffers operates like a *circular array*: the index following the last one, nB-1, is the index 0. This is implemented as follows.

```
for(int n=0; n<nSteps; ++n)
    {
    int k = n%nB;      // k is in range [0, nB−1]
    ..
    // use buffer F1[k]
    ..
    }
```

LISTING 15.4

Operation of a circular array of buffers

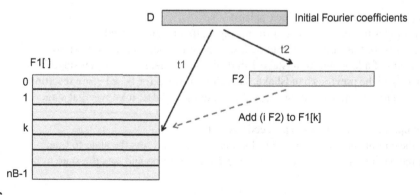

FIGURE 15.6

Data organization in pipelined code.

The circular array is useful because it would be wasteful to introduce as many buffers as time steps. The only requirement is that the first stage, which is leading the computation, does not wraparound and overwrites a buffer before the trailing second stage has finished with it. As we will see, this introduces constraints on the number of buffers nB, which depend on the way threads are synchronized.

One last comment about the data organization adopted in the code. Each one of the arrays F1(k) has size (NM+1), not NM. The first NM complex values are used as before to store the Fourier transforms. The extra complex component is used by the first stage to store the two times being handled in the form t1+it2. In this way, the second stage, when it completes the calculation of the two temperature profiles, knows the time dates to which they correspond.

The listing below shows the additional data items involved in the pipelined codes. The array pointer *F1 is replaced by **F1, a pointer to an array of pointers, allocated as shown in Section 13.7. The remaining data items are related to stage synchronization, and are discussed in the following sections.

```
std::complex<float> **F1;    // array of nB buffers

// Synchronization
// - - - - - - --
OBLock BL;                              // for handshake synch
int     capacity;                       // for producer-consumer synch
tbb::concurrent_bounded_queue<int> Q;   // for producer-consumer synch
```

LISTING 15.5

Additional global data items in the pipelined codes

15.4.2 PIPELINE WITH HANDSHAKE SYNCHRONIZATION

There are two different ways to synchronize the two stages. In the first one, which we call *handshake synchronization*, both threads execute the loop over the time steps shown in Listing 15.2. But the first stage explicitly releases the second one after each iteration, and the second stage waits to be released by the first one to start a new iteration.

This synchronization mechanism, shown in Figure 15.7, is implemented with a Boolean lock, as follows:

- The initial state of the Boolean lock is false.
- Stage 1 toggles the state to true to inform stage 2 that it can proceed.
- Stage 2 waits for true and, when released, sets the state back to false to acknowledge the handshake.
- If, at the end of a loop iteration, stage 1 finds the state true, it knows that stage 2 has not yet acknowledged the previous handshake. Therefore, it waits for false before resetting the state to true.
- If, before starting a new iteration, stage 2 finds the state false, it knows that stage 1 is late and waits for true.
- To sum up, the synchronization proceeds as follows:
  - At the end of each iteration, stage 1 waits for false and sets the state to true.
  - At the beginning of each iteration, stage 2 waits for true and sets the state to false.

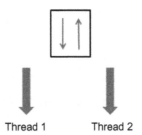

Thread 1   Thread 2

FIGURE 15.7

Thread synchronization with a Boolean lock.

What about the number of buffers nB? Looking back at the synchronization strategy discussed above, we can observe that, if the second stage is operating on F1[k], the first stage can at most operate on F1(k+2) but not beyond. Indeed, if stage 2 operates on F1[k], stage 1 naturally operates on F1(k+1). However, it can happen that stage 1 completes its computation before stage 2, sets the state to true, and moves to F1[k+2]. Therefore, this scenario requires at least nB=3 buffers to operate correctly and avoid overwriting busy buffers. A larger number of buffers will do no harm.

> To avoid data corruption in this synchronization pattern, the number of buffers nB must be larger than 2.

15.4.3 EXAMPLES OF HANDSHAKE SYNCHRONIZATION

There are two examples, HeatOmpB.C and HeatThB.C, using OpenMP or SPool managed threads, and a OBLock or a BLock for synchronization, respectively. We describe next in some detail the OpenMP implementation. The SPool implementation is very similar, with a small number of differences that should, at this point, be familiar to the reader.

```
void HeatTaskFct()
    {
    int k, count, bindex;
    double t1, t2;
    std::complex<float> *F;     // pointer to working buffer
    int Ntot = N*M;

    int rank = omp_get_thread_number();
```

Continued

```
if(rank==0)     // THIS IS FIRST STAGE
    {
  t2 = 0.0;
  for(count=1; count<steps; count++)
      {
      bindex = count%nB;
      F = F1[bindex];    // select working buffer
      t1 = t2 + deltaT;
      t2 = t1 + deltaT;
      F[Ntot].real() = t1;
      F[Ntot].imag() = t2;

      // repeat steps shown in Listing 3:
      // - - - - - - - - - - - - - - --
      // Copy D to F and F2
      // Damp F to time t1
      // Damp F2 to time t2
      // Construct F = F + i * F2.

      // Compute first half of inverse FFT
      fft2h(F, N, M, -1);          // half fft2

      BL.Wait_For(false);  // Release next stage
      BL.SetStare(true);
      }
    }

if(rank==1)    // THIS IS SECOND STAGE
    {
  for(count=1; count<steps; count++)
      {
      bindex = count%nB;
      F = F1[bindex];         // select working buffer

      BL.Wait_Until_True();  // synch with stage 1
      BL.SetValue(false);

      // Complete FFT computation, and print result
      fft2h(F, M, N, -1);
      for(k=0; k<Ntot; ++k) F[k] /= (N*M);
      PrintStatus(F1, N, M, F[Ntot].real(), F[Ntot].imag());
      }
    }
  }
```

LISTING 15.6

OpenMP task function, handshake synchronization

It is easy to see how these task functions implement the protocol discussed above. The first stage starts by determining the next values of the two consecutive time steps $t1$ and $t2$, as well as the index bindex of the next working buffer F1, and initializes the address of the current working buffer F=F1[bindex]. Then, it proceeds as in the sequential code, except that at the end it computes only the first half of the FFT, stores in the last redundant component of F the value of $t1 + it2$, and releases the next stage.

The second stage has been executing the same time step loop and holds the same value of bindex. After being released, it identifies the current working buffer F, completes the second half of the FFT, and passes F, the plate sizes N and M, and the two time dates t1 and t2 to an auxiliary function PrintResult(), which, from the real and imaginary parts of F, prints the two temperature profiles at times $t1$ and $t2$.

The main() function goes through the same initialization steps as in the sequential code, but in addition allocates the Boolean lock BL initialized to false. Then, it sets the number of threads to two and launches a parallel section that executes the task function listed above.

Examples 2 and 3: HeatOmpB.C and HeatThB.C

To compile, run make heatompb or make heathb. Pipelined OpenMP version or SPool version, using handshake synchronization. The input data is read from file fheat.dat.

15.4.4 PIPELINE WITH PRODUCER-CONSUMER SYNCHRONIZATION

The second way of synchronizing the two threads uses a *thread-safe queue of integers*, shown in Figure 15.8. This synchronization pattern proceeds as follows:

- The loop over the time steps that defines the buffer index k on which the stages operates is only executed by the first thread—called in this context the *producer thread*—that drives the computation.
- When the first thread has finished operating on the buffer k, it queues the index k and moves to the next loop iteration.

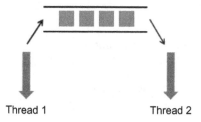

Thread 1   Thread 2

FIGURE 15.8

Thread synchronization with a TBB thread-safe queue.

- The second stage—called in this context the *consumer thread*—executes a very simple code: it dequeues the index k, completes the FFT computation on F1[k], and prints the temperature profiles. The second stage keeps doing this as long as the dequeued index value is non-negative. If the index value is negative, it stops.
- When the time step loop terminates, the first stage stops the pipeline by queuing a negative index.

This is a very loose synchronization. In the absence of handshake, the two threads are not necessarily working on neighboring buffers. Nothing forbids the first stage from running much ahead of the second one in the circular array of buffers. Because of the circular nature of the array indices, it is even possible for the first stage—if it works faster than the second—to make a complete turn, catch up the second stage from behind, and start overwriting a busy buffer. Given the asynchronous nature of the thread operation, this possibility must be excluded to dispose of a thread-safe application.

The solution to this problem is to use a thread-safe queue container, *with a finite capacity*, as was the case of our thread-safe queue class ThQueue<T> discussed in Chapter 9, or the RingBuffer class discussed in Chapter 8. Remember that, when the queue is full, producer threads wanting to queue an element wait for consumer threads to dequeue elements, making space for a new element insertion. In the same way, consumer threads wanting to deque an element from an empty queue wait for producer threads to insert new elements. The queue capacity can then be used to regulate the flow of information from producers to consumers and, in our case, to prevent the producer thread from overwriting a consumer busy buffer.

> To avoid data corruption in this synchronization pattern, the queue capacity must be smaller than nB. The optimum value is, obviously, nB-1.

Rather than using our thread-safe queue ThQueue<T> discussed in Chapter 9, we will use a similar queue container having the same capabilities, provided by the TBB library, to make once again the case for the interoperability of the different programming environments. The listing below summarizes the tbb:concurrent_bounded_queue<T> class interfaces that are needed in our application.

```
#include <tbb/concurrent_queue.h>
...
// Create an empty queue Q of objects of type T
tbb::concurrent_bounded_queue<T> Q;
...
// Set the queue capacity to N
Q.set_capacity(N);
...
// Push an element t of type T to the queue
Q.push(T& t);
...
// Pop an element t of type T from the queue
Q.pop(T& t);
```

LISTING 15.7

Use of the TBB concurrent queue class

15.4.5 **EXAMPLES OF PRODUCER-CONSUMER SYNCHRONIZATION**

As in the previous case, there are two examples, HeatOmpQ.C and HeatThQ.C, using OpenMP or SPool managed threads. As in the previous case, we discuss in detail the OpenMP example.

```
void HeatTaskFct()
    {
    // Same local data as in listing 5
    int rank = omp_get_thread_number();

    if(rank==0)      // THIS IS FIRST STAGE
        {
        t2 = 0.0;
        for(count=1; count<steps; count++)
            {
            ...     // Same as in listing 4
            ...
            // Compute first half of inverse FFT
            fft2h(F, N, M, -1);          // half fft2

            // Send index information to next stage
            Q.push(bindex)
            }
        // Send stop information to next stage
        bindex = -1;
        Q.push(bindex);
        }

    if(rank==1)    // THIS IS SECOND STAGE
        {
        Q.pop(bindex);
        while(bindex >= 0)
            {
            std::complex<float> *F = F1[bindex];
            fft2h(F, M, N, -1);                   // complete fft computation
            for(k=0; k<Ntot; ++k) F[k] /= (N*M);
            PrintStatus(F1, N, M, F[Ntot].real(), F[Ntot].imag());
            Q.pop(bindex);
            }
        }
    }
```

LISTING 15.8

Producer-consumer OpenMP task function

Examples 4 and 5: HeatOmpQ.C and HeatThQ.C

To compile, run make heatompq or make heathq. Parallel OpenMP and SPool versions, using producer-consumer synchronization. The input data is read from file fheat.dat.

For the configuration proposed in the data file fheat.dat, all the versions of the code have similar performance. The speedup is close to 2, as expected. Notice that the pipeline is slightly unbalanced: the first stage computes much more than the second one, but the second one prints data to stdout.

15.5 PIPELINE CLASSES

The previous discussion, dealing with a pipeline with only two stages, showed in detail two different synchronization mechanism between the two worker threads. Dealing with N stages is in principle straightforward: (N-1) Boolean locks or concurrent queues are introduced, providing the synchronization objects between two consecutive stages. However, working with arrays of Boolean locks or concurrent queues soon becomes tedious and error prone. The vath library contains two simple classes that relieve programmers from this burden, by encapsulating the explicit manipulation of arrays of synchronization objects.

These classes are very simple. They have been designed to be used in any programming environment. In fact, they do little more than text processing, and they are declared and defined in the header files listed in Table 15.1. The template parameter T has the following meaning:

- In PipeBL<T>, T is the preferred connector Boolean lock class: either BLock—the idle-wait Boolean lock—or SBlock—the spin-wait Boolean lock— or the OpenMP class OBLock.
- In PipeThQ<T>, the connector is ThQueue<T>, T being type of the data item flowing along the pipeline.

The basic assumption is that these pipeline objects will be used in a context in which the N worker threads implementing the pipeline stages are identified by a set of N consecutive rank indices. This is the case for OpenMP (rank indices start at 0) and the SPool utility (rank indices start at 1). If, as is the case of the NPool pool, worker threads do not have an implicit rank index, it is easy to explicitly attribute each task a rank, as was done before.

These pipeline classes proceed as follows:

Table 15.1 In Column 3, r1 and r2 Are the First and Last Ranks of the Threads Participating to the Pipeline, and c Is the Capacity of the Related Connector Queue

Pipeline Classes		
Header	**Connector**	**Constructor**
PipeBL.h	Any BLock class	PipeBL<T> P(r1, r2);
PipeThQ.h	ThQueue<T>	PipeThQ<T> P(r1, r2, c)

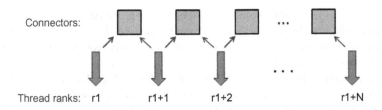

FIGURE 15.9

Structure of the pipeline objects.

- The first and last rank indices of the worker threads are passed as arguments to the pipeline constructors, as indicated in Table 15.1. The pipeline class using a concurrent queue receives optionally the queue capacity as a constructor argument, the default capacity value being 10.
- Once this is done, the pipeline constructor constructs an array of (N-1) connectors, either Boolean locks or concurrent queues. This is shown in Figure 15.9. The (N-1) connectors are identified by indices $(r_1, r_2, \ldots, r_{N-1})$.
- Threads of rank k in the pipeline act both as producer threads (except the last one) by sending synchronization information to the next stage via the connector k, and as consumer threads (except the first one) by receiving synchronization information from the previous stage via the connector (k-1). This is why threads pass their rank to the member functions used for synchronization.

15.5.1 SYNCHRONIZATION MEMBER FUNCTIONS

Table 15.2 shows the synchronization member functions used by the pipeline classes. In the PipeBL<T> class, the WaitForRelease(int r) function connecting with the previous stage returns immediately if called by the first stage. Similarly, ReleaseNext(int r) returns immediately if called by the last stage.

For the concurrent queue class, template parameter T is the type of the data item flowing along the connectors. Our previous example demonstrated how this data item is used to transfer control information to the next stage. Remember that this class implements a very loose synchronization, because threads along the pipeline do not wait for an acknowledgment from the next stage, so nothing prevents them from simultaneously operating on nonconsecutive data sets. We would expect this very

Table 15.2 In Columns 2 and 3, r Is the Integer Rank of the Caller Thread, and Flag Is a Boolean Acting as Output Parameter		
Pipeline Synchronization Functions		
Class	**Previous Stage**	**Next Stage**
PipeBL<T>	WaitForRelease(r)	ReleaseNext(r)
PipeThQ<T>	T GetPrevious(r, flag)	PostNext(T token, r)

loose synchronization to be somewhat more efficient than the one based on Boolean locks, and this seems indeed to be the case in general. Some examples will be shown at the end of the chapter. In any case, we have never found an example in which this loose synchronization is less efficient that the handshake synchronization strategy.

Remember also that the ThQueue capacity must be carefully selected in order to ensure thread safety when there is the danger that producers corrupt consumer data, as was the case with circular arrays. The synchronization functions listed in Table 15.2 work as follows:

- void PostNext(T elem, int rank), called by the producer thread, receives as arguments the data item to be queued in the next connector and the rank of the caller thread (to select the connector).
- T GetPrevious(int rank, bool *flag), called by the consumer thread. This function dequeues and returns the first available element in the connector queue. It receives as arguments the rank of a caller thread (to select the connector) as well as the address of a Boolean flag, which is an *output parameter*. If this flag is true, the returned value is a valid one, queued by a producer. If the flag is false, the returned value is invalid because we are trying to dequeue from an empty and closed queue. We will not need to use this feature in practice.

15.6 EXAMPLE: PIPELINED SOR

We come back to the Sor.C code, discussed in the previous chapter. The purpose of this example is to show in detail how pipelining can efficiently handle the data dependency occurring in the Gauss-Seidel method. Indeed, by pipelining threads it is possible to implement a parallel version of this code *as such*, without using the white-black ordering trick. First of all, complete rows are no longer allocated to each thread. The data set is divided vertically rather than horizontally (see Figure 15.10). Each matrix row is then divided in equal length sectors allocated to successive pipeline stages, and each worker threads *updates its row sector in all the matrix rows*. In fact, the matrix rows are the data items flowing along the pipeline. Each thread controls the activity of the next thread in the hierarchy. In Figure 15.10, the first (black) thread controls the activity of the second (gray) thread, which in turn controls the activity of the third (white) thread.

15.6.1 SOR CODE

This application is identical to the one discussed in Chapter 14: initialization, I/O, result reporting, and all the auxiliary functions used in the code are strictly the same. The only modification is the parallel strategy, which induces some minor modifications in the main() function, and, of course, requires different tasks executed by the worker threads team.

There are several versions of this code, using either OpenMP or SPool class to manage threads, with different choices of the connector classes listed in Table 15.3. Our intention is to compare the relative performance of the different synchronization strategies in a context with significant synchronization contention. There is also a TBB version of the code, using the tbb::pipeline algorithm discussed in the next section. The OpenMP implementation using the queue connectors is discussed next, to show, once again, the interoperability of OpenMP with the vath tools.

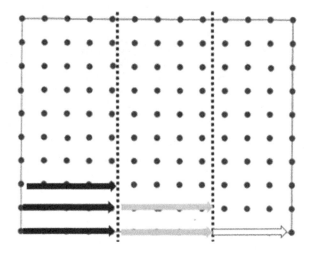

FIGURE 15.10

Pipelining three threads in the Sor code.

Table 15.3 Different Implementations of the Pipelined Sor Code, Using Different Thread Managers and Pipeline Connectors			
Pipelined Sor Implementation			
Source	**Executable**	**Pool**	**Pipeline Class**
SorOmpBL.C	somp_bl	OpenMP	BLock
SorOmpSBL.C	somp_sbl	OpenMP	SpBLock
SorOmpQ.C	somp_q	OpenMP	PipeTh<int>
SorThBL.C	sth_bl	SPool	BLock
SorThSBL.C	sth_sbl	SPool	SpBLock
SorThQ.C	sth_q	SPool	PipeTh<int>
SorTBB.C	sortbb	TBB	tbb::pipeline

The listing below shows the main function in the SorOmpQ.C code. This function initializes a global pointer P to a PipeThQ<int> object. Since we are working with OpenMP, the main thread is included in the worker threads team, and the thread ranks start at 0. The correct thread rank range is passed to the pipeline constructor. The integer data item that flows along the pipeline is the matrix row index being processed. This code adopts a microtasking programming style in which the computation is driven by the main() function, and a parallel region is created each time a lattice update is executed.

```
PipeThQ<int>  *P;        // global data
Reduction<double>  R;
...
main(int argc, char **argv)
   {
   int n, m;
   double resid, error_norm;

   InputData();
   InitJob(M, N);
   CpuTimer TR;

   if(argc==2) nTh = atoi(argv[1]);
   P = new PipeThQ<int>(0, nTh-1);
   omp_set_num_threads(nTh);

   nIter = 0;
   omega = 1.8;
   TR.Start();
   do
      {
      #pragma omp parallel
         { TaskFct(); }
      anorm = R.Data();
      R.Reset();
      nIter++;
      if(nIter%stepReport==0)
         printf("\n Iteration %d done", nIter);
      }while( (anorm > EPS*anormf) && (nIter <= maxIts) );
   TR.Stop();
   // Print results, and exit
   }
```

LISTING 15.9

Main function in SorOmpQ.C

This examples uses the Reduction<double> class to perform the reduction of the partial errors accumulated by the different stages in the lattice update. The TaskFct() task function is defined in the listing below. These tasks are launched every time a new lattice update is required. They start by determining the rank of the executing thread, needed in the synchronization functions, as well as the row subsection under its control. This is done by using the same ThreadRangeOmp(int beg, int end) function used in Chapters 13 and 14 that receives in *beg, end* the global range for column indices, and returns the local range for the calling thread. Since there are N columns, the global column range is $[0, N-1]$. However, boundary values are not updated, so the range to be passed to this function is $[1, N-1)$, as the listing below shows.

- The data item flowing along the pipeline is an integer corresponding to a row index.

- The loop over rows is only executed by the first stage of the pipeline. Once the first stage has updated the row *n*, it queues this value on the next connector. When all rows have been updated, the first stage queues the value (−1) and terminates.
- The following stages dequeue the integer values inside a while loop that keeps running as long as the dequeued values are positive. Then, the corresponding matrix row is updated and, except for the last stage, the row index is queued again in the next connector. When the integer is negative, the while loop ends.

```
void TaskFct()
    {
    int n, m, col, rank;
    int nL, nH;
    double resid, error_norm;
    bool flag;

    rank = omp_get_thread_num();
    nL = 1;                         // determine [nL, nH)
    nH = N−1;                       // for this task
    ThreadRangeOmp(nL, nH);

    error_norm = 0.0;
    if(rank==0)          // This is first stage
        {
        for(m=1; m<(M−1); m++)
            {
            for(n=nL; n<nH; n++)
                {
                resid = U[m+1][n] + U[m−1][n] + U[m][n−1] + U[m][n+1]
                                  − 4 * U[m][n] − F[m][n];
                error_norm += fabs(resid);
                U[m][n] += 0.25 * omega * resid;
                }
            P−>PostNext(m, rank);
            }
        col = −1;
        P−>PostNext (col, rank);
        R.Accumulate (error_norm);
        }
    else        // these are the following stages
        {
        col = P−>GetPrevious (rank, flag);
        while (col>0)
            {
            for(n=nL; n<nH; n++)
                {
```

Continued

```
        resid = U[col+1][n] + U[col-1][n] + U[col][n-1] + U[col][n+1]
                  - 4 * U[col][n] - F[col][n];
        error_norm += fabs(resid);
        U[col][n] += 0.25 * omega * resid;
        }
      P->PostNext (col, rank);
      col = P->GetPrevious (rank, flag);
      }
    P->PostNext (col, rank);  // signal end of iteration
    R.Accumulate (error_norm);
    }
  }
```

LISTING 15.10

Task function in SorOmpQ.C

The negative index value that signals the termination of the pipeline operation must be propagated along the pipeline to ensure the correct termination of all the stages. It is clear that, given the way the code has been organized, there is no flow control problem in this example, and there is no harm in letting a stage to run ahead with its assignment. This is the reason the queue capacity is not specified in the constructor, and the default value is adopted.

The performance of the different implementations of the pipelined Sor code will be presented after discussing the TBB pipeline algorithm.

15.7 PIPELINING THREADS IN TBB

One of the most interesting advanced algorithms proposed by TBB is the pipeline class, whose official documentation is in the topic "Algorithms" in the Reference Manual [17]. The synchronization of the successive stages is implemented by a data item—a token—flowing along the pipeline. Rather than keeping the token type as a template parameter, TBB chooses a (void *) type as a universal token. This is fine, because a (void *) can point to any data type after an adequate cast, so there is no restriction on the nature of the control information flowing along the pipeline. The operation of the TBB pipeline is shown in Figure 15.11.

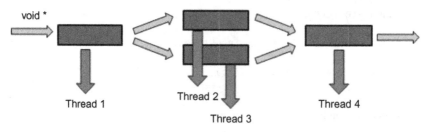

FIGURE 15.11

TBB pipeline.

As shown in the figure, the TBB pipeline algorithm is more sophisticated than the vath pipeline classes discussed before. This algorithm is indeed capable of implementing a nested parallel pattern in which stages can be concurrently executed by more than one thread. In other words: several threads can be put to execute *the same stage*. This is a very interesting feature, because it is possible in this way to accelerate the operation of a particularly slow stage, thereby improving the load balance of the pipeline. This feature is controlled by the user, who decides if a particular stage must be single-threaded or if several threads can execute it in parallel.

The TBB pipeline algorithm is based on two classes: a filter class that describes the operation of a stage, and a pipeline class that connects the filters and runs the pipeline. Note that there are no template parameters here, and that names are relevant: filter and pipeline are classes defined in the tbb namespace.

15.7.1 FILTER INTERFACE CLASS

Here is the declaration of the filter class inside the tbb namespace.

```
class filter
    {
    protected:
     filter(bool is_serial);

    public:
     bool is_serial() const;
     virtual (void *) operator() (void *token) = 0;
     virtual ~filter();
     };
```

LISTING 15.11

Filter interface class

This class defines the task function of a stage via the operator() function. The (void *) argument this function receives is the token coming from the previous stage. The (void *) return value is the token passed to the next stage. The virtual qualifier indicates, as usual, that this class is only *an interface* that defines a behavior to be implemented in derived classes.

This pure base class has a protected constructor accessible by the derived classes that receives a Boolean argument to decide about the parallel nature of the stage: true if the stage is single-threaded, false if the stage can be run in parallel by several threads. The precise level of parallelism will be fixed later on.

To implement a pipeline, filter classes are derived from the filter class. These derived classes may add whatever additional data items and internal support member functions are needed, and define the operator() function that implements the stage operation. Next, we provide a complete example for the pipelined Sor code.

15.7.2 PIPELINE CLASS

Here is the declaration of the pipeline class in the tbb namespace. This class is a packed service provided by the TBB library and is used *as such*.

```
class pipeline
   {
   public:
    pipeline();
    ~pipeline();
    void add_filter(filter\& f);
    void run(size_t max_tokens);
    void clear();
   };
```

LISTING 15.12

Pipeline class

These member functions behave as follows:

- The constructor pipeline() constructs a pipeline without stages. The stages are incorporated later on by another member function.
- The destructor destroys all the filters as well as the pipeline.
- add_filter(filter& f) adds the filter f to the pipeline. This function fails if f is already in the pipeline. Filters are connected in the order they are added to the pipeline.
- run(size_t maxtokens) runs the pipeline. The integer argument is the maximum number of filters that can be executed concurrently. If there are no parallel filters and there is one thread per stage, the optimal value of this argument is the number of threads. This value must be increased if there are parallel filters and enough threads to cope with that.
- clear() removes all the filters from the pipeline

When the run() methods is called, the pipeline starts operation, driven by the first filter (which obviously ignores its token argument). *It is important to keep in mind that the* run() *method keeps repeatedly activating the first filter until it returns* NULL. In writing code for the first filter, programmers must describe the action of the filter on a generic data item, and put some condition that decides when the filter returns NULL and stops the pipeline. But the repeated action of the filter on different objects is automatically fired by the run() method. The remaining filters just react to the token value they receive from the previous stage, and stop operation when they receive the NULL argument, after passing it to the next stage.

15.7.3 TBB PIPELINED SOR CODE

Let us now turn our attention to the TBB version of the pipelined Sor code. We have chosen to focus on this example to illustrate in detail the way the TBB pipeline algorithm works, because it raises more programming challenges than the FFT example involving only two stages. Our purpose is to discuss in some detail the way to write code where the number of stages (equal, of course, to the numbers of worker threads in the TBB pool) is only known at execution time. This is also an excellent example to understand the inner workings of the pipeline algorithm, and to illustrate the inclusion additional data items and member functions in the actual filter class derived from the TBB base class, to ensure its proper operation.

The whole issue here is the definition of the problem-specific filter class—called SorStage— derived from the TBB filter class. Since all filters operate in the same way on the data set—they all update a given subrange of each matrix row—a unique SORstage class can be used to construct all the required chain of filter objects. However, the first filter, having a special role in driving the pipeline operation, needs to be distinguished from the remaining ones.

A microtasking style is adopted for this example: the sequential code runs the pipeline to perform one matrix update and get in return a new value of the global error. Then, main() performs the convergence test and decides if a new iteration is needed, in which case it runs the pipeline again. The fact that the pipeline filters must be reinitialized before each new iteration explains some of the features of the SORstage derived class that follows.

15.7.4 SORSTAGE CLASS

Here is the declaration of the SORstage class.

```
class SORstage: public tbb::filter
  {
  private:
   int beg, end;        // column subrange for this filter
   int rank;            // rank of this filter
   int m;               // row counter in range [2, M-1]
   void *arg;           // argument passed to next stage

   void  UpdateRow(int m);
   void* operator()(void*);

  public:
   double error_norm;  // stores accumulated partial errors
   SORstage() : filter(true), m(2), error_norm(0.0) {}

   void Reset();
      { m = 1;  error_norm = 0.0; }

   void SetFilter(int r, int nst, int NN)
      {
      rank = r;
      beg = 1; end = NN-1;
      StageRange(beg, end, r, nst);
      arg = static_cast<void *> (&nIter);
      }
  };
```

LISTING 15.13

SORstage class

This class has been equipped with several private data items, as well as a few auxiliary functions, to implement the correct operation of the pipeline.

Private data members

The meaning of the private data members is the following:

- error_norm is the internal variable used by the filter to accumulate the errors computed during the lattice swap of its data sector. At the end of the filter operation, this variable holds the partial error value provided by the stage. The global error must be obtained next by a reduction of the values reported by the different stages. This variable is public because its value will be read by main() to compute the global error.
- [beg, end) is the subrange of column indices where the stage operates.
- rank is the rank of the stage, which is equal to the order in which the filter has been inserted in the pipeline. This variable serves two purposes:
  - It distinguishes the first filter from the other ones.
  - It enables the initialization of the filter subrange [beg, end) from the knowledge of the global range [1, N-1) for the column indices.
- m is a running row counter swapping all the row indices to be updated. This counter starts from 1 and runs up to M-1 on successive row updates.
- arg is a void pointer, pointing to a valid address, passed along the pipeline. The pointed value is irrelevant, because we are not in this example sending explicit control information along the pipeline. Each filter knows what it has to do. The pointer is passed just to synchronize the filters.

Member functions

Member functions operate as follows:

- *SORstage()* is the constructor. It creates a filter and initializes the internal working variables m and error_norm. Note that this constructor calls the parent class constructor filter(bool) with a true argument, meaning that the filter is an ordinary sequential filter, and that it does not run in parallel. Then, it initializes the internal working variables.
- *UpdateRow()* is an auxiliary function that updates a subrange of the row defined by the internal row counter m. This function is introduced only to avoid code clutter.

```
void SORstage::UpdateRow(int m)
   {
   for(int n=beg; n<end; n++)
      {
      double resid = U[m+1][n] + U[m-1][n] + U[m][n-1] +
                     U[m][n+1] - 4 * U[m][n] - F[m][n];
      error_norm += fabs(resid);
      U[m][n] += 0.25 * omega * resid;
      }
   }
```

LISTING 15.14

UpdateRow() auxiliary function

- *SetFilter()* is an auxiliary function needed to complete the filter initialization. Indeed, filters have to be created before they are inserted in the pipeline. However, their rank is determined at the moment of its insertion, and this auxiliary function completes the filter initialization at insertion time, determining at the same time the data sector [*beg, end*) allocated to the stage. This is done by calling another auxiliary function StageRange(), identical to the ThreadRange() function we have been using.

- *Reset( )* is needed because the pipeline will be successively run a large number of times. When updating successive rows, the filters keep the memory of the next row to work upon, and the accumulated errors. However, before a new lattice swap starts, these internal working variables must be reset to start swapping rows from m=1 and to start a new accumulation of errors in error_norm.

- *operator( )* defines the filter action. This function discriminates between the first and remaining filters. All filters update the row corresponding to the current value of m (this includes the accumulation of the partial errors), increase m for the next operation, and return a valid void * to the next stage. The only difference is in the way termination is handled.
    - The first filter—which must ignore its argument—terminates when the running row index m gets out of range. In this case, it accumulates partial error in R and returns a NULL pointer to the next filter.
    - The next filters keep running and returning a valid pointer as long as they do not receive a NULL pointer. When this happens, they also perform the global error reduction and return the NULL pointer to the next stages, as shown in the listing below.

```
void* SORstage::operator()(void* p)
    {
    if(rank==1)      // code for first filter
        {
        if(m==(M-1)) return NULL;
        else
            {
            UpdateRow();
            m++;
            return arg;
            }
        }

    if(rank>1)       // code for next filters
        {
        if(p==NULL) return NULL;
        else
            {
            UpdateRow();
            m++;
            return arg;
            }
        }
    }
```

LISTING 15.15

Filter action on data

This completes the discussion of the relevant features of the SORfilter class.

15.7.5 FULL PSORTBB.C CODE

Finally, we list below the main() function code. The auxiliary functions and variable identifiers are the same as those used in the previous versions of this example.

```
int main(int argc, char **argv)
    {
    int n, status;

    InputData();
    InitJob(M, N);

    omega = 1.8;
    if(argc==2) nTh = atoi(argv[1]);      // override nTh
    tbb::task_scheduler_init init(nTh);   // start scheduler

    // construct the pipeline stages
    // – – – – – – – – – – – – – – –
    tbb::pipeline pipeline;
    SORstage ST[16];
    for(n=1; n<=nTh; n++) ST[n].SetFilter(n, nTh, N);
    for(n=1; n<=nTh; n++) pipeline.add_filter( ST[n] );

    tbb::tick_count t0 = tbb::tick_count::now();
    do
        {
        for(n=1; n<=nTh; n++) ST[n].Reset();
        pipeline.run(1);                        // lattice update
        nIter++;
        anorm = 0.0;
        for(n=1; n<=nTh; ++n) anorm += ST[n].error_norm;
        if(nIter%stepReport==0)
            {
            printf("\n Iteration %d performed", nIter);
            printf("\n Current error: %g\n", anorm);
            }
        }while( (anorm > EPS*anormf) && (nIter <= maxIts) );
    tbb::tick_count t1 = tbb::tick_count::now();

    // Print results, and exit
    }
```

LISTING 15.16

Main function

Our purpose in this example is to decide the number of stages at runtime, using as many stages as threads created in the TBB pool. A static array of 16 filters is declared. Then, the requested number (less than 16) is set and inserted in the pipeline. At each iteration, main() resets the filters—which includes the internal error—and runs the pipeline. After running the pipeline, the total error is computed by main() from the partial errors stored in the filters.

15.8 SOME PERFORMANCE CONSIDERATIONS

This section focuses on the relative performance of the different implementations of the Sor code, in order to develop some insight about the efficiencies of the different synchronization strategies. Out the seven codes listed in Table 15.3, we will only report about the three OpenMP versions and the TBB one. Indeed, the code performance is essentially controlled by the pipeline synchronization methods. The three SPool versions have identical performance to the corresponding OpenMP versions, and show the same trends.

The performance tests are carried out in a Unix-Linux environment, because in this case wall, user, and system times are reported. Wall times are, of course, related to the parallel speedup and inform about the scaling quality of the code. In an ideal world with zero synchronization costs, the user time should be equal to the wall time times the number of stages, and equal in turn to the sequential execution time. Values of the user times significantly higher than the sequential execution time indicate significant synchronization overhead in user space, and, as we will see, this is sometimes the case with some implementations.

The cost of synchronization depends only on the internal behavior of the connectors and on the number of stages. Increasing the number of stages, increased synchronization overhead is expected. On the other hand, the ratio of computation to synchronization grows with the system size. Increasing the system size, a decreased impact of the synchronization overhead is expected.

As a first case of low synchronization overhead, we have taken a N=M=1000 configuration, with the optimal value of the over-relaxation parameter ω to benefit from fast convergence (sequential execution time is 27 s). The performance results are given in Table 15.4.

Table 15.4 shows a very honorable behavior of all implementations for two stages. When moving to four stages, the implementations based on the atomic Boolean lock (somp_sbl) and the concurrent queue (somp_q) show a better scaling than somp_bl, based on an idle wait Boolean lock. This was to be expected: the atomic Boolean lock avoid sustained mutex locking, and the concurrent queue implements a more relaxed synchronization.

Table 15.4 1000 × 1000 Configuration, Optimal Value of ω, 3425 Iterations, Sequential Execution Time 26.4 s						
Pipelined Sor, 2 and 4 Stages						
Code	Wall(2)	User(2)	Sys(2)	Wall(4)	User(4)	Sys(4)
somp_bl	15.1	29.2	0.7	10.9	36.7	3.8
somp_sbl	14.4	28.5	0.1	8.5	33.3	0.1
somp_qq	14.5	28.8	0.6	8.9	33.7	1.1
sortbb	16.3	32.4	0.1	11.5	44.1	1.6

Table 15.5 600 × 600 Configuration, $\omega = 1.9$, 27,152 Iterations, Sequential Execution Time 74 s

	Pipelined Sor, 2 and 4 Stages					
Code	Wall(2)	User(2)	Sys(2)	Wall(4)	User(4)	Sys(4)
somp_bl	41.3	81.5	0.9	47.2	123.4	34.2
somp_sbl	40.8	80.4	0.3	21.8	85.2	0.5
somp_q	41.2	81.2	0.9	23.5	90.3	2.5
sortbb	47.2	94.3	0.1	38.0	145.9	6.1

Next, we look at a smaller system (N=M=600), where synchronization overhead is expected to have a more significant performance impact. Using the optimal value of ω, the sequential code executes in only 7 s. In order to have more significant execution times, we used $\omega = 1.9$, slightly away from the optimal value. In this case, the sequential execution time is 74 s. This only increases the number of iterations required for convergence, without changing the ratio of computation to synchronization. The performance results are shown in Table 15.5.

Table 15.5 shows that somp_sbl and somp_q still show correct scaling when moving from 2 to 4 stages, but the behavior of somp_bl is somewhat outrageous. Remember that the idle wait Boolean locks keep preempting the executing thread to a wait state, and that this is a system activity. The significant system time reported in this case is not an accident. This incorrect behavior may seem suspicious, but it turns out that *exactly the same phenomenon happens with the SPool code* sth_bl. It was indeed to be expected that optimized spin locks in which threads are not preempted are much better adapted to a context of high synchronization activity with very short waits.

The TBB implementation does not show the best performance, but remember that the TBB pipeline is much more sophisticated than the simple connector classes, and that it allows a more flexible pipeline strategy with the activation of parallel filters.

15.9 ANNEX: SOLUTION TO THE HEAT DIFFUSION EQUATION

This annex summarizes the three steps that set the stage for the numerical solution of the heat diffusion problem used in the text:

- A finite-difference discretization of the heat diffusion equation.
- Definition of the one- and two-dimensional Fourier transforms.
- Analytic solution for the time dependence of the Fourier coefficients of the temperature distribution.

Finite-difference discretization

As in Chapter 14, the *finite-difference method* is used to obtain numerical solutions of the heat diffusion equation. The continuous (x, y) variables are discretized by introducing a two-dimensional grid, and by representing all continuous functions by their values at the discrete sets of points:

$$x_n = x_0 + (n-1)\Delta, \quad n = 0, \ldots, (N-1)$$

$$y_n = y_0 + (m-1)\Delta, \quad m = 0, \dots, (M-1)$$

where Δ is the *grid spacing*. The point (x_0, y_0) corresponds to the lower-left corner of the rectangular domain, as shown in Figure 15.12. These naming conventions are the same as those used in Chapter 14. Using the notation $T_{m,n}(t)$ for $T(x_n, y_m; t)$, the discretized heat conduction equation becomes:

$$\frac{\partial T_{m,n}}{\partial t} = -\sigma \left(T_{m+1,n} + T_{m-1,n} + T_{m,n+1} + T_{m,n-1} - 4T_{m,n} \right)$$

where $\sigma = \kappa/\Delta^2$. The physical dimension of σ is $1/s$, namely, the inverse of a time. This parameter can be eliminated from the equation by using a dimensionless time variable $t' = \sigma t$. This is what we will do next. The final form of the discretized heat conduction equation is:

$$\frac{\partial T_{m,n}}{\partial t} = \left(T_{m+1,n} + T_{m-1,n} + T_{m,n+1} + T_{m,n-1} - 4T_{m,n} \right) \tag{15.1}$$

where it is understood that time is measured in units of $1/\sigma$, whatever this parameter is.

Fourier transforms

The initial value problem associated with Equation (15.1) can be solved exactly by using the Fourier transform. The original continuous temperature distribution has been replaced by the values of a function sampled on a discrete set of points. It is, however, evident that the periodic boundary conditions we adopted for the temperature distribution mean that $T_{m,n}(t)$ is, for any t, a periodic function of m and n with period M and N, respectively. It is at this point that the Fourier transform enters the stage.

Let us first consider the one-dimensional case, by considering a complex valued function H_n sampled on N values $n = 0, \dots, (N-1)$, and periodic in n with period N. Its Fourier transform h_k is defined as:

$$H_n = \sum_{k=0}^{N-1} h_k \exp\left(\frac{2\pi i k n}{N} \right) \tag{15.2}$$

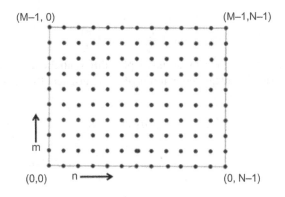

FIGURE 15.12

Discretization of the heat diffusion equation.

This expression defines a linear mapping of N *complex* values H_n into n complex values h_k. It can be immediately verified that $H_{n+N} = H_n$. In fact, this periodic function is being expanded as a superposition of periodic functions of period N (the exponential factors) with smaller and smaller wavelengths $N/2k\pi$. The inverse Fourier transform, that is, the coefficients h_k of the different periodic functions in the expansion, are given by:

$$h_k = \frac{1}{N} \sum_{n=0}^{N-1} H_n \exp\left(-\frac{2\pi ikn}{N}\right) \tag{15.3}$$

Two-dimensional Fourier transforms

The definitions given above can be immediately generalized to two dimensions. The temperature distribution in our problem can be expanded as:

$$T_{m,n}(t) = \sum_{j=0}^{M-1}\sum_{k=0}^{N-1} \tau_{j,k}(t) \exp\left(\frac{2\pi ijm}{M}\right)\exp\left(\frac{2\pi ikn}{N}\right) \tag{15.4}$$

and the inverse transform is given by:

$$\tau_{j,k}(t) = \frac{1}{MN} \sum_{m=0}^{M-1}\sum_{n=0}^{N-1} H_{m,n}(t) \exp\left(-\frac{2\pi ijm}{M}\right)\exp\left(-\frac{2\pi ikn}{N}\right) \tag{15.5}$$

Equation for the Fourier coefficients

Replacing the Fourier expansion (Equation 15.4) of the temperature distribution in the original heat diffusion Equation (15.1), we obtain, with the help of some well-known trigonometric identities, the following simple differential equation for the Fourier coefficients $\tau_{j,k}(t)$:

$$\frac{d\tau_{j,k}}{dt} = -4C_{j,k}\,\tau_{j,k} \tag{15.6}$$

where

$$C_{j,k} = \sin^2\left(\frac{\pi j}{M}\right) + \sin^2\left(\frac{\pi k}{N}\right) \tag{15.7}$$

Equation (15.6) represents a set of single, uncoupled differential equations, one for each Fourier coefficient, which can be trivially integrated in terms of the Fourier coefficients of the initial condition, $\tau_{j,k}(0)$:

$$\tau_{j,k}(t) = \tau_{j,k}(0)\exp(-4C_{j,k}t) \tag{15.8}$$

15.10 ANNEX: FFT ROUTINES

The FFT algorithm optimizes the number of computational steps involved in such a computation. Let us consider first the one-dimensional case. The Fourier transform is a mapping from N complex numbers H_n to N complex numbers h_k, and it is not difficult to convince oneself that, in principle, there are N^2 operations involved in the computation. The FFT algorithm reduces the number of computations to $N \log N$.

The FFT algorithm is particularly simple to use when the sample size N is a power of two, $N = 2^p$. We will henceforth restrict ourselves to this case. The algorithm operates on a vector of size N. After reordering the vector elements, the algorithm performs $\log N$ successive *in-place* modifications of this array. What is left at the end is the required Fourier transform. Full details on the algorithm and on all the issues discussed here can be found in Ref [16].

Since the one-dimensional FFT algorithm is a succession of in-place transformations of a vector, it is by itself a good candidate for a pipelined operation. We have, indeed, written and tested pipelined versions of the one-dimensional routine that we will soon discuss, but we found that one has to go to enormous vector sizes N (several millions) to detect a significant enhancement in computational performance. Pipelining a two-dimensional FFT as a succession of two one-dimensional operations is much more efficient.

The FFT routines we will be using in this example are defined in the include file Fft.h. They are template C++ functions that rely on the std::complex<T> objects of the standard C++ library, T being the type adopted for the components of complex numbers (float or double). Here are the relevant definitions:

One-dimensional FFT

```
template<typename T>
void fft1( std::complex<T> *D, int sz, int isign)
    { ... }
```

LISTING 15.17

One-dimensional FFT

This function is the same that the one-dimensional complex FFT routine of Ref [16], except that it uses directly an array of complex numbers, and that it checks that the data size is a power of two. The conventions for using this routine are as follows:

- D, a pointer to an *offset 0 complex array*, is both an input and output parameter. On input, it contains the original data set, and on output it contains the result of the FFT operation.
- sz is the size N of the complex vector. If sz is not a power of two, the function returns with an error message.
- isign selects the direct or inverse transform. If isign=1, the routine returns the Fourier coefficients of the initial dataset. If isign=-1, the routine performs the inverse transform on the Fourier components.
- To recover the initial data samples from the inverse Fourier transform, the output vector components must be divided by sz.

To check the routine, take a complex vector of size N, perform the direct (isign=1) and the inverse (isign=-1) transforms, and divide the resulting vector by N. You should recover the initial vector.

Two-dimensional FFT

```
template<typename T>
void fft2( std::complex<T> *D, int szx, int szy,
           int isign)
   { ... }
```

LISTING 15.18

Two-dimensional FFT

This routine computes a two-dimensional FFT, on a data set of size szx in the x direction, and size szy in the y direction. The role of isign is the same as before. D is a pointer to an *offset 0 complex array* of size szx.szy that packs the two-dimensional matrix as a one-dimensional vector where the rows are placed one after the other. Again, the routine checks that sizes are powers of two.

It follows from Equations (15.4) and (15.5) that the two-dimensional FFT is just the result of two successive one-dimensional FFTs in the x and y directions. The problem at this point is that the one-dimensional fft1 routine requires the input to be consecutive vector elements. Given the way in which the two-dimensional data set is allocated, this is only true for the FFT in the x direction. In the y direction, column elements are not contiguous. Reference [16] has an in-depth discussion of this issue, with routines that generalize the FFT algorithm to any number of dimensions.

We have adopted here a simpler approach: the two-dimensional fft2 routine uses first fft1 to compute the FFT in the x direction, then it transposes the matrix, then it uses again fft1 to compute the FFT in the new x (old y) direction, and finally it transposes the matrix again to come back to the initial configuration. We have seen that performance is not very different from the refined two-dimensional FFTs of Ref [16]. On the other hand, there is huge benefit because the operation of this routine can be pipelined in a trivial way.

Half of two-dimensional FFT

```
template<typename T>
void fft2h( std::complex<T> *d, int szx, int szy,
            int isign)
   { ... }
```

LISTING 15.19

Half of a two-dimensional FFT

This routine is *half a fft2* routine: FFT in the x direction followed by transposition. Calling it twice, it is equivalent to fft2. This is the routine to be used in the parallel version of this example: each one of the two worker threads will execute half of the two-dimensional FFT computation.

Fourier transform of real-valued functions

We have just stated that the initial array H_n and its Fourier transform h_k are in general complex valued arrays. We can, of course, use these Fourier transforms for real-valued functions H_n, and obtain a set of complex-valued Fourier coefficients h_k, from Equation (15.3). When transforming back to the initial configuration space using Equation (15.2) the initial values are reproduced, namely, complex numbers whose imaginary part is strictly zero within numerical errors. Spending time in computing an already known result equal to 0 is wasteful, and for real-valued periodic functions the Fourier transform computation can be arranged to avoid it. This is discussed in detail in Ref [16]. We will keep in what follows the complex version of the Fourier transform described above because the numerical routines are simpler. Redundant computations will be avoided by using the complex inverse Fourier transform Equation (15.2) *to recover two real functions in a unique computation*, as was discussed in the text.

Fourier transform of real-valued functions

USING THE TBB TASK SCHEDULER

16

16.1 INTRODUCTION

The power and the flexibility of the TBB high-level algorithms, including the task_group interface, have been discussed in Chapter 11. They are expected to operate efficiently in most practical cases. Nevertheless, some more advanced features of the TBB task scheduler may be needed, for example, when the application profile demands specific *event-like synchronizations among tasks*, implemented by the introduction of hierarchical relations among them. A first look at this feature was taken when discussing in Chapter 10 the depend clause recently introduced in OpenMP 4.0. The TBB environment, however, has been in operation for several years and it is more general. Besides task synchronizations, several refined services proposed by TBB—such as thread affinity or task recycling—are only accessible through the basic scheduler API.

This chapter contains rather advanced material, and as such it will probably not be of central interest to all readers. Moreover, this material is well described in the official TBB documentation—TBB tutorial and reference guide—and in James Reinder's book [34]. Nevertheless, a pedagogical effort has been made to summarize it here because these subjects are deeply connected to many other issues discussed in previous chapters, and because we wanted to offer a self-contained discussion of task-centric programming environments. Some of the advanced examples proposed at the end of the chapter are not explicitly discussed in the TBB documentation.

In order to facilitate a selective reading of its content, the different sections are classified as follows:

- Qualitative overview of the operation of the TBB thread pool: Sections 16.1 and 16.2.
- Full scheduler API: Sections 16.3 and 16.4. This is the complete API, based on the task class, that implements a very refined control of the scheduler, like establishing hierarchical relations among tasks that synchronize their activity, bypassing the scheduler by forcing the execution of a specific task, and much more.
- Using the TBB scheduler: advanced examples: Sections 16.6 and 16.7.

16.2 STRUCTURE OF THE TBB POOL

TBB proposes a sophisticated and powerful task scheduler API, inspired by Cilk's programming model. Tasks are registered for execution in a way to be discussed, and refined scheduling algorithms select the task that an available thread executes next, searching to optimize in particular cache memory efficiency

459

and load balance of parallel workloads. TBB also gives programmers the possibility of *bypassing* the scheduler, because a task has the option of enforcing the immediate execution of a successor task without submitting it to the task pool.

16.2.1 TBB TASK QUEUES

The structure of the TBB pool is shown in Figure 16.1. The pool is composed of a fixed number of worker threads, each one run by an available core. There are two kinds of data structures acting as *ready pools*, containing the tasks already submitted for execution:

- *Thread-owned ready pools*—one per worker thread—implemented as deques. Deques are double-ended queues in which elements can be retrieved either from the head (the oldest element) or from the tail (the most recent element).
- *Global task queue*, which looks like an ordinary first-in, first-out (FIFO) queue, where tasks are enqueued at the tail and dequeued from the head of the queue, and are therefore served on a fair FIFO basis. In fact, it would be more appropriate to speak of a quasi-FIFO queue because, for sake of scalability, TBB does not promise exact FIFO order, only fairness that no task will starve. This feature has been incorporated in recent TBB releases to offer programmers a way to deal with simple parallel contexts that do not require more than straightforward fair scheduling, like, for example, a server dispatching single tasks to manage individual client requests.

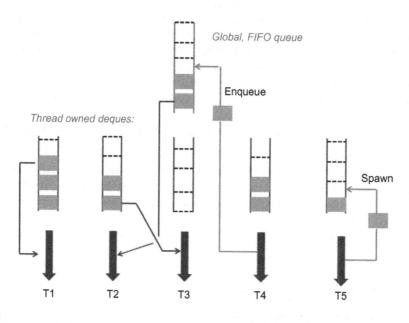

FIGURE 16.1

Structure of the TBB thread pool.

TBB establishes a simple convention for feeding these ready pools:

- A running task *spawning* a new task places it *at the tail of the executing thread deque*, as is the case of thread T5 in Figure 16.1.
- A running task *enqueuing* a new task places it at the tail of the global queue, as is the case of thread T4 in Figure 16.1.

The TBB pool implements therefore two different scheduling strategies. Usage of the global pool emphasizes fairness: tasks are executed in the order in which they are submitted; this is very natural in a throughput computing, embarrassingly parallel context in which tasks are totally independent. Use of the thread's deques, instead, emphasizes locality of memory accesses and optimizes the overall load balance of a parallel application, by activating a parallel treatment whenever there are resources available to implement it. This is the place where the added value provided by the built-in intelligence of the TBB scheduler operates. The operation of the global pool will not be discussed any further in the rest of this chapter.

16.2.2 FIRST LOOK AT THE SCHEDULING ALGORITHM

It is possible at this point to present a first simplified description of the scheduling algorithm by discussing how a thread proceeds to select a task for execution from the ready pools:

- First of all, the thread pops a task *from the tail of its own deque*, as is the case of thread T1 in Figure 16.1.
- If its own deque is empty, it pops a task *from the head of the global queue*, as is the case of thread T2 in Figure 16.1.
- Finally, if the global queue is empty, it steals a task from another randomly chosen thread's deque by popping it *from the head of a neighbor deque*, as is the case of thread T3 in Figure 16.1.

These rules are not exhaustive. Later on, we will see that in some cases the scheduler can be bypassed by forcing a thread to execute next a specific task not popped from the ready pools. This may be decided by the programmer, or it may be done implicitly by the scheduler itself when executing tasks with hierarchical relations among them.

It is not difficult to understand why the thread-owned deques are set to operate in the way described above. Task stealing converts the potential parallelism expressed by the decomposition of a job into tasks, into a mandatory parallel treatment. In the absence of task stealing, a task ends up being executed by the same thread that submitted it. In this case, when the task submission mechanism is undone, it is very natural to select *the most recent task* in the deque, which may benefit from the presence of the local L2 cache of data items recently accessed by the immediate predecessor task. Executing the most recently spawned task exploits data locality and optimizes L2 cache access.

Task stealing, by forking a task to another thread—that is, most probably to another core—gives up all possible cache advantages. Task stealing operates to keep busy idle threads with no target tasks available in their own deques. Since any possible locality advantages are lost anyhow, there is no reason to steal the most recently spawned tasks. This is why task stealing targets the oldest tasks in the victim deques.

16.3 TBB TASK MANAGEMENT CLASSES

The task scheduler API is composed of three basic task management classes, and a few others that implement specific services.

- The task_scheduler_init class, discussed in Chapter 11.
- The task_group class, a high-level programming interface to the scheduler also discussed in Chapter 11.
- The task class, which constitutes the basic, low-level programming interface for task management and synchronization. It incorporates a substantial number of services that enable refined control of the task scheduler.
- A few other subsidiary classes complete the task services (for details, see the Reference Guide) [18]:
  - The task_list class, useful to spawn several tasks at once, rather than doing it one by one.
  - The task_group_context class, a collection of tasks that maintains its identity at execution time. The library allows programmers to set up a common priority level for them all. Tasks in the group can be explicitly canceled by the programmer, or can be implicitly canceled if the code raises an exception.
  - The empty_task class, representing a task that does nothing. This is a very useful tool for task synchronization that will be used intensively in our examples.

16.4 COMPLETE SCHEDULER API: THE TASK CLASS

From now on, we focus on the complete TBB task programming interface, based on the task class. Chapter 11 has shown how the task_group class enables the submission, execution, and possible cancellation of a group of tasks. The task interface provides the programmer with more refined control of the scheduler operation, in particular by enabling the explicit management of task dependencies, which are a key element in the TBB scheduler design.

This section develops the following:

- How to instantiate TBB tasks.
- How tasks are mapped to threads.
- The basic hierarchical relationships among tasks.
- The different ways of allocating TBB tasks, in order to take into account their hierarchical dependencies.
- Two different TBB paradigms for spawning and waiting for a group of child tasks.
- The complete task scheduling algorithm.

16.4.1 CONSTRUCTING TASKS

Task objects are constructed using exactly the same procedures already used in the NPool utility (obviously inspired by TBB):

- Define a class derived from the base tbb::task class.
- This derived class may implement as many data members and auxiliary member functions as needed for the task operation.
- External data arguments needed for the task operation can be captured through the class constructor.
- The derived class must override the execute() virtual function of the base task class. This defines the task operation.
- Task objects are allocated by using overloaded versions of the new operator, in the way described in the following sections.

The listing below shows a task class, the MyTask class that will be used in many simple examples that follow. Task objects of this class have an integer rank and a vath Timer utility as private data members. The rank is a task identifier initialized by the constructor. The Timer is used to block the running thread for a given number of milliseconds, to simulate a long operation. These task objects print an identification message, wait in a blocked state for 1 s, and terminate.

```
class MyTask : public task
    {
    private:
    int    rank;
    Timer  T;

    public:
    MyTask(int r) : rank(r) {}
    task *execute()
        {
        std::cout << "\n Executing MyTask task, rank = "
                  << rank << std::endl;
        T.Wait(1000);
        return NULL;
        }
    };
```

LISTING 16.1

MyTask class

The basic class task has a large number of hidden data items and public member functions that implement all the scheduler services, and which are naturally inherited by the derived class. The execute() function implementing the task operation takes no arguments and, as was the case with the function objects used in the task_group environment, any needed information required for the task operation must be passed via the task constructor.

The execute() function returns a task*, namely, a task reference. *This implements a scheduler bypass*. If the returned task* is not NULL, the executing thread executes the returned task as soon as the execute() function exits. The returned task is not submitted to the pool.

16.4.2 MAPPING TASKS TO THREADS

TBB tasks are executed by threads in the following way:

- *Tasks are mapped to physical threads in a nonpreemptive way.* This means tasks are tied to a specific thread for the whole duration of their lifetime. When the execute() function starts, the task is bound to the thread until execute() returns. There is no task migration across threads (as may be the case of untied tasks in OpenMP).
- When running the execute() function of a task, a thread may suspend its execution and service another task *only when it waits on child tasks.* In this case, the thread may run one of the child tasks or, if there are no pending children, it may steal and run a task created by another thread.
- If a task blocks for some reason other than waiting for children—locking a mutex, or performing a spin or idle wait—the executing thread remains blocked. This is the normal behavior of threads.

Note that this mechanism was borrowed in the NPool utility (except that there is no task stealing in NPool). Suspending tasks is needed to avoid deadlocks that may occur when there are more active tasks than threads in the pool.

16.4.3 HIERARCHICAL RELATIONS AMONG TASKS

The TBB scheduler sets up the tools needed to cope with task synchronizations, by establishing hierarchical relations of the parent-child kind among tasks.

In the vath thread pools as well as in OpenMP, we think of a parent task as a task that spawns a few child tasks, and then, optionally, either terminates or waits for its children. In these cases, the parent-child relationship can be thought of as a describing a transition from a sequential to a parallel region, the child tasks eventually joining the parent tasks if they are waited for.

In TBB, this picture is somewhat different. It is more appropriate to think of the transition from a parallel to a sequential region. Parents are, in fact, identified to successors, corresponding to the continuation task that takes over when a parallel section terminates, and children are called predecessors, corresponding to the parallel region tasks. TBB tasks have, among others, two internal properties:

- *successor* (this property applies to child tasks in a parallel region). This is a pointer to the successor task that will be executed after the current task and its partners terminate. This pointer is either set:
  - When the task is allocated as a child of the successor task (see the next section).
  - By the user code, by calling the set_parent() member function on the target task (see the "synchronization" part of the task class Listing 16.16 at the end of the chapter).
- *refcount* (this property applies to successor tasks). A reference count is an integer that counts the number of tasks that have this one as successor (parent). This reference count is decreased by the scheduler every time one of the child tasks terminates.
  - The successor task reference count is set by the programmer, by a call to the set_ref_count(int n) member function (see Listing 16.16). Indeed, no one else knows how many children have been attached to the successor task.

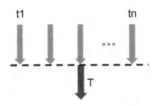

FIGURE 16.2

Successor (parent)-predecessor (children) relationships.

 - Decreasing the reference count is done directly by the child tasks when they terminate. Indeed, the child task knows who its parent (successor) is.

Imagine now that n tasks, t1, t2, ..., tn are allocated as children (predecessors) of a task T. Figure 16.2 shows the predecessor-successor mechanism:

- The reference count of the successor task T must be set to the number n of its children.
- The n predecessor tasks are spawned by some other task, not by T. *We will soon explain the slight change that must be made to this protocol when the children tasks are spawned by T itself.* As they terminate, the reference count of T is atomically decreased.
- The thread executing the last terminating predecessor finds that the T reference count has reached zero, and executes T. *We have here again a scheduler bypass*: the successor task is immediately executed, without being spawned into the task queues.

In Figure 16.2, the parent task is not necessarily the task that spawned t1, ..., tn. It is the task T declared as parent of its children, either when the children were allocated (see next section) or by a call to the set_parent() member function by each one of the child tasks.

16.4.4 ALLOCATING TBB TASKS

Task objects must naturally be created (allocated) before they are activated, and TBB allows programmers to define the hierarchical role of a task at this time. Three hierarchical allocation options are available:

- Tasks can be allocated as root tasks (no parent task). The allocation of root tasks is naturally performed by a static function, not related to any task object. The root allocation of a task reference *T, instance of the MyTask class, is made by the following function call:
  MyTask *T = new(allocate_root()) MyTask(n);
- Tasks can be allocated as children of a given successor task. The allocation of a child task tn as a child of T in Figure 16.2 is performed by a allocate_child() member function called by the successor task T:
  MyTask *tn = new(T.allocate_child()) MyTask(n);

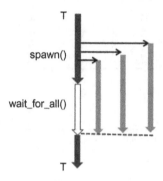

FIGURE 16.3

Task spawning children and waiting for termination.

- Finally, tasks can be allocated as continuations of other tasks. This is a subtle mechanism deployed by TBB to implement a fork-join pattern in which a task spawns several child tasks and terminates, not waiting for children, and is replaced by a continuation task succeeding the child tasks. This mechanism is introduced to enable a continuation stealing like Cilk, instead of the natural child stealing in TBB, as discussed in Chapter 11. This subject is discussed in Chapter 8 of [35]. The allocation of a continuation task Tc is also performed by the task object T that will be replaced, and which *transfers its own parent task to the newly allocated continuation task.* This mechanism is shown in Figure 16.3:

  MyTask *Tc = new(T.allocate_continuation()) MyTask(n);

Why should the task that allocates a continuation task transfer its parent (successor) pointer to the new task? Since the continuation task that takes over when the children terminate is replacing the initial task that spawned them, it is natural that it inherits its successor, in order to preserve the enclosing hierarchical task organization in which the fork-join pattern is inserted.

Listing 16.16 of the task class in Section 16.9 at the end of the chapter shows several allocation functions that return internal data types called proxyN, with N=1, ..., 4. The point is that the TBB library needs to adapt the action of the new operator to the type of allocation requested. New overloaded versions of the new(proxyN) operator are defined, which take these data types as input and perform the memory allocation in the appropriate way. In practice, these data types can be bypassed by directly passing to the new() operator the allocation function call, as shown above.

16.4.5 TASK SPAWNING PARADIGMS

These are the two fork-join TBB paradigms for spawning tasks:

- A task spawns the children and at some point blocks waiting for their termination, as shown in Figure 16.3.
- A task spawns the children and terminates, and a different continuation task is adopted to succeed the children, as shown in Figure 16.4. A number of examples will soon follow.

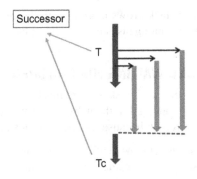

FIGURE 16.4

Allocating a continuation task.

Spawning tasks with no parent (successors) and terminating—as was done in one of the task_group examples in Chapter 11—is also possible, but the problem is that in the low-level task API there is no explicit task_group synchronization pattern that enables a task to wait *for all its descendants*. Only the taskwait pattern, waiting for direct children, is immediately available. Waiting for all descendants can be implemented in this context, using advanced synchronization techniques to be discussed later on.

16.4.6 SPAWNING TASKS WITH CONTINUATION PASSING

Continuation passing is a straightforward application of the predecessor-successor mechanism discussed above. The spawn mechanism—shown in Figure 16.2—proceeds as follows:

- First, the continuation task Tc is allocated as a continuation of T.
- Next, the parallel region tasks tn are allocated as children of Tc.
- The reference count of Tc is set to the number of children n. The successor task will be run directly by the thread executing the last terminating child.
- T spawns the child tasks and terminates.

As the examples will show, this task spawning paradigm requires some tricky coding, and should really be considered as an optimization option, because there are differences that may impact performance. As stated before, this issue is related to the different stealing strategies mentioned in the fork-join discussion in Chapter 11: child stealing in TBB versus continuation stealing in Cilk Plus, which implements a more efficient stack usage. Continuation passing allows TBB to implement the Cilk Plus continuation stealing strategy, at the price of more complex coding.

This is a complex issue, and a complete discussion is available in Chapter 8 of [35]. A simple observation can be given, to give an idea of the issues involved. In continuation passing, the initial task terminates, and its executing thread is released after cleaning all the task local variables from its stack. The executing thread just liberated can proceed to execute another task. If, instead, a task waits for children, its executing thread is not released because the task remains active, and its local data remains alive in the executing thread stack. A thread executing a task waiting for children is not blocked: TBB allows the executing thread to suspend the task, execute another task, and resume later on execution of the initial task. However, the thread stack grows more than in the continuation passing case, and the risk of stack overflow is larger when running tasks that allocate a large number of local variables.

16.4.7 SPAWNING TASKS AND WAITING FOR CHILDREN

TBB also proposes naturally the classical task spawn mechanism: the successor task T spawns its children and eventually blocks waiting for them before resuming execution. This is shown in Figure 16.3. The protocol is now different, because the successor task is already running:

- The reference count of the task T is set to n+1, n being the number of children.
- Then T spawns its n predecessor tasks. At some point, T executes a member function call that waits for them to terminate, and resumes execution.

Setting the successor reference count to n+1 instead of n—by adding +1 for the wait—is critical. In the basic protocol in which the predecessors *are not* spawned by the successor task, the successor is automatically launched when the reference count reaches 0. However, in this case, *another thread is already waiting to run the successor* so the successor cannot be launched by the last child who terminates. Launching a running task crashes the code. The extra value in the reference count takes into account the fact that the successor is waiting for termination of children, not waiting to start execution.

16.4.8 TASK SPAWNING BEST PRACTICES

There are several member functions that can be used to spawn child tasks and eventually wait for their completion, as shown in the "synchronization" part of Listing 16.16. Note that the spawning function are always static: they can be directly called either from the main() function—which is not a TBB task—or from inside a task function code. They are not associated with a particular task object.

When several tasks need to be spawned, the choice is offered of spawning them one at a time, or first encapsulating them in a task_list object, and then spawning them all in a single function call: the spawn() functions take as arguments either a task reference or a task_list reference. Consider the case of a task T that needs to spawn n child tasks t1, t2, ..., tn and wait for their termination. In all cases:

- T must allocate the child tasks t1, ..., tn by using allocate_child() inside the new() call.
- T must call set_ref_count(n+1), to set the initial value of its reference count before spawning the child tasks.

After doing that, T has several options for spawning the n child tasks:

- Pack the n tasks inside a task_list TL, and call spawn_and_wait_for_all(TL).
- Spawn the n tasks—either one by one or via a task list—and then call wait_for_all().
- Spawn directly the first n-1 tasks and then call spawn_wait_for_all(Tn) for the last one.

As emphasized in the TBB documentation, the spawning mechanism just described is not, however, the most efficient way of spawning several tasks and waiting for their termination in the TBB environment. The point is that, as explained in Section 16.2.1, they are all queued in the deque of the running thread that allocates and spawns them. They will, of course, be stolen by other idle threads if available. But it is more efficient, from the point of view of L2 cache reusage, if they are directly created and placed in the deques of other threads that may run them. This is why a recursive task-generation mechanism, in which a task spawns two children and waits, which in turn spawns children and wait, and so on and so forth, is to be preferred if possible.

Examples dealing with these task spawning best practices will be proposed in Section 16.6.

16.5 MISCELLANEOUS TASK FEATURES

16.5.1 HOW THREADS RUN TASKS

When a thread runs a task, the following steps are performed:

- The thread invokes execute() and waits for its return.
- If the task has not been marked by a "recycle" method, requesting that the task is preserved to be reused, as explained in the following Section 16.5.3:
    - The executing thread destroys the task.
    - If the parent task is not null, the thread atomically decrements the successor reference count. If the reference count becomes zero, it executes immediately the successor task.
- If the task has been marked for recycling (as child or continuation) nothing is done. *The successor reference count is not decreased*, and the task is not destroyed.

Keep in mind—for future discussion about task recycling in Section 16.7—that the predecessor-successor protocol of decreasing the successor reference count *only applies if the task is destroyed*; it does not apply if the task is recycled. By default, tasks are destroyed after execution.

16.5.2 COMPLETE TASK SCHEDULING ALGORITHM

Section 16.2.2 presented a first preliminary overview of some of the priorities adopted by an idle thread to select a task to execute next from the available ready pools. The picture can now be completed by listing all the actions taken by a thread to decide on the next task to execute. When a thread finishes executing a thread T, the next task to be executed is obtained by the first rule below that applies:

- The task returned by the execute() method, if the returned pointer is not null.
- The successor of T, if T was the last completed predecessor.
- A task popped from the tail of the thread's own deque.
- A task with affinity for the thread (see the later discussion on memory affinity).
- A task popped from the head of the shared queue, as explained before.
- A task popped from the head of another randomly chosen thread's deque (task stealing).

16.5.3 RECYCLING TASKS

By default, a task object is destroyed when its execute() function terminates. Since TBB is tailored for a microtasking programming style, the memory management overhead related to task creation and destruction can become important in some cases. Consider, for example, the molecular dynamics example MdTBB.C. Lightweight tasks are created and destroyed at each time step in the computation of the particle trajectories: first the acceleration tasks, and then the momentum and coordinate update tasks. It makes sense to try to reuse the same tasks at each iteration, when dealing with a large system with a substantial number of parallel tasks and time steps. This problem is examined in detail in Section 16.9.

16.5.4 MEMORY AFFINITY ISSUES

The importance and relevance of thread affinity issues have been discussed in the OpenMP chapter. TBB provides some support for thread affinity, well described in the documentation, but the memory affinity strategy is different. The OpenMP thread affinity strategy is tailored for a thread-centric environment, where tasks are uniquely mapped to threads. In this case, the thread affinity interfaces select a placement of threads on cores. In a task-centric environment, this approach does not apply. The TBB thread affinity service focuses on establishing a togetherness relation between tasks, by informing the runsystem that they should, in possible, be run by the same thread.

Indeed, a task accessing some global data may want to spawn another task that accesses the same global data. In this case, memory access performance will be enhanced if the task is executed by the same thread. TBB therefore gives the programmer the possibility of defining the *affinity identity* of the initial thread—which can be thought of as some kind identification of the executing core—and passing it to a spawned thread. Then, as discussed before, the affinity identity can be used, if other high-priority criteria fail, to select the task that has the same identity as the terminating task. The TBB documentation insists on the fact that task affinity is a hint for the scheduler: it is not a forcing criteria, and in some cases it may be ignored. Basically, there is a fundamental conflict between affinity and load balancing.

16.6 USING THE TBB SCHEDULER

A few examples follow that illustrate the operation of the TBB scheduler, looking at a few different programming style options for accomplishing some simple tasks.

16.6.1 BLOCKING VERSUS CONTINUATION PASSING EXAMPLES

Consider a code where some initial sequential computation is done first, then a parallel region is activated, and finally the code returns to a sequential region to complete the computation. This example is organized in the way shown in Figure 16.5: the main thread launches the initial sequential task (called B in the figure), which in turn spawns three worker tasks (called M in the figure) that perform some parallel treatment, and finally B takes over after waiting for its children.

Main thread code

Consider first the main thread code. The important observation here is the fact that the main() function *is not running as a TBB task object*. Therefore, this function cannot use the member functions of the task class; it can only access the *static* functions of the class, which behave as ordinary global functions. Taking a look at the task class, we observe that there is not much choice: the only option available to main() is to use spawn_root_and_wait() to spawn either a single task or a task list. Note also that, since tasks must be allocated before being spawned, the main() function can only allocate and spawn root tasks.

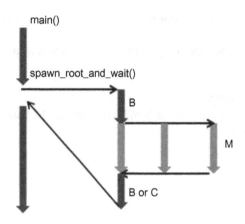

FIGURE 16.5

Forking and joining a parallel section.

We then define a BasicTask class—to be defined later—to construct the object B spawned by main(), which sets the stage for the computation and spawns in turn the three worker tasks of the parallel section as instances of the MyTask class discussed above. Worker tasks are identified by their integer rank. The code for the main() function is given below. This code is generic, and it will be the same for all the examples discussed in this and the following section (as we said, there is not much the main function can do).

```
int main(int argc, char **argv)
    {
    int n;
    if(argc==2) n = atoi(argv[1]);
    else n = 2;
    Timer T;

    task_scheduler_init init(n);
    std::cout << "\nMain starts "<< std::endl;

    BasicTask *B = new ( task::allocate_root() ) BasicTask();
    task::spawn_root_and_wait(*B);
    std::cout << "\nMain ends " << std::endl;
    }
```

LISTING 16.2

Main() code.

The main thread, therefore, spawns the task or tasks that drive the job, and waits. Note that the main thread is in principle doomed to remain blocked doing nothing. For a TBB task, it is possible to spawn the child tasks, and then do some other useful work before waiting for their termination. However, main() is not running as a TBB task. We will see later on how it is possible to modify this context, by setting up a stage in which main() spawns a task, continues to do something else and only then waits for the termination of the spawned task. But this requires advanced synchronization tricks to be discussed later on.

The two examples that follow differ only in the implementation of the BasicTask class that drives the computation.

Example 1: blocking on children

The definition of the BasicTask class is given below, for the case in which the B task waits for its children after spawning the parallel region.

```
class BasicTask : public task
    {
    private:
    Timer  T;

    public:
    BasicTask() {}
    task *execute()
       {
       // Allocate three MyTasks as my children
       // - - - - - - - - - - - - - - - - - -
       MyTask* B1 = new( allocate_child() ) MyTask(1);
       MyTask* B2 = new( allocate_child() ) MyTask(2);
       MyTask* B3 = new( allocate_child() ) MyTask(3);

       set_ref_count(4);   // refcount=(3+1) because I wait

       spawn(*B1);          // spawn childs
       spawn(*B2);
       spawn_and_wait_for_all(*B3);
       return NULL;
       }
    };
```

LISTING 16.3

BasicTask class, blocking style.

This class has a trivial constructor because no data items need to be passed to the tasks. Note that:

- The three MyTask workers are allocated as children of the running BasicTask object, called B. This automatically makes B the successor of the three MyTask workers.
- The reference count of the running BasicTask object is set to 4, one more than the number of spawned children. This is because B waits for its children. If the reference count was set to 3, it would reach zero when all children terminate, and the running task would be automatically spawned. However, spawning a running task crashes the code (try).

In this case, although the thread running task B is not released, it can suspend B while waiting in order to service another thread. This avoids wasting CPU resources on inactive tasks (and avoids deadlocks, as often emphasized before).

Example 1: Blocking.C

To compile, run make block. The number of threads in the pool is passed via the command line (the default value is 2).

Example 2: continuation passing

Next, the definition of the BasicTask class is given for the case in which the B task terminates, and is replaced by a continuation task. The class ContTask is again trivial; the task just writes an identification message and terminates.

```
class BasicTask : public task
  {
  private:
  Timer  T;

  public:
  BasicTask() {}
  task *execute()
    {
    // Allocate the continuation task C
    // - - - - - - - - - - - - - - - - -
    ContTask* C = new(allocate_continuation()) ContTask();

    // Allocate three MyTasks as children of C
    // - - - - - - - - - - - - - - - - - - - - -
    MyTask* B1 = new(C->allocate_child() ) MyTask(1);
    MyTask* B2 = new(C->allocate_child() ) MyTask(2);
    MyTask* B3 = new(C->allocate_child() ) MyTask(3);

    C->set_ref_count(3);  // C is spawned by last child

    spawn(*B1);           // spawn childs
    spawn(*B2);
    spawn(*B3);
    return NULL;
    }
  };
```

LISTING 16.4

BasicTask class, continuation passing style.

- The three MyTask workers are now allocated as children of the continuation task, called C. This makes the continuation task C the successor of the three MyTask workers.
- The reference count of the successor task C object is set to 3, the number of spawned children. The continuation task C is automatically executed when all children terminate and its reference count reaches zero.

Remember that the main() function spawns the initial task B and waits for its termination. In this case, B terminates when the spawned tasks M start execution, and its executing thread is released.

However, in executing the example code you will observe that main() prints its termination message *after the continuation task* C *is finished*. This continuation task, probably run by another thread, is fully playing its role of continuation of B, and taking its place in the wait mechanism of the main thread.

Example 2: Continuation.C

To compile, run make cont. The number of threads in the pool is passed via the command line (the default value is 2).

16.6.2 RECURSIVE COMPUTATION OF THE AREA UNDER A CURVE

The traditional example of the recursive area computation, already discussed in the context of the OpenMP, task_group and NPool environments, is reexamined next, looking at this problem from the point of view of the task API.

The first thing to be observed is that there is no direct way of waiting for all descendants. Therefore, the nonblocking programming style in which tasks either generate child tasks or compute and store partial results in a global variable is not directly accessible here. The next section will discuss how this programming style can be implemented, using more advanced synchronization techniques. For the time being, children have to return partial results to the successor (parent) task. The two options discussed in the simple preceding example are therefore open to us: tasks recursively spawn children and wait for their termination, or tasks recursively spawn children and terminate, being replaced by a continuation task. *It is the continuation task that recovers the partial results returned by the child tasks.*

The main() function, listed below, is the same for the two cases. But there are differences in the recursive task function code.

```
int main(int argc, char **argv)
   {
   double area;
   InputData();     // read Nth and G
   task_scheduler_init init(Nth);
   AreaTask& A = *new(task::allocate_root()) AreaTask(0, 1, &area);
   task::spawn_root_and_wait(A);
   std::cout << "\nArea is : " << area << std::endl;
   }
```

LISTING 16.5

Main function for the recursive area computation.

The first case, in which tasks block waiting for children, has exactly the same structure as the NPool code discussed in Chapter 12. The AreaTask constructor receives as argument the return value address in the parent task. The execute() function declares two local variables x and y where the child partial results are retrieved, and the task returns (x+y) after waiting for its children. The complete listing is in the source file AreaRec1.C.

Example 3: AreaRec1.C

To compile, run make arearec1. The number of threads in the pool as well as the granularity are read from the file arearec.dat.

Continuation passing case

The necessity of handling return values introduces some subtleties in the recursive AreaTask class. These issue are well described in the TBB documentation [18, 34] and the discussion that follows just underlines the main points. The full source code, in file AreaRec2.C, incorporates a number of useful comments. First, a continuation task is defined in the listing below.

```
class AreaContinuationTask : public task
    {
    public:
    double *sum;
    double x, y;

    AreaContinuationTask(double *sum_) : sum(sum_) {}
    task* execute()
        {
        *sum = x+y;
        return NULL;
        }
    };
```

LISTING 16.6

AreaContinuationTask class.

All the continuation task does to collect two partial results from its children (predecessors) and return their sum to its parent. This class has three data items: the doubles x and y, where the predecessor (child) tasks deposit their partial results, and a pointer to a double sum where the continuation task returns its partial result (x+y) to its own successor (parent). This address sum is passed via the constructor when the continuation task is allocated by the task to be replaced, which transfers the return address received when it was allocated by its own successor.

In the initial AreaTask class, the changes to be made are the following (see the source AreaRec2.C):

- The initial task allocates its continuation C, passing the return value address.
- The two child tasks are allocated as children of C, passing the addresses of C.x and C.y, where they have to deposit their return values.
- The two children are spawned, as before. The reference count of C is set to 2, because this task is not waiting: it will run when the children terminate.

Example 4: AreaRec2.C

To compile, run make arearec2. The number of threads in the pool as well as the granularity are read from the file arearec.dat.

16.7 JOB SUBMISSION BY CLIENT THREADS

Our attention moves next to an interesting issue: how to implement, using the TBB scheduler API, the programming style adopted by the task group utilities in OpenMP or TBB, as well as in the NPool task pool: a thread submits a complex parallel job, does something else and, when the time comes, waits for the job termination. This issue is cleanly handled by TBB with the task_group class, as discussed in Chapter 11. However, this class does not provide access to all of the task scheduler services. It is useful to see how a taskgroup-like feature can be implemented by using the task scheduler API. This is possible by using some advanced synchronization techniques, well described in the TBB documentation, which are the subject of this section. The discussion that follows is in fact a refined exercise in task synchronization: how, because of the hierarchical relations, tasks can be used to synchronize instead of compute.

In order to have a clear understanding of the issues at hand, take a look at the "synchronization" part of the task class listing in Annex, Section 16.10, where all the available functions for spawning and waiting for child tasks are declared. Remember that ordinary member functions can only be called by TBB tasks (and not by the main function, which is not running as a TBB task). Static functions, instead, are global functions that can be called by anyone. We observe that:

- For TBB tasks, there are independent spawn() and wait_for_all() function calls available, which implement the standard taskwait mechanism: a task spawns as many tasks as needed, continuing to do something else and then, at the right time, performs the wait call to wait for direct children. *However, there is no immediate way of waiting for all possible descendants.*
- *There are no static functions for an isolated wait call.* Therefore, the main function can only call spawn_root_and_wait(). It cannot directly perform other activities between the spawn and the wait.

It would be useful, instead, to have the possibility for the main function or an arbitrary TBB task, of launching a complex job, eventually doing other things, and waiting when the time comes for the termination of all the tasks generated by the job. The software architecture required to handle this problem, shown in Figure 16.6, is relatively simple and based on the fact that the wait for the end of the job can be delegated to another task—an empty task—whose only role is to wait, and which does not even need to run. This mechanism is a critical part of the TBB design, well advertised in the TBB documentation.

The software architecture shown in Figure 16.6 is implemented in the following way:

- The main thread allocates an empty task E as a root task. *This task will never run.*
- An auxiliary task called B in the figure is allocated by main as a child (predecessor) of the empty task E. Its role is to trigger the parallel job represented by the grey box.
- This auxiliary task B will henceforth be called the *work-holder* task. It encapsulates the gray box parallel job, as a successor of the complete job. This means the initial tasks of the job, spawned by B, will be allocated as children of B.
- The reference count of the empty task E is set to 2=1+1, so that this task *waits but is not executed when its predecessor* B *completes.*
- The empty task spawns its child B task.
- When the time to wait comes, main calls E.wait_for_all(). When this function returns, the gray box has been completed.

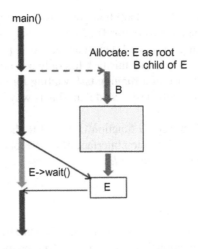

FIGURE 16.6

Job submission by the main thread.

16.7.1 GENERIC INTERFACE FOR JOB SUBMISSION

The previous software organization can be implemented in a generic programming interface allowing the main function of a TBB task to submit a complex job for execution, do something else, and then wait for termination:

- empty_task* Submit(): This is a template function, where the template parameter T encapsulates the submitted job. It returns an empty task reference that acts as a job identifier.
- void Wait_For_Job(empty_task *e): Waits for the job corresponding to the empty task e.

Here is the definition of these functions.

```
template <typename T>
empty_task* SubmitJob()
    {
    empty_task* E = new( task::allocate_root() ) empty_task;
    E->set_ref_count(2);
    T *t = new( E->allocate_child() ) T();
    E->spawn(*t);
    return E;
    }

void WaitForJob(empty_task* E)
    {
    E->wait_for_all();
    E->destroy(*E);
    }
```

LISTING 16.7

Generic functions for job submission.

Note that in defining the generic SubmitJob() function, it is explicitly assumed that the work-holder task class T has a trivial, no argument constructor T(). Note also that, in the WaitForJob() function, once the empty task has finished waiting for the job termination, it is explicitly destroyed by a call to the member function destroy(). The reason is that this task has only one predecessor, and that its reference count has been set to 2, as in the case of a running task waiting for children. However, *this task was never run*, so it was never deleted by the task scheduler. This is why it is good programming practice to explicitly destroy it.

The job ID returned by the SubmitJob() function is passed to the second function to wait for the job. This works exactly like the job submission interface of the NPool utility in Chapter 11. Jobs can be submitted and then waited for later on *in any order*.

16.7.2 SUBMITTING AN IO TASK

The code for this very simple example is in the source file SynchIO.C. The IOTask class submitted for execution has a simple execute() function that writes an initialization message, waits for a given number of milliseconds, and writes a termination message. The time-wait duration is read directly from a global variable iowait, so this class does not need an explicit constructor to capture a data value. Here is the listing of the class.

```
class IOTask : public task
   {
   private:
   Timer  T;

   public:
   task *execute()
      {
      std::cout << "\n IOtask starts " << std::endl;
      T.Wait(iowait);
      std::cout << "\n IOtask ends " << std::endl;
      return NULL;
      }
   };
```

LISTING 16.8

IOTask class.

Since this class already has a default no-argument constructor, it is not necessary to encapsulate it in a work-holder class. It can be passed directly as a template argument to the SubmitJob() function.

The code for the main function is listed below. The main() function launches the IO task, waits for a given number of milliseconds, and then waits for the completion of the IOtask. The wait times, iowait for the IO task and mainwait for the main function, are read from an input file. By modifying these timed waits we can check that the synchronization between the main task and the IO task works properly.

```
int main(int argc, char **argv)
   {
   Timer T;
   InputData();              // read Nth, mainwait, iowait
   task_scheduler_init init(Nth);

   std::cout << "\nMain starts "<< std::endl;
   // - - - - - - - - - - - - - - - - - - - - - - - - - - - - -
   empty_task *e = SubmitJob<IOTask>();     // submit
   T.Wait(mainwait);                        // do something else
   WaitForJob(e);                           // wait for job
   // - - - -  - - - - - - - - - - - - - - - - - - - - - - - -
   std::cout << "\nMain ends " << std::endl;
   }
```

LISTING 16.9

Main() function.

Example 5: SynchIO.C

To compile, run make synchio. The timed waits for the main function and the IO task are read from the file synchIO.dat.

In the vath-based utilities or in OpenMP, the synchronizations required for launching a task, doing some more work, and finally waiting for the child task were handled by using a Boolean lock. This example shows how the same issue can be handled, in the TBB environment, using the built-in synchronization properties of the scheduler, together with empty tasks used as a synchronization tool.

16.7.3 SUBMITTING COMPLEX, RECURSIVE JOBS

In order to present a more sophisticated example of generic job submission, we discuss next how to submit one of the three area computation jobs discussed in Chapter 11: the case in which a recursive AreaTask function, which returns an area value, blocks waiting for children. Internally, the AreaTask function uses task_groups to generate the recursive tasks, but we do not need to be concerned with this issue here. Listing 11.17 shows that the main function blocks on the AreaTask call, waiting for the returned area value. It is shown next how to modify this code in a simple way, in such a way that the main function can now do other work concurrently with the area computation, before waiting for termination and using the result.

The job submission interface provides a simple way of implementing this strategy. A work-holder class encapsulates the AreaTask() call, waits for the return value, and initializes a global result variable, on behalf of the main function. The main function submits the work-holder class, performs other activities, and waits for the job termination before using the value of result.

```
double result;
...

double AreaRec2(double a, double b)
   {
   // Same function as in listing 6, chapter 11.
   }
class WH : public task
   {
   public:
   task *execute()
      {
      result = AreaRec2(0, 1);
      }
   };

int main(int argc, char **argv)
   {
   result = 0.0;
   ...
   task_scheduler_init init(Nth);
   std::cout << "\nMain starts "<< std::endl;
   ...
   ...
   // Launch area job
   // - - - - - - - -
   empty_task *e = SubmitJob<WH>();
   // - - - - - - - - - - - - - - -
   // here main can do other things
   // - - - - - - - - - - - - - - -
   WaitForJob(e);    // e is destroyed here
   std::cout << "\nThird job done. result is " << result <<  std::endl;
   }
```

LISTING 16.10

Submitting a recursive area job.

All main() has to do is to pass the WH class as template parameter to the SubmitJob() function and, when the time comes, wait for the job termination. This example is developed in file Submit.C.

Example 6: Submit.C

To compile, run make submit. The number of threads in the pool as well as the number of tasks are read from the file submit.dat.

Comment on empty tasks

Before moving ahead, it is useful to come back to the role played by the empty task. This task, never spawned and never executed, is in fact acting as a barrier that signals the end of the parallel region computation. Because the empty task is the successor of the work-holder class, its reference count (initially equal to 2) is decreased when the parallel job terminates. The wait_for_all() function, when called on the empty task object, returns when the reference count reaches 1. That is all this empty task is needed for: just synchronization. Using an empty task with a trivial execute() function is very convenient, but not really necessary. Any nontrivial task can also be used to implement the required barrier synchronization. Using the library provided empty task is just a convenient way of remembering that the task is being used only for synchronization purposes.

16.8 EXAMPLE: MOLECULAR DYNAMICS CODE

The original MdTbb.C code in Chapter 13 computes the trajectory of a large number of particles with long-range forces, moving in one dimension. A trajectory sample is computed by iterating a large number of times over small time steps. Then the application prints the final kinetic and total energies of the system, and starts again the computation of a new trajectory sample. The code organization is shown in Figure 16.7. In the initial TBB version in Chapter 13, the code remains in a sequential mode, using the parallel_for algorithm to compute the accelerations and to perform the trajectory updates.

In order to provide a simple example of advanced synchronizations using the TBB scheduler, a new version of the code is now deployed, where the calls to parallel_for are replaced by a direct spawning of a set of parallel tasks. The discussion that follows concentrates on the trajectory computation part of the code, because the occasional energy computations have very little impact in performance. Energies are therefore computed in sequential mode.

Two basic issues are discussed in-depth in this section:

- How to use empty tasks to implement barrier-like synchronizations among tasks.
- How to use empty tasks to recycle computing tasks, avoiding repeated memory allocations resulting from the fact that the computational tasks are created and destroyed at each time step.

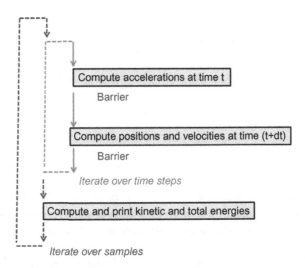

FIGURE 16.7

Code MdTBB: computation of a molecular dynamics trajectories.

16.8.1 PARALLEL TASKS FOR THIS PROBLEM

The programming strategy proceeds as follows: for each time step in the trajectory computation, Ntk tasks are spawned to perform a parallel computation of the acceleration, followed by a successor task whose only role is to enforce a barrier synchronization point among the tasks. Then, Ntk tasks are spawned to update the coordinates and momenta, again followed by a synchronizing successor task. Since there is no sequential work to be performed in the time-step loop, these successor tasks will just be empty tasks.

Here is the listing of the task class used to compute accelerations.

```
class Accelerations : public task
   {
   private:
    int rank;
    int beg, end;

   public:
   // Constructor
   Accelerations(int n) : rank(n)
      {
      int SZ = 3*N;
      int step = SZ/NTk;
      beg = rank*step;
      end = (rank+1)*step;
      if(rank==(NTk-1)) end = SZ ;
      }

   // compute acceleration
   // - - - - - - - - - - -
   task *execute()
      {
      for(size_t n=beg; n!=end; ++n)
         {
         a[n] = 0.0;
         for(size_t j=0; j<SZ; ++j) a[n] += D[n][j] * q[j];
         }
      return NULL;
      }
   };
```

LISTING 16.11

Acceleration task.

The constructor receives an integer rank in $[0, Ntk - 1]$ that identifies the task. Then, from the value of this rank, the constructor computes the range $[beg, end)$ of particle indices that are controlled by this task. The execute() function simply computes the accelerations for all the particles in the subrange allocated to this task.

The task class used to compute the momentum and coordinates updates, called TimeStep, has exactly the same structure.

16.8.2 COMPUTING PARTICLE TRAJECTORIES

The code is basically the sequential code, except that the main() function calls an auxiliary function RunTrajectory that executes the time step loop. When this function returns, a new trajectory sample is available. It is important to observe that the Ntk tasks that compute the accelerations and time steps are all allocated and spawned by main(). This means they are all queued in the main thread personal deque, waiting to be stolen by other threads. This is not the optimal way of using the task scheduler, which is more efficient when, as discussed in Chapter 11, a nested fork-join pattern operates, spreading tasks over different deques. This is what naturally happens when tasks are dynamically generated in a recursive pattern, but in this particular problem we want to address task recycling issues and dynamically generated tasks with a limited lifetime that are not useful. Therefore, we have settled for simplicity in the code structure listed below.

Here is the listing of the RunTrajectory() auxiliary function.

```
void RunTrajectory()
    {
    Accelerations*    x[Ntk];
    TimeStep*         y[Ntk];
    empty_task    *e1, *e2;

    // Allocate empty tasks
    // - - - - - - - - - - -
    e1    = new( task::allocate_root() ) empty_task();
    e2    = new( task::allocate_root() ) empty_task();

    for(int k=0; k<nSteps; ++k)      // time step loop
        {
        // Allocate worker tasks
        // - - - - - - - - - - - -
        for(int n=0; n<NTk; ++n)
            x[n] = new( e1->allocate_child() ) Accelerations(n);
        for(int n=0; n<NTk; ++n)
            y[n] = new( e2->allocate_child() ) TimeStep(n);

        // Set reference counts of successor tasks
        // - - - - - - - - - - - - - - - - - - - - -
        e1->set_ref_count(NTk+1);
        e2->set_ref_count(NTk+1);

        // Spawn NTk Accelerations, and wait for them to complete
        // - - - - - - - - - - - - - - - - - - - - - - - - - - - -
        for(int n=0; n<NTk; ++n) task::spawn(*x[n]);
        e1->wait_for_all();

        // Spawn NTk TimeSteps, and wait for them to complete
        // - - - - - - - - - - - - - - - - - - - - - - - - - - -
```

Continued

```
        for(int n=0; n<NTk; ++n) task::spawn(*y[n]);
        e2->wait_for_all();
        }

    // destroy tasks
    // - - - - - - -
    task::destroy(*e1);
    task::destroy(*e2);
    }
```

LISTING 16.12

Computation of trajectories.

A few comments are useful at this point:

- This function has, as local variables, two arrays of references to Acceleration and TimeStep tasks, as well as two empty tasks. These pointers have yet to be allocated.
- The first thing that happens, before the time step loop starts, is the allocation of the two empty tasks as root tasks. This can be safely done here because these tasks are never spawned, executed, and destroyed. Then, their lifetime is not restricted to each loop iteration.
- The computing tasks, instead, must be allocated, as children of the empty tasks, at each loop iteration, because they are executed and destroyed.
- The reference count of the empty tasks is set to Nth $+ 1$, so that these tasks wait for their children and are not spawned.
- Then, the acceleration tasks are spawned with the empty task e1 waiting for them, which implements the barrier required at this point. The time step tasks follow in the same way.
- When the trajectory computation is finished, the empty tasks are explicitly destroyed.

The rest of the code is straightforward. Performance is comparable to the parallel_for version.

Example 7: MdShed.C

To compile, run make mdsch. Molecular dynamics code using the task scheduler. The input parameters are, as for all the other versions of this code, read from the file md.dat.

Example 8: MdShedBis.C

To compile, run make mdschbis. Same as before, but using an improved recursive spawning of the computational tasks.

16.9 RECYCLING PARALLEL REGION TASKS

When looking at the previous versions of the molecular dynamics code—both high-level algorithms and task scheduler—one observation comes to mind: in this microtasking approach, *the computational tasks are allocated and destroyed at each loop iteration*. For systems of moderate complexity, this may not be a major issue. But imagine the case for a huge number of particles, and a code running on a 60 core Intel Xeon Phi platform, supporting, because of hyperthreading, up to 240 threads. That makes

480 memory allocations per time step. If, in addition, the complete run involves millions of time steps, it is legitimate to explore the possibility of getting rid of memory management overhead by moving task allocations *outside of the time step loop,* as was the already case for the empty tasks. This is, in fact, the most obvious optimization that could justify the use of the task scheduler to squeeze some extra performance for the code.

TBB does provide a task recycling interface. A task that wants to be recycled calls, inside its execute() function, one of the two member functions available for recycling: recycle_as_ continuation() or recycle_as_child_of(task *t). This marks the task for recycling, and prevents the scheduler from destroying it when the execute() function terminates. Then, the task can be spawned again for running. There is an obvious *nonoverlap rule* to be respected when recycling tasks: the recycled task should not be spawned again before the execute() function that marks it for recycling terminates. In other words, the next execution of the recycled task cannot overlap with the current one.

Going back to the molecular dynamics code, let us see how the acceleration tasks could be recycled (the time step tasks would work in the same way). The first thing that comes to mind is to modify the execute() function with one extra line of code, as follows:

```
class Accelerations : public task
    {
    ...
    // compute acceleration
    // - - - - - - - - - - -
    task *execute()
        {
        for(size_t n=beg; n!=end; ++n)
            {
            a[n] = 0.0;
            for(size_t j=0; j<SZ; ++j) a[n] += D[n][j] * q[j];
            }
        recycle_as_child_of(*parent());  // recycling
        return NULL;
        }
    };
```

LISTING 16.13

Attempt to recycle Acceleration tasks.

This extra line of code would, indeed, recycle the acceleration tasks as children of their successor, the empty task e1, returned by the parent() call. Clearly, the nonoverlap rule is respected. Because of the barrier induced by the empty task e1, these tasks will never be spawned again before all the execute() functions that mark them for recycling terminate.

Unfortunately, *this simple scheme does not work, for the reason already mentioned in Section 16.5.1:* recycling the tasks breaks down the implicit barrier mechanism induced by the successor task. If a task is marked for recycling, *the scheduler does not destroy the task when* execute() *terminates, but it does not decrease the parent reference count either.* In this case, the e1 reference count never decreases and reaches 1, the e1 task never returns from the wait, and the code deadlocks at the first loop iteration.

We have concocted a simple example, RecycleBad.C, to show how this happens. Take a look at the source, which is well documented. This code prints the parent reference count, and shows that when the task is recycled the reference count is not decreased.

Example 9: RecycleBad.C

To compile, run make recbad. The number of threads in the pool is 2, and the number of parallel tasks is 4.

16.9.1 RECYCLING PROTOCOL

The previous discussion shows us that the barrier synchronization and the recycling operations do not coexist peacefully when driven by the same task e1. Therefore, *two empty tasks are used, one for synchronization and one for recycling*. The procedure is the following:

- An empty task E is introduced for recycling. The parallel tasks for the parallel region are allocated as children of E, and are recycled as, again, children of E. When these tasks run, the E reference count will not be implicitly decreased, as was shown before. But we do not care, *because E is not used for synchronization, and it never waits*. In fact, E does nothing at all—never waits, never runs—except helping to manage the task recycling protocol.
- Another task P is used for barrier synchronization. It is this task that waits for completion of the N parallel tasks, and its reference count is set to (N+1) before the parallel tasks are spawned. However, now P is not their successor, so P's reference count is not automatically decreased by the scheduler when the worker tasks terminate. For this reason, the worker tasks need to have a reference to P to be able to *explicitly* decrease its reference count before terminating.

The listing below shows how the Acceleration class must adapted to this protocol. The task objects now receive an extra argument in the constructor: a pointer to the fake successor task that will be used for barrier synchronization. Then, there is the execute() function, an explicit call to decrease_ref_count() on the fake successor task.

```
class Accelerations : public task
    {
    private:
    int rank;
    int beg, end;
    empty_task* successor;    // NEW

    public:
    // Constructor
    Accelerations(int n, empty_task *t) : rank(n), successor(t)
        {
        int SZ = 3*N;
        int step = SZ/NTk;
        beg = rank*step;
        end = (rank+1)*step;
        if(rank==(NTk-1)) end = SZ ;
        }
```

```
// compute acceleration
// - - - - - - - - - -
task *execute()
    {
    for(size_t n=beg; n!=end; ++n)
        {
        a[n] = 0.0;
        for(size_t j=0; j<SZ; ++j) a[n] += D[n][j] * q[j];
        }
    successor->decrement_ref_count();
    recycle_as_child_of( *parent() );
    return NULL;
    }
};
```

LISTING 16.14

Modified Accelerations class.

The new version of the function RunTrajectory() called by main(), performing the loop plus sequential region iteration, is listed next. Note that:

- All allocations and deallocations take place outside of the time step loop.
- The same empty task dummy is used to perform the two successive barrier synchronizations.

```
void RunTrajectory()
    {
    Accelerations*    x[NTk];
    TimeStep*         y[NTk];
    empty_task* dummy;
    empty_task* e1, *e2;

    // Allocate tasks
    // - - - - - - - -
    dummy = new( task::allocate_root() ) empty_task();
    e1    = new( task::allocate_root() ) empty_task();
    e2    = new( task::allocate_root() ) empty_task();

    for(int n=0; n<NTk; ++n)
        x[n] = new( e1->allocate_child() ) Accelerations(n, dummy);

    for(int n=0; n<NTk; ++n)
        y[n] = new( e2->allocate_child() ) TimeStep(n, dummy);

    // HERE STARTS THE RECURRENT PART
    // - - - - - - - - - - - - - - - -
    for(int k=0; k<nSteps; ++k)
```

Continued

```
    {
    // Set reference counts of successor tasks
    // - - - - - - - - - - - - - - - - - - - -
    dummy->set_ref_count(NTk+1);
    e1->set_ref_count(NTk+1);

    // Spawn NTk Accelerations, and wait for them to complete
    // - - - - - - - - - - - - - - - - - - - - - - - - - - - - -
    for(int n=0; n<NTk; ++n) task::spawn(*x[n]);
    dummy->wait_for_all();

    dummy->set_ref_count(NTk+1);
    e2->set_ref_count(NTk+1);

    // Spawn NTk TimeSteps, and wait for them to complete
    // - - - - - - - - - - - - - - - - - - - - - - - - - - -
    for(int n=0; n<NTk; ++n) task::spawn(*y[n]);
    dummy->wait_for_all();
    }

// destroy tasks
// - - - - - - -
task::destroy(*dummy);
task::destroy(*e1);
task::destroy(*e2);
for(int n=0; n<NTk; ++n)
    {
    task::destroy(*x[n]);
    task::destroy(*y[n]);
    }
}
```

LISTING 16.15

New version of the RunTrajectory() function.

Example 10: MdRec.C

To compile, run make mdrec. Molecular dynamics code using the task scheduler, with task recycling. The input parameters are, as for all the other versions of this code, read from the file md.dat.dat.

The code works correctly, reproducing the results of the other versions. For a small system, there is not much difference in performance with the versions without task recycling.

16.10 ANNEX: TASK CLASS MEMBER FUNCTIONS

The listing below shows most of the member function of the task class, the ones that are most commonly used. A complete list of member functions and a very detailed description of each one of them is available in the Reference Guide that comes with the TBB release. Note that many of these member functions are qualified as static. Remember that these are ordinary global functions associated with the class and not to a particular object. They must be called by qualifying them with the class name: task::member_function().

```
class task
   {
 protected:
   task();

 public:
   virtual ~task() {}

   virtual task* execute() = 0;

   // Allocation:
   // - - - - - -
   static proxy1 allocate_root();
   static proxy2 allocate_root(task_group_context\&);
   proxy3 allocate_continuation();
   proxy4 allocate_child();
   static proxy5 allocate_additional_child(task\&);

   // Explicit destruction
   // - - - - - - - - - -  -
   static void destroy(task\& victim);

   // Recycling
   // - - - - -
   void recycle_as_continuation();
   void recycle_as_safe_continuation();
   void recycle_as_child_of(task\& new_parent);

   // Synchronization
   // - - - - - - - -
   void set_ref_count(int count);
   void increment_ref_count();
   void decrement_ref_count();
   // - - - - - - - - - - - - - - - - - - - - - - - -
   static void spawn_root_and_wait(task\& root);
   static void spawn_root_and_wait(task_list\& root);
   static void spawn(task\& t);
   static void spawn(task_list\& list);
   // - - - - - - - - - - - - - - - - - - - - - - -
   void wait_for_all();
   void spawn_and_wait_for_all(task\& t);
   void spawn_and_wait_for_all(task_list\& list);
```

Continued

```
// - - - - - - - - - - - - - - - - - - - - - - - - - -
static void enqueue(task\& t);

// Task context
// - - - - - -
static task\& self();
task* parent() const;
void set_parent(task *p);
bool is_stolen_task() const;
task_group_context* group();
void change_group(task_group_context\& ctx);

// Cancellation
// - - - - - -
bool cancel_group_execution();
bool is_cancelled() const;

// Affinity
// - - - - -
typedef (implementation-defined-unsigned-type) affinity_id;
virtual void note_affinity(affinity_id id);
void set_affinity(affinity_id id);
affinity_id affinity() const;

// debugging
// - - - - -
int ref_count();
...
};
```

LISTING 16.16

Task class.

Annex A: Using the Software

This annex provide guidance for compiling and running the support software, which can be downloaded from the book site, http://booksite.elsevier.com/9780128037614/. Before going into the details about libraries and examples, a few words about software installation may be useful.

A.1 LIBRARIES REQUIRED

Pthreads and Windows are native multithreading libraries in Unix-Linux or Windows systems. They are automatically integrated in the operating system. OpenMP is also automatically integrated in the C-C++ compilers (Intel, GCC, VisualC++, etc.). TBB, extensively used in this book, requires separate installation.

Installing and configuring TBB are very simple operations. First, the archive file corresponding to the latest release for Unix or for Windows systems is downloaded from the TBB web site [18]. TBB is installed by expanding the release archive file in some installation directory. Then, the file /bin/tbbvars.sh is modified: the export TBBROOT line must be completed with the full path to the TBB installation directory.

This is all about installation. Every time a new shell is started in which TBB is used, the tbbvars.sh script must be executed (sourced), passing a command line argument corresponding to the platform architecture (ia32, ia64, etc.) and, in Windows systems, the Visual Studio version. This script sets the paths to libraries and include files. Running the script with no command line options lists the set of options available.

At this point, TBB is ready to run. The switch link tbb.lib in Windows or -ltbb in Linux has to be included in the linker, but this is automatically done in the makefiles provided with the codes.

A.2 SOFTWARE ORGANIZATION

The overall software organization is described in Figure A.1. There are two root directories, /msvs for Windows platforms and /linux for Unix-Linux platforms. Here is the typical content and organization of the different library or chapter examples subdirectories:

- */vath_xxx*: library directory:
    - */include*: library include files.
    - */src*: library source files.
    - */test*: sources for library tests.
    - Makefile to build library and tests.
    - Data files (*.dat) required by some of the tests.
- */chxx*: chapter examples directory.
    - */include*: additional include files required by the examples.
    - */src*: examples sources.
    - Makefile to build he examples.

- */linux*
  - */vath_pth* : Pthreads implementation of "vath"
  - */vath_std* : C++11 implementation of "vath"
  - */ch3:* chapter 3 examples
  - */ch4:* chapter 4 examples
  - ...

- */msvs*
  - */vath_win* : Windows implementation of "vath"
  - */vath_std* : C++11 implementation of "vath"
  - */ch3*: chapter 3 examples
  - */ch4*: chapter 4 examples
  - ...

FIGURE A.1

Directory organization of the support software. Each directory under /msvs or /linux includes the corresponding makefile.

- Data files (*.dat) required by the examples.
- Notes: a text file with instructions for compilation and execution of the chapter examples, and eventual comments on the chapter content.

There are obvious redundancies in this code organization. For example, the source, include, and test files for the vath_std implementation of the vath library are identical in the /msvs and /linux directories. Only the makefiles are different. But we have deliberately tried to avoid universal but incomprehensible makefiles, and settled for simple makefiles that can easily be modified by users if needed. Therefore, all the relevant files are reproduced whenever needed.

The same comment applies to the chapter examples. There are, mainly in the early chapters, code examples that target specifically Pthreads, Windows threads, or the C++11 library, and the corresponding files are at the right places. However, most of the examples are portable, and the source files are identical for Windows or Unix-Linux platforms.

A.2.1 BUILDING AND TESTING THE VATH LIBRARY

Each library version directory includes the appropriate makefile for compilation of the library and the compilation and execution of the test codes, as well as data files needed for some tests. Source, include files, and test codes are in the /src, /include, and /test subdirectories, respectively.

To build and test the libraries (in Windows, replace make by nmake):

- Run make libva to build the library.
- Run make all to compile the test codes.
- Run make execall to run all the test codes (which can, of course, also be run individually).

The default compilers are Visual Studio 2013 in Windows and GCC (4.8 or higher) in Linux-Unix. These compilers are fully C++11 compliant, and support all the implementations of the library. The native implementations should work with older compilers. Setting the INTEL_ENV environment variable, when compiling in Linux platforms, selects the Intel compilers. However, Intel compilers are not yet fully C++11 compatible, so they cannot be used to build the C++11 implementation of the library.

A.2.2 COMPILING AND RUNNING THE EXAMPLES

Examples are compiled and run from the corresponding chn directory. Sources are in the /src subdirectory, and the /include sub_directory contains additional include files needed specifically for the chapter examples. Each /chn directory contains eventual data files needed to run the examples, as well as a makefile. The "notes" file in each chn directory provides detailed instructions for the compilation and execution of the chapter examples.

Filename conventions. While most of the examples depend only on portable libraries (OpenMP, TBB, and vath), those in the early chapters target specific libraries (Pthreads, Windows, or C++11). For this reason, a naming convention has been adopted for the sources, ending the source name with a trailing _P, _W, or _S (for "standard") when they run only on Pthreads, Windows, or C++11 environments, respectively. Filenames without these trailing indicators are portable.

Selecting the library. When compiling and running a portable chapter example, different library implementations can be chosen by setting environment variables. This is needed both to set the path to the include files and to the correct version of the library. By default, the native implementations are chosen: Pthreads in Unix-Linux and Windows threads in Windows. Setting instead the CPP11_ENV environment selects the portable C++11 implementation.

- To set in Linux, export CPP11_ENV = 1 or any nonempty string.
- To set in Windows, set CPP11_ENV = 1 or any nonempty string.
- To unset in Linux, export CPP11_ENV = (empty string).
- To unset in Windows, set CPP11_ENV = (empty string).

Running OpenMP codes. Compiling and running OpenMP codes requires an extra switch in the compiler and linker, otherwise the OpenMP directives are ignored. This is accomplished by setting the OPENMP_ENV environment variable.

Running codes using TBB. The tbbvars.sh script must be executed every time a new shell is open. This is sufficient, the makefiles incorporate the -ltbb switch in codes using TBB.

Several examples deliberately mix libraries or programming environments to exhibit interoperability. In those cases, it may happen that more than one environment variable needs to be set. Such is the case, for example, when OpenMP codes use synchronization utilities provided by the C++11 implementation of the vath library. Many OpenMP codes are linked to the vath library just to use the portable CpuTimer class that measures execution times.

All the Windows examples are console applications with command line compilation. Providing a Visual Studio project for each one of them is overkill. A Visual Studio project will eventually be provided on the book web site for the more complex examples of the later chapters. Remember that accessing the CL compiler and the libraries from the command line requires the execution of a varsargs script every time a new console is opened.

A.3 VATH CLASSES

A complete list of all the utility classes provided by the vath library can be found in the vath_status.pdf document, available in the root directory of the software release in the book Web site. This document also summarizes the (few) portability limitations of some of the vath classes, resulting from missing services in the basic libraries or missing features in the different compilers.

The vath_status.pdf document will be updated in the future, if and when improved versions of the library become available.

Annex B: C++ Function Objects and Lambda Expressions

In C++, a *callable* object is an object or expression to which the call operator () can be applied. Functions and—as we will see below—function pointers are callable objects inherited from C. C++ adds two other callable types of objects, *function objects* and *lambda expressions*, which are the subject of this annex.

B.1 FUNCTION OBJECTS

Function objects are heavily used by STL algorithms to incorporate user-defined behavior in the library. They generalize the concept of function pointers, enabling some programming capabilities that are not easily implemented with function pointers alone. We have seen that function objects are used by TBB in the STL-like algorithms implementing parallel patterns, as well as in the taskgroup programming interface, to specify the user-defined task to be executed by a worker thread.

B.2 FUNCTION OBJECT SYNTAX

A *function object*, also called a *functor*, is a C++ object, instance of an ordinary C++ class that has just one particular quality: it defines the function operator() as a member function of the class (possibly together with other more traditional member functions). This particular member function has in turn a specific quality: it is a *no-name* function called with a syntax that mimics an ordinary function call, *using the arbitrary object name as if it was a function name*. Here is the precise syntax:

```
// The function object class:
// - - - - - - - - - - - - -

class MyFunctor
   {
   private:
   // private data and member functions

   public:
   retval operator()(arg1, arg2, ...);
   ...
   // other public data and member functions
   };

// The client code:
// - - - - - - - - -
```

Continued

```
MyFunctor fobj;                  // declare object fobj
retval k = fobj(arg1, arg2, ...); // function call syntax
```

LISTING B.1

Function object syntax

All that happens here is just using the operator overloading capability of C++ to overload the function call operator(). It is important to keep in mind that:

- A functor class is an ordinary class, and a functor object is an ordinary object. It is possible to encapsulate as much data and function members as needed to provide the planned service, and they can all be accessed with the usual C++ syntax for objects: *object name* followed by *member function name*. The only new feature is the presence of the operator() member function, *which is called with the object name only.*
- The signature of the operator() member function is arbitrary: the return value retval can be any type, and there can be as many arguments as needed. Moreover, this member function can be overloaded: it is possible to define *several* operator() functions with different signatures inside the same function object class. The compiler will either select the one that matches the function call, or complain if there is none.

A special operator is then defined as a member function, implementing a function call semantics. We can wonder about the reason for doing this. After all, when services are required from a C++ class, it is always possible to add an ordinary member function, give it a name, and call it in the usual way. However, the fundamental observation here is that function objects implement the same syntax as *function pointers*, which we show in the listing below.

```
retval (*fptr)(arg1, arg2, ...);    // declaration of fptr

// Initialize the pointer: assume that my_function() has the
// correct signature. The function name is also its address.
// We can, but you don't need,  use &my_function to initialize
// the pointer:

fptr = my_function;

// Now, call the function my_function() through the pointer.
// Again, we can use (*fptr) but (fptr) works too: the function
// pointer is also "callable", and dereferencing is not needed.

retval k = fptr(arg1, arg2, ...);
```

LISTING B.2

Function pointer syntax

Function objects and pointers have therefore the same syntax. Function objects can be used at the places where function pointers are expected, that is, at places where a callable object is required. Note that the function pointer fptr is, as the basic types (int, double, etc.), an object not associated with a C++ class. We can therefore say that function objects generalize function pointers in the same way that C++ classes generalize the basic types that are not associated with a class, with the extra bonus that they can solve problems that ordinary function pointers cannot cope with (an example follows later on).

B.2.1 IMPLEMENTING CALLBACKS

As we know, the main utility of function pointers is to implement *callbacks* that customize the behavior of a library. Library functions that implement a service often require from the user a pointer to a function that sharpens its behavior. The classical example is sorting: a function that sorts an array is called, but this function in turn expects that caller to provide—through a function pointer—the function used to compare two array elements. As emphasized before, function objects can be used at every place a function pointer is expected. The STL uses them heavily to customize its behavior.

Many C++ libraries use function objects to implement callbacks. These libraries give the following instructions to the user:

- Define a class XXX (the name of the class is arbitrary) that defines an operator() with such and such signature, which performs such and such service.
- Then, declare an object instance of this class and pass me its name (again, the name is arbitrary).
- Or, if it suits you, just pass me the class name. Since the object name is irrelevant, I can construct it myself (we give an example later on).

In this way, users end up passing behavior to the library *without naming conventions*. Only the function object type is relevant, as well as the implicit existence of an adequate operator() member function in the class.

B.2.2 ABILITIES OF FUNCTION OBJECTS

Let us now examine how function objects enlarge the abilities of function pointers.

Function objects have better runtime performance

It is argued that function objects have better performance than function pointers, because the function call is resolved at *compile time* rather than at *execution time* (as is the case for function pointers). This argument is compelling only if functions are called millions of times.

Easier handling of functions with internal states

Function objects are objects, and they can therefore maintain an internal state between calls that may decide the outcome of the next call (remember the random number generators, etc). Functions can also maintain an internal state through static variables that are preserved between calls, but we know that we cannot have more than one function per process, unless we are prepared to explicitly code several functions with different names, all doing the same thing. With function objects, instead, we can declare as many of them as we want or need. Each one will have its own encapsulated internal state totally independent of the others.

Extending the capabilities of generic programming

C++ templates were initially invented in order to parameterize data types, and write generic code that applies as well to floats or doubles, for example. Since a function object is also a data type, it can also be parameterized by a template parameter. However, in this case, we are doing much more than text processing, because the specialization to a specific class specializes the functions that can be called with the (arbitrary) object name. Therefore, the template parameter is now used to parameterize *behavior*.

This is what the STL does with the algorithms acting on containers. Often, these algorithms admit two template parameters: one for the type of the element stored in the container, and another one for the function object class that completes the specification of the action of the algorithm on the container.

B.2.3 **EXAMPLE**

We present next a simple example that explicitly shows the utility of disposing of an internal state inside function objects to cope with contexts that cannot easily be solved with function pointers. Given an integer array of size N, we want to deal with the following two problems:

- To find the first negative element.
- To find the first element larger than a given value val, not known at compilation time.

   We will look at this problem by using the find_if STL algorithm:

$$\textit{pointer } \text{pos} = \text{find\_if}(\textit{pointer } \text{beg}, \textit{pointer } \text{end}, \textit{predicate } \text{cond})$$

where

- beg is a pointer to the first element of the array.
- end is a pointer past the end of the array.
- cond is a pointer to a function that receives an integer and returns true if the argument verifies the search criterion. In the STL, functions that return a bool are called *predicates*.
- The return value pos is a pointer to the position of the found element. If pos==end, we know the search failed.

In the first problem, the condition is known at compilation time, and it can be managed with a function pointer: it is easy to write a function that decides if its argument is positive or negative. However, the second problem *cannot* be managed as a function pointer, because the function needs to compare the integer elements of the array to a value not known at compilation time, so two arguments must be passed to the predicate function. But this is not possible in this case, because the find_if function expects a predicate signature with only *one* argument.

Here, function objects come to our rescue. A function object can be used, with an internal state that stores val passed as argument when the object is constructed. Then the operator()(int n) function compares n to val.

Example: fctobj_example.C

This file contains the complete code for this example. We give below the main elements of the example.

```
// Function that solves the first problem:
// - - - - - - - - - - - - - - - - - -
bool IsNegative(int& n)
    {
    if n<0 return true;
    else return false;
    }

// Function object class for second problem
// - - - - - - - - - - - - - - - - - - - -
class IsBigger
    {
    private:
    int value;

    public:
    IsBigger(int n) : value(n) {}  // constructor

    bool operator()(int& n)        // the predicate
        {
        if n>value return true;
        else return false;
        }
    };

// client code:
// - - - - - -

int array[N];

// Solve first problem:
// - - - - - - - - - -
int *pos = find_if(array, array+N, IsNegative);

// Solve second problem:
// - - - - - - - - - - -
IsBigger fctobj = IsBigger(3)    // call constructor, value=3
int *pos = find_if(array, array+N, fctobj);

// but, the name of the object is totally arbitrary, so one does not
// really need to pass it. The following code, that passes directly the
// object constructor, also works:

int *pos = find_if(array, array+N, IsBigger(3));
```

LISTING B.3

Using function objects

B.2.4 FUNCTION OBJECTS IN TBB

In the SPool class, tasks were defined by a pointer to a task function. We have seen that the TBB parallelization algorithms like parallel_for or parallel_reduce or the taslgroup construct are functions or class templates that ask the client code to provide, instead, a function object to specify a task to be performed by a thread, through the overloading of the operator() member function.

Clearly, function objects are used to specified behavior, but there is more than that. The basic task scheduling model is a fork-join of children tasks. Let us assume that a thread executing a task divides the target data set into two halves, and forks a child task, executed by a new thread, to perform half of the initial job. This new thread needs to know what specific task to perform on the reduced data set, so it could naturally get a pointer to the same task function the parent thread is executing. However, what happens if we are running a task function *with a persistent but evolving internal state* needed to implement the algorithm requirements? We end up with a nonthread-safe context, with several threads accessing the same nonthread-safe function.

If the task is defined with a function object, we are much better off, *because function objects, being objects, can be copied*. Therefore, the new thread *does not* get the same function object, *it gets instead a brand new function object* totally independent of the initial one, which may be a full or a partial copy of the parent task function object, according to algorithm requirements. C++ is very flexible in allowing the programmer to define constructors that copy objects. A complete discussion is provided in the TBB chapter, where the following issues were discussed in detail:

- The parallel_for algorithm is well adapted to embarrassingly parallel contexts, where there are no partial results coming from different threads to be collected. The function object class required by this algorithm may have a private internal state if that helps to implement the task, but this internal state must be immutable: the operator() function cannot change it. In this case, TBB only requires the standard, implicit, copy constructor.
- The parallel_reduce algorithm applies when partial results must be combined in some way. The function object class *must* have a public internal state used to accumulate or store partial results. In this case, TBB asks you to provide another constructor, called the *split constructor*, which copies the function object but in addition re-initializes the public internal state to the initial default values. In this way, a new thread that is activated to participate in the parallel execution gets a function object in which the history of previous computations by another thread is forgotten.

B.3 LAMBDA EXPRESSIONS

We have seen in discussing function objects that a new type—a C++ class—must always be defined, but the names of the objects instances of this class—in all cases arbitrary—can even be anonymous, as in the example above in which we passed directly the class constructor rather than the function object name.

Lambda expressions—introduced in the C++11 standard—push this idea much further. They can be seen as an *inlined, "on the fly" definition of an unnamed function object*. When the compiler meets a lambda expression, it certainly creates a new type, but the class name—as well as the function object it instantiates—do not need to be known by the client code. This avoids the necessity of explicitly defining the function object class, making the code much less verbose. The other essential property of lambda expressions is the "on the fly" definition, which means that a lambda expression can be defined *at the place it is needed, inside a enclosing function*, which is not the case for traditional inlined functions. We have used lambda expressions in Chapter 11 to define "on the fly" task functions passed to a thread manager utility.

The lambda expression syntax provides all the information the compiler needs to define the overloaded operator() in the implicit function object. The most basic syntax is [ ][...}, where the initial brackets identify a lambda expression, defining a callable unit of code between the following braces. The simplest lambda expression, defining a function that takes no arguments and returns void, is:

```
// A simple lambda expression taking no arguments, with
// no return value
// – – – – – – – – – – – – – – – – – – – – – – – –

[] { // function body; }
```

LISTING B.4

Very simple lambda expression

The function so defined, like an ordinary function, can reference the global variables in the application, and call global functions. If return type and parameter lists are required, the following general syntax is used:

[capture list] (parameter list) –>return type { function body }

Let us examine the different items in the expression above:

- *Return type*:
  - If the function body contains only a return statement, the return type does not need to be specified. It is taken directly from the type returned in the function body.
  - If, instead, the function body contains more than a single return statement, the return type must be explicitly specified. Otherwise, the lambda expression ignores the return statement and returns void.
- *Parameter list*: This is the set of arguments to be passed to the operator() function
- *Capture list*: Defines the way local variables in the enclosing environment are accessed (captured).

  - A lambda expression can use a local variable from its surrounding function *only* if it captures that variable in its capture list.
  - A totally empty capture list means that no local variables from the surrounding environment are used.
  - Local variables captured by the lambda expression become data members in the implicit function object class.
- *Capture codes*: Local variables can be captured by value (their values are copied) or by reference (a reference to the local variable is defined in the implicit class). The capture codes are:
  - [ ]: This lambda does not use any local variable from the surrounding function.
  - [=] Any surrounding local variable is captured by copy.
  - [&] Any surrounding local variable is captured by reference.

- [=, &a, &b] Default is copy but a and b are captured by reference.
- [&, =a, =b] Default is reference but a and b are captured by value.

Using these conventions, it is very easy to rewrite the complete Listing B.3 as, follows, avoiding the explicit definition of predicate functions and function objects.

```
// Solve first problem, n>0:
// - - - - - - - - - - - -
int *pos = find_if(array, array+N, [](int& n)->bool {if n>0 return true;
                                                      else return false; });

// Solve second problem, n>value:
// - - - - - - - - - - - - - - -
int value;
int *pos = find_if(array, array+N, [=](int& n)->bool
                                        {if n>value return true;
                                         else return false });
```

LISTING B.5

Listing 3, using lambda expressions

In the first case, we are dealing with a simple function with no internal state, and no local values are captured. Since the body function is not just a return statement, the bool return value must be specified. In the second case, a function object with internal state is needed, and the integer value to be compared to n needs to be captured.

A another example of lamba expressions, we can reexamine the listing 6.11 of the TimedWait_S.C example in chapter 6, where a timed wait in the C++11 environment was discussed. Here is a new version of this example, using a lamba expression instead of a function pointer.

```
using namespace std;

condition_variable CV;
mutex my_mutex;
bool predicate = false;

void worker_thread()
   {  // same as in the original code }

int main(int argc, char **argv)
   {
   bool retval;
   chrono::duration<int, milli> delay(1000);
   thread T(worker_thread);
   T.detach();
   do
      {
      unique_lock<std::mutex> my_lock(my_mutex);
      retval = CV.wait_for<int, milli>(my_lock, delay,
                                       [](return predicate;} );
```

```
        if(!retval) cout << "\n Timed out after 1 second" << endl;
        }while(!retval);
    cout << "\n Wait terminated " << endl;
    }
```

LISTING B.6

TimedWait_S.C, new version

In the original code, an auxiliary function bool Pred() was defined that returned the predicate. Now this is done on the fly with a simple lambda expression. No local variables are captured no arguments are passed and, since the function body is just a return statement, the bool return value does not need to be specified.

More examples of the usage of lambda expressions can be found in Chapter 11, dealing with the TBB taskgroup utility.

Bibliography

[1] Intel. Intel CilkPlus; 2013. URL: http://cilkplus.org.

[2] Microsoft. Microsoft Parallel Patterns Library; 2015. URL: https://msdn.microsoft.com/en-us/library/dd492418.aspx.

[3] MIT. M.I.T. Cilk; 2013. URL: http://supertech.csail.mit.edu.

[4] Dennard R, Gaensslen F, Yu HN, Rideout L, Bassous E, LeBlanc A. Design of ion-implanted MOSFET's with very small physical dimensions; 1974. URL: www.ece.ucsb.edu/courses/ECE225/225_WOBanerjee/reference/Dennard.pdf.

[5] Kirk D, Hwu WM. Programming massively parallel processors. Waltham, MA: Morgan Kaufmann; 2013. ISBN 978-0-12-415992-1.

[6] Wilt N. The CUDA handbook. Waltham, MA: Addison-Wesley; 2012. ISBN 978-0-321-80946-9.

[7] Sanders J, Kandrot E. CUDA by example. Waltham, MA: Addison-Wesley; 2011. ISBN 978-0-13-138768-3.

[8] Jeffers J, Reinders J. Intel Xeon Phi coprocessor. Waltham, MA: O'Reilly; 2012. ISBN 978-0-12-410414-3.

[9] Intel. Intel Xeon Phi documentation; 2013. URL: http://intel.com/software/mic.

[10] Gove D. Multicore application programming. Boston, MA: Addison-Wesley; 2011. ISBN 978-0-321-71137-3.

[11] Butenhof D. Programming with POSIX threads. Reading, MA: Addison-Wesley; 1997. ISBN 978-2-7440-7182-9.

[12] Nichols B, Buttlar D, Proulx Farrel J. Pthreads programming. Sebastopol, CA: O'Reilly; 1998. ISBN 1-56592-115-1.

[13] Microsoft. Windows API home page; 2015. URL: https://msdn.microsoft.com/en-us/library/ff818516(v=vs.85).aspx.

[14] Williams A. C++ concurrency in action. Shelter Island, NY: Manning Publications; 2012. ISBN 978-1-933988771.

[15] GNU compiler collection site; 2015. URL: http://gcc.gnu.org.

[16] Press W, Teukolsky S, Vettering W, Flannery B. Numerical recipes in C. 2nd ed. New York, NY: Cambridge University Press; 1992. ISBN 0-521-43108-5.

[17] Intel Threading Building Blocks. TBB reference manual; 2015. URL: http://software.intel.com/en-us/node/506130.

[18] Intel Threading Building Blocks. Download and documentation TBB site; 2015. URL: http://www.threadingbuildingblocks.org.

[19] Boehm HJ. Threads cannot be implemented as a library; 2004. URL: http://www.hpl.hp.com/2004/HPL-2004-209.html.

[20] Adve S, Boehm HJ. Memory models: a case for rethinking parallel languages and hardware. Commun ACM 2010; 53(8):91–101.

[21] Adve S, Boehm HJ. Memory models: a case for rethinking parallel languages and hardware; 2002-2001. URL: http://rsim.cs.uuic.edu/Pubs/10-cacm-memory-models.pdf.

[22] Boehm HJ. Threads basics; 2009. URL: http://www.hpl.hp.com/2009/HPL-2009-259.html.

[23] Lamport L. How to make a multiprocessor computer that correctly execute multiprocess programs. IEEE Trans Comput 1979; C-3(9):241–248.

[24] Patterson D, Hennessy J. Computer organization and design: the hardware/software interface. 4th ed. Burlington, MA: Morgan Kaufmann; 2009. ISBN 978-2-7440-7182-9.

[25] Herlijy M, Shavit N. The art of multiprocessor programming. Waltham, MA: Morgan Kaufmann; 2012. ISBN 978-0-12-397337-5.

[26] Chapman B, Yost G, van der Paas R. Using OpenMP: portable shared memory parallel programming. Cambridge, MA: The MIT Press; 2007. ISBN 978-2-7440-7182-9.

[27] ARB. Official Architecture Review Board (ARB) OpenMP site; 2013. URL: http://www.openmp.org.

[28] ARB. OpenMP application programming interface; 2013. URL: http://www.openmp.org/mp-documents/OpenMP4.0.pdf.

[29] ARB. OpenMP application programming interface–examples; 2014. URL: http://www.openmp.org/mp-documents/OpenMP_Examples_4.0.1.pdf.

[30] de Supinski B, Klemm M, Stotzer E, Terboven C, van der Paas R. Advanced OpenMP: performance and OpenMP4.0 features; 2014. URL: sc14.supercomputing.org/program/tutorials.

[31] Terboven C. SC14: a short stroll through OpenMP4.0; 2014. URL: http://terboven.com.

[32] Intel Threading Building Blocks. TBB getting started (tutorial); 2015. URL: https://www.threadingbuildongblocks.org/intel-tbb-tutorial.

[33] Intel Threading Building Blocks. TBB user guide and flow graph; 2015. URL: http://software.intel.com/en-us/node/506045.

[34] Reinders J. Intel Threading Building Blocks. Waltham, MA: O'Reilly; 2007. ISBN 978-0-596-52480-8.

[35] McCool M, Robison A, Reinders J. Structured parallel programming. Waltham, MA: Morgan Kaufmann; 2012. ISBN 978-0-12-415993-8.

[36] Intel. Guide to vectorization with Intel C++ compilers; 2013. URL: http://tinyurl.com/intelautovec.

[37] Lamport L. The parallel execution of DO loops. Commun ACM 1974; 17(2):83–93.

Index

Note: Page numbers followed by *f* indicate figures and *t* indicate tables.

Printed in the United States
By Bookmasters